THE FOLDS OF OLYMPUS

The Folds of Olympus

MOUNTAINS IN ANCIENT GREEK
AND ROMAN CULTURE

JASON KÖNIG

PRINCETON UNIVERSITY PRESS
PRINCETON & OXFORD

Copyright © 2022 by Princeton University Press

Princeton University Press is committed to the protection of copyright and the intellectual property our authors entrust to us. Copyright promotes the progress and integrity of knowledge created by humans. By engaging with an authorized copy of this work, you are supporting creators and the global exchange of ideas. As this work is protected by copyright, any reproduction or distribution of it in any form for any purpose requires permission; permission requests should be sent to permissions@press.princeton.edu. Ingestion of any IP for any AI purposes is strictly prohibited.

Published by Princeton University Press
41 William Street, Princeton, New Jersey 08540
99 Banbury Road, Oxford OX2 6JX

press.princeton.edu

GPSR Authorized Representative: Easy Access System Europe - Mustamäe tee 50, 10621 Tallinn, Estonia, gpsr.requests@easproject.com

All Rights Reserved

First paperback printing, 2025
Paperback ISBN 978-0-691-23848-7
Cloth ISBN 978-0-691-20129-0
ISBN (e-book) 978-0-691-23849-4
Library of Congress Control Number: 2022934720

British Library Cataloging-in-Publication Data is available

Editorial: Ben Tate and Josh Drake
Production Editorial: Jill Harris
Jacket/Cover Design: Kimberly Castañeda
Production: Danielle Amatucci
Publicity: Alyssa Sanford and Charlotte Coyne
Copyeditor: Jennifer Harris

Jacket/Cover image: Jason König

This book has been composed in Arno

For Eliza, Rory, and Serena

CONTENTS

List of Illustrations   xi

Map   xiv

Preface   xvii

Acknowledgements   xxix

PART I. MOUNTAINS AND THE DIVINE

1　Summit Altars   3
　　Divine Presence and Human Culture   3
　　Memory and Embodied Experience   7
　　Mediterranean Mountain Religion   9
　　The Summit Altars of Mainland Greece   12

2　Mountains in Archaic Greek Poetry   20
　　The Homeric Hymns   20
　　Hesiod and the Muses on Mount Helikon   26
　　Mount Olympus and Mount Ida in the Iliad   30
　　Mountain Similes: Natural Force and Human Vulnerability   35
　　Mountain Similes: Divine Vision and the Sublime   40

3　Pausanias: Mythical Landscapes and Divine Presence   47
　　Euripides to Pausanias   47
　　Arkadia   53
　　Boiotia   57
　　Phokis   64

4 Egeria on Mount Sinai: Mountain Pilgrimage in
   Early Christian and Late Antique Culture   69
   Biblical Mountains   69
   Mountain Allegories in the Writings of the Emperor Julian 73
   Mountain Pilgrimage   77
   Egeria on Mount Sinai   81
   Egeria and the History of Travel and Mountaineering   84
   Egeria on Mount Nebo   90

PART II. MOUNTAIN VISION

5 Mountain Aesthetics   95
   Mountains as Objects of Vision   95
   Aesthetic Categories and the Classical Tradition   97
   Beautiful Mountains   100
   Ancient Mountains and the Sublime   105

6 Scientific Viewing and the Volcanic Sublime   107
   Volcanic Knowledge and Human Vulnerability   107
   Observing Etna   109
   The Pseudo-Virgilian Aetna *and the Language of Vision* 113
   Literary Ambition and Philosophical Virtue:
   Etna in Seneca's Letters   115

7 Mountains in Greek and Roman Art   119
   Miniaturised Mountains   119
   Mountains in Roman Wall Painting   126
   Enigmatic Mountains   135

8 Mountain Landmarks in Latin Literature   144
   Mountain Symbolism   144
   Mountains in Latin Epic   149
   Mountains and Gender in Ovid and Seneca   152
   Mountains in Horace's Odes   155

9	Mountains and Bodies in Apuleius' *Metamorphoses*	160
	A Stage-Set of Mount Ida	160
	Rhetorical and Symbolic Mountains in the Metamorphoses	163
	Mountain Terrain and Haptic Experience	168
	Landscapes of the Goddess Isis	174

PART III. MOUNTAIN CONQUEST

10	Warfare and Knowledge in Mountain Territories	181
	Mountains and Modernity	181
	Rock-Walkers: Specialist Expertise in Mountain Warfare	183
	Local Knowledge: Control and Resistance in Mountain Terrain	186
	Representing Mountain Conquest	191
11	Mountain Narratives in Greek and Roman Historiography	199
	Landscape Narratives	199
	Herodotus	200
	Xenophon and Arrian	204
	Plutarch	205
	Polybius	212
12	Strabo: Civilising the Mountains	218
	Human-Environment Relations in Strabo's Geography	218
	Strabo's Cartographic Perspective	220
	Spain and the Alps	222
	Italy and Greece	224
	Pontus	227
13	Ammianus Marcellinus: Mountain Peoples and Imperial Boundaries	230
	The Isaurians in the Res Gestae	230
	Natural-Force Metaphors	233
	Bodily Immersion: Mountains, Rivers, Sea	236
	Viewing from Above	238
	'Like a Snowstorm from the High Mountains': The Huns and the Goths	240

PART IV. LIVING IN THE MOUNTAINS

14 Mountain and City — 247
   Mountain Communities — 247
   Environmental History in the Mountains of the Mediterranean — 249
   Mountains and Identity — 251
   Mountains and the Ancient Economy — 254
   Mountain Pastoralism — 257
   Plato's Laws *and the Mountains of Crete* — 262

15 Dio Chrysostom and the Mountains of Euboia — 267
   Idealising Mountain Communities — 267
   A Mountain Idyll — 269
   Visiting the City — 274
   Urban Perspectives — 280

16 Mountain Saints in Late Antique Christian Literature — 283
   Human-Environment Relations in Early Christian Hagiography — 283
   Narrating Mountain Asceticism — 288
   Theodoret and the Mountains of Syria — 290
   Pseudo-Nilus' Narrations *and the Massacres at Mount Sinai* — 293
   The Life of Symeon the Mountaineer — 297
   Mountain Retreats in Jerome's Life of Hilarion — 300

Epilogue — 305

Notes 313
Bibliography 383
Index Locorum 419
General Index 433

ILLUSTRATIONS

1.1. Ruined columns from the temple of Zeus Lykaios, with the summit of Mount Lykaion behind.   5
1.2. View from the summit of Mount Lykaion looking northeast towards the stadium and hippodrome.   7
1.3. View south from the summit of Mount Ithome over ancient Messene.   13
1.4. Mount Apesas with its flat top from the stadium at Nemea.   14
1.5. View from the summit of Mount Arachnaion, looking west to Argos.   16
2.1. View to the west from the summit of Zagaras, easternmost peak of the Helikon range.   29
2.2. Mytikas summit, Mount Olympus.   31
3.1. Summit ridge of Mount Kithairon.   60
3.2. Hippokrene spring, Zagaras, Mount Helikon.   63
4.1. Moses receiving the Ten Commandments on Mount Sinai. Mosaic from the Basilica, Saint Catherine's Monastery, Sinai, sixth century CE.   80
7.1. Prometheus bound to a rocky arch, being freed by Herakles. Apulian calyx-krater, ca 340s BCE, attributed to the Branca Painter. Berlin, Antikensammlung, Staatliche Museen zu Berlin.   121
7.2. Muse sitting on the rocks of Mount Helikon. White-ground lekythos, ca 445–435 BCE, attributed to the Achilles Painter. Munich, Staatliche Antikensammlungen, SCH 80 (formerly Lugano, Schoen Collection).   122

7.3. The Judgement of Paris. Red-figured hydria, ca 470 BCE. London, British Museum. 123

7.4. The Judgement of Paris. Terracotta pyxis, attributed to the Penthesilea Painter, ca 465–460 BCE. New York, Metropolitan Museum of Art. 124

7.5. Silver stater, Arkadian League, 363–362 BCE. Reverse: Pan sitting on rocks. Berlin, Münzkabinett der Staatlichen Museum, Altes Museum. 125

7.6. Coin showing head of Vespasian (obverse); Roma seated on the seven hills (reverse), 71 CE. London, British Museum. 125

7.7. Trajan's Column, Rome, completed 113 CE. Scene LXII: Roman forces advancing through forested, mountainous scenery. 126

7.8. Wall painting of a villa with mountains, from the House of Lucretius Fronto, Pompeii; detail of the south wall of the tablinum, first century CE. DeAgostini Picture Library / Scala, Florence. 127

7.9. Narcissus at the fountain, from the House of Lucretius Fronto, Pompeii, bedroom, first century CE. Photo Scala, Florence / Luciano Romano. 129

7.10. Nineteenth-century watercolour of a wall painting from Pompeii showing the Rape of Hylas, from the House of Virnius Modestus, IX.7.16, early first century CE(?). DAI-Rom, Archivio, A-VII-33-088. 131

7.11. Wall painting showing Odysseus' companions in the land of the Laestrygonians, from a house in the via Graziosa, Rome, mid-first century BCE. Musei Vaticani. 134

7.12. Bacchus and Mount Vesuvius, Lararium of the House of the Centenary, Pompeii, first century CE. Naples Archaeological Museum. 136

7.13. Euthykles Stele. Found in the Valley of the Muses, late-third century BCE. Height 1.19 m, width 0.50 m. National Archaeological Museum, Athens, NAM 1455. 138

7.14. Marble relief showing the apotheosis of Homer, Archelaos of Priene, from Bovillae, second century BCE(?). Height 1.15 m. London, British Museum. 141

10.1. Route of the Persian outflanking move at the battle of Thermopylai, Mount Kallidromos, looking west towards Eleftherochori from above Nevropoli. 188

10.2. Peutinger Table, section 5: Dalmatia, Pannonia, Moesia, Campania, Apulia, Africa. 194

14.1. Coin showing the head of Julia Maesa, grandmother of the emperors Elagabalus and Severus Alexander (obverse), and Mount Argaios (reverse), 221–224 CE. Caesarea, Cappadocia. 254

This map includes some of the most important mountains, mountain ranges, and regions discussed in the book, but it is not intended to be exhaustive. For more detailed mapping, see Talbert (2000).

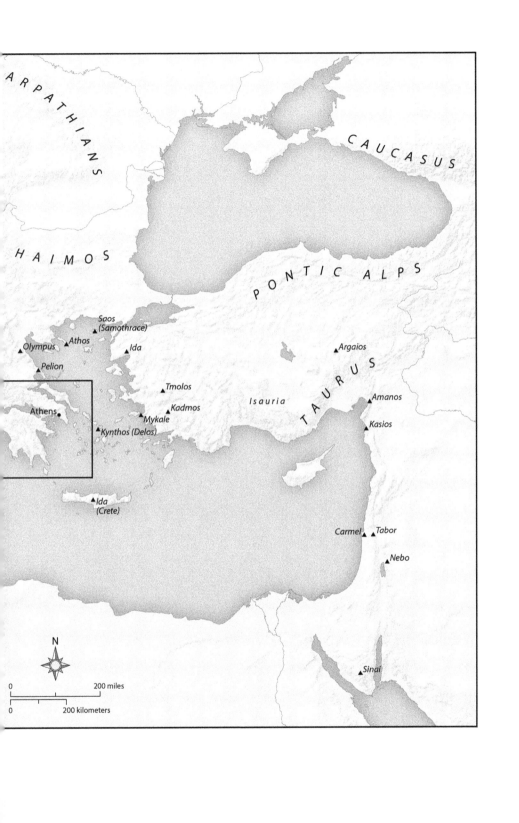

PREFACE

IF YOU WANT to see how mountains mattered in ancient Greece, there is nowhere better than Mount Lykaion in Arkadia. I went there with my family one morning late in May in 2014. We drove most of the way up, past the village of Ano Karyes, to the stadium and hippodrome a couple of hundred metres below the southern peak, slightly the lower of the mountain's two summits. I went up from there on foot while the others stayed down below; they were on the lookout for snakes, having tripped over one in the fort at Acrocorinth the day before. A track curves upwards around the west side of the mountain. The slopes were green and covered with late-spring flowers. Just below the summit you come to a wide plateau; then you go up a steep conical mound to the top. It's hard not to be distracted by the view. You get an amazing sense of height. The southern peak is at 1,382 metres—not much by Greek standards, but it stands high up above the industrialised plain of Megalopolis with its giant smoking chimneys. And then beyond that you can see the ripples of other mountains on all sides far into the distance, with the snow-covered summit of Mount Taygetos through the haze away to the south, and Mount Ithome, and the temple of Apollo at Bassai covered in its protective tent to the west.

But it was the summit itself that I had come to see. The top section of it (about the top metre and a half above the bedrock) is the remains of the ash altar of Zeus Lykaios. It was one of many altars on mountain summits across the Mediterranean world. But this one is special, in part because it has been excavated more extensively than any equivalent site. There was not a vast amount to see when I went there, outside the excavation season: some shallow trenches, covered over with plastic sheeting, and overgrown with grass. And yet the contents of those trenches can help us to draw a remarkably rich portrait of the way in which the summit was used by the area's inhabitants. Initial excavations over 100 years ago uncovered in the fabric of the altar (among other things) lots of burnt animal bones, hundreds of fragments of fifth- and fourth-century BCE pottery, and also various metal objects used as dedications, including two coins, a knife, and two miniature bronze tripod cauldrons dating from the eighth or seventh century BCE. The most recent excavations (since 2004) have turned up more animal bones, in enormous numbers (nearly all of them burnt; mainly femurs, patellas, and tails from sheep and goats, with small numbers of pig bones in addition). It is clear now that the fill of the altar site is largely made up of bone fragments. These burnt remains date from as early as 1600 BCE. Also found were thirty-three more coins, dating from the sixth to fourth century BCE, from right across mainland Greece; more tripods (roughly forty in total); and other dedications too, including a small bronze hand, holding a silver lightning bolt, broken from a statuette (the hand of Zeus, presumably), eleven lead wreaths from the seventh century BCE, and a glass-like substance called fulgurite which is formed when lightning strikes sand or soil. It is not clear whether this was brought to the altar as a dedication, the product of Zeus's lightning returned to its source in his honour, or whether it was formed by a lightning strike on the mountain itself, a reminder of the presence of the god at his sanctuary. The excavations also found some human and animal figurines in terracotta, and the remains of hundreds of Mycenean drinking vessels (ca 1600–1100 BCE), which suggest that the site was a place of feasting, and even, unexpectedly, a considerable number of pottery fragments dating from the final Neolithic period (ca 4500–3200 BC). Most astonishing of all is the recent find of a human body buried within the altar: the remains of a teenage boy with the upper part of his skull missing, dating from the eleventh century BCE. Whether that gives us evidence to back up the rumours of human sacrifice at the site that we find in a number of ancient texts[1] is at the time of writing not yet clear, and even if it did, there would probably be no reason to think that that was a widespread practice, given that no other human remains have been uncovered. But this certainly was a place where countless animals met their deaths: sacrificial victims were slaughtered on the summit of the mountain by the people of Arkadia in honour of the god Zeus for many centuries, even millennia. And when you look more closely at the ground, you can see that it is covered with a scattering of bone pieces under the grass—charred grey splinters and scraps, the remains of animals who were killed and burned up there thousands of years ago.[2]

The Mediterranean is a place of mountains, but you could read a lot of books and articles about classical antiquity without realising that. There are some exceptions. Fernand Braudel famously claimed that the mountainous character of the region was one of the shaping factors in ancient Mediterranean history.[3] And yet the mountains of ancient Greek and Roman culture are often hidden in plain sight. We can get glimpses of their economic, religious, and social importance from some inspiring studies of individual sites and regions,[4] many of them based on remarkable archaeological initiatives, but for many classicists, with our predominant focus on urban, elite history, these are still marginal territories. That is all the more so for tourists. One of the things that amazed me most about Mount Lykaion on that May morning was just how empty it was: there was no one else there all day.[5] Mountains are everywhere in ancient literature too—the mythical landscapes of ancient poetry, from Homer's Olympus onwards, the hostile mountain terrain that forms the backdrop to so many accounts of military campaigning in ancient historiography, or the harsh mountains of the desert, the spiritual battleground for the Christian ascetics in the early Christian saints' lives—but publications on the mountains of ancient literature are even more sparse. Richard Buxton has done more than anyone to expand our view in a series of pioneering works on the mountains of ancient Greek myth.[6] He has shown among other things how ancient mythical narrative reflected but also transformed its audiences' real-life experience of mountains. However, his work focuses above all on classical Greek tragedy; it leaves huge swathes of material from other genres and other periods still open to analysis. Very few people have so far taken up the invitation to explore further.[7]

One of the challenges is that ancient literature, with a few important exceptions,[8] tends to avoid the kind of extended, often aesthetically inflected set-piece representations of landscape that we are so familiar with from the Romantic period onwards. Ancient images of mountains tend to be individually briefer than their modern equivalents. That does not mean that they are any less consequential. Typically they are threaded into the background of the works they are a part of, showing themselves over and over again with a cumulative 'intratextual' sophistication—'intratextuality' being the phenomenon of internal interrelationship between different parts of a single text—which is easy to miss if we are used to more explicit, modern ways of reflecting on landscape.[9] One of my aims in this book is to contribute to the history of ancient mountains, by bringing together a vast amount of material on ancient mountain life that has not generally been viewed as a coherent whole, and drawing out the importance of a series of key themes for our understanding of it, which I hope will help even specialist readers to see some of this material freshly. But that historical and archaeological material is intended above all to give context to my main objective, which is to understand the role played by representations of mountains in ancient Greek and Roman literature, and in the process to generate a series of original readings of the texts and authors I discuss. With such a vast subject it is simply not possible to cover in the depth they deserve all of the ancient works where mountains play an important role, or all of the mountains of the Mediterranean, so my procedure here has been to focus on a series of case studies, exposing some key texts to questions that I hope will stimulate engagement with other material too.[10] I look at four different themes in turn: the relationship between mountains and the divine; the role of mountains as objects of vision in ancient culture; the role of mountains in ethnographic and geographical writing and in military history, as places both subjected to and resistant to conquest and civilisation; and last the status of mountains as places of work and habitation, on the edges of urban culture. What kinds of pleasure and fascination do ancient writings about mountains offer to their ancient audiences (and indeed also to us)? How do they engage with their audiences' understanding of mountains as real places in projecting their own distinctive images of landscape? What do these texts tell us about ancient understandings of the relationship between human culture and the natural world? If we want to have any hope of answering those questions, we need to read these texts from end to end, staying alert to the way in which successive passages project distinctive, cumulative images of the mountains of the Mediterranean and of their relationship with human culture.

In the process one of my goals is to bring the study of ancient mountains more into dialogue with its modern equivalents. There is now a huge volume of work on mountains in the modern world, ranging from scientific and geographical studies on issues as diverse as geology, environment, climate, heritage, and human geography[11] to cultural-historical studies of the development of modern mountaineering and landscape depiction, most of it focused on the past 250 years or so. Mountain studies has emerged as a vibrant and diverse cross-disciplinary field over the past few decades. But there has been almost no interest among classicists in engaging with that material, and very little inclination in turn among modern mountain historians to think seriously about the premodern history of the places and questions they study.

One of the factors in that lack of communication is the widespread belief that human responses to mountains in Western culture underwent an abrupt change from the late eighteenth century onwards, with the development of mountaineering as a leisure pursuit and the development of the concepts of the picturesque and the sublime. The conventional story is that mountains had been viewed in premodern culture as places of fear and ugliness, to be avoided at all costs; now they came to be appreciated as places of beauty and sublimity.

That narrative has its origin in the Alpine writing of the nineteenth century, for example in the work of Leslie Stephen, who was the father of Virginia Woolf and one of the leading figures in English Alpinism in the mid- to late nineteenth century.[12] Those views were then influentially restated and contextualised in Marjorie Hope Nicolson's book *Mountain Gloom and Mountain Glory*, published in 1959, which has been one of the foundational works of twentieth-century mountain history. Nicolson's reading of classical texts about mountains is quite cursory and at second-hand, perhaps not surprisingly given that her main aim was to understand changes in writing about mountains from the eighteenth century onwards.[13] Her conclusions have been repeatedly cited in an oversimplified form, as if the watershed summed up in her title, and her explanations for it, are undisputed facts.[14] I suspect that many people, when they walk or climb in the hills, even if they have read only a little of the history of mountains and mountaineering, have a sense, perhaps not consciously expressed, that the pleasure they experience in moving through the landscape and admiring it is something distinctively modern.

Nicolson's gloom and glory narrative is starting to be challenged more and more,[15] but it is still astonishingly tenacious. Clearly many things did change in the eighteenth century: that would be hard to deny. Mountaineering in particular developed in quite unprecedented ways from its beginnings in the late eighteenth century through the nineteenth century—that story has now been studied from many different angles.[16] But if we give too much weight to the idea of a watershed, it can bring all sorts of negative consequences. It can stop us from seeing the many continuities between modern and premodern.[17] At the same time it can prevent us from understanding what made premodern responses different and distinctive: if we are interested only in the question of whether the ancient world did or did not have precedents for modern ideas of the sublime, or for modern mountaineering culture, we ignore the challenge of understanding Greek and Roman responses to mountains on their own terms.[18] The habits of mountaintop sacrifice referred to earlier are just the most striking example of how alien some aspects of ancient uses of mountains could be.[19] Either way, whether we emphasise the similarities or the differences between ancient and modern, it is clear that mountains mattered in the ancient world, and that ancient responses to mountains were vastly more sophisticated and varied than the standard narrative suggests. It is bewildering, when you take the trouble to look, to think that anyone would ever have doubted that.[20]

In this book, by contrast, I draw every so often on modern mountain studies to ask new questions of the ancient material, while also using the mountains of the ancient world to give new depth and nuance to the stories told within many different corners of mountain studies about the long history of human engagement with mountains. One precedent for that approach is the work of Veronica della Dora,[21] who ranges very widely across many different periods and places, the ancient Mediterranean included, in seeking to understand what mountains have meant for their human viewers over many millennia. In what follows I do not make any attempt to match the chronological breadth of her work. My focus in this book (which is one of my contributions to a wider project on the history of mountains generously funded by the Leverhulme Trust) is above all on the ancient world, and especially Greek and Roman antiquity, from archaic Greece in the eighth century BCE to late antiquity in the fifth century CE, although I also discuss at various times parallels from Jewish and Near Eastern traditions.[22] But I do share with della Dora a belief that the story of human engagement with mountains needs to be told with a much greater chronological depth than is currently the case.[23] Other publications from our project accordingly take a collaborative and comparative approach to mountain history over many centuries, with a special focus on the influence of classical texts and concepts in writing about mountains from the early modern period onwards.[24]

One theme above all unites the diverse material that follows—that is the tendency for mountains to be both places of human engagement and at the same time objects beyond human control. The tension between those two possibilities was one of the key driving forces for human interest in mountains in the ancient Mediterranean, as it is also in the modern world.[25] We often assume that mountains were places of wilderness in Greek and Roman antiquity, defined by their position outside the city, linked with divine presence and primitive human populations, and that clearly was one element in their fascination. But in fact mountains were often intimately tied to the cities they were close to.[26] Ancient writing about mountains often dramatises the struggle to bring mountains under control either literally or imaginatively. How do we bring these spaces into human civilisation? How do we make them knowable? Those questions have been central to modern responses to mountains, which have often involved attempts to dominate or incorporate mountain territories and mountain peoples for political, sometimes imperial goals.[27] Gaining knowledge about mountains has often been central to those processes. That was the case for ancient Greek and Roman culture too.[28]

Looking at the relationship between mountains and human culture can also bring new insights into the history of human interaction with the environment more broadly. Many of the texts I look at in this book have powerful resonances with recent thinking about human relationships with the more-than-human world in the environmental humanities, especially within the cross-disciplinary field of ecocriticism, with its focus on literary representations of human-environment relations.[29] Of course there is always a risk of anachronism in approaching ancient literature through the framework of modern environmental thinking. There is a long history of oversimplified attempts to fit ancient responses to the environment into narratives about the development of modern attitudes and modern problems.[30] Attempts to ascribe some kind of 'environmental consciousness' to ancient authors, or to argue that the ancient world experienced human-caused environmental degradation equivalent to our own, have often drastically underestimated the complexity of the ancient evidence.[31] One thing we can gain from re-examining the ancient sources in all their diversity is the chance to challenge and complicate these narratives. We need an approach that respects the variety of ancient responses:[32] that involves reading ancient representations of human-environment relations from end to end, with an alertness to their internal correspondences and contradictions, rather than focusing on isolated passages out of context. We also need an approach that respects the alienness of many aspects of ancient interaction with the environment, even as it seeks points of resemblance.[33]

Nevertheless, it has become increasingly clear that there are ways in which ecocritical perspectives can raise new questions about ancient culture, and also ways in which ancient Greek and Roman literature can offer us images of relationships between human culture and the environment that are potentially valuable as resources for us today. Exploring those points of connection is still a work in progress.[34] Until quite recently there has been very little explicit engagement with the environmental humanities within Classics, especially among those who work on classical literature. That has begun to change, helped perhaps by the move away from an exclusive focus on 'nature writing' in ecocriticism: any text can be open to an ecocritical reading, as a means of shedding light on its underlying assumptions about human-environment relations.[35] That shift opens up new possibilities for analysis of classical texts, given that extended descriptions of the natural world tend to be less prominent in ancient literature than in their modern equivalents. From at least the late eighteenth century, that reticence has been taken as a sign that the ancients were simply not interested in nature, just as they were thought not to have been interested in mountains.[36] We are in a better position now to understand the sophistication and fascination of ancient environmental thinking.

There are many possible ways of approaching the relationship between ancient and modern engagement with the environment. Perhaps most importantly, ancient literature repeatedly presents us with alternatives to anthropocentrism in its portrayal of human-environment interaction. 'New materialist' approaches within Classics have begun to shed light on the way in which ancient texts explore the entanglement between human actors and their environments, and the way in which they emphasise the agency of the non-human world, with the effect of questioning anthropocentric hierarchies of value.[37] There is a high concentration of those phenomena in ancient depictions of mountains, with their interest in the tension between human control and human disempowerment.

Ancient representations of landscape and environment also offer us models for thinking about the relationship between global and local perspectives in our understanding of human-environment relations. A number of recent studies have drawn attention to the way in which modern genres often struggle to represent environmental problems on a global scale. Most prominently, Amitav Ghosh in his book *The Great Derangement* has argued that the modern Western prose fiction tradition, with its tendency to be obsessed by autonomous individuals inhabiting clearly bounded landscapes, is not well suited to dealing with the global challenge of climate change.[38] By contrast the combination of local and global scales comes quite naturally to a lot of ancient writing about human relations with the environment. We see that in texts like the *Iliad*, with its interwoven network of similes that allow us to view countless other places side by side with the battlefield at Troy, or in the intricate structures of ancient historiographical and geographical writing, which juxtapose images of human-environment interaction from right across the Mediterranean world and beyond. In that sense there is more at stake in the choice to read classical depictions of mountains intratextually than a judgement about the aesthetic priorities and compositional habits of ancient narrative: it can also be a way of opening ourselves up to the potential of Greek and Roman literature as a resource for new modes of environmental imagination in the present.

There is also now a vast body of theory on the question of how we should understand the idea of 'landscape'. As it developed from the Renaissance onwards that concept was linked with the idea of viewing from a distance, and associated with elite control over geographical space.[39] In some of its manifestations that was a very modern concept, for example in the development of landscape painting and landscape gardening, but it was also founded in classical precedents. As we shall see, the motif of viewing from mountain summits was a very widespread one in ancient Greek and Roman literature, and it was linked with authority of various kinds—divine, military, authorial.[40] For many people, however, and in many contexts, the experience of landscape is never as detached as that image implies. Landscape is always a human construct, a product of human imagination.[41] Landscapes also matter for identity, and the images created by humans for understanding the landscapes they inhabit and encounter are often experienced viscerally. Different meanings are imprinted on landscapes palimpsestically over time by the communities that interact with them, often in a way that reflects particular power relations and ideologies, and often through a process of contestation and negotiation between competing visions. Many analysts have found 'place' a more helpful term than 'landscape' for articulating that grounded quality of human interaction with the earth's surface, and the way in which certain locations over time accumulate powerful symbolic and historical resonances.[42] Another strand within modern scholarship, associated with the 'phenomenological' tradition, has made it clear that the human experience of landscape is often a bodily one that involves a sense of being immersed in the landscape quite different from the more detached styles of viewing that we associate with more traditional, visual conceptions of landscape appreciation.[43]

One of the things we can gain through giving attention to ancient writing about mountains is an understanding of the way in which that whole range of possibilities for human engagement with the earth's surface was there already in classical antiquity.[44] The tension between visual and bodily ways of making sense of landscape is one of the recurring themes of this book: it was central to ancient thinking about mountains just as it has been in modern mountaineering culture from at least the early eighteenth century onwards,[45] and just as it has been to modern writing about landscape more broadly.[46] These are two different ways of making mountains knowable, or at least partially and imperfectly knowable, two different ways of understanding the relationship between mountains and human experience. Their dual importance is implied by the 'folds' of this book's title,[47] which is intended to draw attention to some of those conflicting resonances (the original phrase is from Homer's *Iliad*,[48] which will make an appearance early on in the book, in chapter 2). On one level that title suggests a focus on the physical textures of the landscape of the ancient Mediterranean, asking us to imagine a close-up view of mountain terrain, where the valleys and ravines and gullies on a mountainside can be obstructive, claustrophobic, concealing, or perhaps protective, as the folds of a garment or even of flesh, impinging on the traveller's experience in a very physical way. At the same time it points us towards a detached way of viewing from a distance, where the roughness of mountain terrain at ground level is smoothed away. It might make us think about a geological timescale, which can be appreciated only from a position of detachment. It points also to the textuality of ancient mountains, fixed in book form, on paper. The folds of Olympus are places of bodily experience and dwelling and at the same time places of the imagination, both solid ground and literary fantasy. Those different possibilities are repeatedly juxtaposed and in some cases inextricably intertwined with each other in ancient Greek and Roman literature.

Of course all of the mountains I talk about in what follows still exist (apart from a few that are imaginary or unidentifiable), and you can go and visit them if you are free to travel, and if you have the time and the money, and the energy and capacity to climb uphill. This is a book about real places: especially the mountains of mainland Greece, but also their counterparts in Italy, in Turkey, in Egypt and elsewhere. One of the great sources of the fascination with mountains in ancient culture, one of things above all that made them human places, was their association with the past. They were places of memory, linked with history and myth and with the celebration of communal identity, in the rituals of sacrifice that took place on Mount Lykaion and on so many other summits. The dominant fantasy of modern mountaineering culture is of the individual standing alone on the summit, where no one has trodden before.[49] Looking at the mountains of the ancient world can help us to see more clearly the power of an alternative and equally inspiring fantasy, that is the idea of the mountain as a place of history and repeated human presence over many generations and millennia. When we stop to think about it, that link between mountains and the past is at the heart of their fascination for us too.[50] That is true even for the great mountains of the Alps and the Himalayas, where part of the thrill is to follow the routes that others have climbed before. For those who do not climb it may be hard to understand why anyone would still want to go to Everest, as a place that it is not just extremely dangerous, but also (at least in the popular imagination) crowded with guided climbers and covered with litter and dead bodies. But the people who go up that mountain do so partly to see for themselves those iconic places from the history of mountaineering where others have climbed or died before them. The mountains of the Mediterranean offer a different kind of thrill, but one which is equally grounded in human history. You can still go to the places of myth, the famous mountain battle sites of the ancient world, the summit altars where ancient worshippers sacrificed for millennia. That is one of the reasons why mountains matter: every time we walk on a mountain or read about it or imagine it, we have the opportunity to experience a sense of connection, albeit sometimes a tenuous and precarious one, with those who have visited it and inhabited it in the past. That role of mountains as places of memory is one of the things that unites ancient and modern responses most powerfully. The mountains of Greece in particular are some of the most wonderful places I know to walk.[51] I hope that this book will in a small way encourage more people to visit them—or to explore them in other ways, if that option is not available. Visiting these places in person has helped me to understand the texts and the history better. It can give you a sense of the scale of particular slopes and summits and their spatial relationship with the cities beneath them. I have tried to make that clear through the occasional first-person passages scattered through the book, especially in part I. It has also given me opportunities to reflect on how we can write the history of mountains in the ancient world from the perspective of our own culture, where mountains are standardly viewed as places of sport and leisure: I have tried to explore some of the challenges involved in that process in the epilogue.

But this is also above all a book about the way in which mountains have been represented and imagined. Some sections were written during the first stages of the coronavirus pandemic in 2020, at a time when going to any of these places in person was a very distant prospect. I spent a lot of time then travelling through places in my memory or in my imagination. I also spent a lot of time reading about ancient mountains and thinking about what these texts have to say to us today, at a time when our understanding of the relationship between humans and the environment has been challenged so starkly. My aim in the chapters that follow is not just to communicate some of the pleasure and fascination of that material, but also to convey something of the way in which ancient portrayals of mountains can confront us with powerful images against which to measure our own relationships with the world around us.

ACKNOWLEDGEMENTS

THIS BOOK is one of a series of publications from a project titled 'Mountains in Ancient Literature and Culture and Their Postclassical Reception', funded by the Leverhulme Trust. I am grateful to the Trust for their generous support. Thanks especially to Dawn Hollis, who has been a wonderful collaborator on the project. My own ideas about the history and representation of mountains in ancient Greek and Roman culture have taken shape in dialogue with Dawn's research on the history of mountains in early modern Europe and beyond. I am grateful to the many colleagues, from a range of different disciplines, who have taken part in the project's workshops and shared their ideas and expertise so generously over the past five years. Special thanks also to Nikoletta Manioti, who co-organised with me a conference on mountains in classical antiquity in St Andrews in 2017 just before the start of the project, and to the contributors to that event.

I have been thinking about ancient mountains for at least a decade, probably longer than that. Many people have helped during that time, too many to list in full (not least the many audiences for papers I have given on related subjects at conferences and research seminars over the past ten years or so), but I would like to thank in particular Gianfranco Agosti, Joanne Anderson, William Bainbridge, Elton Barker, William Barton, Alexis Belis, Carla Benzan, Daniel Berman, Harry Boyd-Carpenter, Chloe Bray, Andrea Brock, Roger Brock, Richard Buxton, Ernest Clark, Jon Coulston, Eleri Cousins, Koen De Temmerman, Veronica della Dora, Tim Duff, Katharine Earnshaw, Lucy Fletcher, Barbara Graziosi, David Greenwood, Stephen Halliwell, Peter Hansen, Tom Harrison, Johannes Haubold, Jon Hesk, Dan Hooley, Sean Ireton, Fergus King, Alice König, Myles Lavan, Achim Lichtenberger, Jeremy McInerney, Georgia Petridou, Alexia Petsalis-Diomidis, Beppe Pezzini, Jonathan Pitches, Verity Platt, Ruben Post, Elaine Rankin, Betsey Robinson, David Gilman Romano, Christopher Schliephake, Sophie Schoess, Rebecca Sweetman, Richard Talbert, Matteo Taufer, Mark Usher, Abigail Walker, John Weeks, Jonathan

Westaway, Tim Whitmarsh, Nicolas Wiater, Gareth Williams, and Greg Woolf, all of whom have helped through inspiring conversations, advice on points of detail, help with images, comments on draft chapters, invitations to give talks, and in some cases by spending time with me in the mountains.

I am grateful to all at Princeton University Press, especially to Ben Tate, Josh Drake, Lisa Black, Jill Harris, Jennifer Harris, and to the anonymous readers for their encouragement and wise advice.

Above all, thanks to Alice, Eliza, Rory, and Serena.

PART I

Mountains and the Divine

1

Summit Altars

Divine Presence and Human Culture

When the god Zeus comes down from Mount Olympus[1] to Mount Ida above the city of Troy in Book 8 of the *Iliad*, he installs himself in a space that is poised strangely between the human and divine spheres. The poet tells us that Zeus 'came to Ida with its many springs, the mother of wild beasts, to Gargaros, where his sanctuary (τέμενος) was and his smoking altar' (*Iliad* 8.47–48).[2] Later, in Book 14, he is seduced here by his wife, Hera. The earth on the mountain's summit sends up a growth of new flowers as a bed for them to lie on: that passage has repeatedly been taken as an allegorical one, to describe the bounty that springs from the union of different natural forces.[3] 'Do not be afraid', Zeus says, 'that any god or man will see us, for I will cover us with a golden cloud' (14.342–44). Only the poet's divinely inspired voice can pierce that cloud and allow us to spy on the opening moments of their lovemaking, just as the voice of the poet is the only source that can give us access to the charmed life of the gods on Mount Olympus. And yet in other ways Mount Ida is a place of regular human presence. The word 'sanctuary' or 'precinct' (τέμενος) in the passage quoted earlier implies a clearly delineated, presumably human-made space surrounding Zeus's altar on the summit. And then in the climactic battle scene of the poem, as Achilles is chasing Hector round the walls of Troy, closing in on him, the poem slows for a moment to give us a divine perspective. All the gods are watching, but it is Zeus who speaks first: 'my heart is mourning for Hector, who has burned the thighs of many oxen in my honour on the peaks of many-valleyed Ida' (*Iliad* 22.169–71). It seems that Hector has been himself, many times, to this place of divine mystery and pleasure, to sacrifice to the gods.

Those passages are typical of a tension that runs right through the long history of representing mountains in ancient Greek and Roman literature. The mountains of the Mediterranean were both divine and human places. Part I of this book explores the intertwining of those two different perspectives in a selection of texts written over a period of more than 1,000 years, from the epic poetry of archaic Greece[4] through to the Christian pilgrimage writing of late antiquity. In order to understand those portrayals, however, we need to look first at the wider context of ancient religious practice.[5] Mountains were dwelling places of the gods within mythical narrative,[6] and places associated with divine epiphanies and miracles beyond human understanding, but they were at the same time places of human presence where one might gain special access to the gods via sacrifice.

Those practices are in many respects quite alien to what we are familiar with from modern Western culture. The eighteenth and nineteenth centuries did see an increase in 'sacralisation' of the mountains, for example in the increasingly common use of religious language to describe mountain experience.[7] In many cases that involved seeing divine presence in nature through an encounter with the sublime.[8] Mountains have a power to inspire awe and astonishment that can transport us momentarily beyond our usual human perspective on the world. This idea in itself had ancient precedents.[9] From the very late eighteenth century onwards it became common to erect crosses on peaks in the Alps and elsewhere in Europe,[10] partly in imitation of earlier practices of mountain pilgrimage which had their origin in the Christian culture of late antiquity. But those strands of religious thinking in postclassical culture do not help us much in entering into the experience of those involved in the processions and sacrifices that wound their way to the hilltops and peaks of the Mediterranean over many hundreds and even thousands of years. It takes a certain effort of the imagination, along with close attention to the still patchy and inaccessible archaeological record, to be able to understand what that might have been like.

Let us go back first to Mount Lykaion to look a little more closely at what lies on the slopes beneath the summit. This was a site that mattered for Arkadian identity.[11] It must have been viewed as significant partly because it stood beyond the boundaries of normal human civilisation. We should probably imagine hundreds of people travelling out from the cities to the mountain for fairly short periods for festival occasions, before returning to their homes. Sacrifice at this kind of location was a way of integrating wilderness within the culture of the city and a way of asserting control over the whole of a city's territory (or in this case cities in the plural, since Mount Lykaion seems to have been a focus for the region of Arkadia as a whole). And the idea of encountering space outside civilisation may have had a particular significance in an

FIGURE 1.1. Ruined columns from the temple of Zeus Lykaios, with the summit of Mount Lykaion behind. Photo: author.

Arkadian context. The Arkadians had a reputation in the ancient world, like many mountain communities, for being a very ancient people, and for being distant from the norms of urban civilisation, not least because of the poverty of the region—for example in the common image of them as 'acorn eaters'. That image of a wild culture took on a more idealised form in the poetic stereotype of Arkadia as a pastoral paradise.

And yet we need to be cautious about an excessively romanticised view of the ancient Mount Lykaion as wilderness. The peak itself was very far from being wild, especially in the later centuries of its history. This was a built environment. Just below the summit stood the precinct of Zeus, which seems to have been more than 100 metres in length and 50 metres wide. Two column bases still stand there (figure 1.1), not far from the base of the summit cone.

Zeus was not the only god worshipped here: we know from the second-century CE travel writer Pausanias (who will feature again in a later chapter) that there were two other sites, in honour of Pan and Parrhasian Apollo, also on the mountainside.[12] Close to the latter was a place thought by some to have been the birthplace of the god Zeus.[13] Large numbers of surviving coins produced in the fifth and then again in the fourth century BCE show images of Zeus Lykaios, perhaps a depiction of a throned statue of Zeus which stood as a cult object in the shrine. These coins seem to have acted as expressions of Arkadian identity, although the political unity of the region as a whole was always fragile.[14] Further down, at a height of roughly 1,200 metres on the mountainside, is the stadium and the hippodrome (figure 1.2), roughly 300 metres long, the only fully visible example of a horse-racing track in the whole of Greece; also a row of stone seating or steps, a fountain house, a bathhouse, a stoa 67 metres in length, and another building commonly identified as a hotel, but which is more likely to have been an administrative building for the sanctuary and a venue for dining, with a partly subterranean passage leading from it towards the stadium and hippodrome.[15] Most of these buildings date from the second half of the fourth century BCE; by this stage the summit altar seems to have dropped out of use as a place of sacrifice, as the main focus for ritual activity shifted a little way down the mountainside. They were constructed primarily for the great festival of the Lykaia, which had been held there (probably every four years, but perhaps every two) also through much of the archaic and classical periods.[16] Some scholars think that it may even have predated the games at Olympia, just over 20 miles to the west (in line with the claims of the Elder Pliny, who describes Mount Lykaion as the site of the very first athletic contests in Greek history).[17] It was a famous festival. Pindar refers to the Lykaia repeatedly in his victory odes, in lists of the festivals where his patrons have won victories.[18] Two inscriptions recovered from the site, both dating from the late fourth century BCE, list victors in the standard range of ancient Greek athletic and horse-racing events—the majority of them local athletes from Arkadia, but also including a number of famous competitors from much farther afield, as far away as Macedonia and Rhodes and Sicily.[19] Like all ancient athletic festivals it would have been viewed as an opportunity to celebrate the communal identity of the city or region that hosted it. In the victory lists from the festival we find unusually frequent use of the regional identifier 'Arkas' ('Arkadian'), in contrast with the usual custom of identifying oneself with one's city, which suggests that Mount Lykaion was viewed as a particularly appropriate place for displaying Arkadian identity.[20] Presumably hundreds or even thousands of spectators attended. It is hard to think of a more vivid illustration of the fact that going up mountains could be a regular and important activity for the inhabitants of the ancient world.

FIGURE 1.2. View from the summit of Mount Lykaion looking northeast towards the stadium and hippodrome. Photo: author.

Memory and Embodied Experience

Mountains like Mount Lykaion were thus places of memory. They were widely viewed as ancient places, linked with pre-human events in mythical narrative.[21] It seems likely that those involved in mountain rituals would have felt a sense of engagement with that past in their ascents, a thrill at being momentarily close to the places of myth, even as they knew that that old world of divine presence was hard to access in everyday experience. Equally important, however, was the way in which the mountains linked communities with their own human pasts, as locations of repeated sacrifice over many generations. One function of mountain ritual was to assert control over the edges of a city's territory, and to win divine support for the city's land and institutions.[22] For many cities the visibility and proximity of their mountains would have helped to maintain those links. It was not only the view from the summit that mattered in mountain ritual, with its ability to encompass the territory down below, but also the view upwards from the city. When you see the smoke of sacrifice on the mountain you know that you are seeing a view that generations of others have seen before.

These were also places of bodily engagement. As we have seen already in the preface, there has been a reaction over the past few decades against approaches that envisage landscape as terrain viewed from a distance, with their implications of an outsider or elitist viewpoint. Some scholars have emphasised instead the way in which human experience of landscape involves a bodily immersion appealing to all of the senses, where landscape and the body are mutually intertwined and give meaning to each other. Tim Ingold has used the phrase 'taskscape' to describe the way in which particular spaces become marked by repetitive human actions, often over many generations, and in turn give meaning and direction to those who pass through them in their day-to-day lives.[23] The mountains of the Mediterranean must have been taskscapes in exactly that sense—not only their lower slopes, which were used for farming and other kinds of productive activity, as we shall see further in part IV, but even their remote summits, with their paths and their altars, where worshippers toiled their way upwards in procession, and where the detritus of centuries of sacrifice was piled together, as a feature of the landscape that was fixed but also nevertheless grew year by year with each sacrifice. The physical experience of the mountain's slopes and summit must have helped to make the experience of memory and the sense of access to the divine more intense and more personal. At the same time these mountains were places of performance, associated with kinds of bodily engagement set apart from normal day-to-day life, as mountains still are, albeit in different ways, in the present, not least in the cultures of mountaineering.[24]

Of course it is difficult to reconstruct those experiences precisely. That is the problem we face. Detailed accounts of involvement in mountain ritual from the ancient world are very rare. There has been a tradition over the past two centuries of interpreting that absence in rather patronising terms as a sign of the relatively primitive nature of Greco-Roman interactions with landscape, on the assumption that people who live close to mountains are less likely to describe them and engage with them with the sophistication that comes from elite detachment.[25] It is easy to see why that is a tempting view, but in some manifestations it can lead us to endorse a self-congratulatory exceptionalism, which sees modern engagement with landscape as uniquely sophisticated. How do we move beyond that explanation? Seeing these places for ourselves can help. You get a sense of the scale of the mountains, a sense of what it might have been like to move through them on paths that in some cases must be largely unchanged today, of their proximity to and intervisibility with communities on the plain and with each other, and even something of the thrill of standing in places where others have stood before over many millennia. But we also need to be aware of the distance between modern and ancient. There is a risk of imposing an outsider viewpoint on spaces that we cannot possibly experience exactly as they were experienced in the ancient world.[26] The alternative, I suggest, is to try to read the textual evidence with more alertness to the theme of embodied experience. When we do that, we begin to see traces of the kind of corporeal engagement with landscape and with the divine that I have been describing, side by side with more detached ways of interacting with mountain terrain.

Mediterranean Mountain Religion

Before we turn to the texts, however, it may be helpful to set out in a bit more detail some of the range and variety of mountain religion in the ancient Mediterranean. When we do that, we see some remarkable continuities across centuries and across cultures, but also lots of local variations—just as the surviving literary depictions of mountain religion project their own distinctive visions against a background of shared assumptions and practices.

There are similar sites to Mount Lykaion right across the Mediterranean.[27] We know of nearly 100 ancient shrines in Greece on or near mountain summits, some of them just from literary sources, but many with identifiable archaeological remains.[28] There must be others not yet identified. Mountain shrines rarely included monumental buildings, so their traces are often inconspicuous. Some important summits in Greece have military installations on them, and that has hindered investigation too. Occasionally the process of building those installations has led to new discoveries, as on Mount Parnes in Attica: a rescue excavation conducted there in 1959 during the construction of a military barracks uncovered a 100-square-metre ash altar very similar to the one on Mount Lykaion (including among other things around 3,000 iron knives, along with the usual pottery and bone fragments), apparently confirming ancient literary reports of a pair of altars to Zeus on the summit.[29] And yet even with those problems of neglect and inaccessibility there is more than enough for us to see just how widespread the practice of mountaintop ritual was. Despite their architectural modesty these are some of the most spectacular and undervisited ancient sites in the whole of Greece.

Summit sanctuaries were most often in honour of Zeus,[30] but there were also countless sanctuaries on the lower slopes, in honour of many different gods. Artemis is a good example: her sanctuaries tended to be located not on summits but in border territories and in passes, in line with her role as a goddess who watched over places associated with danger and threat.[31] In many cultures around the world, including some ancient Near Eastern cultures, mountains have themselves been sacred objects of worship,[32] but there is very little sign that the same was true for the ancient Greeks and Romans,[33] although we do see occasional traces in Greek poetry and art of what are probably quite ancient traditions of personifying mountain gods.[34] Of the summit altars, not all are ash altars—in fact we know of only ten securely identified examples in Greece. In other cases, the altars for sacrifice were made of stone or rubble, or in some cases were even cut into the rock.[35] The finds at Mount Lykaion are fairly typical: bone fragments, pottery, votive offerings of many different types, often including figurines. And it is typical too in chronological terms: the number of sanctuaries with clear evidence for extensive use as early as the Mycenaean period is small; it often seems to be the case that these sites flourished as places of sacrifice, like Mount Lykaion, above all in archaic Greece. Nevertheless there is a lot of variation even in chronological terms, and in several cases, as we shall see, there are even signs of a revival of ritual activity at pagan mountaintop shrines in the Christian centuries of late antiquity.

When we look beyond mainland Greece and the islands of the Aegean some things change and some things stay the same. Crete, for example, has its own distinctive culture of mountaintop religion, in the remains of dozens of what are usually referred to as 'peak sanctuaries' from the Minoan period, most of them dating roughly from 2000–1500 BCE.[36] Most of the evidence for ritual activity is in the form of votive offerings, often figurines, some of them apparently representations of worshippers at the shrines themselves, and also large numbers of pottery fragments which suggest that feasting and the pouring of libations were important. Sacrifice, however, seems to have been very scarce, and that sets the Cretan sites apart from their Greek equivalents. Even more so than in mainland Greece, these sites tend to have been situated on relatively low summits close to communities, rather than remote mountaintops. Visibility between sanctuary and community and between different sanctuary sites was clearly very important.[37]

Asia Minor too is rich with mountain shrines.[38] Strabo talks about the large number of sanctuaries maintained by the Paphlagonians in the remote territory of Mount Olgassys (modern Ilgaz Dağları), which is part of the Pontic

Alps, the chain of mountains, rising to more than 2,000 metres, that stands to the south of the Black Sea in northern Turkey.[39] A little farther east the temple of Zeus Stratios on the summit of Büyük Evliya, east of Amaseia, was a place of sacrifice and dedications from communities in the whole surrounding area of Pontus. Mithridates, the great enemy of Rome, is said to have offered a victory sacrifice there.[40] All of this is in line with what we find in the Greek sites farther west, but Asia Minor is also a good place to see the influence of the rather different Near Eastern traditions which viewed mountains themselves as sacred, rather than just as places connected with particular divine figures. The worship of the so-called Mother Goddess was widespread across Asia Minor. She seems to have been equated with some of the mountains of the region rather than just worshipped on them—for example with the various mountains named Dindymos in Phrygia, Tmolos above the city of Sardis, Ida in western Asia Minor above Troy, all of which gave water to the plains and life to the flocks which were driven up onto their pastures in the summer.[41] Farther south, Mount Kasios, modern Jebel Aqra (Kel Dağı in Turkish), is another place where we can see glimpses of a pre-Greek history of mountaintop ritual. Here again the mountain itself was an object of worship. It was a sacred place for the Hittites to the north in the late Bronze Age: their name for the mountain was Hazzi, and the mountain god who occupied it was Teshub. To the south the Caananites worshipped the storm god Baal and named the mountain Sapuna. We know from texts discovered in Ras Shamra, the ancient port city at the foot of the mountain, just north of Latakia in northern Syria, that Baal is said to have lived on the mountain summit in an ornate palace built for him by the gods, along with the goddess Anat. When the mountain began to be a place of sacrifice for the Greek populations in the area—the first attested example is from the late fourth century BCE—they inherited a site that had already been used for hundreds of years by the cultures that preceded them. And those many centuries of sacrifice have left their mark on the mountaintop, which is the site of the biggest ash altar surviving from the ancient world: 55 metres wide and 8 metres deep, more than five times head height—although now the site of a Turkish military base.[42]

In Italy and the western Mediterranean too mountains and hills were places of the gods. There is evidence for a distinctive religious culture in the Alps, which increasingly combined local religious tradition with Roman influences as Roman involvement in the region intensified. For example, the temple of Jupiter Poeninus stood at a height of 2,472 metres above sea level on the Great Saint Bernard Pass; it was previously a site sacred to a local deity Poeninus.

Surviving from there is a remarkable series of fifty-one bronze votive inscriptions, most of them dedicated by Roman soldiers, asking the god for safe passage.[43] Farther south, perhaps the most important mountain site of all in mainland Italy was Mount Albanus (modern Monte Cavo), thirteen miles southeast of Rome. It is the highest point of the Alban hills, and the site of a famous shrine consecrated to Jupiter Latiaris. This was a place of memory for the Roman people. Celebrated there every year was the festival of the Feriae Latinae, where all the members of the old Latin League (a grouping of communities in Latium which first formed to resist Rome, but later came under Roman leadership) would offer sacrifice as a way of reaffirming their loyalty. Officiating was one of the most important tasks given to the consuls and other senior Roman officials—in fact every magistrate of Rome was required to attend. You can still see the remains of the road that led up to the summit temple. In 44 BCE, Julius Caesar, after celebrating the Feriae Latinae on Mount Albanus, entered the city in a solemn procession, and was proclaimed by some sections of the population as king. At the centre of the ritual was the sacrifice of a pure white heifer which had never been yoked, provided by the Romans. The representatives of the Latin cities would receive a share of the sacrificial meat in return for their gifts of lamb and cheese and milk. Once a year, then, this mountain would be the focus of an extraordinary display of power and community, attended by some of the most important political figures in the city of Rome, using that space outside the city and elevated above it in order to celebrate their history and their cohesion.[44]

The Summit Altars of Mainland Greece

But it is mainland Greece where we see the greatest concentration of these sites, and the ones that are most relevant to the texts that I want to look at in most of the rest of this chapter. The Peloponnese is full of evocative and surprisingly accessible mountain sites (many of them with roads or dirt tracks leading almost to the summits). The vast majority have had little or no archaeological attention by comparison with Mount Lykaion. To the south of Mount Lykaion, for example, and visible from it, is Mount Ithome,[45] which stands at just 800 metres above sea level, closely above the extensive remains of the ancient city of Messene (figure 1.3); the relatively low altitude of the summit is a sign that prominence was more important than absolute height in the categorisation of mountains in ancient Greece.[46] We know from Pausanias that there was a sanctuary of Zeus there.[47] Plutarch tells us that Philip V of

FIGURE 1.3. View south from the summit of Mount Ithome over ancient Messene. Photo: author.

Macedon climbed to the summit temple in the late third century BCE, after a bloody intervention in the civil conflict within the city, 'in order to sacrifice to Zeus and to see the place'.[48] The word θεωρήσων ('in order to see') is the standard word for the kind of viewing that accompanies visits to religious sites and festivals (the gap between tourism and pilgrimage was much less clear in the ancient world than it is for us). But there is almost no sign of the ancient cult on the summit plateau today: most of the space is taken up by deserted monastery buildings. It is possible that the ancient sanctuary had an altar cut out of the rock, but if so it has now been built over, and the stone tripod base which is said to have been built into the walls of the monastery is hard to find. But what you can still experience is the ancient descent from the top of the mountain to the city below. As you start down from the summit on the dusty track to the east, you see a faded sign pointing off into the undergrowth to the right, leading to a path that winds through undergrowth over rocky ground all

FIGURE 1.4. Mount Apesas with its flat top from the stadium at Nemea. Photo: author.

the way down the mountainside. It is not much used: when I went down by that route on a visit in 2014 it was overgrown, with spiders' webs stretched across the path; sometimes the way ahead was hard to spot. It brings you out finally opposite the tavernas in the village of Mavromati, at the Clepsydra spring with its mulberry tree. Pausanias tells us that water was carried every day up to the summit from that same spring in a ritual designed to commemorate the washing of the infant Zeus by the two Nymphs, one of them named Ithome, who nursed him.[49] (Ithome was one of many mountains, including Mount Lykaion, which were claimed as Zeus's birthplace or his place of upbringing). Presumably this is the path they took, or another one very much like it.

Farther north and east in the Peloponnese is Mount Apesas (modern Phoukas),[50] which stands above the stadium at Nemea, the site of one of the four great athletic festivals of mainland Greece (figure 1.4). It seems likely that the cult of Zeus on the summit and the festival below were linked with each other. According to some ancient accounts there is an etymological connection between the name of the mountain and the Greek word *aphesis*, the starting area for horse races at the games. The mountain's distinctive flat top is recognisable from a great distance, and well placed also for viewing many of the other religiously important summits of the Peloponnese. There is no way of telling for sure, but it seems likely that this kind of 'intervisibility' enhanced the sense that mountaintop worship gave one access to a community which stretched right across the Greek world. You can still see today the remains of a huge ash altar at the eastern edge of the summit plateau: ashy soil, the usual mixture of pottery and bone fragments. It may have been as much as 50 metres wide.

And then to the east again is Mount Arachnaion,[51] close to the ancient site of Epidauros near Argos. Pausanias mentions the existence of two altars, of Zeus and Hera, on the summit, where people made offerings for rain.[52] Throughout much of the nineteenth and twentieth centuries these altars were associated with stones found on the saddle between the two summits, but that identification has since been corrected: in fact the altars were situated on the western summit, which stands at around 1,200 metres. This too seems to have been a very ancient site: as at Mount Lykaion, there have been extensive finds of Mycenean artefacts, including large amounts of pottery, and more than 100 fragments of terracotta figurines.[53] The mountain dominates the view to the east from Argos and Nafplio: you can spot it straight away by the wind turbines on the summit ridge. It is not much visited, but it is a strangely evocative site despite that. You get to the top by a wide, ugly track, carved out of the mountainside for the wind farm. It was empty of people when I went there, apart from some engineers mending one of the huge turbines away in the distance. There was just a fox sitting on the path ahead of me, and some swifts and ravens in the breeze at the summit. Once again, there is not a vast amount to see: some desultory plastic sheeting from the last excavations, lots of rubbly rock, and a couple of brick foundations, one unidentified, one from a ruined chapel to Prophet Elias. But on the ground there are hundreds of pottery fragments, concentrated in two patches just to the south of the summit marker. It feels now like a place outside civilisation. And yet people did come here, trudging up the mountainside to make their offerings and sacrifices, for hundreds if not thousands of years, and what they left is still there for you to see. As they stood on the summit they would have seen the cities of the coast spread out to the view before them (figure 1.5), with the knowledge that their fellow citizens were looking up to the smoke of sacrifice from below.

If you are in Athens, the easiest mountains to reach are the ones that you can see ringing the city on all sides. These too were places of regular human

FIGURE 1.5. View from the summit of Mount Arachnaion, looking west to Argos. Photo: author.

presence. Attica seems to have had particular enthusiasm for the worship of Zeus. Pausanias tells us that

> the mountains of the Athenians also have statues of the gods on them. On Pentelikon is a statue of Athene, on Hymettos, one of Zeus, along with altars of Zeus Ombrios [Zeus of the rain] and Apollo the Foreseer. And on Parnes is a bronze Zeus Parnethios, and an altar of Zeus Semaleos [sign-giving Zeus]. There is also on Parnes another altar, and they sacrifice on it, sometimes invoking Zeus Ombrios and sometimes Zeus Apemios [Zeus averter-of-evil]. Anchesmos is not a large mountain; it has a statue of Zeus Anchesmios. (Pausanias, *Periegesis* 1.32.2)

The archaeological evidence backs up Pausanias' account. The most important sanctuary, close to the summit of Mount Hymettos, which stands just ten miles or so to the east of Athens, is surrounded by antennae and military buildings. Access was forbidden for several decades in the late twentieth century, but these days you can drive right up to it: it stands on the left, a few hundred metres before the end of the road. As you go up, you pass cyclists and walkers, first through the trees but then emerging onto the bare upper slopes of the mountain. The remains of the altar stand in a natural depression about half a mile north of the highest peak, without a view. Findings included a large volume of pottery fragments inscribed with some of the earliest surviving examples of written Greek from the whole of Attica, dating from the seventh to late sixth centuries BCE. It seems likely that the majority of offerings brought to Zeus at the altar were offerings for rain, probably for the whole of the Athenian plain to the west of the mountain rather than just Athens, in line with Pausanias' report of an altar to Zeus Ombrios ('Rainy Zeus') on the summit. That is no doubt in part because of the mountain's status as a weather indicator: clouds on the summit tend to indicate approaching rain. The role of Zeus as rain god is widely paralleled, both in Attica—at the sanctuary of Zeus Ombrios on Mount Parnes—and beyond, on the island of Aigina, at Megara, and also on Mount Lykaion according to Pausanias.[54] We have an inscription from the island of Kos, dating from about 200 BCE, recording a decision made by 'the association of those who process together to Zeus of Rain (Zeus Hyetios)'.[55] On Mount Hymettos we should probably imagine not just formal processions of that type, but also visits by individuals to bring dedications to the mountaintop without sacrificing: the usual combination of ash and burnt animal bones is mixed with a strikingly large volume of pottery fragments. The bulk of the material dates from between the twelfth and sixth centuries BCE, but there is some later material as well, from the Hellenistic period, and even fragments of 120 lamps from the fourth to fifth centuries CE.[56] Those signs of a revival of attention to mountain sanctuaries in the imperial period and late antiquity have a number of parallels in sites from mainland Greece.[57]

And then when you go north, you come very quickly to some of the most famous and most sacred of all mountains of ancient Greek culture. Some of these mountains are bigger and higher than their counterparts in the Peloponnese, and it is striking that they often show fewer signs of mountaintop ritual. It does seem to be the case that lower and more accessible mountains were more likely to be places of sacrifice, especially when they had an intimate spatial relationship to particular communities: Mount Ithome is a good example of both. The huge bulk of Mount Parnassos, for example, with its double summit, shows no sign of an altar, even though it was such a crucial place of divine presence in mythical narrative: to some extent mythical and ritual engagement with the divine seem to have been separate from each other, at least in this case.

For many years it was assumed that the same was true for Mount Olympus, and even now the evidence for mountaintop sacrifice there is little known. The textual evidence is brief and obscure, and the archaeological finds have been unspectacular. Their implications, however, are fascinating. People did come to these summits, regularly and religiously, for centuries on end, to offer sacrifice. That fact is almost unacknowledged within modern scholarship on the Homeric and Hesiodic Olympus. Solinus, writing probably in the third century CE, talks about an altar on the summit, and tells us that offerings left there are found again undisturbed a year later.[58] We find a similar view ascribed to Plutarch by an ancient commentator on Aristotle, and also in one of the works of Augustine: both explain that phenomenon by the claim that Olympus is above the clouds, and so windless.[59] All three are presumably writing from hearsay, and Solinus in particular seems like a doubtful source, given that so much of his work is taken up with the collection of marvels, many of them even more implausible than this one. But the material evidence for sacrifice is unequivocal. Traditionally the cult to Zeus which all of these texts refer to was associated with the chapel of Saint Elias on the northernmost peak, Profitis Elias, but the only significant remains are those which were found on the southern peak of Agios Antonios (which stands at 2,817 metres, just 100 metres lower than the highest summit Mytikas) between 1961 and 1965 during the building of a meteorological station: among other items ash, bone fragments, fragments of pottery, and three inscriptions to Zeus Olympios, two of them Hellenistic, one of them perhaps later, from the imperial period.[60] The third mentions a priesthood, which suggests an organised cult of the kind usually associated with important sanctuaries. Perhaps the most remarkable discovery of all was a set of coins, some of them Hellenistic, from the fourth century BCE onwards, but many of them from the fourth or even fifth centuries CE, which suggests that the sanctuary may have been visited most of all in late antiquity, even after the christianisation of the Roman Empire.[61] The worship of Zeus was widespread in the surrounding area, too, especially in the city of Dion on the northern slopes of Olympus, where the sanctuary of Zeus Olympios is still visible. It seems to have been important in the Hellenistic period in particular. This was also the venue for the festival of the Olympia which took place every four years from the late fifth century BCE onwards, with musical and athletic contests, the former in honour of the Muses. The festival of the Olympia at Dion is not the same as the original Olympic games at Pisa, hundreds of miles away in the Peloponnese: dozens of other festivals in the Greek world tried to share something of the prestige of the Olympics by taking on their name, but Dion, unlike those others, clearly had a good excuse for doing so. Regular processions of people and animals for sacrifice must have wound their way from the city up the mountain, on the same tracks that are used still today, as they did in so many other parts of the Greek world too.[62]

2

Mountains in Archaic Greek Poetry

The Homeric Hymns

Some of the most exhilarating fantasy images of mountains from classical antiquity come from the Homeric hymns—from Mount Ida, 'mother of wild beasts', where Aphrodite seduces the mortal Anchises in the *Homeric Hymn to Aphrodite*, to the image of Pan racing over the 'peaks of the mountains and the rocky tracks' in the *Homeric Hymn to Pan*. These texts seem to have been composed over the course of several centuries, mostly between about 700 and 500 BCE, so it would be misleading to read them as if they are part of an intricate single design. Nevertheless they do clearly respond to each other and to the Homeric epics, whose even more complex portrayal of mountains I will turn to later. The combined body of archaic epic—Homer, Hesiod, the remains of the Epic Cycle, the Homeric hymns—tells a broadly coherent story about the developing relationship between the gods, and between gods and humans. They tell first of the formation of the world, and the struggles between divine powers before the existence of humans, and then of the formation of the Olympian pantheon, which involves the absorption of new gods into the community on Olympus. They also tell of the heroic age, where the gods and mortals are separated by a huge gulf which may nevertheless be bridged occasionally by personal contact; and then last of its aftermath in the present day, the world of these poems' original audiences, where that kind of contact is a distant memory, and where access to the gods comes only through prayer and sacrifice, and through established rituals and routines of cult worship linked with particular locations.[1] The mountains play a key role in the unfolding of that story. They also function as a particularly appropriate setting for the Homeric hymns' explorations of the interplay between mortal and divine.[2]

There are two main strands in the hymns' representation of human-divine contact. The first is in the poems' stories about divine presence in the mountains, and especially epiphanies (that is, appearances of gods to humans). The community of the gods on Mount Olympus is impossibly distant from human presence, but just occasionally on other mountains, and in some other special places at lower altitude, the gods can show themselves to mortals. By far the longest example is from the *Homeric Hymn to Aphrodite*, which fits closely with Richard Buxton's characterisation of mountains in Greek myth as places where 'things normally separate are brought together'.[3] The hymn tells the story of how the goddess Aphrodite falls in love with Anchises, who is pasturing his cattle on the slopes of Mount Ida, near to Troy. And yet the poem also includes an inbuilt reminder of the impossibility of any equivalent encounter in the present day. Aphrodite's divine status is very prominent in the description of her journey to the mountain: she goes to her sanctuary at Paphos, where she is bathed by the Graces with divine oil, and clothes herself luxuriously, and then travels with magical speed: 'high up among the clouds, making her way swiftly, she came to Ida with its many springs (Ἴδην... πολυπίδακα), the mother of wild beasts and she went straight across the mountain to the farmstead' (*Homeric Hymn to Aphrodite* 67–69), with wolves, lions, bears and leopards fawning on her and mating in her wake. Mount Ida was particularly marked by erotic connotations. The phrase 'Ida with its many springs (Ἴδην πολυπίδακα), the mother of wild beasts' is also used among other things in introducing Hera's seduction of Zeus on Mount Ida in *Iliad* 14.283. The detail of Aphrodite's beautification in lines 59–63 also repeats almost word for word sections from Hera's preparations for that encounter in *Iliad* 14.169–72, and Aphrodite's journey to the mountain echoes Hera's at *Iliad* 14.225–30 and 280–85.[4] Those parallels—whether we assume that the *Hymn to Aphrodite* is imitating those Homeric passages or drawing on a common formula of divine adornment—emphasise the way in which Anchises is being exposed temporarily to the divine sphere.[5] Anchises and Aphrodite sleep together, like Zeus and Hera, in this place outside the usual boundaries of human civilisation, lying on the skins of lions and bears Anchises has killed in the mountains. Then when Anchises awakes, Aphrodite reveals her identity, towering above him now from her true, divine height, and gives parting instructions that their child, Aeneas, is to be brought up by the Nymphs on the mountainside. The hymn thus offers us a fantasy image of the mountain as a zone where the boundaries between gods and humans can be breached. At the same time, however, the poet repeatedly draws our attention to the gap in status between Aphrodite and Anchises. He also makes it clear that such encounters belong to the past. One of the text's functions—one of its contributions to the story of the development of divine and human relations that all archaic epic participates in—is to dramatise the moment of rupture between the heroic age and the present, for the poet implies that Aphrodite's desire is part of Zeus's plan to put an end to the couplings of gods with mortals which have led to the birth of heroes: Aphrodite's humiliation is such that she will never again impose desire for mortals on her fellow divinities.[6] In the *Homeric Hymn to Aphrodite*, then, the mountain is a place where human association with the divine becomes at least fleetingly and temporarily imaginable, but we are also made aware that it is in practice a distant and unlikely prospect.

Side by side with narratives of divine epiphany are details of a second, very different way of accessing the divine, through ritual. We hear repeatedly that the mountains are the territory of one or other of the gods.[7] One way of fleshing out that notion is to tell stories of what they have done in particular mountain locations, or to celebrate the mountains as divine birthplaces,[8] or in some cases to describe the gods in general terms ranging over unnamed mountain and hills.[9] The alternative is to describe the human act of establishing and maintaining rituals in honour of the gods in particular locations. That is not to say that we should view the Homeric hymns as celebrations of specific local cults:[10] it is clear that these are in many respects very Panhellenic texts, concerned with the shared culture that united the many different communities of Greece, and that their interest in the absorption of individual divinities into the pantheon on Mount Olympus is a way of expressing the development of a Panhellenic vision of religious and poetic identity in the centuries during which the hymns were composed.[11] But they do nevertheless repeatedly show an interest in the real experience of mountaintop ritual. There is one glimpse of that in the *Homeric Hymn to Aphrodite*. On seeing Aphrodite, Anchises responds at once to her more-than-mortal beauty, before he knows her true identity (although of course we cannot know for sure how much he really suspects and how much of this is flattery): 'perhaps you are one of the Nymphs who inhabit the beautiful groves, or one of those Nymphs who live on this beautiful mountain.... For you on some mountaintop, in a place which is visible all around (περιφαινομένῳ ἐνὶ χώρῳ), I will set up an altar, and I will make beautiful sacrifices to you at all the proper seasons' (*Homeric Hymn to Aphrodite* 97–102).[12] The word translated here as mountaintop (σκοπιῇ) can be used for a lookout post, so Anchises may be imagining how it is to look down from this imaginary shrine, but this passage also reminds us of the importance of making mountaintop sanctuaries visible from below: the implication is that the shrine will act as a substitute for the beauty that Anchises is gazing on as he speaks. It is unlikely that the poet has a specific cult of Aphrodite or any other divinity on Mount Ida in mind.[13] But these verses are clearly composed for a world where the general principle of mountaintop sacrifice was commonplace. At least this way of being close to the gods will remain.

There are other examples too. In the *Homeric Hymn to Demeter* we see Demeter giving orders for a temple to be built in honour of Persephone by all the people of Eleusis on a 'projecting hill' above the spring of Kallichoros (*Homeric Hymn to Demeter* 272). The *Hymn to Delian Apollo* twice tells us that 'all peaks and tall promontories of the high mountains and rivers flowing to the sea are dear to you' (*Homeric Hymn to Delian Apollo* 144–45, repeating almost identical lines at 22–23). But it also makes clear Apollo's special affection for 'rocky Kynthos' (*Homeric Hymn to Delian Apollo* 141), the mountain on the island of Delos where he was born, and refers to the festivals the people of Delos hold there in his honour. Earlier the poet has described the various places Apollo's mother Leto visited while she was in labour, many of them mountains—'Thracian Athos . . . Pelion's high peaks . . . the shady mountains of Ida . . . the steep mountain of Autokane . . . rocky Mimas . . . the steep peaks of Mykale' (*Homeric Hymn to Delian Apollo* 30–46)—before she is finally received by Delos, coming to rest on Mount Kynthos, in return for a promise that the island will be able to host sacrifices to her son in future. In one remarkable passage we hear that 'all Delos blossomed with gold as does a mountaintop with woodland flowers' (χρυσῷ δ' ἄρα Δῆλος ἅπασα . . . ἤνθησ', ὡς ὅτε τε ῥίον οὔρεος ἄνθεσιν ὕλης) (*Homeric Hymn to Apollo* 135–40). This passage too might recall for some readers the atmosphere of divine presence in *Iliad* 14, where the summit of Mount Ida blossoms spontaneously with flowers in accompaniment to Hera's seduction of Zeus. The gold of Delos stands as an earthly, human substitute.

Those two ways of accessing the divine correspond to the two spheres of myth and ritual whose complex interrelation is one of the most distinctive features in the long history of ancient Greek and Roman thinking about the gods.[14] But do these texts reflect in other ways too—beyond these fantasies of divine epiphany, and beyond their interest in the existence of mountain rituals—on what it might have meant for human actors to experience divine presence in mountain landscapes? And is there any sign of the kind of embodied engagement with landscape that I have suggested must have been part of the ancient experience of mountains, both in religious contexts and otherwise? I want to explore those questions, finally, through a discussion of one much shorter and less well known text, the *Homeric Hymn to Pan*. This hymn seems to have been composed later than many of the others, probably in the fifth century BCE,[15] but for all that it encapsulates many of the most typical features of mountain representation in the hymns. It portrays the mountains as divine playgrounds which are at first sight utterly apart from human presence, but which also turn out on closer inspection to raise the possibility of contact between human and divine perspectives. We meet Pan on the peaks that he loves:

> he goes (φοιτᾷ) through wooded meadows, together with the dancing Nymphs who tread (στείβουσι) on the summits of some sheer cliff (κατ' αἰγίλιπος πέτρης . . . κάρηνα). . . . He has as his territory every snowy crest (πάντα λόφον νιφόεντα) and the peaks of the mountains (κορυφὰς ὀρέων) and the rocky tracks. He goes here and there (φοιτᾷ δ' ἔνθα καὶ ἔνθα) through the thick undergrowth, sometimes drawn by the gentle streams, but sometimes he wanders (διοιχνεῖ) among the high rocks (πέτρῃσιν ἐν ἠλιβάτοισι), climbing up (εἰσαναβαίνων) to the highest flock-spying summit (ἀκροτάτην κορυφὴν μηλοσκόπον). Often he runs through (διέδραμεν) the long shining mountains (ἀργινόεντα . . . οὔρεα μακρά) and often on the shoulders of the hills (ἐν κνημοῖσι) he charges along (διήλασε) killing wild beasts, keen-sighted. (*Homeric Hymn to Pan* 2–14)

There is a thrilling sense of freedom in this passage: an impression of agility and restless movement, but also sure-footedness and control.[16] And yet part of the excitement the poem generates comes from the way in which it measures those things on a human scale. Pan's movements here are speeded-up versions of the kinds of movement that we would expect from a shepherd or goatherd, or even a goat, in mountain pastures.[17] The poet uses a wide range of terms for mountain topography—hills, crests, peaks, summits, mountains, cliffs, ridges—as if Pan is replicating in his movement, through its encyclopaedic quality, human attempts to categorise and represent mountain territory. The many, varied verbs of motion stand in implicit contrast with the standard human experience of mountain terrain as obstructive and hard to move through, and in that sense they set this passage apart from the more threatening mountain scenes in the similes of the *Iliad*, which as we shall see often include foresters, hunters, or herdsmen in situations of struggle and work, or else imply static human observers who are passive in the face of the natural powers they are encountering. In the *Iliad* and the *Odyssey*, where the gods often travel over mountain terrain in ways that are beyond human comprehension, as they do also in some of the other Homeric hymns, scenes of divine movement are more likely to confront us with the impossibility of transcending that very earthbound way of encountering high places. In the *Homeric Hymn to Pan*, by contrast, the god acts out an exaggerated, fantasy version of kinds of freedom and even pleasure that are at least imaginable for human actors in the mountains.[18] To take just one example, we hear that Pan 'wanders among the high rocks' (πέτρῃσιν ἐν ἠλιβάτοισι διοιχνεῖ). The adjective ἠλίβατος meaning 'sheer', 'high', 'steep' tends to be used in the *Iliad* and *Odyssey* in quite negative contexts in situations of stress or threat for human actors: it is the word used for the rock that the Cyclops rolls in front of his cave to trap Odysseus and his fellow crew members in *Odyssey* 9.243.[19] For Pan, by contrast, the steep rocks are places under his control, places of delight. Through his use of the word ἠλίβατος, the poet thus emphasises the difference between divine and human, but also at the same time maintains a human scale, allowing his audience a fantasy of identification with a much freer way of moving through mountain terrain that is usually associated with obstruction and threat.

At the same time the poem also shows us, conversely, how a divine figure might be trapped temporarily into a more earthbound experience of mountain territory. The second half of the hymn recounts Pan's origins and birth. We hear that Pan's father, Hermes, came to Arkadia: 'there, despite being a god, he used to tend rough-haired sheep for a mortal man; for melting desire came upon him and bloomed, desire to be united in love with Dryops' beautiful-haired girl' (*Homeric Hymn to Pan* 32–34). Hermes is usually a figure associated with mobility and freedom,[20] very much like Pan in the first half of the poem. That is clearly on show in the *Homeric Hymn to Hermes*, which the *Homeric Hymn to Pan* seems to refer to,[21] and which tells the story of how Hermes, on the day of his birth, travels from his cave on Mount Kyllene to the meadows of Pieria around Olympus, to steal the cattle of Apollo.[22] In the *Homeric Hymn to Pan*, however, Hermes finds himself in a quite different position, undertaking human labour and submitting to human control within what should be his own territory, 'there where he has his sacred place (τέμενος) as god of Kyllene' (*Homeric Hymn to Pan* 31). The knowledge that Pan's origins are underpinned by a story of a god subjected to the mortal experience of herding might makes us more inclined to see resonances of human, pastoral activity in Pan's own movements in the first half of the poem. There is thus an implicit contrast running right through the poem between divine freedom and human constraint, but the text also raises fleetingly the possibility that that contrast might sometimes be temporarily eroded, perhaps even within the experience of human movement through mountain terrain.

Hesiod and the Muses on Mount Helikon

The poems of Hesiod, composed probably in the eighth or perhaps seventh century BCE, help us to add to this inventory of possibilities for the representation of divine and human involvement with the mountains in archaic epic. That is partly because Hesiod's poems tend to focus on different epochs of cosmic history from the Homeric hymns. In the *Theogony*, which focuses on the creation of the universe and the initial stages in the emergence of the Olympian pantheon, mountains are among the most ancient places of the earth, and the events which are said to have played out on their slopes and summits are even more distant from human experience than the activities of the gods in the Homeric hymns. The poem describes the creation of the world from chaos: 'Gaia [Earth] first bore starry Ouranos (Heaven) to be equal to herself, in order that he should cover her on all sides, and so that she should be a safe dwelling place for the blessed gods forever. And she bore the long mountains, the pleasant haunts of the divine Nymphs, who live in the wooded mountains' (Hesiod, *Theogony* 126–32). Later the poet tells us how the gods 'first took control of many-folded Olympus' (*Theogony* 113). The mountains of Greece are also places where some of the brutal formative moments of divine history are played out. You might think of Kronos, son of Gaia, who learns that he will be usurped by his son, and so swallows all of his children at birth. His sister-wife Rhea, overcome with grief, conspires with her parents Ouranos and Gaia to conceal Zeus in Crete after his birth: 'Gaia took him in her arms and concealed him in a deep cave down in the secret places of the holy earth on thickly wooded Mount Aigaion' (*Theogony* 482–84). Later the Titans base themselves on Mount Othrys in their struggle against the gods of Olympus and the battle rages over these two mountains at the south and north of the plain of Thessaly. Repeatedly we hear that Olympus shakes with the charging of the gods and with Zeus's thunder. And then when those power struggles are over, Zeus rules on Olympus without any challenge to his power, welcoming the other gods. Hesiod pays special attention to the presence of the Muses, the goddesses of poetry, telling us how they went to Olympus after their birth, and how they entertain the other gods with their song: 'Their sweet voice flows untiring from their mouths; and the houses of loud-thundering father Zeus laugh at the lily-like voice of the goddesses as it spreads around; and the peaks of snowy Olympus echo, and the homes of the immortals' (*Theogony* 39–43). Over and over again Zeus and the other gods are referred to as living on Olympus, with a consistent use of the present tense.

In the *Works and Days*, by contrast, Hesiod's subject is the post-heroic world of the present day. The poem conjures up an image of humans immersed in and entangled with their environment, and in contrast with a lot of present-day environmental discourse, views that not as something to be celebrated, but as a reason for pessimism.[23] Famously Hesiod charts the successive ages of humankind: golden, silver, bronze, then the age of heroes, and finally a fifth age, the age of the present, where humans have no escape from toil and sorrow. The rest of the poem, which gives instructions for farming, is anchored in that very human world of work, and the mountains of this text are mundane, inhabited spaces. The poet identifies his own village by its position near to Helikon, but it could hardly be further removed from the luxuries of the homes of the gods on Olympus: 'near Helikon in a miserable village, Askra, bad in winter, unpleasant in summer, never good' (Hesiod, *Works and Days* 639–40). The mountains can be benign. We hear that people who are just will avoid famine: 'to them the earth bears much life, and in the mountains the top of the oak tree bears acorns, and the middle bees' (*Works and Days* 232–33), and there is one reference to wood-cutting on the mountains, at line 428. Elsewhere the mountain can be a hostile landscape, for example when the north wind brings storms: 'falling upon many oak trees with high foliage and thick pines in the mountain glens he brings them down to the much-nourishing earth' (*Works and Days* 509–11). All of this is very distant from the mythical landscapes of the *Theogony*.

Those two images of the mountains seem at first sight quite incompatible with each other, but there is one moment where Hesiod bridges the divine-human divide, in the prologue to the *Theogony*. That passage uses divine epiphany as a way of conceptualising poetic inspiration,[24] and in doing so makes one of the most memorable and influential contributions to the history of mountain imagery in all of classical literature:

> From the Helikonian Muses let us begin to sing, who hold the great and holy peak of Helikon, and who dance around the violet-coloured spring and the altar of all-powerful Zeus with soft feet, and having washed their delicate bodies in Permessos or in the Hippokrene spring or sacred Olmeios, make their beautiful, lovely dances on highest Helikon, moving

nimbly with their feet.... One day they taught Hesiod beautiful song, while he was shepherding his sheep beneath holy Helikon. (Hesiod, *Theogony* 1–8, 22–23)

Here, if nowhere else in Hesiod, we seem to have a fantasy of human contact with the gods—the Muses are imagined descending to the lower slopes where Hesiod is watching his flocks—and also at the same time an acknowledgement, comparable to what we find in the Homeric hymns, of the way in which mountains were used as places of worship in the real, human culture of the eighth and seventh centuries BCE. If we give too much weight to those aspects of the passage, however, there is a risk that we will miss its primary metaphorical and poetic function.[25] It would be misleading, for one thing, to see this a clear reflection of archaic cult worship on the mountain. Clearly Hesiod does refer in general terms to the practice of mountaintop worship in his reference to the altar of Zeus. Many scholars have worked hard to identify the places Hesiod refers to, and to reconstruct the cult of Zeus and the Muses at the time when Hesiod's poem was composed. It is not impossible that the remains of a small building on the summit of Zagaras, the easternmost peak of Mount Helikon (figure 2.1), above the Valley of the Muses, are the remnants of an altar to Zeus that was in use in the eighth century and before, but the evidence for that is very inconclusive, and the general consensus is that it is more likely to have been a watch tower because of the roof tiles that have been found there. Nor do we have any other reliable evidence for worship of Zeus or the Muses on this mountain from the archaic period.[26] Certainly it was not until much later that the cult of the Muses on Helikon came to have a high degree of prominence: it was developed by the city of Thespiai, together with an agonistic festival, the Mouseia, with musical competitions in the Valley of the Muses on the lower slopes of the mountain. Most of the building remains there seem to date from the Hellenistic period,[27] and all the evidence suggests that the shrine and the festival flourished above all under Roman rule, and even thanks to Roman sponsorship, from the late first century BCE onwards, like so much of the Greek festival calendar, which underwent a huge revival in that period. It seems likely that the development of the shrine of the Muses, or at least its expansion into a famous and prominent site, was a response to this famous passage of Hesiod, rather than something pre-existing that the opening of the *Theogony* reflects.[28]

We run into similar problems when we take the image of Hesiod receiving divine inspiration on the mountainside too literally. For a long time it was a

FIGURE 2.1. View to the west from the summit of Zagaras, easternmost peak of the Helikon range. Photo: author.

common view that Hesiod himself was a member of precisely the type of peasant community he describes at Askra in the *Works and Days*. Some scholars have assumed that the opening of the *Theogony* does reflect assumptions within that kind of peasant society about mountains as numinous places of divine presence, in contrast with the countless later imitations of this passage, where the image of encountering the Muses on Mount Helikon becomes a deeply literary motif, a shorthand for the process of poetic inspiration.[29] Some even go so far as to assume that Hesiod really did have a vision on the mountainside.[30] Even if we do not want to go that far we could read this as a proto-Romantic moment of inspiration in the natural environment which could prompt others to imagine their own movement through the landscape in similar terms. But the consensus among most Hesiod scholars now is that we need to be extremely cautious about taking Hesiod's first-person claims in his poems as reliable autobiographical data, and that the motif of the shepherd as poet gaining knowledge from the Muses was a highly literary image even at the time Hesiod was composing, paralleled by a wide range of other surviving and probably also non-surviving texts.[31] Among other things, it is clear that Hesiod is equating his own progression as a poet from local to Panhellenic (that is, as a representative of the whole of Greece) with the journey the Muses themselves make, on Hesiod's account, from local deities associated with Mount Helikon to Panhellenic divinities welcomed by Zeus on Olympus.[32] Here, then, the mountain setting allows Hesiod to gain access to a kind of divine presence not just through a fantasy of epiphany, and not just though an acknowledgement of the importance of mountain ritual, but above all as an imaginary frame for his poetic self-definition.

Mount Olympus and Mount Ida in the *Iliad*

We have seen, then, that mountain ritual was a widespread feature of archaic and classical Greek culture, and also that mountain settings played a very varied role in framing the interplay between divine and human spheres in archaic Greek epic. Against that background I want to turn now to the *Iliad*, which was probably composed before any of the texts we have looked at so far, in the eighth century BCE, drawing on centuries-old traditions of oral poetry. My aim is to show how it manipulates those assumptions in the service of one of the most complex and intricate depictions of mountains in ancient literature. The poem juxtaposes divine and human ways of engaging with mountains and invites us to think about how they relate to each other. That is a story that has not been told before except in passing. In the process the poem presents us with productively conflicting images of the relations between humans and the environment. In that sense the *Iliad* offers us one of the most powerful of all examples of ancient environmental thinking, and a classic instance of the way in which ancient mythical narrative could function as a vehicle of environmental reflection.[33]

Mount Olympus is the most prominent mountain of the *Iliad*.[34] It is a place utterly apart from human presence: the poet's powers of imaginative access through the inspiration of the Muses are the only exception.[35] No human treads on the summit to sacrifice to the gods. Is it possible that the Greeks of the eighth century would have seen it as different from other mountain summits, perhaps as a place where the gods really were in residence in some physical sense? On the face of it that seems unlikely. Going up to mountain summits for sacrifice was such a familiar activity in archaic culture that it is hard to believe anyone would have taken Homer's vision of the gods feasting in ornate

FIGURE 2.2. Mytikas summit, Mount Olympus. Photo: author.

palaces literally. It is striking, however, that the finds from the Agios Antonios peak on Olympus are much later than for most other peaks where we have archaeological evidence for mountaintop ritual, where the evidence usually stretches back through the archaic period even to much earlier centuries. By contrast the Olympus evidence, as we have seen, is Hellenistic and then late antique (with a gap of many centuries between the two). Olympus is also unusual in that two of its three highest peaks—Mytikas and Stefani—are jagged rock formations which stand above the grassy slopes of the rest of the mountain and are not easily accessible on foot. Mytikas is not known to have been climbed before 1913, and Stefani not before 1921 (although the certainty with which that 'fact' is usually reported is of course misleading, and typical of the way in which modern accounts of mountaineering exploits tend to ignore any possibility of premodern precedents).[36] These days the climb to Mytikas (figure 2.2) is relatively straightforward: you can scramble over the rocks without a rope, following the paint splashes that mark the best route. It would have been perfectly possible to get animals up there for sacrifice: the dogs from the Agapitos Refuge sometimes follow walkers up over the rocks all the way to the summit, so presumably a goat would have been able to manage just as well. But there is no evidence that anyone ever tried it: no ancient dedications or remains of sacrifice have ever been found on the Mytikas summit. Maybe the special role of Olympus in the *Iliad* does reflect an archaic perception that there was something different about this mountain, something that made it especially well suited to be free of human footprints, as a separate place for the gods[37] (although as we have seen there is a precedent in Mount Lykaion for using a lower summit as a centre of cult worship).

The *Iliad* itself certainly avoids describing Olympus as a mountain which could be accessible to human presence. In some passages Olympus is described with adjectives appropriate to a mountain; there is even one passage (*Iliad* 14.225–30) where the poet does seem to be envisaging a geographically accurate Thessalian location for Olympus, in describing Hera's journey from Olympus to Pieria, Emathia, Thrace, Athos, and Lemnos on her way to Mount Ida.[38] Elsewhere, however, we can lose sight of the fact that this place of the gods is on a mountain summit at all: some passages refer to the home of the gods as 'heaven' or 'the sky' (*Ouranos*), either instead of or in combination with 'Olympus'.[39] The poem's vivid but rather vague descriptions of the palaces of the gods are almost unconnected with any realistic mountain topography.[40] At the end of *Iliad* Book 1, to take the most famous example, the gods return to Olympus from twelve days away feasting with the Ethiopians. Zeus is described 'sitting apart from the others on the highest peak of many-ridged Olympus' (*Iliad* 1.498–99), which seems to be his own private territory. There he receives the goddess Thetis, who asks him to intervene in favour of her mortal son Achilles. He nods his assent, and Olympus 'quaked' (1.530). Hera suspects a plot, and a quarrel is close to erupting, until her son the lame god Hephaistos intervenes and begs her to be happy, reminding them of how Zeus once hurled him from 'the divine threshold' (1.591) so that he plunged all day long down through the air to the island of Lemnos. Then the gods feast, far removed from the suffering of the Greeks and Trojans down below, and they all laugh together at Hephaistos as he limps around the banqueting hall serving. Finally they go away each to their own home, in the houses Hephaistos has made for them, with Zeus and Hera sleeping side by side. There are similar scenes repeated over and over again in the *Iliad* and also a little less frequently in the *Odyssey*, sometimes with similarly detailed descriptions, but more often through a kind of shorthand, with reference to 'the gods who have their homes on Olympus',[41] or 'high Olympus',[42] 'the heights of Olympus',[43] 'many-ridged Olympus' (although of course that last phrase, for all its brevity, does in some respects suggest a real-life view of the mountain's complex topography).[44] Zeus's occupation of the highest summit is also repeatedly linked not just with his high status, but also his superhuman powers of vision. Nor is it only Zeus who looks down, from Mount Olympus; other gods watch too, and from other places.[45] The gods also travel from Olympus, and across other mountains, with superhuman speed. At the beginning of Book 13, for example, we get a glimpse of Poseidon sitting on the highest mountain of the island of Samothrace (more than 50 miles from Troy), admiring the fighting. He takes pity on the Trojans and decides to intervene: 'straight away he came down from the rugged mountain, striding ahead swiftly with his feet, and the high mountains and the woods trembled beneath the feet of Poseidon as he travelled' (*Iliad* 13.17–19). In three strides he has reached his home at Aigai in Euboia.[46]

There are also, however, important strands in the poem which portray mountains on a more human scale, most prominently Mount Ida.[47] As we have seen, Zeus spends much of the poem not on Olympus, but on the Gargaros peak of Mount Ida giving assistance to the Trojans, and his presence there is linked with the existence of an altar in his honour; later he refers to the fact that Hector has sacrificed regularly to him there (*Iliad* 22.169–71).[48] Zeus's loyalties, it is clear, are divided and complicated: he sits on Mount Ida in part as protector of the Trojans and as recipient of Trojan worship.[49] It is not necessarily the case that the poet or his audience would have been closely familiar with the cult of Mount Ida (for which there is extensive evidence, although most of it is post-Homeric), nor is it obvious exactly which peak within the Ida range Zeus is sitting on.[50] But clearly these lines are composed for listeners entirely familiar with a culture of mountaintop sacrifice. And they take us momentarily into the world of Homer's eighth-century audience, who know that regular personal contact between gods and heroes lies unreachably in the mythical past and that their only reliable channel to the gods is through sacrificial ritual. From there Zeus intervenes in the fighting in ways which at times seem to be directly visible and comprehensible to the Greeks and especially the Trojans below. At 12.252–54, for example, he sends a blast of wind and a dust cloud from Mount Ida, bewildering the Greeks and giving the upper hand to the Trojans.[51] Mount Ida is also the place where Zeus's own powers are temporarily constrained, in a way which undermines the absoluteness of the gulf between mortal and divine control. Here, on the mountain summit which is so dear to him, even Zeus's vision is clouded; he is also forced increasingly to accept that his own love for the Trojans cannot overcome the fated direction of the war.[52] His wife, Hera, seduces him there, in the passage we encountered at the beginning of chapter 1, having persuaded the god Sleep to bring slumber to the eyes of Zeus, so that Poseidon can work unhindered against the Greeks: 'Sleep went up a very tall pine tree, the one which at that time grew tallest on Mount Ida, and he broke through the air to the *aithēr*. There he sat, covered by pine branches, in the likeness of a clear-voiced bird' (14.287–90). The detail of the *aithēr* implies a parallel between Ida and Olympus: Olympus too was supposed to be above the weather, free from storms and snow.[53] At the same time the presence of the pine makes this, by contrast with Olympus, into a recognisable mountain landscape.

Elsewhere we see human populations living on the slopes of mountains or close to mountains, which are important for the identity of particular communities.[54] That is clear especially in the Catalogue of the Ships in Book 2. Listed first among the Greeks are the Boiotians, 'who inhabited Hyrie and rocky Aulis, and Schoinos and Skolos, and mountainous (πολύκνημόν) Eteonos' (2.496–97); later 'those who inhabited Arkadia beneath the high mountain of Kyllene by the tomb of Aipytos, where the men are good at fighting hand-to-hand' (2.603–4); 'next was Odysseus, leading the great-hearted Cephallenians, who held Ithaca and Mount Neriton with its windswept woods' (2.631–32); then 'Prothous son of Tenthredon led the Magnetes who lived around the river Peneus and Mount Pelion with its windswept woods' (2.756–58). These passages share the perspective of later writers like Pausanias—the subject of my next chapter—who are interested in the way in which the landscape of Greece is marked by mythical heritage that matters for local identity.[55] Other examples are threaded through the poem. Andromache, the wife of the Trojan hero Hector, is described in Book 6 as 'the daughter of great-hearted Eëtion, Eëtion who lived below the wooded hill of Plakos in Thebe-under-Plakos, as ruler over the men of Kilikia' (6.395–97). In some respects these details enhance the distinction between divine and human experience of mountains, but there is also a sense in which they imply connections. The poem paints a picture of an orderly relationship between landscape and community, with the gods inhabiting the upper slopes and humans inhabiting the lower slopes of mountains. We see a similar dynamic in the *Odyssey*, for example in repeated references to the importance of Mount Neriton for the identity of the Ithacans and Odysseus.[56] Once again, in the *Iliad*, it is above all on Mount Ida that divine and human community come closest. At one point the Trojan hero Aeneas refers back to a time when 'sacred Ilion had not yet been built as a city of mortal people on the plain but they still inhabited the slopes of Mount Ida with its many springs' (*Iliad* 20.216–18).[57] One of the Trojans killed early on in the poem is Simoeisios, 'who was born by the banks of the river Simoïs when his mother was coming down from Mount Ida, where she had gone with her parents to see their sheep' (*Iliad* 4.476–78). The Trojans go about their day-to-day activities of herding just below the summit of Mount Ida that Zeus will occupy later in the poem; and Simoeisios' identity and even his name are inextricably tied to that landscape.[58] Mount Ida thus stands in contrast with Mount Olympus, as a place linked with human presence and identity.

Mountain Similes: Natural Force and Human Vulnerability

But it is the similes of the poem which bring an extra level of complexity and fascination to the *Iliad*'s portrayal of mountains. These extended comparisons occur throughout the poem, but most often in the scenes set on the battlefield. Some of them have more or less harmonious domestic or agricultural settings, but the majority are set in the natural world beyond or on the edges of human civilisation.[59] A very large proportion of that latter category have mountain settings. Oddly their relationship with the mountains of the main narrative has received almost no attention.[60] Similes that are close together within a single sequence of action are particularly likely to be read in connection with each other,[61] but the whole cosmos of the similes can also stand in our minds as a single, multi-faceted image, which is sketched out cumulatively for us as the poem proceeds. One of the functions of these scenes is to bring home the marginal nature of the battlefield, which similarly stands outside normal human civilisation.[62] At the same time, they offer us a vision of a separate and distinctive world that stands almost entirely apart from the world of the Greek and Trojan heroes and confronts us with a very different vision of mountains and their relationship with divine and human culture.

The variety and sophistication of the similes' panoramic portrayal of human-environment relations has also been very little discussed. There is a growing body of work on ecocritical themes in the Homeric poems—for example on the way in which these texts challenge anthropocentric worldviews and assert the agency of more-than-human objects[63]—but very little of that work pays attention to the similes.[64] My argument here is that the similes contribute perhaps more than any other aspect of the poem to the *Iliad*'s place as a major landmark in the Western environmental tradition. What we tend to find in the similes is an oscillation between a sense of human control over landscape and a much more precarious, vulnerable relationship, where human actors are often under threat and struggling for control and safety,[65] and cut free from any identifiable idea of landscape as a carrier of cultural memory linked with specific communities. Some of these latter images even have haunting resonances with present-day images of environmental disaster, especially in a series of descriptions of destructive floods or forest fires, usually set in mountain terrain.[66] The similes also remind us of the vast range of possibilities for human-environment relations across a very wide geographical scope. They repeatedly disrupt the surface of the main narrative, confronting us with a global image of the hierarchies between human beings and natural forces even as we focus intensely on particular localised moments of action on the battlefield. Those abrupt switches of location and perspective are precisely the kind of shifts that modern ecocritical discourse tends to value so highly for their ability to make us aware of the global scale lying behind local environmental phenomena.[67] It seems odd in that context that the *Iliad*, and especially the similes of the *Iliad*, have not had a higher profile in the history of ecocritical thinking, or been used more widely as a resource for creative responses to the theme of human-environment interaction in the present.

To begin from the beginning: if we read the *Iliad* through its mountains, we are likely to notice first the Olympus scenes in Book 1, followed by the links between mountains and identity in the Catalogue of the Ships in Book 2. In the process we might reflect not only on the enormous differences between them but also on the way in which they represent two aspects of a shared culture, both divine and human, where mountains are linked with order and community. We might notice also the way in which Achilles, in his quarrel with the Greek commander Agamemnon, swears an oath by a sceptre cut from a tree 'in the mountains' (1.235), a product of wild nature brought within civilisation as a symbol of kingly authority, or the way in which Nestor in his speech describes some of the great heroes of a previous age and their conflict against 'mountain-dwelling wild beasts whom they destroyed utterly' (1.268) (a reference to the war between the Lapiths and the half-horse, half-human centaurs), again bringing the mountains under the sway of heroic civilisation.

But side by side with those details is a groundswell of very different mountain images. First we see a series of five similes, before the Catalogue of the Ships, which compare the mass of Greek troops with various awe-inspiring natural phenomena: in the one mountain simile of the five, the poet describes the glitter of the soldiers' armour, 'as when destructive fire burns up unlimited woodland, on the heights of a mountain, and the bright light is visible from far away' (2.455–56). Then immediately in Book 3 when they join battle, we encounter another image which combines that sense of vast scale with a much more intimate impression of bodily immersion in a mountain landscape:

> As when the south wind pours down mist over the tops of the mountains, mist that is not loved by shepherds but is better than night for a thief, and you can see as far as you can throw a stone, in just the same way a cloud of eddying dust rose up beneath the feet of the soldiers as they advanced. (3.10–14)

The visually restricted quality of that image, which stands in contrast with the quasi-divine sense of vision from a distance in the similes of Book 2, seems particularly appropriate to this moment of descent into the more claustrophobic experience of battle. The reference to the throwing of a rock conveys the distance of the shepherd from the heroic world: it is not clear whether that action has a purpose at all beyond measuring the shepherd's difficulty of seeing, but either way it clear is that it is very different from the function of that motif in the various battlefield scenes to follow where we see heroes throwing stones at each other in combat.[68]

In fact the expected clash between the Greeks and Trojans does not come, because the two armies agree to a truce and a duel, which turns out to be inconclusive, between Menelaus and Paris. It is not until more than a book later that the two sides prepare again to meet each other. At that point another remarkable mountain simile articulates a similar tension between distant vision and human vulnerability: the Greek warriors arm themselves for battle

> as when from a mountain summit a goatherd sees a cloud approaching over the sea, driven by the blast of the west wind, and from a distance as it comes over the sea, bringing a great storm, it seems blacker and blacker like pitch, and the goatherd shudders as he watches, and drives his herds into a cave. (4.275–79)

Here we have an image of human and animal bodies at risk which is strikingly different from the depictions of divine and human control over mountains that we have encountered in Books 1 and 2. The sense of fearfulness and corporeal vulnerability looks at first glance very different from the more confident, celebratory version of bodily immersion in mountain terrain that we have seen in the *Homeric Hymn to Pan*, where human, pastoral movements are grafted onto an idealised imagining of divine movement (although there are other facets of the passage from *Iliad* 4 which have the potential to complicate that initial impression, as we shall see later). In those opening books, then, the poem's vision of human engagement with mountains builds gradually towards a more pessimistic, less anthropocentric set of images as we move into the poem's first battle scenes.

The impulse to depict human domination of nature in the mountains is never suppressed entirely. There is one particularly fascinating example in Book 23 when the Greeks go to Mount Ida to collect wood for the funeral of Patroklos under the command of the hero Meriones. For the most part the landscapes of the similes are quite separate from the experience of the Greek and Trojan heroes on the battlefield, but in this case, very unusually, we do see the Greeks entering the simile world:[69]

> They set out carrying woodcutting axes in their hands and well-plaited ropes, and the mules went ahead of them. They travelled a great distance uphill and downhill, sideways and across (ἄναντα κάταντα πάραντά τε δόχμιά τ' ἦλθον); but when they reached the shoulders of Ida with its many springs, immediately they began to cut down the high-leaved oaks in haste with their long-bladed bronze, and the trees fell with a crash; and then the Achaeans split them and tied them to the mules; and the mules tore up the ground with their feet, striving to reach the plain through the thick undergrowth. (23.114–22)

It is perhaps no accident that this incident comes after the fighting has halted, as if it is only then that the distinction between battlefield experience and the more normal world of work drops away. The Greeks' use of a space associated with labour and economic productivity for the Trojans too seems especially appropriate to a time of truce: it was common for the peoples of several different neighbouring cities to share the resources of a single mountain.[70] The poet is fascinated here with the bodily experience of travelling through mountain terrain, for example in the singsong phrase 'uphill and downhill, sideways and across', or in the detail of the mules 'tearing up the ground'. This is the kind of tactile detail which in other circumstances might contribute to a pessimistic view of human and animal immersion in the environment, but in this case it seems to be intended to have a more celebratory effect.[71]

More often, however, even initially positive images of anthropocentric dominance tend to be undercut. Here I want to focus especially on the first two-thirds of Book 11 as a case study. This is a key turning point in the poem: first Agamemnon is dominant, and then the Trojan Hector once Agamemnon withdraws from the battle. It also has one of the poem's richest concentrations of similes.[72] What we see in these passages is once again an oscillation between images of human control and human vulnerability in relation to mountain landscape, with an increasing move towards the latter.

The first series of mountain scenes in Book 11 begins with Mount Olympus. The Greeks and the Trojans are cutting each other down in battle. The goddess Eris is the only immortal with them on the battlefield: 'The others were not there with them, but sat at ease (ἔκηλοι) in their own halls, in the beautiful homes that had been built for each of them in the folds of Olympus (κατὰ πτύχας Οὐλύμποιο)' (11.75–77). Just a few lines later we find another, much more human example of rest, in a passage which is not strictly speaking a simile but which is set in precisely the kind of mountain landscape that the similes are full of:

> at the time when a woodcutter prepares his meal in the mountain glens (οὔρεος ἐν βήσσῃσιν), when he has tired his arms in cutting down tall trees, and weariness comes to his spirit, and desire for sweet food seizes his mind, then by their bravery the Greeks broke through the battle lines. (11.86–90)

The connection between the reposing woodcutter, in the glens of the mountains, and the gods sitting apart[73] in their homes in the folds of Olympus ought to be immediately clear, but it has not to my knowledge ever been remarked on. The woodcutter's is of course a very different kind of relaxation, earned through hard toil, but we might nevertheless perceive similarities between the two, and so view the woodcutter's experience of mountain repose all the more in positive terms.[74] That passage is followed in the next hundred or so lines, however, by a series of three similes with related settings that present a much bleaker vision of the destructive force of nature,[75] most terrifyingly in a forest fire description: 'As when a destructive fire falls on a wood that is thick with trees, and the whirling wind carries it everywhere, and the bushes fall root and branch as they are overpowered by the rush of the fire; so beneath Agamemnon, son of Atreus, the heads of the Trojans fell as they fled' (11.155–59). Here the poet exposes the precariousness of the anthropocentric image of work and rest in the woodcutter scene, and portrays the power of the natural world as so overwhelming that it drowns out any mention of human presence or human agency.

There is another example later in the book of that kind of progression towards an increasingly stark image of human vulnerability and even irrelevance in relation to natural forces, in a set of three similes very close together, first describing Odysseus alone against the Trojan forces and then the arrival of Aias to back him up. In the first passage Odysseus is compared with a wild boar crashing out of the undergrowth: the hunters stand their ground despite being afraid (11.414–20). Then a few lines later, we see the Trojans crowding round the Greek general Odysseus on the battlefield

> like tawny jackals in the mountains (ὄρεσφιν) around a horned stag that has been wounded, that a man has shot with an arrow from the string; the stag has escaped from him, fleeing by foot, so long as his blood is warm and his limbs have the power to move, but when the swift arrow subdues him, then the raw-flesh-eating jackals devour him in the mountains (ἐν οὔρεσι) in a shady grove; but some god brings a plundering lion; the jackals run away, and he devours the prey. (11.474–81)[76]

Here an initial impression of human control, in the wounding of the stag, is completely sidelined as the simile goes on, with the jackals and the lion competing for mastery. The final simile of the three once again discards human presence entirely, in another image of environmental disaster in the mountains (the word ὄρος is repeated here for the third time in twenty lines, as if to emphasise the connection and progression between the two similes).[77] Aias falls on the Trojans:

> As when a river in flood comes down to the plain, a winter torrent from the mountains, forced onwards by the rain of Zeus, and carrying with it dry oaks and pines, and casting much debris into the sea, so then did shining Aias rush over the plain driving the enemy before him, slaying horse and man. (11.492–97)

This natural force imagery leaves an impression of human insignificance. It also potentially has dehumanising implications, both for the victims of violence and for its perpetrators.[78]

Mountain Similes: Divine Vision and the Sublime

The dominant impression, then, is of the difference between the tentative and vulnerable human actors of the similes and the divine and heroic engagement with mountains that we see in the main narrative. The similes in many cases encapsulate the capacity of the more-than-human world to overwhelm human control and human identity and presence.[79] That contrast is never a straightforward one, however. My argument in this final section of the chapter is that even in the most violent of these natural-force similes there is still an intense interest in celebrating human dominance—and not just because they do sometimes present successful images of human woodcutting or hunting in the mountains. In some cases we might even be left with the impression that it is possible for humans to perceive or experience quasi-divine ways of interacting with landscape even within the post-heroic mountains of the similes.

One factor in that effect is of course the way in which these powerful forces of nature that overwhelm the humans of the simile world are themselves associated with the heroes on the battlefield. The flood image used for Aias is not only insistent in its portrayal of human insignificance within the mountains of the simile world, and potentially dehumanising for the hero himself, but at the same time wildly and extravagantly assertive of human mastery. It is that paradoxical combination that potentially makes many of the mountain similes of the *Iliad*—and equivalent natural-force similes in other settings, especially at sea—so powerful as models for ecocritical thinking, given that that kind of oscillation or ambivalence is so central to our own modern ways of thinking about the environment too.

Not only that, but wild-nature similes are also often used to defamiliarise human characters and human capacities, in a way which stretches our understanding and in some cases deliberately leaves us struggling to make sense of the full implications of the comparison.[80] The image of Aias as a mountain stream in flood has obvious implications for his strength and his momentum in this particular moment of the battle, but it also has certain features that are hard to map on to human experience, particularly in the final detail about the carrying of silt into the sea. Many of the most memorable examples of this kind of estranging function are in mountain similes in the *Iliad* and also in the *Odyssey*,[81] appropriately so given that one powerful strand in the Greek imagination of mountains involved a perception of the mountain's inhuman status, on the edge of human understanding. The most famous, and famously puzzling example is a description of Hector at one of his most dominant moments as he approaches the Greek ships, with the backing of Zeus on Mount Ida: 'He spoke, and then he rushed on like a snowy mountain, shouting, and he flew through the Trojans and their allies' (13.754). How can a mountain be a good point of comparison for someone moving rapidly?[82] One solution has been to emphasise the snow on the peak, and to see this as an image of the flashing of Hector's armour, although his armour is not mentioned explicitly. Another little-noticed passage earlier in same book makes that reading more plausible: Idomeneus put on his armour and 'set off just like a lightning bolt which the son of Kronos takes in his hand and shakes from dazzling Olympus, revealing a sign to mortals, and its light is conspicuous; in the same way the bronze around his breast shone as he ran' (13.242–45). The obvious alternative is to take it as a sign of Hector's size and his strength and also his status as a rallying point and landmark for the troops around him.[83] Near Eastern and Indian traditions do associate heroes with mountains, sometimes even mountains in motion, in very similar contexts,[84] and even in the Greek poetic tradition there are other passages too which suggest that mountains could be personified as divine figures.[85] But whether or not we view any of these explanations as plausible, we should surely also see the dissonance between the simile and what it describes as part of what makes it so powerful and memorable.

Mountain similes can thus associate human characters with more-than-human natural forces in ways which are deliberately hard to grasp. In some cases they are used with similarly estranging effect to characterise not just human strength but also human passion. There are two particularly powerful examples together at the beginning of Book 16. The Greek army is in terrible straits. Patroklos goes to the tent of his friend, the great warrior Achilles, whose withdrawal from the fighting after a quarrel with Agamemnon is one reason for the disastrous reversal on the battlefield, and begs Achilles to lend him his armour, 'shedding hot tears, like a black-watered spring that sheds its dark water down over a sheer rock-face'.[86] Achilles agrees; he also prepares his Myrmidon troops to fight:

> and they were like raw-flesh-eating wolves in whose hearts is unspeakable strength, wolves who have killed in the mountains a great horned stag, and devour him, and the jaws of all are red with blood; and in a pack they go to lap with their slender tongues the surface of the black water from a black-watered spring, belching out blood and gore, and the spirit in their breasts is fearless, and their bellies distended. (*Iliad* 16.156–63)

This is another of the great turning points of the poem, which will lead eventually to Patroklos' own death and Achilles' return to the battlefield to take revenge against the Trojan leader Hector. The two similes are tied together not just by their mountainous setting, but by the repetition of the 'black-watered spring'.[87] The passions unleashed here prefigure what is to follow: Achilles' bitter mourning for his friend, for example, or the scene where he and Hector's father Priam weep together when Priam comes to Achilles to retrieve Hector's body;[88] also the savagery of his mutilation of Hector's corpse: the 'raw-flesh-eating wolves' anticipate Achilles' wish that he had the appetite to eat Hector's flesh raw,[89] or his many threats to feed Hector's body to his dogs. It is striking here that the poet reaches for mountain imagery in seeking to characterise the more-than-human passions and sufferings of his characters. Once again these similes are in themselves utterly dismissive of human presence, asking us to imagine a scene which is alien to any anthropocentric understanding of the world; at the same time they also offer us extraordinary images of the intensity of human capacities and passions, which gain much of their power precisely by stretching our understanding beyond normal human experience.

Equally remarkable is a set of mountain similes which describe human actors viewing the natural world with a striking clarity which has a certain amount in common with the poem's representations of divine viewing from Olympus and elsewhere, or indeed with modern associations between mountains and the sublime. In fact a strikingly large proportion of the poem's similes do offer us a distant perspective:[90] in that sense the mist simile from the beginning of the first battle scene in Book 3 is far from typical. We have seen one example already of mountaintop viewing, in the image of the goatherd sheltering in a cave after seeing an approaching storm from his mountaintop vantage point in 4.275–79.[91] There is another similar example in the book following: Hera has been to talk to Zeus on the highest peak of Olympus; she whips her horses into action: 'as far as a man sees through the haze with his eyes as he sits on a mountain summit, looking over the wine-coloured sea, so far do the loud-sounding horses of the gods leap' (5.770–72). This human viewer sees much less than the gods, who have the whole of the inhabited world spread out before them, but it still comes closer than we might expect to divine vision if we come to it from other similes where human capacity is treated more pessimistically.[92] Another simile at the end of Book 8 famously opens up a very distant viewpoint from ground-level up, in describing the fires of the Trojans on the plain at night:[93]

> As when in the sky the stars shine brightly around the radiant moon, and when the upper air has become windless and all the mountaintops stand out and the tops of the headlands and the glens, and the vast expanse of the upper air is split apart from heaven above, and all the stars are visible, and the shepherd rejoices in his heart. (8.555–59)

The presence of the shepherd reminds us that this is an earthbound view,[94] but it nevertheless seems able to access at least temporarily a cosmic scale of perception.[95] We might even feel that these passages anticipate modern representations of the experience of the sublime in response to awe-inspiring natural landscapes, of the kind that were widespread from the eighteenth century onwards.[96] One important recent account has argued forcefully for the existence of that phenomenon even within ancient literature long before Longinus' famous treatise *On the Sublime*, and has cited Homer as a key example;[97] and the description of mountaintop viewing over the sea in association with Hera's horses at 5.770–72 was itself mentioned by Longinus as one example of the sublime in Homer.[98]

Do the similes allow us to see glimpses of the divine in the overpowering natural phenomena they describe to us? And in that sense do they raise the possibility of a different way of accessing and perceiving the divine within a post-heroic experience of the mountains which is rather different from the poet's inspired perception of the divine community on Olympus? Certainly there are passages in the poem which make it clear that Zeus at least causes or perhaps even in some sense inhabits certain natural phenomena, particularly in association with the weather, which was one of his traditional spheres, and especially rain and thunder and lightning.[99] That connection is articulated at most length in one remarkable simile describing the din of the fleeing Trojan cavalry:

> There are days in autumn when the whole countryside lies darkened and oppressed under a stormy sky and Zeus sends down torrential rain as a punishment to men. . . . In consequence their streams all run in spate, hillsides are scarred by torrents, and the rivers, wrecking the farmlands in their way, rush down headlong from the mountain with a great roar into the turbid sea. (16.384–92)[100]

That passage raises the possibility that we should see an encounter with the divine in some other similes too, especially in those which mention rain and thunder without explicit mention of Zeus, or which envisage human spectators confronted with rivers in flood and rough seas.

The reactions of those human spectators in the similes reinforce those impressions.[101] In the storm simile of Book 4, the goatherd sees the clouds approaching from his mountain-top lookout: 'the goatherd shudders as he watches, and drives his herds into a cave' (4.279). At first sight we might imagine that this kind of negative reaction to the sight is incompatible with any appreciation of nature's sublime or divine power, but of course fear is a key ingredient in the eighteenth- and nineteenth-century sublime, and in some of its ancient equivalents.[102] The verb used here ('shuddered': ῥίγησεν) occurs only eleven times in the *Iliad*. Five of those passages explicitly involve gods or humans reacting to gods or to divine events.[103] By contrast, in the simile from the end of Book 8 describing the fires of the Trojans, we hear that 'the shepherd rejoiced in his mind' (γέγηθε δέ τε φρένα ποιμήν) (8.559) at the sight of the mountaintops and the stars. That reaction too is appropriate as a response to the sublime, at least as it is defined within the later European tradition. Like ῥιγέω, γηθέω is another verb that is used regularly in the Homeric poems to describe human responses to the divine.[104]

The *Iliad* is typical of ancient representations of mountains partly because of the way in which it juxtaposes so many different images, and challenges us to make sense of their interrelations. Among other things it offers us many different ways of thinking about the relationship mountains have with the divine and with the human. On the one hand Homer lets us see Olympus, with its remote community of gods accessed through his divinely inspired poetic vision, which leaves us with the impression of a vast gulf between gods and mortals. Side by side with that he presents Mount Ida, which is closer to human society, as a place of mountaintop ritual, a focus for Trojan identity, and an exemplar of the relationship between mountains and human community that we glimpse also through the Catalogue of the Ships. Those images stand side by side with an alternative strand, in the similes, where the more-than-human world has the capacity to overwhelm or even submerge human agency in mountain environments. Even in the similes, however, we see anthropocentric perspectives resurfacing repeatedly. That effect comes partly from the way in which they celebrate heroic prowess precisely through these images of more-than-human agency, with reference to wild animals, rivers in flood, forest fires. In addition, however, and perhaps more surprisingly, the poet's emphasis on the vulnerability of human bodies in mountain environments exists side by side with more detached, empowered ways of perceiving mountain landscapes, where we every so often see hints of quasi-divine, even quasi-sublime ways of viewing ascribed to the otherwise vulnerable and anonymous human actors, hinting at the capacity for a kind of elevated human perceptiveness in relation to inhuman and overwhelming natural landscapes. A very large proportion of the similes that are important to those effects are similes involving mountains. In that sense the poet is articulating already in the *Iliad* one of the key tensions that runs through representation of mountains right into the modern world, that is the tension between embodied and detached perception. It also anticipates the tension between mountain 'gloom' and mountain 'glory' that has been so important for the later history of human responses to mountains: versions of both of those images exist with each other already side by side in the poem, as they do in other ancient texts too. The poem's juxtaposition between a kind of claustrophobic, immersive, pessimistic vision of human-environment relations and sometimes almost in the same breath the extravagant, exhilarating celebration of human control and perceptiveness in relation to landscape is one of the things that makes the mountain images of the *Iliad* so powerful, as an imaginative resource against which to measure our own similarly conflicted experiences of human-environment relations.

3

Pausanias: Mythical Landscapes and Divine Presence

Euripides to Pausanias

The traditions of mountaintop sacrifice were still flourishing throughout the eastern Mediterranean when the Homeric poems were composed, probably in the eighth century BCE. In the centuries that followed they seem to have become less widespread. They were supplemented, however, by other forms of religious expression in mountain landscapes. Mount Lykaion is once again a good example: there are relatively few finds dating later than the fourth century BCE from the ash altar on the summit, but we know that the athletic festival continued to flourish on the slopes of the mountain for many centuries afterwards, and that it received new investment, in the form of new buildings, in the second half of the fourth century around the time when the record of offerings on the summit dies away. The slopes of Mount Helikon similarly gained a new identity as a place of festival and pilgrimage from the Hellenistic period onwards. The mountains of Greece, and of Asia Minor and Italy too, continued to be dotted with shrines and statues of the gods into the imperial period. Some places, where those markers of the past were packed together with unusual density, became the object of what has been called 'topophilia', the collective cultural obsession with key places of memory.[1]

The tension between divine and human control over the mountains also continued to play a central role in writings on Greek and Roman myth. For example, in the Greek tragedy of the fifth and fourth centuries BCE, as in the earlier epic tradition, the mountains of myth continued to be represented as places of divine presence and at the same time of embodied human experience. They also continued to be envisaged at least in some cases as real, identifiable places, rather than conventional and purely literary landscapes. Mount Kithairon is the best example. It was crowded with narratives associated with the myths of the city of Thebes: Oedipus, taken to the mountain as a child to be abandoned; Aktaion, torn apart by his dogs on the mountainside in punishment, according to the most common account for having set eyes on the goddess Artemis bathing. The most horrifying depiction of the mountain comes in Euripides' *Bacchae*.[2] That play dramatises the irruption of divine presence and bodily experience into a landscape that initially appears to be under rationalising control.[3] It also sets the play within a recognisable landscape: many Athenians would have known Mount Kithairon from personal experience, having tramped across the slopes on their way to Delphi for the Pythian festival or for visits to the shrine of Apollo at other times, or else for trade, for shepherding, or on guard duty at the edges of the territory of Attica.[4] The play tells the story of Pentheus, king of Thebes, and his refusal to accept the worship of the god Dionysus within his city. His attempts to maintain rational control over the city's territory are swept away through a horrifying act of divine vengeance. The god imposes a divinely inspired madness on Pentheus' mother, Agaue, and other women of the city, prompting them to move out of the city to the slopes of the mountain, and when Pentheus comes to spy on them Dionysus reveals Pentheus' hiding place to them and they kill him with their bare hands, thinking he is a mountain lion. The play is full of passages which conjure up powerful images of Dionysus' impact both on the mountain itself and on the human and animal bodies that inhabit its slopes.[5] The first is the scene where a messenger tells Pentheus about how he came upon the sleeping women as he was grazing his flocks. The women wake when the cattle approach: 'One of them taking her thyrsus hit a rock, from which a spring of water came leaping out; another dug her reed into the ground and right there the god sent up a spring of wine' (Euripides, *Bacchae* 704–8). The herdsman and his companions hide behind some bushes and try to ambush the women, but they are lucky to escape with their lives: soon the trees are dripping with the raw flesh of the cows, which have been torn apart by the women in their frenzy. Next the women rush to 'Erythrai and Hysiai, villages beneath the rocks of Kithairon, and falling on them like an enemy army they turned everything upside down, grabbing children out of their houses' (*Bacchae* 751–54): these were real villages to the south of Thebes on the slopes of Kithairon. Later they return to the peak of the mountain and Dionysus once again produces clear springs of water for them from the earth. And then most powerfully of all, we come to the place where Pentheus meets his end. Here the messenger's description of leaving Thebes once again has a certain topographical precision: 'after we walked past all the Theban houses, we crossed over the streams of Asopos and made our way up into the rocks of Kithairon' (*Bacchae* 1043–45). Dionysus guides them to the maenads and they spy on them. Initially it looks like an idyllic place, a place for the human body to be at rest:[6] 'We were in a glen with cliffs all around, watered by streams, shaded by pines; the maenads were sitting there occupying their hands with pleasant labour' (*Bacchae* 1051–53). Very quickly, however, it becomes a place of defilement, of bodily immersion in the landscape in the most grotesque sense imaginable, which is contrasted with the initial theme of detached viewing as Pentheus is dragged down from the high tree he has hidden in; soon the mountain echoes with his screams, and the flesh of his body is scattered over the rocks and bushes: 'some beneath the rough rocks, some in the deeply wooded foliage— not an easy task to find it' (*Bacchae* 1137–39). If you had seen this play in Athens (its first performance in Athens was after Euripides' death around 406 BCE)[7] and then found yourself travelling across Mount Kithairon, perhaps on your way to the Pythian festival, would you have looked at the rocks and the bushes as you walked and imagined them hung with lumps of Pentheus' flesh? Would you have seen the mountain streams as remnants of the gifts of Dionysus? Mount Kithairon in the *Bacchae* is thus a place of a place of bodily immersion, both for the characters of the play, in the most horrifying sense, and also for its audience. It was associated with divine power, and linked with the very distant, mythical past; at the same time it was a landscape that was still accessible to Euripides' contemporaries.

Later centuries saw a proliferation of geographical and mythographic writing, which collected local stories into vast works of compilation: texts like Pseudo-Apollodorus' *Library* or Pseudo-Plutarch's *On Rivers and Mountains and Things Found in Them* are full of mythical stories with mountain settings. By writing about mountains and other non-urban landscapes these authors brought wilderness space within human civilisation, encompassing it safely within the boundaries of their texts. In some cases that involved rationalising mythical stories in order to give more plausible explanations for apparently miraculous events. Did that process necessarily involve losing touch with the status of mountains as places of embodied experience and divine presence?

That is certainly not the case for Pausanias. The *Periegesis* of Pausanias is one of the greatest of all ancient compilations of mythical material. It was written in the second half of the second century CE. It consists of a region-by-region account of the places of mainland Greece, especially temples with their statues, and of local history and myth. It is also one of our most detailed surviving accounts of a living culture of mountains as religious spaces in Greco-Roman culture. Pausanias repeatedly emphasises the way in which mountains could act as markers of local identity, and as important landmarks on the roads which joined the territories of different cities. In his account they are covered in temples and statues and sacred caves and springs, each with its own rituals and stories.[8] Pausanias sometimes takes on a sceptical persona, rejecting what he sees as unreliable reports of divine intervention and replacing far-fetched mythical accounts with rationalising alternative versions.[9] And yet this is also a profoundly religious text. Pausanias repeatedly emphasises his own piety and his own commitment to religious observance.[10] And every so often we do come across moments where he is willing to accept stories from the past about marvellous manifestations of divine power, in ways which disrupt his rationalising, antiquarian approach.[11] It is striking that some of the most powerful of these moments are set on mountains: it as if these are particularly numinous places for Pausanias, where the normal laws of rational assessment are more likely to be suspended, and where reports of divine presence are hard to explain away or ignore.

Grasping those effects requires us to read the text from end to end, in order to see how these productive inconsistencies in Pausanias' approach play out within the detailed textures of his writing.[12] That in turn requires us to put aside certain preconceptions about Pausanias and about the genre he is working in, and to recapture some of the fascination that ancient readers felt for this kind of knowledge-ordering writing. There has been an increasing realisation in recent decades that the encyclopaedic styles of compilation that Pausanias relies on are likely to have been viewed by ancient readers as much more pleasurable and prestigious than they are for us; also that ancient knowledge-ordering works often invited consecutive reading rather than just piecemeal consultation of the kind we usually associate with reference works.[13] Pausanias, in other words, is an exhaustive compiler of information, but that does not mean that the *Periegesis* is just a collection of facts and anecdotes to be mined for information; it is also a gradually unfolding work of the imagination.[14] It offers a mental map of the territory of mainland Greece as a space that is saturated with thrilling traces of the mythical and historical past. The past is accessible through the network of stories and memories that attach themselves to the landscape of the present. Mountains play a significant role within that vision, as places of temporal fluidity, where different zones of myth and history co-exist with each other: that is an idea which is shared by a lot of modern writing about mountains too.[15] That image is built up cumulatively, over many books, which present us with recurring common threads but also in some cases disjunctions between Pausanias' treatments of myth in different contexts. For the nineteenth century, Pausanias was one of the most important of all classical authors. The dozens of nineteenth-century travellers who left accounts of their journeys around mainland Greece modelled themselves on Pausanias. They took his text with them everywhere. Pausanias' attempt to catalogue the traces of the Greek past as they appeared to him under Roman rule inspired and made possible their own encounters with the Greek heritage and their own obsessive attempts to understand the traces that heritage had left under Ottoman rule. The twentieth century lost interest, or at least came to view Pausanias mainly as a not consistently reliable source for understanding archaeological sites. But the tide seems to be turning again, as more and more people rediscover the *Periegesis* not just as one of our key texts for understanding Roman Greece, but also as a rich and sophisticated work in its own right. The tension between rationalising and epiphanic ways of understanding the divine in the *Periegesis* is one important aspect of the challenging reading experience the text offers us.

I also aim to show that Pausanias is acutely aware of what it means for the human body to be exposed to mountain landscapes, and to the landscapes of Greece more generally. Pausanias' work, I argue here, is one of the most intensely bodily of all works of imperial Greek literature. That claim may at first sight be a surprising one. Certainly it is at odds with the impression that Pausanias is a very self-effacing narrator with very little interest in recording his own responses to the terrain he passes through.[16] That makes him very different from the voices we are used to from modern travel writing: he does regularly mention things he has seen or stories he has heard, and he regularly imagines an anonymous human traveller moving through space, but almost never with any day-by-day details of his impressions or encounters on the road. But when we look more closely it becomes clear that Pausanias' work is in fact a powerful example of the potential for literary representations of travel to convey an impression of bodily immersion. There are bodies everywhere in the text. They help to represent corporeal engagement—at least imagined corporeal engagement—as a key part of the experience of travel and antiquarianism:[17] Pausanias delights in taking his readers to places where things have happened to human bodies in the past, or where that continues to be the case in the present-day rituals he describes, inviting us to imagine our own bodies in contact with the earth and trees and rocks of Greece. Moreover, the many scenes of bodies embedded or buried in the landscape contribute to Pausanias' representation of the continuing, physical presence of the mythical and historical past in the places of Roman Greece. To take just one example, we might look at his account of the myth and ritual associated with Trophonios, which is just one example from a series of descriptions of buried bodies and bones and their associated graves and hero cults closely clustered together in Book 9 on Boiotia.[18] Pausanias first tells the story of how Trophonios was swallowed up by the earth: 'then the earth opened and received Trophonios at the point in the grove at Lebadeia where we find the pit called the pit of Agamedes, with a block of stone beside it' (9.37.7). A few pages later he describes at length the ritual associated with the oracle of Trophonios, which involves descending beneath the earth:

> The oracle is beyond the grove on the mountain. . . . Inside the enclosure is a chasm in the earth, not naturally occurring, but constructed with the skills of masonry. . . . The one who is descending lies down on the ground, holding barley-cakes kneaded with honey, puts his feet into the hole first and then follows along himself, trying eagerly to get his knees into the opening. The rest of his body is at once pulled in, rushing in after his knees, just as the biggest and swiftest river will cause a person to vanish when caught up in a whirlpool. (9.39.9–11)

This description guarantees through its corporeality the continuing presence and power of the mythical past: Pausanias emphasises that the place of Trophonios' descent is still visible, and Trophonios himself is still in some sense present there in his oracle. In the process he invites his readers to imagine their own claustrophobic immersion along with the worshipper into the earth itself.

The theme of bodies at risk also plays a major role in a series of passages, many of them set on mountains, where environmental forces and manifestations of divine power overwhelm human actors, in a way which disrupts Pausanias' predominantly rationalising persona. In some cases those are stories of metamorphosis or other divinely inspired punishment. Most often Pausanias rejects any divine explanation, but there are some exceptions, as we shall see, and even when he is sceptical he usually accepts some aspects of the underlying story. In doing so he represents Greece as a land where the humans of the past have over and over again been confronted with their corporeal vulnerability in their encounters with the environment. Pausanias has had a lot of attention in recent decades for his attitudes to the Greek past and the Roman present, and as a source for the history of Greek religion. The idea that he might be a significant figure for our understanding of ancient environmental thinking might look bizarre from those perspectives. But in fact the *Periegesis* offers a distinctive vision of human interrelations with the more-than-human world, where human bodies always have the potential to be immersed in and overcome by the numinous landscapes of Roman Greece.[19]

Arkadia

What was it like to travel through the fabled mountains of mainland Greece in the second century CE? Here I want to focus on a reading of the final three books of the *Periegesis*: Book 8 on Arkadia, Book 9 on Boiotia, and Book 10 on Phokis. These three books deal with some of the most mountainous areas of Greece, and some of the Greek mountains with the richest concentration of mythical associations. Book 8, perhaps more than any of the other books of the *Periegesis*, offers us a traveller's-eye view of Greek territory.[20] Here, more frequently than anywhere else in the work, Pausanias uses phrases in the first person.[21] He also uses third-person phrases which suggest the perspective of the traveller even more frequently than in most of the rest of the work: 'someone who travels along such-and-such a road will see . . .'[22] That is clear as soon as Pausanias enters the territory of Arkadia, after an introduction to the region's history:

> There are two ways of entering Arkadia on the Argive side, one in the direction of Hysiai and one over Mount Parthenion into the territory of Tegea, and also two others on the side of Mantineia, one through what is called Prinos and the other via the Ladder. The latter is wider, and its descent had steps which had once been cut into it. (Pausanias 8.6.4)

Pausanias does not describe his own particular journey, but he does prompt us to imagine the dimensions and contours of the route as we would experience it if we chose to follow his directions, over these various passes.[23] As we read on we are regularly invited to envisage mountains as landmarks on the road and as boundary markers between the territories of different cities.[24] At 8.12.8, he tells us that one of the roads to Orchomenos from Mantineia goes via Mount Anchisia, and that the border between the two cities runs across the mountain, and from Orchomenos one of the roads to Kaphya runs beneath Mount Trachys (8.13.4). Alternatively if you go from Orchomenos to the north:

on the road to Pheneos a mountain will greet you. On this mountain meet the boundaries of the land of the people of Orchomenos, Pheneos and Kaphya. Above the boundaries rises up a high cliff; they call the cliff the Kaphyatic rock. After the boundaries of the cities I have mentioned is a ravine, and the road to Pheneos goes through it. (8.13.6)

Moving on from there, 'if you go from Pheneos towards the rising sun you get to the heights of a mountain called Geronteion with a road on it' (8.16.1). This is a traveller's-eye view of the mountains of the Peloponnese, from ground level. Mountains in the ancient world were not isolated spaces, cut off from the surrounding world: they could be zones of connectivity, territories that could join the communities on either side of them as much as dividing them.[25]

Through those descriptions of roads and routes is threaded a whole series of references to mountains that are marked by stories from the past. Some of these references are to historical events,[26] and some to natural happenings,[27] but the vast majority refer to mythical events, often involving local traditions and distinctively Arkadian versions of well-known stories.[28] A mountain called Three Springs is the home of the Nymphs who washed Hermes when he was born (8.16.1). Mount Viper is the scene of the death of the hero Aipytos, son of Elatos, from a snake bite (8.16.2). Pausanias tells us that the snakes still exist in his own time and that he has even seen one himself (8.4.7): that detail hints characteristically at links between the distant past and the present, where just occasionally present-day bodies may be at risk in precisely the same way as the bodies of figures from the heroic past. Nearby is Mount Chelydorea, where Hermes first made a lyre from a tortoise shell (8.17.5). Farther on are the Aroanian mountains, where the daughters of Proitos took refuge in their madness until they were cured by Melampous (8.18.7). Embedded within this landscape at every turn are tombs, shrines, and statues. Mount Anchisia is not just a landmark on the road; it also holds at its foot the tomb of Anchises, from whom it is named (8.12.8), and on the mountainside a sanctuary of Singing Artemis, which is shared by the cities of Mantineia and Orchomenos (8.13.1). At 8.15.9, we hear that 'On Mount Krathis is a Sanctuary of Pyronian Artemis, and in the even more distant past the Argives used to bring fire from this goddess for the festival of the Lernaia'. Farther north, 'beyond the tomb of Aipytos is the highest mountain in Arkadia, Kyllene, and there is a ruined temple of Kyllenian Hermes on the summit of the mountain' (8.17.1). When Pausanias comes later to the city of Kleitor, he tells us that 'on the summit of the mountain about thirty stades from the city a temple and statue of Korian Artemis have been built' (8.21.4). Later we hear that Mount

Mainalos is sacred to the god Pan, and that some people even claim to be able to hear him playing on his pipes there: that detail appeals to our senses and invites us to imagine ourselves there straining our ears into the wind to catch a distant echo of the god's music (8.36.8).

Clearly there was a culture of religious tourism of some kind lying behind these descriptions. It is hard to reconstruct completely. We cannot know for sure how many of these places Pausanias went to himself. Did he climb to the summit ridge of Mount Kyllene (Mount Ziria in modern Greek; the summit is at 2,376 metres above sea level) to see the statue for himself, or was he relying on written information or local informants? Was Pausanias typical of long-standing habits of religious travel in Arkadia, or was he trying to create or re-create something that was far from commonplace when he was writing in the mid-second century CE?[29] How many of these sites were still commonly in use? He describes the shrine of Hermes on Kyllene as ruined, but that need not necessarily imply neglect: for Pausanias a site in ruins seems often to have been more powerful as a marker of the way in which the past stands tantalisingly out of reach for an observer in the present.[30] If others did travel to these sites regularly too, what kinds of religious observance were they involved in, and how did they envisage their own travel? We have seen already that tourism and pilgrimage were much less clearly distinguished in ancient Greek and Roman culture than they are for us.[31] But despite his lack of detail on those questions, Pausanias' work does conjure up an impression of a living culture of engagement with the religious landscape, and there are some sites in the work where Pausanias does describe his own presence in the first person.

Pausanias even refers several times to his own association with the city of Magnesia beneath Mount Sipylos in Asia Minor, which was probably his home city. It is striking that several of these fleeting moments of self-definition involve references to the mountains that stood nearby. For example, in his account of the worship of the mythical hero Pelops at the great festival site of Olympia he tells us that 'signs remain even today of the fact that Pelops and Tantalos dwelt in my part of the world. In the case of Tantalos, there is a lake called after him, and a tomb that is not inconspicuous; and there is a throne of Pelops on Mount Sipylos, on the peak of the mountain' (5.13.7). The 'throne', a chair cut into the rock on the very summit of the mountain, standing directly above a 300-metre precipice, is still visible today. Some scholars think it may have been associated with worship of Zeus or some other divinity: there are parallels right across the Mediterranean world for other rock-cut mountain thrones, some of which have inscriptions to named gods.[32] Earlier on in the

Periegesis, in his account of Athens, Pausanias refers to a representation of Apollo and Artemis killing the children of Niobe, and explains that he has himself seen the famous rock on Mount Sipylos (still visible today) where she was said to have been turned to stone: 'I myself saw this Niobe when I went up Mount Sipylos' (1.21.3). These references to Mount Sipylos seem to mark out Pausanias' belonging to a particular community,[33] as well as giving us an example of his interest in the experience of mountain tourism close to home.

But are these passages just antiquarian records of old buildings and old stories? Or does Pausanias represent the sites he visits as numinous places in any sense? Towards the end of Book 8, Pausanias visits Mount Lykaion. His account of the mountain includes all the ingredients we have already seen for the rest of Arkadia: stories about the mythical past,[34] and sacred places dotted around not just on the summit itself but also elsewhere on the slopes lower down.[35] Pausanias hints that he has been up to the summit himself, but characteristically without quite making that explicit: 'on the highest summit of the mountain is a mound of earth, which is an altar of Zeus Lykaios, and the Peloponnese is for the most part visible from there' (8.38.7): this is one of very few passages in his work where he mentions any kind of view.[36] In some respects, however, his description of Mount Lykaion stands out from the rest of the book, because of the way in which it raises the possibility, although without endorsing it unequivocally, that this may be a place which even now sees divine or supernatural happenings. He tells us that no one is allowed to enter the *temenos* ('precinct') of Zeus on the summit, and that anyone who does will be dead within a year; also that no living creature within the *temenos* casts a shadow—although in that latter case he hedges his bets with the phrase καὶ τάδε ἔτι ἐλέγετο ('these things too were told') (8.38.6).[37] Pausanias also says cryptically 'There was no pleasure for me in inquiring into the sacrifice, but let everything be as it is and as it was from the beginning' (8.38.7).[38] Here the summit has an air of mystery. Whatever his motives, Pausanias chooses not to subject Mount Lykaiion's sacrificial rituals to his rationalising, antiquarian gaze.

In order to make sense of that passage we need to join it up with another discussion of Mount Lykaion much earlier in Book 8, which is one of Pausanias' most important expressions of his cautious but also ultimately decisive faith in the possibility of divine impact over human actors in certain special times and places. There he tells us how Lykaon

> brought a human child to the altar of Zeus Lykaios, sacrificed it and poured its blood on the altar, and they say that at the sacrifice he was immediately

turned into a wolf from a human. I for my part am convinced by this story; it has been told by the Arkadians from a long time ago, and it has the additional advantage of probability. (8.2.3)

In the past, he says, when humans and gods lived close to each other, some human beings were even turned into gods, so it is perfectly possible that Lykaon became a wolf and Niobe a rock. In the present day, by contrast, no one becomes a god except by flattery (a dig at the deified Roman emperors) and people who enjoy listening to wonders mix up the truth with a lot of rubbish, believing for example that now someone becomes a wolf for nine years at every sacrifice to Lykaian Zeus (8.2.6), or that 'Niobe on Mount Sipylos weeps in summer' (8.2.7). Pausanias' acceptance is thus limited, and he maintains his scepticism about the possibility of similar marvels happening in the present. But there seems to be something about the antiquity of Arkadia[39] and especially Mount Lykaion that makes him more inclined to accept these ancient reports of divine intervention as reliable.[40]

Boiotia

In Book 9, Pausanias moves north to Boiotia. Here we find again very frequent mentions of mountain shrines and rituals, but also a more reserved attitude towards claims about divine happenings. The relationships between human and divine, between bodies and environment, are different here. His first stop is Mount Kithairon. Here it turns out to be unusually difficult to locate some of the most famous mythical and historical stories of bodily vulnerability. Pausanias comes first to the ruins of Hysiai and Erythrai, and then on returning to the road he sees the memorial to the Persian general Mardonios, who was killed at the battle of Plataia that took place on the slopes of Mount Kithairon in 479 BCE, but he also makes it clear that Mardonios' body itself disappeared on the day of the battle. Pausanias then tells us that 'whereabouts on Kithairon the disaster happened to Pentheus, the son of Echion, or where they exposed Oedipus after his birth, nobody knows' (9.2.4). It is striking that Pausanias passes up the opportunity to tell the story of Pentheus' dismemberment in detail.[41] Does that amount to a rejection of the vision of divine intervention that the *Bacchae* offers us?

There is, however, one story of bodily dissolution that Pausanias does succeed in locating, and that is the story of Aktaion:

> As you travel from Megara there is a spring on the right, and then as you go on a little further there is a rock. They call this the bed of Aktaion, and they say that Aktaion slept on this rock whenever he was tired from hunting, and they say that he looked into the spring while Artemis was bathing there. Stesichoros of Himera wrote that the goddess threw a deerskin around Aktaion and so prepared for him death by his hounds, to stop him from taking Semele as his wife; but I believe that an illness consisting of a mad frenzy overcame the dogs of Aktaion; they went mad and would have torn to pieces whoever they came across without telling them apart from each other. (9.2.3–4)

Pausanias clearly sees rabies as the more plausible explanation, even if he leaves open the possibility of some divine involvement.[42] But even if this does not match the full-on miraculous quality of the events on Mount Lykaion, it is still striking that Pausanias does not dispute the basic fact of Aktaion's death by his dogs. He makes it clear that this has been a place of human suffering in the past. And by describing to us the slab of rock on which Aktaion is said to have rested he prompts us to imagine our own immersion in that mythical landscape: he invites us to imagine stretching out in that place for ourselves, re-creating the mythical past, fitting ourselves into the contours of the bed as Aktaion himself did (an ominous prospect, perhaps).

Above all, however, Mount Kithairon for Pausanias is a place of ritual. Book 9 includes one of our most important and extensive surviving descriptions of mountaintop sacrifice, in Pausanias' account of the festival of the Daidala, which he tells us was celebrated regularly on the summit of Kithairon by the city of Plataia. He explains first that the festival celebrates a story of reconciliation between Zeus and Hera: Hera had gone off in a sulk; Zeus pretended to be about to marry a mortal woman; he wrapped a wooden statue in a dress and set out in a wagon for the marriage procession; Hera appeared and tore the dress off, discovered the trick, and was pleased. He then tells us how the festival is conducted. That description is so remarkable that it is worth quoting at length:

> There is a grove not far from Alalkomenai. The trunks of the oak trees there are the thickest in Boiotia. The Plataians come to this grove and set out portions of boiled meat. The other birds hardly come near, but they keep a careful watch on the crows, which do keep coming. Whichever crow grabs the meat, they look out to see which of the trees it lands on. And whichever tree it settles on, they cut it down and make the *daidalon* from it; for the statue too, like the festival, is called a *daidalon*. (9.3.4)

Here Pausanias offers us a fairly harmless, symbolic version of bodily dissolution on Mount Kithairon very different from the horrifying dismemberment of Pentheus in the same location.

Pausanias then moves on to a detailed account of the festival's processions:

> This festival the Plataians celebrate by themselves, calling it the Little Daidala. But as for the Great Daidala, the Boiotians celebrate it with them, and they celebrate it every fifty-nine years, for that is the period they say the festival lapsed for, when the Plataians were in exile. They have fourteen statues ready, which have been prepared each year at the Little Daidala. These are allocated by lot to the people of Plataia, Koroneia, Thespiai, Tanagra, Chaironeia, Orchomenos, Lebadeia, and Thebes. ... The less important towns contribute jointly. They take the statue to the river Asopos and put it on a wagon, together with a woman to act as bridesmaid. Then they draw lots again to determine their order in the procession. After this they drive the wagons from the river up to the summit of Kithairon. On the peak of the mountain an altar has been prepared for them. This is how they make the altar: they fit together squared blocks of wood and put them together just as if they were building a house with stones, and having raised the altar to a great height they pile on brushwood. The cities and their magistrates each sacrifice a cow to Hera and a bull to Zeus, and burn the victims on the altar, full of wine and incense, together with the statues. Private individuals sacrifice the victims one would expect from rich men; those who are less wealthy sacrifice smaller victims, and all the offerings are burned together. The fire seizes and destroys the altar along with them. I know of no other flame that reaches so high or is seen from so far off. (9.3.5–8)

As always it is hard to know how far this represents a straightforward reflection of real practices and how far it represents an attempt by Pausanias or his informants to conjure up an image of festive continuity with the past. Pausanias' passing mention of a 'local guide' (ὁ τῶν ἐπιχωρίων ἐξηγητής) (9.3.3) gives us one possible source, and also incidentally hints at an established industry of sacred tourism around Mount Kithairon.[43] If the great Daidala takes place only every fifty-nine years Pausanias is unlikely to have seen it, and each new version is likely to have been a reinvention of barely remembered practices from two generations before. No one has ever reported remains of an altar on the summit of Kithairon.[44] Still this passage does give us one of the most vivid surviving descriptions of what a mountaintop sacrifice and procession might have been like, and especially of the way in which it could join city and

FIGURE 3.1. Summit ridge of Mount Kithairon. Photo: author.

mountain together. The processional details—different communities each contributing to the sacrifice, and each on display in a pre-arranged position within the parade—are consistent with what we know of other kinds of urban sacrificial processions, from the evidence of other inscriptions from the Hellenistic and Roman world. At the same time the oddity of some of the details here, especially the crows and the meat, reminds us of the vast variety of local ritual in the ancient world.

Also striking is this passage's representation of vision and visibility. The views from the top today are impressive, if you can tear your eyes away from the huge wind turbines that line the ridge (figure 3.1). From the summit, which forms a natural boundary with Attica and Megaris to the south, you can see much of Boiotia laid out before you. The visibility of many of the cities participating in the festival must have contributed to the ceremony's enactment of community. But that is not what Pausanias says: what interests him is the fact that 'no other flame reaches so high or is seen from so far off'. Once again this passage reminds us that it was not just the view from summit sanctuaries that mattered for the Greeks; just as important was the visibility from below (or indeed from other mountains). It may be the case that relatively few worshippers made the journey to the summits to sacrifice in this and other festivals in honour of Zeus, but on a clear day even those down below would have been able to follow with their eyes the smoke of sacrifice rising up from the peak of Kithairon. If you go to Plataia (modern Plataies) today, you can see just how close the city lies to the base of the mountain: the scale of that relationship is surprisingly intimate.

From Plataia, Pausanias goes north to Thebes, and then on to northwest Boiotia, taking sideways glances at a series of lesser mountains along the way.[45] Standing tall between these much briefer passages is Mount Helikon, the mountain that dominates the second half of the book. This too, like Mount Kithairon, is a place of religious observance, but not a place associated by Pausanias with direct, miraculous interventions of the gods. He makes it immediately clear that the mountain with the territory around it is a special place of safety and fertility, and our first instinct might be to take that as an index of its divinely protected character,[46] but oddly Pausanias chooses not to ascribe that phenomenon explicitly to divine presence or divine involvement. For example, he tells us that even snake bites on Mount Helikon are less dangerous; he then offers us a lengthy account of the way in which a snake's venom is affected by 'the pasture where the snake grazes' (9.28.2). Here too, as on Mount Kithairon, Pausanias is downplaying both bodily threats and miraculous dangers.

This is still a sacred place, of course, but the marvels here are human creations in honour of the gods rather than marvels brought into being by divine intervention. Pausanias makes that clear in a long account that once again allows us to glimpse the outlines of a culture of tourism, in this case associated particularly with the sanctuary of the Muses, which stood at the head of the valley to the east of the mountain. This was for many centuries an important site, the venue for the great festival of the Muses with its musical competitions under the control of the city of Thespiai.[47] The Valley of the Muses has a distinctly rustic feel now, with very few remains of ancient buildings, and that makes it hard to guess at its former glories. If you visit today, you will see lots of columns scattered around the ground at the head of the valley, and very little else. But even in Pausanias' time it was not an architecturally monumental place: there was a theatre and an altar and a long colonnade, but not much else. What marked it out, instead, was its extraordinary collection of statues and paintings. And it is this that makes it, for Pausanias, one of the great highlights of Boiotia. We know from surviving inscriptions that the site was packed with statues of leading Roman benefactors, especially members of the Roman imperial family.[48] Other inscriptions give victory lists from the games, dating back to the third century BCE.[49] But what Pausanias notices above all is the images of music and poetry. On the approach road he notes an image of Eupheme, nursemaid of the Muses, and another of Linos, son of Poseidon, whose singing was unparalleled among mortals, and who was killed by Apollo as a rival. Later come (among others) images of the Muses by famous artists; an image of Apollo and Hermes fighting over a lyre; two images of Dionysus, one of them dedicated by the Roman general Sulla; and then a series of statues of great poets, Hesiod (along with a tripod he is said to have won in competition) and Orpheus foremost among them.[50] The whole site, on Pausanias' account, is a celebration of musical inspiration. There was heavy investment in the site in the third century BCE. We know from other texts too that the Valley of the Muses was a place of pilgrimage and tourism in the imperial period. Plutarch describes a visit there in the late first century CE: 'on Helikon, at the home of the Muses, while the people of Thespiai were celebrating the festival of the Erotidia. For they celebrate the festival every four years, in honour of Eros as well as the Muses, very ambitiously and splendidly' (Plutarch, *Amatorius* 1, 748f). The festival Plutarch refers to here seems to have been celebrated in the city: Plutarch brings his wife to sacrifice to the god Eros and to ask him to intervene in a quarrel between their parents; they tire of the festival and go off to camp, along with friends, in the Valley of the Muses.

That culture of tourism seems to have extended even to the higher slopes of the mountain. Here too Pausanias shows strikingly little interest in the idea of divine presence and divine power on the mountainside. The key passage is his account of his visit to the Hippokrene spring, which was an important site not only because of its appearance in Hesiod's *Theogony* but also because of the way in which it was imagined as a place of inspiration in Hellenistic and Roman poetry:[51]

> If you ascend about twenty stades from this grove you get to what is called the Horse's Fountain (Ἵππου ... κρήνη). They say that the horse of Bellerophon made it by striking the ground with his hoof. The Boiotians who live around Helikon have a tradition that Hesiod wrote nothing but the *Works*, and even from that work they reject the prelude to the Muses, saying that the beginning of the poem is the account of the Strifes. They showed me also a piece of lead where the spring is, mostly defaced by time, on which is engraved the *Works*. (9.31.3–4)

You can still see the Hippokrene spring today. It stands just below the summit ridge of Zagaras, which is the peak at the eastern end of the Helikon range. I

FIGURE 3.2. Hippokrene spring, Zagaras, Mount Helikon. Photo: author.

climbed up there in June 2015. You follow a wide track to the west from the head of the Valley of the Muses. There were beehives everywhere and bees buzzing in the trees, and no one else in sight all day apart from a goatherd in the distance. After a couple of miles you turn steeply uphill. The climb to the summit ridge is about 500 metres of ascent, and then it's an hour or so west from there to the summit of Zagaras, scrambling along the big outcrops of rock which line the ridge. The Hippokrene spring is at the edge of a steeply sloping pasture just before you get up to the ridge. There is a gap in the rocks with water three or four metres below and clouds of flies buzzing just above it (figure 3.2). Fixed to the rocks is a rusty chain and a plastic bucket: you can throw it down so that it splashes into the water. I had not realised how far up the spring would be. Pausanias must have climbed all the way up the long slope to see it. His brief use of the first-person pronoun ('they showed me') gives us a precious glimpse of the culture of mountain climbing as tourism which is implied, but not firmly attested in the rest of his work. That shadowy 'they' is intriguing too: presumably these are local guides again, who would accompany the steady stream of visitors who must have come here even outside festival time. It is also striking here that the Boiotians have such a stripped-down, divinity-free version of Hesiod's poems, not including the *Theogony*, and not including the preface to the *Works and Days*, which calls on the Muses to give inspiration to the poet—a more conventional version of divine inspiration than the story of personal encounter with the Muses that we find in the opening lines of the *Theogony*. Theirs is a very human vision of Hesiod's work, which ignores the old mythical stories of the gods and focuses on the day-to-day portrayal of post-heroic life that dominates the *Works and Days*. That seems all the more odd given that the whole of the sanctuary down below, at least on Pausanias' account, is a celebration of the power of the Muses, and given that the *Theogony* preface itself talks about the presence of the Muses at the spring: it would seem like an ideal place for the *Theogony* to be on display. The inhabitants of Boiotia, on Pausanias' account, are inclined to strip away stories of divine presence from their mountains, and his portrayal of Helikon is part of that wider pattern.[52]

Phokis

Last, in Book 10, after Kithairon and Helikon, we move to the third of the three ancient summits to the north of the Corinthian Gulf, Parnassos, and to the sanctuary of Apollo at Delphi that lies beneath it. Here once again, as in Book 8, Pausanias seems to be more open to the idea of divine presence within sacred landscapes and its impact on human bodies. His narrative slows to indicate the special mythical and historical significance of the site he is dealing with.[53] Delphi, even more so than Mount Lykaion, was a built space, a supreme example of the kind of human presence within divine mountain landscapes that we have seen already in the previous nine books of the *Periegesis*. Like the Valley of the Muses on Mount Helikon, it was a place of pilgrimage and tourism, and an object of ancient topophilia. It thrived throughout the imperial period right into late antiquity. It offered an encounter with the classical past, which had left its marks everywhere in the monuments and dedications which were scattered across the site. It must also have offered a powerful sensory experience, especially at festival time, with the looming cliffs above, and the sounds of the musical contests and the spectators echoing across the sanctuary.[54] In that sense it was a very human place.

Pausanias, however, also represents the summit of Parnassos as a place which is in some respects beyond human understanding and separate from the built-up and enclosed terrain of the sanctuary. That is clear especially in his account of the Korykian cave. The cave is several hours walk above Delphi. It is an enormous space: around 60 metres long, with a high, echoing roof. It was sacred to the Nymphs and to Pan. It seems to have been a standard stop on the Delphi tourist trail. Excavations have revealed tens of thousands of terracotta figurines. Cut into the walls of the cave are niches that would have held some of these dedications. Archaeologists have also found 22,000 knucklebones, mainly from sheep and goats, which may have been used for divination, perhaps particularly by local shepherds and goatherds.[55] Much of this material is from the classical period, and the finds decline in the second century BCE, but we then see an increase in material from the first century CE onwards, especially finds of lamps (some of them from as late as the fourth century CE), perhaps provided for visitors who wanted to explore the back sections of the cave where the sunlight barely reaches.[56] Plutarch in one of his dialogues mentions that a visitor to Delphi, who is described as 'a lover of sights' (*philotheamōn*), has been escorted up to the Korykian cave.[57] Pausanias went there himself: 'As one goes from Delphi to the peak of Parnassos, there is a bronze statue about sixty stades [that is, about seven miles] from Delphi, and the path up to the Korykian cave is easier for an active person than it is for mules and horses ... of all the caves I have seen this one seemed to me to be worth seeing most of all' (10.32.2). The cave itself is not up in the high mountains. The initial path up from Delphi is steep, just as Pausanias says, but once you are above the cliffs you emerge onto level pastureland that stretches on for many miles to the north and the east, with the sound of sheep- and goat-bells all around. The Korykian cave stands just above it, a short climb up a steep hill opposite the main Parnassos peaks. Pausanias makes it clear, however, that the cave stood on the edge of much wilder territory: 'from the Korykian cave it is difficult even for an active man to reach the summit of Parnassos; the peaks are higher than the clouds, and the Thyiades rave there in honour of Dionysus and Apollo' (10.32.7).[58] The summit of Parnassos can be a forbidding place even now in the summer: bleak and rocky, and sometimes covered in mist, with only the ski-lift machinery to break up the monotony of the huge slopes. There is no evidence for sacrifice on any of the summits:[59] many of the peaks where we have most extensive evidence for mountaintop ritual were considerably lower than the giants like Parnassos and Olympus, and so more accessible to the communities around them. But what we do know about is the worship of Dionysus that Pausanias refers to. The Thyiades were a society of women who worshipped at a regularly occurring winter festival through a kind of ritual frenzy on the mountainside, a less murderous version of the madness of the Bacchic women who rip Pentheus to pieces at the end of Euripides' *Bacchae*. Their activities are widely attested. Other ancient sources too stress the way in which their ritual involved an encounter with the mountain as a hostile space, distant from normal human experience. The philosopher Plutarch was active in the late first and early second century CE and was himself a priest of Delphi. We know that one of his addressees, the priestess Klea, who seems to have been a member of the educated elite, acted as leader of the Thyiades. Plutarch records an occasion—the best example we have of an ancient mountain rescue operation—when the Thyiades had to be rescued from Mount Parnassos after being trapped there in a snowstorm so severe that the clothes of the rescuers froze solid and split apart when they were straightened.[60] We have evidence for similar rituals of *oreibasia* (mountain-going) from elsewhere in the Greek world too, most famously from Miletos in Asia Minor. No doubt the reality was more mundane than we sometimes assume. But it is clear nevertheless that this was not just a dispassionate antiquarian commemoration of famous events from Greek myth. It involved a trance-like state; it involved real dangers; it was an attempt to experience or at least enact divine presence and divine inspiration in a mountain environment.[61] In representing Parnassos as the territory of the *oreibasia* Pausanias depicts it, like Mount Lykaion, as a space which lies beyond the reach of his rationalising gaze.

That image of Mount Parnassos as a space which is beyond human understanding, and inaccessible to normal human presence, is reinforced much more extensively in another passage later in Book 10 where Pausanias describes how Mount Parnassos itself resisted the invading forces of the Gauls in 279 BCE. That narrative portrays the failure of masculine, military control over divine territory, implicitly in contrast with the more successful, ritualised, female engagement associated with the *oreibasia*: human conquest, or attempted conquest of mountain terrain does tend to be represented as a masculine prerogative, as it often has been in the modern world too.[62] It is a story he has already touched on elsewhere in the work, most importantly early on in his account of Athens in Book 1, the very first mention of a mountain in the work, in response to a painting of Kallippos, the Athenian who commanded the Greek forces: 'When they joined battle, then thunderbolts were hurled at the Gauls, and rocks torn away from Mount Parnassos; nightmare figures stood as hoplite soldiers against the barbarians' (1.4.4). He returns to this incident again in Book 8, as a parallel for a Mantineian story that the god Poseidon had fought for the Arkadians in a battle against the Spartans: 'most clearly of all the army of the Gauls was destroyed at Delphi by the god, openly destroyed by divine powers (ὑπὸ δαιμόνων)' (8.10.9).[63] In Book 10, finally, he tells the story of the invasion at more length. The Gauls, under their commander Brennos, manage to bypass the Greek resistance at Thermopylai and march on Delphi, motivated in part by a desire to plunder the treasures at the sanctuary. Apollo through his oracle tells the Delphians that he will look after them. And when the army arrives 'Brennos and his army were faced by those of the Greeks who had assembled at Delphi, and portents from the gods were revealed to the barbarians quickly, and more clearly than any other case I know of' (10.23.1). That sentence perhaps explains why Pausanias gives so much prominence to this story, as the very best available example he knows of divine intervention, to stand in tension with his more sceptical approach to what he views as less plausible stories elsewhere in the *Periegesis*. He tells us that the Gauls were terrified by lightning and earthquakes, and by supernatural sightings of divine heroes from the Delphic past.[64] In the night there was a fierce frost, and snow and 'great rocks slipping down from Parnassos and broken-off bits of cliff headed straight for them' (10.23.4). In the next night comes the fatal blow as they are infected with 'panic', the madness of the god Pan, so that they begin to hallucinate about being under attack and kill each other. Pausanias' summing up is insistent: 'I assure you that is how it happened' (10.24.1). Here Pausanias offers us an image of mountains as places of supernatural power of a much more immediate and more terrifying kind than the image of divine presence through ritual which has predominated through much of the rest of the work. The mountains have their own agency here: a capacity to resist mistreatment and to submerge the bodies of their invaders.[65]

Reading Pausanias' *Periegesis* can help us to understand the mountains of the ancient world, and especially their continuing role as religious landscapes in Greece even in the Roman period. The mountains of the text can help us in turn towards a fresh understanding of Pausanias' work and particularly of his representation of the relationship between the human and the divine. Pausanias is in some respects a rationalising author, but he also has an acute awareness that the landscapes he travels through have been places of divine presence. He is fascinated by the presence of human bodies in the places he describes, to a far greater degree than we usually realise. His work is packed with stories of bodies embedded or buried in the landscape; he represents corporeal engagement with the landscape, or at least imagined corporeal engagement, as a key part of the experience of travel and antiquarianism; most importantly for this chapter, he is acutely aware of the way in which divine and other more-than-human forces can overwhelm human actors, through stories of the human body at risk in particular places. It is striking that two of the most prominent manifestations of that combination of divine presence and bodily vulnerability are set on the ancient mountains of Lykaion and Parnassos, which stand on either side of his more rationalising treatment of the mountains of Boiotia. Reading Books 8, 9, and 10 together allows us to experience Pausanias' oscillation between different attitudes to the divine in different contexts. In the process we are confronted with the challenge of disentangling his approach for ourselves and forming our own views about how one can distinguish between true and false reports of divinely inspired events. Mountains are not the only landscapes in the text where those kinds of effects come into view. The whole of Pausanias' work is about reporting the way in which present-day landscapes are marked by the associations of the past. All of the territories Pausanias explores, both urban and rural, are covered with religious buildings and local rituals. There are other locations at ground level where we see Pausanias accepting stories about divine presence in a way which disrupts the rationalising surface of his narrative. And yet it is surely no accident that two of the most powerful of those moments are set in mountains that had very ancient religious and mythical associations. In exploring those incidents so conspicuously Pausanias is typical of a much wider tendency in ancient literature, which is so often fascinated by tension between two different ways of imagining mountains, on the one hand as landscapes that can be brought within human culture, and on the other as places that are resistant to human control and beyond human understanding; places that confront us as humans with our own bodily vulnerability in relation to divine and natural forces.

4

Egeria on Mount Sinai: Mountain Pilgrimage in Early Christian and Late Antique Culture

Biblical Mountains

How did the associations between mountains and the divine develop in early Christian and late antique culture? In this final chapter of part I, I turn to the pilgrimage narrative of Egeria, who travelled in the Holy Land in the late fourth century CE and left one of the most extensive travel narratives surviving from the ancient world. We have her accounts of ascending Mount Sinai, on the Sinai peninsula in what is now Egypt, and Mount Nebo, in modern Jordan. We know from a summary of her work, which survives only in part, that the full text included other mountain ascents too. Egeria shows us perhaps more vividly than any other ancient author how the divine could be accessed through human knowledge and through the human routines and rituals associated with certain sacred mountain landscapes. Her vision is both typical of late antique responses to mountains and the divine and in some ways quite idiosyncratic. She also stands out as an unusual example of female involvement in ways of spending time in the mountains that more often had masculine associations.

Egeria's text has a certain amount in common with the long tradition of representing Greco-Roman mountain religion that stretches back through Pausanias to Homer and beyond, but it is also shaped by Jewish and Christian antecedents that were quite distinct. Mountains are everywhere in the Hebrew and early Christian scriptures (there are around 500 references).[1] As in the Greco-Roman tradition, they are repeatedly represented as places of divine presence and divine revelation, on the edges of human control and understanding. Most influential of all was the scene from Exodus 19–34, where Moses receives the law on Mount Sinai. Moses has led the Israelites out of Egypt into the mountainous wilderness, a space that represents freedom and escape from exile, while also exposing them to threats of warfare and hunger. Early on in their journey they come to Mount Sinai. When they arrive there God tells Moses to forbid the Israelites from approaching the mountain while they purify themselves: anyone who touches even the foot of the mountain is to be stoned to death or shot with arrows.[2] Only on the third day are they allowed to approach: 'Now Mount Sinai was wrapped in smoke, because the Lord had descended upon it in fire; the smoke went up like the smoke of a kiln, while the whole mountain shook violently. . . . When the Lord descended upon Mount Sinai, to the top of the mountain, the Lord summoned Moses to the top of the mountain, and Moses went up' (Exodus 19:18–20).[3] In what follows Moses makes a number of other ascents of Mount Sinai; he receives God's commandments there, and in one case stays on the mountain for forty days. For the most part he perceives only God's voice, as is usual in the Hebrew tradition, but in one famous passage he is able to see God on the summit, albeit with severe restrictions:

> And the Lord continued, 'See, there is a place by me where you shall stand on the rock; and while my glory passes by I will put you in a cleft of the rock, and I will cover you with my hand until I have passed by; then I will take away my hand, and you shall see my back; but my face shall not be seen'. (Exodus 33:21–23)

The limits to Moses' knowledge and perception are made completely clear here. This passage is one of the most influential of all examples of the way in which mountains can force us to confront the unknowability of the divine.[4] It stands in contrast with the later moment where Moses gazes down on the promised land from Mount Nebo just before his death in the book of Deuteronomy: the distant vision he has there could hardly be more different, although even in that case it is clear that he is seeing only what God allows him to see.[5] That contrast is another powerful example of the tension between distant mountaintop viewing on the one hand, associated not just with Zeus in the *Iliad* but also with various human actors in positions of authority, and on the other hand an image of mountains as places where human vision is restricted or where humans see sights that are puzzling and hard to decipher.

The other great mountain narrative of the Hebrew bible is the story of Elijah from 1 Kings. There too mountains are places of divine presence. They are also places of conflict between different religious traditions, between old and new. That kind of conflict has parallels in the Greco-Roman tradition, for example in the clashes between old and new gods in Greek mythology over particular mountain territories,[6] and also outside religious discourse in a text like Dio Chrysostom's *Euboian Oration*, discussed in more detail in chapter 15, which dramatises the differences between old and new ways of living in the mountains.[7] 1 Kings is also a classic example of the kind of cumulative, intratextually challenging portrayal of landscape that I have suggested is typical of ancient Greek and Roman literature too. It would be easy to focus just on the key moments of the narrative, in all their cinematic and bloodthirsty detail, but that would miss the way in which those high points are set in the context of a lengthy exploration of mountains as places of divine worship and divine communication. The first half of 1 Kings is an account of the reign of Solomon; the second tells the story of his various successors and their increasing wickedness and rebellion against God. A significant part of the first half of the book is taken up with a detailed description of the building of Solomon's Temple, which is presented as a place of special access to the Lord through prayer. In the late chapters of the book, however, the role of the Temple is increasingly challenged by the continued devotion of Solomon and his successors and their people to the 'hill-shrines', which are linked with false gods.[8] Before the building of the temple these places are viewed as acceptable, but afterwards they become places of impiety, in line with Deuteronomy 12:2–3, which had commanded the destruction of mountaintop shrines and the institution of a single place of worship. First Solomon himself turns to false gods, under the influence of his 700 wives: 'Then Solomon built a high place for Chemosh the abomination of Moab, and for Molech the abomination of the Ammonites, on the mountain east of Jerusalem' (1 Kings 11:7). After Solomon's death Jeroboam builds hill-shrines to stop the people from sacrificing in the Temple, which he fears would revive their loyalty to the family of Solomon. An unnamed prophet predicts the destruction of the priests of the hill shrines,[9] but Jeroboam goes on giving his support to these sites,[10] and Rehoboam does the same in Judah: 'For they also built for themselves high places, pillars, and sacred poles on every high hill and under every green tree; there were also male temple prostitutes in the land' (1 Kings 14:23–24). It is against this background that Elijah comes on the scene to reclaim the mountains as places of communication with the true God. First he defeats the 450 prophets of Baal on Mount Carmel (the mountain range that juts out into the Mediterranean above the modern city of Haifa in Israel): he rebuilds the altar of the Lord on the mountain and prays for a response, and the fire of the Lord falls and consumes the sacrifice. The prophets of Baal, by contrast, can get no response from their own god. Elijah has the prophets of Baal seized and slaughters them in the valley.[11] And then immediately afterwards comes a much more private moment of divine presence, in a scene that echoes Moses' encounters with God:[12] Elijah flees to Mount Horeb (which is generally thought to be an alternative name for Mount Sinai) and sleeps in a cave; a voice comes to him and tells him to go and stand on the mountain before God; first a great wind will pass by, Elijah is told, then an earthquake, then fire, but the Lord will not be in any of those; then will come the sound of silence. At that point Elijah hears the voice of the Lord, who orders him to go down to Damascus.[13] The mountains of 1 Kings are places of drama and conflict, then, but it is a drama that builds gradually to a climax over many generations. Nor is it fully resolved by Elijah's spectacular and vengeful behavior: at the very end of the book the situation under the pious rule of Jehoshaphat in Judah has improved, but even so the hill-shrines are allowed to remain,[14] and it is hard to avoid the impression that the formulaic claims, which have been repeated over and over again through the narrative,[15] about monarchs who have challenged the exclusivity of the Temple in Jerusalem, may continue indefinitely into the future. The mountains, in this text, are never fully under control.

One of the other distinctive features of mountains in the Hebrew Bible is their symbolic function. That often involves portraying mountains in positive terms, which stand in tension with their association with danger and isolation elsewhere. For example, they are imagined as places for the proclamation of good news.[16] They are personified (much more frequently so than in Greek and Latin literature) and imagined celebrating, especially in the Psalms: 'Let the floods clap their hands; let the hills sing together for joy' (Psalms 98:8); 'When Israel went out of Egypt . . . the mountains skipped like rams, the hills like lambs' (Psalms 114:1–4). They are used as illustrations of the power of God, who can bring blessing or destruction even to mountains at will: 'I will make the land a desolation and a waste, and its proud might shall come to an end; and the mountains of Israel shall be so desolate that no one will pass through' (Ezekiel 33:28); 'the mountains shall drip sweet wine, and all the hills shall flow with it' (Amos 9:13). The mountain of the Lord, sometimes associated with Mount Zion, which came to be used as the name for the hill on which the Temple in Jerusalem was built, is represented repeatedly as a place of refuge and comfort to which the people of God will come.[17]

These passages from the Hebrew Bible are imitated and recast over and over again within the New Testament, where mountains similarly stand as places of contact between the everyday human world and the other world of the divine.[18] Most important is the Gospel of Matthew, where Jesus has six major mountain scenes:[19] for example, he delivers the Sermon on the Mount,[20] in a way which equates him with Moses speaking to the assembled Israelites after his receipt of the law; and in Jesus' Transfiguration he is accompanied by Moses and Elijah (we hear only that this takes place on 'a high mountain'; it was later associated with Mount Tabor, but the text's vagueness about location makes it easier for us to see it is as a replay of the encounters on Sinai and Horeb).[21] The first scene in Acts is Jesus' ascent to heaven from the Mount of Olives.[22] These mountain scenes are there partly to emphasise the interconnection between Jesus and his predecessors from the Hebrew Bible.[23] Here again mountains are powerful places of the imagination in part because of their associations with memory and history and the past, just as they have been in modern mountain writing too. They are also associated with experiences that come close to modern notions of the sublime, as places of height and solitude that have an overwhelming, awe-inspiring impact on Jesus' disciples.[24] When Jesus stands on the mountaintops he takes on a very ancient kind of authority and holiness, and the divine sphere becomes at least temporarily open to mortal apprehension, as it had been also in those famous scenes from Exodus and 1 Kings.

Mountain Allegories in the Writings of the Emperor Julian

The symbolic function of mountains took on even greater prominence in the centuries that followed, as part of a broader increase in allegorical thinking both in religious discourse and in travel and pilgrimage writing in late antiquity.[25] When Methodius wrote his *Symposium* in the late third century CE, with its dialogue between ten holy virgins on the subject of chastity, in imitation of the speeches in praise of love from Plato's *Symposium*, he set it in a garden paradise on a mountaintop and described the virgins toiling up the rough path from below, past terrifying reptiles and steep precipices. The precise significance of the mountain is never made explicit, but the way up clearly stands for the rough path to salvation, and the summit paradise clearly has afterlife connotations.[26] There is a parallel in Isaiah 25:6–8, which similarly imagines a mountaintop banquet as an image for the final reward that comes after death: 'On this mountain the Lord of hosts will make for all peoples a feast of rich food, a feast of well-aged wines, of rich food filled with marrow, of well-aged wines strained clear. And he will destroy on this mountain the shroud that is cast over all peoples, the sheet that is spread over all nations; he will swallow up death forever'. Moses' climb of Mount Sinai was also used in a number of passages by early Christian theological writers as a metaphor for spiritual ascent. Gregory of Nyssa's *Life of Moses*, from the late fourth century CE, slips abruptly from a vivid account of the terrifying sight of the smoke covering the mountain, and of Moses' fear, into a more allegorical mode:[27] 'he teaches, I think, by his deeds that the one who is going to be together with God must withdraw from all that is visible, and lifting up his own mind to what is invisible and incomprehensible, as if to the summit of a mountain, must believe that the divine is there in that place where understanding does not reach' (Gregory of Nyssa, *Life of Moses* 1.46). And then later: 'knowledge of the divine is a mountain which is truly steep indeed and difficult to access, and most people hardly get as far as the foothills' (*Life of Moses* 2.158).

Those interests were not confined to Christian writings. The pagan emperor Julian, who ruled briefly in the mid-fourth century BCE, was fascinated both by real mountains as sites of divine relevation and by the challenge of reshaping classical and Christian traditions of mountain symbolism. In that sense he represents a good example of the cross-fertilisation between pagan and Christian responses to landscape in late antiquity, and of the continuing interest in mountains as places on the very edge of human understanding. In the spring of 363 CE, Julian saw a vision on the summit of Mount Kasios (Jebel Aqra), the great mountain of the gods on the Turkish-Syrian border. As we have seen already, that mountain had a long sacred history even before Julian travelled there, as the home of the Canaanite god Baal and his Hittite equivalents, and was later colonised by Christian monks. But Julian would not have been interested in that: his devotion was to Zeus. He travelled to the mountain from the city of Antioch, twenty miles or so to the north, where he spent much of the last year of his life. The trip seems to have been a much anticipated and in some respects quite public event. The orator Libanius, one of Julian's supporters and an important figure in Antiochean society, wrote a letter to one of Julian's officials, Anatolius, several months before the event, wishing him a successful sacrifice and encounter with 'the god who protects the mountain', and explaining that he himself would be coming too were it not for ill-health.[28]

Presumably, then, we should imagine Julian travelling with a sizable retinue, and also with very public preconceptions about the mountain as a place of divine communication. In a later work Libanius tells us that 'having gone up Mount Kasios to Kasian Zeus in the very middle of the day, he saw the god, and having seen him stood up and received some advice, by which he later avoided an ambush again'.[29] It did not do him much good in the long run. Just a few months later Julian was dead, fatally wounded in battle against the Persians; in fact Libanius' account is itself part of a funeral oration for Julian, delivered a year or two later. But it is nevertheless a remarkable moment in the continuing history of mountains as places of divine communication.

What kind of relationship does this story have with Julian's own religious beliefs and practices and those of his contemporaries? The Roman Empire had been increasingly christianised since the conversion of the emperor Constantine in 312 CE. Greco-Roman rituals and beliefs were able to exist side-by-side with the new Christian faith in some contexts, but their popularity weakened as the century went on. When the emperor Julian came to power in 361 CE, he embarked on an extraordinary campaign to restore the old faith, not so much by suppression of Christianity (although he attempted to curtail the power of the Christian schools), but more by a massive effort of revival of and personal participation in ancient pagan rituals. Above all he was famous for his obsession with sacrifice.[30] He sacrificed regularly, and on a vast scale. Libanius, earlier in the same funeral oration, tells us that 'everywhere there were altars and fire and blood and the smell of sacrifice and smoke and rituals and prophets freed from fear and piping on the mountain-tops and processions' (Libanius, *Oration* 18.126).[31] He seems to have taken particularly seriously the role of emperor as priest, sacrificing on behalf of his subjects. Sacrifice seems to have mattered to Julian above all because it was a way of opening up a channel of personal communication to the divine. The scene on Mount Kasios, which seems to have involved sacrifice on the altar of Zeus, is part of this wider pattern.

So should we see Julian's encounter with Zeus as a very traditional moment? Or does it reflect new ways of thinking about the gods and about landscape? Of course divine epiphany goes a long way back into earlier classical culture, to Homer's Olympians and Hesiod's Muses. There are hundreds of surviving stories about the appearance of gods to humans in later centuries too, not just in mythical narrative but also in reports of present-day epiphanies, many of them recorded in inscriptions, and many of them linked with particular religious sites.[32] If anything we see an intensification of interest in divine appearance in the second and third centuries CE.[33] Midday is often represented, as it is in this passage, as a specially numinous time, when the gods are particularly likely to show themselves.[34] Mountains are common places for epiphany, along with other marginal landscapes removed from human civilisation, and not only in mythical texts like the *Homeric Hymn to Aphrodite*; mountaintop appearances are reported as having happened in historical time too.[35] Herodotus famously tells us of an encounter between the Athenian messenger Pheidippides and the god Pan on Mount Parthenion on the borders of Arkadia, where Pan promises his support in the Battle of Marathon.[36] It is relatively rare in the classical tradition of epiphany to see Zeus in person (and the text does insist that Julian's encounter is a visual one), but here too there are precedents.[37] In many of these cases Zeus is in disguise, especially in erotic epiphanies, involving the seduction of beautiful mortal women, and in stories where Zeus receives hospitality from humans, or where he brings help in battle. But Julian's intimacy with Zeus goes one step further. The most obvious classical precedents for this passage come in stories where an individual's regular access to conversation with Zeus is used is a sign of political status, for example in the story that we find already in the *Odyssey* where the Cretan ruler Minos converses with Zeus every nine years, in some accounts on Mount Ida.[38]

Julian is reaching back to very old models of divine presence, then. And he is not unusual in doing so. And yet he is also doing something very new with those ideas. The novelty of this scene on Mount Kasios comes partly from the way in which it is underpinned by philosophical theorisation of the mechanisms for connection between mortal and divine. An interest in that problem, together with an increasing interest in allegory, was one of the distinctive features of Neoplatonic thinking, which became prominent especially in the later third and fourth centuries CE.[39] Julian also boasts repeatedly about the way in which the gods have guided him and been close to him throughout his life. One of the most fascinating manifestations of that claim is his letter *To the Cynic Herakleios*.[40] He talks about the way in which the god Hermes took him in hand early in his life and brought him to the foot of 'a great and high mountain'. On the summit, says Hermes, dwells the father of the gods; Julian must be careful to worship him piously. The young Julian acknowledges that he does not yet see the father of the gods clearly; then he prays: 'Father Zeus . . . show me the path that leads upwards to you'. Finally Zeus reveals to him the god Helios, who takes him up to a high summit flooded with light and offers him the chance to rule. It is hard to avoid the conclusion that those allegorical associations must have been in Julian's mind that day on Mount Kasios. Did

Julian view that sacrifice and the vision that accompanied it as manifestations of his own philosophical ascent to the divine?[41]

But the newness of Julian's divine encounter does not come just from the influence of late antique pagan philosophy. This is surely also a response to Christian images of revelation by the one God on the mountaintops. Julian had had a Christian education and had lived much of his adult life as a Christian, and the Gospel narratives must have been burned into his memory. The surest sign comes in that scene from *To the Cynic Herakleios*, where Helios offers Julian earthly power: that passage is not just a late echo of the Homeric association between mountain summits and divine vision and authority. It is also much more precisely an allusion to the famous scene in Matthew 4:8–10 where Jesus is led up to a high mountain by the devil, who offers him all the kingdoms of the earth. Jesus of course refuses; Julian, in his parodic imitation of the Gospel text, accepts.[42] As so often in his writings he attempts to combat Christianity by mockery. And yet that passage also shows us that it is very hard, by the fourth century, even for the arch-pagan Julian, to think about mountains and the divine purely in Greco-Roman terms.

Mountain Pilgrimage

The other distinctive development in late antique responses to mountains and the divine was the development of a new culture of Christian pilgrimage.[43] That had a great deal in common with the proliferation of pagan mountain rituals and holy places which we have seen already in Pausanias and which continued to be important even after the christianisation of the Roman Empire in the fourth century. In that sense Julian's visit to Mount Kasios is far from being an isolated incident. Some of the mountaintop shrines from mainland Greece underwent surprising late antique revivals: for example Mount Hymettos in Attica,[44] or Mount Olympus,[45] both of which give evidence for a surprising revival in dedications, after a long gap, in Christian late antiquity.[46] One very fragmentary surviving inscription, probably from the fourth century CE, seems to give evidence for visits to the Cave of Pan on Mount Parnes, also in Attica: it tells us that one elite worshipper Nikagoras has undertaken the 'difficult ascent' to the cave 'for the eleventh or twelfth time'.[47]

But these instances are sparse by comparison with the vast body of evidence for early Christian pilgrimage which emerges quite suddenly from the mid-fourth century onwards. At precisely the period when Gregory of Nyssa and Julian were writing, new pilgrimage routes were emerging in the eastern

Mediterranean. Some of this travel was focused on the ascetics who took up their places in the mountainous deserts of Egypt and Palestine and Syria, and who attracted disciples and pilgrims in vast numbers. Saints' lives, which were written in ever larger numbers from the late fourth century onwards, record the extravagant devotions of holy men, and the miracles and divine communications that those devotions made possible.[48] These texts reflected and contributed to new ways of understanding the connections between wilderness and the divine, and helped to attract new recruits to the ascetic life, as well as the many travellers who came to marvel and to be blessed.

But equally important, and to some extent intertwined with that phenomenon, was the growth in pilgrimage to biblical sites across the Holy Land. The famous mountains of the Hebrew Bible were favoured destinations within that new industry, which flowered above all on the Sinai Peninsula, where it has continued right through the Byzantine and medieval periods into the present.[49] The pilgrims who travelled there seem to have gone partly in order to stand themselves in the places of scripture. In many of those sites visitors could take part in liturgy; some sites also held the relics of saints. The identity of the biblical Mount Sinai was (and still is) much debated.[50] But the identification with Jebel Musa in the southern Sinai Peninsula was very widely accepted from the fourth century onwards. Quite quickly, a complex infrastructure sprang up to cater for all the visitors, reaching its peak in the sixth and seventh centuries. There were three standard tourist routes from Jerusalem. The desert towns of the Negev, to the east of the Sinai peninsula, seem to have catered for large numbers passing through. The small town of Nessana, for example, had two caravanserais, one of which is described in a surviving papyrus document for the region as having an upper storey with space for 96 rush mats.[51] Monasteries and churches were built in large numbers around Jebel Musa, although not on the summit itself, and the monks seem to have spent much of their time guiding visitors around the sites. Prayer niches were built along the routes, many of them with a view of the summit of Mount Sinai, to help the pilgrims to focus their devotions,[52] and the 'Stairway of Repentance' was built into the mountainside, with almost 4,000 steps, to be climbed as an act of ritual preparation.[53] The climax of these developments was the emperor Justinian's building of a monastery and basilica, the famous monastery of Saint Catherine, by the site of the burning bush, in the mid-sixth century. And the pilgrims continued to come, in ever larger numbers. Anastasius of Sinai, writing around 700 CE, records a visit by 800 Armenian pilgrims to the summit at the same time—sixteen coachloads, by a modern count.[54]

This activity involved subjecting the landscape to human control through the accumulation of claims about the identity of particular places and through the imposition of rituals and routines. At the same time, however, it left space for more miraculous, mystical ways of thinking about divine presence, just as Pausanias did. For example, the summit of Mount Sinai was said to have repeated its manifestations of divine presence regularly for its pious visitors. Anastasius' Armenians got more than they bargained for: fire descended and covered the whole summit; no one was harmed, but the tips of their staffs were scorched and they cried out for mercy for about an hour before the vision finally receded. That is just one of a selection of stories in Anastasius about miracles on the summit.[55] The sixth-century historian Procopius stresses the wildness of Mount Sinai, and claims that no one can spend the night on the summit because of the lightning crashes and other terrifying manifestations of divine power.[56] Theodoret, who was writing much closer to the time of Egeria, in the first half of the fifth century, tells us about one monk who knelt for a whole week in fasting at the site associated with Moses' encounter with God, until he finally heard a divine voice.[57]

The imagery of ascent was also used within these places of pilgrimage to give expression to ideas of spiritual progress which were on the edge of human understanding. At the very centre of the monastery's collection of mosaics was an image of Jesus' transfiguration which allowed its viewers to imagine themselves side by side with the apostles on the summit of Mount Tabor. Above that image stood two images of Moses at Sinai. On the left he stands before the burning bush. On the right he receives the law on the summit of the mountain (figure 4.1). In that right-hand image Moses is hemmed in between two rocks; he averts his eyes as God passes down the laws to him, with his hands covered by his cloak. Like the transfiguration mosaic this is not a spectacular mountain depiction: we see two rocks, one of them in front of Moses, reaching up to about his waist, and the other behind him, stretching just above his head; presumably they are intended between them to stand for the cleft in which God places Moses in Exodus 33:22. However, the very restrictedness of the image allows us to imagine ourselves on the summit with Moses, sharing his own constrained viewpoint. And it stands as a symbol of ascent to the divine of the kind that many pilgrims would have been familiar with from Gregory of Nyssa and others, and which they would have acted out in their own experience of climbing to the summit. John Climacus was abbot of Saint Catherine's Monastery in the sixth or seventh century, and wrote a devotional work titled the *Ladder of Divine Ascent*. The closing sentences of the work sum up all that

80 CHAPTER 4

FIGURE 4.1. Moses receiving the Ten Commandments on Mount Sinai. Mosaic from the Basilica of Saint Catherine's Monastery, Sinai, sixth century CE. The Picture Art Collection / Alamy Stock Photo.

has gone before, drawing on the language of the Psalms, where mountains are celebrated as places of divine glory: 'Climb, brothers, climb eagerly, focusing on the ascent in your heart, and hearing him who says: "Come, let us go up to the mountain of the Lord and to the house of our God, who makes our feet like the feet of the deer, and sets us up on the high places"' (John Climacus, *Ladder of Divine Ascent* 30, *Patrologia Graeca* 88, 1160D–1161A). For the pilgrims of late antiquity, allegory was a way of imagining and conveying the experience of divine encounter.[58]

Egeria on Mount Sinai

Egeria too records the experience of accessing holy ground on Mount Sinai and Mount Nebo, but she does that in a way which is in some respects quite different from these other authors. That makes her a fascinating and challenging figure for the history of ancient and modern responses to mountains. Most strikingly, for Egeria there is no sign of the fire of God's presence on the mountain, and perhaps more remarkably no expectation of it. Instead she is preoccupied with the human rituals of prayer and eucharist and reading from scripture in the holy places she visits. In that sense Egeria's text is perhaps the most consistent of all ancient examples of the idea that mountaintop access to the divine can come through human activity and human knowledge-ordering. We have seen versions of that idea in a series of Greek and Roman texts, for example for Homer's Mount Ida, which is a place of human presence and sacrifice in contrast with the inaccessible summits of Olympus, or in Pausanias' Arkadia, with its networks of local cults and stories. The difference is that both of those texts also leave room for a more unpredictable image of divine presence manifesting itself in ways which overwhelm human control. The same goes for the wider tradition of representing Mount Sinai, which is one of the archetypal places for thinking about the unknowability of the divine.[59] In all of these cases there is a degree of separation between human ritual and divinely inspired miracle, as if the two are different ways of experiencing and accessing the divine. Egeria, by contrast, seems to have very little interest in the idea of a sphere of holiness which stands outside daily human experience. She is of course very much aware of the importance of Moses' divine encounter on Mount Sinai as the foundational moment for the pilgrimage she is undertaking, but she shows very little interest in the detail of that event, and she does not seem to need the prospect of the miraculous in the present in order to feel that she is in God's presence.[60] There is a fascinating parallel in another text set on Mount Sinai, the *Narrations* of Pseudo-Nilus, dating probably from the early fifth century CE.[61] That text describes the massacre by barbarians of some of the monks living around Mount Sinai. The work as a whole is unequivocally and extravagantly pious, but it does at the same time raise the possibility of a disillusioned reaction to a life of asceticism in the desert.[62] At one point the narrator escapes to the summit of the mountain, and prays to

God, asking why the mountain did not unleash its power to stop the killings (*Narrations* 4.8).[63] Pseudo-Nilus is acutely aware of the difficulties of understanding and submitting to divine will, and for his narrator the absence of divine signs on the mountaintop is a source of anguish and temporarily at least of complaint.[64] For Egeria, by contrast, it is not a matter for comment. Even when she does mention God's appearance to Moses she does so only briefly, for example in describing the central peak, 'on the summit of which is the place where "the Glory of God came down", so it is written' (*Itinerarium Egeriae* [hereafter *IE*] 2.5).[65]

Egeria's interest in rituals and in stories is clear from the very opening lines of the text as we have it. Her account seems to date from the 380s CE, just a couple of decades after the emperor Julian's death. We know very little about her. She may have been a nun (her work is addressed to readers she refers to as 'sisters'). She was presumably relatively wealthy, although her journey may have been financed by her community in exchange for a first-hand account of the holy sites. She probably came from the west of the Roman Empire.[66] Her Latin is not particularly polished or sophisticated, and some have taken that as a sign that she may have had only a limited education, although as we shall see there are some respects in which her use of language plays an intricate role in conveying the impressions she wants to convey. Her account of the Sinai region takes up six chapters out of forty-nine in the text as it survives and is followed by a wide range of other sites throughout the Near East, including an account of Jerusalem, and especially the liturgy of Jerusalem, which takes up most of the second half. The opening of Egeria's text is lost, but we know from a later abridgement that the Sinai sections come fairly near the beginning.[67] The text as it survives begins precisely at the moment of her first glimpse of Mount Sinai. Their guide advises them that it is customary to pray on first seeing the mountain, and they do so. Egeria identifies the valley as the one in which the Israelites waited while Moses was on the mountaintop for forty days and forty nights. They reach the mountain and are given a bed for the night, and then the next morning they set out early for the summit, accompanied by the priests and monks from the monastery. They are met on the summit by other monks, who read a passage from the book of Moses, give them communion, and then show them the places of scripture, including a cave Moses is said to have passed time in during his ascent up the mountain to receive the tablets a second time. On the way they pause at Mount Horeb (here understood as the neighbouring mountain to Mount Sinai) to see the cave where Elijah hid from Ahab, and the stone he set up as an offering to God, and then they camp overnight next to the burning bush, which is still alive, Egeria tells us, and still sends out green shoots. At that point her text becomes more crowded, as if the richness of these places overwhelms her narrative, clamouring for her attention: the place where the calf was made ('in that place a large stone is fixed to this day' [*IE* 5.3]); the rock on which Moses smashed the tablets in his anger; 'the place where manna and quails rained down for them' (*IE* 5.8), and so on. In all of this it is striking that Egeria almost never expresses any doubt about the identity of these sites, in contrast with Pausanias, who is constantly interrogating local stories for their reliability. For Egeria, by contrast, the identification of particular sites with their scriptural equivalents by her monastic informants seems to be unfailingly reliable.

Over and over again throughout this narrative Egeria stresses the fulfilment of her desire and of her expectations. These holy places with their rituals of reading and prayer and eucharist seem to have given her what she came for: 'and so we decided, having first seen all the things we desired, to descend from the mountain of God and to come to the place where the bush is' (*IE* 2.3); 'after your desire has been fulfilled and you descend from there' (*IE* 2.7); and so on. In the valley below, before she comes to the mountain, she pauses to set out her plan, which is both a literal route plan and at the same time a textual itinerary which leaves her readers in no doubt about what they are about to see:

> This was our route: we would first of all ascend the mountain of God, since the ascent was best by the direction from which we were approaching, and then we would descend again to the head of the valley, that is where the bush was, because the descent of the mountain was better from there. And so that was what we decided, that once we had seen all we desired to see, and descending from the mountain of God, we would come to the place where the bush is, and from there we would return right through the middle of the valley itself lying ahead of us to the road with the men of God, who would show us each of the places mentioned in the Bible, and thus it was accomplished. (*IE* 2.3)

She then proceeds to take us through that itinerary site by site. In doing so she exercises control over the landscape she passes through, just as the Christian populations of the Sinai peninsula did in appropriating the area's heritage from its Hebrew biblical heritage.[68] There is a sense of comprehensiveness in her account ('each of the places mentioned'), and also a remarkable impression of transparency and predictability, which puts each experience in its expected place, mapped out in advance.[69] Later, in commenting on the size of the central summit, which she tells us is not clear from below, she explains similarly that she knew in advance what to expect: 'I realised this already, before we reached the mountain of God, since the brothers had informed me, and when I got there, I saw plainly that it was so' (*IE* 2.7). Then as she takes her leave of the mountain, with an escort of holy men from Mount Sinai on her onward journey to Pharan, thirty-five miles to the north, she talks yet again of the fulfilment of her desires, but now in a way that stresses her humility: 'And so having seen all the holy places that we desired to see . . . unworthy and undeserving as I am . . . I cannot sufficiently thank all those holy men who willingly deigned to receive my humble self into their monastic cells' (*IE* 5.11–12). That expression of humility suggests that she sees even the blessings that have been given to her as beyond her deserts; an encounter with the divine like the one Moses received—and which the mountain is said to have conjured up for the Armenian pilgrims several centuries later—would by implication be beyond her most ambitious expectations. What she has is enough. Moreover, the odd repetitiveness of her account makes it clear to the reader that everything she sees has its own clearly defined place and identity.[70] She is interested not so much in recording detailed impressions of the sites (and sights) themselves, but in the fact that she has reached the places that are identified by her guides with particular biblical places.[71] In her account, physical places and scriptural passages become one and the same: the Latin word for place, *locus*, is used by Egeria to refer to both.[72] The other reason this way of thinking about encounters with the holy is valuable is because of the way in which it allows that experience to be transferred and experienced vicariously. In particular the sense that reading an account of an activity can somehow bring you closer to it—that is the logic of Egeria's repeated reading of scripture in the desert—presumably applies equally to the recipients of her letters in her community back at home.[73] By reading, by working through a mental inventory of each site, each relic, each story in its proper place, they too can fulfill their desires without any need for direct experience of the miraculous. In all of this she seems entirely satisfied with the idea of accessing the divine through human routines.

Egeria and the History of Travel and Mountaineering

Some accounts of Egeria's work have focused on the question of whether we should see her as a precursor of modern ways of interacting with landscape. There is obviously a risk of oversimplification in that kind of approach. Some aspects of Egeria's account anticipate modern ways of writing about mountain ascents quite closely; others feel quite alien to their modern equivalents. We need to find ways of talking about the text which acknowledge the significance of both of those strands. On the one hand Egeria's text is often viewed quite rightly as an important landmark in the history of travel writing. She talks about her travels in the first person, in a way which is very unusual for ancient accounts of mountain climbing and for ancient travel writing more generally. In doing so she always returns sooner or later to the question of why these places matter to her.[74] For example, she describes in several places the effort of the climb to the summit. The climb is hard:

> And so I went up with great toil, because it was necessary for me to go up on foot, since it was not possible to ascend in the saddle, and yet I did not feel the toil, on that side of the mountain I did not feel the toil, because I had the impression that I was fulfilling my desire, at God's command; and so at the fourth hour we arrived at the highest summit of Sinai, the holy mountain of God, where the law was given, that is, the place on which the glory of the Lord came down on the day when the mountain smoked. (*IE* 3.2)

In Egeria's text, then, the mountains have become not only places of divine presence but also places of individual experience, as landscapes that need to be written in the first person.

Her first-person account of viewing the mountain, and viewing from the mountain, plays a powerful role in her text, as it does in so many modern reports of mountain ascents, whereas in most other ancient literature summit views tend to be reported in the third person. For Egeria, that involves looking at the mountain from a distance: 'In the meantime we came by walking to a certain place where the mountains through which we were travelling opened out and formed an infinitely large valley, very flat and extremely beautiful, and across the valley appeared Sinai, the holy mountain of God' (*IE* 1.1). It also involves looking down from above,[75] once they have received communion in the church on the summit: the other mountain summits below them are like little hills; she also claims (implausibly, given the limits of human viewing from the summit)[76] that 'Egypt and Palestine and the Red Sea and the Virgin's Sea that extends as far as Alexandria, and also the unbounded lands of the Saracens: all these seemed so far below us that we could scarcely believe it' (*IE* 3.8). Egeria's first-person appropriation of long-standing classical and biblical traditions of mountaintop viewing, which as we have seen are usually associated with authoritative or sometimes divine viewing, is remarkable, and in some respects feels very modern, for example in its emphasis on the way in which the view is earned through the toil of the ascent ('those mountains which we scarcely managed to climb in the first place.... From there we were able to see beneath us...' [*IE* 3.8]). Despite her humility, she has gained access to this immensely authoritative subject position through God's will and through the routines and rituals of pilgrimage. Of course Egeria and her contemporaries were not interested in mountain climbing as a competitive pursuit, or as an expression of individuality, and in some ways that sets her apart from modern mountaineering discourse.[77] What matters to her instead is precisely that she is standing in a place where others have stood before, and that she is able from there to access a view that encompasses vast swathes of biblical geography and history. But in fact that kind of approach to mountain summits, as places of history, does have plenty of modern parallels. It was particularly important in the nineteenth-century travel-writing from the Mediterranean, much of it written by classically educated antiquarians travelling with Pausanias in hand. In many of those travellers' accounts we see a pattern whereby the visibility and prominence of the classical past intensifies the higher up the narrator climbs, as if the ascent sweeps away from view the day-to-day realities of the lowlands and allows the ancient world to come more clearly into view.[78] We see exactly the same thing for Egeria: the view of biblical lands that she gets from the summit is made possible by her exertions.

Egeria thus does have a certain amount in common with modern conventions of writing about mountain experience. At the same time, however, there is a tendency to remark on the absence of detailed descriptions and personal impressions in Egeria's writing, along with its heavily allegorical quality, as if these things make her work unsatisfying by the standards of modern travel writing.[79] Those reactions replicate intriguingly the debates that have swirled around Petrarch's famous account of ascending Mont Ventoux in 1336. That text is often taken as a first step, but also a missed opportunity, in the development of modern mountaineering literature.[80] Petrarch climbs 'solely to admire the mountain's conspicuous height', and he admires the view ('I stood like someone who is stupefied') but he then moves into a series of allegorical reflections on the theme of spiritual ascent: 'If only I may accomplish that journey of the soul for which I sigh both by day and by night in the same way as I have accomplished today's journey with the feet of my body, overcoming all the difficulties at last' (Petrarch, *Epistolae familiares* 4.1, 313). For some readers that turn to allegory is a sign that Petrarch is not truly modern, even if he seems to come close in the opening part of the account.[81] Are Egeria and Petrarch modern? Or are they actually not as modern as they initially appear?

Ultimately that kind of teleological approach, which judges these authors according to how far they measure up to or fall short of an idealised image of a more highly developed modern sensitivity, seems unproductive. Better is an approach that recognises the complexity of that relationship between ancient and modern. We may see aspects of these texts that can help to nuance self-congratulatory ideas of modern exceptionalism; at the same time we need to try and understand them in relation to their own worlds as well as our own. From that point of view we can start to see that allegorical language might actually have seemed quite compatible with a personal, corporeal response to landscape for classical and medieval readers.[82] The heavily symbolic nature of Egeria's account is hard to miss in the depiction of her own ascent of the mountain quoted earlier, which would have recalled instantly for its readers the allegorical use of the language of ascent that was so widespread in early Christian culture. But for an audience so familiar with that language, allegorical imagination and bodily experience would surely have been viewed as cross-fertilising with each other in the actual experience of climbing.

Egeria's text is also fascinating for what it can reveal to us about ancient conceptions of gender in mountain landscapes. In that respect too it represents a challenging point of comparison for modern mountain experience. For the most part in Greek and Latin literature climbing mountains is something done by men. The exceptions are female goddesses, who are often depicted on mountains, and also women involved in Bacchic ritual. In the latter case female presence in the mountains is often associated with precisely the kind of visible divine intervention that Egeria tends to sideline in her work. Egeria's interest in the 'summit position', by contrast, is an appropriation of ways of interacting with landscape that are more usually linked with masculine authority, for example with Moses in the biblical tradition. In modern mountaineering discourse too, mountain conquest has often been associated with masculine self-presentation, but even from very early on in mountaineering history female climbers have challenged that stereotype, in ways we have become increasingly aware of.[83]

Egeria does not show any particular self-consciousness about her appropriation of masculine mountain experience, but one of her late antique readers is much more blatant about it, and in the process presents us with a set of images which curiously both bring Egeria closer to modern mountain experience and also at the same time make even clearer her distance from it. The text in question is a later summary of her work, composed by a seventh-century monk from Galicia, Valerius. His letter reveals even more clearly than the surviving portions of Egeria's text the importance of mountains for her account, in mentioning a string of other peaks from the non-surviving sections:

> Another was the very high mountain that stands above Pharan, on whose summit Moses prayed with his arms stretched out while the people fought, until victory came; also the overhanging ridge of the fearful Mount Tabor, where the Lord appeared in glory with Moses and Elijah; and another equally vast mountain, which is called Hermon, on which the Lord used to rest with his disciples; and another very high mountain called Eremus, on which the Lord taught his disciples the Beatitudes; and another similarly exceptionally high mountain, which is called the mountain of Elijah, on which the Prophet Elijah himself lived, and where the hundred prophets were hidden; and another like it which looms over Jericho and which like the others was sanctified by the Lord. (Valerius, *Letter in Praise of the Life of the Most Blessed Egeria* 3)[84]

That passage leaves no doubt about the centrality of mountains to Egeria's conception of pilgrimage. Valerius' account of the ascent of Mount Sinai casts her as a heroic explorer figure making her way into the hostile wilderness and joyfully experiencing God's presence there:

> going on to the holy Mount Sinai . . . forgetting her female weakness, she hastened on with unflagging steps, supported by the right hand of God, to the steep heights of this mountain, whose peak stands up at the height of the clouds. Thus driven on by the resources of her divine piety, she reached the holy summit of that rocky mountain, where the divine glory itself, almighty God, condescended to dwell in giving the holy law to blessed Moses. (2)

He tells us, in a passage that is both more allegorical and at the same time more corporeal than anything we find in Egeria's account of Mount Sinai, that 'the challenge of travelling through the whole world did not weaken her, the stormy seas and the vast rivers did not confine her, the vastness and terrible roughness of the mountains did not threaten her, the ferocious savagery of the impious tribes did not terrify her' (4).[85] Valerius also emphasises repeatedly the importance of the summit position for Egeria: 'carrying herself untiringly to the inaccessible summits of so many mountains, with the help of God and through the burning desire in her heart she bore lightly the barrenness of such a great altitude' (3). That makes her into a figure who anticipates much more clearly than Egeria's own account later traditions of mountaintop self-representation most commonly associated with mountaineering literature. It is also the language that is more often associated with male authority figures, especially the victorious generals and culture heroes who are celebrated for their conquest of mountain territory.[86] The phrase 'forgetting her female weakness' makes Egeria's subversion of gender expectations particularly clear. In a sense it is precisely the allegorical intensity of Valerius' language that enables this characterisation of Egeria. In early Christian culture women may not have literally undertaken masculine feats of physical and military prowess in the mountains, but they were are able to be heroic figures of piety and devotion in the disciplines of spiritual ascent. In that sense Egeria's appropriation of male ways of interacting with mountain terrain, especially in Valerius' account of it, makes her an inspiring precursor of later pioneering figures in female mountaineering, while also showing how she is embedded in early Christian modes of representation quite alien to modern ways of describing mountains.

Another way of bringing Egeria into dialogue with our own contemporary preoccupations, finally, is through an ecocritical frame. What images does Egeria give us of the relations between humans, the divine and the natural environment? In some respects landscape is a very prominent feature of the text, and mountains in particular loom large in her work.[87] That is the case even syntactically: the valley by which Egeria approaches Mount Sinai and then later the mountain itself are either subject or object of a large proportion of her sentences in the opening pages of the work as it survives.[88] And yet despite that the mountain environment is astonishingly absent as a force independent of Christian narrative and Christian religious observance. Early Christian culture has sometimes been portrayed as the source of the anthropocentrism that has ultimately allowed the destruction of our resources in the modern world.[89] As we shall see later in this book, that claim is often made in bizarrely oversimplified terms, which vastly underestimate the variety of ancient Christian environmental thinking. But certainly Egeria shows little interest in exploring potential weaknesses in the predominantly anthropocentric image she projects. There is very little here to match the depiction of overwhelming, destructive natural forces, either divinely controlled or otherwise, in Homer or in Pausanias. In that sense she stands apart from the tensions between wild nature and human control which I have argued is one of the central themes of both ancient and modern writing about mountain landscapes. Or perhaps we should say instead that her doubts about the possibility of human control over landscape are more firmly suppressed than they usually are in mountain writing. The dream of an orderly, controlled relationship with the mountains is one that many texts, from many different eras, are tempted by. Is the odd repetitiveness of her Latin, and her repeated insistence that all is as we would expect it to be, and that her desire has been fulfilled exactly as she hoped it would be, in itself an attempt to shut down the ever-present potential for sacred mountain landscapes to slip away from our grasp, through their overwhelming, unpredictable, sometimes miraculous associations, and with their history of being subjected to variant readings in a process of struggle for control over correct interpretation?[90]

Egeria on Mount Nebo

Egeria's experience on Mount Sinai is replayed in very similar form a few chapters later when she visits the summit of Mount Nebo soon after her arrival in Jerusalem. Mount Nebo stands in modern Jordan, just to the northeast of the Dead Sea, with a view of Jerusalem from its summit; it is a place of pilgrimage and tourism still today. Egeria travels with several holy men from Jerusalem. They stop at various Old Testament landmarks along the way to pray and to read from scripture. As for Mount Sinai, Egeria tells us that the ascent was hard work (although in this case she seems to have done most of the climb on the back of a donkey). And here too, once they reach the summit (just over 800 metres above sea level) they find all the trappings of religious tourism: a small church, with the tomb of Moses, where they pray, and holy men on hand to show them round (although it is not always clear whether Egeria is talking about the monks from the summit or those who have travelled with her, who seem to be familiar with the place from previous visits).

As on Mount Sinai it is only when they have prayed that they are invited by their guides to turn their attention to the view:

> 'If you wish to see the places which are described in the Books of Moses, come outside the door of the church and observe and look from the summit itself, from the place where these things can be seen, and we will tell you one by one what these places are which can be seen'. Then we being very pleased went outside. For from the door of the church itself we saw the place where the river Jordan runs into the Dead Sea, which was right below us. . . . And the greater part of Palestine, which is the Promised Land, was visible from there too, and the whole land of Jordan, as far as the eye could see. (*IE* 12.3–5)

They see the place where Lot's wife was turned into a pillar of salt (but not the pillar itself: that used to stand near the sixth milestone from Zoar, so the Bishop of Zoar has told them, but was later submerged in the Dead Sea). They see Heshbon, the city of Sehon, king of the Amorites, and Safdra, the city of Og, king of Bashan, and a whole series of other biblical sites. And then they return to Jerusalem back on the road by which they came.

This passage is another memorable illustration of just how much mountain summit views could matter in the ancient world. It is also another illustration of how Egeria accesses the holy through her exposure to ritual—it is only when they have prayed that they look at the view—and through the human exercise of biblical history. There are suggestions of pleasure in Egeria's account, particularly in the word 'pleased' (*gavisi*, in Latin) in response to the invitation to view from the summit: presumably this is at least in part the pleasure of anticipation. But perhaps most striking again is the way in which the view from above confers authority.[91] That is in part because it offers Egeria access to knowledge: she takes on here the rational persona of the geographer, mapping out the land below her as precisely as she can, particularly in her careful, almost pedantic account of the location of Lot's wife's pillar. But it is also a divine, religious authority: as Egeria makes clear right at the start of her account of the visit, this is the mountain Moses was told by God to climb in order to see the Promised Land laid out before him, in the knowledge that he would die on the mountain without setting foot there.[92] By that parallel, the view from above confers ownership and belonging, albeit of a tentative and partial kind, if we follow the comparison with Moses to its conclusion.

Mountains in the ancient world had a deep-rooted connection with the divine, but there were many different ways of giving expression to that connection. In some cases, especially for Olympus, it involved imagining mountains as places of divine dwelling cut off from human contact or human knowledge. In other cases it involved the perception of awe-inspiring natural phenomena which might be represented quite explicitly as divinely inspired, as on Mount Sinai, or in Pausanias' account of Mount Parnassos during the invasion of the Gauls. In other cases again it involved various kinds of human ritual and human routines, which were often linked with sacred stories about the past, both in the pagan summit altars that were scattered right across the eastern and central Mediterranean and in the Christian equivalents that developed into famous stops on the pilgrimage trail throughout the Holy Land. Different texts handle the tensions between those possibilities in different ways, especially the tension between mountains as places within and beyond human control. Of course mountains are not the only kinds of landscape these authors care about. Homer in his similes, Pausanias, and Egeria all explore many other kinds of terrain, and the mountains of their texts need to be viewed within those wider networks of landscape images. However, mountains do tend to be exposed in particularly conspicuous ways to the techniques of representation that matter most for each of these authors individually in their explorations of the relationship between the human and divine spheres: they tend to stand out from the textual ground around them. Moreover, the way in which these authors represent the divine in mountain landscapes tends to be linked in turn with their varied representations of the relationship between humans and the environment. The texts we have looked at oscillate between anthropocentric views of that relationship, and acceptance of the overwhelming power and incomprehensibility of the more-than-human world. Egeria is in some respects a limit case, in the sense that she accesses the divine on Mount Sinai and Mount Nebo almost exclusively through the human phenomena associated with pilgrimage, and in some respects that makes her work appear more anthropocentric and less interested in the way in which humans can be subjected to forces beyond their control. But we should not for that reason take her as less interested than those other authors in the capacity for particular places to be imbued with divine presence: the mountains she visits are for her enormously numinous places. The point is rather that for Egeria there is no separation between the sacred and its human markers and manifestations. In her writing the mountain summits of the Mediterranean become places of holiness and desire in a more personal and more human way than ever before, to be accessed through her intense and intimate experience of the divine in mountain pilgrimage.

PART II
Mountain Vision

5

Mountain Aesthetics

Mountains as Objects of Vision

Mountains are places associated in particularly intense ways with vision, both in ancient and in modern culture. We look *at* mountains: they draw our gaze even from a great distance, standing above and apart from the land around them, dark with rock and storm clouds or white with snow. That was true for ancient viewers too. Egeria's first glimpse of Mount Sinai across the huge and 'extremely beautiful' valley by which she approaches is an important moment in her narrative. The experience of looking up at the smoke of sacrifice on mountain summits was a crucial part of the communal experience of mountaintop sacrifice. There is a different type of mountaintop fire in the opening lines of Aeschylus' *Agamemnon*, the first play of his great tragic trilogy the *Oresteia*: a series of mountain beacons brings news of the fall of Troy and of Agamemnon's impending return, first on Mount Ida, then on a chain of others including Mount Athos and Mount Kithairon and other peaks beyond. In this case the visibility of the mountaintops has been harnessed and enhanced by human ingenuity. Agamemnon's wife Clytemnestra compares the light to a human herald, leaping from beacon to beacon, bringing from her husband the message they had prearranged: she describes the guards who have been posted for long years at the site of each beacon precisely for this moment.[1] We also look *from* mountains. We have seen already that the fascination with the act of looking from mountain peaks was just as powerful for ancient authors and readers as it is for us, and that mountaintop viewing was repeatedly associated with territorial knowledge and authority: that goes for Egeria gazing from Mount Nebo as much as for Zeus looking down from Olympus; we will see other examples too in relation to military and geographical authority in part III. Mountaintop viewing was a central feature of ancient imaginative engagement with the earth's surface just as much as it has been in the modern world.[2]

There is still, however, a tendency to assume that ancient visual descriptions of mountains fall short of their modern equivalents, on the grounds that the classical world did not have any idea of mountains as aesthetically pleasing, and more specifically that there was no ancient notion equivalent to the sublime or the picturesque,[3] concepts which were associated especially though not exclusively with mountain scenery from the mid-eighteenth century onwards, for example in the writings of the Romantic poets which still tend to be viewed as decisive landmarks in the development of a distinctively modern landscape sensibility. One of my arguments in this chapter is that that distinction between ancient and modern has been overstated: there are approximate parallels for the mountain sublime and the mountain picturesque scattered everywhere across the slopes of ancient literature, and in many cases postclassical writers who have been important in the development of those concepts were influenced by classical precedents.[4]

At the same time, and perhaps more importantly, I want to give attention here to the question of what makes ancient representations of mountains and visuality distinctive. If we think about ancient mountains only in relation to modern aesthetic categories, we can end up with an inadequate picture of the richness of classical thinking on these issues. Perhaps most strikingly, there is a tendency within ancient literature to see mountains as objects that are cryptic, enigmatic, hard to decipher, and charismatic for precisely that reason. That opaqueness is often presented in highly visual terms. In other words the widespread association between mountains and clarity of vision often stands in tension with an alternative strand in ancient thinking. Sometimes that involved seeing mountains as fully visible but at the same time difficult to comprehend. That goes for natural-scientific investigations of volcanoes, Etna especially, which is on one level vastly visible but also hides within it secrets that are hard to fathom, or for some of the mountains of ancient art and poetry, where powerful and vivid, often miniaturised images of mountains take on allegorical or symbolic significance that may be hard to decipher. In other cases the difficulty of comprehending mountains may be articulated instead quite literally through images of visual obscurity and restriction. The simile image from *Iliad* 3.10–12 is a memorable example: 'As when the south wind pours down mist over the tops of the mountains, mist that is not loved by shepherds but is better than night for a thief, and you can see as far as you can throw a stone'. That passage stands in contrast with the poem's many images of divine and mortal clear-sightedness in mountain contexts. There is a similar contrast often in Greek tragedy: the clarity of the mountain beacons in the *Agamemnon* stands in contrast with the theme of concealment and incomprehension, which gathers momentum as the trilogy goes on.[5] And in Euripides' *Bacchae* the initial atmosphere of visual control increasingly gives way to scenes of misperception on the slopes of Mount Kithairon, especially in the horrifying moments where Pentheus' project of spying on his mother and other Bacchic women, looking down on them from his detached treetop viewpoint, gives way to the misidentification whereby Pentheus is mistaken for a mountain lion and torn to pieces. We shall see in part III that similar images of obstructed vision, standing in contrast with occasional interludes of clear-sightedness, are very common in ancient military accounts of mountain campaigning.

Often in these cases the visual is overwhelmed by other senses, and especially by the sense of touch, as we see mountain terrain impinging on human bodies in very tactile ways. That is not to say that those tensions are unique to ancient literature. There are many modern parallels, for example in the motif of restricted vision in mountaineering literature, or in the procedures of route-planning in mountaineering practice, where climbers will scan the rock faces and ridges they plan to climb in order to find the right line,[6] or in the notion that mountain appreciation requires a special perspective, linked with education and social distinction.[7] But those themes are particularly intense and particularly frequent in ancient texts. In that sense the visual representation of ancient mountains is shaped by many of the same tensions that run through the other chapters of this book too: the tension between mountains within and beyond human control, and the tension between detached engagement and bodily immersion. Mountains encourage detached ways of viewing; they also confront us with the difficulties of maintaining that kind of detachment, in the face of the immersive, bodily quality of human encounters with mountain environment.

Aesthetic Categories and the Classical Tradition

How exactly do ancient Greek and Roman practices of landscape description compare with their modern equivalents? It may be helpful first to map out some of the main categories of eighteenth- and nineteenth-century landscape appreciation. Much of the groundwork for modern understanding of the sublime was laid during the course of the eighteenth century, among others by authors like John Dennis, Edmund Burke, and Immanuel Kant.[8] But perhaps the most influential attempt to bring the sublime into dialogue with other aesthetic categories was Uvedale Price's *Essay on the Picturesque*, published first in 1794, and then in expanded form in 1810. For Price the beautiful and the sublime stand at two ends of a spectrum of aesthetic possibilities, with the picturesque halfway between the two. By that account both the picturesque and the sublime were valued for the way they stood apart from the formal beauty of human-made, crafted landscapes (for example Price criticised Capability Brown's landscape gardens and their domestication of nature). The picturesque came to be associated with the idea of natural scenes that imitated art more or less spontaneously, not necessarily completely without human intervention, but always in a way that valued the casualness and roughness of nature. That preference was further extended in the concept of the sublime: sublime landscapes stood out for their ability to induce feelings of awe; they were often associated with a vertiginous sense of fear and threat, and with a sense of indescribability, which contrasted with the more controlled aesthetic responses to merely beautiful landscape.[9] Not surprisingly it was the picturesque and the sublime, rather than the beautiful, that came to be associated most often with mountain scenery. Of course we should not imagine that these categories were always clearly separated from each other. These were contested terms, used in a wide variety of different ways by different commentators from the early eighteenth century onwards, sometimes tendentiously, sometimes imprecisely. These different approaches to landscape appreciation also had a certain amount in common, not least their association with high social status: the ability to take a detached view of the natural world, to see it as if through the frame of a painting, to make judgements of taste about landscape—all of these things were viewed as capacities that went hand in hand with social and literary authority.[10]

The obsession with these concepts in eighteenth- and early nineteenth-century intellectual culture was quite new, but many of the authors who were responsible for that development were themselves heavily influenced by classical authors. The concept of the picturesque was initially shaped by representations of the relationship between nature and human culture in ancient and modern traditions of pastoral poetry and art,[11] where the natural world tends to be relatively benign but also often with elements of roughness and danger. Later versions tended to be more attracted to images of nature that were wilder, but they too found classical parallels. Uvedale Price, for example, took Pausanias, and especially Pausanias' description of artworks, as one of the main precursors for his ideas about the picturesque.[12] On the face of it that is odd, given Pausanias' lack of interest in landscape description, but it is partly explained by Pausanias' fascination with the historical associations of the Greek landscape, especially his fascination with ruins,[13] which were often a prominent feature of picturesque depictions both in art and literature.[14] Price writes, for example, that 'a temple or place of Grecian architecture in its perfect entire state, and with its surface and colour smooth and even, either in painting or in reality is beautiful; in ruin it is picturesque'.[15] Perhaps for that reason the idea of the 'picturesque' was often taken as particularly appropriate to the landscape of Greece.[16]

The sublime, too, was rooted in the past. The rediscovery of the sublime was largely due to the increasing interest in Longinus' work *On the Sublime*. It has sometimes been suggested that Longinus' primary focus on literary or rhetorical sublimity makes him relatively distant from eighteenth- and nineteenth-century interests in the 'natural' sublime. However, recent accounts have tended to stress instead the connections between Longinus' text, and its eighteenth- and nineteenth-century equivalents.[17] There is also one section in Longinus' work which deals with the presence of the sublime in nature directly, at *On the Sublime* 35.4:

> Thus stirred by some natural instinct we marvel not at the small streams, even if they are clear and useful, but at the Nile and the Istros [that is, the Danube] or the Rhine, and all the more at the Ocean; nor do we admire this small flame, that is kindled by us ourselves, because of the way it maintains a clear light, more than the fires of heaven, even though they are often darkened; nor do we think it more deserving of wonder than the craters of Etna, whose eruptions throw up rocks and whole hills from the depths, and sometimes pour out rivers of that earthborn and spontaneous fire.

This passage had a wide influence even from the late seventeenth century onwards, in the work of Thomas Burnet (whose *Sacred Theory of the Earth*, published in 1681 in Latin and then in 1684 in English, famously rethought the natural history of mountains) and then in the work of later theorists of the sublime over the next hundred years or more.[18] Recent work has also made it clear that the past was a much more important feature in Romantic characterisation of particular landscapes as sublime than has usually been understood.[19] Travellers in Greece in the eighteenth and nineteenth centuries often seem to have viewed the presence of the classical heritage as a constituent feature of the sublime and picturesque landscapes they describe. Moreover, in judging the value of landscape in part according to its historical and cultural associations they are often heavily influenced by ancient authors, like Strabo and Pausanias, who do the same.[20] Clearly the intellectual ferment around these categories was viewed as something quite new: much of the writing on mountain and landscape aesthetics from the late eighteenth and nineteenth century has an air of exploration and novelty, as if their authors are revelling in their freedom to open up new ground in their understanding of human aesthetic experience. But it would be quite wrong to characterise the relationship with classical and early modern ways of thinking about landscapes as one of discontinuity: what we see instead is a tension between novelty and tradition.

Beautiful Mountains

Many ancient texts do portray mountain landscapes in negative terms, as frightening or inauspicious places.[21] But mountains could also be beautiful to ancient viewers. Extended description of beautiful landscape is most common in the *locus amoenus* ('pleasant place') tradition which was so prevalent throughout both Greek and Latin literature (primarily but not exclusively in verse). That tradition was often invoked as a precedent for beautiful landscapes from the Renaissance onwards, but most often in relation to the crafted, garden-type landscapes against which the devotees of the picturesque and the sublime were reacting in their insistence on the incorporation of wild nature. The ancient *locus amoenus* was often a human-made space—the foundational *locus amoenus* passage in Western literature is the garden of Alcinous in *Odyssey* Book 7, which was imitated obsessively throughout the next millennium—or at any rate a naturally occurring scene that had a garden-like scale, usually a meadow or woodland grove with a stream running through the middle. It is not surprising, then, that mountains are not described so frequently as some other kinds of landscape in the *locus amoenus* tradition.

Nevertheless there are plenty of exceptions which demonstrate that it was perfectly commonplace in the ancient world to think of mountains as sources of aesthetic pleasure.[22] In some cases that involves squeezing mountain landscapes, often with a certain amount of ingenuity, into a *locus amoenus* frame. Mountain settings often had an important role in the pastoral tradition: the herdsmen of Theocritus' *Idylls* and Virgil's *Eclogues* often pasture their animals on the mountain slopes, or choose mountain settings for the idealised landscapes they describe in their songs, although they avoid the highest peaks.[23] That convention is reimagined quite extensively in later prose writing. Dio Chrysostom's description of the home of the hunters who give him hospitality in the mountains of Euboia (which we will return to in part IV), is a particularly seductive example, not least because it avoids the impression of artifice and idealisation that we sometimes find in *locus amoenus* descriptions elsewhere, in a way that roughly corresponds to the picturesque interest in spontaneous nature. Dio tells us that they live in 'a deep and shady ravine, and running through the middle of it was a river that was not rough, but was easy to wade through, for both cows and calves, and the water was abundant and pure, rising as it did from a nearby spring, and there is always a breeze blowing through in the summer . . . and there are many very beautiful meadows stretching out beneath tall and sparse trees' (Dio Chrysostom, *Euboian Oration, I* 7.14–15).

In some early Christian texts the *locus amoenus* mountain motif is combined with images of terrestrial paradise. Basil of Caesarea writes to his friend Gregory of Nazianzus in the late fourth century describing his new mountain-top retreat in Cappadocia:[24]

> For there is a high mountain, covered with a deep forest, intersected on the north side by cool and clear waters, and from its foot stretches out a flat plain, which is continuously enriched by the moisture from the mountain. A forest grows spontaneously around it with varied trees of many kinds, acting almost as a fence [that is, as around a garden], so that even the island of Calypso, which Homer seems to have admired more than any other place for its beauty, seems insignificant by comparison. (Basil of Caesarea, *Letter* 14)

Twice in the long description that follows he mentions explicitly the pleasures the view provides to him.[25] Gregory (*Letters* 4–6) replies sceptically, effectively accusing Basil of romanticising, and substitutes much more wild and threatening imagery:[26] he seems to be self-conscious about the limitations of the ways of representing mountains within the frame of the *locus amoenus* that Basil has chosen. For both of these authors, their engagement with rhetorical and poetic conventions of landscape description is not an inert, decorative frame; instead both of them use these resources in original ways in order to project their own distinctive visions of the ascetic relationship with landscape.[27]

In parallel with that *locus amoenus* tradition, and to some extent cross-fertilising with it, stood the rhetorical practice of ekphrasis: extended set-piece descriptions of vivid scenes of many different types.[28] There seems to have been plenty of space within that tradition for wild landscapes of various kinds. The rhetorical theorist Aelius Theon, in an essay *On Ekphraseis* (*Progymnasmata*

11), lists 'places, such as meadows, seashores, cities, islands, deserted places (ἐρημίας) and other places like that'.²⁹ Techniques of ekphrastic description were widely used in speeches of encomium. Pseudo-Hermogenes tells us that 'there have even been encomia of plants and mountains and rivers' (*On Encomium, Progymnasmata* 7).³⁰ Menander Rhetor suggests that a formal speech of encomium for a city might include description of the mountains which surround it, along with its plains, rivers and harbours.³¹ Clearly, then, the idea of a mountain ekphrasis was perfectly conceivable, although no example survives of a full-scale description of a mountain along those lines in any ancient rhetorical text.³²

That passage from Menander Rhetor gives us a clue to one of the features that unites many of our best surviving ancient images of mountain beauty, that is the tendency for mountains to be viewed as beautiful when they are integrated or at least partially integrated into a domesticated, often urban frame: that effect is much more common than in modern descriptions of mountains as objects of aesthetic admiration. A good example is Plato's description of the mythical island city of Atlantis in *Critias* 118b: 'the mountains that surrounded the plain were celebrated for their number and size and beauty (κάλλος)'.³³ There are several similar passages in the work of the orator Dio Chrysostom, who lived in Asia Minor in the late first and early second century CE: he announces that he has no intention of offering the expected praise of the mountains around the city of Tarsos (33.2) and later in the same speech suggests that the beauty of Mount Ida, along with the many other advantages of the city, did not in the end bring any benefits for Troy (33.20). In another speech he praises the beauty of the mountains surrounding the city of Kelainai in Phrygia: 'I see that this city is inferior to none of the first rank of cities. . . . For you occupy the strongest, most fertile spot on the continent; you are situated among the most beautiful plains and mountains (πεδίων δὲ καὶ ὀρῶν μεταξὺ καλλίστων)' (35.13).³⁴ The orator Libanius, in his praise of the city of Antioch delivered in the second half of the fourth century CE, gives a prominent place to Mount Silpios, the mountain that stood to the south of the city and partly within the city walls.³⁵ For Libanius it is a 'shield' protecting the city and a source of pleasure, with its trees, gardens, flowers and birdsong (Libanius, *In Praise of Antioch, Oration* 11.200).

One of the most extensive examples comes from Strabo's account of Rome and its hills (a passage that might conceivably be influenced by the kind of formal praise traditions Menander Rhetor refers to, although Menander's work dates from several centuries later than Strabo's):

They have also constructed the roads that run through the country, by adding cuts to the hills and embankments to the valleys.... The ancient Romans paid no attention to the beauty (τὸ κάλλος) of Rome, because they were occupied with other greater and more necessary matters; but those who came later, and most of all those who live in our time, have not fallen short in this respect either, but have filled the city with many beautiful ornaments.... And the works of art that are situated all around the Campus Martius, and the ground, which is covered with grass all through the year, and the crowns of the hills beyond the river which stretch down to the river, presenting the appearance of a stage-painting, all these things provide a spectacle that is hard to draw away from (δυσαπάλλακτον).... The most noteworthy of the city's tombs is the one called the Mausoleum, a great mound by the river built on a foundation of white marble, covered right up to its summit with evergreen trees.... Such is Rome. (Strabo, *Geography* 5.3.8)

We will see more later of Strabo's obsession with the distinction between the wild edges of the empire and the tamed, built landscapes in the centre of it, but what is so striking here is the way in which he depicts the latter through the language of beauty. The noun he uses at the beginning of the passage (τὸ κάλλος) is often reserved for eroticised, human beauty. Here it is associated with the kinds of viewing that take place only at a late stage in the process of taming the natural world: the Romans have no time for it at the start. Rome is beautiful in this passage above all as an urban landscape, and the hills and mountains share that beauty insofar as they are absorbed into the city or at least made complementary to it. Not only do the Romans cut roads through the hills in order to facilitate that process of urban adornment, not only do they construct the artfully naturalistic summit of the Mausoleum within the boundaries of the city, but they also situate the artwork of the city in such a way that it is framed by the crowns of the hills above.[36] The image of the stage-set adds to that impression of domestication within the context of urban display. And for Strabo, at least momentarily, the scene seems to be almost overwhelming in aesthetic terms. The word 'hard to draw away from' (δυσαπάλλακτον) is an odd word to use—it is usually applied to things that are unpleasant and hard to escape from, like diseases—but it does nevertheless convey an impression of almost irresistible personal engagement with the beauty of the view. This is closer to the crafted landscapes of the Renaissance villas and the country estates of the eighteenth century, which celebrated the domestication and adornment of nature, than it is to the untamed landscapes of the picturesque. But it is nevertheless a striking example of the way in which mountains in the ancient world could be appreciated for their art-like qualities and for their beauty.[37]

For another example along similar lines, where the natural fertility and autonomy of the natural world gets more prominence, we can look at a letter by Pliny the Younger. Pliny is writing in 105 CE to his friend Domitius Apollinaris, inviting him to stay in his Tuscan villa. He mentions the nearby Apennine mountains repeatedly, partly for their healthiness—'the healthiest of our mountain ranges'—but above all because they exemplify the beauty of domesticated nature.[38] The appearance of the region, he boasts, is

> most beautiful. Imagine to yourself a huge amphitheatre, of the kind that only nature could create. A broad and extensive plain is surrounded by mountains; the mountains on their summits have tall and ancient forests. There is abundant and varied hunting there. From there, woods ready for felling stretch down together with the mountain slopes. Interspersed between these are rich and earthy hills . . . which are not inferior to the most level plains in fertility. . . . You would take great pleasure, if you could view this layout of the region from the mountain. For you would think you were looking not at the earth, but at a view painted to the highest level of beauty; such is the variety, such is the arrangement that wherever the eyes fall they will be refreshed. (Pliny, *Letters* 5.6.7–13)

The villa is artfully constructed to give different views from different angles, and the mountain view is part of that design: 'At the end of the cloister is a bedroom cut out from the cloister itself, which looks over the hippodrome, the vineyards, and the mountains' (5.6.28). This passage anticipates to a remarkable degree many of the common motifs of modern landscape appreciation: beautiful mountains as part of a crafted backdrop combining human cultivation with the spontaneity of nature, assessed by the criteria of landscape painting, all in a way that seems to guarantee the good taste and social status of the letter writer.[39]

Side by side with those passages we also find others that imagine mountains viewed from even more of a distance. In Cicero's *De natura deorum*, for example, one of the speakers, Balbus, takes the beauty of the world as an argument for divine creation. He invites us to 'gaze as it were with our eyes' on the beauty of creation, and to imagine the whole world spread out before us: 'Add to these the endless cool flow from the springs, the transparent river waters, the bright green clothing of the river banks, the concave heights of the caves, the roughness of the rocks, the height of the towering mountains, the immensity of the plains. . . . If we were able to see these with our eyes as we can in our minds, no one seeing the whole earth would have any doubts about divine reason' (Cicero, *De natura deorum* 2.98–100). There is no sign here of human impact on nature, but this passage too, and others like it, has a lot in common with the postclassical idea of landscape appreciated from a distance by an elite viewer with the taste and the vision to appreciate it.[40]

Ancient Mountains and the Sublime

The sublime too is a staple feature of ancient descriptions of the natural world. Recent research has made it even clearer than before that Greek and Latin literature contain examples of the mountain sublime just as powerful as anything in postclassical literature, and that they had a formative influence on their modern equivalents. The elision of that classical history of the sublime is another odd feature of the oversimplified narrative of modern exceptionalism that still prevails in a lot of writing about the history of landscape ideas. In parallel with the welcoming landscapes of the *locus amoenus* was another strand of ancient landscape description that focused on awe-inspiring and sometimes threatening terrain. We have already seen how the dizzying scale and power of some of Homer's landscapes—both in the similes and also in the scenes of Zeus on Mount Olympus—anticipate many of Longinus' concerns.[41] *Prometheus Bound*, a Greek tragedy dating from the fifth-century BCE and usually ascribed to Aeschylus, which describes Prometheus suffering punishment from Zeus in the Caucasus mountains, is another foundational text for that tradition. In the opening lines, for example, the mountain to which Prometheus is being fastened is described with reference to its 'high-cliffed rocks' (πέτραις ὑψηλοκρήμνοις) (*Prometheus Bound* 4–5), and as a 'terrible stormy chasm' (φάραγγι... δυσχειμέρῳ) (15), a 'crag remote from humans' (ἀπανθρώπῳ πάγῳ) (20).[42] Shelley drew heavily on the *Prometheus Bound* for his own *Prometheus Unbound*: Mary Shelley wrote in her notes on the play that 'the sublime majesty of Aeschylus filled him with wonder and delight', although he was also clearly interested in Prometheus as a model for resistance to tyranny.[43] There are scenes of awe-inspiring mountain description also in Latin verse texts, the work of Lucretius in particular,[44] and in accounts of Hannibal's crossing of the Alps.[45] These too were influential on eighteenth- and nineteenth-century authors on the sublime. Thomas Gray, in letters to his mother describing his crossing of the Alps, together with Horace Walpole, in 1739, quotes both from the accounts of Hannibal's crossing in Livy and from the epic poetry of Silius Italicus.[46] Gray's account, and also Walpole's writings on the same experience, are often taken as one of the earliest manifestations of an interest in sublime landscape, stimulated among other things by William Smith's translation of Longinus, which had appeared earlier in the same year.[47] There are differences between ancient and modern. It is hard to find any ancient passage which theorises explicitly the paradoxical idea that such places might give pleasure, even though the possibility of thrill and fascination in the reader is clearly implied in many cases. Nevertheless, ancient Greek and Latin literature are packed with passages which convey the vertiginous fascination of high cliffs and peaks. One of the fundamental peculiarities in the conventional narrative of a watershed between pre-modern mountain 'gloom' and modern mountain 'glory' is the way in which it treats fear: in ancient and medieval texts fear in mountains is viewed as a symptom of primitive sensibility; in writing on the history of mountains from the late nineteenth century onwards it is taken as a sign of an exclusively modern sensitivity to the aesthetic fascination of mountain landscape. In fact there are clear continuities between the two.[48]

6

Scientific Viewing and the Volcanic Sublime

Volcanic Knowledge and Human Vulnerability

The active volcanoes of the Mediterranean played a very special role in ancient ideas about mountains as aesthetic objects. Mountains were always in some respects outside human experience, but that was true in particularly powerful ways for volcanoes. At the same time they were also in some cases very close to human habitation and able to impact on urban life in a much more direct and implacable way than any of the other mountains we have looked at so far. Greek and Latin literature at least from the fifth century BCE onwards is full of attempts to make sense of them.[1] Etna especially is a recurring topic in many of the texts which have been cited as the closest parallels for modern images of the natural sublime. These are some of the most extravagant, awe-inspiring descriptions of mountains surviving from the ancient world. In that sense we should see Longinus as just one representative of a common ancient motif, rather than as a rare exception or outlier in a culture immune to the aesthetic power of mountains. Mount Etna is for him one of the outstanding examples of the sublime in nature: he describes the volcano's eruptions, which 'throw up rocks and whole hills from the depths, and sometimes pour out rivers of that earthborn and spontaneous fire' (Longinus, *On the Sublime* 35.4). It seems likely that he was drawing on earlier accounts in that choice of Etna as an example side by side with the Nile and other great rivers; at any rate we find the same cluster of natural phenomena in Lucretius, in a passage which probably shares a common source with Longinus' account.[2]

In addition to being charismatic examples of ancient aesthetic engagement with mountains, these texts also exemplify the ever-present tension between knowledge and incomprehension in relation to ancient mountains, between visual control and confusion, between decipherment and obscurity. Many ancient writers were fascinated by the challenge of interpreting volcanoes rationally and scientifically.[3] In modern mountaineering culture too, and not just in relation to volcanoes, scientific curiosity has been a major motivation and justification for climbing.[4] They attracted sophisticated speculations over many centuries. In many cases that involved using the wonder associated with the sublime as a spur to analysis. Side-by-side with that impulse, however, was an awareness of the extreme difficulty of understanding them. Even the most resolutely scientific approaches tended to slip into mythical styles of description which seem to emphasise the limitations of rationalising human explanations.[5] These ancient ways of making sense of volcanoes were very influential over eighteenth- and nineteenth-century accounts, many of which quote extensively from classical texts and in some cases also oscillate between scientific and mythical styles of depiction.[6]

In that sense ancient volcano descriptions tend to challenge anthropocentric understandings of the world. The same goes potentially for depictions of sublime landscape in any context, given the way in which they tend to disturb notions of human mastery over nature by confronting us with natural phenomena of breathtaking bulk and power almost beyond perception and comprehension (although of course the claim to be able to identify the sublime, like the equivalent notion of the picturesque, is also in itself an assertion of human perceptiveness used often to reinforce claims to intellectual and social distinction). But that phenomenon is particularly stark for volcanoes, which almost inevitably raise questions about human vulnerability in the face of the natural world. What kinds of mastery or understanding are available to us in relation to volcanoes? Our ancient sources tend to be quite optimistic about the capacity for human understanding to make sense even of these most inhuman objects, but nearly always with an awed awareness that any such understanding is likely to be difficult and partial.

Ancient attempts to come to terms with volcanic landscapes also tend to be very much aware of their shifting, unstable quality. In that sense they have a certain amount in common—perhaps as much as any other Greek and Roman responses to landscape—with our own attempts to come to terms with a changing planet today, particularly in the parts of the world that are having to absorb most rapidly the impacts of global warming. Story-telling was one resource for that; sometimes the traditional stories about particular landscapes had to change in the light of new events, for example in the aftermath of the eruption of Vesuvius, which led to a reimagining of some of the oldest mythical stories about the landscape around the Bay of Naples, and to new appropriations of images of volcanic activity in mythical and historiographical writing.[7] Elsewhere we see signs of an urgent desire to observe and to process new information. Ancient scientific approaches to volcanic landscapes could be relatively detached and abstract, but there was also often an awareness of their importance for real human populations. Modern discourse about climate change can be abstract too, but in much the same way it tends to gain extra power when it focuses on real human consequences.[8] Seneca, in his *Natural Questions*, written not long before the eruption of Vesuvius, discusses the importance of that kind of human context in response to the earthquake that took place in the region in 62 or 63 CE:

> It is necessary to find solace for distressed people and to remove their great fear. Yet can anything seem adequately safe to anyone if the world itself is shaken and its most solid parts collapse? Where will our fears finally be at rest if the one thing which is immovable in the universe and fixed, so as to support everything that leans on it, starts to waver; if the earth loses the characteristic it has, stability? (6.1.4–5)

The relation between landscape and human population is represented here as a dynamic one: the ground itself is shifting both metaphorically and literally beneath their feet;[9] the same goes for human understanding of those phenomena, which is developed and adapted urgently in response— although Seneca's consolation is not in the end based on any very precise, scientific knowledge but on the assumption that one may be vulnerable to natural disaster of this kind anywhere in the world.[10] No one knew for sure that Vesuvius was a volcano liable to inflict disaster at any time: the eruption of 79 CE was the first for 700 years or so.[11] But Seneca's text is just one in a long line of ancient attempts to understand the oddities of the terrain around Naples, and in many cases that involved edging towards an understanding of its volcanic quality by comparison with other active volcanoes like Etna.[12]

Observing Etna

With Vesuvius lying dormant for many centuries of classical history it is hardly surprising that it is Mount Etna that gets the greatest share of attention in our ancient sources,[13] shared every so often with accounts of the volcanoes of the

Aeolian islands. The volcano is consistently described as an object of wonder. The story of Etna's presence in classical literature begins[14] with Pindar,[15] whose description may well have influenced Longinus' *On the Sublime* 35.4.[16] In *Pythian* 1, Pindar tells the story of Zeus's imprisonment of the giant Typhos (sometimes referred to instead as Typhon or Typhoeus) beneath the volcano

> from whose innermost parts are discharged very holy springs of unapproachable fire. During the day rivers of lava pour out a stream of fiery smoke, but at night the red flame whirls up rocks and carries them into the depths of the sea with a crash. That monster sends forth the terrible streams of Hephaistos; it is a portent amazing to see, a wonder even to hear of from those who were present; such is the creature bound within the dark-leafed peaks and the plain of Etna. (Pindar, *Pythian* 1.21–8)

Pindar is probably responding here to an actual eruption of Etna in the 470s BCE just before the poem was composed.[17] It is striking that Etna is awe-inspiring even at second hand ('even to hear of from those who were present'): by implication Pindar's description potentially shares in the power and sublimity of its subject.[18]

Other sources, by contrast, emphasise the ways in which human observers can make sense of the mountain scientifically.[19] A culture of volcanic tourism grew up around Mount Etna. One passage from Strabo, from the first half of the first century CE, gives us a particularly remarkable glimpse of the importance of mountain tourist guides, to parallel what we have seen of religious mountain tourism in Pausanias more than a century later:

> Near to Centoripa is the town of Aitna ... which receives and escorts those who go up the mountain, for the mountain ridge begins there. The high regions of the mountain are bare and ash-like and covered in snow during the winter, whereas the lower slopes are divided up by thickets and plantations of many different types. The tops of the mountain appear to undergo many changes because of the distribution of the fire, which sometimes will cluster together in a single crater, but at other times divides itself, sometimes sending out streams of lava, sometimes flames and sometimes fiery smoke, and at other times ejecting red-hot stones. It is inevitable as a result of these happenings that not only the underground passages will undergo changes but also the openings which are sometimes numerous all around on the surface. (Strabo, *Geography* 6.2.8)

That passage is dominated by language of careful observation ('the tops of the mountain appear to undergo many changes') and inference ('it is inevitable as a result of these happenings'). Strabo's rationalising persona is reinforced in what follows, where he passes on to a detailed account recently given to him by some acquaintances who have made the ascent. They report 'a vertical cloud rising up to a height of about two hundred feet, motionless (for it was a windless day) and like smoke' and they debunk the common story about the philosopher Empedocles committing suicide by jumping into the volcano, on the grounds that the wind and heat arising from the crater would have made it impossible to approach closely enough.[20]

Other mountain tourists on Etna would have explained their journeys in rather different terms, as motivated by wonder at the marvels of the natural world, rather than a desire to conduct anything resembling scientific research. But in fact the two cannot be clearly separated in ancient thinking, since wonder was regularly represented as a starting-point and spur for scientific and philosophical investigation. Pliny the Elder (who lost his life in the eruption of Vesuvius in 79 CE, tempted by his scientific curiosity, according to his nephew's account, into staying within range of the eruption for too long)[21] puts Etna at the head of his list of what he calls 'mountain marvels': 'Etna always burns at night, and has enough fuel to supply its fires for a vast period, even though it is snowy in winter, when it covers its output of ash with frosts'.[22] The emperor Hadrian, too, seems to have made a habit of climbing mountains. He travelled through his territory perhaps more widely than any other Roman emperor. One account tells us that 'he sailed to Sicily, where he climbed Mount Etna in order to see the sunrise, which is said to be multi-coloured like a rainbow' (*Historia Augusta, Hadrian* 13.3).[23] It is hard to draw any very clear conclusions from these brief reports about Hadrian's real motives. But we can at least say that the text represents him as having an interest in the spectacle of nature: there is a hint in that passage that he wants to see whether or not the reports of the odd multi-coloured sunrise are true.

Strabo makes no mention there of the mythical context for Etna; he also tends to take a fairly matter-of-fact approach to the awe-inspiring forces that other authors describe as manifestations of the sublime. Other authors, however, use those elements of the Etna tradition to enrich their own scientific accounts. Pseudo-Aristotle's *On the Cosmos*, which dates probably from the mid-first century CE, is a good example.[24] The opening section gives us the first recorded use outside of literary criticism of the Greek word ὕψος (*hypsos*) in the Longinian sense of 'sublimity'.[25] Disciplines other than philosophy, the author claims, have shunned any contemplation of the universe precisely because of 'its sublimity and its extensiveness' (διὰ τὸ ὕψος καὶ τὸ μέγεθος). The author then goes on to reject commonplace habits of natural description:

> and so those who have earnestly described for us the character of a particular place, or the shape of a single city, or the size of a river, or the beauty of a mountain, as some have done in the past, some of them speaking of Ossa, some of Nyssa, some of the Corycian cave, some of whatever other point of detail it happens to be—one might well pity them for their meanness of spirit. (Pseudo-Aristotle, *On the Cosmos* 391a)

The author here seems to be rejecting the standard encomiastic tradition of mountain description that I discussed at the beginning of the chapter. The mountain descriptions that follow are on a different scale, described from a grander, cosmic viewpoint, rather than being focused on specific places.[26] For example the author describes the earth as follows: 'This region is adorned with innumerable green plants, high mountains, deep-shaded woodland, and cities established by the wise creature, man' (392b).[27] Later he describes openings in the earth's surface that release underground wind and fire 'like Lipara and Etna and the volcanoes in the Aeolian islands. These often flow like rivers and throw up fiery, red-hot lumps' (395b). For this author at least, the sublime is the proper object of scientific enquiry, and the author accesses it through his sweeping vision of the universe and of the world. The vast mountains and volcanoes of the earth are a key part of that vision.

In other cases scientific observation is combined with mythical imagery. Just a few decades after Pindar, and perhaps influenced by him,[28] *Prometheus Bound* at lines 351–72 describes the imprisonment of Typhon beneath Mount Etna as a parallel for the punishment of Prometheus in the Caucasus.[29] The play carries many traces of engagement with fifth-century volcanic theory, for example the belief that eruptions were caused by storms of underground winds,[30] and it uses that imagery to draw a connection between volcanic upheaval and civic strife.[31] Lucretius, several centuries later, overlays his rationalising account of Mount Etna with extravagant poetic celebration of the power of the volcano.[32] He is one of the authors most often cited as an 'exception' to the standard story about the absence of sublime mountain description in ancient literature,[33] and as we have seen already, he and Longinus may have a common source for their account of the volcano.[34]

The Pseudo-Virgilian *Aetna* and the Language of Vision

The Pseudo-Virgilian *Aetna* anticipates modern versions of the mountain sublime perhaps more extensively than any other ancient text. It analyses in more than 600 lines the causes of Etna's wonders: 'what strong causes make the fires billow out' (*quae tam fortes volvant incendia causae*) (*Aetna* 2). The poem's answer to that question is itself quite conventional[35]—the earth is hollow, with channels running through it like veins,[36] and those hollows are filled by underground winds and fire that burst through particular points of weakness, and burn with special force in a place like Etna which has the necessary fuel—but the language the poet uses to describe those processes has an unusual intensity and extravagance. He paints a picture of powerful motion, with surging movements of vast bodies of matter both upwards and downwards, projecting an intense impression of chaos and fear: 'for very many marvels are visible on that mountain. On one side vast openings terrify and plunge into the depths. . . . Elsewhere thick cliffs block the path, and the confusion is enormous' (*Aetna* 180–83). It is now commonplace to point out that this text too combines science with myth, rejecting mythical versions while also indulging in them and harnessing mythical imagery for scientific themes.[37] The poet rejects mythical themes in the opening lines of the text,[38] but he then repeatedly teases his reader by hinting that the phenomena he is describing might have mythical explanations after all: 'From far away in his hiding place Jupiter himself marvels at the great fires and trembles silently lest new Giants should rise up to renew their buried war, or lest Dis [that is, Pluto] should be feeling ashamed of his kingdom and swapping Tartarus for heaven' (*Aetna* 203–6).[39] For all his rationalising persona, those old stories are clearly still powerful vehicles for conveying the grandeur of the phenomena he is describing.

What is less often discussed is the language of vision in the work.[40] The text conveys an extraordinary image, influenced by Lucretius,[41] of the poet's capacity to reveal the inner workings of the earth. In the process it uses the language of viewing repeatedly, especially in a striking series of references to the role of the eyes in scientific observation.[42] In that sense it is one of our best examples of the way in which mountains were represented obsessively as objects of vision in some ancient contexts. One of the most intense clusters of visual language comes about a third of the way through the text, at the point where the poet returns to Mount Etna specifically after some generalising discussion of the structures of the earth. What he wants to stress here is just how unmissable the evidence is: the causes 'will themselves confront your eyes (*occurrent oculis*) and force you to acknowledge them' (*Aetna* 179); and later: 'the things and your eyes teach you (*res oculique docent*): the things themselves force you to believe' (*Aetna* 192). Those pronouncements seem particularly appropriate for a mountain like Etna, which stands up from the land around it so prominently that it is visible from much of the eastern half of Sicily.

Only a little later, however, there is a fascinating change of emphasis where the poet moves on instead to stress the challenges of looking. One crucial issue in his representation of those challenges is what he sees as the difference between passive, bovine gazing at the wonders of nature and the more discriminating vision that he has mastered himself, which draws inferences from natural phenomena and leads to an understanding also of hidden things beneath the surface of the earth.[43] The key passage comes not much later, at the moment when the poet turns to what he represents as the much more difficult challenge of working out where the winds themselves come from. He tells us that there is a divine pleasure available to humans 'not to gaze on wonders only with the eyes like cattle' (*non oculis solum pecudum miranda tueri more*) (*Aetna* 224–25), but instead to understand the heavens, and even more 'to know the earth and mark the many wonders that nature has bestowed' (*cognoscere terram et quae tot miranda tulit natura notare*) (*Aetna* 252–53).[44] Later he describes the process of eruption, and imagines a viewer standing on a hilltop to watch from a distance: 'Then you will think it appropriate to flee in terror and yield to divine things: from the safety of a hill (*e tuto . . . collis*) you will observe (*speculaberis*) everything' (*Aetna* 465–66). This passage manipulates the common motif of mountaintop viewing in fascinating ways: of course the viewer here gains something of the authority associated with that motif in other contexts, but the previous line, with its emphasis on panic and flight, undercuts the dignity of that association, and reminds us too of the viewer's distance from the things he is observing.[45] That difficulty of approaching close to the evidence has also been discussed earlier in the text, in a passage where the poet discusses the unavailability of the sense of touch for his observations. The facts, he tells us, teach the eyes, and they would also 'inform you by touch, if it were possible to touch safely; the flames forbid it, and the guardian of its activity is the fire that prevents approach; and the divine care for these matters is without any witness; all these things you will see from far off' (*Aetna* 193–96). In many ancient representations of mountains vision is associated with control, whereas the sense of touch is invoked in contexts where human actors are immersed in mountain landscapes in confusing and overwhelming ways.[46] In this case, by contrast, vision from a distance is presented as a second-best option, a substitute for close-up bodily engagement.

That is not to say that the poet aims to undermine his own claims to authority in any sustained way. This is still a remarkable celebration of the power of human perceptiveness, not just in giving attention to the visual wonders of Etna's flames, which we can hardly help responding to, but also in using that sight as a spur to deeper understanding. The emphasis on visuality intensifies still further in some of the final scenes—'A host of sparks flash forth at every blow: the glowing rocks—look, you see the flashes in the distance; look, raining down in the distance! (*scintillas procul ecce vides, procul ecce ruentes*) fall with undiminished heat' (*Aetna* 505–7)—and in the poet's claim that Mount Etna is far more valuable as an object of vision than all the standard tourist sites associated with mythical stories: 'look at (*aspice*) the vast work of the artist nature; you will see no spectacles so great belonging to the human masses' (*Aetna* 601–2).[47] Ultimately the poet is enormously confident in the effectiveness and the value of his viewing of the mountain. But that confidence is nevertheless veined with reminders of the opacity and inaccessibility of Mount Etna as an object of analysis.[48]

Literary Ambition and Philosophical Virtue: Etna in Seneca's *Letters*

We have had a glimpse of the natural philosopher and dramatist Seneca already. He too was fascinated by Mount Etna, which features in two intriguing discussions in his *Letters*. In some ways Seneca is unusual in his representation of Etna. By contrast with most of the other authors we have looked at, perhaps with the exception of Strabo, he tends to downplay its physical grandeur. However, he does represent the mountain as powerfully enigmatic in other respects, in drawing attention to its symbolic potential, as an image of literary practice and philosophical virtue.

Both letters are addressed to his friend Lucilius, who served as procurator of Sicily in the early 60s CE. *Letter* 51 is written from the city of Baiae in the Bay of Naples, which was known for its luxury. It opens as follows:

> Everyone does his best, my dear Lucilius! You over there have Etna, that elevated and most renowned mountain of Sicily (*editum illum ac*

nobilissimum Siciliae montem); although I cannot understand why Messala called it 'unique'—or was it Valgius? for I have been reading both—since very many regions vomit out fire. . . . I do the best I can; I am satisfied with Baiae. (Seneca, *Letters* 51.1)

The words *editum* and *nobilissimum* both suggest dignity and social distinction; *editum* can also simply mean 'high'. The mountain is clearly being represented here in positive terms, by contrast with Baiae, with its moral laxity. But this nevertheless falls short of the kind of awed, overwhelmed response to the volcano that we see from so many other ancient authors, and the sentence following rejects the idea that there is anything unique in Etna's landscape ('very many regions vomit out fire'); it perhaps also hints at scepticism towards the kind of claim about literary originality that we have seen in the opening lines of the *Aetna*. Seneca thus seems quite underwhelmed by the volcanic phenomena in themselves. However, the image of the mountain—both this mountain and others—as symbolic of virtue and moral elevation turns out to be very important for Seneca in his denunciation of Baiae in the rest of the letter. Later, for example, Seneca introduces Hannibal as an example of the softening effect of the area around Baiae, which is again contrasted with an image of the mountains as places of virtue: we hear that his time in Campania 'weakened that man who had been unconquered in the snows and the Alps' (51.5). He also tells us that Marius, Pompey, and Julius Caesar all built villas near to Baiae, 'but they placed them on the topmost ridges of the mountains (*summis iugis montium*). This seemed more military, from an elevated place to look down on places spread far and wide below them' (51.11).[49] The dignity that is associated with Etna in the opening lines, and with other kinds of mountain dwelling and experience, in contrast with the laxity of Baiae, turns out to be far more interesting in Seneca's eyes (at least in this text) than any observation of natural wonders.

In *Letter* 79, Seneca takes a much closer interest in those natural wonders—as one might expect from the author of one of the greatest surviving works of ancient natural science, the *Natural Questions*[50]—although even in this case he tends to avoid elaborately grand description of them.[51] He writes to say among other things that he is contemplating asking Lucilius to climb Etna for him to answer some questions:

> Some people deduce that the mountain is gradually subsiding and being consumed, because in the past it used to be visible to sailors from farther away. It is possible that this is happening not because the height of the

mountain is decreasing, but because the fire has faded and is discharged less strongly and less copiously, and because for the same reason the smoke is also more sluggish during the day. However, neither of these other two possibilities is unbelievable: either that the mountain is growing smaller through being swallowed up day by day, or that it stays the same, because the fire does not consume the mountain itself, but having been produced in some subterranean valley it boils out and is fed by other sources: in the mountain itself it has not a source of fuel but a way out.... But let us put these things aside for further discussion once you have written to me about how far the snows lie from the crater, the snows that even the summer does not melt, so safe are they from the neighbouring fire. (*Letter* 79.2 and 79.4)

This is another important testimony, alongside Strabo's, to the possibility of scientific tourism on Mount Etna in the Roman period.

The passage also presents us with quite a modern image of the mountain ground down over vast time periods—another indication of the way in which volcanic landscapes were viewed as dynamic terrain. We tend to think of that interest in the deep time of mountain landscapes as a distinctively modern interest, inherited from texts like Thomas Burnet's *Sacred Theory of the Earth*, which was published in the late seventeenth century and which according to many accounts laid the ground for later understanding of geological time.[52] We also tend to think that ancient writers had very little understanding of the vast timescales involved in the formation of mountain landscapes. But in fact that topic has an extensive ancient pedigree, in Seneca and many others, especially in ancient writing on volcanoes. Already for ancient observers these were places of unstable and shifting ground rather than permanently fixed terrain, and places with a geological history, albeit a very enigmatic one.[53]

Seneca then switches suddenly to the literary possibilities Mount Etna offers. Lucilius, it seems, is planning to write a poem about the mountain anyway (some have even suggested that Lucilius is the poet of the *Aetna* itself). The subject, Seneca says, is 'a traditional one for all poets' (79.5). As in *Letter* 51 he gives a very different account of the uniqueness of the subject from the one we find in the *Aetna*, but he does not go so far as to suggest that the long tradition of Etna writing makes this an unworthy topic: 'It makes a big difference, whether you come to a topic that has been worn down or one where the ground has only been broken; in the latter the topic grows each day and the things that have been discovered already do not prevent future discoveries'

(79.6). Lucilius' literary plans are rescued here from negative judgement by a metaphor that looks back to Seneca's earlier description of the ground of the volcano itself. Poetic ambition, when you have the right subject, in other words when it is built on ground that has not already been 'worn out' or 'consumed' (*consumptam*) and so is able to 'grow each day' (*crescit in dies*), is favourably contrasted with the mountain itself, which is suspected of being gradually reduced in size over time.

And then in the second half of the letter Seneca shifts his attention abruptly once again to focus now on human virtue and wisdom.[54] Etna is once again an important point of comparison:

> I do not know whether your Mount Etna could collapse and fall in on itself, or whether this lofty peak, which is conspicuous over the vast stretches of the sea, could be worn down by the continual power of the fires; but there is no flame, no ruin that can bring down virtue. This is the one kind of grandeur that cannot be suppressed; it cannot be carried further or forced back. The magnitude of virtue, like that of the heavenly bodies, is fixed. Let us therefore try to raise ourselves upward to that level. (79.10)

Here Seneca once again contrasts the evanescence and instability of Etna with the things of higher value, and praises the much more sublime goal of virtue,[55] which, like Lucilius' literary activity, but in a more powerful and important way, cannot shrink and will endure. Etna is thus an enigmatic object for Seneca: we are challenged to make sense of it as we read, within the dense and challenging texture of the letter. He too is deeply interested in the mountain's volcanic effects, but for him Etna also has a more important and deeper significance, as an image against which to measure the value and endurability of human virtue.[56] That makes *Letter* 79 quite unusual in the landscape of ancient writing about Etna, but also at the same time typical of a wider tendency in ancient literature—and in ancient art, which is the subject of chapter 7—to treat mountains as charismatic, multi-dimensional objects in need of decipherment.

7

Mountains in Greek and Roman Art

Miniaturised Mountains

Mountains were objects of fascination in Greek and Roman art, although in ways quite different from anything we are familiar with in modern landscape painting.[1] Often they were compressed and miniaturised. That was partly because of the restrictions of the media within which they were depicted—it could hardly be otherwise for a mountain on a coin, for example—but it was also a consequence of their symbolic function, which allowed the image to stand as a shorthand for a particular place or a particular kind of place. It would be tempting to dismiss this kind of symbolic quality, just as some critics have dismissed the allegorical, symbolic function of mountains in ancient and early modern poetry, as a sign of a lack of any serious interest in mountains.[2] In fact the opposite is often true: in many cases the symbolic power of mountains was precisely the source of their fascination for ancient readers and viewers.

The situation is rather different with the mountains that recur frequently in Roman mythological wall paintings. These too often tie images from myth to particular places with powerful, centuries-old narrative associations, just like their more compressed equivalents in Greek vase paintings and coins, helping us to identify particular scenes and stories. At the same time their greater realism leaves open the possibility of a more visceral response. They tempt the viewer into a fantasy of identification with the scenes on display, conveying a paradoxical atmosphere of pleasure and threat, as settings for stories of human risk and suffering. In that sense these images, very much like the mythological compilation of Pausanias, draw on the ever-present potential for mountains to be experienced as landscapes of risk where human agency is liable to be overwhelmed. One of the things that all of these different images hold in common, however, is the status of mountains as objects that demand decipherment and pose challenges to human understanding.

There is an obvious contradiction in the fact that these most vast of all landscape features were so often depicted in miniaturised form. We could take that as a sign that ancient artists and viewers were simply unmoved by the awe-inspiring scale of mountains, which modern viewers are inclined to take as one of the defining features of the natural sublime. But it seems equally possible that they would have delighted in that paradox, and in the ingenuity with which mountains could be compacted within a human scale. The mountains of archaic and classical Greek vase painting are typical examples.[3] They may have been influenced in part by the stylised conventions of ancient stage-sets, where a mountain could be signalled by a rocky background: we have a series of surviving images that depict characters set against a 'rocky arch', which may have been a standard piece of stage equipment. Figure 7.1 depicts Prometheus attached to his mountain, represented by a squiggly line, which stretches a little above head height: there are several parallels in other vase paintings.[4] In many other classical vase paintings, mountains are depicted by relatively unobtrusive rocks set in one corner of the image. There is an explicitly signposted version of the convention, whereby a rock can stand in for a mountain, in a white-ground vase from the mid-fifth century BCE which depicts the Muses relaxing at home. The rock on which one of the Muses is seated is labelled by the artist as 'Helikon' (figure 7.2).[5] Depictions of Paris's judgement of the beauty contest between Hera, Athene, and Aphrodite in archaic and classical vase paintings routinely show the hero sitting on rocks which are clearly meant to stand for Mount Ida as a whole (for example, figures 7.3 and 7.4). The earliest examples date back to around 520 BCE, and there are many examples from the fifth century.[6] That brief, conventional detail of iconography would have been enough for most viewers to activate a rich array of mythological and poetic associations for Mount Ida.[7] And that mountain setting, far from being an inert adornment, is in fact central to the story these images tell, in the sense that it helps to explain why Paris chose Aphrodite ahead of the other gods. As a member of the royal family of Troy, one would expect him to be more interested in the gifts of military might and power offered to him by Athene and Hera, but his identity as a shepherd, brought up on Mount Ida after being abandoned there as a child, explains his lack of interest in those prizes and his preference for Aphrodite, the goddess of love. That preference unleashes the theft of Helen, and the assault of the

FIGURE 7.1. Prometheus bound to a rocky arch, being freed by Herakles. Apulian calyx-krater, ca 340s BCE, attributed to the Branca Painter. Berlin, Antikensammlung, Staatliche Museen zu Berlin. bpk Berlin / Antikensammlung, SMB / Johannes Laurentius.

Greek army against the unbreachable walls of Troy, and ultimately the fulfilment of Zeus's plan to solve the problem of overpopulation in the world through the Trojan War.[8]

These kinds of miniaturised, stage-set mountains are depicted over and over again over many centuries and in many different artistic contexts. There are lots

FIGURE 7.2. Muse sitting on the rocks of Mount Helikon. White-ground lekythos, ca 445–435 BCE, attributed to the Achilles Painter. Munich, Staatliche Antikensammlungen, SCH (formerly Lugano, Schoen Collection). Photo: ArchaiOptix, Wikimedia Commons. Licence: CC-BY-SA-4.0.

of numismatic examples. An extensive series of Hellenistic coins from Arkadia has the bust of Zeus Lykaios on the obverse, and on the reverse the god Pan seated on a rock which is clearly meant to stand for Mount Lykaion, where he had a sanctuary (figure 7.5). In a coin minted in 71 CE, we see a female personification of the city of Rome sitting on seven rounded hills (figure 7.6).[9]

FIGURE 7.3. The Judgement of Paris. Red-figured hydria, ca 470 BCE. London, British Museum. © The Trustees of the British Museum.

There are many similar examples of miniaturised mountains in coin depictions of Mount Argaios from Caesarea in Cappadocia.[10] There are also numerous examples of rocky backgrounds standing for mountains on Trajan's Column, which was constructed in the early second century CE in the centre of Rome. Spiralling up the outside of the column are intricately carved images celebrating Trajan's triumph in the Dacian Wars, in modern-day Romania. Here too, in the restricted spaces of the column's spirals, the artists repeatedly resort to stylised rocky stage-sets as a shorthand for the mountainous territory of the Carpathians (figure 7.7).[11] Ancient maps, too, often depicted mountains in stylised, compressed form.[12]

If we jump forward by several centuries to Justinian's Basilica at Saint Catherine's monastery, in the image of Moses on Mount Sinai (see figure 4.1), we

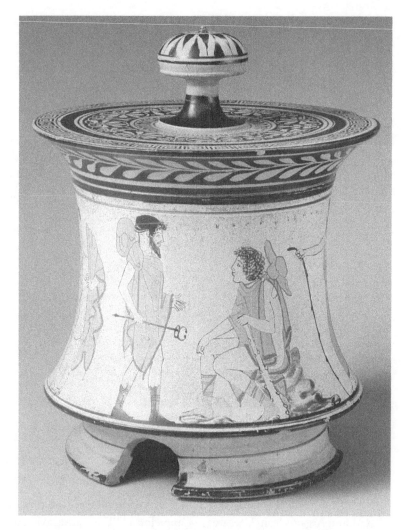

FIGURE 7.4. The Judgement of Paris. Terracotta pyxis, attributed to the Penthesilea Painter, ca 465–460 BCE. New York, Metropolitan Museum of Art. Rogers Fund, 1907.

see there again a relatively restricted rocky background, designed to fit neatly into a small mosaic panel, standing as a shorthand for the rugged mountain that visitors would have seen standing above them from outside the monastery. Here too it would be quite wrong to suggest that the simplicity of the depiction of Mount Sinai implies a lack of interest. The mountain was already crowded with symbolic and narrative associations; it would have taken only a

FIGURE 7.5. Silver stater, Arkadian League, 363–362 BCE. Reverse: Pan sitting on rocks. Berlin, Münzkabinett der Staatlichen Museum, Altes Museum. Photo: ArchaiOptix, Wikimedia Commons. Licence: CC-BY-SA-4.0.

FIGURE 7.6. Coin showing head of Vespasian (obverse); Roma seated on the seven hills (reverse), 71 CE. London, British Museum. © The Trustees of the British Museum.

FIGURE 7.7. Trajan's Column, Rome, completed 113 CE. Scene LXII: Roman forces advancing through forested, mountainous scenery. Image: J.C.N. Coulston.

cursory representation of the summit to activate those associations for viewers whose purpose in visiting was in many cases precisely to climb the mountain for themselves. In the face of this image—whether it is viewed before or after the pilgrim climbs the Stairway of Repentance—we find ourselves together with Moses in the presence of the divine. The sense of confinement in the mosaic's depiction of the summit by these two rocky cliffs if anything enhances that sense of identification, reproducing as it does the restrictions in Moses' vision throughout his encounters with God on Mount Sinai.[13]

Mountains in Roman Wall Painting

In Roman wall painting, mountains and landscapes generally tend to be depicted in much more detail, although here too we often find relatively small-scale rocks and cliffs with a stage-set quality, intended to stand for mountainous

FIGURE 7.8. Wall painting of a villa with mountains, from the House of Lucretius Fronto, Pompeii; detail of the south wall of the tablinum, first century CE.
DeAgostini Picture Library / Scala, Florence. © Photo SCALA, Florence.

territory without the need for full-scale depiction of it. Some of these mountains appear in scenes that have a decorative function rather than a narrative one.[14] This style of landscape painting seems to have emerged in the early imperial period: Pliny in his *Natural History* 35.116 records that an artist named Studius, working in the reign of Augustus 'first introduced the very pleasant habit of painting walls, depicting villas and porticoes and landscape gardens, groves, woods, hills, fish-ponds, canals, rivers, coasts'.[15] In some cases images of this type back up the impression we have gained already from the literary sources that mountains are more likely to be viewed with pleasure when they are in the background to an urban or villa setting. The best example is from the house of Lucretius Fronto in Pompeii (figure 7.8).

The image is painted on a solid wall as if it is the view through a window. The foreground is a landscape of water with boats and a villa, but in the background stand three peaks, bare of vegetation, sloping steeply up so that their peaks almost bump against the border of the image. Another villa image stands facing this one on the opposite wall, more faded, but again with mountain slopes in the background. Just like Strabo's hills of Rome, standing in the background to the artwork of the city, these mountains seem to be appealing precisely because of the way in which they can be framed and domesticated as a background to buildings. At first glance they look like very big mountains, but at the same time they also seem close to the buildings in front of them; the left-hand peak appears on further inspection little higher than the trees that stand in front of it; and their absorption into the near symmetricality of the picture as a whole suggests that they are valued because of the way in which they can, for all their vastness and barrenness, be contained within a human, architectural framework.

More often, however, mountains in Roman wall painting have a narrative context, as settings for depictions of famous moments in Greek myth. There is a wonderful example in one of the other rooms of the house of Lucretius Fronto, in an image of Narcissus admiring his reflection against a backdrop of cliffs (figure 7.9).[16] It is a very different image in some respects, in the sense that it is set far outside the bounds of urban civilisation, but it does nevertheless raise some of the same questions about the relationship between nature and human culture. These are the high mountains: the cliffs in the background are sheer or in some cases overhanging, and they seem to stand over a vast abyss which would not be out of place in Romantic representations of the Alps. And yet Narcissus is there. He seems oddly oblivious to the harshness of his surroundings: there is no anxiety in his face, no awareness of the breathtaking peaks behind him, or of the cold of the high mountains, signaled by the dark sky, as he sits with his clothing slipping from his shoulders, in the distinctive sloping pose in which he is depicted in many other Pompeiian paintings too[17]—only a complete absorption in the image of the human face that is the object of his fascination. The pool at Narcissus' feet, which is small like a mirror, might remind us of precisely the kind of trompe-l'oeil artwork which is visible all over Pompeii, not least in the window-like mountain images already discussed from the same house: if so, Narcissus' absorption, focused on the illusory rather than on natural landscape, parallels the viewer's own. The slope of Narcissus' body corresponds to the shape of the cliff behind him that stretches up above his waist. The two peaks on the left-hand side of Narcissus

MOUNTAINS IN GREEK AND ROMAN ART 129

FIGURE 7.9. Narcissus at the fountain, from the House of Lucretius Fronto,
Pompeii, bedroom, first century CE. Photo Scala, Florence / Luciano Romano.
© Photo SCALA, Florence.

as we look, and even more the peak to his right, are rounded and roughly level with the rounding of own head, as if hinting at the possibility of personification. Has he adapted his pose to the landscape, or is the landscape itself inherently sympathetic to human presence, wrapping itself protectively around him, and imitating the rightward slant of his body? Is that similarity of shape a sign of the pre-eminence and mastery of the human figure in this image. Or does it remind us rather of the landscape's dangerously seductive quality, which is of course exactly the thing that turns out to be Narcissus' downfall? The ledge or platform on the left is also odd. Most of the other Narcissus images from Pompeii are set on the lower slopes of mountains, framed in standard fashion by human-sized rocks and stage-set cliffs. In that context we often see flat rocks, often with other characters sitting on them, most often the god Eros.[18] In this case, by contrast, the emptiness of the platform emphasises Narcissus' isolation. It looks entirely inaccessible. The prospect of looking down from it, if one were able to reach it, is a dizzying one. It would surely leave one with the impression of human insignificance in the face of the vastness of nature. And yet in its perfect flatness it does also look like the kinds of platforms and projections that we find in ancient architectural wall paintings, as if it would serve as a building place for a clifftop villa.[19] Do these mountains dwarf and enfold Narcissus? Or are even they inextricably marked by the idea of human dominance and control?

The high mountains of this Narcissus image are quite unusual. More often in mythological painting the mountain backdrops are on a smaller scale, depicted primarily as low cliffs and rocks. There are dozens of examples from Pompeii and beyond.[20] In the house of Virnius Modestus (IX.7.16),[21] for example, there are two separate, small rooms at the front of the house, both of which had three paintings on mythological subjects. In the slightly smaller of the two rooms, to the north, there are images of Perseus and Andromeda, Hylas and the Nymphs (figure 7.10),[22] and Cassandra and the Trojans with the Trojan horse below a small, stylised Mount Ida; and in the larger, south room images of Diana and Actaeon, Pegasus and Bellerophon, and the fall of Icarus. Five of these images have a strikingly similar structure, with a mountain or cliff of some sort on the right-hand side. The last (Diana and Actaeon) cannot be reconstructed clearly enough to be sure, but it seems likely that that painting too would have had a rocky background, given the setting of the story on Mount Cithaeron, and given the use of rocky settings in other depictions of the Actaeon story from Pompeii. That repetitive structure is surely an invitation to interpret these images together,[23] and a reminder that they come from a single mythical world, where humans immersed in wild landscapes are at risk at the hands of the gods. There are similar effects in other assemblages too. In house V.2.10, for example, there are four images all with mountain backgrounds.[24] Hercules with the Hesperides faces an image of Hippolytus at the shrine of Diana; both images focus on enclosed spaces with mountain

FIGURE 7.10. Nineteenth-century watercolour of a wall painting from Pompeii showing the Rape of Hylas, from the House of Virnius Modestus, IX.7.16, early first century CE(?). DAI-Rom, Archivio, A-VII-33-088.

backdrops.[25] The other pair of facing images is Marsyas playing the flute on Mount Helicon, and the fall of Icarus again, both of which depict the violent consequences of excessive pride; both are set against a harsher landscape of jagged cliffs and crags.

The mountain backgrounds are significant not just for these stories individually, but also for the way in which they respond to each other. The similarity and cross-fertilisation between images is perhaps not surprising. The repetition of common subjects over and over again in the houses of Pompeii shows just how popular Greek mythical narrative was as a subject for villa decoration. Each of these paintings responds to local but also wider Mediterranean fashions of representation: presumably most viewers of these images would have seen other related images before, and would have been inclined to draw comparisons with that wider series,[26] as well as with other paintings in the same room.[27] Nor is it surprising that mountain scenes were common, given the important role of mountain landscapes in the narratives themselves: the story of Diana and Actaeon unfolds through Actaeon's experience of hunting on Mount Cithaeron beyond the limits of urban civilisation;[28] the story of the love of Polyphemus for the nymph Galatea is structured around the contrast between two realms, the liquid sea and the bleak, rocky landscape of the shore, drawing on Homer's description of the mountain-dwelling Cyclops. As many commentators on these images have pointed out, that effect has a lot of in common with the mountain backdrops that are woven through literary representations of mythological narrative, especially Ovid's *Metamorphoses*.[29] The prevalence of mountains in the visual record is also backed up by literary descriptions of mythological painting, especially by Philostratus, who repeatedly mentions mountains in the background to the pictures he describes in his *Imagines*.[30] Different images between them thus had a cumulative effect that would have encouraged the viewer to imagine a varied world of mythical landscape, comprising mountain landscapes, but also pastoral settings, and seashores and groves, in a way that had something in common, although on a smaller scale, with the composite world conjured up by Homer's similes in the *Iliad*.

These images also gain part of their attraction by their capacity to draw their viewers in, offering a fantasy of absorption.[31] The relatively small scale of the mountain scenes they present us with, which are so welcoming to human presence, are, I suggest, crucial to that effect. In some cases, even mythological paintings are set in panels, rather like the frame that surrounds figure 7.8 from the House of Lucretius Fronto, that make it look as though they are views from windows.[32] In some cases these pictures might stand near to real views of the sea or mountains and gardens from the doors or windows of a house, hinting at the possibility that the viewers would encounter mythological terrain if they were to step outdoors themselves.[33] Moreover, the landscape backgrounds in these paintings are sometimes so dominant that some viewers might not have realised initially that they were looking at depictions of specific mythical stories:[34] the recognition of particular narratives emerges from the act of contemplation and decipherment. The recurring presence of cliffs and crags conjures up an impression of a shared world on the edges of human civilisation, and it is a world where the original viewers of these images could easily have imagined themselves—unlike the Narcissus image from the House of Lucretius Fronto, with its high-mountain wilderness setting—precisely because of their preference for smaller-scale hills and rocks rather than vast mountain landscapes that would dwarf their human actors entirely. In that sense these images raise questions about how the landscapes of everyday experience shared the atmosphere of risk and foreboding that was central to so many of the mythical scenes.[35]

We find very similar conventions in painted landscapes elsewhere in Italy too. For example, the famous *Odyssey* landscapes from the Esquiline hill in Rome,[36] which predate the Pompeii images, are full of rocky terrains as a setting for mythological narrative: it is the mountainous backgrounds that tie together the images and make them into a coherent series. They are rugged, threatening landscapes. In some cases we do see hills and cliffs in the middle distance, but even in these cases the images are dominated by rocks and crags in the foreground, as immediate settings for the human or divine figures. Those landscapes recur in very similar form in successive pictures, with the light always falling from the top left[37] in order to tie them together:[38] the surviving pictures represent in turn a series of Odysseus' adventures from Books 9–12 of the *Odyssey*. In figure 7.11, for example, Odysseus' companions encounter the daughter of the Laestrygonian king and queen, unaware that the cannibalistic Laestrygonians will soon be hunting them down.

The image picks up on the mountainous character of Odysseus' description in *Odyssey* 10: 'on the seventh day we came to the steep city of Lamos'; 'around the harbour on both sides were cliffs of sheer rock'; 'I climbed up and stood on a rugged peak to reconnoitre'; his companions meet the wife of the king and find that she is 'as big as the peak of a mountain, and they felt hatred towards her'; 'from the rocks the Laestrygonians bombarded us with boulders as big as a man can carry'.[39] In the painting the Laestrygonians and the terrain

FIGURE 7.11. Wall painting showing Odysseus' companions in the land of the Laestrygonians, from a house in the via Graziosa, Rome, mid-first century BCE. Musei Vaticani. Album / Alamy Stock Photo.

they inhabit are reduced in size: there is a suggestion of a mountainous landscape, but the two prominent cliffs that flank the Laestrygonian princess are not very many times higher than the figures themselves. And yet there is still a remarkable sense of menace in the landscape, with its dark shadows and sheer rock faces, perhaps even more so than in the original, where the poet's descriptions of the terrain are consistently brief. Once again the human scale and detail of the landscape increases the sense of threat and fascination rather than diminishing it, and makes it easier for the viewer to imagine her- or himself into the painting.[40] That distinctive scaling-down of the mountainous background, far from being a sign of a lack of interest, is one of the things that marks these landscapes as places on the edges of human civilisation, rather than utterly outside it—hospitable to human presence, but hostile and dangerous too.

Enigmatic Mountains

Every so often, however, mountains are present in ancient images not as backgrounds but as primary objects of depiction. Unlike the mythological mountains in the Pompeii and Esquiline wall paintings, the three examples I turn to now are in different ways highly stylised and non-realistic. All three offer their viewers intriguing puzzles of interpretation. In all three cases those puzzles are linked with the challenge of understanding the way in which particular mountains were places of divine presence.

For the first (figure 7.12), we stay in Pompeii. The image, from the so-called House of the Centenary, seems to have been situated in the house's *lararium*, the domestic altar used for worship of the gods. The god Bacchus, clothed in grapes, stands beside what is almost certainly Mount Vesuvius, which has plants and terraces depicted on its slopes. Next to him is a coiling snake and a leopard cub, animals particularly linked with his powers. This is not remotely realistic as a depiction of the mountain (although it may not be so far different from the real view of Vesuvius as we initially think: the mountain has two summits now, but may have had just one, as in the image, before the eruption of 79 CE). Its location suggests that it would not have had large numbers of viewers, but it nevertheless seems to be designed as a complex portrayal that would repay contemplation and decipherment, and as an image that had a certain symbolic significance encoded with in it, which would have brought the satisfaction of understanding to those who were familiar with it. Above all it seems to signify the local identity of Vesuvius as a place rich in vines, nourished by the presence of the god. The Latin poet Martial says that 'These ridges Bacchus loved more than the hills of Nysa' (Martial, *Epigrams* 4.44): Nysa was the unidentified mythical mountain of the east famed as the birthplace of Bacchus-Dionysus. Strabo offers a more scientifically inclined version of that same claim:

> Mount Vesuvius lies above these places. It is inhabited all around with beautiful farmlands, except on the summit. For the summit is mainly flat, and entirely fruitless, and looks ash-like, and it reveals porous indentations in the rocks, which are soot-coloured on the surface, as if they have been eaten away by fire, so that one might assume that this place was in the past burnt and had craters of fire, but then was quenched when the fuel gave out. Perhaps this is the cause also of the fruitfulness of the area, just as in Katana, they say, the areas covered by ash, from the hot ash carried up into the air by the fire of Etna, made the land well suited for vines. (Strabo, *Geography* 5.4.8)[41]

FIGURE 7.12. Bacchus and Mount Vesuvius, Lararium of the House of the Centenary, Pompeii, first century CE. Naples Archaeological Museum. Photo: Carole Raddato, Frankfurt, Germany, Wikimedia Commons. Licence: CC-BY-SA-2.0.

The Pompeii image is not necessarily presenting Vesuvius' slopes as beautiful in the way that Strabo does, but it matches Strabo's celebration of the richness of the mountain slopes, and in that sense the image is yet another example of the way in which ancient mountains tended to be represented in positive terms when they were benign, fertile, made compatible with human civilisation and human cultivation. As so often, the peak is reduced to a manageable human scale: it is little bigger than the figure of Bacchus and the animals that accompany him, and the trees on its slopes are far larger relative to the overall size of the mountain than they would be in a real view of Vesuvius. And yet the mountain is very far from being under human control: it is still a place of mystery. Bacchus here stands almost as an equivalent of the mountain itself: both are of roughly the same size and shape, with the downward slope of the god's shoulders matching the upper slopes of Vesuvius; both are cloaked in vegetation, with the regular patterning of the grapes matching the regular pattern of the terracing on the slopes, as if the mountain is in itself a personification of the divine presence.[42]

This is a miniaturised, stylised mountain, then, but it is not for that reason abstract or detached from human experience: the reduction in size contributes to the impression of a landscape that is accessible and helpful to its human inhabitants. At the same time, however, it facilitates the artist's attempts to present us with a rich, enigmatic, even mysterious fantasy of divine protection and divine presence.

The second image, the so-called Euthykles stele (figure 7.13), takes us back to mainland Greece.[43] It is one of the most extraordinary surviving examples of personification of a mountain from the ancient world. This is the face of Helikon, staring out at us from behind the mountain's ridge. The image is a votive relief, dedicated at the sanctuary of the Muses beneath Mount Helikon, probably in the late third century BCE.[44] The monument as a whole stands just over one metre high. Set above and below the image it has three short texts in verse. The first, in three lines, tells us that it has been dedicated by someone called Euthykles, son of Amphikritos, in honour of the Muses, and asks them to safeguard his descent and his reputation. It seems likely that the dedicator is associating himself with his great poetic predecessor Hesiod: the crown engraved at the bottom of the relief may be meant to signal that he has won a victory in a local poetic contest.[45] The third, also in three lines, records the fact that Hesiod celebrated 'the Muses and Helikon': the claim that Hesiod has celebrated not only the Muses but also the mountain itself seems appropriate given the prominence of the mountain in the sculpted image. And sure enough

FIGURE 7.13. Euthykles Stele. Found in the Valley of the Muses, late third century BCE. Height 1.19 m; width 0.50 m. Athens, National Archaeological Museum, NAM 1455. © Hellenic Ministry of Culture and Sports / Hellenic Organization of Cultural Resources Development.

in the middle text, in four verses, it is the mountain itself that speaks (like many ancient epigrams, this one invites the viewer to give voice to the mountain by reading the text aloud): 'In this way I, Helikon, not unskilled in the art of the Muses, aged like a mortal, face to face cry out this oracle: "For mortals who obey the instructions of Hesiod there will be order and land rich with fruits"'.

The monument offers us quite an unusual image of Hesiod's work. One might expect that these verses would be accompanied by an image of the poet encountering the Muses on the mountainside, but instead Hesiodic poetic authority is guaranteed by the mountain itself, in a way that has no precedent either within Hesiod's poems or in any other surviving text from classical antiquity. In the process the relief offers us an image of the relationship between Hesiod's two poems that not everyone shared. We have seen already that Pausanias, who visited the shrine in the second century CE, reported a local tradition that Hesiod wrote nothing but the *Works and Days*, and that even in that work the prefatory address to the Muses was not genuine.[46] The Helikon relief resists that tradition. The oracle clearly refers to the maxims of the *Works and Days*, where Hesiod gives instructions on how to farm and how to live.[47] But at the same time the wild, aged figure of the mountain, and the reference to his life-span in the middle epigram, are surely intended to recall the representation of mountains as some of the most ancient places of the earth in the *Theogony*;[48] he also insists on the importance of the Muses for Hesiod's poetry. In that sense the monument offers a more unified image of Hesiod's achievement than the tradition reported by Pausanias.[49]

But those details do not capture in full the oddity of the monument. The shortage of parallels for visual personifications of Helikon or indeed of most of the other mountains of Greece[50] is the thing that contributes perhaps most of all to making this a puzzling, surprising image. It challenges us as viewers to make sense of the unfamiliar. There is a good comparison point in a surviving fragment by the Greek poet Korinna, where she describes a competition between Mount Kithairon and Mount Helikon: Kithairon wins, having gained the support of the Muses, and Helikon in his fury tears off a piece of the mountainside and flings it down below to shatter into 10,000 stones.[51] That text, like the image, is unusual in its choice to personify the mountains: Helikon is there a primitively powerful figure.[52] However, there are also striking differences from the Euthykles stele, partly because Korinna's text gives us a very different version of the relationship between Helikon and the Muses.[53] The relief resists that image of conflict, representing Helikon in harmony with the Muses and humbly acknowledging their mastery, appropriately so for a dedication to the goddesses in their sanctuary. And the face itself reflects something of that atmosphere of reconciliation. There is no doubt that we are in the presence of a wild figure: the hair is neat, almost symmetrical, but not for that reason human; if anything it seems organic, lush and plant-like.[54] But this is the figure who is prophesying prosperity for humans (a richness of growth that will perhaps match the plant-like richness of his hair), and his position behind the mountain ridge is non-confrontational, almost as if he is himself sheltering, or at any rate revealing his presence reluctantly or shyly. The image seems to be asking us what it means to think of the mountain as a place of divine presence. And the answers it gives us are arrestingly different from most of the familiar alternatives, in its vision of the mountain itself as a wild divinity, who in other contexts might be threatening or vengeful, but who here guarantees the fertility of the landscape for human use. In that it has something in common with the combination of divine power and human order that we have seen also in the Pompeii Vesuvius painting.

The third image is the famous Archelaos relief (figure 7.14). It was found in the remains of an ancient villa to the south of Rome. It dates from sometime between the third and first century BCE.[55] More than any of those other images, this relief sets a puzzle to the viewer.[56] As for the Euthykles stele, it is a puzzle that prompts us to think among other things about the role of mountains as vehicles for poetic inspiration. This clearly is a mountain. Zeus sits enthroned on the summit slopes. Some modern scholars have argued that it is Mount Helikon, given the presence of the nine Muses below Zeus—Mnemosyne ('Memory'), the mother of the Muses, stands at the top right—although it might equally be Olympus, given the Hesiodic tradition of the Muses' transfer to Olympus. The presence of Apollo in the centre left, seated and playing his *kithara* next to the *omphalos*, the rounded stone that is said to have marked the centre of the world at Delphi, suggests Mount Parnassos. One option is to think of it as an imaginary composite of the three.[57] One recent study has argued convincingly that Olympus is by the far the most plausible candidate,[58] but even if we accept this view it is surely the case that many ancient viewers too would have had to puzzle over the image in order to work that out; and even if we feel we have solved that problem, it is only the beginning of the interpretative difficulties the relief presents us with.

The bigger puzzle is about what exactly this relief is aiming to convey about the processes of poetic inspiration. No one quite knows why the image was carved, but it seems possible that the monument was designed to celebrate the victory of a poet in competition in one of the festival contests that proliferated

FIGURE 7.14. Marble relief showing the apotheosis of Homer, Archelaos of Priene, from Bovillae, second century BCE(?). Height 1.15 m. London, British Museum.
© The Trustees of the British Museum.

across the eastern Mediterranean in the second and third centuries BCE: standing on a plinth in the centre right is a figure with a tripod of the kind that was regularly awarded as a prize for musical competition. The presence of the Muses in the upper levels suggests that the poet wishes to associate himself with Hesiodic models of inspiration, as many Roman poets did, but he also draws even more explicit links with Homer, who sits at the bottom left of the image (he is labelled, as many of the other figures also are).[59] He is being crowned by *Chronos* ('time') and *Oikoumene* ('the inhabited world') as a sign of the chronological and geographical extent of his fame. Personifications of the various literary genres are sacrificing a bull in his honour. In the upper half we see a remarkable network of gazes: Zeus exchanges glances with Mnemosyne; to her right, one of the other Muses hurries down a rocky path as if with a message. We might see Apollo as the recipient of the inspiration that is being passed from Zeus on the summit downwards, but it seems equally to lead to the poet figure on the right, even though he is a little isolated, on his platform, from the divine scenes around him. The poet is iconographically linked with Homer: both of them hold scrolls. Homer in turn is linked with Zeus: both are enthroned, bearded, and carrying a scepter; Homer is portrayed here in the position of a deity receiving sacrifice in a sanctuary.[60] The implication is that Homer too, like the unnamed poet, has access to the divine world on the mountaintop above, both because of his own quasi-divine qualities and also no doubt because of his powers of vision and imagination. The human actors are blocked off from the scenes above them by the thick border over their heads which gives their location almost a subterranean feel. Only Homer, the implication is, can see above and beyond. If that is correct, the unknown victor is surely being invited to imagine himself in Homer's own position, scaling the mountain of the gods in his mind's eye. The image is a reminder of the rich variety of ways in which mountains could be linked, through the idea of divine presence, with poetic composition. And it offers a sophisticated variation on the Hesiodic tradition of depicting mountainside poetic inspiration via a personal encounter with the Muses.

All three of these monuments thus share an interest in the human value of mountains, where mountains are sources of poetic inspiration and prosperity. At the same time all three, in presenting us with puzzling images in need of decipherment, portray mountains as places of mystery on the edge of human understanding; in all three that status is envisaged as a consequence of their connections with the divine. They explore those tensions in a less realistic mode than many of the other literary and artistic images we have looked at.

They are quite different from the painted cliffs and crags from the walls of Pompeii, with their very personal, human scale, or from the remote mountain settings of Homer's similes, but that would not have made them any less powerful or any less compelling for their original audiences: for ancient viewers that rich symbolic potential of mountains was itself precisely one of the things that made them so fascinating. In many literary depictions, symbolic and realistic aspects of mountain landscape were interwoven with each other if anything in even more complex and challenging ways than they are here, as we shall see now in turning to the mountains of Latin poetry, and then last to the *Metamorphoses* of Apuleius.

8

Mountain Landmarks in Latin Literature

Mountain Symbolism

One of the most famous mountains in ancient literature is also one of the most briefly described. Mount Soracte stands about 30 miles north of Rome. It is not particularly high: the summit stands at 691 metres above sea level, not a long walk from the village of Sant-Oreste on its slopes. It is a spectacular place, visible from a long way off—it stands up from the plane like a giant fin, with no other hills anywhere near it—but that in itself does not explain its fame. The crucial factor is the Soracte ode by Horace (*Odes* 1.9), written in the late first century BCE, which has been one of the best known and most loved of all Latin poems at least over the last two or three centuries. The initial image in that poem is of the mountain covered in snow, followed by a description of drinking wine in front of a warm fire, and then a set of reflections on youth, old age, and love: 'You see how Soracte stands white with deep snow (*vides ut alta stet nive candidum Soracte*), and the labouring woods can no longer hold the weight, and the rivers have stopped from the sharp cold' (*Odes* 1.9.1–4). After those four lines, the mountain fades from view: Soracte is not mentioned again in the poem. Those four lines have been enough for literary immortality. It was the opening line of this poem that Patrick Leigh Fermor's German captive, General Kreipe, quoted to him in looking at the sunrise on Mount Ida in Crete in 1944; Leigh Fermor claims to have quoted the rest of the poem to him from memory in response, an incident which united the two men temporarily in their shared mastery of the classical heritage.[1] It was also an important landmark for the classically educated northern Europeans who travelled in Italy in the nineteenth century. The Victorian travel writer Augustus Hare, in his *Days*

Near Rome, published in 1875, gives a long account of his visit to Mount Soracte. In the process he not only describes Soracte himself repeatedly; he also quotes over and over again from others who have done the same. In *Days Near Rome*, and one of his other guide-books, *Walks in Rome* (1871), he quotes at length from twelve different nineteenth-century authors (including novelists like Amelia Edwards, Nathaniel Hawthorne, and Charlotte Dempster, as well as travel writers and scholars) who had previously described the mountain, including a famous passage from Byron's *Childe Harold's Pilgrimage* IV, 74. That fascination with Mount Soracte is a good example of the dominance of the classical tradition, for nineteenth-century travellers, over their real-life encounters with the Italian landscape. It is also a response that many ancient readers would surely have understood. In the mountains of Latin verse symbolic landscapes of the imagination were grafted on to fantasies of real-life engagement, with an effect that is often both charismatic and enigmatic. Horace's Soracte is just one of many examples.

We will see more of Horace's Soracte later. But first it needs to be framed within a wider discussion of the way in which particular named mountains could take on an intense symbolic significance, in Greek and Latin verse texts especially, acting as markers of both regional and poetic identity. The prevalence of symbolic or allegorical summits in classical, medieval, and early modern verse has sometimes been taken as a sign of a lack of interest in mountains in premodern culture, as if symbolic representation is automatically dry and formulaic.[2] What we see in the Latin poetic tradition, to the contrary—and also in some prose texts, as the Mount Etna of Seneca's *Letters* shows—is that symbolic mountains could stand as powerful landscapes of desire and fantasy; also that their symbolic properties could be manipulated creatively in many different ways.[3] Brevity need not imply insignificance. Latin verse mountains also often had intratextual resonances: many mountains are mentioned only in a few lines or even a few words, as in the case of Soracte, but they often gain added force when we read them as part of a series of mountain references threaded through the works they are a part of. Not all of the mountains I look at in this section are represented as objects of human vision, as Soracte is, but many of them do share a conspicuous quality which makes them not unlike the three enigmatic mountain images we have just looked at, standing out from the textual ground around them and demanding attention and decipherment.

For the poets and readers of later Greek and Latin verse, Hesiod's encounter with the Muses on Mount Helikon was a particular object of fascination and imitation: it was replayed and reimagined obsessively. Perhaps the most famous version was that of Callimachus in his *Aitia*. Only fragments of that text survive, but it seems to be the case that Callimachus recounts a dream in which he conversed with the Muses on Mount Helikon.[4] That may have been a response not just to the growth in the cult of the Muses at Helikon in the third century BCE, but more specifically to interest in the site from the Ptolemaic rulers of Alexandria, where Callimachus was based.[5] The motif was then in turn widely adapted in Republican and early imperial Latin poetry.[6] There was a later tradition that Hesiod was awarded the prize of victory in a competition against Homer, not because of his superior skill but because of the greater usefulness of his poetry, which was dedicated to agriculture and peace rather than war and slaughter.[7] In that sense Helikon and the Hesiodic persona it implies were particularly appropriate to Latin poets keen to resist the temptation of writing about military subjects.[8] The mountain landscape which the Muses inhabit, and especially the springs where they dance and bathe, also became associated with a particular kind of poetics, associated with delicacy, tenderness, in some cases femininity: this is one of the foundational passages for the prevalent later use of the spring as an image of poetic inspiration.[9] Intriguingly the proliferation of these poetic treatments of Helikon roughly coincided with the further expansion of the sanctuary of the Muses on the slopes of Mount Helikon in the Roman period, which seems to have taken place at least partly under Roman sponsorship, to judge by the large number of statues dedicated to members of the imperial family and other wealthy Romans: literary fantasy and a culture of real-life tourism seem to have gone hand in hand.[10]

Propertius in particular returns several times to the scene of poetic inspiration on Helicon.[11] 'My page,' he boasts, 'has carried down this work by an undefiled track from the mountain of the sisters [that is, the Muses], so that you can read it in peace' (Propertius 3.1.17–18). There he combines the Hesiodic Muses of his Callimachean model with another famous feature of Callimachus' *Aitia* prologue, that is its recommendation of the kind of poetry that follows 'unworn tracks (κελεύθους ἀτρίπτους)' (Callimachus, *Aitia* fr. 1, lines 27–28). In a later poem Propertius' rejection of epic becomes more explicit, with the difference that in this case Helicon is itself associated with the epic tradition: 'I had dreamt I was reclining in the soft shade of Helicon, where the water of Bellerophon's horse flows, and that I was able to sing to the strings of my lyre about your kings, Alba, and the deeds of your kings, a great task' (Propertius 3.3.1–4). He is about to drink from the Hippocrene spring, from which the Latin epic poet Ennius also claimed to have drunk as inspiration for his epic poem on the history of Rome.[12] Just at that moment the god Apollo tells him to leave behind epic poetry, and shows him instead the cave of the Muses, one of whom, Calliope, confirms Apollo's advice, and advises him instead to write love poetry.

It is not only the preface to the *Theogony* that shapes the mountain symbolism of later Greek and Latin literature, but also one other Hesiodic passage, from his *Works and Days*—which may have had some influence over Callimachus' 'unworn tracks' in the *Aitia* prologue—where he famously sets out a choice between two paths, the rough and the smooth:

> Baseness is there to be grasped in abundance, easily, for the road is smooth (λείη μὲν ὁδός), and she lives very close by; but in front of excellence the gods have placed sweat; the path to it is long and steep and it is rough at first (μακρὸς δὲ καὶ ὄρθιος οἶμος ἐς αὐτὴν καὶ τρηχὺς τὸ πρῶτον); but when one comes to the top (εἰς ἄκρον), then excellence is easy, though before that it was hard. (Hesiod, *Works and Days* 287–92)

These lines are quoted more extensively than any other passage of Hesiod in surviving ancient literature.[13] They are manipulated in a huge variety of different ways for the purposes of poetic, philosophical, literary-critical, and theological self-definition.[14] Some of the earliest and most powerful examples comes from the work of Pindar. There is a close Hesiodic echo at *Olympian* 9.107–8, where he tells us that 'the ways of wisdom are steep' (σοφίαι μὲν αἰπειναί).[15] He also makes frequent use of summit imagery to visualise the idea of outstanding achievement without any particularly conspicuous reminiscence of Hesiod. For example, in *Nemean* 1 he claims that 'the summit of absolute glory (πανδοξίας ἄκρον) lies in success' (Pindar, *Nemean* 1.10–11); his theme, he says, is 'in the great heights of virtue (ἐν κορυφαῖς ἀρετᾶν μεγάλαις)' (*Nemean* 1.34). His subject in the first passage is the chariot race victory by Chromios, the general Hieron, tyrant of Syracuse, at the Nemean festival, while the second passage refers to Herakles, whose deeds are the subject of the second half of Pindar's song. These moments are related to a wider series of images, running through his work, which link various kinds of elevation fleetingly and enigmatically with his own poetic achievement.[16]

In other cases Hesiod's passage is used to describe educational and philosophical progress.[17] Galen, in the opening lines of *On the Composition of the Art of Medicine*, draws on Hesiodic imagery in representing his work as an aid to the addressee, Patrophilos, who has started on the difficult path to medical knowledge but cannot complete the journey on his own 'because of its height and its length and its roughness' (δι' ὕψος τε καὶ μῆκος καὶ τραχυτῆτα)

(K1.224).[18] The imagery of ascent, and sometimes Hesiod's passage specifically, were also used extensively by early Christian writers, as we have already seen, in their attempts to envisage the process of spiritual ascent.[19] Many later appropriations also give Hesiod's words moralising connotations.[20] The lyric poet Simonides tells us about a tale that 'Virtue lives on rocks that are difficult to climb (δυσαμβάτοισ' ἐπὶ πέτραις)' and is seen only by those who reach 'the peak of manliness' (ἄκρον ἀνδρείας) (Simonides fr. 579). More than eight centuries later the orator Libanius cites Hesiod in moralising terms in praising the emperor Julian for avoiding the temptations of 'drinking, gambling, and sex' as a young man and instead setting out 'on the steep and rough path (ὄρθιον καὶ τραχὺν οἶμον)' (Libanius, *Oration* 12.28). The rough mountain track also becomes a standard image within literary criticism.[21] In these cases the fantasy mountain landscapes associated with certain kinds of prose style become linked with good taste and high status and in some cases envisaged as particularly masculine spaces.[22] Ancient poets and readers and critics thus often found themselves moving through mountain landscapes in their mind's eye as a way of conceptualising different kinds of literary activity. Portraits of intrepid individuals toiling up rugged mountain tracks and scaling high peaks may have been rare within Greek and Roman records of day-to-day experience, but their metaphorical importance meant that they were nevertheless ubiquitous as fantasy images within the ancient imagination.

The second-century CE comic writer Lucian parodies these conventions in a number of ways. For example, in his *Hermotimus* he satirises the idea of philosophical progress.[23] You cannot be far from reaching happiness, says Lykinos, Lucian's alter ego in the dialogue, for you have been studying for twenty years. No, only on the lower slopes, Hermotimus replies, quoting this passage from Hesiod in explanation (*Hermotimus* 2). Lykinos proceeds to quiz him literal-mindedly over exactly how long the journey will take. Will you be at the summit by next year, he asks, or after one Olympic cycle or two? That kind of imagery takes on literary, rhetorical connotations, rather than philosophical ones, in another of Lucian's works, *A Professor Public Speaking*, where he satirises a speaker who offers a route to philosophical success which involves an easy, pleasant route, and who criticises those who are 'still at the foot of the ascent, creeping up with difficulty over crags that are slippery and hard to climb, sometimes rolling off on to their heads, and getting many wounds from the rough rocks' (Lucian, *A Professor Public Speaking* 3).[24] The association between mountain-tops and authority also takes on a special significance for Lucian (although not in a way which is explicitly tied to that Hesiodic precedent) in a series of scenes where looking down from a mountain summit is used as an image for his distinctive satirical gaze, allowing him to mock human pretensions by being distanced from them.[25]

Mountains in Latin Epic

Side by side with those developments was a more Homeric strand of mountain representation in Greek and Latin epic, where mountains were settings for divine or heroic action and for similes. These texts are not shaped to the same degree by the traditions of metapoetic thinking we have just looked at,[26] but they are nevertheless aware of the symbolic potential of mountains, and their capacity to mark identity, for example in the use of mountains as images for envisaging Roman adoption and adaptation of Greek culture.

In some cases these symbolic and identity-forming functions are also combined with more realistic practices of representation borrowed from the geographical writing that we will look at in more detail in part III. The *Argonautica* of Apollonius of Rhodes is a good example: the poem has some memorable mountain similes; there are scenes on Mount Olympus; in both of these senses Apollonius is close to the Homeric tradition. More innovatively, mountains are also used every so often through the poem as an index of the Argonauts' progress eastward towards the wild lands of the Colchians in their search for the golden fleece.[27] In Book 1, for example, Mount Pelion, the place of their departure, and the mountain from which the wood for the ship *Argo* was taken, is described as a benign landscape of divine protection: the gods look down on them from heaven, while the Nymphs watch their departure from the summit and the centaur Cheiron comes down from the mountain to wave them off.[28] They sail northeast, with a boat's-eye view of Olympus and Ossa and Athos. But soon they pass through the Hellespont and reach more unfamiliar territory, most importantly the great mountain of Dindymon (which has not been convincingly matched to any real mountain on the Black Sea), where they must fight against the six-handed earthborn monsters. They win, and climb the mountain, gaining a view of the unfamiliar lands around them, which is described in careful, geographical detail. They also win the favour of the Mother Goddess particularly associated with the mountain by means of a mountaintop sacrifice, a sign of their control over the new and initially threatening territory they have entered.[29]

One of the most extensive examples of this kind of evolving landscape narrative in ancient verse is from Virgil's *Aeneid*. Virgil uses landscape, and mountains specifically, in a great variety of different ways; it would be hard to capture the richness and range of those phenomena in a short summary.[30] Nevertheless it is clear that these many different scenes have a cumulative effect, which invites us to draw links between different parts of the poem. One of the best places to start is at the very end of the poem, at the famous duel between the Trojan Aeneas, ancestor of the Roman emperors, and his enemy Turnus. Just before their combat begins, Virgil offers us one remarkable mountain simile:

> Now father Aeneas (*pater Aeneas*), hearing the name of Turnus, abandons both the walls and the high citadel, throwing aside all delays and breaking off from all his tasks; exulting with happiness he makes a terrifying noise of thunder with his weapons; he stands huge as Mount Athos or Mount Eryx, or father Apennine (*pater Appenninus*) himself when he roars through the quivering oak trees and takes pleasure in lifting his snowy head to the winds. (Virgil, *Aeneid* 12.697–703)

Even out of context it is clear that this image ascribes enormous dignity and grandeur to Aeneas: the stature of the mountains matches his own. But the richness of this image only becomes clear in full when we set it against the lines around it, and against the many other mountain references that accumulate in the rest of the poem. For example, it becomes clear that the first two of these three mountains have been introduced in part as symbols of the divine protection that Aeneas is about to receive, from Jupiter (the Roman equivalent of Zeus, who is said to have been worshipped on Mount Athos), and Venus (who was worshipped on Mount Eryx in Sicily). The intervention of these two deities in Book 12 makes possible Aeneas' victory over Turnus in the lines that follow.

Two other series of mountain imagery stand out in particular. The first is geographical (and has much in common with Apollonius' text, which Virgil imitates repeatedly in the *Aeneid*). In the first half of the poem especially—in the scenes set in Troy, or during the Trojans' westward journey as refugees— there are several mentions of the mountains of Troy, especially Mount Ida. As the city of Troy burns, Aeneas' father Anchises prays to Jupiter for help, and in response they see a comet streaking through the sky to bury itself in the forests of Mount Ida (*Aeneid* 2.696). At the funeral games after Anchises' death in Book 5, Aeneas offers as a prize in the ship race a cloak with an image of Ganymede 'tiring the swift deer on leafy Ida with running and javelin' (*Aeneid* 5.252–53), and then snatched up from the mountainside by Jupiter's eagle; and later in the boxing match Entellus collapses to the ground 'as a whole pine tree falls sometimes, torn up by the roots either on Erymanthus [a mountain in Arkadia] or on great Ida' (*Aeneid* 5.448–49). We cannot be entirely sure that this is the Trojan Mount Ida rather than the Cretan one, but the latter too has a special connection with the Trojans, as we learn in Book 3, when they contemplate settling in Crete on the grounds that this is the home of their first ancestors.[31] Those references to Mount Ida and the mountains of the east recur every so often in the second half of the poem, as if to remind us of where the Trojans have come from. In Book 10, for example, Aeneas' ship carries images of Phrygian lions, with 'Mount Ida towering above them, a great pleasure to the exiled Trojans' (*Aeneid* 10.158). But increasingly they come to be supplemented by mention of Italian mountains, as an index of Aeneas' progress westwards and of his increasing appropriation of Italian territory.[32] As they sail northwards past the Bay of Naples their companion Misenus is drowned and the Trojans bury him 'beneath a high mountain, which is now called Misenus after him and holds his eternal name through the centuries' (*Aeneid* 6.234–35), embedding their own memories into the mountain landscape of Italy from their first arrival. There is a steady accumulation of mentions of Italian mountains in the books that follow. The simile applied to Aeneas at the beginning of the duel is the climax of that series. Aeneas is portrayed, through the repetition of the word 'father', almost as an embodiment of the mountain itself, which stands here in all its grandeur as a patriotic symbol of the land the Trojans are fighting for.

The second dominant strand of mountain imagery centres around the familiar contrast between civilised and uncivilised mountain landscapes. The *Aeneid*, like the *Iliad*, is packed with mountain similes which are used to describe the power of heroes on the battlefield as equivalent to the forces of nature. In some cases those similes have positive connotations, but in other cases they seem to signify excessive passion or lack of control. Some individuals associated with mountains are dangerous or threatening, especially in the case of the most monstrous of all characters in the poem, the mountain-dwelling Cacus, whose defeat at the hands of Hercules (*Aeneid* 8.193–267) is recounted to Aeneas on the site of the future city of Rome. The setting for that encounter has a certain amount in common with other ancient precedents for sublime mountain description, although there is no suggestion that it is a view we might take pleasure from: it takes place within a mountain landscape that is overwhelming, with terrifying depths and heights; it also seems to draw on Virgil's familiarity with descriptions of volcanic eruption.[33] Turnus himself is particularly associated with that complex of threatening and uncivilised mountain scenes. In one of his first appearances, for example, we hear that 'his tall helmet, crested with a triple plume, holds up a Chimaera, breathing out the fires of Etna from its jaws' (*Aeneid* 7.785–86). In the central battlefield scenes of Book 12, Aeneas and Turnus share a destructive mountain simile: they rage across the battlefield 'as when foaming streams make a crashing sound in their fast rush down from the high mountains and run into the sea, each of them leaving devastation in its wake' (*Aeneid* 12.523–25). But later in the book this kind of imagery applies only to Turnus:

> just as a rock rushes down headlong, ripped from the peak of a mountain by the wind, whether loosened by a wild storm or by the creeping passage of the years; and the relentless mountainside is carried steeply down at enormous speed and leaps from the ground rolling along with it woods and herds and men; so Turnus rushed to the city walls, through the scattered ranks. (*Aeneid* 12.684–90)

The dignified description of Aeneas as father Apennine, which comes just a few lines later, stands in contrast with this image of unrestrained power and destruction, which is in itself only one of a long series of related images running through the poem as a whole.[34] The mountains of the *Aeneid* thus have an intricate symbolic significance, and a structural importance for the narrative as a whole, which make sense only when we see each landscape as part of a wider series.

Mountains and Gender in Ovid and Seneca

There are similar effects in many later Augustan and imperial Latin verse texts, along with some powerful reflections on the relationship between gender and mountain experience. Some of the richest examples come from the work of Ovid. In his love poetry the mountains of Greece occur regularly as symbols of his poetic self-definition. In the opening of his *Ars amatoria*, in a variation on the Hesiodic personas of Propertius and others, Ovid insists that his poem springs from experience rather than the inspiration of the Muses: 'nor did Clio and the sisters of Clio appear to me, while I was guarding the flocks in your valleys, Ascra. Experience is what prompts this work: pay attention to an expert poet' (Ovid, *Ars amatoria* 1.27–29). Repeatedly too he refers to mountain narratives in Greek myth, using them as images against which to measure up his own experience, as defamiliarising pointers to the wildness that can be found even within the civilised, urban relationships he charts in the poems.

For example, in *Amores* 1.7.13–14 he compares the beauty of his beloved with the mythical huntress Atalanta in the Maenalian hills. He uses the same example in *Ars amatoria* Book 2, in reassuring his readers that even the most resistant target for seduction will yield to a patient approach in the end: 'What could be harsher than Atalanta from Nonacris? Despite her savagery she submitted to the merits of a man' (*Ars amatoria* 2.185–86). Sometimes he uses stereotypes of harsh mountain landscapes on the geographical edges of empire to similar effect: for example, at *Amores* 2.16.19–20 we hear that 'then even if I had to set foot shivering with cold on the windy Alps, so long as I had my mistress with me, my journey would be easy'. And then in Ovid's *Metamorphoses*, his fifteen-book epic recounting mythical stories of transformation, mountains are common narrative backdrops: they form a fantasy landscape which is intimately familiar to his readers as a terrain of the imagination but also at the same time exotic and distant from real experience. One of the first incidents Ovid narrates is the story of the Arkadian king Lycaon and Jupiter's punishment of him for his cannibalism.[35] We see Jupiter coming down from Olympus against the backdrop of the Arkadian mountains: 'I descended from high Olympus and travelled over the earth as a god in human form. . . . I had crossed Maenala, bristling with the lairs of wild beasts, and Cyllene, and the pinewoods of frozen Lycaeus' (Ovid, *Metamorphoses* 1.212–17).[36]

The *Metamorphoses* also offers us a distinctive view of the relationship between mountains and gender, especially in the opening books of the poem. Repeatedly the mountains are represented as female spaces, associated with the female goddess Diana, Roman equivalent of the hunter-goddess Artemis, and with her Nymphs. Over and over again we see these spaces invaded by male figures threatening sexual violence.[37] In Book 1, for example, Ovid tells the story of Syrinx, who is pursued by Pan and transformed into a reed: 'On the cold mountain slopes of Arcadia, among the wood Nymphs of Mount Nonacris, one Nymph was the most sought after of all: the Nymphs called her Syrinx. . . . Pan, his head garlanded with sharp pine needles, sees her coming back from Mount Lycaeus . . .' (Ovid, *Metamorphoses* 1.689–91, 699–700). In Book 2, Jupiter rapes Callisto in the mountains of Arcadia, and then Diana banishes her when she discovers the shame of Callisto's pregnancy: 'No Nymph who set foot on Mount Maenalus was dearer to Diana, goddess of crossroads, than she was. . . . Diana, accompanied by her chorus of companions, approaching along the slopes of Mount Maenalus, taking pride in the death of the wild beasts she has hunted, catches sight of her . . .' (Ovid, *Metamorphoses* 2.415–16, 441–43). Admittedly masculine control is often precarious in these spaces. Actaeon's death by his own hounds after his metamorphosis into a deer is a good example: 'the whole pack, driven by desire for their prey, follow him over crags and cliffs and trackless rocks, where the path is difficult or there is no path at all . . . he fills the slopes that are so well known to him with mournful protests' (Ovid, *Metamorphoses* 3.225–27, 239). Here the mountain spaces that he had mastered through his hunting become suddenly threatening to him, just as the mountain landscapes of the Pompeii Actaeon paintings combine familiarity with danger. But Ovid's text does nevertheless offer us many opportunities for thinking through the way in which male control over passive female bodies can be equated with human intrusion into pristine landscapes beyond the normal limits of human civilisation, just as it can in modern thinking about gender and the environment.

In Seneca's tragedies mountains similarly form a recurring backdrop to his horrifying retellings of Greek myth, most extensively so in the *Phaedra*, which retells the story of Euripides' *Hippolytus*, where Phaedra falls in love with her hunting-obsessed stepson Hippolytus. One of the striking things about Seneca's version is the way in which it reverses the gender assumptions we find in Ovid. In the *Phaedra* the mountains are masculine places. In the opening scene, Hippolytus addresses a group of fellow huntsmen, calling to them to hasten to the mountains. He oscillates between mentioning the local hills in Attica—'the high ridges of the mountains of Cecrops' (Seneca, *Phaedra* 2), 'the places that lie spread out beneath rocky Parnethus [that is, Parnes]' (4–5), the 'crags of sweet Hymettus' (22)—and other mountains much farther afield that he presumably knows only by hearsay: the 'ridges of the wild Pyrenees' (69). And he presents these as places away from female company: he appeals to the virgin Diana as 'masculine goddess' (54). It is Phaedra who is represented as an intruder into that space. She fantasises about the idea that she can follow her beloved into the hills: 'he is the one I want to follow, through the deep forests and across mountains, even clinging to the ridges of snowy hills, and treading the harsh rocks with agile feet' (233–35); and later 'I would not be ashamed to go through deep snows if you order me to, nor to scale the frozen ridges of Mount Pindus' (613–14).[38] Her language in those passages recalls the image of the shepherd-god moving through rocky landscapes from the *Homeric Hymn to Pan*,[39] or Valerius' representation of Egeria as a female mountaineer taking on heroic roles that one would more naturally associate with male subjects.[40] Between them, Ovid and Seneca help us to see not just that the mountainside was a gendered space in the ancient imagination, as it is also for us, but also that that gendering could be imagined in a range of different possible ways: mountains could be represented as female spaces that acted as a challenge to male control, but equally as spaces of male heroism where female intrusion would be out of place.

Mountains in Horace's *Odes*

Horace too uses mountains, and landscape description more generally, in a rich variety of different ways. Many of his mountains are enigmatic: they hint at symbolic and metapoetic depths while also resisting any straightforward decipherment. Horace's portrayal of mountains is also intratextually sophisticated. Acres of paper have been consumed in debate about the Soracte ode: it must count as one of the most heavily analysed twenty-four lines in the whole of ancient literature. But to my knowledge there has never been any sustained attempt to relate it to the wider context of mountains in ancient literature and in the rest of Horace's work. That relationship is one of the things that gives the poem its complexity. The mountains of the *Odes* are not frequent enough or lengthy enough to form what one might call a landscape narrative of the kind we find in Virgil, or in the text we will look at in the chapter following, Apuleius' *Metamorphoses*, but they are still a recurring presence, with a cumulative force.

Above all mountains for Horace are imaginary spaces. But that does not mean they are any less powerful for him; on the contrary they tend to be represented as numinous places, distant and exotic at the same time, but accessible even so through the powers of poetic imagination. Often, for example, Horace refers to mountains as places of wilderness. There is an implied contrast between these rough places beyond the bounds of civilisation and the poet's own privileged, civilised location, which allows him to view them dispassionately as objects of conventional poetic contemplation. At the same time, however, those same images often stand in exaggerated form, for the threats and challenges of the poet's own urban life, in much the same way as for Ovid in the *Amores* and *Ars amatoria*. In *Odes* 1.23, for example, Horace uses a mountain simile to achieve precisely this kind of effect: he criticises a woman, Chloe, for fleeing his advances 'like a fawn seeking its terrified mother in the trackless mountains' (Horace, *Odes* 1.23.1–3). The deserted wastes of the mountainside can be contemplated pleasurably and dispassionately as objects of poetic fantasy, but they give us a slightly unsettling, very personal image of the struggles of love. In 1.22, similarly, we hear that the man of upright life needs no weapons to defend himself, 'whether he is about to make a journey through the sweltering Syrtes or the inhospitable Caucasus, or the lands that are lapped by the fabled Hydaspes' (*Odes* 1.22.5–8). Here the journey through the Caucasus is conjured up in very economical fashion as an extravagant, exaggerated image of human vulnerability.

In other cases mountains are linked especially with divine presence. Some of these references are very brief and allusive, so much so that they are easy to miss on a first reading. A typical example is his passing reference to Venus as 'Erycina', alluding to her cult on Mount Eryx in Sicily (*Odes* 1.2.33); or to Cybele as 'Dindymene', because of her cult at Mount Dindymon or Dindymus in Phrygia (*Odes* 1.16.5). In 1.21, he praises the goddess Diana in the second stanza: 'she who delights in rivers and in the foliage of the trees which stand out on cold Algidus or in the dark forests of Erymanthus or the green forests of Gragus' (*Odes* 1.21.5–8). Algidus is in the Alban hills in north-central Italy, Erymanthus is one of the mountains of Arkadia, and Gragus is a mountainous area in Lycia in modern Turkey, so the wide spread of these three mountains is an index of the extent of Diana's power; it also perhaps symbolises the extent of Roman dominion, given that the final stanza of the poem celebrates the gods' support for Augustus and his empire, asking Apollo to drive away diseases beyond the boundaries of the empire, diverting them to the Persians and the Britons. Other references are a little more extensive and less cryptic, though still very complex in their literary resonances. In 1.12, for example, Horaces debates which god or human to praise: 'Which man or hero do you choose to celebrate, Clio? Which god, whose name the playful echo will sing back either on the shady face of Helicon or on Pindus or on frozen Haemus, from where the woods blindly followed tuneful Orpheus' (*Odes* 1.12.1–8). Horace is letting his poetic imagination range over some of the archetypal mythical places of divine presence: Clio, as one of the Muses, is associated especially with Mount Helicon, while the reference to Mount Haemus allows him equate his own poetic voice with that of Orpheus, who was particularly associated with that mountain.[41] Those opening lines are then paralleled in the final section of the poem in the poet's praise of Jupiter–'you will shake Olympus with your heavy chariot' (*Odes* 1.12.58)—under whose protection, Horace tells us, Augustus will rule with justice. Horace's mountains are thus understated and often heavily compressed and difficult, relying on readers who know their mythology back to front; they are also far more frequent than a casual reading might suggest.

Most complex, and most important, are the passages where Horace draws on the traditional images of mountainside inspiration in order to make statements about the poetic and cultural identity of his own writing. At 3.4, for example, he paints the mountains of Italy as his inspiration, and as Roman equivalents of the great poetic mountains of Greece, using them as symbols of the cultural transfer from Greece to Rome which his own poetry represents. He tells a story of being lost as a child on the slopes of Mount Vulture in southern Italy, and draped by wood pigeons with a covering of leaves; then he addresses the Roman muses, the Camenae, directly: 'I am yours, Camenae, yours as I climb the steep Sabine hills' (*Odes* 3.4.21–22). The Sabine hills, with their Roman version of the Muses, the Camenae, are Roman equivalents of Helicon, and Horace himself is a Roman Hesiod.[42] Similarly at 1.17, Horace tells us that the pastoral god Faunus (an Italian god, but often associated with the Greek Pan) often 'swaps Lycaeus [that is, Mount Lykaion] for pleasant Lucretilis' (*Odes* 1.17.1–2) (a mountain in the Sabine hills whose precise identification is debated, but which may be Monte Gennaro northeast of Rome) and Ustica (another, unidentified mountain in the same area) in order to protect Horace's goats. Once again Horace is using the mountains here as symbols of the poetic transfer of pastoral from its archetypal home in Arcadia to his own home region of Italy and to his own poetry,[43] just as Virgil had invited Pan from Mount Lycaeus at the beginning of his *Georgics*—a closely related image of cultural and poetic appropriation.[44]

How then does the Soracte ode relate to these very literary but also at the same time powerfully personal uses of mountain imagery? It has in common with all of those earlier works a sense of mountains as places to visit above all in the imagination. But it is also different in some respects, or at any rate it does not fit neatly into any of the categories I have just outlined. For example, it resists any explicit link with the divine-poetic summits in the rest of the *Odes*, where mountains stand for particular literary traditions or particular varieties of inspiration. One might argue that Soracte symbolises again Horace's transfer of Greek lyric to Rome, and any reader who comes to this poem with those other passages from the *Odes* in mind is likely to be alert to that possibility. The ode is based on a poem by the archaic Greek poet Alcaeus, which similarly contrasts the coldness of winter with the comfort of the symposium, although without any mention of a mountain.[45] Does Horace appropriate that Greek tradition by transferring it to the Roman countryside and to Latin verse? But the poem certainly does not draw our attention to the idea that the mountain is intended to symbolise that process. Even by the standards of Horace's other enigmatic mountains Mount Soracte is hard to fit into any standard category.

The clarity and simplicity of the opening lines enhance that challenge of interpretation. The famous initial image is of the mountain covered in snow: 'You see (*vides*) how Soracte stands white (*candidum*) with deep snow, and the labouring woods can no longer hold the weight, and the rivers have stopped from the sharp cold' (*Odes* 1.9.1–4). This opening image is a powerfully visual one, as the opening word of the poem, *vides* ('you see') makes clear,[46] and Horace's starting point seems to be a real view of the mountain. However, it becomes almost immediately clear that his view here is primarily an imaginative one: it is just about possible to see Soracte in the far distance from Rome (about twenty miles away), but there is no way anyone could see the trees labouring under the weight of the snow on the mountainside itself (and the same goes even if one imagines Horace in a nearby villa). And even this imaginary mountain landscape soon fades from view: Soracte is not mentioned again in the poem. It seems extraordinary that such a brief glimpse could have haunted the imagination of centuries of later readers. But one reason for that is simply that it haunts the rest of the ode, despite the lack of any explicit mention, as we struggle to work out its significance for everything that follows.

In the stanza following, Horace turns away from the mountain and the winter harshness that it stands for:[47] 'Melt away the cold by heaping wood on the fire abundantly, and more generously still pour out the four-year-old Sabine wine, Thaliarchus, from its jar' (*Odes* 1.9.5–8). There may be another image of cultural transfer here: the local, Sabine wine of Latin poetry within the Greek-style wine-jar of Alcaeus' model (*diota*). More importantly for now, this stanza suggests that Soracte is acting in much the same way as the Caucasus and other wild peaks elsewhere in the *Odes*, as an image of hardship in contrast with the urban companionship and pleasure of the drinking party. The heaping of logs on the warm fire stands in contrast with the heaping of snow on branches. Horace rejects the mountain and looks inwards towards this more domestic scene.

The third stanza complicates matters, however: 'Leave the rest to the gods, who have at the same time stilled the winds battling with the seething sea, nor are the cypresses or the ancient mountain-ashes shaken any longer' (*Odes* 1.9.9–12). Here we have an image of calmness following on from the disturbances and threats of the natural world. That serenity parallels the serenity of the drinking party in the preceding lines. But it is also linked with the opening description of Soracte by the mention of the trees: are the unmoving ash and cypress related to the trees that now stand calm under their weight of snow in the opening stanza?[48] And if so, is the scene on the summit of Soracte in fact equivalent to the calm Horace longs for, rather than inimical to it?

And then finally the second half of the poem introduces yet another resonance. Horace recommends that we should not fret at what tomorrow brings; while you have youth—'while grumpy white hair (*canities*) is absent for you in your youth' (1.9.17–18)—you should give yourself over to pleasures, and especially the pleasures of love. There are surely hints of a parallel between the white hair of old age and the whiteness of Soracte's summit,[49] both of which Horace tries to push aside. The closing symbol of erotic engagement in the poem—the playful, half-resisting finger of the beloved, with its connotations of the small-scale, vulnerable, ephemeral quality of human experience—stands in contrast with the bulk and permanence of the ancient mountain. Here again the mountain reverts to being a symbol of what is to be rejected or ignored. Horace may even be equating his own position with the situation of the snowy mountain, and in contrast with the experiences of youth, representing himself as a poet who writes from a position of middle age, when the first grey hairs start to come (Horace was 42 when the poem was published). Alternatively, should we see the snow on the summit of the mountain as the first dusting of autumn, if we translate *nec iam* as 'not yet', and take *alta ... nive* to refer not to 'deep snow' but to snow that is 'high up' on the mountain, covering only the highest summit?[50] If so, Soracte's first coating of snow, before the full arrival of winter, which the poet turns away from in the opening stanza, is equivalent to the very first onset of old age, which Horace rejects in giving attention while he still can to the pleasures of youth.

Like many of the other mountains of the *Odes*, then, Soracte is remote from Horace but also at the same time highly personal, in the sense that we are invited to read it among other things as a starting point for envisaging the poet's own situation.[51] Or perhaps it is better to say that it oscillates between remoteness and intimacy. Is Soracte a symbol of what the first-person voice of the poem rejects—wild nature and laborious old age—in his drinking party and in his reflections on the civilised pleasures of youth? Or is it intended as a more intimate image of the speaker's own experience, in a way which makes it harder to shut out than that straightforward contrast implies? By that reading the poem prompts us to leave open the possibility that the cold snowy peak parallels the poet's awareness of the encroaching prospect of 'grumpy white hair', or that the stillness of the mountain, coated in snow, parallels, through the linked pair of images of trees still after a storm, the calm that comes with trust in the gods, and the serenity of the drinking party. It is impossible to give a clear answer to those questions.[52] But that, of course, is precisely the point. It would be hard to see the mountain of this poem as an object of aesthetic assessment.[53] The language of beauty is entirely absent in those opening lines, despite their powerfully visual character. But it is nevertheless an object of contemplation in a rather different sense. Horace's Soracte is one of the supreme ancient examples of the mountain as an enigma, as an object whose significance is precisely to be puzzled over, and that is something we respond to still.

9

Mountains and Bodies in Apuleius' *Metamorphoses*

A Stage-Set of Mount Ida

Apuleius' *Metamorphoses* is one of the most mountainous texts, certainly the most 'rocky' text, in the whole of ancient literature.[1] It also includes what must be the most extensive and most bizarre ancient depiction of a stage-set mountain. The novel is a first-person narrative, told by a narrator called Lucius. At the beginning we see him travelling to Thessaly in northern Greece in search of magic. He gets more than he bargained for. The wife of his hostess in the town of Hypata turns out to be a witch. In Book 3, Lucius hides and watches her turning herself into a bird, assisted by the slave-girl Photis whom he has seduced. He then wants to try for himself, but gets the wrong potion, and turns into a donkey. Photis leaves him overnight in the stables, telling him that the antidote is rose petals, and that she will fetch some for him the next day, but in the night he is stolen by robbers and driven away to their mountain hideout. In the next seven books, he goes from one owner to the next, being repeatedly humiliated and mistreated. His last owners discover that he has human understanding and appetites, and arrange for him to be displayed in the arena to have sex with a condemned woman in front of the crowds, but he manages to escape, and runs away to the beach. In the night he has a vision of the goddess Isis, who tells him that he will find rose petals in a procession of her worshippers the next day. Lucius follows her instructions, is turned back into human form, and then spends the rest of Book 11 undergoing a series of initiations as a worshipper of Isis. There is a strong contrast between Lucius' flawed character in Books 1–10, with his inability to see beyond earthly pleasures—he is gluttonous, lustful, excessively curious—and the disorienting change in Book

11, where he claims to have access now to higher, divine wisdom. This is not a pious religious tract. If anything, it is a parody of narratives of conversion, given that Lucius has absurd qualities even in Book 11: most obviously his gullibility in giving away vast amounts of money to fund his successive initiation ceremonies matches his uncritical craving for magic in Books 1–3. But the contrast between earthly in Books 1–10 and divine in Book 11 is nevertheless important for the structure of the novel.[2]

In the moments leading up to Lucius' appearance in the arena, at the end of Book 10, he is momentarily distracted from his own troubles by a dance performance of the judgement of Paris, which takes place in an elaborately crafted setting:

> There was a wooden mountain constructed with lofty workmanship on the model of that famous mountain which the poet Homer sang of, Mount Ida. It was planted with greenery and living trees, pouring out river water from a spring, made by the hands of the craftsman, on the highest summit. (Apuleius, *Metamorphoses* 10.30.1)

Paris and the goddesses come on stage: Lucius' description of them stretches over several pages; he is engrossed especially by the sensuous dancing of the goddess Venus. And then very suddenly at the end of the dance the stage-set is cleared away:

> From the highest summit of the mountain, through a hidden pipe, saffron dissolved in wine bursts up high into the air, and falling to the ground, scattering, it rains down on the goats who are pasturing all around with a sweet-smelling shower, until, dyed to a greater beauty, they swap their natural whiteness for a yellow colour. And then, when the whole theatre was filled with a pleasant fragrance, a chasm in the earth swallowed up the wooden mountain. (*Met.* 10.34.2)

What role does this mountain play in Apuleius' narrative? Why does Apuleius choose to describe it in so much detail and at such a conspicuous moment in the narrative? If we want to make sense of it, we need to set it against a long series of other mountain descriptions in the work. The *Metamorphoses* is packed with rocks, peaks, and precipices, many of them dangerous and threatening, marked out by imagery of steepness and roughness and jaggedness. Those passages alternate with more welcoming landscapes—valleys and plains, streams and meadows.[3] Not all of those features are Apuleius' invention. The *Metamorphoses* is a highly embellished adaptation, in many sections a translation, of a Greek original. That original does not survive, but we do have another version of the story—usually known as the *Onos* (*Ass*)—which seems to be based on that same original version, and which is very close to Apuleius' version in many respects. It shares some features of Apuleius' representation of mountains, especially in its many descriptions of painful mountain tracks, but its portrayal of the mountains is nothing like so extravagant or so frequent. For example, the *Onos* does not show any signs of the stage-set mountain of Book 10 (or the conversion scenes of Book 11 that follow it), or of the many inserted stories, told to each other by characters in the novel, which are one of the key sources of the complexity of Apuleius' text, and which include some important references to mountain landscape.

Two strands of mountain depiction stand out particularly in Apuleius' account. The first is a series of strikingly rhetorical, and in some cases symbolic descriptions of mountains and other kinds of landscape, which have obvious resonances with the examples of visual and figurative representations of mountains that we have already looked at. These scenes often involve a degree of self-consciousness about the artificial or illusory quality of Lucian's perceptions. The other strand is a much more bodily way of interacting with landscape. Over and over again we read about scenes of injury or death where the human or animal body is in contact painfully with rocky mountain terrain. Both of those ways of perceiving landscape are represented ultimately as symptoms of the human subjection to earthly experience that Lucius is stuck with throughout Books 1–10; both are swept away from view with the stage-set mountain of the arena at the end of Book 10, as the novel moves into its final phase where Lucius comes under the protection of Isis.

Those themes make Apuleius' novel a powerful resource for reflection on the history of human engagement with the environment. For one thing it is striking that those two strands in Lucius' perception of mountains correspond to two major strands in modern thinking about landscape. As we have seen already, some modern accounts see landscape primarily as a human construct, as an object of viewing and also a product of human imagination and memory. Others stress instead or as well the way in which landscape is experienced immersively and corporeally, not just through visual engagement but through the full range of our senses.[4] Apuleius seems already to be very much aware of those different possibilities and fascinated by the question of their relative validity. Not only that, but these scenes also offer us a memorable vision of human disempowerment in the face of landscape. Lucius attempts to assert his intellectual accomplishment and his detachment from the difficult situation in which he finds himself by resorting to conventional rhetorical techniques of landscape description, but over and over again the text confronts us with his lack of control, as we see him, and other characters of the novel too, subjected to painful, bodily encounters with the terrain they travel through. Lucius' transformation into animal form, which is also equated at various moments in the novel with the experience of slavery,[5] is crucial to that effect: it shows us a nightmare world where anthropocentric assumptions about human mastery over landscape are repeatedly exposed as illusory, displaced by the bodily realities of an animal relationship with the environment.[6]

Rhetorical and Symbolic Mountains in the *Metamorphoses*

Often Apuleius depicts the landscapes of the *Metamorphoses* as places of fantasy and fabrication. Much of that literary-rhetorical embellishment seems to have been Apuleius' innovation, rather than something taken from his Greek source, given that it is not present in any sustained form within the *Onos*.[7] For example, his landscapes often have allegorical connotations—although it would be misleading to suggest that they articulate any simplistic message: what we find instead is a playfully imprecise engagement with moralising language.[8] They also often have an allusive, literary character, which in some cases draws on rhetorical traditions of landscape description associated particularly with the techniques of ekphrasis.[9] The connotations of artificiality associated with those techniques were not straightforward. Ancient theories of ekphrasis—by which I mean the practice of producing *enargeia* or clarity, in Greek rhetorical theory—view it as a technique which aims to bring to life the scene being described, making absent things present.[10] However, there is also a strong strand within these ancient discussions which acknowledges the gap between the fabricated scene and the original on which it is based,[11] and Apuleius is clearly aware of that (as we shall see later in looking at his description of the bandits' lair at 4.6).[12] The *Metamorphoses* is full of stylised terrains, which draw heavily on recognised literary and rhetorical motifs. In some cases Apuleius actively hints at the inadequate, fabricated, unreal character of those representations. Those effects are enhanced by the geographical imprecision of the central books of the novel.[13]

What has not been pointed out before, however, is the way in which this awareness of artificial landscape keys into the wider theme of false perception which is so important for the work as a whole. Apuleius was not just a novelist; he was also a Platonic philosopher. In his surviving philosophical work, especially his *De Platone*, he takes a particular interest in the contrast between mortal and divine realms that he finds in Plato, for example in the *Gorgias* and the *Phaedrus*. That theme is important for the *Metamorphoses* too, where the sublunary, earthly discourse of Books 1–10, which is concerned above all with trickery and appearance and associated with things which are literally visible in the world of senses, is contrasted with the higher discourse of Book 11.[14] At the same time the unreliable landscapes of Books 1–10 also play an important role in Apuleius' depiction of the conversion process Lucius undergoes. It has been pointed out that the *Metamorphoses* parallels other ancient (and also modern) conversion narratives where conversion is preceded by an impression of disintegrating reality. The unstable and untrustworthy character of the physical world as Lucius represents it contributes to that impression.[15]

The first symbolic mountain of the text comes very early on, in just the forty-eighth word of the novel's prologue. The prologue is a riddling statement, which offers among other things a set of cryptic images of the speaker's identity and challenges us to work out whose voice we are listening to.[16] The answer to that question is debated—is this Apuleius, is it his character Lucius, is it even the book itself?[17] Early on he tells us that 'Attic Hymettos and Ephyrean Isthmos and Spartan Taenaros are my ancient stock, fruitful soils preserved for ever in more fruitful books' (*Hymettos Attica et Isthmos Ephyrea et Taenaros Spartiaca, glebae felices aeternum libris felicioribus conditae, mea vetus prosapia est*) (*Met.* 1.1). The precise significance of the mention of Mount Hymettos is unclear,[18] but one of its effects is to affiliate the speaker with Athens, perhaps in part as a reference to the fact that Lucius was educated there, as we learn from a chance remark later in the text;[19] presumably also by an association with Attic eloquence, which was traditionally associated with the famous Hymettian honey, and based on underlying Hesiodic assumptions about mountains as vehicles for conceptualising literary inspiration.[20] This mention of Mount Hymettos is inconspicuous, especially for a first-time reader—it is a very much more understated version of the enigmatic mountain motif than the extravagant stage-set of Book 10—but it nevertheless sets the scene for the many mountain scenes that follow, and alerts us to Apuleius' awareness of the traditional association between mountains and literary symbolism.

Lucius' story begins just a few lines later, immediately after the end of the preface. The very opening sentences of his narrative immediately give us a good example of Apuleius' fascination with rhetorical techniques of landscape description. He tells us first of all that he was travelling to Thessaly on business. The second sentence is as follows:

After I had emerged from the steep paths of the mountains (*ardua montium*) and the slippery paths of the valleys and the wet paths through the meadows and the cloddy paths of the fields, riding on a native white horse, because he too was very tired, and in order that I might also myself shake off my saddle-soreness by the invigorating act of walking, I jumped down to my feet, attentively rubbed away the sweat from my horse's forehead, caressed his ears, detached his bridle, and led him forward at a gentle pace, until the accustomed and natural operations of his stomach removed the discomfort of his weariness. (*Met.* 1.2.2)

The opening group of four phrases—'steep paths ... slippery paths ... wet paths ... cloddy paths'—is carefully crafted.[21] It draws heavily on epic language;[22] it also has a heavily rhetorical feel, as if ticking off in turn the different categories of landscape description one might use in a rhetorical exercise.[23] At the same time it hints at the literary and moral symbolism associated with the Hesiodic tradition of the steep path of excellence, although without making it clear what the precise significance of that language is.[24] If we read the first of the four phrases, 'the steep paths of the mountains' (*ardua montium*), with those symbolic traditions in mind we might take it as a claim that Lucius has traversed morally challenging terrain in the pursuit of virtue. Lucius is offering, in other words, an elevated and idealised vision of his own travel. It is also striking, however, that the air of detachment and even idealisation or aggrandisement implied in the opening words of the sentence is not maintained. Most obviously, anyone coming to this passage as a second reader will know that Lucius is about to be have a more brutal set of confrontations with the *ardua montium* than he is bargaining for here[25]—although the word 'emerged' (*emersi*) at the same time strikes a more optimistic note, in anticipating Lucius' final emergence from the oppressive world of rocky slopes, slippery paths, and false perceptions which holds him in its grip throughout Books 1–10.[26] Even within this opening sentence there is a move from elevated language downwards to very mundane, physical concerns: the wiping of the sweat, the horse's digestion problems.[27] Here then, in the very opening section of the narrative, Apuleius presents us with a rhetorical vision of landscape while also hinting at its inadequacy as a representation of the real, bodily experience of travelling: Lucius is quite literally brought down to earth as the sentence goes on.

That passage is followed, in Books 1 and 2, by Lucius' first impressions of the town of Hypata. Here the text repeatedly returns to the image of landscapes which are formed or altered by magic. Landscape, on that account, is malleable, open to fabrication, untrustworthy. The following passage is just the most prominent of several examples:[28]

> Nothing of what I saw in that city seemed to me to be what it was, but everything had been completely transformed into another shape by deadly muttering; the result was that I believed that the stones I stumbled over were hardened humans, that the birds I heard were feathered humans, that the trees which ran around the city wall were in the same way foliated humans, and that the waters of the fountains were liquefied human bodies. (2.1.3–4)

That sentence—and especially the phrase 'nothing seemed to me to be what it was'—foregrounds the theme of untrustworthy perception.[29] Here we clearly are seeing events through Lucius' eyes as he experienced them at the time.[30] The surface appearance of the city's landscape, in Lucius' view, is not reliable; it hides behind it a sinister, magical reality. Equally Lucius' own perception of the ubiquity of magic seems suspect in itself: this is a highly literary landscape, imbued with precedents from Ovid's *Metamorphoses* and elsewhere, as if Lucius has read Ovid too literal-mindedly and fabricated a vision of the landscape of Hypata on that basis.[31]

It is also hard for Lucius to maintain his detachment from these metamorphic landscapes. A few pages later he visits the house of his aunt Byrrhena and takes great pleasure in gazing at a sculpture of the goddess Diana and of Actaeon being devoured by his own dogs against a rocky background (*Met.* 2.4–5). That image prefigures vividly Lucius' own sufferings later in the novel: he is several times at risk of attack by dogs after his transformation.[32] The passage offers us a remarkable image of the power of the kind of mythical narratives we saw from the Roman wall paintings of Pompeii and elsewhere, and of the statuesque representations of myth that were also common in elite villas. Those images offered fantasy images of risky, numinous landscapes; they invited their viewers to imagine themselves being absorbed into the scenes in front of them.[33] Here Lucius succumbs to that risk of absorption in the most literal way possible in being sucked into a landscape that resembles the dangerous landscapes of myth.

The link between landscape and false perception becomes even more prominent after Lucius' transformation. There are, for example, several scenes[34] which use the poetic conventions of the *locus amoenus* to describe apparently idyllic landscapes which later turn out to be deceptive and dangerous.[35] The most striking example comes very soon after Lucius' metamorphosis scene.

Having been led away from his host's house in Hypata he is convinced that he has found some roses:

> a little further off I saw a glen full of the shade of a leafy wood; and in the middle of its various little plants and luxuriant shrubs, shone the bright red colour of gleaming roses. And now in my heart, which was not wholly bestial, I thought that it was a grove of Venus and the Graces, within whose dark recesses the royal splendour of this festive flower was gleaming. (*Met.* 4.2.1–2)

His hopes are dashed. The flowers turn out to be not roses but oleanders, which are poisonous. Lucius resolves to eat them anyway, but at that moment the gardener and several others approach him and begin to beat him. Lucius' ability to identify this site as a *locus amoenus*—marked as such among other things by the association with Venus and by the imagined presence of the rose, the archetypal flower of such spaces—is represented as a sign that he has not lost his educated, human identity entirely ('and now in my heart, which was not wholly bestial . . .'). It turns out to be a mirage, a place of violence and threat, populated by a much more mundane flower, which is described by the narrating Lucius in pointedly realistic, almost scientific terms.[36] Once again it is clear that Lucius is inhabiting a world of illusion.

That theme of fabricated, fantasy landscape is treated in more extended form in a number of passages in the work which draw on the rhetorical traditions of ekphrasis we looked at earlier in this chapter. The most extravagant of all of these is Lucius' description of the bandits' mountain hideout:

> The subject and occasion demand that I should offer a description of the region and the cave which the robbers inhabited. For I shall at the same time put my abilities to the test and also make sure that you gain a clear insight into the question of whether I really was a donkey in my understanding and my faculties of perception. The mountain was rough, shady with forest foliage and exceptionally high. Its very steep slopes, where it was surrounded by jagged and hence inaccessible rocks, were encircled by hollow, pitted valleys. . . . From the highest peak a spring gushed down abounding in giant bubbles, and pouring down the steep sides, it vomited out silvery waves. (*Met.* 4.6.1–4)

One of the first things that stands out here is the elaborately crafted nature of this description. Its rhetorical character is enhanced by the address to the reader, a common feature of ekphrasis, which draws attention to the way in which the scene is being brought to life in front of our eyes.[37] The literary quality of the mountain is also clear. The language of jaggedness and steepness, which is a recurring feature of the work as a whole, draws heavily on stereotyped poetic language of mountain description.[38] Moreover, the passage is full of carefully crafted language, packed, for example, with alliteration and assonance.[39] A number of scholars have seen this as a key passage in the history of what have sometimes been called *locus horridus* traditions in Latin literature, pointing out how Lucius systematically inverts the motifs of the *locus amoenus* in Virgil and Seneca and others.[40] In addition, the passage has a historiographical character: for example the opening phrase—'the subject and occasion itself demand'—echoes a number of passages of Sallust and Tacitus.[41] Not only that, but it is also clear on closer inspection that the passage has a strong air of exaggeration and inconsistency, almost absurdity, and that Apuleius goes out of his way here to draw attention to the artificiality of the description.[42] For one thing, the jaggedness of the hideout as it is described here contradicts Lucius' account of their arrival at the hideout just a few lines before: 'we then climbed a gentle slope and arrived at our destination' (*Met.* 4.5.7).[43] The grand, imposing quality of the passage—appropriate to epic or historiography—is undermined by a final bucolic detail, just after the passage quoted earlier, where we hear that the mountain was topped with a 'tiny hut carelessly thatched with cane', which recalls various passages describing modest, rustic huts in earlier Latin literature.[44] And the passage's historiographical pretensions have an obvious absurdity when we note the incongruity between the serious tone and the identity of Lucius, at the time of gathering his material, as a donkey.[45] All of those factors contribute to the impression of a fantasy mountain, almost a carboard cut-out, patched together rather inconsistently from conventional rhetorical and poetic motifs. Apuleius is highly self-conscious about the constructed nature of his narrator's landscape description.

Mountain Terrain and Haptic Experience

Mountains are objects of vision, given significance by the human imagination. They also have the capacity, perhaps more than any other type of landscape—with the possible exception of the sea—to reveal the precariousness of idealised human attempts to control and impose meaning on the environment. The mountains of the *Metamorphoses* are no exception. Lucius' rhetorical persona, by which he seeks to assert his continued mastery of elite techniques of landscape appreciation, is undercut brutally by his physical experience of the mountain terrain that he passes through. That development is part of a broader effect whereby Apuleius stresses the physicality of landscape, and its ability to impinge on human and animal bodies in ways which produce suffering.[46] The sheer frequency of that motif in the *Metamorphoses* is quite remarkable.[47] Some aspects of this interest in the physicality of landscape are present in the *Onos*, as part of that work's obsession with the harshness and brutality of non-elite life,[48] but it is also clear that Apuleius has very much extended those themes in his own version. One function of that awareness of the physicality of landscape is to debunk the unrealistic, idealised, rhetorical versions of landscape we have just been looking at. At the same time, however, it draws attention to another aspect of the limitation of Lucius' understanding of the world: it stands as a sign of his earthliness, and his inability to see beyond bodily experience to higher spiritual truths.

The most straightforward manifestation of that theme, and the one where Apuleius is closest to the *Onos*, comes in the many scenes where Lucius is concerned about the way in which the ground digs into his feet as he walks, or otherwise impedes his progress.[49] There is a cluster of these scenes in Book 9. At one point, Lucius describes his journey with a set of false priests: 'the road was pitted with puddle-filled channels, wet in places with stagnant swamp-water, and in other places slippery with filthy slime. In addition, my legs were battered by frequent obstacles and continual slipping' (*Met.* 9.9.1–2). Later, having passed into the ownership of a baker, Lucius is having trouble with his feet again: 'Immediately . . . he led me along a steep path which was threateningly full of sharp stones and bushes of every kind' (*Met.* 9.10.5).[50] And then winter brings a particularly unpleasant version of the same problem: 'In the morning, stepping with my naked feet on the freezing mud and the extra-sharp fragments of ice, I was tormented to death' (*Met.* 9.32.4).[51]

An even more brutal version of this kind of encounter with rocky landscapes comes in the many scenes where people are attacked and in some cases killed with rocks. Earlier in the work, a girl who is being held by the robbers in their hideout with Lucius explains that she has dreamt of her new husband being killed: 'one of the robbers, provoked to a state of fury at his relentless pursuit, having a grabbed a stone which lay at his feet, struck my poor young husband and killed him' (*Met.* 4.27.4). Later, Lucius and those he is travelling with suddenly find themselves under attack for no apparent reason, in a scene which replays Odysseus' encounter with the stone-throwing Laestrygonians in *Odyssey* 10.121–32: 'For from the rooftops and from the nearest hill those farmers quickly rolled down rocks on top of us. . . . In fact, one of the stones suddenly smashed against the head of the woman who was sitting on my back' (8.17.4–5). At one point one of Lucius' owners attacks a Roman soldier who has accosted him on the road: 'immediately he began to pound him on his face and his hands and his sides, with his fists, his elbows, his teeth, even with a rock grabbed from the road' (9.40.2).[52]

Most horrifyingly of all, there is a succession of scenes in the central books set in the robbers' hideout where individuals are thrown over cliffs to die on the rocks beneath, or else are threatened with that fate. In 4.5, one of Lucius' fellow donkeys is thrown over a cliff 'even now still breathing, off a very high precipice down into the next valley' (4.5.4) as punishment for collapsing out of exhaustion, moments after Lucius had contemplated doing the same.[53] Here, the physical impact of landscape is made horrifyingly clear, although even at such a moment of physical brutality Apuleius is reluctant to abandon a rhetorical style of presentation: these phrases have a highly crafted, alliterative character.[54] In 4.12, some of the newly returned robbers give an account of the death of one of their comrades, Alcimus, who was pushed out of a window by an old woman: 'quite apart from the great altitude, he fell on top of an enormous rock which was lying nearby, and his ribcage was shattered and scattered' (4.12.8). One of Psyche's sisters, in the story Lucius listens to in the hideout, dies by being dashed on the rocks after jumping off a cliff, mistakenly expecting to be carried by the wind: 'her limbs were tossed and scattered by the rocks of the cliff' (5.27.3); her other sister meets with the same fate not long afterwards (5.27.5). In 6.25, Lucius is taken out to collect some stolen goods which have been stashed in a cave and collapses with exhaustion: 'battering me and shoving me with frequent blows they made me fall on top of a rock at the side of the road' (6.25.4). When they return to the hideout they threaten to dispose of him, given his weakness, by throwing him over a cliff,[55] and he contemplates his fate in a soliloquy:[56] 'Do you see those nearby ravines and the sharp rocks which stick out into them, which will penetrate you before you reach the bottom and rip you apart limb by limb?' (*Met.* 6.26.6). Ironically that is precisely the fate that awaits many of the robbers themselves after their capture in 7.13.6.[57] The *Metamorphoses*, then, has an obsessive and gruesome fascination with the extreme vulnerability of human and asinine bodies to the physicality of rocky landscape.[58]

One particularly outlandish manifestation of those concerns is in the many scenes where Apuleius presents us with bodies which are immured in the landscape or trapped by it, so as almost to become a part of it.[59] Lucius' perception of the magical quality of the landscape of Hypata, quoted earlier, is a good example from early in the work: 'I believed that the stones I stumbled over were hardened humans' (*Met.* 2.1.4). In 2.5.7, similarly, Lucius is warned about the magical powers of his wife's host, who transforms her lovers 'instantly into rocks or sheep or any other sort of animal' if they offend her. Metaphorical petrification also recurs often in the work. In 6.14.6, for example, Psyche, overwhelmed by the terrors of the inaccessible cliff from which she has been instructed to fetch water, is 'turned into stone by the impossibility of it', becoming, metaphorically at least, a part of the landscape she fears. And in 4.5.3, mentioned already earlier, the exhausted donkey is described in similar terms: the robbers agree among themselves 'not to delay their flight too long for the sake of a dead, or rather petrified, donkey', as if he has already become a part of the jagged mountain landscape in which he is about to meet his death. There are even hints that Lucius himself envisages his metamorphosis as a process which has similarities with this experience of being absorbed or entrapped by landscape.[60] In 3.23 he expresses his desire to take to the air as an owl, but his transformation into a donkey in 3.24 keeps him firmly tied to the earth.[61] He is acutely aware of the coarseness of his new body: 'my hair was thickening into bristles and my delicate skin was hardening into hide (*duratur in corium*)' (*Met.* 3.24.4). That word *duratur* echoes the similar phrase used in 2.1.4 to describe 'rocks transformed [literally 'hardened'] from men' (*lapides... de homine duratos*). The similarity between these passages stands out all the more given that this usage of *durare* to describe metamorphosis is unique to Apuleius in surviving Latin.[62]

Apuleius' sensitivity to the encounter between body and landscape is particularly acute in Book 7, in the scenes which follows Lucius' liberation from the bandits' hideout. Lucius eagerly anticipates the rewards he has been promised for helping the girl Charite in her attempted escape from the robbers. He is to be allowed 'to run free in the country fields' (*Met.* 7.14.5) and he is at last happy: 'I was now about to give up loads and burdens, and having gained my freedom was sure to find some roses at the beginning of spring in the flowering meadows' (*Met.* 7.15.1).[63] Predictably enough, however, this turns out to be another one of the novel's false *locus amoenus* scenes, and Lucius is soon plunged back into a nightmare world of discomfort and danger. The wife of the herdsman assigned to look after him, 'a greedy and utterly wicked woman' (7.15.3), attaches Lucius to a mill and puts him to work, driving him mercilessly. The claustrophobia of his endless 'circling steps' (*ambagibus*) (7.15.5) stands in contrast with the freedom he has anticipated. Not only that, but the harsh, painful, rocky landscapes which have been so much of a torment to him before now infect even Lucius' food: we hear that she used to give him 'bran which was unsifted and dirty and rough with much gravel' (*furfures incretos ac sordidos multoque lapide salebrosos*) (7.15.5). Not only does the rocky landscape impinge on him painfully from the outside; here it also works its way inside his body through his consumption of the gravel.[64]

There is no relief in view. Soon afterwards, Lucius is assigned to carry wood down from the nearby mountain, and the boy given the task of supervising him turns out to be a monster of cruelty:[65]

> Not only was I exhausted by the steep ridge of the high mountain, not only did I wear down my hooves by knocking them against rocky spikes, I was also beaten into shape even on the downward slope by frequent blows from a stick to such an extent that the pain from the blows penetrated even into the marrow of my bones. By always striking his blows against my right hip, and always hitting the same place, he wore away the hide and inflicted on me a very wide wound, making a hole—or rather a pit or even a window (*immo fovea vel etiam fenestra*). (Met. 7.17.3–4)

The mountainous vocabulary here is entirely familiar by this stage to anyone who has read the rest of the novel—the steep slopes and spiky rocks, which trip Lucius and dig into him. What makes this passage stand out is the extraordinary description of the pit in his skin: the physical impact of Lucius' enslavement is so extreme that his body almost becomes a landscape, to be dug up and hollowed out. Worse is to come. Whenever Lucius' load becomes unbalanced, the boy evens out the load by adding stones rather than moving sticks from one side to the other (7.17.5): Lucius is being pressed down by rocks from above as well as tormented by them underfoot. Moreover, the boy offers him no help 'if by some chance, where the edge of the bank was slippery with muddy slime (*limo caenoso*), I collapsed because of my inability to bear my burden and slid down' (7.18.2). Finally the boy sets fire to Lucius and he has to throw himself into a 'puddle of muddy water' (7.20.2), coating his body in grime in order to save himself, in a way which undermines any impression of his own detachment from the physical world: the mud and rocks and gravel of the earth's surface become part of his body, ingrained in his skin and digging into his feet.[66]

On one level this attention to the suffering of the body in its encounter with landscape is ostentatiously 'realistic'. It is a sign that Lucius undergoes a very visceral confrontation with the 'real world'. In that sense it debunks the 'false rhetoric' of the idealised, stereotyped landscape scenes laid out in the previous section. At the same time, however, it also reveals other limitations in Lucius' viewpoint. Most importantly it reminds us that he inhabits a world where bodily concerns are so overwhelming that it is hard to see beyond them to higher spiritual truths.[67] This is another rather different aspect of the 'earthliness' that traps Lucius in Books 1–10. Moreover, the theme of the body's confrontation with landscape also contributes to the impression of Lucius as a figure who is disoriented and confused, forced by his new situation to experience the world in ways which are alien to him. There has been a tendency in ancient novel scholarship to categorise Apuleius' *Metamorphoses*, along with Petronius' *Satyrica* and some of the Greek fragments, as a 'comic-realistic' novel, in contrast with the more idealised Greek novel tradition.[68] That is partly, and justifiably, because of Apuleius' interest in portraying, in some respects very convincingly, the experience of non-elite life in Roman Achaia.[69] It is also, however, due in part to the novel's obsession with grotesque physicality. In practice, however, close attention to the physical working of the human body and to the grotesque aspects of the body, can often have a disconcerting, defamiliarising effect, rather than contributing to an impression of realism. Such representations gain their power precisely by their ability to undermine and unsettle any sense of the naturalness of the way we experience our bodies in day-to-day life.[70]

Lucius' encounter with landscape is a case in point, in the sense that it draws attention to the alienness of his own body, which he comes to experience in unfamiliar, unsettling, almost dream-like ways. That is one of the effects which makes this novel such a powerful resource for ecocritical thinking. The novel returns obsessively to issues that have been central to 'posthumanist' approaches to the relationship between humans and the environment.[71] Those approaches challenge traditional images of the individual as a clearly bounded, autonomous subject detached from the natural world and able to observe it dispassionately. They emphasise instead the way in which humans are inevitably entwined with the world around them; often too they emphasise the difficulties of drawing clear dividing lines between human and animal identity. Apuleius anticipates those concerns, in exposing the vanity of anthropocentric conventions of representing human bodies and selves who are confident of their own mastery over landscape and of their own separateness from the more-than-human world.

Often in those scenes, Lucius seems to be struggling to find exactly the right way of describing his peculiar experiences, as his sense of his own elite detachment and his own separateness from the physical world melts away: the image of the 'pit or window' in his skin from 7.17.4 is an extreme but in some ways typical example. These defamiliarising effects are also linked with ideas of status. Lucius' uncomfortable, bewildered awareness of his own body and its vulnerability is closely linked with his drop in status, from elite to non-elite, from human to animal (that latter fall being conceptualised as equivalent to the fall from free to slave).[72] It is hardly surprising that this change is dramatised through the confrontation with harsh and uncivilised terrain. Wild landscapes—and particularly mountain landscapes—were widely viewed as places for bandits and outcasts who stood apart from normal human culture, and for prodigies who overturned the normal rules of the natural world, as Lucius does in his metamorphosed state.[73] Lucius' perception of the physicality of landscape in Books 1–10 thus has an air of unreality and disorientation hanging over it, even when it pays attention to the gritty details of corporeal experience. That in turn may also be linked with the work's representation of conversion. As we have seen, it is a common pattern in ancient conversion narratives that the moment of conversion is preceded by a period of estrangement from one's familiar experience of the world which makes the future convert open to the changes that are to come.[74] The defamiliarising quality of Apuleius' highly physical descriptions of landscape in Books 1–10—where even the boundaries between living bodies and inert mud and rock are not secure—makes a significant contribution to his portrayal of unstable reality before conversion.

Landscapes of the Goddess Isis

Book 11 changes everything. The strange landscape experiences of Books 1–10, which are both excessively rhetorical and excessively physical at the same time, are banished from the novel together with the other aspects of Lucius' former self, replaced by the higher realities Lucius claims to perceive (albeit, we might suspect, with a degree of self-delusion even here) through his devotion to Isis.

The climax of the novel's extraordinary accumulation of mountains and rocks comes in the arena scene from the end of Book 10. Here, finally, we come back to the mountain we started with. At 10.29, Lucius is led inside the arena. As he waits, he watches the judgement of Paris scene on the stage-set Mount Ida, which is described in intricate detail.[75] Even more so than for the other mountains of Books 1–10, Apuleius goes out of his way to stress its artificial character: the mountain is described as 'constructed with lofty workmanship' (*sublimi instructus fabrica*). We hear that it was 'planted with greenery and living trees, pouring out river water from a spring, made by the hands of the craftsman, on the highest summit' (10.30.1). The themes of fabrication are deeply ingrained here.[76] The mountain is literally brought alive through the hands of the artificer, through the living plants and trees which grow on it. Its fake, theatrical quality is pointed up all the more prominently in the passage already quoted from the end of Lucius' description where a shower of saffron-infused wine erupts from the summit of the mountain (10.34.2). Here, in a literalised version of the Golden Age of Virgil, *Eclogues* 4.43–5, the goats become coloured by saffron, but through human, theatrical ingenuity, rather than the workings of nature.[77] The juxtaposition of that allusion with two distinct references to moralising discussions of theatricality in Seneca only points up the theme of artificial fabrication all the more.[78]

In that sense the wooden mountain seems to stand broadly speaking for all the other extravagant, theatrical landscapes Lucius has moved through in his travels. Its similarity with the mountain which houses the robbers' hideout in 4.6 helps to cement that association: for example, the Mount Ida of the arena is described as 'pouring out river water from a spring on the highest summit' (*summo cacumine ... fonte manante fluviales aquas eliquans*) (*Met.* 10.30.1), in much the same way as the mountain of the bandits ('from the highest peak a spring gushed down'; *de summo vertice fons affluens* [*Met.* 4.6.4]).[79] Its character as a stage-set is also surely significant: it stands for the way in which Lucius (although he may not be aware of it at the time) is about to discard the world of artifice and illusion he has been in thrall to up till now. Here, with Lucius on the brink of his conversion, the text says goodbye to theatricality, and indeed to theatrical landscapes, sweeping them into oblivion,[80] along with the sensual, voyeuristic pleasures of the 'earthly Venus' which are given such prominence in the description of the dance itself.[81]

It is striking, too, that this mountain, unlike all of the others we have encountered so far in the work, is described in strikingly pleasant terms. Gone now is the language of fearful precipices and rocky paths.[82] Perhaps the point is that Lucius' viewing brings him temporarily into the position of a member of the elite at leisure in the audience, able to watch and enjoy without fear. For once Lucius' attempt to view the mountain with a degree of rhetorical detachment is not thwarted, and in this case the disappearance of the assumption that mountains are places of fear and dread anticipates his imminent release: only now, with the power of Isis taking over his life, can he step back and understand that the landscapes he has passed through are no longer to be feared. It is as though Apuleius is prompting us as readers, in the moment leading up to the conversion scene, to discard the association of landscape with suffering and to see it for what it really is—as a stage-set, a prop of the sublunary world of illusion which Lucius will be freed from by his forthcoming devotion to Isis.

In Book 11 mountain landscape and mountain imagery disappear abruptly from view, along with the frequent descriptions of travel by road.[83] They are replaced by new images of water and the sea. Admittedly there is a fair amount of water imagery sprinkled through Books 1–10, but in contrast with the water of Book 11 it usually involves rivers rather than the sea, and water which is dangerous and frightening rather than calm.[84] In 11.1, Lucius, after his escape from the arena, bathes on the beach at Cenchreae in order to purify himself. In 11.3, he sees a vision of the divine face of the goddess Isis rising from the sea. In 11.7, having sprinkled himself with seawater, he makes his way to the festival of Isis, and admires the sea, now lapping calmly against the shore after a storm. After his retransformation the water imagery persists—for example, another bath and purificatory sprinkling in 11.23, and a journey by sea to Rome in 11.26.

Mountains in Book 11 are marked above all by their absence or, in the few passages where they do intrude, by their difference from the mountains of Books 1–10. In 11.13, for example, at the moment of Lucius' transformation back into human form, we see a reversal of the earlier hint that Lucius has experienced his body as a kind of landscape, hard and lapidary: the long list of changes to his body includes the detail that 'my lofty neck shrank (*cervix procera cohibetur*)[85] ... my rock-like teeth went back to their human smallness (*dentes saxei redeunt ad humanam minutiem*)' (*Met.* 11.13.5). Later, Lucius' emotional prayer of thanksgiving to Isis includes a celebration of her powers over nature: 'The birds travelling in the sky are in awe of your majesty, the beasts wandering on the mountains, the snakes hiding in the ground, and the monsters swimming in the sea' (*Met.* 11.25.3–4). Lucius is now able to view his earlier experience—as 'a beast wandering on the mountains'—with a sense of detachment which is utterly different from his own suffering immersion in mountainous landscape in Books 1–10, and to see with hindsight what he had been blind to before, that all of the world is imbued with the power of Isis.[86]

One other particularly important passage, finally, is the speech given by the priest of Isis in the moments after Lucius' re-metamorphosis: 'on the slippery path of vigorous youth (*lubrico virentis aetatulae*) you slid into servile pleasures and gained the perverse reward of your unfortunate curiosity' (*Met.* 11.15.1). 'At once', Lucius tells us, 'I joined the ceremonial procession and walked along accompanying the shrine' (11.16.2). Looking back at Books 1–10 with this passage in mind we can see that the harsh and slippery roads Lucius has travelled on[87] are among other things literalised versions of the metaphorical slippery path the priest draws attention to here.[88] Here Lucius is finally in a position, if he pays attention to the priest, to step back from his earlier concern with bodily discomfort, and to understand landscape in a more sophisticated, metaphorical fashion thanks to his newly acquired religious knowledge. The disappearance of slippery roads in Book 11 is also an emblem of Lucius' move from the paths of error to the straight road of righteousness. It is no accident that we see Lucius, immediately after the priest's speech, joining the straight and orderly procession of the goddess, an experience of walking utterly unlike what he has been through in the novel up till now.

Mountains were routinely imagined as objects of vision in the ancient world. Sometimes that involved aesthetic assessment and appreciation. There are substantial overlaps between ancient and modern treatment of mountains in that respect: concepts like the picturesque and the sublime do have ancient parallels, and even ancient roots, even though those ideas developed in new directions in the eighteenth and nineteenth centuries. However, if we consider ancient viewing of mountains only in relation to its connections with modern aesthetic categories, we can end up missing what is distinctive about it—we need to understand it on its own terms too. One particularly important aspect of ancient mountain depiction was its symbolic function. There has been a tendency to assume that the fascination with symbolic and allegorical mountains in premodern writing implies a dependence on formulaic poetic and rhetorical clichés. On the contrary, symbolic mountains in the ancient world were often objects of fascination and fantasy, for example in the Hesiodic tradition of poetic inspiration on the slopes of Mount Helikon, which was imitated obsessively for more than a millennium following. In many cases that fascination was enhanced by the enigmatic, cryptic quality of both literary and artistic mountains, which posed challenges of decipherment to the viewer. There are examples in the sculpture and wall paintings of the late Hellenistic and imperial periods. There is also a scientific equivalent of that phenomenon in the vast body of ancient writing about volcanoes, which combined spectacle and mystery: volcanoes were among the most visible of all natural objects in the ancient Mediterranean, but also among the hardest of all to decipher and understand, particularly because their inner workings were hidden from human perception.

Human ability to impose meaning on mountains could also be challenged and undermined by their overwhelming physicality. Apuleius' *Metamorphoses* offers us one of the ancient world's richest and most complex reflections on that process. The novel is another example of the importance of reading ancient landscape portrayals intratextually: mountains and rocks occur over and over again in the text; if we want to make sense of them, we need to read from end to end in a way which acknowledges their relationship with each other. Apuleius draws on the full range of traditions of symbolic thinking about mountains, including moralising, literary resonances drawn ultimately from the Hesiodic tradition. At the same time he juxtaposes those traditions self-consciously with a very different, more physical way of thinking about landscape, in drawing attention to the way in which mountain terrain impinges on his characters' bodies and impedes their movement. That combination is one of the things that makes the *Metamorphoses*' reflections on landscape and the environment resonate so richly with modern thinking about those subjects. Lucius' haptic encounter with the terrain he travels through undercuts his attempts to represent landscape according to conventional rhetorical means, for example in his description of the robbers' mountain hideout in Book 4. His travels in the mountains in the central section of the book also brutally expose the fragility of anthropocentric thinking about the environment: in that section of the novel in particular mountain terrain impacts on both human and asinine bodies irresistibly, in a way which forces Lucius to abandon any pretence of human control or elite detachment from the landscape around him. We will see the similar effects in part III for the unruly mountain landscapes that are so conspicuous in ancient historiographical accounts of military campaigning.

PART III
Mountain Conquest

10

Warfare and Knowledge in Mountain Territories

Mountains and Modernity

Mountains were also places of warfare in the ancient world. Often they had great strategic significance: control over key mountain passes had military and economic advantages.[1] They also posed distinctive challenges of leadership: mountain battle sites were often unpredictable, and mountainous regions on the edge of civilised territory could be desperately hard to conquer and control. In many cases the distinctive topography of particular mountain regions led to a situation where the same patterns of warfare repeated themselves over and over again in successive campaigns, in some cases even into the twentieth century.[2] The sites of mountain warfare thus shaped military history through their very real and enduring physical form. They were places of real suffering and bravery. At the same time they were territories of the imagination. In many cases it is hard to discover exactly where in the mountains particular military campaigns or battles unfolded:[3] some ancient authors make an attempt at topographical precision, but often those efforts are overwhelmed by their interest in portraying mountains in battle as places of confusion and fear, where each individual mountain battle scene resonates with others that have come before.

Conquering the mountains was also a way of acting out a vision of progress and modernity, as it has been also for us. The represented, imagined mountains in ancient historiographical and geographical writing are marked by the same basic tension that we have seen already for other genres, as places both beyond and subject to civilised control.[4] That opposition manifested itself in various ways: different authors tend to handle it quite differently depending on their broader goals, celebrating or doubting human capacities for dominance over mountain terrain to different degrees. The representation of mountain peoples is a powerful tool in those reflections: highland populations were often denigrated as uncivilised in ways which justified conquest. In many cases we see a contrast between scenes of successful control, which involve the assertion of particular kinds of knowledge and expertise in relation to mountain terrain and mountain peoples, and on the other hand scenes which give prominence to the frustrations and failures of military and administrative engagement with mountain regions. In those latter cases mountains are sometimes represented as places of great antiquity, with their own more-than-human agency,[5] able to resist whatever reshaping human actors might attempt to impose on them:[6] Pausanias' account of Mount Parnassos' resistance to the invading Gauls is a good example. Mountain peoples too are often viewed as remnants of more ancient ways of being human.[7] We see a similar phenomenon in twentieth- and twenty-first-century representations of mountain terrain: control over mountains is linked with ideas of progress for us too; at the same time we too tend to see mountains as territories which have the capacity to resist modernity, for example because their incorporation into visions of national identity or scientific progress is often uneasy or incomplete.[8] That similarity between classical and post-Romantic responses has implications for the way we understand the history of mountains. The tendency to celebrate—albeit sometimes precariously and unconvincingly[9]—the dominance of 'modern' ways of interacting with mountains, by contrast with what are viewed as more primitive, 'pre-modern' responses, has often been taken as a defining feature of our own understanding of mountains from the nineteenth century onwards, but it is in fact a very ancient phenomenon, paralleled by and even originating in Greek and especially Roman ways of interacting with the Mediterranean environment.

In other cases, especially in ancient battle narratives, scenes where generals interpret mountain terrain clear-sightedly are in tension with images of mountains as places of obscurity and bodily immersion in the environment, where it is hard to perceive anything beyond the rough, icy ground, the clouds, the looming cliffs and rock-falls. Bodily, haptic engagement with mountain landscapes is a crucial part of modern mountaineering practice, and modern mountaineering narratives: that was the case even in the early days of nineteenth-century mountaineering culture,[10] and even more so from the late nineteenth century, which saw the development of new kinds of self-representation among mountaineers increasingly fascinated by physical endurance and risk and even suffering.[11] Those attitudes have parallels within ancient writing about mountains—although it is harder in the ancient material to find representations of physical engagement with mountains as source of pleasure, to be welcomed and celebrated. In that sense mountains in ancient historiography, like the mountain paths and hideouts of Apuleius' *Metamorphoses*, are good places for seeing the richness of ancient engagement with ideas about the fluidity of the boundary between individual and environment. The human body has a special vulnerability in these landscapes; the desire to exercise control from a position of detached mastery is often frustrated; in some cases, as we shall see for the work of Ammianus Marcellinus in particular, characters from the civilised centres of the Mediterranean are even themselves infiltrated by the unruliness of the landscapes and peoples they encounter in those mountain terrains beyond the edges of the empire.

Rock-Walkers: Specialist Expertise in Mountain Warfare

Before we turn to those texts, however, I want to look in more detail at some of the ancient evidence for mountain warfare; also at the role of mountains in processes of territorial mapping and political image-making. Are there modern parallels that can help us to envisage ancient military engagement with mountains? Mountain warfare has played a strategically and symbolically important role in military campaigning over the past century or more, and military practice has had a formative influence over modern ways of imagining and interacting with the mountains. The twentieth century in particular saw the development of distinctive kinds of expertise in mountain warfare, which influenced and were in turn influenced by leisure mountaineering. The fighting that took place in the Dolomites between 1915 and 1917 on the Italian-Austrian front led to huge numbers of casualties: around 10,000 troops died just from avalanches in December 1916. In places you can still see the wartime tunnels and the remnants of the old barracks wedged between the rocks, and the remains of rusted cans, bullet casings, pieces of wood, and bones scattered over the mountainsides. Some of the soldiers who fought there were mountain guides who had made their living in the mountains and now used their skills to fight.[12] In the decades following, the Himalayan expeditions of the 1920s and 1930s were profoundly influenced by the experiences of World War I: they provided a substitute for the dangers and the companionship of the trenches, and the desire for conquest of the mountains was motivated in part by the desire to reassert national pride.[13] In World War II military and sporting engagement with mountains cross-fertilised to an even greater extent. The US Army's 10th Mountain Division was formed in 1943, partly to counter the already existing mountain warfare divisions in the German army, but it was also inspired by the new interest in winter sports in North America, and recruited heavily from accomplished skiing and mountaineering enthusiasts. It played a major role in the Apennine mountains in Italy, most famously in its night-time attack on the German position on Mount Belvedere, which involved more than 1,000 soldiers climbing a steep 500-metre cliff-face, the Riva Ridge, in winter conditions in February 1945.[14] The technological advances that supported that kind of activity led in turn to important developments in the history of leisure climbing: the large-scale production of cheap nylon ropes and other equipment helped to make mountains and cliff faces accessible to more and more people in the years after the war. Himalayan exploration continued to be influenced by military experience into the 1950s and beyond: for example, John Hunt, leader of the successful 1953 Everest expedition, had spent some of World War II as chief instructor at the Mountain Warfare School in Braemar before commanding a battalion on active service in Italy.

In our ancient sources too, there is some evidence for particular categories of troops with special skills of mountain warfare.[15] In classical Greece fighting in the mountains was relatively uncommon thanks to the dominance of heavily armed hoplite warfare and codes of conduct which required battle on the plains. In the Hellenistic and Roman periods, by contrast, accounts of mountain battle are common, associated with attempts by Hellenistic kings and then by Roman armies to conquer and maintain order in upland territories on the edges of their empires. Perhaps the most famous example is from the spring of 327 BCE. Alexander the Great was in Uzbekistan, camped below the Sogdian rock and its seemingly impregnable fortress (which sheltered among others the Bactrian royal family, including the beautiful princess Roxane, whom Alexander would later marry). Arrian tells us the story of its capture:

> Then Alexander announced that twelve talents would be the prize for the first man to climb to the top, eleven talents for the second, and so on for the third, with 300 gold darics as the final prize for the last. This announcement spurred on the Macedonians, who were already keen, all the more. Three hundred men assembled, the ones who had experience of rock-climbing in sieges (ὅσοι πετροβατεῖν ἐν ταῖς πολιορκίαις αὐτῷ μεμελετήκεσαν). They prepared small iron pegs, used for securing tents, for driving into the snow where it seemed firm, or into patches of ground not covered by snow,

and securing these with strong ropes made of flax, they set off, when night fell, to the steepest and therefore least guarded section of the rock. And driving in these pegs either into the earth, where it showed through, or into the patches of snow which were least likely to give way, they hauled themselves up by a variety of routes up the rock. Thirty of them died during the climb: their bodies fell in various places in the snow, and were not recovered for burial. But the rest of them, reaching the top of the rock around dawn, waved linen flags in the direction of the Macedonian camp, as Alexander had ordered them to do. (Arrian, *Anabasis* 4.18.7–19.3)

There is no reason to see the competitive element of Alexander's challenge as evidence for a conception of climbing as sport: there are not to my knowledge any ancient parallels. But Arrian does tell us clearly that some of Alexander's men have built up expertise in climbing from previous engagements.

The verb πετροβατεῖν (literally 'rock-walk') is particularly intriguing. It is used, along with related forms like the adjective πετροβάτης ('rock-walker'), only about ten times in surviving Greek literature. It is applied in two cases to the god Pan, and in one case to mountain goats. But the other usages are nearly all equivalent to what we find in the Arrian passage. In one passage, from the work of Appian, Arrian's near contemporary, the African prince Arabio attacks the camp of the Roman general Cornificius unobserved 'with rock-climbers (πετροβάταις ἀνδράσιν) who crept up through the cliffs' (*Civil Wars* 4.7.56).[16] In another, from the late Hellenistic historian Diodorus Siculus, the Assyrian queen Semiramis captures a besieged city 'taking with her those of the soldiers who were accustomed to go over rocks (τῶν στρατιωτῶν τοὺς πετροβατεῖν εἰωθότας), and ascending with them through a narrow ravine' (*Bibliotheca* 2.6.8). The word ὀρειβάτης ('mountain-walker', 'mountain-goer') and equivalents is also used every so often in similar terms—for example in Plutarch's *Life of Cato the Elder*, Cato is in the mountains above Thermopylai attempting to lead his troops in a surprise attack at night; he gets lost, and leaving his troops sets off alone to find the way, 'taking with him a certain Lucius Manlius who was an accomplished mountain climber (ἄνδρα δεινὸν ὀρειβατεῖν)' (Plutarch, *Cato the Elder* 13.2).[17] All of these passages suggest previous experience: the rock-walkers of these texts seem to be ancient specialists in mountain warfare.

There is no evidence for specialist mountain units in the Roman army, but it seems likely that auxiliaries recruited from mountainous regions would often have been viewed as particularly well suited to mountain warfare.[18]

There is a good example in Polybius' account of the expedition of the Seleucid king Antiochos III against Arsakes II of Parthia, which culminated in Seleucid victory at the battle of Mount Labus in what is now northern Iran in 209 BCE. Arsakes thinks his position guarding the pass is an impregnable one, but Antiochos realises that he will have a chance if his light-armed troops can climb the rocks to attack the pass from above, and he divides up his soldiers accordingly: 'Having made this decision, he assigned the first division to Diogenes, giving him archers and slingers and those of the mountain soldiers (τῶν ὀρείων) who had the ability to throw javelins and stones, and who did not fight in formation, but instead faced danger individually, whenever time and place called for it, and gave very effective service on difficult ground' (Polybius, *Histories* 10.29.5). The plan works: they attack from above and the barbarians flee. That word ὀρείων is a difficult one to translate here. It may be meant to refer to a special category of troops. Often, however, it is a geographical word, meaning 'mountain people'. It may be that in this case it implies a combination of those two senses, in order to indicate a special sub-group within the army particularly suited to fighting on mountainous ground. There is a Latin parallel in Sallust's *Jugurtha* 93–94. The Roman Republican general is besieging a mountaintop fort. One of his auxiliary troops, from the mountainous region of Liguria in northwest Italy, goes in search of water and finds himself at the back of the mountain, which has a sheer, unguarded cliff. He notices snails on the rocks and begins to collect them, climbing higher and higher until he reaches the plateau at the top. Later he leads a small light-armed detachment by the same route, fastening ropes to rocks or projecting roots, and they capture the fort.

Local Knowledge: Control and Resistance in Mountain Terrain

This kind of generalised expertise in particular kinds of terrain was not the only kind of knowledge that mattered for mountain warfare: local knowledge of people and places could be even more important. One of the most famous examples is from the battle of Thermopylai in 480 BCE where a tiny contingent of Spartan soldiers held out against the vast forces of the Persian army down at sea level, guarding a narrow neck of land with the sea on one side and cliffs on the other. Finally the Persians managed to outflank them by following a path over Mount Kallidromos behind, guided by a Greek, Ephialtes; they brushed aside the Phokian troops stationed there to defend it, and attacked the Spartans from behind. That Persian victory was won by their control over mountain territory, achieved in this case through their access to local knowledge. Other battles were fought in later centuries where that route was similarly decisive.[19] The challenge of deciphering the complicated topography of Mount Kallidromos has been taken up eagerly by modern scholars: the question of what route exactly the Persians took to get up into the mountains has been a matter of debate over many decades and ancient historians with particular interests in topography have painstakingly retraced the possible routes on foot in order to choose between them. Even if you do not feel you have anything original to contribute on that question, experiencing the Persian route through the mountains can be a powerful way to understand the way in which the battle unfolded. The high-altitude valley the Persians passed through, which runs from the village of Eleftherochori eastwards to Nevropoli and beyond, is a surprising place (figure 10.1). The historian A. R. Burn wrote two short articles in the 1950s on high-altitude routes in the Greek mountains which have been used repeatedly in both ancient and modern warfare to move large bodies of soldiers quickly and secretly.[20] He describes the path as follows:

> The upper Asopos valley runs along the top of the Anopaia or Kallidromos mountain, with the ridge of Liathitsa rising in gentle, grassy slopes on its north or right bank, and a lower parallel ridge, rising only just enough to make the place a valley at all, on the south. Between the two runs the valley, a furlong wide, flat-bottomed, full of silt, a couple of miles long (with a kink half-way, where you walk round the corner of the steep rocks of Liathitsa summit); so nearly level from end to end that the stream has cut itself deep meanders as though in an English meadow; and in April, when the snow is just melting, so full of white and purple crocuses that it is impossible to walk otherwise than on them.[21]

It is easy to understand, when you see it, why Ephialtes' knowledge made all the difference. The route is protected by very steep ground, especially to the north—from sea level you would never guess it is there—but once you get up there it is a perfect high-altitude highway for a detachment of many hundreds of troops marching at night.

Mountain terrain also often allowed hostile forces to retreat into strongholds and hiding places that were hard to find and hard to capture. Here too local knowledge was crucial, for both sides. Sometimes that could involve the retreat of whole populations.[22] The Messenians were specialists. In a series of

FIGURE 10.1. Route of the Persian outflanking move at the battle of Thermopylai, Mount Kallidromos, looking west towards Eleftherochori from above Nevropoli. Photo: author.

wars with Sparta they retreated over and over again to mountain fortresses. In the First Messenian War, in the eighth century BCE, they held out for several years behind their fortifications on Mount Ithome.[23] They were at war again forty years later, between 685 and 668 BCE. After an initial defeat they fled to Mount Eira, north of Messene, and holed up there for eleven years before the site was finally captured thanks to information passed to the Spartans by a deserter.[24] And then more than two centuries later, these earlier conflicts were replayed yet again. An earthquake devastated Sparta and a group of helots (the subjugated population who were kept under Spartan control effectively as slaves) of Messenian descent broke free and fortified Mount Ithome once again. They held out for ten years before they finally struck a deal with Sparta to be allowed safe passage out of the Peloponnese.[25]

Particularly common was a situation where light-armed troops would melt away into the mountains after harassing their enemies on the plains below:

variations of that kind of guerilla warfare are of course still in use in mountainous warzones today. That was one of the things that made mountainous frontier territories notoriously difficult to control. In addition, mountain regions tended to be quite fractured, with many different tribes loosely connected with each other but without any central organisation. The only reliable response was to combine military activity with a painstaking and gradual process of building up local knowledge. That kind of process was followed with varying degrees of success and completeness by the Roman army right across the Mediterranean world.

In some cases, ambitious plans for military dominance were simply too complicated and resource-intensive to enforce, and the Romans relied instead on a strategy of forging alliances with local rulers in mountainous territory, who maintained order while preserving their own autonomy. The Roman Empire's relationship with the Isaurians, in southern Turkey, is a good example of the difficulty posed by mountain populations for plains-dwellers right through Mediterranean history:[26] the region of Isauria was dominated by a southern spur of the Taurus mountain range, with peaks as high as 3,000 metres.[27] We see a glimpse of that difficulty in the letters of Cicero during his time as governor of Cilicia, which included both the mountains of Isauria and the adjacent plains. Cicero describes vividly the challenges of maintaining control over the mountains with inadequate military resources. Every so often he leads punitive expeditions into the interior of the province, as pre-Roman rulers of the region had often done too, but their value is mainly symbolic, with very little chance of bringing about permanent subjection.[28] In that context it is not surprising that the Romans at times gave up on military conquest and resorted instead to negotiated relationships with local bandit leaders who were allowed almost complete autonomy outside the structures of the Roman Empire in exchange for keeping peace.[29] Strabo summarises that approach in *Geography* 14.5.6: 'For the place was naturally suited to piracy, both by land and by sea: by land because of the size of the mountains and the peoples living beyond them, who have plains and fields that are large and easily attacked'. For that reason, Strabo suggests, it was thought better for the region to be ruled by local kings rather than Roman commanders.[30] Every so often that equilibrium broke down, in periods of extended conflict in the late first century BCE and early first century CE, and then again in late antiquity. It is important to stress that this is not a case of the Romans struggling to control a primitive barbarian population which was entirely alien to them. In fact we see signs of very deep-rooted acculturation of the region to the Roman norms of urban life, much of it actively encouraged by the Romans during the calmer period from the mid-first to the mid-third century, which saw flourishing civic activity, extensive road building in the mountains, and recruitment of Isaurians into the Roman army.[31] Some of these changes may even have facilitated the increasing wealth and influence of Isaurian warlords and so prompted the increasing resistance to Rome which led to a series of revolts from the 260s CE onwards.[32] In all of these different ways, and over a period of many centuries, it is clear that the region's topography was one of the main factors that shaped Isaurian intransigence, and in turn made it hard for the Roman army and successive Roman governors in the region to do anything about it.[33]

Other mountain territories in the Roman Empire had a similarly protracted history of resistance, although in some cases their ultimate pacification was more successfully achieved. One of the most complex versions of that process took place in the Alps. Hannibal's crossing of the Alps in the Second Punic War in 218 BCE was only the most high-profile invasion of Italy from the mountains. The second century BCE especially saw repeated incursions by Alpine tribes; it also saw increasingly clear articulations of the principle that the Alps should stand as a frontier protecting the edges of the Roman Empire, or at least a barrier under Roman control that allowed Roman troops and merchants to cross but prevented unwanted invasions.[34]

We can get a glimpse of the painstaking and protracted processes by which that principle was enforced by zooming in on the region of Liguria in the far northwest of Italy where the northern Apennines merge into the far southwestern arm of the Alps.[35] The mountains rise up almost straight from the sea, leaving a narrow coastal strip which was an easy target for raids, but also a crucial transit route for any attempt to connect Italy with the northwestern Mediterranean.[36] Throughout the late third and second centuries BCE, there were repeated incursions by the Ligurians from their mountain strongholds. The Romans won multiple victories against them, but those successes tended to evaporate quickly as their enemies retreated to the hills to regroup, using the intimate knowledge of the mountains gained from their pastoral activities.[37] The Ligurian population was fragmented between different groups without a common leadership so that defeating one group could still leave others untouched.[38] The last recorded wars against the Ligurians were in 118–117 BCE: the whole process of pacifying the region had lasted over a century. Lasting success came only when military engagement was supplemented by other measures like road building, the foundation of both native and colonial settlements in the mountains, and also the relocation of some Ligurian populations to the plains.[39] Another crucial factor in that success was improved local knowledge, which eventually allowed the Roman army to outmanoeuvre the mountain populations of Liguria on their own terrain.[40]

However, that still left the bulk of the Alps outside reliable Roman control: it was many decades before there was any significant change. There were sporadic Roman raids against Alpine tribes through the second and first centuries BCE, but they only ever brought temporary and incomplete control. In 57 BCE, Julius Caesar sent an expedition with the aim of opening up and securing the Great Saint Bernard Pass to enable trade, but that too was unsuccessful.[41] It took a concerted campaign in the reign of Augustus over several decades, between 35 and 7 BCE, to pacify the tribes of the Alps more decisively.[42] Once again this was a project not just of military dominance but also of cultural change: the consolidation and expansion of the road network[43] and the development of a Roman urban culture in the mountains was just as important in the long run as the operations of the Roman army.[44]

Representing Mountain Conquest

The knowledge accumulated within these processes of conquest was used in a range of different ways. It was displayed, sometimes in monumental form, in order to advertise imperial and military achievements. It also found its way into geographical texts that were in most cases not explicitly celebratory of empire but which nevertheless had a certain amount in common with other kinds of display that were. The difficulties of conquering mountain terrain help to explain why the mountains often had a prominent role in these processes of image-making.[45] The boasts of the emperor Augustus, in his *Res Gestae*, a biographical account of his achievements which was inscribed on stone monuments across the empire, are perhaps the most famous example: 'I pacified the Alps, from the region which is closest to the Adriatic, as far as the Tuscan Sea, without waging war unjustly on any tribe' (*Res Gestae* 26).[46] Augustus' enormous victory monument at La Turbie, just north of Monaco, commemorating his conquest of the western Alps, is still standing.[47] It included a list of about fifty subjugated tribes,[48] which can be reconstructed with the help of a passage in Pliny the Elder's *Natural History* 3.24. The heroic work of opening up the Alps, and especially the achievement of road-building across the mountains, was widely associated with the mythical story of Hercules as the first to bring civilisation to the region,[49] and his achievements were routinely contrasted with what was represented as the impiety of Hannibal.[50] Visual depictions of mountains could also be used to celebrate conquest, as we have seen already, for example in the triumphs which made their way through the streets of Rome to celebrate successful military campaigns. Tacitus tells us that 'in the consulate of Gaius Caelius and Lucius Pomponius, Germanicus Caesar, on 26 May, celebrated his triumph over the Cherusci, the Chatti, the Angrivarii, and the other tribes who inhabit the territory as far as the Elbe. Spoils and captives were carried in procession, along with images of mountains and rivers and battles' (Tacitus, *Annals* 2.41).[51] Trajan's Column in Rome depicts Roman victories in the Dacian Wars and is full of images of mountains, as we saw in chapter 7, as a sign of their dominance over the Carpathian mountains in what is now Romania.[52]

Is there any sign that military knowledge-gathering and the habits of imperial celebration had a close relationship with the depiction of mountains and other landscape features in maps in the Roman world[53] as has been the case repeatedly in modern colonial projects?[54] The answer is cautiously yes, but with very many caveats. There are numerous passages that describe generals climbing hills and mountains to gain a better view of the terrain down below, so at least in that sense the gathering of cartographic knowledge had military associations.[55] Vegetius in his *De re militari* 3.6 suggests that generals need to have accurate itineraries for all the regions in which they are campaigning, including information about mountains and rivers, and adds that 'the more conscientious generals reportedly had itineraries of the provinces in which the emergency occurred not just annotated but illustrated as well'.[56] It is clear that maps were nothing like as widely available in Greek and Roman culture as they have been in the modern world, and it has been common to argue that the ancient Greek and Roman spatial imagination was overwhelmingly dominated by a hodological (that is, road-level) perspective focused on the tracing of itineraries, and with very little interest in cartographic ways of imagining space. However, that view has been increasingly nuanced in recent work which reasserts the importance of cartographic thinking and map-making traditions at least in some contexts.[57] Some surviving maps, and surviving descriptions of maps, do give considerable prominence to mountains, even if not in explicitly imperial or military contexts.[58] For example, Ptolemy's *Geography*, a mathematical treatise on mapping dating from the second century CE, includes hundreds of mountains as cartographical reference-points. In very broad terms his enterprise presumably reflects the expansion of geographical knowledge that came from the Hellenistic and Roman imperial projects, although he makes no explicit mention of the Roman Empire.[59] At any rate it represents a confident assertion of geographical command over the landscape of the inhabited world: Ptolemy almost never expresses doubt about the locations that he lists.[60]

Most famous of all is the Peutinger Table, which survives in just a single, medieval copy, derived from a late antique original possibly dating from the late third century CE. It divides the Mediterranean world into a set of fourteen different north-south segments, from Britain in the west to India and Sri Lanka in the east. Each segment is then subjected to severe horizontal compression so as to be represented in stylised form in a strip just 13 cm high. By the standards of modern cartography that approach massively distorts the exact shape of particular land masses and the seas that separate them, but it does nevertheless offer a very vivid view of the interrelation between different cities and landmarks within each of the map's fourteen regions, as well as an ideologically charged vision of the centrality of Rome, which stands at the centre of the map in a way which makes Italy look much larger than it should. Mountains play an important though fairly understated role on the map.[61] It includes about 140 mountain ranges overall. They are represented in entirely uniform terms, with no distinctions of height, and generally running in very straight lines, as shown for example in figure 10.2.

The central strip of land in that image is Italy, with the Bay of Naples below and the saw-like line of the Apennines running horizontally above it, first in white on the left, that is, northern side, and then filled-in in black for the southern part of the range to the right. The makers of the map are more interested in ranges than in individual mountains—for example it is striking that Mount Vesuvius is given very little prominence. The mountains on the map also go unnamed for the most part, and in that sense these images are very different from the triumphal representations mentioned earlier, or from their equivalents in geographical writing, where inventorising and naming key features of Mediterranean landscape is an important goal. The kinds of intricate local knowledge which would have been crucial both in campaigning and in imperial administration, and which we see traces of in ethnographic and geographical writing, are flattened out almost entirely. That may be partly because the map seems to be focused among other things on helping its viewers to understand the routes between different locations, although probably not in a way that was designed for practical use.[62] In that sense it seems to be heavily influenced by hodological ways of thinking about space, despite its cartographical form. Nevertheless it is clear that the map conjures up an image of the world that is very idealised: it gives the impression of an ordered world, where rough landscapes have been smoothed over and made uniform, and where they no

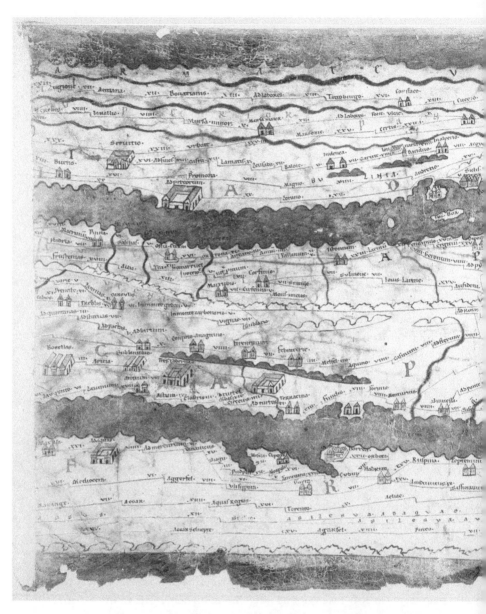

FIGURE 10.2. Peutinger Table, section 5: Dalmatia, Pannonia, Moesia, Campania, Apulia, Africa. Ancient World Mapping Center © 2021 (awmc.unc.edu). Used by permission.

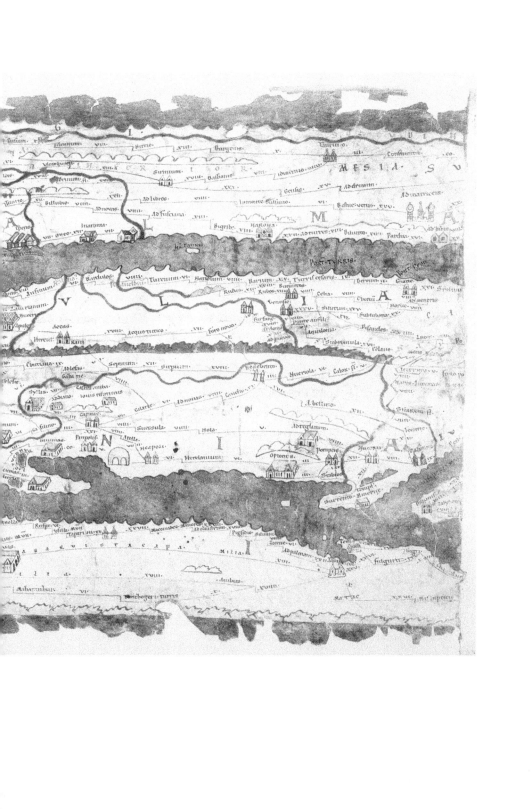

longer impinge upon civilised territory. The map's preference for a schematised representation of mountains does not imply a lack of interest: like the miniaturised mountain images of chapter 7, these compressed depictions have their own distinctive symbolic resonances.[63]

To what extent did depictions of mountains in geographical and historiographical works share the triumphal goals of artefacts like the *Res Gestae* or the La Turbie monument? Pliny the Elder's vast encyclopaedic work the *Natural History* is a good test case. It has often been seen as a document that both celebrates and is enabled by empire. Mountains, like rivers, played a crucial structuring role in both historiographical and geographical writing, for example in helping to delineate the boundaries of particular regions, and Pliny is no exception.[64] His text is full of mountains, many of them mentioned in the context of Roman imperial conquest: Pliny's reference to the tribes of the western Alps is just one of many similar passages where the incorporation of territory into the empire and of territorial knowledge into his encyclopedia are represented as parallel processes.[65] In some cases Pliny seems to be offering us an imagined view from above, as if from a mountaintop,[66] envisaging the lands within and beyond the Roman Empire spread out as on a map before the authorial gaze. Even though we do not have many examples of physical maps reflecting the imperial worldview, the view from above was nevertheless used repeatedly as an image for geographical knowledge-gathering and geographical authority:[67] we will see other examples in the course of the next three chapters.

Many ancient works of history also included extensive sections of ethnographic information which similarly had the potential to reinforce an imperial worldview. Ancient ethnographic thinking was dominated by environmental determinism—in other words the assumption that particular climates and terrains shaped the character of the people who inhabited them. In many cases those habits of thinking led to the belief that inhabitants of mountain regions were inherently uncivilised and violent.[68] One of the foundational texts for that approach, Hippocrates' *Airs, Waters, Places*, maps out at enormous length the relationship between character and landscape for many different regions. He tells us that 'those who inhabit a region which is mountainous and rough and high and well watered, where the changes of the seasons bring big differences, are likely to have large figures well adapted to suffering and courage; and natures of this kind have not a little wildness and savagery' (*Airs, Waters, Places* 24). It is not difficult to see how those kinds of claim might have had a mutually reinforcing relationship with projects of imperial conquest. That is not to say that the characterisation of mountain peoples was always negative. Ancient ethnographic ways of thinking about mountain populations have had a long afterlife in postclassical and especially nineteenth- and twentieth-century nation-building: the classical roots of those interests have not always been acknowledged. In those later responses the tendency to denigrate 'mountaineers' (in the traditional sense of people who live in the mountains), and to see mountains as barriers against invasion, is often in tension with an alternative possibility, where mountain inhabitants are valued for their distinctive virtues and even in some cases taken as emblematic figures of national identity.[69] There are plenty of traces of that latter attitude in our ancient sources too, not least in the hint of admiration in the Hippocrates passage just quoted, and in the way in which the mountain populations of Italy were absorbed and assimilated as valued constituents of the Roman Empire and Roman identity after a period of initial conflict with Rome, for example in the images of admirable ruggedness and austerity associated with the people of the Apennines.[70] But either way, ethnographic stereotypes were being manipulated for the purposes of national and imperial self-definition.

We do need to be cautious, however, about assuming that geographical and other kinds of knowledge were straightforwardly intertwined with imperial goals and institutions.[71] Certainly that connection seems to have been much looser than it has been for many modern European empires.[72] Many individual authors turn out to be quite inconsistent in their representations of territorial subjugation when we look at them more closely. In some passages, for example, Pliny is actually quite negative about human exploitation of mountain terrain:

> Nature made the mountains for herself as frameworks (*compages*) for holding together the inner parts of the earth, and at the same time for subduing the onslaughts of rivers and weakening the force of the waves and restraining the least calm parts with her hardest material. We cut into these mountains and drag them away purely for pleasure, mountains which once it was amazing even to have crossed. Our forefathers viewed the scaling of the Alps by Hannibal and later by the Cimbri as something marvellous; now these same Alps are quarried for a thousand types of marble. (Pliny, *Natural History* 36.1–2).[73]

We will see a series of other examples in what follows where images of human control are in tension with much more negative or unflattering portrayals of engagement with the mountains in political and military contexts. The conquest of mountain terrain was routinely associated with modernity and imperial control, as it has been also for the empires of the modern world, but that was rarely a straightforward process. The mountains were often represented as obdurate places resistant to outside impositions. Even where that was no longer the case, as this passage from Pliny shows, extravagant exploitation of mountain terrain could be taken as a sign of hubris and human overreaching.

11

Mountain Narratives in Greek and Roman Historiography

Landscape Narratives

Three figures above all overshadow our view of mountain generalship in ancient historiography: Xerxes, the Persian king whose vast forces were repulsed by the Greeks in the Persian Wars of the 480s BCE; the Macedonian Alexander the Great, whose sweeping campaigns brought about the conquest of vast swathes of territory in the Near East; and last the Carthaginian Hannibal, whose crossing of the Alps in 218 BCE was the most famous example of foreign invasion in Roman military history. The stories of these three campaigns were told over and over again not just in historiography but also in many other genres. They were also used as images against which other later military campaigns were measured: they were powerful exemplars of the rewards and hazards of human dominance over the earth's surface. In all three cases—and for many other ancient leaders too—mountain-battle scenes were used by later historians as arenas for characterisation: the decisions generals make under great pressure in threatening terrain help to mark out their special qualities, or in some cases their failures.

But if we really want to understand the way in which mountains mattered for ancient historiography, we need to read those battle scenes, with their intense focus on specific moments and specific places, side by side with other passages of landscape depiction. There is evidence for a rhetorical strand of landscape description in some ancient historiography, but it is nevertheless quite unusual to find extensive and elaborate depictions of landscape setting even for important battle narratives. The satirist Lucian complains about one historian 'who gives, according to his own idea, the clearest, most convincing descriptions of every town, mountain, plain, or river' (*How to Write History* 19). Later he tells us that 'it is helplessness about the real essentials, or ignorance of what should be given, that makes them take refuge in word-painting—landscapes, caves, and the like' (20). He recommends instead 'restraint in descriptions of mountains, walls, rivers, and so on' (57).[1] The vast majority of our surviving texts do adopt precisely the kind of understated way of describing landscape that Lucian recommends (Lucian might not have been surprised about that, since he is portraying the objects of his satire as untalented imitators of great predecessors, and so presumably not destined for literary immortality). That restrained technique, where landscape descriptions tend to be relatively brief, even in cases where their authors value topographical precision highly,[2] requires us to read intratextually, with careful attention to passages that might at first glance look individually rather underwhelming, rather than just lurching from one spectacular set-piece to the next. In some cases that might involve reading a set of mountain battle scenes as an interconnected series; in other cases it involves giving attention to representations of mountains as regional boundaries, or ethnographies of mountain people. It also involves looking for the gradual but insistent development of recurring themes, for example the value of human alteration of the environment, or the difficulties of human perception and calculation in politics and warfare. Typically those themes ebb and flow, dropping away and coming back into view, offering us cumulative images of human interaction with the natural world. In some cases successive passages reinforce each other, offering us a relatively consistent vision; in other cases we find inconsistencies and internal contradictions which can challenge us to think about the significance of landscape for ourselves, and help us to envisage more clearly the sophisticated, multifaceted nature of ancient environmental thinking. Reading intratextually also allows us to see how ancient writers represented human interaction with the environment on a global scale by juxtaposing images from right across the Mediterranean world.

Herodotus

Herodotus' *Histories* is a foundational example of these intratextual techniques of landscape representation. His *Histories*, an account of the origins and unfolding of the Persian wars in the 490s and 480s BCE, was written in the second half of the fifth century BCE. Mountains are everywhere in his work. Often they stand in the background as understated settings for the campaigning that unfolds around them. But when we read these passages as a series we can begin to see how they contribute between them to a sustained reflection on the relationship between human communities and their environments.

One of the features of Herodotus' work that is particularly influential is his treatment of geography and ethnography. He uses mountains repeatedly to map out the shape and the boundaries of particular regions or routes.[3] His depiction of the boundaries of Egypt is a good example:

> From Heliopolis, as you travel up, Egypt is narrow; for on one edge a mountain-range belonging to Arabia stretches alongside, from the north towards midday and the south wind . . . ; in it are the stone-quarries which were quarried for the pyramids at Memphis. On this edge the mountain ends where I have said, and then turns back; where it is at its widest, so I was told, it is a journey of two months from east to west, and the border regions in the east are said to produce frankincense. Such then is the character of this mountain-range; and on the side of Egypt towards Libya stretches another mountain-range, rocky and covered in sand: in this are situated the pyramids, and it runs in the same direction as those parts of the Arabian mountains which stretch towards the south. (Herodotus, *Histories* 2.8.1–2)[4]

In other passages Herodotus' gaze falls more on the inhabitants of the mountains, with far from flattering results: 'The Caucasus runs along the side of this sea that stretches westward. It is of all mountain-ranges the biggest in extent and the highest. The Caucasus has many and various races of people living within it; most of them live wild in the forests . . . and they say that these people have sex in the open like cattle' (1.203.1–2). Or later, and even more exotically:

> As far as the country of these Scythians the whole land which has been described is a level and deep-soiled plain; but from this point on it becomes rocky and rough. When one has passed through much of this rough country, there live in the foothills of some high mountains a people who are said to be universally bald, both men and women alike, and snub-nosed with big chins, and who are said to speak their own language, wearing Scythian clothes, but living from the produce of trees. . . . Each person lives under a tree, covering it in winter with waterproof white felt, and in summer without felt. . . . Now as far as these bald people are concerned there is a lot of clarity about their land and about the peoples on this side of them . . . but for the territory beyond them, no one is able to say for sure, for it is cut off

by high and inaccessible mountains, and no one passes over them. These bald people say (but I do not believe them) that these mountains are inhabited by goat-footed men; and that after one has passed beyond them there are other people who sleep for six months of the year. (4.23–25)

In that passage the oddity of the populations is proportionate to the ruggedness of their terrain and their distance from the centres of Greek civilisation,[5] although Herodotus also introduces a note of caution in raising the possibility of inaccuracy in these accounts: unfamiliar and inaccessible lands are more likely to be subject to fabricated reports.

These passages are not just inert digressions: they are also closely linked with Herodotus' wider themes. They are connected with his wider exploration of the way in which geographical and ethnographic knowledge can facilitate imperial conquest, while incomplete or flawed knowledge can undermine it. They also help to raise questions, which Herodotus never answers for us directly, about how far these exotic peoples measure up against the Persians, and even against the Greeks. The very closing paragraph of the work refers back to a debate among the Persians, back in the sixth century, long before their attempted invasion of Greece. A Persian advisor suggests moving all their people from the 'rough' land of Persia to somewhere 'softer' and more pleasant. King Cyrus is unimpressed: rough lands, he says, breed strong and free peoples (9.122). Here we have a much more positive vision of the connections between harsh terrain and national character, informed by beliefs about environmental determinism that were still at an early stage in their evolution at the time when Herodotus was writing.

In addition to these functions of mapping and ethnography, which became so conventional in the later historiographical tradition, Herodotus also returns repeatedly to one theme which gives his representation of mountains a special complexity—that is the theme of human alteration and domination of the land, and the land's (and the sea's) resistance to that. Herodotus is one of the most important early representatives of a tendency to be ambivalent about those processes in ancient historiographical and geographical writing; he is also acutely aware of the impact of environmental alteration on human populations.[6] In places he seems to admire the technological accomplishments he describes—for example at one point he praises the people of Samos for digging a passage through a mountain to bring water into their city (3.60)—but he sees also that this kind of landscape alteration can be associated with hubris and with tyranny.[7] Later in the same book we hear about a plateau in Asia 'surrounded on all sides by a wall of mountains, broken by five gorges' (3.117), each one inhabited by a different tribe. The Persian king has dammed up all five gorges, making the plateau into a sea, and opens the gates only when the desperate, water-starved tribes come to plead with him and bring tribute.[8]

That theme becomes more prominent in the final three books, which turn to the details of Xerxes' invasion, in an extraordinary series of passages describing attempts to tame and enslave the natural world. Most famously, Xerxes whips the Hellespont and throws a pair of shackles into it when his first attempt at a pontoon bridge is destroyed in a storm (7.35),[9] but that is only one of many related incidents. In an earlier Persian expedition, a huge number of ships—Herodotus says 300—had been destroyed by a storm when they were passing around Mount Athos (6.44). Xerxes therefore spends three years digging a canal through the isthmus on the inland side of the mountain so that the same will not happen again. There are some positive overtones,[10] but also a strong impression of tyrannical behaviour—for example we hear that 'men of all nations who were part of the army worked at digging, under the whip' (7.22.1).[11] Here human oppression and environmental alteration go hand in hand.

One important element in Herodotus' treatment of this theme is the way in which the mountains, along with other natural features like the sea and the wind, are animated as agents of resistance—divinely inspired, so Herodotus sometimes implies—to the Persian invasion.[12] None of them is humanised quite so vividly as the shackled Hellespont, but they share with that seascape the capacity of being autonomous, unpredictable, beyond Xerxes' control. The deadly storm off Mount Athos is just one in a series of mountain storms that bring destruction to the Persians.[13] Before Xerxes reaches the Hellespont, large numbers of his men are killed by a thunderstorm at the foot of Mount Ida (7.42). Two other huge storms shipwreck the Persians against Mount Pelion (7.188 and 8.12), leaving dead bodies floating in the sea and getting tangled in the oars of the surviving ships. When the Persians approach Delphi, they are terrified by thunderbolts and two massive crags break off from Mount Parnassos and crash down in their path (8.37) (Pausanias knew Herodotus' work back to front and clearly had that passage in mind in describing the resistance of Mount Parnassos to the Gauls).[14] Xerxes' uncle and advisor Artabanos has earlier named the land and the sea as the two greatest enemies the Persian army must face (7.49), while the Greeks have been told by the oracle at Delphi that the winds will be their greatest allies (7.178).

Right in the middle of that complex of incidents comes the battle of Thermopylai. One way of looking at the Persians' famous outflanking movement along the path on Mount Kallidromos would be to see it as another example of their success in controlling mountainous terrain,[15] like Xerxes' exercise of control over Mount Athos, not least because of its links with Herodotus' many other illustrations of the necessity of local, geographical knowledge for imperial conquest.[16] At one point Herodotus describes how the Phokians guarding the path heard the leaves crunching beneath the feet of the Persians as they marched ('the air was still, and there was a lot of noise, as was likely with all the leaves spread out beneath their feet' [7.218]). We might read that detail as an image of the way in which the Persians are intimately and sensuously immersed in the environment that is finally now yielding to their control. Alternatively, we might read it as a sign of the challenge of moving through the mountains undetected, as if the ground itself is attempting to betray them even at this turning point in the narrative. At the same time we might see Leonidas' defence of the pass at sea level as another example of the way in which human bravery, reinforced by natural forces, in this case the destructive power of the sea, succeeds in resisting the hubristic might of Xerxes, at least in the heroic first phases of battle. Herodotus tells us that many Persian soldiers 'fell into the sea and died; many more were trampled by their fellow soldiers while still alive; and it was not possible to count the numbers of the dead' (7.223), just as the storms from Mount Pelion and Mount Athos have scattered their bodies over the waves.

Xenophon and Arrian

Herodotus is relatively uninterested in characterising military leaders according to their powers of perception and ingenuity in relation to landscape, but in a series of later history writers that theme becomes very important.[17] Battle landscapes were regularly associated with confusion and difficulty of perception,[18] and that association is often enhanced at high altitude by the difficulties of rough terrain and challenging atmospheric conditions. For example, Xenophon, in his *Anabasis*, describes his own leadership of a group of Greek mercenaries returning home across Asia Minor. A key part of his self-characterisation in that work is his ability to interpret the mountainous terrain they are passing through. That characterisation has a cumulative impact: over and over again we see Xenophon seeing what others are unable to see, in a way which brings a military advantage to the Greek soldiers in their encounters with hostile forces.[19]

Arrian's *Anabasis* is another good example. Alexander's capture of the Sogdian rock at *Anabasis* 4.18–19 is just one of a series of different mountain battles and sieges designed to celebrate Alexander's dominance over the landscape. Most strikingly, it is the first of three mountaintop sieges that come in very quick succession in the narrative. Immediately afterwards, Arrian takes us to the rock of Chorienes, a mountaintop site surrounded by a deep ravine on all sides, which Alexander captures by building ladders to descend into the ravine, and then building up a huge earth causeway from the bottom of the ravine upwards (4.21). Finally he captures the rock of Aornos by building an artificial mound of earth beside it (4.28–30). In Arrian's narrative, Alexander's ingenuity and boldness give him an extraordinary and consistent dominance over mountains and other landscape features (rivers too are repeatedly overcome). This characterisation is haunted by the memory of Xerxes, through occasional hints that Alexander's conquests of landscape might be viewed as hubristic.[20] For example in the Chorienes passage Arrian tells us that Alexander 'had advanced to such a degree of daring and success that he thought all places should be accessible and available to him' (Arrian, *Anabasis* 4.21.3). However, the overall effect is to suppress those worries beneath an overwhelmingly celebratory veneer. One famous story, from the work of Vitruvius, who was writing more than a century before Arrian, similarly resists the temptation to characterise Alexander as a hubristic conqueror of landscape, while also drawing attention to that risk. The architect Dinocrates proposes to carve Mount Athos in the likeness of the king and to build a city on the mountainside, but Alexander rejects his suggestion, on the grounds that it will be difficult for the city to have an adequate water supply (Vitruivius, *De architectura* Book 2, preface). There, Alexander's restraint stands in contrast with Xerxes' willingness to do violence to Mount Athos two centuries before.[21]

Plutarch

One of the richest uses of this theme of military perceptiveness in mountain-battle scenes comes in Plutarch's *Lives*.[22] Plutarch is not necessarily the first author one would think of looking at for an image of mountain warfare, but his *Lives* are in fact full of scenes where generals grapple with the difficulties of fighting in the mountains, often successfully, and often in a way which involves inflicting confusion on their enemies. Plutarch's recurring use of that motif is another example of the intratextual approach to depiction of mountains that I have outlined, if we assume that the *Lives* is to be read as an interconnected text, rather than a disjointed string of individual biographies.[23] In *Publicola* 22, the Sabines set an ambush near Fidenae, but Postumius Albinus learns about the plan from deserters: he sends troops up into the hills to keep them under observation; they then attack successfully in heavy fog from that high ground at daybreak. In *Fabius Maximus* 6–7, Hannibal finds himself trapped, because of an error of communication with a local guide, in difficult ground at Casilinum, surrounded by mountains and blocked by marshy ground near to the sea. The Roman commander Fabius Maximus uses his knowledge of the topography to surround Hannibal. Hannibal's soldiers are despondent, but Hannibal leads them to safety through trickery: he orders burning torches to be tied at night to the horns of 2,000 oxen; they rush wildly over the mountain slopes, and the Roman soldiers guarding the pass wrongly assume that the Carthaginians are attacking them from all sides and withdraw. In *Aratus* 22, Aratus leads a night-time attack on the hill of Acrocorinth that stands at the south edge of the city of Corinth. The darkness brings confusion at first, but they are eventually successful, and in the end it is the enemy who is afflicted by sensory difficulties: the light of the moon and the echoes make it seem as though there are more troops than there are. There are many other examples.[24]

What is distinctive about Plutarch's use of that theme is the way in which he takes on the standard presentation of mountains as visually enigmatic places in need of decipherment and makes it a part of his project of biographical characterisation. Some of Plutarch's subjects are unable to cope with the challenge of mastering the landscapes they encounter, but more often they are portrayed on the contrary as heroes of perception, who stand out for their ability to decipher the conditions in which they find themselves.[25] This focus on the perceptiveness of his heroes resonates with Plutarch's philosophical interests in the problems of ignorance and his emphasis on the way in which those problems can be overcome through good judgement and moderation of the passions. The wise man, for Plutarch, will show his wisdom by his ability to act rationally and with good judgement under pressure.[26]

We can see those effects on show in detail in another battle at Thermopylai, in Plutarch's *Life of Cato the Elder* 13–14, this time from 191 BCE, nearly 300 years after the Greek encounter with Xerxes. The Roman army is at war against the Macedonian Seleucid king Antiochos III. Antiochos has blocked up the pass at Thermopylai, and thinks that he has blocked out the war from Greece. The Romans despair of getting through, but then Cato realises that an outflanking movement is possible over the mountain path used by the Persians. Mentions of the Romans' initial confusion recur several times in the course of that manoeuvre, but gradually Cato's control over the situation becomes more and more secure:[27]

After they had climbed up, the prisoner of war who was guiding them lost his way, and wandering about in impassable and precipitous places filled the soldiers with terrible despair and fear. Cato, seeing the danger, ordered them all to remain stationary and to wait, while he himself, taking with him a certain Lucius Manlius who was an accomplished mountain climber, went ahead with much toil and much danger, in the profound darkness of the moonless night, suffering many interruptions to his vision and lack of clarity because of the wild olive trees and the crags that stretched out in front of him, until they came upon a path which, so they thought, led down to the enemy camp, and there they put signs on some conspicuous cliffs that towered up above Mount Kallidromos. They then made their way back and collected their troops, and going forward again to the signs they turned on to the path and began to move along it; but when they had gone a little way the path failed them and they found a ravine in front of them, and once again they experienced perplexity and fear, not knowing and not being able to see that they happened to have got very close to the enemy. But then the day began to dawn, and some of them thought they heard voices, and soon they were able to see a Greek camp beneath the cliff. (*Cato the Elder* 13.2–4)

From then on it is the Greeks who are subject to fear and uncertainty. Cato captures one of the enemy soldiers, and learns from him that it is only a small detachment guarding the route over the mountain, and so launches an attack which routs them easily: 'but when the enemy saw them rushing down from the cliffs, they fled to the main army, and filled all of them with confusion' (13.7), and the Greeks all take to their heels, submitting themselves to 'impassable roads and wanderings that were useless for flight' (14.1). In all of this Plutarch's emphasis on the mental processes and emotional responses of Cato and others is striking. The initial confusion experienced by the Romans and at times also by Cato himself is passed on to the enemy, while Cato shows his mastery of the situation, and his ability to overcome initial error and uncertainty by the acquisition of hard-won knowledge.

It seems likely that Plutarch has added much of this material to what he found in his sources in order to enhance his characterisation of Cato.[28] Certainly none of the details of Cato's night-time route-finding are in the other surviving texts that discuss this incident. Livy (36.18.8) describes Cato's outflanking movement only in very cursory terms.[29] One other obvious point of comparison is the genre of military strategy writing, for example the *Strategemata* of Plutarch's approximate contemporary Frontinus (the father-in-law of

Plutarch's dedicatee Sosius Senecio). Certainly it is striking that Frontinus (like other ancient writers on military strategy) has a large number of mountain-battle exempla where mountains are linked with trickery and uncertainty.[30] At the same time the brevity of the *Strategemata* stands in contrast with the more expansive character of Plutarch's mountain descriptions, with their focus on the mental experience of his human actors. Frontinus' account of this incident at Thermopylai—like Livy's, which he seems to be imitating—is brief, and lacks Plutarch's interest in mental states of fear and confusion: 'he dislodged the Aetolians who were guarding the ridges of Mt. Callidromus, and then appeared suddenly from the rear on a hill overlooking the camp of the king. Antiochus' forces were thus thrown into confusion, and the Romans rushed at them from both sides, and having dispersed and routed the enemy they captured the camp' (Frontinus, *Strategemata* 2.4.4).[31]

In other cases Plutarch's scenes of mountain campaigning are overlaid with an awareness of the role of mountains as objects of scientific curiosity, which provides a parallel for the perceptiveness of his biographical subjects.[32] There is a good example in Plutarch's *Life of Sertorius* 17. Sertorius is fighting in Spain against the Characitani, who live in caves on a hilltop. The country at the base of the hill is covered in a crumbly soil. In time of war they are accustomed to retreat to their caves, where they assume themselves to be safe from attack. Sertorius rides up to inspect their position, and notices dust from the soil being blown up towards the caves. He orders his soldiers to make a pile from the dust, and when the wind comes they stir it up: 'And [the Charicatani], since their caves had only that one inlet for air, against which the wind was blowing, were soon blinded, and soon afflicted with choking breath, from breathing in air that was harsh and mixed with much dust' (17.12). After three days they surrender.

This narrative shares with the *Life of Cato the Elder* and many other passages an interest in the ability of the good general to 'read' mountain landscape, and to inflict sensory and mental confusion on the enemy. It is a very brief account, and it has the kind of self-contained quality which would make it well-suited to the anecdotes of cunning generalship that we find in the military strategy tradition. There is presumably a good chance also that Plutarch is drawing on earlier historiographical accounts, perhaps Sallust especially.[33] But the incident is not in any other surviving ancient text, and once again that makes the precise degree of Plutarch's invention hard to pin down. However, there are two features of this passage which I suspect Plutarch is using in quite original ways, even if he has not necessarily invented them. The first is the way in which he shows us Sertorius overcoming his initial *aporia* and inflicting blindness, in this case quite literal blindness, on his enemies, and the way in which he focalises much of his account through Sertorius, giving us access to Sertorius' mental processes.[34] That is done with a light touch, and with relatively few words, but nevertheless in a way that allows us to imagine Sertorius' gradually dawning realisation that there is an alternative to conventional conflict:

> There was no route of attack anywhere, but as he was wandering about at random and indulging in empty threats, he saw that a great quantity of dust from that soil was being carried up against them by the wind.... So drawing inferences from these things and listening to the reports of local inhabitants, Sertorius ordered... (17.5–8)

Plutarch here stresses Sertorius' use of rational judgement through the term 'drawing inferences' (συλλογιζόμενος) (17.8).[35] We then see the barbarians wrongly 'conjecturing' (ὑπονοοῦντες) (17.8) that this is a mound for attacking the hill, and jeering at Sertorius' soldiers, before finally succumbing to the dust clouds in the passage already quoted.[36]

The second feature is the way in which Plutarch supplements these themes of confusion and perception with the use of scientific language. The first relevant passage is Plutarch's initial account of the crumbly limestone dust (powdered lime has a corrosive, burning effect on human eyes and lungs):

> The whole region beneath the hill yields a clay-like earth and a soil that is easily crumbled because of its porousness, nor is it strong enough to bear the weight of people walking on it, and it disperses widely, like unslaked lime or ashes, if it is touched even lightly. (17.3)

There is a good parallel for geographical-scientific discussion along similar lines in Strabo, *Geography* 12.8.17, which explains the winding path of the river Maeander by the crumbliness of the soil in the surrounding area. The other passage is Plutarch's account of the winds:

> For the caves, as I have said, faced north, and the wind which blows from the north, which some call Caecias, is the most prevalent and strongest of the winds in that place, being a mixture of winds from the moist plains and from the snow-covered mountains; and at that time, at the height of summer, it was particularly strong, and nourished by the melting snows of the northern mountains it blew delightfully and kept on blowing, bringing refreshment both to them and to their grazing animals during the day. (17.6–7)

The wind Caecias is mentioned three times by Aristotle, for example in *Meteorology* 363b17; also in *Problems* 26.1 (940a19) where the Aristotelian emphasis on moisture ('Why is the Caecias the only wind that draws moisture to itself?') matches Plutarch's mention of the 'watery plains and snow-covered mountains'.[37]

One of the functions of this material is simply to characterise this as an odd, significant landscape. It is a memorable and unusual place, outside normal human experience: an arena for testing out the mental operations of Plutarch's biographical subject.[38] Once again Plutarch is not alone in that technique. There is no shortage of landscapes defined by their scientific peculiarities in ancient historiography and geography, from Herodotus onwards. But it seems likely that Plutarch is at the very least enriching and giving a special prominence to this scientific material here, given how closely it is related to the scientific material of some of his non-biographical works, for example in the drinking-party conversations of his *Sympotic Questions*.[39] These details seem to be included in part precisely to conjure up an image of intellectual enquiry. If the crumbly soil of the Characitani or the moisture-carrying wind Caecias were raised in the intellectually curious context of the symposia of the *Sympotic Questions* we would expect them to be followed by a whole series of explanations and conjectures.[40] That is not what happens here, but we do see something related: Sertorius similarly reflects on these phenomena and deciphers them. In other words the insertion of scientific language at this point prompts us to think about enquiry as an intellectual virtue. And it paints Sertorius once again as a hero of perception, whose decipherment of the mountain landscape in which he finds himself is different from but in some respects parallel to the decipherment that Plutarch and his intellectual companions attempt in their philosophical and scientific discussions.[41]

There is a similar set of passages in Plutarch's account of the battle of Pydna in the *Life of Aemilius Paulus*. Aemilius is portrayed repeatedly both there[42] and elsewhere in the work[43] as a good interpreter of the environmental conditions in which he and his troops find themselves. Several times that kind of detail about Aemilius' tactical intelligence is supplemented by references to scientific knowledge, both his own and that of others.[44] For example, Plutarch at one point quotes an epigram in which Xenagoras records his calculation of the height of Mount Olympus: 'and yet the geometricians say that neither the height of a mountain nor the depth of the sea can surpass ten stades. Xenagoras, however, seems to have taken his measurement not in a cursory way, but following a method and with instruments' (15.11). In that case the details of the measurement do not have any bearing on the decisions Aemilius makes as general, nor does Plutarch even suggest that Aemilius is aware of them. Nevertheless the insertion of this scientific material does offer us an image of careful observation which is parallel to Aemilius' own observational virtues, not least because Aemilius shares Xenagoras' refusal to go along with the majority view without good basis.[45]

The longest example comes at the moment when the Romans are settling into their position in the foothills of Mount Olympus. The soldiers are annoyed by the lack of drinking water, and Aemilius solves the problem by ordering the digging of wells.[46] Plutarch describes his reasoning at length, and includes an extended discussion of alternative views on whether there are stores of water underneath springs:[47]

> Aemilius, therefore, seeing (ὁρῶν) that the tall and tree-covered mountain of Olympus lay nearby, and judging (τεκμαιρόμενος) from the greenness of its trees that there were sources of water flowing deep underneath, dug many wells at the foot of the mountain which acted as vents for the water. These were immediately filled with clear streams which rushed all together into the newly empty space by the weight and impulse of the water's pressure. (*Aemilius Paulus* 14.1–2)

Some people, he says, deny that there are stores of water beneath the ground where we find springs:

> for, they argue, just as women's breasts are not, like vessels, full of ready milk that flows out, but instead produce milk by converting the nourishment they contain, and filter it through; in the same way those places in the ground that are very cold and full of springs do not have water concealed beneath them, nor cavities that send out streams and deep rivers of such great size from a ready and underlying source, but rather they convert vapour and air into water by compressing and condensing them under pressure. (*Aemilius Paulus* 14.5–6)

Plutarch then offers a number of reasons for being sceptical about that view. This is a long discussion, much longer than the scientific material of the *Sertorius*—only part of it is quoted here—and once again it would not be out of place in one of the scientific discussions in Plutarch's philosophical works. It has sometimes in the past been treated as a digression, but in fact it plays a central role in Plutarch's account. One way of reading it is to see it in the context of Plutarch's characterisation of Aemilius as someone engaged with

Greek learning: the question whether springs were caused by underground reservoirs of water had a long history in Greek philosophical writing.[48] But even if we do not assume any detailed engagement with earlier writings on that subject on the part of Aemilius—and Plutarch never explicitly suggests that we should—it still offers us an image against which to measure up Aemilius' observational and intellectual astuteness. It conjures up an image of perceptiveness and enquiry which offers us a parallel for Aemilius Paulus' ability to see beneath the surface where others are unable to do so,[49] very much like the ancient writers who asserted their ability to see the inner workings of Etna and the other volcanoes of the Mediterranean in their hidden depths. Aemilius reads the landscape of Mount Olympus in a way that allows him to fulfil his military goals.

Polybius

In 218 BCE, the Carthaginian general Hannibal crossed the Alps with a huge army, including about 40 elephants, in what is surely the best known of all ancient mountain expeditions. It has been used for centuries following both as a comparison point for other literal mountain crossings and conquests and as a metaphor for various other kinds of achievement: Napoleon, for example, was repeatedly compared with Hannibal after his crossing of the Alps through the Great Saint Bernard Pass in 1800.[50] In ancient texts Hannibal's invasion is represented repeatedly as an example of military daring and ingenuity, in much the same way as the exploits of Plutarch's generals in their mountain battles, though often at the same time with overtones of hubris.[51] It also gives us some of our most powerful ancient examples of high mountains as hostile and challenging landscapes, characterised by extreme cold and steepness, and as places of sensory confusion and even bodily immersion. That is perhaps not a surprise in the case of Livy,[52] who shares Plutarch's fascination with the experience of confusion in battle situations in other passages too.[53] My main focus is therefore on our other most extensive surviving historiographical account, by Polybius, who ostentatiously takes a more rationalising, unspectacular approach to narrating Hannibal's crossing.[54] That makes it all the more interesting to see how the overwhelming bodily impact of Alpine terrain takes over his narrative at various points: Hannibal is often in control of the situation in Polybius' account, but there are several moments where we see that control slipping (sometimes quite literally slipping, on the icy ground of his Alpine crossing).[55] Those passages often have a strikingly 'haptic' quality, focused intensely on the impact of mountain landscape on the human body, and especially on the sense of touch, which is not unlike the very tactile, immersive mountain experience we encounter in Apuleius' *Metamorphoses*. Polybius also stands out for the way in which he uses the theme of military care and perceptiveness in the mountains for the purposes of authorial self-definition: he juxtaposes images of Hannibal's military leadership with an account of his own authorial control over his subject in a way which invites us to measure them up against each other.[56]

Modern mountaineering literature is similarly fascinated by the painstaking details of bodily engagement and immersion in high-altitude environments, and also at the same time by dreams of human conquest and control over challenging landscapes. Mountaineering literature, especially from the late nineteenth century onwards, depicts varieties of risk and exhaustion that involve close physical contact with the mountain; at the same time they celebrate the sense of exhilaration and mastery associated with overcoming those challenges.[57] The tension between those two strands is one of the things that make the genre so compelling for modern readers. The resemblance with writing about military expeditions in ancient Greek and Roman historiography is not accidental. We have seen already that a lot of modern mountaineering practice has been closely intertwined with military experience. Many twentieth-century accounts of mountaineering expeditions similarly have strongly military resonances, for example in their repeated use of the language of conquest.[58] That is partly precisely because of their reliance on traditions of writing about military campaigning that stretch back ultimately to ancient Greek and Roman literature. Those traditions would have been much more widely familiar a century ago than they are now, when generations of schoolboys had an intimate acquaintance with campaign narratives by Caesar in Latin or Xenophon in Greek, or indeed Livy's account of Hannibal in the Alps. That link makes it all the more bizarre that the narrative of modern exceptionalism, where mountaineering and especially mountaineering writing are viewed as uniquely modern practices without premodern parallels, still has so much traction in popular discourse. Modern mountaineers often climb for leisure rather than for military purposes, and that is hard to parallel in the ancient world, but many of the structuring themes and motifs of modern writing about mountain expeditions are nevertheless rooted in ancient precedents.

Polybius' authorial presence is conspicuous right from the start of his account, where he rails against writers who attempt to 'astonish their readers by their description of wonders associated with these places ... assuming that the strength and roughness of the Alps is such that not only horses and troops and elephants, but even light-armed footsoldiers, would not easily be able to cross them' (Polybius, *Histories* 3.47.6–9). They represent Hannibal as reckless—but do they really believe, Polybius asks, that Hannibal would have risked his whole expedition without knowing anything about the route? They have not taken the trouble to learn that groups of Celts had crossed the same mountains even not long before in order to fight against the Romans together with their allies in northern Italy.[59] The astonishment of those historians is matched by the astonishment of the Romans, who have a similarly incredulous attitude to his undertaking, presumably because they too are uninformed about what it really involves: Hannibal makes the most of his enemies' lack of perceptiveness in order to inspire panic in them.[60] Polybius, by contrast, understands the rational basis for Hannibal's strategy:

Hannibal did not act as they say, but proceeded very sensibly in

> this enterprise. ... For the difficulties of the terrain he employed local guides and leaders. ... And I can speak with confidence on these matters because I have made inquiries about them from those who were present at the time, and because I have seen these places for myself, and because I have personally made the journey through the Alps, in order to understand and see for myself. (3.48.10–12)

Earlier Polybius has told us that Hannibal 'had informed himself accurately about the fertility of the land at the foot of the Alps and near the river Po, the denseness of its population, the bravery of the men in war, and above all their hatred of Rome ever since that former war with the Romans which I described in the preceding book to enable my readers to follow all I am about to narrate' (3.34.2–3). The parallel between Hannibal and Polybius in these passages is hard to miss. Both of them need to know the real, concrete details of the land. The care of the general and the care of the historian blend into one.

However, Polybius' claim to be offering a realistic account does not manifest itself just in detached topographical precision; it is also articulated precisely through his attention to the tactile, corporeal elements of the Carthaginian experience which in places drown out any attempt at an accurate topographical account.[61] It is very hard to reconstruct Hannibal's route exactly from Polybius' account, much to the frustration of generations of modern scholars. Debate about that question was one of the most vehement controversies of nineteenth-century and twentieth-century topographical scholarship,[62] but none of the countless attempts to work out exactly which route he took has been decisive. It is surely more productive to focus instead on the status of Polybius' account as a work of the imagination, based of course on a real event, but powerfully reshaped and reimagined for later audiences.[63] Seeing Polybius' account in those terms does not mean, however, that we should view it as unrealistic: one of his achievements is to create a kind of 'reality effect' precisely through his portrayal of the claustrophobic visual and physical limitations that the Carthaginians experience.

Polybius pays particular attention to the terrain and its corporeal impact on the bodies of Hannibal's men and animals. The first action comes very soon after the Carthaginians begin their ascent. The tribe of the Allobroges sends troops to occupy the route by which Hannibal will have to ascend. Hannibal finds out about their plans and deals with the situation efficiently, launching a raid to take over their positions at night when they have retreated to a nearby town. The Carthaginians continue upwards. At first it is the pack-animals that are most at risk; indeed it is the sight of them toiling slowly upwards that inspires the Allobroges to attack once again: 'since the path was not only narrow and rough but also precipitous, the slightest movement or disturbance caused many of the pack animals to fall over the cliffs together with their packs' (3.51.4). Hannibal considers the problem carefully—he is described as 'seeing' (βλέπων) and 'reflecting' (συλλογιζόμενος)[64]—and rescues the situation by climbing up with a select group of troops to attack the Allobroges from above at night, then attacking the town they had been using as a base, regaining some of the captured pack-animals in the process.

Hannibal's control over the situation is threatened once again, however, when his native guides turn against him and attack the Carthaginians in a narrow gorge:

> for the barbarians, who occupied higher ground, skirted along the mountainside and rolled down boulders (τὰς πέτρας ἐπικυλίοντες) on to some of them, or struck them with stones thrown by hand (ἐκ χειρὸς τοῖς λίθοις τύπτοντες), and threw the Carthaginians into universal confusion and danger, so much so that Hannibal was forced to pass the night, together with half his force, in a position protected by bare rock (περί τι λευκόπετρον ὀχυρόν), and without his horses and his pack-animals, watching out for them, until with difficulty, after a whole night of struggle, they extricated themselves from the ravine. (3.53.4–5)

Here human as well as animal bodies are at the mercy of rock, at risk from the boulders rolled down from above, or hemmed in by cliffs in their place of shelter, just as they over and over again are in Apuleius' *Metamorphoses* three centuries later.

Finally the Carthaginians reach the summit. At that point those claustrophobic images of bodily restriction and obstructed vision are once again in tension with an idealised image of Hannibal's clear-sightedness. His soldiers are despondent, so he shows them

> the clear view of Italy; for it lies so close under the mountains that when both of them are examined together the Alps appear to have the position of an acropolis to the whole of Italy. And so showing them the plains around the river Po and reminding them of the goodwill of the Gauls who inhabited that region, and at the same time showing them the position of Rome itself, he made his troops somewhat bolder. (Polybius, *Histories* 3.54.2–3)

Hannibal's plan seems to be only partially effective: it can only go a certain way towards lifting their minds from the sufferings they are still enduring in the difficult terrain of the Alps. But it is nevertheless a striking assertion of his military and cartographical command over the situation, after so many pages of struggle.[65] Once again it invites us to measure Polybius' authorial far-sightedness against Hannibal's military equivalent: he has already drawn attention to the fact that that his own knowledge of the Alps is in some sense parallel to that of Hannibal; like Hannibal, only in vastly more detail, he too is committed to showing his readers 'the position of Rome' in its wider geographical and historical context.[66]

The worst is still to come. As any reader of twentieth-century mountaineering literature knows, the greatest dangers lie on the way down. The path is narrow and obscured by snow, and those who step wide of it are dashed down onto the rocks below. The Carthaginians are used to this by now, Polybius says, and they go on slowly. Once again the real trouble starts with the animals: 'when they got to a place where it was impossible for the elephants or the pack animals to pass, because of the narrowness, an earlier landslip having broken off about one and a half stades of the face of the mountain, and a further landslip having occurred recently, then the soldiers once again became disheartened and discouraged' (3.54.7). A fresh fall of snow causes problems for the narrative's human actors too—and here Polybius shows an extensive interest in the precariousness of their contact with the ground:

new snow had recently fallen on top of the already existing snow which had survived from the previous winter, and it so happened that this was easy to slip through, both because it was freshly fallen and so soft, and because it was not yet deep. But whenever they had trodden through it and set foot on the congealed snow underneath they no longer sunk into it, but slipped along with both feet, as happens to those who travel over ground coated with mud. But what followed on from this was even more difficult. For the men, being unable to pierce the layer of snow underneath, whenever they fell and tried to get a grip with their knees or hands in order to stand up, then they slipped all the more, precisely because they were pressing down, the ground being exceptionally steep. (3.55.1–4)

One of the most striking things about these passages is again their haptic quality—in other words the way in which they appeal to the sense of touch in order to communicate an impression of human bodies obstructed by a real landscape. The animals even fall through the layers of snow and remain stuck there as if frozen into it, immersed in the mountainside. Only a concerted engineering project extricates the Carthaginians from this impasse. Polybius here makes conspicuous use of the vocabulary of construction in a way which looks at first sight quite incongruous with Hannibal's mountain surroundings, drawing attention to Hannibal's use of skills associated with urban civilisation: he 'builds up' (ἐξῳκοδόμει, 3.55.6) a path over the cliffs; later he sets his Numidian soldiers to work on further 'building' (οἰκοδομίαν, 3.55.8). Only then, once they are past this crux in their descent, are they able to limp down to the plains of northern Italy, fifteen days after beginning their climb.

Ancient mountaineering literature thus celebrates human mastery over landscape, but that mastery tends to be partial and precarious; in Hannibal's case it is far less secure than Polybius' own geographical grasp of the territory of Italy and the Alps. Variations on those themes recur over and over again in ancient geographical and historiographical writing about mountain conquest. Some of those accounts are broadly optimistic about the capacity for individual generals, or armies and empires, to dominate mountain terrain; others project a much more pessimistic vision; we will see examples of both in the two chapters that follow. But either way there are nearly always traces of an underlying tension between those two possibilities, between control and vulnerability, conquest and disaster, just as there are also in so much modern writing about mountains and mountaineering.

12

Strabo: Civilising the Mountains

Human-Environment Relations in Strabo's *Geography*

Two authors dominate the second half of part III. Strabo's *Geography*, written in the early first century CE, either during the reign of the emperor Augustus or under his adopted son and heir Tiberius, or both,[1] when their conquest of the Alps was still a recent memory, offers a breathtakingly wide-ranging picture of the regions and communities of the Mediterranean world: their topographies, their histories, their local cultures.[2] Ammianus' *Res Gestae*, composed around three and a half centuries later in the late fourth century CE, gives us one of the most sensationalistic and emotionally powerful accounts of the infighting of the imperial elite and the constant threat of external invasion in the newly Christian empire of his own lifetime. These two texts are among the most intricate and extensive portrayals of mountains surviving from the ancient world, but in both cases that phenomenon has to my knowledge never been explored except in passing. In looking at them side by side one of my aims is to examine in more detail the variety of ways in which ancient traditions of writing about mountains and other kinds of landscape could be used. Both of them draw on widespread conventions of depicting mountain warfare and mountain conquest, Ammianus especially. Both of them also draw repeatedly on negative ethnographic stereotypes of mountain peoples. Those similarities attest to the continuity of ancient thinking about mountains over many centuries and many genres. In some respects, however, they are also quite different. Strabo offers us a remarkably confident vision of human mastery over mountain landscapes in the Roman Empire. Ammianus, by contrast, is much more conflicted, and much more aware of the way in which the uncivilised world of the mountains can overflow and infect the heart of empire. Those differences remind us of the hazards of generalising about ancient attitudes to and representations of human control over the environment.

Both works are also classic examples of intratextually sophisticated mountain narratives that unfold gradually over the space of hundreds of pages, juxtaposing many different images of human-environment relations. In Strabo's case one of the pleasures his texts offers us is the chance to experience an unfolding narrative, one might even say to be part of a journey that takes us in turn through a series of different human places and human cultures and explores in turn their relationship with the landscapes they are a part of. The thrill of reading Strabo comes in part from the control exercised by his authorial persona, which views that variety as if from above, laying out different regions and peoples and cities before our gaze with extraordinary confidence and precision.[3] It is only when we read the text from end to end that we can appreciate those effects in full.[4]

There are two distinct strands of mountain depiction in Strabo's work: the first one links mountains with wild, uncivilised peoples; the second stresses the domestication of mountains. That contrast is part of an overarching division between civilised and uncivilised territory within the text.[5] In the first category, for example in Spain or the Alps, he is interested in the standard ethnographic association between mountains and lack of civilisation; he is also interested in the way in which mountains can be brought under political and military control. By contrast in the second kind of landscape, which is concentrated especially in Italy and mainland Greece and to some extent Asia Minor, we see a very different use of mountains: here mountains are characteristically associated with cities, and often enclosed within city walls; they are also associated with economic advantage and with local religious traditions.[6] In that sense the state of a territory's mountains is one of the measures Strabo uses to define its position on the spectrum from savage to civilised. And yet that process of categorisation is never straightforward for Strabo, especially when one is immersed in the experience of travelling through his text: the text also includes many passages that complicate or even undermine that basic civilised-uncivilised dichotomy.

How much does that vision have in common with current ecocritical perspectives on human relationships with the environment? At first sight, very little. The *Geography* has often been taken as work that celebrates the Roman and specifically Augustan image of peace and civilisation as consequences of imperial conquest and assimilation.[7] Like much ancient ethnographic writing it does repeatedly show us human populations living close to nature, even in harmony with nature, but generally from a highly anthropocentric perspective that glorifies human control over the natural world and denigrates cultures that lack that kind of control: there is very little sign that Strabo values respect for the more-than-human world on its own terms. Even for Strabo, however, his celebration of civilised and economically productive exploitation of the environment is not completely uniform: the long-standing tradition of associating landscape alteration with hubris is not suppressed entirely.[8] The vast scope of his work also gives us access to powerful ways of imagining the variety and complexity of human-environment relations on a global scale. Each of the regions and places he takes us to has its own way of living with the land around it. Moreover, in Strabo's vision of the inhabited world the land often takes an active role in shaping human culture, or at least shaping the possibilities and opportunities that human populations have available to them.[9]

Strabo's Cartographic Perspective

Strabo mentions mountains with remarkable frequency. The word ὄρος ('mountain') and other related forms recur over and over again. To take just one example, he is single-handedly responsible for more than 10 percent of occurrences of the word ὀρεινός in surviving ancient Greek literature (meaning 'mountainous' or 'of the mountains', and used especially to describe mountain peoples): it is used 129 times in the surviving books of the *Geography*, out of a total of just 1,141 in surviving Greek literature. That count is surpassed to my knowledge only in the more heavily mathematical work of Claudius Ptolemy, who focuses much more exclusively than Strabo on the exercises of mapping and measuring the earth's surface.[10]

Some aspects of Strabo's mountain depictions are very much in line with what we find in other geographical and historiographical authors. That is most obvious for the ethnographic association between rough mountains and uncivilised peoples, which dates back at least to Herodotus and Hippocrates and others in the fifth century BCE.[11] Also typical is Strabo's use of mountains to divide the inhabited world and to outline the shape of particular regions. Strabo's authorial perspective is often a cartographic one, focused on the shapes and sizes of particular regions. That characteristic viewpoint is often contrasted with the resolutely road-level, traveller's vision of Pausanias.[12] Spain, he says:

> resembles an ox-hide stretched along its length from west to east, having its forward parts in the east, and with its breadth running from north to

south. Its length is six thousand stadia altogether, and its breadth is five thousand stadia at the widest point, although in some places it is much less than three thousand, especially near to the Pyrenees, which form its eastern boundary. (3.1.3)

In some of these passages Strabo names earlier predecessors, especially the Hellenistic geographer Eratosthenes, who seems to have used mountains repeatedly in his attempt to divide the earth's surface into different regions and to measure the distances between them.[13]

At the same time Strabo's use of those traditions also has some very distinctive features. For example, there is one fascinating passage where his virtuosic deployment of a cartographic perspective is explicitly equated with the view from a mountaintop.[14] Plenty of other authors hint at the same kind of connection, but there are very few parallels for the way in which Strabo endorses that link through a first-person account of his own experience. The passage in question is his account of his own ascent of Acrocorinth, the hill that stood on the southern edge of the city of Corinth:[15]

> The position of the city [that is, Corinth], from the report of Hieronymos and Eudoxos and others, and as I have seen myself, when the city had been recently restored by the Romans, is more or less as follows. A high mountain, about three and a half stadia in vertical height, and about thirty stadia in ascent, ends in a sharp summit. It is called Akrokorinthos. The northern side is the steepest, and the city lies below it on level trapezium-shaped ground near to the foot of the hill. ... The summit has a small temple of Aphrodite, and below the summit is the spring Peirene, which has no overflow, but is always full of clear and drinkable water. ... From the summit Parnassos is visible to the north, and Helikon—high, snow-covered mountains—and the Krisaian gulf that lies beneath them, surrounded by Phokis and Boiotia and Megaris and the parts of Korinthia and Sikyonia which lie across the gulf opposite Phokis. (8.6.21)

The references here to religious culture and mythical stories and their place in the landscape bring Strabo in line with the traditions of local history we find in Pausanias a century and a half later. But it is mapping above all that interests him here. The passage suggests that climbing mountains could have been a practical help to geographical writers like Strabo. But surely more important than the data he can gather when he is standing on the summit is the fact that it gives him a way of imagining the world, spread out before him, and particularly the other mountains, which are so prominent and so helpful as boundary markers and regional landmarks. The use of shapes—the trapezium shape of Corinth—is one he returns to for much vaster regions which without space travel could only ever be seen from the mind's eye. And perhaps most important of all is the way in which he drifts immediately after this paragraph into an account of the plains around Corinth, in a way which makes it momentarily hard to be sure whether he is still on the mountaintop, or whether he has just reverted to his usual technique of mental mapping as if from on high:

> The beginning of the coastal district on the two sides is on the one side Lechaion, and on the other Kenchreai, a village and harbour which is about seventy stadia away from Corinth.... Lechaion lies beneath the city, having few residents, but walls about twelve stadia in length have been built on both sides of the Lechaion road. (8.6.22)

Strabo is also distinctive, however, not just because of the ambition and explicitness of his oroskopic viewpoint. He also stands out for his tendency to give mountains, along with seas and rivers, an unusually active role in the division of the earth's surface.[16] In one passage he tells us that 'it is the sea more than anything else that defines and shapes (γεωγραφεῖ καὶ σχηματίζει) the land, forming gulfs and oceans and straits; also isthmuses, peninsulas, and promontories; and rivers and the mountains give their assistance in that' (2.5.17). There, remarkably, in a metaphor Strabo repeats elsewhere in the text too,[17] the land itself does the geographer's work for him: the word 'defines' (γεωγραφεῖ) might be translated more literally as 'does geography'; it is used for the activity of the geographer elsewhere in Strabo's work.[18] Strabo draws attention to his own control over his material, for sure, but he also reminds us that human claims to mastery can only go so far: the mountains and the rivers too are 'geographers', 'earth-writers', which shape the earth's surface rather than simply describing it.

Spain and the Alps

One of the other things that makes Strabo stand out from his predecessors is the complexity of his treatment of the human domestication of mountainous territories. The first high places we reach as we follow Strabo on his clockwise journey around the Mediterranean are the mountains of Spain. Here perhaps more than anywhere in the work, Strabo (and apparently also the polymathic late Hellenistic Syrian writer Posidonius, who seems to have been his source for some of this material)[19] is obsessed with the process whereby Rome has pacified brigands and brought political and military control to wild populations. Occasionally he reports setbacks and defeats for the Roman army, but the overarching story is one of successful taming. He talks, for example, about the tribes around the river Tagos:

> even though the land was blessed with fruits and cattle and an abundance of silver and gold and other similar metals,[20] nevertheless most of the people had given up on getting their livelihood from the soil, and spent their time in banditry and continual war ... until the Romans stopped them, humbling them and turning most of their cities into villages, although some they improved by joining them together. It was the mountain people (οἱ ὀρεινοί) who began this lawlessness, as one would expect; for since they occupied inferior land and possessed very little, they desired what belonged to others. (3.3.5)

Here there is a direct link between mountain identity and warlike behaviour.[21] But Strabo also stresses that it can be brought under control—for example at one point he describes the way in which the Romans have subdued the Cantabrians; Tiberius, by assigning to them an army of three legions 'has succeeded not only in making some of them peaceful but also in accustoming them to life as citizens' (οὐ μόνον εἰρηνικούς, ἀλλὰ καὶ πολιτικοὺς ἤδη τινὰς αὐτῶν ἀπεργασάμενος τυγχάνει) (3.3.8).

Later Strabo moves on to the Alps, and the story is similarly celebratory:

> Most of the territory of the Salassi lies in a deep glen, shut in by mountains on both sides, but a part of it stretches up to the summits above. ... Until quite recently ... they were still powerful, and as is customary for brigands they inflicted much damage upon those who travelled through their mountains. ... Once these men robbed even Caesar and threw rocks on his soldiers. ... But later Augustus overthrew them completely ... and now the whole of the neighbouring country as far as the highest parts of the passes over the mountain is in a state of peace. (4.6.7)[22]

One might argue that Strabo's repeated reference to Roman conquest of the mountains is a celebration of the triumph of empire, given that mountains are the limit case of inhospitable terrain and hostile humanity. That view is not self-evident, given that he also spends a lot of time describing territories which are far beyond the reach of Rome.[23] However, his mountain depictions certainly have a great deal in common with other celebrations of Roman imperial dominance over the landscape in the centuries before and after, for example with the boasts of the emperor Augustus in his *Res Gestae*.[24]

Strabo sums up that civilising mission explicitly in one programmatic passage early on in the work, even before he launches into the detailed account of Spain:

> Of the inhabitable part of Europe, the wintry and mountainous areas are by nature miserable places of habitation, but even regions of poverty and banditry become tamed (ἡμεροῦται) once they get good administrators. That is the case for the Greeks, who inhabit rocks and mountains but lived well because of their interest in political life and in the arts and because of their knowledge of the art of living in other respects too. The Romans too took over many peoples who were naturally untamed (ἀνήμερα) because they inhabited regions that were rough or harbourless or cold or for other reasons difficult to inhabit, and they brought into communication with each other peoples who had previously been isolated, and they taught the wilder people how to live as citizens. (2.5.26)

This passage is programmatic for the rest of the work:[25] the vocabulary Strabo uses here is echoed again and again in the books that follow. And the repeated metaphor of taming suggests that he has no doubts about Rome's capacity for benevolent dominance over the mountains.

Italy and Greece

Strabo's depiction of the mountains and hills of Italy and Greece, as that passage might lead us to expect, could hardly be more different. When we come down from the Alps into Italy at the beginning of Book 5, or from the wild country of Thrace into mainland Greece in Book 8, we enter a different world. For Strabo, mountains can be obstacles to civilisation, but they need not necessarily be so. Here they are integrated within human culture in a much more ancient and more careful way. That is partly a reflection of how things were: the hills of north-central Italy simply were more urbanised than the Alps. But we should not doubt the artfulness of Strabo's portrayal of that fact.

Most strikingly, mountains in Italy come to be linked with civic identity. A very large proportion of the cities Strabo describes are built close to mountains or even more strikingly on or around mountains. That theme is not completely absent even in his account of Spain.[26] But its frequency for mainland Italy and Greece is extraordinary. For example in sections 2 and 3 of Book 5,

Strabo describes thirteen different settlements (more than half the total number of cities he mentions in that part of the text) built on or around mountains or hills.[27] Take Praeneste, for example: 'it has for a citadel a high mountain above the city. . . . And in addition to its natural strength, hidden passages have been cut through the mountain from all sides as far as the plain, some for water supply, and some as concealed exits' (5.3.11). In passages like these, as for Herodotus' Samians, there is a striking absence of any link between alteration of landscape and hubris.

Strabo's account of the seven hills of Rome is part of that wider narrative of the domestication of mountain landscape.[28] One immediately striking feature of the texts is Strabo's frequent use of the word ὄρος ('mountain') to describe the Caelian and Aventine hills.[29] More often in other Greek authors the hills of Rome are described by the word λόφος ('hill'). Peaks did not necessarily have to be particularly high to be referred to as ὄρος—prominence from the land around seems to have counted for more—but most of the hills of Rome are joined with each other, rather than being isolated summits, which may explain the standard usage.[30] Strabo's unusual preference is an invitation to read this passage in relation to the many other mountains of the *Geography* as a whole. And once again he returns repeatedly to the theme of domestication. He tells us, for example, that:

> The first settlers walled the Capitolian and the Palatine and the Quirinal Hill. . . . And Ancus Marcius took in the Caelian mountain (ὄρος) and the Aventine mountain (ὄρος) and the plain between them . . . for it was not a good thing to leave such strong hills outside the walls for any who wanted to get hold of fortifications, nor was he able to fill out the whole circle as far as the Quirinal. Servius, however, detected the gap, for he filled it by adding both the Esquiline Hill and the Viminal. . . . In the beginning, then . . . there was nothing fortunate in their position that could be expected to bring blessings to the city; but when the region had become their own property, through their virtue and their hard work, then there was an accumulation of blessings that went beyond all natural advantages. (5.3.7)

From there he moves on to describe the city and its landscape with the language of beauty, in the passage already discussed in chapter 5. This is partly a human-made landscape, then: threatening mountains, which could shelter enemies, are made benign through being absorbed into the space of the city.

That sense of integration of city and nature is often combined with an emphasis on the fertility of the mountains of Italy which is precisely opposite to

Strabo's representation of sterile mountains elsewhere. Tusculum, he says 'is adorned by the plantations and villas that surround it, and particularly by those that extend below the city towards Rome; for here Tusculum is a fertile and well-watered hill, with many gentle summits and magnificent palace constructions. Next to it are also the foothills of Mount Albanus, which has the same kind of fertility and the same kind of buildings' (5.3.12). We hear later that Mount Vesuvius and Mount Etna are fruitful places too, surrounded by farmland which is nourished by the ashy soil.[31] Those passages are typical of the way in which the mountains of Italy are associated, on Strabo's account, with economic advantage, very much unlike their Spanish and Alpine equivalents. Later, for example, in his list of the advantages which Italy's geography has produced, he tells us that 'since the Apennine mountains stretch along the whole length of Italy, leaving on both sides plains and hills that bear abundant fruit, there is no part of the country that does not share in the advantages of both mountain and plain (6.4.1).[32] He also regularly lists religious and mythical traditions associated with particular mountains and their nearby communities, in a way that reminds us how profoundly embedded they are within a local culture that had been built up over many hundreds of years.[33]

Admittedly many of these Italian cities did have their own moments of resistance to Rome, and Strabo does acknowledge that, in a way that might remind us of the mountain conflicts of Books 3–4; but he also makes it clear that they lay firmly in the past, standing as occasional moments of disruption in a much more orderly history.[34] By contrast, when Strabo leaves mainland Italy briefly in 5.2.7 to take us in turn to Corsica and Sardinia, we see a fleeting recurrence of the motif of unruly mountain tribes guilty of large-scale brigandage and pacified in the very recent past by the Roman army. The same goes for his portrayal of Sicily in 6.2.6, where Strabo describes how he saw a famous brigand from Mount Etna executed in the arena in Rome by being placed on a stage-set version of the mountain which then collapsed into a cage of wild animals underneath. That image encapsulates the difference between the wild bandit country on the edges of Roman civilisation and the domesticated mountains of the mainland: the stage-set Etna is a miniaturised version of the crafted landscapes Strabo has described over and over again for Italy itself.[35]

Strabo's Greece, too, is full of cities built around mountains.[36] Corinth is an obvious example: he tells us that even Acrocorinth itself was incorporated within the wall that used to surround the city (8.6.21). Book 8 also regularly associates mountains with local, religious history.[37] Just occasionally Strabo does mention examples of banditry in the mountains of Greece, in a way which recalls his repeated obsession with that motif for Spain and the Alps, and also for the mountains of Thrace in Book 7 (Mount Haimos in Thrace was the archetypal home of bandits in the ancient imagination). For example at 9.1.4 he describes the Skeironian rocks, and reminds us that this was the setting for the stories about the bandits Skeiron and Pityokamptes who were killed by Theseus. But the whole point here is the antiquity of that episode. In Greece the pacification of the mountains lies in the very distant past: this territory is firmly separated from the rough zones of the world where that process of integration is either very recent or ongoing.

Pontus

In practice, however, the distinction between civilised and uncivilised territories sometimes becomes blurred in the text. Civilised territories can contain motifs associated with uncivilised ones, and vice versa, and some regions in particular seem to stand as marginal zones which do not fit comfortably into one category or the other. That becomes clear especially when we move to Asia Minor, from the Greek islands, in Book 11; and even more so when we get to Strabo's home territory of Pontus,[38] and the other territories of central and northern Anatolia, in Book 12. That halfway status of Pontus is partly a reflection of the topography of the region, which consisted of a narrow coastal strip to the south of the Black Sea containing a number of Greek cities, and the mountainous zone of the Pontic Alps in the interior. As we move into these regions in Book 11, we start to see a recurrence of ethnographic descriptions of uncivilised mountain populations,[39] of the kind which have been largely absent in the previous few books set in Greece, along with a renewed interest in mountain brigands and anecdotes about their pacification. It is clear that we are back in rough and threatening territory. We also start to see more and more frequent references to Mithridates and his wars against the Romans between 88 and 63 BCE, and especially to the campaign against him led by the Roman general Pompey. Once again, as in the Alps, the Roman forces do not have it all their own way. For example, in 12.3.18 Strabo tells the story of a wild mountain people called the Heptakometai who drug Pompey's soldiers with madness-inducing honey and then cut them down. But as our journey goes on more and more signs emerge of Pompey's success in bringing the east and its mountains under control.[40]

However, the focus on Mithridates also complicates Strabo's portrayal of the region.[41] For one thing he makes it clear that he has a family connection with Mithridates, through his grandfather, who served as one of Mithridates' commanders, as Strabo tells us (although he also handed over some of Mithridates' fortresses to the Romans towards the end of the war).[42] Presumably Strabo himself grew up in the area in the aftermath of Pompey's defeat of Mithridates. In Strabo's account of it, the region of Pontus and around turns out to be full of precisely the kind of intricately crafted rock-built towns and fortresses that function as signs of civilisation in Italy and Greece, although in this case they are used as strongholds against the Romans, who usually get the better of them sooner or later.[43]

The most important of those rock-built settlements is Strabo's home city of Amaseia, which is built into the rocky landscape around it:

> it is a marvellously constructed city both by human foresight and by nature,[44] since it can offer at the same time the advantage of a city and a fortress; for it is a high and sheer rock, which descends precipitously down to the river. It has on one side the wall that runs along the edge of the river, where the city is settled, and on the other side the wall that runs up from both sides to the summits. . . . Inside this circuit are both palaces and monuments to the kings. . . . The rock also has inexhaustible reservoirs of water inside it, since two tube-like channels have been dug out, one of them running to the river and the other towards the neck [that is, the ridge between the two peaks]. (12.3.39)

This is another much discussed passage, but as for Strabo's account of the hills of Rome its links with Strabo's wider narrative of mountain domestication have not been discussed at length.[45] Strabo seems to be challenging us to draw our own conclusions about the implications of those links. Clearly Amaseia resembles the rock-built cities of Italy and Greece: there are details here which recall the water channels and palaces of Praeneste and Tusculum. But should we therefore see it as a place that stands apart from the unruly mountain strongholds of Mithridates, which are halfway to the disorderly savagery of the rough mountain people who have been brought under Roman control right across the Mediterranean world, and so perhaps as an elegant compliment to his home city? Or should we see both Amaseia and those other strongholds as a sign of the sophistication of Mithridatic Pontus, whose intricate symbiosis between mountain landscape and urban architecture is very close to what we find in Italy, in a way which complicates any simple opposition between the two?

If we really want to understand Strabo and his mountains, we need to read the text from end to end, and we need to be alert to the extraordinarily rich and complex network of internal correspondences between successive sections. Those correspondences contribute to a strong, basic dichotomy between civilised and uncivilised, but they can also complicate it and undermine it. It is important to stress that the volume of information Strabo accumulates within the text is vast: the passages I have collected here represent just a tiny proportion of the text's references to mountains. They follow each other relentlessly, one peak after the next, with the same familiar motifs endlessly repeated and reconfigured. And as we move through that immensely complicated terrain, the transitions from rough landscape to civilised landscape are sometimes equivocal and hard to perceive, just as they are in any physical journey, as we try to sense the changing character of the land we are passing through, until we step back and contemplate it from a distance.

Strabo celebrates human control over mountain landscapes, then, perhaps more so than any other ancient author, but even for Strabo that control is very far from absolute. In some regions sophisticated and primitive markers of landscape use are intertwined with each other, in a way which reminds us that the civilising process is often partial and incomplete. Strabo is also acutely aware that human communities must work with the landscapes they inhabit, taking the opportunities the land offers them, moulding their cities and their cultures to fit the terrain around them, rather than simply shaping the landscape at will. As we shall see in part IV, a very high proportion of the people of the ancient Mediterranean did live in or around mountains, responding to their surroundings productively and creatively, and defining themselves in relation to the terrain which formed the backdrop to their day-to-day lives. In that sense Strabo is an important precursor of the increasing modern interest in viewing the history of mountains as a global phenomenon that needs to be approached comparatively, with an understanding of the continuities between different mountain regions as well their distinctive features.[46] One of Strabo's achievements, in other words, is to show us how mountain cultures develop in countless different regions and different cities through the intertwining of human culture and physical environment. In doing so he offers us a dazzling image of the variety and richness of human-mountain relations on a global scale.

13

Ammianus Marcellinus: Mountain Peoples and Imperial Boundaries

The Isaurians in the *Res Gestae*

The work of Ammianus Marcellinus offers perhaps the most sensationalistic of all ancient portrayals of mountain peoples and mountain warfare. Ammianus' *Res Gestae* covers the period 353 to 378 CE. It is based in part on his own experience: he describes at length his involvement in fighting against the Persians in what is now eastern Turkey, and his experience of being besieged in the city of Amida. It includes detailed accounts of campaigning in mountainous country, and other kinds of difficult terrain, both there and in many other border territories, for example in Gaul and Germany, and in Cilicia.

Ammianus is very similar to Strabo and to many other ancient history writers in seeing a strong distinction between the civilised centre of the Roman Empire and the barbarian territories outside it. That involves regular descriptions of mountain tribes who threaten the security of the empire. These descriptions include some of the most extreme surviving examples of ancient denigration of mountain populations: Ammianus uses traditional ethnographic stereotypes in vivid and extravagant ways, with very little sign of the kind of flexibility that some have seen in, for example, Herodotus, who leaves open the possibility that barbarian cultures might in some respects compare favourably with their Greek equivalents.

In other respects, however, Ammianus does undermine the boundaries between uncivilised mountain peoples and civilised plains-dwellers, much more so than Strabo does. That is partly because he is less optimistic about the prospect of taming those threatening outside forces: they are a current and ongoing threat in his text, always threatening to overflow the boundaries of the empire, in a way that largely reflects the fourth-century situation, although Ammianus also foregrounds that problem in distinctive ways. It is also because the kind of natural-force imagery he applies to barbarian peoples is also repeatedly attached to the Roman army and also to a series of elite individuals within the civilised heart of the Roman Empire, an effect which prompts us to question the distinction between Roman and barbarian identity. That impression is enabled in part by the structure of his work, which (not unusually for ancient historiography) shuttles backwards and forwards between events in the imperial court and accounts of campaigning on the edges of the empire.

Ammianus is in that sense a distinctive, but neglected figure in the history of the ancient environmental imagination. Mountains and mountain peoples play an important role in his powerful exploration of human-environment relations, especially through his use of imagery. Ammianus' use of natural-force imagery involves a vast range of metaphors referring to animals, storms, and floods among other things: in that sense the mountains are not just the home to many of the populations whose restless violence drives so much of the action of the text, and venues where campaigning armies must face up to threatening landscapes; they also provide some of the guiding images which Ammianus uses to describe the many kinds of threat and turmoil that the Roman Empire faced in this difficult period.

We get our first glimpse of savage mountain populations very near to the beginning of the work as it survives (Books 1–13 are missing). Ammianus shows us the Isaurians 'bursting out' (*proruperunt*) (Ammianus, *Res Gestae* 14.2.1) into open war, a change from their usual pattern of peaceful behaviour interspersed with occasional plundering raids.[1] Ammianus represents them as bestial in their savagery and secrecy: 'in the words of Cicero, as even wild beasts (*ut etiam bestiae*), warned by hunger, return usually to the place where they were once fed, in the same way all of them, coming down from the steep and inaccessible mountains like a whirlwind (*instar turbinis degressi montibus impeditis et arduis*), sought out the regions near to the sea, concealing themselves there in pathless hiding places and enclosed valleys' (14.2.2). They 'creep on all fours along the anchor ropes' (*per ancoralia quadrupedo gradu repentes*) and kill the sailors in their sleep.

The Isaurians then withdraw to the mountains, and use the terrain to their own advantage to frustrate the Romans' attempts to bring them under control.

That process is described with a characteristic emphasis on the difficulties the Roman army faces in the mountains:

> the soldiers were overcome by the strength and numbers of the Isaurians; having been born and brought up among the steep and winding terrain of the mountains (*inter editos recurvosque ambitus montium*), the Isaurians leapt over it (*persultat*) as if it was flat and gentle ground, harming their exposed enemy with missiles from a distance, and terrifying them with savage howling (*ululatu truci perterrens*). Sometimes our infantry, in pursuing them, were forced to climb high slopes; even if they managed to reach the summits, with slipping footsteps (*lapsantibus plantis*), and by grabbing on to undergrowth and thorn-bushes, nevertheless among such narrow and pathless places they were unable to take up their line of battle or to keep their footing, even by a strenuous effort; and while the enemy ran in all directions above them and threw down rocks they had torn off from the cliffs (*rupium abscisa*), they made their way down steep slopes, in great danger; or else if they fought bravely, out of desperate necessity, they were thrown into confusion by vast masses of falling debris. (14.2.5–6)

The Isaurians are in their natural habitat here. They are also described once again through animal imagery, leaping and howling through the rocky ground; earlier they have been described as 'creeping more widely' (*serpentes latius*) (14.2.5). By contrast the Romans are subjected here to all of the standard motifs associated with armies out of their element in the mountains. Like the Carthaginians in the Alps they have difficulty with their feet on the slippery ground: Ammianus' description of the way in which they haul themselves up precariously with their hands by the undergrowth enhances the vividly haptic qualities of the passage, making it clear that the Roman soldiers are immersed in this landscape, close up to it, in a way that involves their whole bodies. They are also at risk from vast rocks rolled down from above, again just like Hannibal's soldiers in the Alps,[2] or even Odysseus and his men fleeing from the Laestrygonians. We are in familiar territory here in literary terms, even as Ammianus draws attention to its alienness for the soldiers themselves. As soon as the Isaurians come down to level ground, however, the tables are turned and they are slaughtered 'like defenceless sheep' (14.2.7), appropriately for pastoral mountain-dwellers. Eventually, after a number of other encounters, the Isaurians 'scattered, as they usually do, and made for the trackless places in the high mountains' (*dispersique, ut solent, avia montium petiere celsorum*) (14.2.20).

But that is not the end of the matter. The Isaurians reappear later in the work, and their tendency to raise their heads over and over again after periods of recovery is represented, again, in animal terms, for example with the imagery of hibernation: 'gradually reviving, just as snakes burst out of their holes in the spring, they came down from their rocky and inaccessible gorges, gathered together into dense bands, and harassed their neighbours with robbery and banditry, eluding the frontier-posts of our soldiers, as one would expect of mountain people (*ut montani*), and easily, by their experience, running through the rocks and thickets' (19.13.1).[3] Here very little seems to have changed: the Isaurians are in their element in the mountains, just as they had been before.

Natural-Force Metaphors

Ammianus' use of natural-force imagery in his depictions of the Isaurians is of course not his invention, but he does use it distinctively and with unusual frequency and intensity. We find similar metaphors in Tacitus, who was one of Ammianus' key models, in his many descriptions of provincial revolt.[4] The same goes for descriptions of revolt in other contemporaries of Ammianus.[5] But one of the things that makes Ammianus' version stand out is his fascination with the recurring rhythms of revolt, where hostile tribes hide away and regain their strength, before bursting out again, in a relentless rhythm of containment and release. He is fascinated not only by images that equate human populations with storms or rivers or wild animals, but also by descriptions of hidden lairs, and by verbs of bursting or overflowing. That pattern implies a kind of restless, insatiable energy, an impression which is often then enhanced by the description of hostile populations roaming or wandering at will in search of plunder.[6] And it becomes particularly frequent in the last third of the work: over and over again we see barbarians retreating to the mountains,[7] where the Roman army is cautious about following, knowing that their opponents have the advantage of local knowledge.[8] Images of eruption also intensify in the closing sections of the work,[9] in a way which prepares for the climactic and disastrous overspilling of the Huns and the Goths into Roman territory in Book 31 which we will see more of later on.

Ammianus is also distinctive for the way in which he applies that kind of imagery widely, not only to barbarian tribes but also to Romans, including even members of the Roman elite. Again there are precedents for that. Most obviously one might think of the *Iliad*, where soldiers from both sides of the conflict are associated over and over again with animals and storms and rivers in flood. One effect is to celebrate the strength and bravery of individual heroes, but those similes also at the same time create an impression of battle as an overwhelming, more-than-human force that overpowers and threatens all the human actors indiscriminately, not least in the similes that apply to vast bodies of troops collectively rather than to particular warriors.[10] In Ammianus' text too, this kind of overwhelming natural-force imagery can be applied to Roman and barbarian alike. But what makes Ammianus stand out is the way in which he extends that so frequently to members of the imperial family and the imperial court whose actions are characterised by Ammianus in negative terms, even in contexts far removed from battle situations,[11] as if he is interested in all those wild populations in part because they give him a metaphor for what is happening in the centre of Roman politics. Here too we often see a distinctive oscillation between concealment and destruction.[12]

To take an example again from the very beginning of the work as it survives, those encounters with the Isaurians are not the first use of natural-force imagery and animal imagery in Book 14. Ammianus has already used equivalent metaphors in the very opening pages, in describing Gallus, who had recently been given the title of Caesar by his cousin the ruling emperor Constantius II. Ammianus tells us first that the empire was exposed to new 'storms' (*tempestates*) by the 'gusts of raging fortune' (*fortunae saevientis procellae*) (14.1.1), through Gallus' misdeeds. After an initial survey of those crimes, which include the encouragement of informers and the execution of innocent men, Ammianus returns to that storm imagery in his final summary, in a structure of ring composition: Gallus, he says, 'rushed forward with irreversible force, like a fast-flowing river' (*instar rapidi fluminis, irrevocabili impetu ferebatur*) (14.1.10). The phrase *instar rapidi fluminis* ('like a fast-flowing river'), with its epic simile connotations, comes just a few lines before the equivalent phrase *instar turbinis* ('like a whirlwind') used for the Isaurians.[13] It is hard to avoid the conclusion that Gallus' actions are equivalent in their destructiveness to the incursions of the Isaurians, and that he carries within him something of the natural savagery and violence that we might more usually associate with barbarian populations who are shaped, according to ancient ideas about environmental determinism, by the harshness of the landscape they inhabit.

Those effects are enhanced by the allusiveness of Ammianus' writing at this point. We might notice that the animal imagery Ammianus uses to introduce the Isaurians is drawn from a domestic context, rather than a military one, from Cicero's description of a case of judicial corruption in his *Pro Cluentio*

(25, 67–68). For readers who recognise the reference it may be no surprise when Ammianus, like Cicero, uses related metaphors for wrongdoing and untrustworthiness within the Roman elite. Ammianus' metaphors here also recall the long series of force-of-nature images that characterise the conflict between Aeneas and Turnus in *Aeneid* 12, for example at *Aeneid* 12.523–28, where both Aeneas and Turnus are described as rapid rivers pouring down from the mountainsides and bringing destruction in their wake.[14] At *Aeneid* 12.923, Aeneas' spear is described as being like a black whirlwind (*atri turbinis instar*) as it pierces Turnus' defences in that final decisive blow of the poem. The fact that the destructive powers of Aeneas are being transferred here to the Isaurians in that phrase *instar turbinis* points us to the common ground between barbarians and Romans that runs right through Ammianus' work.

That initial description of Gallus, and its juxtaposition with the savagery of the Isaurians, sets the standard for everything that follows. Over and over again images of storm are applied to the actions of fate in order to describe disastrous developments within the imperial court, just as they are in those opening lines of Book 14.[15] We also see Isaurian-style animal imagery applied to individual Romans who attract Ammianus' contempt, especially the imagery of snakes and other creeping animals hiding away in their lairs until the moment when they can burst out into open view. Soon after the incident with the Isaurians—and after a brief introduction to the external threats posed by the Persians, who would have caused devastation 'like a thunderbolt' (*fulminis modo*) if they had been successful in their plans (14.3.2), and the Saracens, who have brought destruction 'like rapacious kites' (*milvorum rapacium similes*) (14.4.1)—Ammianus introduces the *notarius* Paulus, who is described as 'a kind of viper' (*coluber quidam*), who was 'extremely clever in scenting out hidden means of danger (*vias periculorum occultas*) for others' (14.5.6). Ammianus tells us that he brings about the arrest of many innocent people, and 'like a river, suddenly inundated the fortunes of many' (*fluminis modo fortunis complurium sese repentinus infudit*).[16] Later Arbitio makes false accusations against the general Ursicinus, and is compared with 'an underground snake, sitting in ambush beneath its hidden entrance-hole, watching each passer-by and attacking him with a sudden assault' (15.2.4). And after the death of Julian one of the pretenders to the imperial throne, Procopius, is described in similar terms: 'These things Procopius observed secretly. . . . He lay in ambush like a beast of prey, ready to leap out straight away on seeing anything which could be taken' (26.6.10). These storms and rivers in flood and wild beasts are not exclusively mountain images, of course, but they are often associated with mountain contexts and mountain peoples, as in the Isaurian passages. The image of the hiding place in particular is characteristic of Ammianus: he returns to it over and over again both to describe barbarian tribes regathering their strength in the mountains and members of the imperial court biding their time, on the lookout for the chance to spread their poison.

Metaphors of natural violence are also applied repeatedly to both Roman and barbarian forces in the long series of campaign narratives that follow. There are lots of scenes along those lines in the successive scenes of campaigning set in Gaul and in Germany around the Rhine. Many of Ammianus' most extravagant uses of that imagery are reserved for barbarian forces. At 16.5.17 the barbarian tribes who break out into violence are 'like wild beasts (*utque bestiae*) accustomed to live by plundering', who continue in their habits even when new and stronger guards are put in place: that metaphor recalls the repetitiveness and persistence of the bestial Isaurians (*ut etiam bestiae*) (14.2.2). In some cases, however, it is the Roman troops who are compared with overwhelming natural forces.[17] At 15.4 the Romans are ambushed by the Alamanni, who 'spring out from their hiding places unexpectedly' (*improvise e latebris ... exsiliunt*) (15.4.8). The next day, however, in response, it is the Romans who pour out 'like a river on their enemies' (*more fluminis hostibus superfusi*) (15.4.11). At 17.8.4, the Romans under Julian are attacking another tribe farther north: we hear that he 'struck them like a thunderstorm' (*tamquam fulminis turbo perculsit*).

Bodily Immersion: Mountains, Rivers, Sea

Both Roman and barbarian armies are also often at risk of being overwhelmed by threatening landscapes, often in ways that emphasise their bodily entanglement and immersion in the environment.[18] We have seen already that in the mountains both the Romans and their enemies blend with the landscapes they are operating in: the barbarians like animals completely at home in the rocks, the Romans fighting for each step, clinging on to the undergrowth, with their bodies exposed to the slippery ground and the rocks thrown down from above. That kind of scene is repeated in other passages too. The conflict with the Alamanni in Germany resurfaces sporadically even after the death of Julian in battle against the Persians in 363. Five years later, in 368, the emperor Valentinian launches a concerted campaign against them, hoping to stamp out the threat once and for all, and succeeds in defeating them in battle at Solicinium. That success comes despite the fact that the enemy, 'putting trust in their knowledge of the ground', have retreated to 'a very high mountain, precipitous and impassable with rough hills on all sides (*montem... praecelsum, per confragosos colles undique praeruptum et invium*), except on the north, where it had an easy and gentle slope' (27.10.9). Valentinian is nearly killed while inspecting the cliffs, having arrogantly assumed that he would be able to find a route to the summit other than the one the scouts had picked out: 'as he was making his way by a winding route through unknown ground and swampy marshes (*per ignota... et palustres uligines devius tendens*), he would have died by the sudden assault of an ambushing band concealed in a hidden spot, had he not as a last resort spurred his horse and retreated through the slippery mud (*per labilem limum*)' (27.10.11). Finally and laboriously the Romans take the summit, despite being out of their element: 'brandishing their spears, they approached the rocks that lay in their path, and tried to get up to the higher slopes, while the Alamanni tried to push them back; and then the whole weight of the army came up, and with the same troops in the front rank, through places that were rough and overgrown with thickets, with a huge effort of strength, they forced their way on to the high ground' (27.10.12). The dominant impression here once again is of the desperate difficulty of mountain warfare. Conquest of the Alamanni and of the summit are entangled with each other: victory comes only from the painstaking process of dragging themselves upwards step by step to the top of the mountain. In another incident soon afterwards, a group of Roman soldiers is killed while fortifying Mount Pirus on the far side of the Rhine (28.2.5–9): the barbarians 'leapt out' (*prosiluit*) from the fold of a nearby hill; the Romans are half-naked and 'still carrying earth' (*humum etiam tum gestantes*) (28.2.8). Both Romans and barbarians here are immersed in the environment. In this case that state of closeness to the earth brings disaster for the Romans.

Images of immersion in threatening environments, both in this kind of successful manoeuvre and in incidents of military disaster, are common for other kinds of landscape too, especially for rivers, again for both Romans and barbarians. For example, the metaphors of natural force that Ammianus loves are literalised in one remarkable passage from Julian's campaign against the Alamanni. The enemy are described fleeing, like sailors and passengers rushing to get away from a stormy sea (16.12.51); and then are quite literally overwhelmed and drowned as they try to swim across the river: some are carried along like logs, and their blood mingles with the water of the river (16.12.57). We might feel that this is an appropriate end for barbarians, absorbed back into the harsh landscape which has shaped them in the first place. Elsewhere, however, Roman soldiers are subject to the same fate, for example in an encounter in Persia where a detachment of Roman troops on their way to Samosata, including Ammianus himself, are ambushed and forced to swim in flight across the river Tigris. The images of bodily absorption in the waters—'some hurled themselves from there headlong, but got stuck in the shallows, with their weapons entangled; others were swallowed up, dragged down in the eddying pools' (18.8.9)—are closely reminiscent of that earlier account of the flight of the Alamanni.[19] Those two scenes are one of a series of drowning and flooding images in Ammianus' work, the most famous of which is his account of the tsunami of 365 CE, which inflicts indiscriminate damage and drowning on a vast scale (26.10.15–19). That passage has resonances, as much as any other passage of ancient historiography, with modern experiences of and representations of environmental disaster. It also forms one of the climactic examples of Ammianus' sustained exploration of the universal vulnerability of human populations in their relationship with the environment.[20] Edward Gibbon famously said of this passage that 'such is the bad taste of Ammianus ... that it is not easy to distinguish his facts from his metaphors'.[21] That seems precisely the point: here the metaphors of flooding that recur so frequently in the rest of the work become literalised in a way which gives expression to the indiscriminate power of nature.[22] In Ammianus' worldview barbarians and Romans alike can embody and be overwhelmed by the violence of the natural world.[23]

Viewing from Above

That is not to say that Ammianus has no interest in images of control over mountain landscapes. Perhaps the most famous example comes in his account, just a few pages before those chaotic ambush scenes on the banks of the Tigris, of one of his first experiences of campaigning against the Persians in Mesopotamia, in the mountainous terrain that stretches from what is now southern Turkey through the east of Syria and into northern Iraq. On arrival in the region Ammianus, serving under the command of the Roman general Ursicinus, rushes to the city of Nisibis, just as the Persian forces are closing in. He is nearly captured, but rides on, with Persian soldiers in pursuit, to alert the Roman forces at the fortress of Amudis; they hide from the Persians in the mountains and then go on to the city of Amida. From there Ammianus is sent on a secret mission to the region of Corduene farther east, which is ruled by a Persian satrap with Roman sympathies:

I travelled over pathless mountains and through steep gorges to get there (*per avios montes angustiasque praecipites veni*).... Then with one silent companion who knew the country I was sent to some very high cliffs (*ad praecelsas rupes*) a long way from there, from where, if human eyesight was not fallible, even the tiniest of objects would have been visible from fifty miles away. (18.6.21)

At dawn of the third day, Ammianus tells us, 'we saw the whole circuit of lands spread out below us ... filled with countless columns of troops, with the king leading the way, glowing brightly with the splendour of his clothing (*vestis claritudine rutilantem*)' (18.6.22). Ammianus claims to be able to identify also the leaders riding to the left and right of the king. He then returns to his commander, 'through deserted and solitary places' (18.7.2), with news of the Persian forces. The implausibility of Ammianus' account has often been pointed out, with his claim to be able to see in extraordinary detail from a vast distance, but the passage nevertheless gives us a powerful image of Ammianus' use of mountain terrain to gain military advantage, and also at the same time a metaphor for his authorial control.[24]

The military incidents he describes in these books stand side by side not only with a number of other occasions when knowledge of the mountains and ability to navigate through them is used for military and personal advantage but also with a series of geographical passages which lay out Ammianus' knowledge of the terrain and the populations of the various regions he is dealing with, and which include extensive reference to the mountains, in the manner of Herodotus and Strabo and others.[25] For example, the second half of Book 23 includes a long account of the different regions and peoples of the Persian Empire, followed by a detailed account of the emperor Julian's campaign against them, in which Ammianus also participated. Over and over again in this account mountains are used as landmarks for situating particular tribes: 'All the inhabitants of these lands are spread out over a very wide area, and very great mountain heights stand over them, which they call Zagrus, Orontes, and Iasonius. Those who inhabit the western side of the very high mountain Coronus are blessed with abundant fields of crops and vineyards' (23.6.28–29). And similarly later:

Next the Sogdiani inhabit the foot of the mountains which they call the Sogdii.... Next to these are the Sacae, a savage tribe, who live in a rough land which is fruitful only for cattle, and is therefore not adorned with cities. The mountains Ascanimia and Comedus stand over it.... Along the slopes and spurs of the mountains which they call Imavi and Apurii, there are various Scythians within Persian territory . . . (23.6.59–61)

Ammianus' sketch of the Persian empire is typical: it seems to imply that he can see the whole of that territory laid out in front of him. His cartographical perspective here, as if from above, projects an image of authorial control and far-sightedness.[26]

'Like a Snowstorm from the High Mountains': The Huns and the Goths

However, this kind of control over mountain territory is always at risk of being drowned out by more pessimistic images of threat. We see both strands in the extraordinary final book, Book 31, jostling against each other for the upper hand in the narrative. In some respects Book 31 is quite different from what has come before,[27] but for all those differences Ammianus clearly intended his readers to be alert to its relationship with the rest of the work.[28] As it stands, the greater extravagance of this book's ethnographic sections represents a climactic intensification of the ways of writing about barbarian peoples[29] that we have encountered in earlier books, rather than a radically different approach. Ammianus first introduces the Huns, 'who were barely known from ancient records', and tells us that they 'exceeded every limit of savagery' (31.2.1). They are an object of terror even for other barbarians around them: the other Gothic people decide that they need to move away when they hear about the appearance of 'a previously unfamiliar race of men, who had recently risen from some hidden cavity, like a snowstorm from the high mountains', which 'was seizing or destroying everything in its way' (31.3.8). The Huns live without homes and without cooking; they are monstrously ugly and misshapen, but tough: 'wandering haphazardly through the mountains and woods, they grow accustomed to cold and hunger and thirst from their cradles' (31.2.4). Ammianus exercises a kind of limited control over this new threat through his cartographic and ethnographic knowledge.[30] At the same time he draws attention to their potential to exceed any kind of order that he or the forces of the Roman Empire more broadly can impose. That difficulty is conveyed by his repetition of many of the motifs of natural violence which have been used over and over again both for external threats like the Isaurians and for dangerous forces within the Roman elite itself, for example in that image of the snowstorm in 31.3.8 bursting out from its place of concealment.

The sense of uncontainability intensifies in what follows. As the book goes on, we see the Huns and the other barbarian tribes threatening and at times overrunning the edges of the empire. The Goths are given permission to cross the Danube by Valens, precisely in order to escape from the Huns, a decision that Ammianus represents as disastrous. Their crossing of the Danube goes wrong: many of them are drowned in the process (31.4.5). That scene clearly has negative connotations, not least because it sets them so far apart from the traditions of heroic river crossing scenes.[31] But its function is not straightforwardly to separate the Goths from the more civilised peoples within the Roman Empire: this is another in the long series of drowning scenes in the work, which threaten Greeks and Romans as much as barbarians. It is immediately followed by the use of natural-disaster imagery to describe not the Goths themselves but those who are urging their acceptance within the bounds of empire: 'in this way by the stormy eagerness (*turbido ... studio*) of insistent men was the destruction (*pernicies*) of the Roman world advanced' (31.4.6). As so often, natural disaster is not just something that comes from without; it also infects the heart of empire. The subsequent disturbances caused by the Goths are themselves described in similarly elemental terms. We hear that 'the barriers of our frontier were unlocked and the realm of savagery was spreading far and wide columns of armed men like glowing ashes from Aetna' (31.4.9). There is more fighting in the mountains, for example between the Goths and the Romans around Mount Haimos in Thrace: the Romans hope to trap them there in the narrow gorges by building huge barricades. The Roman general Saturninus then arrives and decides to relax the blockade and withdraws.[32] The barbarians break free, 'like beasts that had broken their cages' (31.8.9), overwhelming the plains of Thrace with atrocities. A little later we see the Roman Frigeridus fortifying the Succi pass in the Haimos mountains to prevent the barbarians from overflowing like 'torrents foaming with molten snow' (31.10.21). Later the Gothic cavalry, combined with forces from the Halani, 'burst out like a thunderbolt near high mountains (*ut fulmen prope montes celsos*)' (31.12.17). They make for the city of Adrianople 'like wild beasts made more cruelly savage by the stimulus of blood' (31.15.2).[33] They go on to inflict one of the Roman army's most disastrous defeats there at the Battle of Adrianople in 378 CE, killing the emperor Valens, in the last major action of Ammianus' history.

This gathering storm of trouble that spills over the edges of the empire makes for an unsettling conclusion to the work. The book ends with this barbarian flood held at bay by the Roman army. The Goths lose confidence and head northwards 'as far as the foot of the Julian Alps (*ad usque radices Alpium Iuliarum*), formerly called the Venetic Alps' (31.16.7), their restless aggression transformed as often in these accounts into restless and aimless wandering. At the same time all the Goths living in Roman cities are slaughtered on a single day: 'this sensible plan was carried out without uproar or delay, and the eastern provinces were thus snatched from great dangers' (31.16.9). That horrifyingly casual endorsement of genocide is the closing incident of the work, apart from a brief three-sentence epilogue. The narrative progression that culminates in this final book is nevertheless both unmissable and disturbing—a story of increasing threat from the barbarian forces beyond the edges of the empire, much of it emerging from mountain territories. The recurring patterns of containment and eruption that we have seen throughout make that ending rather ominous, even pessimistic, despite the fact that our final glimpse is of the Roman forces in control. It is only when we read these mountain scenes as part of a series that we can appreciate their full significance. The events of Book 31 finish in 379, but Ammianus seems to have been writing later, and certainly after the Roman signature of a treaty with the Goths in 382.[34] Others have suggested before that Ammianus may have been opposed to or at any rate unconvinced by that treaty.[35] Presumably the important point is that he approves of the radical approach to eliminating the capacity of the Goths to harm the Roman Empire, in contrast with the more tentative alternative of offering them a treaty which might allow them to return as a threat in future.[36] Certainly for anyone who has read the text from beginning to end the retreat of the Goths to the Julian Alps has ominous undertones beneath its reassuring surface.[37] There is a sense of inevitability in these endless cycles of suppression and overspilling which recur right through his narrative, and most conspicuously of all in this final book. If we have learnt one thing from the rest of the text it is that mountain peoples are always liable to burst back out of their hiding places, like the savage and elemental forces of nature they are repeatedly associated with.

Mountains—like the people who inhabit them—are regularly represented in ancient historiography as wild and barely controllable places on the edges of civilisation. That pattern is often in tension, however, with an interest in celebrating human control over mountain terrain, albeit usually in a way that is precarious and partial. The best way to appreciate those effects is to read these texts from beginning to end, staying alert to the way in which they weave together distinctive landscape narratives from their shared motifs. Different texts handle the balance between those different elements differently: some are more optimistic and more celebratory than others about the prospect of bringing the mountains within civilisation; in others the sense of mountains as places beyond control is more insistent. The same is true for modern mountaineering literature, which originates in part from traditions of military campaign narratives rooted ultimately in ancient Greek and Roman literature. Many ancient texts articulate those tensions through their juxtaposition of a range of different viewpoints: they give us examples of cartographic viewing, which implies the exercise of authorial and military control over landscape, along with instances of outstanding ingenuity and perceptiveness on the part of generals in mountain terrain, side by side with a more close-up, restricted viewpoint, where the human body is vulnerable to or even immersed in the landscape. That kind of immersion is generally not viewed positively in ancient texts; neither is the closeness of barbarian populations to the harsh landscapes they inhabit. Nevertheless many of these texts share with modern environmental writing an awareness of the prevalence and even the inevitability of entanglement between humans and their environment. Ammianus is a classic case of that: it is not only the barbarian peoples of the text who are shaped by and vulnerable to the natural forces associated with the mountains, but also the Roman soldiers who have to encounter those threatening landscapes in very bodily ways in battle situations, and who have to fight incessantly to prevent hordes of barbarians from overrunning the empire from the mountain territories on its margins, like swollen mountain torrents. Ammianus gives us a global view of the Roman struggle to contain these threats, which are represented as environmental as much as human dangers. Even members of the imperial court and the imperial family, who are often far removed from the arenas of provincial revolt, are marked by and at risk from the forces of animal cruelty and natural disaster, which are associated repeatedly with mountain landscapes from the very beginning of the text as it survives, and which overflow into all corners of the work.

PART IV
Living in the Mountains

14

Mountain and City

Mountain Communities

The Cyclops Polyphemus is one of the first mountain people of European literature. In the *Odyssey* he is a figure far removed from urban civilisation. When Odysseus introduces the Cyclopes to the audience of his story, the hyper-civilised Phaiacians, he tells us that 'they do not have council meetings or laws, but they inhabit the peaks of the high mountains in hollow caves, and each of them rules over his children and wives, nor do they pay any attention to each other' (Homer, *Odyssey* 9.113–15).[1] How exactly Odysseus knows all of this from his brief visit is not clear, but it is striking that this sketch anticipates the ethnographic language that was so common in later centuries: if the Cyclopes are the first people of the mountains, then Odysseus is ancient literature's first ethnographer. The Cyclopes' way of life is pastoral, like all of the odd communities Odysseus visits in the travels he recounts in Books 9–12, none of whom have any signs of agriculture. After their first night in his cave Polyphemus eats two of Odysseus' companions for breakfast and then sets out to pasture his sheep: 'with much whistling, he turned his flocks towards the mountain' (9.315). It is clear that he shares the inhuman quality of his surroundings: 'He was a monstrous marvel; he was not like a grain-eating human, but like a wooded peak of the high mountains, which is visible isolated from the others' (9.190–92).[2]

The association between mountains and uncivilised populations was very widespread in ancient Greek and Latin literature—that is immediately clear from authors like Strabo and Ammianus, among many others—but that image conceals a much more complex reality. In many parts of the Mediterranean we are now in a position to look beyond the negative images that dominate Greek and Roman literature, thanks in part to important developments in the archaeology of mountain regions, in order to recapture something of the highly developed local cultures of those who inhabited the mountains of the ancient Mediterranean. Mountains were also often connected both economically and culturally with the cities that lay close to them.[3] Even texts that indulge in negative stereotypes of mountain populations often acknowledge the possibility of more positive versions of mountain life and recognise the entanglement between mountain territories and urban fabric. The Homeric poems, especially the *Iliad*, stress the importance of mountains for local identity, both for the Trojans and for many of the communities that make up the Greek army.[4] Strabo shows us how mountains can be incorporated within urban space in the territory of Greece and Italy, in contrast with the barely tamed uplands (as he represents them) of the Alps and Spain. The region of Isauria in some respects exemplifies the split between mountain-dwellers and plains-dwellers which has often been seen as crucial to Mediterranean history,[5] but it has become increasingly clear nonetheless that Isaurian society in the Roman imperial period was wealthy and sophisticated, and deeply influenced by elite Greco-Roman culture, despite its reputation for unruliness.[6]

The influence of urban life over mountain economies and cultures has been a constant feature of European mountain history through the medieval world into the present.[7] At the same time we have learned more and more to put aside our own urbanised frameworks of understanding, and our assumption that climbing to summits is the only proper subject for mountain writing, in seeking to understand the day-to-day histories of those who live and work in mountain territories.[8] A major part of the cross-disciplinary field of mountain studies now devotes its energy to giving a voice to mountain peoples across the world, aiming to understand their distinctive histories and the distinctive challenges they have to deal with in the face of cultural and environmental changes, linked for example with depopulation and climate change.[9] The history of Nan Shepherd's book *The Living Mountain* over the past few decades exemplifies that shift. It was written in the 1940s, but not published until 1977, and it is only recently that it has gained an international reputation. Shepherd shows very little interest in the summits; instead her book offers an intricately observed picture of the Cairngorms in Scotland in all their different moods and seasons and at all altitudes, and of the people of the Cairngorms and their organic link with the environment they inhabit: 'the crofts and small hill-farms wrested from the heather and kept productive by unremitting labour'.[10]

In the mountains of the Mediterranean, Northern European visitors in the nineteenth century largely replicated ancient dismissiveness about mountain populations. It was not until the second half of the twentieth century that outsiders began to write about Mediterranean mountain communities from a more anthropological perspective, using knowledge built up in some cases from many years of living and observing in mountain communities: anthropologists like John Campbell, who lived and worked for years among the pastoral Sarakatsani in the far northwest of Greece, and showed in painstaking detail how their distinctive notions of honour and kinship were related to their pastoral practice;[11] or Juliet du Boulay, in her account of life in a mountain village in Evia (Euboia).[12] That is not to say that ancient mountain-dwellers were exactly like their modern counterparts. The idea that mountain communities have a special antiquity, that they represent almost a living link with the very ancient past, unaffected by changing political boundaries and practices, is in itself a long-standing and in some cases belittling stereotype, linked with the idea of mountains themselves as places of great antiquity and isolation. But what the anthropological work of Campbell and others does allow us to glimpse is the likelihood that ancient mountain communities would have had a similar complexity to those modern mountain societies, even if it is not frequently acknowledged or understood by ancient elite authors.[13]

Environmental History in the Mountains of the Mediterranean

Throughout human history there has been an enormous variety in human responses to mountain environments. One factor is environmental variation, but just as important is the way in which different communities have responded differently to similar environmental conditions. That is clear for present-day upland populations,[14] just as it is for their counterparts from Greek and Roman antiquity. Mountains dominate the topography of the Mediterranean world, and shape the activities and identities of its inhabitants, but there are limits to how far we can generalise about them. One of the distinctive features of Mediterranean landscape is in fact its huge regional variation, even down to the level of small microregions which can face distinctive challenges very different from those in other microregions just a few miles away.[15] This geographical variation is accompanied by a wide range of different forms of economic activity. That is not to say that landscape shapes society straightforwardly and inevitably: local environmental knowledge brings different solutions in different places, and particular local economies are shaped by their interaction with a network of other microecologies around them.

The material evidence has been crucial in helping us to understand this variety better for mountain regions. Archaeological data from survey projects, and scientific studies of the palaeoenvironmental evidence, allow us to reconstruct chronological and geographical variations in landscape use in a degree of detail which would have been almost unimaginable just a few decades ago.[16] That evidence points to the existence of pastoral activity in the mountains even quite early in the human history of the Mediterranean, in the fifth millennium BCE.[17] It also shows us, however, that the fluctuations in the degree of human activity in high-altitude zones over time were far from uniform, even in regions which seem to have been quite similar to each other in environmental terms. Forms of environmental determinism have continued to influence modern accounts of the ancient Mediterranean, in studies which assume that human populations are constrained or even shaped by their environments. It is certainly true that zonation in mountain landscapes, where variations in altitude and slope orientation lead to sharp variations in temperature and weather conditions over a very short horizontal distance, impose limits on the possibilities for productive activity at different levels which will tend to be replicated more or less in adjacent valleys and slopes.[18] However, more recent work has emphasised by contrast the contingency and variability of local responses, even in communities relatively close to each other.[19]

That evidence helps to show how difficult it is to generalise about the similarities and differences between ancient and modern environmental problems. Clearly ancient mountain communities did at various times face relatively rapid oscillations in climate conditions, which would have challenged them to develop new forms of local knowledge of their environments,[20] but those developments were not uniform: changes in climate might sometimes have had quite different effects even in adjacent valleys,[21] and there is certainly nothing comparable to modern awareness of climate change as a rapidly developing phenomenon caused by human intervention. In other respects too, the parallels that have often been claimed between instances of human degradation of the environment in the ancient world and its modern equivalents are quite precarious. To take just the best known example, the Roman period on some accounts saw massive deforestation, which is sometimes taken to prefigure the kinds of environmental change brought about by modern industrialised societies. It has become increasingly clear that the evidence for that claim is patchy. In fact some of the most significant clearance of forests seems to have happened centuries if not millennia before,[22] and the degree of regional variation in later deforestation and regrowth is so pronounced that any generalisation about environmental damage comes to seem very unreliable.[23] Attempts to take ancient attitudes to the environment as precursors to their modern equivalents on the basis of oversimplistic readings of a few key texts have increasingly been exposed as inadequate.[24] That is not to deny that there are important parallels between ancient and modern environmental challenges, or that ancient environmental thinking can be a valuable resource for our own responses to ecological problems in the present. But that relationship is never a simple one, nor can it ever be understood just from the evidence of ancient literature: if we want to understand ancient literary representations of environmental damage, they need to be viewed side by side with the material evidence in all its complexity.

Mountains and Identity

Let us return again for a moment to where we started, to Mount Lykaion in Arkadia. Arkadia is an obvious place to look if we want to see behind the stereotypes of mountain populations.[25] The region tends to be represented in ancient texts either as an idyllic pastoral landscape or as a poverty-stricken backwater. The material evidence, archaeological and coin evidence in particular, exposes the inadequacy of those images. There is no reason to assume that levels of poverty were exceptional: because of the fact that its economy depended heavily on natural resources, Arkadia had a limit to the size of population it could support. It did, however, have a surprising amount of agricultural land, and lots of timber, in addition to its flocks. It also seems to have had a good wagon-road network (traces of it survive in eastern Arkadia), and lots of thriving and interconnected cities, which were themselves closely integrated with the rural territories that surrounded them. Paradoxically, the mountainous topography seems to have made Arkadian identity more cohesive rather than less. The political system we see in places like Attica, with one big city, Athens, acting as a focal point for a big surrounding area, tends not to work well in somewhere like Arkadia, where different communities are necessarily more split up from each other by geographical realities. Instead, ethnic identity, the idea of shared membership of a common *ethnos* ('people' or 'tribe'), is a better way of drawing together so many separate microregions.[26]

In Arkadia, Mount Lykaion itself played a major role in that interconnectedness.[27] We have seen already how the festival of the Lykaia on the slopes of Mount Lykaion was a focus for Arkadian identity. It was celebrated in coin issues by the Arkadian league in the fourth century BCE with images of Zeus

Lykaios (compare figure 7.5). Processions from the city of Megalopolis, and other cities too, would have wound their way through the long miles to these shrines, acting out the inclusion of the mountains within the territory of the city and the wider region.[28] Pausanias also mentions a sanctuary of Apollo on the eastern slopes of Mount Lykaion, facing Megalopolitan territory: 'At the annual festival celebrated for this god they sacrifice a boar to Apollo the Helper in the market-place, and then once they have slaughtered it they take it straight to the sanctuary of Parrhasian Apollo in procession with piping, cut out and burn the thighs, and consume the victim there and then' (Pausanias, *Periegesis* 8.38.8). Like so many of the rituals Pausanias reports, the precise significance of this one is a mystery—it may even have been a mystery to those who carried it out by the time Pausanias was writing—but one of its functions is clearly to link the *agora*, as the symbolic centre of the city, with the mountain. There is evidence for many other similar cults in Arkadia where mountaintop worship is closely duplicated in a nearby city.[29]

In many modern countries and cultures too, mountains have been bound up with a sense of national and local identity.[30] Mountains have been important most often as borders. The notion of distinct populations developing within plains surrounded by mountains was prominent especially in the late nineteenth and early twentieth centuries.[31] In other cases mountains are envisaged as backbones or centres around which a country or region is formed. In some cases both conceptions are combined, as in the example of France, which is bounded by the Jura, the Alps, and the Pyrenees, but also centred on the mountains of the Massif Central.[32]

What is less often acknowledged in contemporary mountain studies is the fact that those phenomena have countless premodern and especially classical precedents. Herodotus in his *Histories* frequently takes mountains as boundaries for the territory and identity of particular peoples;[33] Roman writers repeatedly represent the Alps as a frontier and a barrier to invasion.[34] The notion of mountains at the heart of a region's territory was common too. As already noted, fragmentation often paradoxically drove mountain communities to construct and maintain relations of interconnectedness.[35] In that regard the strong sense of regional identity in Arkadia was typical of what we find in other ancient mountain areas too. For example, Phokis, the region around Mount Parnassos in northern Greece, like Arkadia developed a strong sense of ethnic rather than civic identity, uniting diverse and separated communities, precisely because of the dominance of the mountains.[36] The Arkadian use of religious ritual to enhance the shared identity of mountain communities also has many parallels. One recent publication uses viewshed analysis to analyse the regional significance of the sanctuary of the god Zeus Stratios, on a mountain summit near to Amaseia in north-central Turkey, to show that the territory from which the smoke of sacrifice could be seen very closely corresponded to the territory on whose behalf those sacrifices were carried out.[37] The same was true equally at the edges of Greek and Roman civilisation. For example, excavations at a sanctuary at the Gurzuf Saddle Pass in the mountains of Crimea on the Black Sea have shown how the site acted as a focus for communal identity for the fragmented mountain populations of the region.[38]

Mountains could also be important for cities, which in the ancient world, in the absence of any modern notion of the nation-state, tended to act as autonomous political entities, especially in classical and Hellenistic Greece. For example, the role of mountains as boundary markers was frequently important, and in some cases was the subject of dispute. An inscription from the third century BCE describes the decision of arbitrators from Megara called in by the city of Epidauros in the Peloponnese in order to redefine its borders with neighbouring Corinth: '... from the peak of Korduleion to the peak of Halieion; from Halieion to the peak of Keraunion; from Keraunion to the peak of Korniatis; from Korniatis to the road on the ridge of Korniatis ... from the peak of Phaga to the peak of Aigipura ...' (*Sylloge inscriptionum graecarum*, 3rd edition, 471), and so on at great length.[39] There are many modern parallels for that process of negotiation and arbitration in relation to mountainous borders between countries, made necessary by the fact that the principle of a 'natural boundary' has often been hard to apply in practice, for example because ridge lines and watersheds, two of the most obvious markers one might use to determine the position of a boundary line in the mountains, do not necessarily coincide.[40]

Mountains were also depicted commonly on ancient coins, as symbols of civic or regional identity. The most frequently represented mountain in the whole of classical antiquity is Mount Argaios (today Mount Erciyes), a massive volcanic mountain in Cappadocia in eastern Turkey, which stands at a height of just below 4,000 metres, and is visible from a vast distance. There are hundreds of surviving coins struck by the nearby city of Caesarea that depict the mountain. The example here (figure 14.1) is from the early third century CE. These coins tend to show the mountain in stylised form, often with a star above the mountain; others have personified figures on the summit, or wreaths or eagles; some show trees on the slopes or a u-shape to indicate the crater.[41]

FIGURE 14.1. Coin showing the head of Julia Maesa, grandmother of the emperors Elagabalus and Severus Alexander (obverse) and Mount Argaios (reverse), 221–224 CE. Caesarea, Cappadocia. The Picture Art Collection / Alamy Stock Photo.

There are other examples too, many of them depicting religious buildings on hills or mountains close to the city, for example in surviving coin images of Acrocorinth, or of the Acropolis at Athens, of the mountain sanctuary of Venus Erucina from the Sicilian town of Eryx, of the rocky landscape of Strabo's home city of Amaseia, or of the sanctuary of Zeus on Mount Gerizim above the Samarian city of Neapolis (modern Nablus).[42]

Mountains and the Ancient Economy

Not only were they markers of identity, but mountains also made a major contribution to the ancient economy, and were often closely integrated in economic terms with the territories around them.[43] Our elite sources tend to ignore that situation (in fact they tend to suppress the importance of the countryside as a whole), preferring to celebrate elite interaction within the city rather than non-elite activity outside it.[44] The use of mountains for hunting is an exception: it has a strong literary presence. However, most ancient depictions of hunting perpetuate the stereotype of separation between urban civilisation and mountain wilderness: hunting is a way for members of the elite to conquer temporarily the wild spaces outside the city walls.[45] But in fact the mountains were very far from being empty, unmanaged landscapes. Instead they were places of exploitation. Farmland on the lower slopes of mountain territory was often highly prized, because of the access to good water supplies and the moderate temperatures in summer.[46] The mountains were important as sources of timber, both for local use and for trade: wood was exported on a vast scale across the Mediterranean world. The Hellenistic philosopher Theophrastus gives an exhaustive account of the different kinds of trees that flourish in different regions. He talks over and over again about their building uses, and about the superiority of timber from mountains.[47] Charcoal burners seem to have been viewed with suspicion as another mountain group who functioned on the very edges of civilisation, but they too played a significant role in the ancient economy: a large proportion of urban inhabitants, without time or opportunity to gather wood for themselves, would have relied on their work for fuel.[48] Fuel may have made up as much as 20 percent of ancient Roman GDP.[49] Mining, for example in marble quarries, produced important exports.[50] We have to work quite hard to piece together the evidence for all these activities from inscriptions and from scattered literary references—for example there are many passing mentions to gathering timber in Greek mythological narrative. But the overall picture is clear: mountains were often places of economic productivity.

Athens' relationship with its mountains is a good example. They provided the forests for the shipbuilding which was so important for Athens as far back as the fifth century BCE. The marble quarries of Mount Pentelikon and Mount Hymettos supplied the fabric of the city and its artistic exports. If you walk in those hills today, you can still see the remains of the quarry roads built to bring down huge blocks of marble to the city and to the sea.[51] Particularly distinctive are the rectangular holes cut into the bedrock on either side of these tracks, used for wooden stakes; tied to these were ropes, used to reduce the speed of the marble blocks as they were brought downhill on their sledges. Mount Parnes supplied water to the city via an aqueduct constructed by the emperor Hadrian. In the classical and Hellenistic periods these were also places of defence, garrisoned with fortresses against invaders. The Attic hills seem to have been more neglected during the late Hellenistic and early Roman periods, but in late antiquity, especially from the fifth century CE onwards, the mountains regained their importance.[52] There are some signs of the reactivation of their quarries, presumably to fuel the building boom in the city itself. Abandoned residential and agricultural sites were reoccupied. Defensive positions in the hills were brought into use again, to protect against barbarian invasion. Hand in hand with all of that was a revival of mountain religion. We have seen already that the sanctuary of Zeus on Mount Hymettos had a striking increase in dedications during these late antique centuries. That is paralleled by an upswing in traditional pagan cultic activity at a number of other hillside and cave sites in Attica in the fifth and sixth centuries—surprisingly so, given that Greece was becoming more and more heavily christianised at the time.[53] Attica was typical of the way in which mountain borderlands, far from being neglected wastelands, often exhibited complex patterns of land use and land ownership. They were lucrative spaces for individual landowners. For cities, economic exploitation of marginal spaces on the edges of their land was a way of acting out territorial control.[54]

The economic importance of mountains reinforced their status as zones of connection, rather than zones of primitive isolation. Different communities often shared the resources of a single mountain. Sometimes that could lead to dispute, as we shall see in a moment for the phenomenon of conflicts over pastureland.[55] But just as often mountains were zones of co-operation and communication.[56] The cities located on the slopes on the opposite sides of Mount Kadmos in the Maeander valley shared the territory of the mountain as a common source of pasturage and timber. The degree of interaction between members of the elites in these cities is striking, and much more prominent than their relationship with the more accessible cities of the plains below. Their shared use of the mountain, where their shepherds and timber-gatherers would have crossed paths with each other repeatedly, is surely one of the reasons for that.[57]

Presumably these zones of contact and conflict would have been envisaged in most contexts primarily as masculine spaces. There are many stories in ancient texts of female worshippers at risk of attack in sanctuaries in borderlands on the edges of their city's territories, which were often associated especially with the goddess Artemis.[58] But once again it is very hard to generalise, and very hard to be sure about what a gendered experience of mountain borderlands might have looked like at different times and places. The fact that some border areas were more densely inhabited[59] than we might initially expect suggests that these could be spaces which women lived and worked in too.

Mountain populations also sometimes had more long-distance connections with other regions of the Mediterranean world. One important factor was the widespread phenomenon of out-migration from mountain populations. The traditional model assumes that this was a response to the unsustainable expansion of population density in mountain regions with very limited carrying capacities. That model is now viewed more sceptically than it used to be, and it is clear that it was often just as much a natural result of economic interconnectedness. But either way it is clear that Greek and Roman cultures were impacted quite widely by the mobility of mountain peoples, for example through the recruitment of large numbers of mercenary troops from mountain regions.[60]

Mountain regions were also influenced in turn by economic and technical innovations in the plains, although not evenly and uniformly so.[61] We have seen already that Isauria was home to a wealthy and sophisticated culture despite its resistance to Roman rule. There are countless other examples. For all the prevalence of premodern stereotypes of impoverished and isolated mountain populations, there are good reasons to think that the differences in wealth between mountains and plains have been much more stark in the modern world than they ever had been before, especially from about 1800 onwards, albeit with a great deal of local variation.[62] Mountain regions in the ancient Mediterranean may often have been more open to the penetration of relatively low-level agrarian technologies than they are for more complex farming techniques today.[63] Even the relatively isolated mountain populations of Crimea were heavily influenced by Roman culture in the region, as far as we can judge from the prominence of Roman coins and military equipment at the Gurzuf Saddle sanctuary from the middle of the first century BCE onwards.[64] An inscription surviving from the Pyrenees, set up by two men who claim to be the first to have quarried and exported twenty-foot marble columns from the area, honours 'the god Silvanus and the mountains of Numidia'. That mention of the marble-bearing mountains of North Africa gives a vivid impression of the way in which mountains could be seen as connected to a wider global economy.[65]

Mountain Pastoralism

Where does pastoral culture fit into that picture? What were the pastoral cultures of the ancient world really like? Two features particularly stand out: their variety, and their surprising degree of connection with the non-pastoral world.

First: variety. It has often been suggested that there is a standard, 'Mediterranean' style of transhumance involving movement of animals over large distances between winter base and summer pastures. That has long been the practice of the Vlachs and Sarakatsani of northwest Greece. Long-distance transhumance took place on a particularly large scale in medieval Italy. There is some evidence for it in Latin literature too. It seems to have become a widespread practice in Italy from the second century BCE onwards. It was practised particularly by wealthy aristocrats, who could afford huge flocks, sometimes of thousands of animals, and the many shepherds needed to accompany them often hundreds of miles across Italy. We can trace the likely route of the drove roads that led up and down from the mountains. Varro tells us that he himself owned flocks who 'spent their winters in Apulia [in southeast Italy] and spent their summers in the mountains of Reate [north of Rome], these two distant pasturages being connected by public trails, just as a yoke holds together baskets' (Varro, *De re rustica* 2.2.9). Varro may have been motivated partly by the fact that he owned pastures in Reate, and wanted to avoid pasturing his flocks for a fee closer to their base in Apulia.[66] Transhumance may even have left some precarious traces in the archaeological record. For example archaeological survey in the Biferno valley in the Apennines in east-central Italy, precisely on the route that Varro mentions, has found evidence for temporary settlements which look as though they might have been the annual overnight camps of transhumant shepherds, with lots of broken pottery but no tiles.[67] That said, it is hard to be absolutely sure that these are not the relics of more local pastoralism, which involved movement of much smaller flocks across very much smaller distances. It seems likely that the local population in the Biferno valley would have practised precisely this kind of small-scale transhumance, moving their flocks just 500 vertical metres up and down the slopes of the valley. The consensus now is that this more local, less eye-catching kind of 'vertical' transhumance, in many different variants, was much more widespread in Mediterranean culture than its larger-scale, long-distance equivalents.[68] There is evidence too that substantial flocks were also kept permanently at low levels. One incentive for that practice was the desire to make sure of a good supply of manure for arable land.[69] Nor should we assume that pure pastoralism was the norm. Probably the overwhelming majority of the pastoral population mixed small-scale use of mountain pastures in the summer with various kinds of agricultural activity, in a wide variety of different combinations.[70] Here again the Apennines are a case in point: modern scholars have in the past tried to characterise this as an exclusively pastoral area, but it has become increasingly clear that pastoralism for most inhabitants was just one activity of many.[71]

Second: connectivity. The idea of pastoral communities as necessarily and drastically isolated is equally dubious. As we have seen there is evidence for pastoral activity in the mountains of the Mediterranean as early as the Neolithic period, but despite that pastoralism is generally speaking a relatively sophisticated activity that evolves at a late stage in human agrarian history.[72]

Local transhumance over very small distances might often have been a fairly insular experience, but even medium-range movement of flocks (perhaps over dozens of miles rather than the hundreds of miles travelled by Varro's flocks across Italy) would have required quite complex co-operation with individuals and authorities in other territories beyond one's own home.[73] We have a number of inscriptions recording agreements for the flocks of one city to pass through the territory of another.[74] Cities also often entered into agreement for use of each others' pastures, and common pasture land could sometimes be shared under a formal agreement between two or more cities.[75] Mountain foothills are often hard to travel through, but summit plateaus very much less so,[76] and summer pastures were accordingly often places of interaction for people who saw themselves as part of the same community, in contrast with their separation in the plains during the winter. John Campbell describes a similar phenomenon for the Sarakatsani as he observed them in the 1960s:

> quite apart from the greater geographical dispersion of the community in winter, the problems of weather and lambing isolate the shepherds of each flock whose only concern during these months is the care of their animals. In summer, although the Sarakatsani are still dispersed over 390 square miles of mountainous country, there is time to visit kinsmen who live at a distance, weddings and festivals are celebrated, and in general there is greater awareness of the community and its honour.[77]

In that kind of situation the power of ethnic rather than civic identity becomes clear: that more flexible kind of allegiance could unite shepherds who lived in relatively small, separate communities in their winter bases.[78] The summer pastures could be meeting places in the ancient world too. The classic example is a passage from Sophocles' *Oedipus the King* 1133–39, where a shepherd from Thebes recalls how he passed the baby Oedipus to a colleague from Corinth when they met in the summer on Mount Kithairon: 'when we were in the region of Kithairon, he with two flocks and I with one, I was in this man's company for three whole periods of six months, from spring to the rising of Arktouros; and then in winter I would drive my animals back to their folds, and he to the farmsteads of Laios'. The Cyclopean stereotype of isolated families who 'pay no attention to each other' has some grounding in the realities: no doubt the shepherd's life could often be a lonely one. But it misses the way in which pastoral regions developed their own distinctive models of communal identity, different from the dominant city-based model of community, but not for that reason any less cohesive.

In some cases, however, the pressure from neighbouring cities on the same pastureland led to conflict. For example, one surviving source records war between the Phokians and the Lokrians over pasture on Mount Parnassos:

> The cause of their hostility was this. There is for these peoples a disputed region on Parnassos, over which they had fought also in the past. Often it is used for pasturage both by the Phokians and by the Lokrians, and when either of the two sees the others there, they gather together many people and take their flocks. There had been many incidents like this already on both sides, but they had always been resolved through trial and negotiation, but on this occasion, when the Lokrians took back animals to replace the ones they had lost, the Phokians . . . invaded Lokria under arms. (*Hellenica Oxyrhynchia* 13.3)[79]

Nor were cities the only bodies that struggled for control over valuable pastoral territory. The sanctuary at Delphi, under the control of the governing body known as the Amphiktyony, needed vast supplies of sheep and cows for sacrifice: every request for an oracle had to be accompanied by sacrifice; the Pythian festival must have consumed many hundreds if not thousands of animals. One of the consequences of the so-called First Sacred War in the early sixth century BCE was to bring the fertile Krisaian plain under Delphic control, presumably in order to ensure a steady supply of sacrificial animals. These pressures lasted for many centuries: a border treaty from the second century BCE with the nearby city of Ambryssos similarly brought under Delphic control large areas of pasturage on Mount Parnassos and Mount Kirphis.[80] There is extensive epigraphic evidence from the Hellenistic period for officials and groups, often in Asia Minor called *orophylakes* ('mountain guards'; or perhaps *horophylakes*: 'border guards'), with equivalent terms in other regions, who were tasked with controlling their cities' mountainous boundaries, as well as dealing with brigands and runaway slaves.[81]

One fragmentary inscription from the city of Thebes in the Maeander valley in Asia Minor makes the connection between pastoral activity and urban culture clear with remarkable vividness.[82] It is a sacrificial calendar, from the fourth century BCE, describing the offerings to be made by shepherds and goatherds from Mount Mykale to a set of local deities, including the mountain itself. The start of the inscription is lost; the surviving text begins as follows, halfway through a sentence:

... and hand over to the *hieropoioi*, having sworn the oath on Mykale, and to make an offering on the 13th of the month Taurion to the Nymphs even as to Mykale.... And to make a shearing offering to Hermes of a kid to be sacrificed for each herd from their own herd—it is not permissible to purchase an animal—along with half-choinix cakes and two *hemitessera* of wine for libation. And those who pasture sheep are also to make the offering from each flock of a lamb if [at least] five are born, and they are to contribute the other things just like those who pasture goats. And those who bring [a shearing sacrifice] are to have the hide and leg and kidney and intestines of the shearing sacrifice, but the *hieropoioi* are to take the meat of the shearing sacrifices and that (of the animals) they themselves sacrifice and they are to deal out portions, per person, to all the Thebans and the citizens as many as [are present?]. (*Inschriften von Priene* 362)[83]

Another text (*Inschriften von Priene* 361 and 363) inscribed on the reverse of the same stone confirms the boundaries of the territory of the city of Thebes, with frequent mention of rocks and slopes and cliffs as landmarks.

Mount Mykale stands on the very edge of the Aegean Sea, on a promontory which projects out towards the island of Samos. Thebes was a small town on the southern slopes of the mountain, standing at the very mouth of the Maeander, facing Miletos, which stood on the other side of the river to the south. We know that Thebes was under the control of Miletos during the fourth century BCE.[84] It is hard to be sure exactly what motivated the inclusion of these shepherds and goatherds in the city's religious life. Was this an acknowledgement of their importance to the city, in a region which relied heavily on the textile industry for its wealth? The profits derived by Miletos from its control over Thebes were probably based on wool, which would have been fed into Miletos' renowned wool-working industry.[85] Or was it an attempt to keep the shepherds under control? The answer may be both: there is an element of coercion here, in the instructions about the oath and about the required contributions; at the same time they are involved in the city's life as central members of the Theban community.[86] It is also hard to be sure about the social status of these men, but presumably many of them were poorly paid employees or even slaves, working for wealthy masters, rather than independent farmers, and if so that makes their absorption into the rituals of the city all the more striking.

The inscription may also have been intended as an attempt to advertise to the surrounding area Thebes' claim to the pasture lands on the mountain.

Mount Mykale was renowned for its resources, not just pasturage, but timber too. We know from other surviving documents that there was a long-running rivalry for half a millennium between the island of Samos and the city of Priene (which stood a little to the east of Thebes) over rights to territory on the mountain slopes.[87] You can still see some of the boundary markers laid down on the mountain by arbitrators from Rhodes in the second century BCE if you walk there today. It is striking that the Samians claimed those rights despite the intervening stretch of water, but the forests were such a rich resource that they tempted islanders over the straits in much later centuries too. Did the Thebans feel pressured by those claims into a conspicuous assertion of their own connection with the mountain, as a much smaller community? Or should we view this as part of a strategy by the much larger city of Miletos to assert their own claim to the mountain via their smaller neighbour north of the Maeander river. Pausanias claims that a spring arising on the slopes of Mount Mykale flows under the sea to the harbour at Panormos.[88] That story may have been an attempt to link the mountain with the sacred geography of Miletos: Panormos was close to Didyma, Miletos' main cult site, ten miles or so to the south of the city. It is hard to be sure.[89] But whatever the motive is for the setting up of this inscription, it is clear that the pastoral and the urban are closely entwined in the image of orderly ritual observance this inscription conjures up. In distributing their offerings to the people of the city down below, the shepherds of Mount Mykale act out their relationship with urban culture and identity. It is hard to imagine a more vivid refutation of the stereotype of pastoral isolation.

Plato's *Laws* and the Mountains of Crete

The standard ancient (and modern) image of mountain populations as primitive and unconnected with the wider world is thus very misleading. If we want to have any chance of reconstructing ancient mountain life as it was lived, we need to look beyond literary depictions to the increasingly rich archaeological and scientific evidence. Famously there are only two accounts in the whole of surviving Greek and Latin literature of the practice of vertical transhumance: the passage already cited earlier from Sophocles' *Oedipus the King*, and another from Dio Chrystostom that we will look at later.[90] Does that mean that literary depictions simply have no value for any attempt to understand the experience of mountain dwelling in Greek and Roman antiquity?

As a way into thinking about that question I want to look now at a famous passage from Plato's *Laws* against the background of the evidence for mountain life both in the Mediterranean generally and in Crete specifically, which is the setting of Plato's dialogue. As the title suggests, the work is a conversation about different possible laws and constitutions, involving a Cretan, Kleinias, a Spartan, Megillos, and an unnamed Athenian. The crucial passage comes at the beginning of Book 3 of the work, in a discussion about the development of political systems in human society.[91] It has often been quoted, without much reference to the wider context of the work, to back up the perfectly convincing claim that the ancient Greeks saw mountains as places of great antiquity.[92] The Athenian, who is leading the conversation, raises the topic of the destruction of human society during the great flood, and suggests that the mountaintops were a place of refuge for the survivors. Let us imagine, he says 'that those who at that time escaped from the disaster would have been mainly mountain people engaged in shepherding, sparse embers preserved from the human race somewhere on the mountaintops' (Plato, Laws 677b). He imagines these primitive survivors living on harmoniously without any knowledge of the tools and inventions and arts that had been mastered by their counterparts in the now destroyed cities of the coast:

> In the first place, because of their isolation they were well-disposed and friendly to each other. Secondly, there was no need for them to fight over food. For there was no lack of flocks—except perhaps for some of them at the beginning—which is what they mainly lived from at that time; for they were not short of meat or milk, and they obtained further good and abundant food supplies by hunting. (678e–679a)

They had no need of any complex system of government, he says, but lived like the Cyclopes,[93] with each family under paternal authority.

That description looks very simplistic compared with what we know now about the evolution of ancient mountain life.[94] A charitable reader might perhaps find ways of linking the Athenian's account with some aspects of that history. For example, it seems just about conceivable that the idea of the descent from the mountains back down to the plains after the post-flood restoration of civilisation might be a reflection of the widespread phenomenon of outward migration from mountain regions already discussed earlier.[95] In Cretan history specifically we find an intriguing parallel for the notion of populations retreating to the mountains if we look at the events of the late Bronze Age, probably around the late thirteenth century BCE, which saw a large refugee population move into the mountains of Crete, away from the coastal plains. We can reconstruct something of their life there through archaeological investigation, which gives us a glimpse of their reliance on easily defensible sites at high altitude, and of their initially sparse and improvisatory survival economy, which must have involved among other things an increased focus on pastoral activity.[96] But it seems very unlikely that Plato would have been aware of that.

In most other respects the evidence from Crete points to the oversimplified, idealised quality of the Athenian's formulation. That is not meant to imply any negative judgement on Plato or his character: the Athenian's sketch is carefully represented as a hypothetical thought experiment, with no particular claim to be historically accurate. The problem arises only if we try to use it as the basis for a reconstruction of ancient mountain history. The mountains of Crete are heavily associated with the island's early Bronze Age history in the third millennium BCE, so in that sense they are among the island's very ancient places, but certainly not as zones of primitive, 'early' agrarian activity. The peak sanctuaries that were in use across the island seem to have functioned as important focal points in that period for the identities of particular communities.[97] Not only that, but it is possible that they also had a considerable economic significance, in allowing local elites to articulate a sense of regional authority and group identity, which in turn made it possible for them to pursue their own interests with co-operation from an extensive labour force and from neighbouring regions.[98]

The epigraphical evidence for pastoral activity in Crete also shows it to have been a very sophisticated activity and a relatively late development in Cretan history, dependent on complex systems and agreements negotiated between different cities on the island.[99] For example, we have surviving regulations for shared use of pasture between adjacent cities,[100] and for the allocation of fines for damage, payable to the city who owns the land.[101] A third-century BCE inscription gives the text of a treaty between the neighbouring cities of Hierapytna, towards the eastern end of the south coast of Crete, and Praisos in the hills inland: 'The Hierapytnian shall have the right to graze (his flocks) on the land of the Praisians, with the exception of the sacred enclosures at Ardanitos and Daros, and similarly the Praisian on the land of the Hierapytnians, on the condition that they will do no damage and will return each to his own land'.[102] The decree goes on to specify that anyone taking advantage of this opportunity will need a citizen of the other city to act as mediator, presumably someone with good local knowledge and able to arbitrate in any conflicts between the outsider and local families with long-established rights of land use in the area.[103] Measures outlined in other inscriptions involve rules for customs duties[104] and procedures for ensuring road safety and preventing animal theft, all clearly aimed in part at transhumant shepherds.[105] The bulk of this evidence comes from the Hellenistic period; it explains the widespread portrayal of Crete as a place of animal husbandry in Hellenistic poetry.[106] It is possible that these developments were a response to an overpopulation crisis in certain cities, which drove many Cretans to seek new forms of livelihood,[107] rather than the high point of a gradual shift towards increasing agrarian sophistication, but even if that is right it does not alter the fact that large-scale pastoralism comes late in Cretan mountain history, rather than being a primitive, ancient activity as Plato's Athenian suggests.

Plato's portrayal of the mountains comes to look at least a little more complicated, however, when we view this passage from Book 3 against the mountain setting of the dialogue itself: the two passages are not often read together. The conversation opens with a question from the Athenian about who is responsible, god or human, for the respective law codes of Crete and Sparta. Among us Cretans it is Zeus, Kleinias replies, and Apollo for the Spartans. They discuss the tradition that the great lawgiver of Crete, King Minos, used to consult with Zeus every nine years, presumably on Mount Ida, although that is not specified (624a–b).[108] Then they propose to walk from Knossos near to the coast to the cave of Zeus on Mount Ida while they talk about 'government and laws' (625a). In making that suggestion they appropriate the Minos tradition as a model for their own philosophical conversation, representing it as a modernised, rational, collaborative version of Zeus's mountainside inspiration.[109] In the process the Athenian offers an extraordinary image of the pleasures they can expect to experience en route: 'certainly the road from Knossos to the cave and temple of Zeus is a long one, and there are likely to be shady resting-places (ἀνάπαυλαι… σκιαραί) along the road among the tall trees (ἐν τοῖς ὑψηλοῖς δένδρεσιν) in this stifling weather' (625b). The local, Kleinias, backs up that impression: 'Indeed, sir, there are as you go on cypress trees in the groves of amazing height and beauty, and meadows where we can spend time resting' (Καὶ μὴν ἔστι γε, ὦ ξένε, προϊόντι κυπαρίττων τε ἐν τοῖς ἄλσεσιν ὕψη καὶ κάλλη θαυμάσια, καὶ λειμῶνες ἐν οἷσιν ἀναπαυόμενοι διατρίβοιμεν ἄν) (625b–c). Kleinias then proceeds to describe the way in which the mountainous terrain of Crete has helped to form the island's distinctive ways of training and fighting: 'For you see the nature of the whole island of Crete, which is not flat like the territory of the Thessalians. For that reason they use horses more, whereas we train by running. For our terrain is uneven, and more suited to exercises that involve running on foot' (625c–d).[110]

In many ways of course this passage is no more realistic than the later image of the high-altitude survivors of the flood. Others have pointed out before that Plato is not a reliable witness to the forestation levels of classical Crete.[111] It is most likely that Plato is referring here to the Idaian cave southwest of Knossos, around 1,500 metres above sea level. If so, the description here is exceptionally optimistic: that is a tough hike, probably around twelve hours of walking each way.[112] Plato not only describes Mount Ida with the kind of idealised imagery which is common in *locus amoenus* descriptions in classical verse, but also more specifically makes it resemble the shady resting-place outside the city walls of Athens which is used by Socrates and Phaedrus as a space for philosophical discussion in Plato's own earlier work the *Phaedrus* (230b–c), and which was an archetypal landscape of philosophy in centuries of later writing too. Here the mountain becomes a very modern-sounding place of elite leisure, free from anxiety and discomfort. This is clearly not an eyewitness account—or if it is, it is a very selective one.

But what these passages from the *Laws* do draw attention to, for all their lack of realism, is the fact that the relationship between the mountains and human culture, especially urban culture, can never be summed up in a single image. Books 1 and 3 are not necessarily incompatible: we might see the situation described at the beginning of Book 1 as a late moment in the development of the mountain history, whose very early days are then sketched in Book 3, as if Plato is tracing an evolution from early, primitive inhabitation to more modern, sophisticated ways of interacting with landscape. One function of that evolutionary view is presumably to imply an optimistic vision of the possibilities for human social and political organisation that the speakers are exploring in the work. Even so it is hard to avoid the impression of enormous difference between the two passages. Both Plato's description of primitive life and his portrait of urban engagement are fantasy images, at the two far ends of the spectrum of possibilities for envisaging mountains in relation to human society. But they do nevertheless suggest an understanding of the basic tension between two conceptions of mountains that lay at the heart of a lot of ancient mountain writing and presumably also ancient mountain experience, that is the tension between mountains within and beyond urban civilisation.

15

Dio Chrysostom and the Mountains of Euboia

Idealising Mountain Communities

Throughout the Western literary tradition, the countryside has often been idealised as an unspoiled space set apart from the problems of urban life. That image has also repeatedly been exposed as a mirage that disguises the reality of close connectedness between city and country. Raymond Williams, in his 1973 book *The Country and the City*, drew attention to the artificiality of nostalgic images of rural life in English literature from about 1600 onwards, many of which posited a strong separation between rural and urban.[1] We have learned to understand that the idea of pristine nature free from human interference is a fabrication: even in imagining and pursuing that ideal we undermine it. Even the most remote rural environments carry the marks of human presence and human activity, and the origins of that situation stretch far back into human history. The same goes for images of primitive rustic community free from urban corruption, which often turn out on closer inspection to reveal more about urban fantasies and urban priorities than about the real experience of their inhabitants.

There are ancient precedents both for those kinds of mirage and for the desire to expose them to scrutiny. It is usually Virgil who gets the blame for the dominant idea of separation between country and city that has had such a powerful hold over the European imagination. William Cronon has written that 'such beliefs are deeply embedded in Western thought. We learned our city-country dichotomy from the nineteenth-century Romantics, who learned it in turn from the pastoral poets stretching back to Virgil'.[2] It is certainly the case that this view of the structure of space has a great deal of prominence in ancient Greek and Roman writing. However, we also have ancient texts which reflect on the legitimacy of the city-country dichotomy self-consciously, and in ways which every so often anticipate strands of contemporary thinking on that problem.[3]

One of the most brilliant examples of that kind of reflectiveness is in Dio Chrysostom's *Euboian Oration* (*Oration* 7).[4] Dio depicts a remote mountain community in idealising, pastoral terms, but also challenges us to think about the validity and value of the images he is presenting us with. The text dates from around 100 CE.[5] It is a work in two halves. The first half is a narrative in the first person: Dio describes being shipwrecked on the island of Euboia, and receiving hospitality there from a rustic hunter and his family who live and hunt in the mountains. In the course of Dio's stay the hunter recounts his experiences of a trip to the city to answer demands for money. The second half switches abruptly to a discussion of which jobs are most suitable for the urban poor: their miserable lifestyle is implicitly contrasted with the rustic contentment of the hunters.[6] It is tantalising, but also misleading, to think that we may be getting a glimpse here of real life in the mountains of Euboia. Anthropological work on the island in the mid-twentieth century revealed a traditional peasant society which is not without parallels in Dio's portrayal.[7] The portrayal of depopulation in the Greek countryside for which this text is famous has an intriguing reflection in the archaeological evidence for changing land-use in the nearby Bouros-Kastri peninsula in southern Euboia, which does seem to have seen a drastic reduction in the number of rural sites in the late Hellenistic and early imperial periods.[8] In practice, however, it seems unlikely that this is an eyewitness account. Dio's knowledge of the topography of Euboia seems to be very imprecise,[9] and his account probably owes more to literary stereotypes of decline in the Greek east in general than to the situation on the ground in Euboia specifically.[10] In Dio's other writings too he is a brilliant self-dramatiser, with an interest in experimenting with a wide range of different personas and different first-person voices, and in that context the idea that this is an autobiographical account comes to look even more precarious.

What we do find in Dio, however, as for Plato, is a more general understanding of the dynamics of city-mountain relations in Hellenistic and Roman culture, and of the legal and economic pressures involved in that relationship, even if it is not anchored in detailed understanding of a specific location.[11] This text is unusual in the degree to which it idealises the inhabitants of the mountains, but it is in other respects quite typical of a wider interest in ancient literature, in Dio's dramatisation of the uneasy relationship between two competing conceptions of mountain landscape. The mountains of Euboia are represented by Dio as spaces far removed from urban culture, but he also repeatedly shows how precarious that freedom is, and how hard it is to escape from an urban perspective in viewing and valuing them. Is the mountain separate from the city? Or is it a part of the city? The tension between those two possibilities is central to the story Dio tells. His text stands apart from the dominant tendency to denigrate mountain peoples in ancient historiography and ethnography. However, the history of modern urban engagement with mountain regions has taught us that idealisation and denigration are often two sides of the same coin—and in fact Dio's text does juxtapose his own positive assessment of the hunter's lifestyle with more traditionally negative characterisations of them as bandit figures by the people the hunter encounters in the city. There are countless modern examples not just of negativity about the backwardness of mountain communities, but also of fetishisation, where mountain customs are presented and preserved in their 'authentic' form for the urban, touristic gaze of those who visit from the cities.[12] Dio's text offers us an unusually self-conscious ancient version of that phenomenon.

A Mountain Idyll

The first action of the text is Dio's shipwreck and his subsequent encounter with the hunter, who is down at sea level with his dogs. One of the striking features of this section is the way in which it represents the hunter as a very ancient figure closely linked with the land he inhabits. In the opening sentences of the work, for example, Dio assures his readers that the story he is about to tell comes from his personal experience: 'I shall describe the kind of men I met in almost the centre of Greece (ἐν μέσῃ σχεδόν τι τῇ Ἑλλάδι), and the life they were living' (Dio Chrysostom *Oration* 7, 1). That opening depicts Dio as an ethnographer, and more specifically as an Odysseus figure,[13] describing an unfamiliar population, emphasising his detachment and distance from the people he encounters. In describing the setting of the tale as 'practically the centre of Greece', Dio seems to be suggesting that the hunter has a special link with Greek identity and the Greek past.[14] Then when he sees the hunter for the first time Dio immediately reaches for a reference to Homer: 'A short time later, I saw a man, a hunter, to judge by his appearance and his clothing; he was healthily bearded, rather than just having hair at the back of his head in the miserable and sordid style that Homer says the Euboians used when they came to Troy' (4). This odd passage[15] does not suggest an exact equivalence between the hunter and the Euboian warriors of the *Iliad*, but the comparison nevertheless shows us that the narrator's first instinct is to view this figure in Homeric terms. As so often, mountains are envisaged here as zones of connection with an ancient past. The hunter seems also to have an understanding of weather signs, and an ability to read the mountains which are the backdrop to his day-to-day life, a detail which suggests his closeness to the land: '"these conditions now are not suitable for sailing. . . . I would be happy if the wind died down within the next five days, but that is not likely", he said, "whenever the peaks of Euboia are enclosed by clouds to such an extent as you see them now"' (6).

The portrayal of time in relation to mountain populations, and especially the association of mountain-dwellers with antiquity, whose ancient identity stands in opposition to modern attempts to control mountain territory, has a long and troubling modern legacy. In some cases mountain primitivism has been idealised, as it is by Dio in this work. For some eighteenth-century writers, Jean-Jacques Rousseau among them, 'the primitive character of the mountaineer, protected from the world, is a guarantee of happiness'.[16] The virtue of mountain-dwellers has even been viewed at various times as a force that can regenerate the populations of the plains:[17] Dio too seems to assume something along those lines at least in taking the hunter and his family as a model against which to measure urban society. In many other contexts, however, a reputation for antiquity has been disempowering, used as an excuse for conquest and domination by outside powers, or else as an excuse for the imposition of an elitist, anthropological gaze by outside viewers in a way which can deprive native communities of their own distinctive voices and perspectives.[18] Mountains within the last two or three centuries especially have been places for performing modernity, for example in the way in which the completion of particular mountaineering challenges have been viewed as distinctively modern achievements, or in the way in which mountains have been given a prominent role in newly formed states as symbols of nationhood. At the same time mountains have been viewed as places of great antiquity, with their own much older histories and cultures which are always to some extent resistant to these efforts of modernisation.[19] That tension is present already in Dio's portrait of the mountains of Euboia.

In what follows we discover that the hunter and his family have in fact had some experience of a more modern way of living and working in the mountains. They go back to the hunter's hut, and on the way Dio listens to his story. The hunter explains that he lives with a friend—each is married to the other's sister—and that they have sons and daughters. Their fathers used to work for a rich man

> who owned many droves of horses and cattle, many flocks, many good fields too and many other possessions together with all these mountains (ξύμπαντα δὲ ταῦτα τὰ ὄρη).... In the winter we grazed our cattle in the flat lands, where we had plenty of pasturage and a good deal of hay put up; but in the summer we would drive them into the mountains (ὄρη) (11, 13).

Euboia is a narrow island with a high mountain backbone, reaching up to just over 1,700 metres at its highest point, but the word ὄρη refers here not just to mountain peaks; instead, as often in Greek, it signals mountainous territory in more general terms, including the pasture-rich lands on the mountains' slopes. The word 'all' (ξύμπαντα) emphasises the thoroughness with which formerly common land has been appropriated for private wealth. When the rich man died, executed by the emperor, his property was confiscated and the cattle taken away to be butchered, but the hunters' fathers stayed in the huts they had built as their summer base, and turned to hunting, on finding that they could not get work in the villages and the city down below. The rich man's ownership of the mountains is an early reminder in the text of the way in which mountain landscapes could come under the control of the wealthy urban elite. There is evidence from the Roman period that pastoralism—far from being a primitive activity—could be used by rich landowners as a relatively easy source of income, difficult to assess for tax, and as a way of dominating marginal land and maintaining control over subordinate populations.[20]

By contrast, the formation of the hunters' community which follows the wealthy man's death is implicitly presented as a return to an older, more organic way of interacting with the landscape, associated with a time before organised animal husbandry, and based on subsistence farming, which is described in more or less realistic terms. The hunter makes it clear, for example, that they do not own the land: 'for the place is not ours, nor did we inherit it' (11). They seem to stand outside all the systems of civic and private control which as we have seen were so common in mountain borderlands, reaching back to an older system of common use which predates the private ownership associated with their former employer.[21] After the cattle were driven away, he says, 'no one has ever paid us our wages' (τὸν μισθὸν οὐδεὶς ἀποδέδωκε: 12). That detail makes it clear that their position outside a monetary economy was not freely chosen. Their decision to stay in their summer huts even through the winters similarly puts them outside the norms of pastoral life, where the transhumant shepherd's isolation from the life of the plains is always temporary. However, they do not abandon animal husbandry completely. We learn later (47) that at the time of the hunter's trip to the city they have a few goats and cows; and the hunter mentions that the land they had under cultivation there was sufficient for them partly 'because it had a lot of manure in it' (ἅτε κόπρου πολλῆς ἐνούσης) (16). That mention comes in the course of an account of the life their fathers lived after the confiscation of their cattle, and it may be a reference primarily to the fertile quality of the land in the years immediately after the departure of the herds, but it is possible that the hunter is thinking just as much of the advantages his own current collection of animals brings. One of the advantages of animal husbandry in mixed farming was in the fertilisation it provided for the fields.[22] They also grow a variety of crops, and in that sense the description of their food stores that the hunter gives in response to his accusers in the city is relatively realistic in the context of our other evidence for peasant production in this period: the hunter mentions millet and barley as well as wheat (45).[23]

The hunters' dogs share in that move back to an older way of interacting with their environment. They have been trained for herding, but they develop an appetite for hunting gradually and by their own instincts, without needing to be taught:

> late in life they learned the new taste (μεταμανθάνοντες) for eating meat rather than barley-mash, filling themselves up on it whenever an animal was caught, and going hungry if not, and so now they began to give more attention to this kind of thing, and they began to pursue equally everything that was visible, and began to pick up the scent and tracks in one way or another, and so became instead of shepherd dogs a kind of late-learning (ὀψιμαθεῖς) and rather slow hunting dogs. (17)

This description is overlaid with the characteristic language of literate, human education that is so typical of Dio. Words like μεταμανθάνω ('to learn something new or different') or ὀψιμαθής ('late-learning') are more appropriate to sophists or students than dogs—for example the former is sometimes used to describe adopting a new language.[24] But it is nevertheless a powerful image of the dogs' increasing attention to tiny details of the mountain landscape. And it describes a process of evolution in mountain life which is quite different—despite the superficially similar mention of hunting in both texts—from Plato's version of primitive mountain shepherds transforming their culture gradually and painstakingly over many centuries into something more modern. For

Dio the evolution is quick and spontaneous; it also goes backwards, to a much older way of living in the mountains that is represented by him as far more desirable than the life of city. Meanwhile the men find that hunting becomes easier in the winter, since they can follow the footmarks of animals more easily in the snow (19). Here we see them adapting resourcefully to their environment, as mountain communities have often done in other periods and other cultures too.

Their domestic situation is similarly idealised, and cut off from the sophisticated culture of the city. They are not completely isolated from the outside world, or from relations of borrowing and exchange: we hear that one of the hunter's daughters is married to a rich man in the village, who lent them seed to sow wheat last year, and which they stress they repaid after harvest time (68–69), the hunter's friend's son has swapped a wild boar in the village for a pig, which he is fattening up as a sacrifice for his approaching wedding with the hunter's daughter (73), and they talk about borrowing some more wine from the village for the wedding (76); the hunter also at one point mentions passers-by (οἱ παριόντες) taking the grapes from the vines they have planted (46). Nevertheless this is a largely self-contained community. The two families have intermarried (20). They seem to live here under patriarchal or at least family authority. Plato had made the same point for his mountain-dwellers, comparing them with the Cyclopes, but Dio here goes out of his way to give a positive view of that situation, in his depiction of the humorous and harmonious[25] interactions between the two families (65–80), for example in their good-natured discussion of their plans for the wedding, which Dio witnesses two days later, before he leaves. Their diet, too, is both idealised and down-to-earth, and contributes to the sense that the hunter and his family have an organic connection with the land they inhabit. When Dio and the hunter arrive at the huts they feast together on good but simple food (75).[26]

Here then we have a high-altitude community described in remarkably positive terms, with a memorable mixture of idealisation and realism which makes it very different from Plato's more negative version in the *Laws* of primitive life in the hills after the flood. At first sight this looks like an important exception to the usual ancient denigration of mountain life. Clearly Dio has some basic understanding of the rhythms of pastoral life here, with its move from winter on the plain to higher pastures in the summer: he is very rare among ancient authors in paying any attention to that phenomenon.[27] And his description of the people who give him hospitality suggests an admiration for this kind of life close to the land, which is implicitly contrasted with the miserable life of the urban poor, and clearly worth preserving, in Dio's view, from the threat of encroachment by the city.[28]

Visiting the City

These opening pages also show us, however, the difficulty Dio has in moving beyond his own urban perspective in his attempts to share or describe their way of life. That is clear, for example, in his description of their dwelling place with the conventions of poetic and rhetorical *locus amoenus* motifs. We have seen one glimpse of this passage before, but it is worth repeating. The place where they built their summer steadings, where they now live all year round, is

> a deep and shady ravine, and running through the middle of it was a river that was not rough, but was easy to wade through, for both cows and calves, and the water was abundant and pure, rising as it did from a nearby spring, and there is always a breeze blowing through in the summer... and there are many very beautiful meadows stretching out beneath tall and sparse trees (πολλοὶ δὲ καὶ πάγκαλοι λειμῶνες ὑπὸ ὑψηλοῖς τε καὶ ἀραιοῖς δένδρεσιν ἀνειμένοι). (14–15)

That is a powerful counter-example to the assumption that mountains were always viewed as wilderness spaces in ancient culture. It adapts standard *locus amoenus* conventions by overlaying them with all the pragmatic concerns one would expect from a cattle-herder, in a way which suggests that Dio has made a real effort to understand his subjects, in his report of the hunter's description rather than just imposing an inappropriately romanticising literary template. But it is also nevertheless a product of Dio's own literary perspective, in a way that would have been unmissable for Dio's readers. It even has philosophical overtones that are particularly appropriate to the philosopher Dio, in the detail of the shady spaces between the trees, which resemble the route up to Mount Ida in Plato's *Laws*.[29] Is Dio weighing this up as a possible place for philosophical discussion?

Dio's distance from the culture he describes even impacts on his bodily experience of the landscape of Euboia. For example, the shipwreck scene recalls Odysseus' arrival on the island of Circe in *Odyssey* Book 10. Dio, like Odysseus (*Odyssey* 10.146) climbs up to see what is going on: 'I carried on and with difficulty climbed up to a high place, and from there I saw the dogs in confusion and running backwards and forwards, and from those signs I inferred that the animal they were chasing had been forced up by them against the cliff edge and had jumped off' (4). He falls comically short of Odysseus, who single-handedly kills and carries off a stag (*Odyssey* 10.156–71), whereas Dio has to leave the butchering of the deer to the hunter (he tells us that 'I helped as much as I could': 5), who in that sense takes on the Odyssean resonances that are initially associated with Dio himself. It is clear, in fact, that Dio is an accidental visitor to the mountains, a misfit. The hunter tells him at one point that he looks like a weak city-dweller:

> For now you shall rest after your difficult experience, but tomorrow, as far as it is possible for us, we will take care to make sure you get to safety, now that we have got to know you. You look to me like one of those men from the city, not a sailor or labourer; in fact you seem to be suffering from some great bodily weakness, to judge by your thinness. (7–8)

That passage draws on comic stereotypes of the philosopher to present Dio as a weakling unsuited to the rigours of rustic life.[30] It is as though Dio's stereotypically philosophical impracticality and weakness almost literally disqualify him from the rural lifestyle that his philosophical outlook predisposes him to idealise.[31] Can Dio really have a chance of understanding or participating in this rustic community given that characterisation?

The gulf in understanding between city-dwellers and mountain-dwellers becomes all the more clear when the hunter launches into an account of a visit he made some years ago to the city. It turns out he has been only twice in his life, the first time as a child with his father, and then the second time when a man came to their dwelling demanding money. The hunter tells Dio that he followed the man willingly into the city, presumably the city of Karystos, which stands at the very southern end of Euboia, beneath the slopes of Mount Ocha. On arrival he is bewildered and can describe what he sees only with reference to the features of the natural world he is familiar with. For example he tells Dio that 'the theatre is hollow like a ravine (φάραγξ), except that it is semicircular rather than long in two directions, and built of stone rather than natural' (24). The echo of the 'ravine' in the hunter's earlier description of his dwelling place in the mountains enhances the sense of incongruity between these two environments. It is striking also that the hunter uses quite visceral, bodily language to describe the impact the city has on him. Within his own environment in the mountains he seems to be unfazed by the natural forces he must encounter daily, but in the city, he tells us, 'I myself was once nearly knocked over by the shouting, as though a wave or a thunderbolt had broken over me' (25–26), using the kind of language others might use in relation to wild landscapes in the mountains or at sea.

The city-dwellers find it equally hard to understand the hunter's perspective and his experience. Their initial hostility towards him is portrayed in very negative terms, as one of the targets of Dio's satire,[32] but it is based on negative stereotypes of mountain populations that were very commonplace. The hunter is brought in front of the crowd—clearly the city's assembly—and he is accused of appropriating public property:

> This, gentlemen, is one of the men who profit from the public land (τῶν καρπουμένων τὴν δημοσίαν γῆν), for many years now, not just him, but his father before him. They use our mountains as grazing land (κατανέμουσι τὰ ἡμέτερα ὄρη), and they farm and hunt and they have built many houses and they have planted vines, and they have many other advantages despite the fact that they have paid nothing to anyone for the land, nor have they received it as a gift from the people. What would they have received it for? They occupy what is ours (ἔχοντες δὲ τὰ ἡμέτερα) and are wealthy, but they have never performed any public service, nor do they pay any portion of their wealth as tax, but they live free from taxes and obligations for public service, as if they were benefactors of the city. (27–28)

What kind of example will it set, he asks, 'if you allow these beasts (τοῖς θηρίοις τούτοις) freely to hold more than 1,000 *plethra* [that is, 250 acres] of the best land (πλέον ἢ χίλια πλέθρα γῆς τῆς ἀρίστης)?' (29). That question paradoxically combines negative and positive stereotypes of mountain territory. The hunter and his family are represented as uncivilised, even bestial, figures not qualified for normal human society. At the same time the speaker draws attention to the value of the land they occupy, in a way which is represented of course as absurdly incongruous, given what we know of the hunter's lifestyle, but which also at the same time picks up on urban anxieties about controlling valuable mountain terrain on the borders of city territory. Later the accusations become even more vehement: 'I have learned that there are two ringleaders of the people who have seized almost all the land in the mountains (ἅπασαν σχεδὸν τὴν ἐν τοῖς ὄρεσι χώραν)' (30). That claim characterises the hunter as a bandit figure, one of the kinds of mountain people most commonly represented as outside the norms of human civilisation in texts like Apuleius' *Metamorphoses*.

The underlying assumption here is that the mountains are the property of the city, to be administered by the city, and that claim had some basis.

Standardly there was a division, in Greek cities, between several different categories of productive land beyond the city itself—including cultivated land, grazing land, woodland, sacred space—each of which had its own dedicated laws and officials. Outside those spaces was the category of wilderness, which is what the hunter and his family occupy.[33] However, cities often asserted their control over wilderness too, given the valuable resources it could contain.[34] We know that the Euboian public lands had been appropriated by Rome after the Achaian War in 146 BCE, but it seems likely that they had been returned to local control as a gift at some later date,[35] so it seems that the hunter and his family could plausibly have been viewed as intruders in territory that the city saw as its own.[36] Renting of public land was fairly common in the Greek cities of the Roman Empire, but rarely for free.[37] The speaker's claims about their exploitation of the city's territory for vast personal gain might conceivably have been valid for the hunters' former master,[38] and might well reflect a background of conflict between cities and wealthy individuals for control over land on the edges of the city's territory,[39] although it is also clear that they are absurdly inappropriate for the frugal community we have already been introduced to through Dio's eyes. The vocabulary the accuser uses is the language used in legal contexts for possession of land without lawful ownership.[40]

A second speaker then steps forward: he is on the hunter's side, but still speaking from an urban perspective, if anything even more so than the first speaker. He argues, in the hunter's defence, that the city's lands are neglected, and that they should be grateful to anyone who uses them productively:

> 'At the moment, gentlemen,' he said, 'almost two-thirds of our land is wilderness (ἔρημα), because of neglect and underpopulation. I too own many acres, as I think some others do also, not only in the mountains but also in the plains (οὐ μόνον ἐν τοῖς ὄρεσιν, ἀλλὰ καὶ ἐν τοῖς πεδινοῖς). If anyone were willing to farm them I would not only give them for free, but would gladly offer them money in addition. For it is clear that they are of more value to me like that, and land which is inhabited and under cultivation (χώρα οἰκουμένη καὶ ἐνεργός) is a pleasant sight, whereas wilderness (ἡ δ' ἔρημος) is not only a useless possession to its owners, but also very pitiable, and a sign of the misfortune of its owners'. (34)

This image may be a reflection of the increasing concentration of large estates in the hands of a few landowners in this period, one of the consequences of which could be neglect,[41] although it is also clearly influenced by ancient stereotypes of decline within the Greek countryside. The speaker then proposes incentives to encourage citizens, and even non-citizens, to farm public land:

> So let them have it for free for ten years, and then after that time let them agree to pay a small portion from their crops but nothing from their livestock. And if any foreigners cultivate the land, let them too pay nothing in tax for the first five years, and then after that let them pay twice as much as the citizens. And if any foreigner brings 200 plethra [that is, 50 acres] under cultivation, let him be made a citizen, in order to encourage as many as possible. (37)

There is epigraphical evidence for schemes of this sort, offering initial exemption from rent in exchange for cultivation.[42] The speaker's goal seems to be to bring as much of the city's wilderness territory as possible into the category of cultivated land. In pursuing that goal, he seems to be acting in sympathy with the hunter's point of view, but in fact his solution is just as much rooted in a civic perspective as the first speaker's proposal.[43] He seems to have only a tenuous grasp on the question of what might motivate the hunter: most of his suggestions seem more likely to appeal to the audience of city-dwellers. Moreover, when we look more closely at the legal context it turns out that several of his proposals—the redistribution of vacant land, grants of the right to farm rent-free, and grants of citizenship—were not straightforwardly in the city's gift, and would have needed confirmation from Rome. In his way the second speaker is just as demagogic as the first, in his tendentious assertion of the city's autonomy over questions of land allocation.[44] Last his lament for the neglect of the city's territory leads him to deplore the current situation which even sees cows and sheep—including sheep belonging to the first speakers—being grazed inside the boundaries of the city (39). The problem for this second speaker is not, as the hunter might put it, that the city is overflowing its boundaries and intruding on the mountains, but rather that the mountains and the rural landscapes of animal husbandry are overflowing into the city. The second speaker wants more urban control, not less.

The hunter then speaks himself. He speaks naïvely, by comparison with the previous speakers, but also in a way that draws on some more positive traditions for representation of mountain people. He gives a full inventory of his food stores and possessions, which seem comically meagre by comparison with the inflated accusations of the first speaker. He offers them freely to the city. The watching citizens laugh at him: he has become a source of comedy rather than danger, although no less an outsider for that. He does, however, make it clear to his listeners that he has citizen status himself: he tells them that his father once came to the city when a grant was being made to all citizens, and got some along with the rest.[45] He also offers the service of his sons in fighting for the city (49). As we have seen already for the shepherds of Mount Mykale, the inhabitants of the rural borderlands were envisaged as figures who needed to be controlled and regulated, but they were also valid, and in some contexts valued members of the citizen community. Mountain peoples also played an important military role in the ancient world.[46] The hunter, for all his innocence, and for all his reluctance, or inability, to see things from the perspective of the city, nevertheless does seem to be aware that there are positive personas available to him, beyond the figure of the brigand, as a citizen mountain-dweller.

The situation, which had initially seemed so threatening, ends happily, but even in the moments of resolution there are details that seem ominous. The decisive moment comes when a third speaker stands up, and attests to the fact that he was (like Dio) cared for by the hunter and his family after being shipwrecked. The crowd, which is represented as absurdly volatile, is now on the hunter's side, and they vote that he and his family should be allowed to enjoy free use of the land, and that 'no one should disturb them' (μηδένα αὐτοῖς ἐνοχλεῖν) (61), a standard formulation for protection of property rights.[47] They also vote that he should be treated like a benefactor and invited to one of the city's public meals, reversing the first speaker's complaint, discussed already earlier, that the hunter and his family have been treated like benefactors in living free from tax liabilities. The hunter initially wants to attend wearing the animal skin he is dressed in, and expresses a preference for going without dinner rather than changing his clothes, but in the end is persuaded to throw a tunic and cloak over the top. That absurd detail is yet another example of the way in which the people he encounters in the city try to integrate the hunter into urban culture even when they treat him positively. Finally he sets off for home, having refused the money they offer him: 'And from then on nobody has bothered us (ἀπ' ἐκείνου δ' ἡμᾶς οὐδεὶς ἠνώχλησε)' (63). For now at least the hunter's lifestyle may be intact, but despite that impression of security we surely cannot help being aware that the arrogant incomprehension of the city-dwellers may erode that freedom in future, especially when we read on into the depressing barrage of examples of the miserable life that awaits poor people absorbed into the city.

Urban Perspectives

Dio thus juxtaposes two different images of harmonious human interaction with the mountains. The first image is the hunter's model of self-sufficient adaptation to a life of subsistence. The second is the model of larger-scale exploitation of the mountains in the interests of the city and under the control of the city. It is striking that even the second speaker who supports the hunter is unable to see beyond a city-based solution, which will ultimately involve the hunter and his family in paying taxes.[48] Of course Dio's representation of the city is in many respects a negative one. It is important to stress, however, that this second image might have seemed a very attractive one to many of Dio's readers and even to Dio himself. Dio's text is in fact unusual in acknowledging so clearly the integration of mountains into the economic life of the Roman Empire's cities. He seems to know why mountains mattered so much for ancient cities. These speakers have a plan for bringing the mountains back under control. In other contexts it is not hard to see how this might be an attractive idea: what they have in mind is an ideal of harmonious, economically productive interaction between the city and the natural world.

To put that in more generalising terms, this text holds two different images of mountain life in tension with each other. One is an image of mountain populations living outside urban civilisation and close to nature. That is an unusually positive version of the standard stereotype of unsophisticated mountain peoples. The other is an image of the mountain as an economically productive place under the control of the city. The work as a whole dramatises an unresolved tension between those different worldviews. Dio seems to express a preference for the first of those, but we can never quite lose the suspicion that his perspective is closer to that of the city-dwellers who find it so hard to think beyond their own fixed ideas about what the relationship between city and country should be.[49] It is worth remembering that the wealth and prestige of the cities of the Greek east is a major preoccupation of much of Dio's other surviving work, especially his speeches in praise of various cities of Asia Minor. We have already glimpsed in an earlier chapter Dio's praise of the beauty of the mountains and plains around the city of Kelainai.[50] That detail is combined with an encomium of the landscape's productiveness: 'For you occupy the strongest, most fertile spot on the continent; you are situated among the most beautiful plains and mountains; you have very abundant springs and very fertile land, bearing countless products ... and you tend and pasture many herds of cattle and many flocks of sheep' (Dio Chrysostom, *Oration* 35.13). The mountains of Kelainai are beautiful, but they matter also because they contribute to the city's prosperity.[51]

We might even suspect that the rural idyll of the hunter and his family is offered to us quite deliberately as a mirage. Certainly Dio draws attention to the stylised character of some aspects of his description of it, and the difficulty he has, as a city-dweller, in accessing or understanding what he sees. Does that realisation explain why he turns his attention to the realities of life in the city in the second half? He does raise the possibility of removing all the urban poor from the city out to the countryside (107–8),[52] but only very briefly, as if acknowledging the fact that this is hardly a pragmatic solution. In that sense Dio's work anticipates present-day recognition of the impossibility of any abstract sphere of pristine nature or idealised rural isolation beyond the reach of urban culture. One response to that recognition has been an increased attention to city landscapes in ecocritical discourse. We have also come to understand that an obsession with the preservation of purely natural spaces can lead us to ignore the demands of environmental justice, in other words to miss the way in which concern for the natural environment also needs to go hand in hand with solutions that support marginal and disadvantaged communities, not just the indigenous populations who inhabit these protected spaces, but also the much larger communities who live in the urban, industrialised spaces around them. Dio's narrative gives us an intriguing set of precedents and parallels against which to measure up our responses to those challenges, in his turn away from rural life in the first half of the work to a more realistic interest in the realities of urban poverty and inequality in the second. That is not to say that his concerns are exactly equivalent to those of modern environmental commentators. Dio is not talking specifically about environmental justice. His prescriptions in the second half of the work have an elitist, moralising character, influenced by his Stoic philosophy, that is in some respects quite unlike anything we are likely to encounter today. In that sense his work has the odd mix of the familiar and the alien that is so often apparent in ancient precursors of modern environmental themes. Nevertheless this text can, I suggest, be a powerful resource for thinking about the inadequacies of an approach that fetishises pristine, rural environments at the expense of urban populations, and for helping us to see that versions of that worry have a very long history.[53]

The mountains of the ancient Mediterranean were thus fruitful places for thinking through the question of how different varieties of human relationship with the environment were to be valued. Are mountains places outside civilisation? Or are they part of the city, always under human control? The tension between those two possibilities is a major strand in ancient thinking about mountains, and we can see that if we read texts like the *Euboian Oration* from end to end, with attention to the way in which they offer a complex, gradually unfolding narrative about human engagement with landscape. Dio shows us how difficult it is to find a clear-cut answer to those questions.

16

Mountain Saints in Late Antique Christian Literature

Human-Environment Relations in Early Christian Hagiography

The *Euboian Oration* is unusual, for the literature of the Roman Empire, in the way it envisages life in the mountains in such close-up, personal terms. When we look ahead to the fourth century CE, however, we start to see much more frequent descriptions of inhabiting mountain territory, in the saints' lives that survive in such huge numbers from late antiquity right through the medieval period, many of which have mountain settings.[1] That is not to say that these works are primarily interested in life at the very highest altitudes, any more than Dio is. The flexibility of the Greek term *oros* ('mountain') becomes particularly clear in this context. It can refer to mountain peaks, and some holy men are said to have occupied sites on or near the summits. But for the most part it applies more generally for the rocky expanses of wild terrain at lower altitude, especially in late antique Egypt, where it is used almost interchangeably with the Greek word *erēmos*, meaning 'desert'. In some late papyrus texts from the seventh and eighth centuries it comes to mean 'monastery', or in some cases even refers to a concentration of monasteries in the same region.[2]

Like Dio—although in some respects very differently—the authors of the saints' lives offer a broadly positive vision of isolated mountain lifestyles cut off from urban civilisation (or at any rate a positive vision of Christian versions of mountain life: we will see more of how these texts treat the pagan populations of the mountains later). Asceticism, in other words the practice of self-denial, especially sexual and dietary abstinence, both by individuals and within monastic communities, had been a part of Christian life from the very beginning, but from the middle of the fourth century onwards it came to play an even more prominent role within Christian identity. The men and women who practised asceticism most extravagantly became, through the texts that presented them to the wider world, heroes of holiness. They were thought to have special powers of healing. Their stories circulated widely as sources of inspiration for Christians right across the social spectrum. Many of them chose to live their lives away from human habitation, in the wild spaces of the mountain and the desert,[3] initially in Egypt, and in Syria and Palestine, and then more and more widely across the Mediterranean. Isolation aided their lives of prayer and spiritual discipline, away from the temptations of the city. And by taking over places usually associated with those who lived beyond the bounds of civilisation—bandits and wild animals—they advertised the power of Christianity to transform humiliation paradoxically into a sign of Christian power and victory.[4] Of course there were precedents. Many of the prophets of the Hebrew Bible lived harsh lives in the desert. Jesus and John the Baptist did the same.[5] There were also non-Christian precursors for ascetic withdrawal in Roman Egypt, for example in the account given by Philo of the Jewish ascetic group the Therapeutai.[6] We have some surviving stories of Greek and Roman philosophers in the mountains: Diogenes Laertius tells us that Heraclitus used to wander in the mountains, eating grass and plants.[7] But the Christian occupation of those territories was on a completely different scale. The saints' lives are crucial sources for these developments: in many ways they reflect the realities of the explosion of monasticism asceticism that began to gain momentum particularly during the late fourth and fifth centuries.

It is also clear, however, that the idealised images of ascetic isolation that the saints' lives present us with sometimes give a distorted picture of the realities of monastic life. Just like the Greco-Roman portrayals of isolated mountain communities—both negative portrayals of barbarian populations beyond civilisation and positive portrayals of pastoral solitude—early Christian hagiography often conceals the fact that the *oros* could be a place of work closely tied to the economy and society beyond.[8] That has become more and more clear over recent decades thanks in part to extensive archaeological excavation in monastic sites, especially in Egypt.[9]

One factor was the influx of visitors, especially once desert asceticism had become more established in the fifth century and after. The narrator of one important text, the *History of the Monks in Egypt*, which we will see more of later, represents himself as a visitor from a monastic community elsewhere travelling with a large group of companions to see the famous holy men of

Egypt. That phenomenon is related to the sacred tourism we have seen already in the case of Egeria, whose travels took place probably in the 380s. Her primary goal is to see the iconic mountain sites described in the Old Testament, but the monks who are assigned as guides to Egeria and her party are also objects of interest in themselves. When she reaches the church on the summit of Mount Sinai, 'here was the priest who was assigned to the church coming out from his cell towards us, a morally upright old man, a monk from early in his life, and, as they say, an ascetic and—what more can one say—the kind of man who is worthy to be in that place' (*Itinerarium Egeriae* 3.4). The phrase 'as they say' suggests a certain lack of familiarity: ascetic culture is still in its early days at the time Egeria is writing. But it is clear that the man is an object of admiration for his virtue; also that his holiness is in Egeria's view appropriate to the landscape he inhabits.

The prevalence of images of isolation in hagiographic writing also conceals the fact that communal monasticism, much closer to civilisation, was the norm.[10] Clearly some ascetics did take the extreme route of isolating themselves from the surrounding world. Often, however, they had a much closer relationship with the surrounding villages than the saints' lives suggest.[11] Monks would often trade their produce with the local inhabitants: there is evidence for the production of mats, baskets, plaited ropes, sandals, linen cloth, and books. We also have evidence for monasteries keeping detailed records of these transactions, and for the appointment of stewards within individual monasteries to oversee them.[12] Some monastic communities were so large that they came to be like villages or towns in their own right. Ascetics were also regularly involved in the life of the urban churches.[13] That seems to have been the case especially for the ascetics of Palestine, where close relationships with surrounding communities were more common than in Egypt, at least, in the fifth and sixth centuries.[14] For one thing most of the Palestinian monasteries were close to each other, linked by networks of paths. Many were also close to Jerusalem, in most cases within just a day's journey. Monastic communities were closely integrated into the church life and economic life of other cities, especially Scythopolis in northern Palestine,[15] where ascetics and church leaders enjoyed close relationships, and where thriving monasteries received the patronage of wealthy citizens, as well as ministering to the urban poor.

The tension between these two different poles of ascetic inhabitation of the mountains—between isolation from and engagement with the outside world—is central to many of the stories the saints' lives tell. For some texts we have to work hard to see behind their idealisation of ascetic solitude. Others, for example Jerome's *Life of Hilarion*, which I turn to at the end of this chapter, draw attention to that tension quite self-consciously. The tension between solitary and communal monasticism has been a major theme of work on late antique hagiography in recent decades. That phenomenon is usually discussed, however, only within the frame of early Christian monasticism. My goal is to set it in addition within the much wider context of mountain history, both ancient and modern, in order to understand more clearly how it relates to patterns of representation that stretch across many centuries of human engagement with mountains.

Dealing with that tension has a certain amount in common with the challenge we face in understanding the constructed, artificial nature of idealised images of wilderness in post-Romantic culture. The modern notion of wilderness as a space outside human culture is a mirage: the very act of conjuring up wilderness as a category is itself an imposition of human frameworks onto the more-than-human world.[16] Attempts to preserve and protect wilderness tend in practice to involve human intervention in and alteration of the territory that is being preserved. The ideal of the human encounter with wild landscape—often a solitary encounter that involves a degree of danger and distance from the familiar territory of human civilisation—is a powerful ingredient in the self-identification of millions of people around the world, but it is of course encouraged and enabled by a massive industry of adventure writing and outdoor equipment manufacture, and often creates situations where apparently wild places turn out on closer inspection to be heavily shaped by human presence. On the face of it the early Christian saints, with their shrivelled and anti-athletic bodies, could hardly be further removed from the kinds of physicality associated with the mountaineer in the modern imagination. And yet they are described repeatedly with athletic metaphors that celebrate their endurance and their feats of holiness.[17] They give us some of the closest parallels from the ancient world for our own thrilling narratives of solitary, even heroic encounter with wilderness landscapes. And those late antique narratives, like our own versions, turn out on closer inspection to conceal a much more complex story about the difficulty of separating wilderness from human culture.

There are other ways too in which the saints' lives—for all their oddity and alienness[18]—anticipate modern thinking about mountains and the environment. Like Dio's text, and like so much thinking about mountains in the modern world, they are often acutely aware of the way in which mountains can have a distinctive temporality.[19] The wilderness places that the ascetics inhabit are often attractive partly because of their status as very ancient places, linked with the past, as mountains so often were in the ancient imagination.[20] That is partly of course because they were places of Christian memory, associated in some cases with the biblical past,[21] and also increasingly as the centuries went on with the lives of earlier saints.[22] But they were also places that carried traces of a pre-monastic heritage. For example solitary ascetics are often represented as inhabiting tombs, partly as a way of signalling their own voluntary removal from the world of present-day civilisation.[23] At the same time, the actions of the saints asserted Christianity's claims to utterly new and unfamiliar ways of interacting with these ancient spaces. Christian occupation of the mountains often involved the displacement of pagan rituals and cult centres.[24] The representation of the ascetics' feats of abstinence and miracle-working as mountain performances enhances that impression.[25] Communal, pagan performances of mountain ritual, with their tendency to privilege civic self-representation even when they involved processions and sacrifices well beyond the territory of the city, give way to performances based, at least according to the saints lives, on the heroic, charismatic acts of individuals. The Christian ascetics of the saints lives thus performed their occupation of mountain and desert territories in ways that were both ancient and startlingly new.

These texts also parallel in many ways modern environmental thinking in their challenge to conventional hierarchies between human culture and the more-than-human world. It has been for many decades commonplace to claim that early Christianity bears much of the responsibility for modern anthropocentrism in relation to the environment,[26] but in many ways the saints' lives point in quite the opposite direction, for example in presenting us with lives that foreground the difficulty of separating human actors from their environment, and the inadequacy of a worldview that sees a sharp dividing line between human and animal.[27] The saints' lives in fact had a significant, but rarely acknowledged influence over early environmental writing in the nineteenth century.[28] One factor in that influence is their interest in the theme of human immersion in landscape, which tends to be valued very highly in hagiographical writing, to a degree that is unusual for ancient literature.[29] The saints' lives offer us a vision of mastery that is quite distinct from its Greco-Roman ancestors, in its paradoxical acceptance of the way in which human bodies and identities can be overwhelmed by desert and mountain terrains, so that they become almost inextricable from their environments.

Narrating Mountain Asceticism

The mountain territory, the *oros*, played a central role in Christian hagiography right from the start. The genre was invented in the *Life of Antony*, written in the mid-fourth century by the bishop and theologian Athanasius. The text's idealised representation of Antony and his asceticism (both in the original Greek, and in Evagrius' Latin translation which followed soon after its publication) had a vast influence over later hagiographical writing, and over the Christian communities of the fourth century and after. To take just the most famous example, Augustine in his autobiographical work the *Confessions* describes how he was converted by hearing a story about two other men being converted after reading the *Life of Antony*.[30] The final decades of the fourth century and the first few decades of the fifth saw an explosion of hagiographic writing along similar lines. The prevalence of mountain territory in those works is partly a response to the landscape of the *Life of Antony*.[31] It also influenced real-life ascetic practice, helping to fix the idea that mountainous landscapes were the proper venue for the harsh struggles and joys of ascetic devotion.

As so often in hagiography, the *Life of Antony* begins in civilisation, but within just a few lines we leave it behind. Antony, we hear, was from a wealthy, Christian family of Egyptian descent. After the death of his parents, he hears in church Jesus' exhortation to the apostles to sell all they have and give to the poor, and he resolves to live a life of poverty and spiritual devotion. At first he does not go far: 'for there were not yet many monasteries in Egypt, nor did any monk yet know the distant desert; but all those who wished to give attention to themselves practised asceticism in solitude not far from their own village' (*Life of Antony* 3.2). Repeatedly he resists the attacks and temptations of demons. He intensifies his dietary self-denial and moves himself to more and more lonely locations. But the decisive moment—in a sense the founding moment for the whole idea of desert asceticism—is when he finally decides to go 'to the mountain' (εἰς ὄρος) (11.2). There he finds a deserted fort, full of snakes, which leave immediately on his arrival. He shuts himself up in the fort and lives there for twenty years, receiving a supply of bread just twice a year. Finally he emerges when some of his followers attempt to break in to gain access to him. Later he goes even farther away, into the more remote 'inner desert':[32] 'And having travelled for three days and three nights . . . he came to a very high mountain (εἰς ὄρος λίαν ὑψηλόν); and there was very clear water under the mountain, sweet and very cold, and outside there was a plain and a few untended palm trees' (49.17). Here once again we see the traditional motifs of the *locus amoenus*, with its trees and stream, adapted for a mountain setting. Athanasius makes it appropriate for this hagiographical context by stripping away the traditional associations of abundance and characterising it instead as a place of precarious subsistence.[33] Antony chooses to settle there (the place is the Galala Plateau in the northeastern Egyptian desert). He is beset by demons and wild animals, but he resists them and begins to cultivate the land so that it produces meagre crops. He stays on the mountain until his death, visited by an increasing number of suppliants in need of healing, still alone in the 'inner mountain' (τὸ ἔσω ὄρος) (51.1) with just two fellow ascetics as helpers in his old age, but with a community of monks settled closer to human habitation in the 'outer mountains'.

The disciplines of Antony, and the harshness of the landscape he inhabits, are relatively understated. Later texts go much further. The *History of the Monks in Egypt* is one of several works of collective hagiography from the early fifth century, dealing in turn with the lives of many different ascetics. One of them is the monk Elias:

> No report can describe that harsh desert in the mountain as it deserves, in which he sat never going down to the inhabited region. The path taken by those who went to him was a narrow one, so that even those who pressed themselves forwards could only just get along it, because of fierce rocks on either side. He used to sit beneath a rock in a cave, so that even the sight of him was greatly terrifying. . . . And in his old age he ate three ounces of bread in the evening and three olives. In his youth he was consistent in eating just once a week. (*History of the Monks in Egypt* 7)

Here the monk has almost blended into the landscape he inhabits, sharing its fearful and inaccessible qualities, with the sparseness of his diet matching the infertility of the land itself.[34]

Other passages in these collective hagiographies, by contrast, are more interested in exploring the extensive contacts between monastic communities, some of them in mountain settings, and urban or village cultures. For example, one passage from Palladius' *Lausiac History*, written in the early fifth century, gives a vivid picture of the scale and economic complexity of the monastic community at Nitria, where he lived for nine years:[35]

> And so having journeyed to the monasteries around Alexandria and having spent time there for three years, with their 2,000 or so excellent and zealous members, I returned from there and came to the mountain of Nitria. . . .

Next to this mountain is the great desert, which stretches as far as Aithiopia and the Mazicae and Mauretania. On the mountain live around 5,000 men, with different ways of life, each one living as he is able and as he wishes: they are allowed to live alone, or in pairs, or with a large number of companions. On this mountain there are eight bakeries, which serve both the men who live there and the anchorites in the desert, 600 of them.... There is a guest house next to the church, where they receive anyone who comes to visit until he leaves of his own accord, without any time limit, even if he stays for two or three years. Having allowed him to stay for one week in idleness, for the rest of the time they occupy him with work, either in the garden or the bakery or the kitchen.... In this mountain there are also doctors living, and confectioners. And they use wine and wine is sold. All these men work at linen manufacture with their hands, so that they are all self-supporting. (Palladius, *Lausiac History* 7)

Here the monastery is integrated into the surrounding economy, and protected to some extent from the harshness of the mountainous territory that surrounds it.[36]

Theodoret and the Mountains of Syria

Theodoret's *Religious History*, probably written around 440 CE, transposes those narrative traditions of collective hagiography to the rather different landscape of Syria.[37] That is not to say that Syrian monasticism in itself grew directly out of its Egyptian equivalents: it seems likely that some aspects of it developed independently.[38] But in generic terms Theodoret's work follows those earlier precedents, not least in its interest in mountain settings.[39] There are also differences, however. Generally speaking the ascetics of Theodoret's text situate themselves in places which give them more opportunities for contact with the outside world than their counterparts in the Egyptian texts.[40] Many of his lives open by locating their subject on mountains set close to particular cities or villages. Theodoret tells us, for example, that 'Rhosos is a Cilician city, on the right as one sails into the Cilician Gulf. To the east and south of it is a high mountain [that is, Mount Amanos, north of Antioch], densely wooded and shady; it nourishes wild beasts in its thickets. Finding here a valley sloping towards the sea, the great and celebrated Theodosius, having built a small cell, embraced the evangelical way of life in solitude' (Theodoret, *Religious History* 10.1).[41]

Theodoret also tells us that he has himself visited the dwelling place of the ascetic Thalelaios: 'At a distance of twenty stades from Gabala [that is, the modern town of Jableh on the coast of northwestern Syria]—which is a small and pleasant city—he occupied a hill on which there was a sanctuary dedicated to demons and honoured with many sacrifices by the impious people of the past' (28.1). Thalelaios drives away the demons. We hear later that 'the local inhabitants said that many miracles have occurred through the prayer of this man' (28.5). The saint has taken over a mountain associated with religious rituals that were presumably linked with the communal life of the city, and lives there, close to civilisation, as a local landmark.[42]

Some of Theodoret's saints do spend time in more remote territory in the higher mountains,[43] but even in these cases they generally come down to ground level either temporarily or permanently to help the local populations.[44] For example, James of Nisibis left the city and 'embraced the solitary and quiet life, and occupying the peaks of the highest mountains lived on them, making use of the thickets in spring, summer, and autumn, and having the sky as his roof; in the wintertime a cave received him, providing sparse shelter' (1.2). He lives off wild food and uses clothing made of goats' hair. He also, however, descends every so often to perform miracles, mainly involving the infliction of curses on wrongdoers, and is later compelled to accept the office of bishop: 'having exchanged that way of life on the mountains (τὴν ὄρειον ἐκείνην διατριβήν) and having against his inclination to spend his time in the town, he did not change either his food or his clothing' (1.7). There is a similar narrative pattern in the life of Macedonius, who 'had as his *palaistra* [in other words his 'exercise ground' or 'gymnasium'] and stadium the peaks of mountains, not living in a single place, but now living in one location and now moving to another' (13.1). He lives a nomadic lifestyle apart from civilisation, but Theodoret also makes it clear that this pattern of living in itself reflects his closeness to human society: he tells us that Macedonius moved continually in order to escape the crowds of visitors; also that Theodoret's own mother supplied him with food and became his friend. At one point the bishop Flavian tricks him into coming down from the mountain and into being enrolled as a priest: Macedonius pursues him with a stick, afraid that 'the ordination would deprive him of the mountaintop (τῆς τοῦ ὄρους κορυφῆς) and of the way of life he desired' (13.4). In a later incident he 'descended from the mountain' (13.7) voluntarily to intervene on behalf of the city against a verdict from the emperor.[45]

These open-air, mountaintop ascetics seem to anticipate in some ways the kinds of freedom that we often associate with wilderness experience, with its positive connotations of detachment from civilised urban life, but one fascinating moment in the text reminds us that we need to be careful about an anachronistic reading of that phenomenon. Theodoret's life of Eusebius of Teleda opens by signalling a transition from the world of the desert, in the first three lives, to the 'inhabited land' (τὴν οἰκουμένην) (4.1), with the intention of showing that more populated terrain is no hindrance to virtue. Once again the setting is a mountain that stands close to civilisation, east of Antioch, with a 'precinct of demons' on its summit. A plain stretches to the south with many villages,[46] and 'at the very edges of the high mountain there is a very large and well-populated village, and in the local language they call it Teleda' (4.2). There can be no doubt here that we are in distinctively Syrian mountain territory, close to human habitation. Here, in a valley above the foot of the mountain, an ascetic Ammianus builds a retreat. Eusebius has been living a life of devotion immured in a windowless hut several miles away, but Ammianus persuades him to come to join him at Teleda as a teacher for the community there. Eusebius is not there to enjoy the view: 'Eusebius and the wonderful Ammianus were sitting on a rock, and one of them read aloud the history of the holy Gospels, while the other laid bare the meaning of the more obscure passages. Some farm labourers were ploughing the land in the plain below them, and the great Eusebius was distracted by this sight', so that he has to ask Ammianus to repeat some of the Gospel reading. Later, dismayed by his own weakness, Eusebius 'made a rule never to look at that plain with his eyes nor to feast upon the beauty of the heavens and the choir of the stars' (4.6). In order to enforce that rule on himself he attaches iron collars to his waist and his neck and a chain joining them together so as to keep his eyes on the ground. This is the kind of image that can every so often stun us into reassessing too-easy images of continuity between ancient and modern patterns of response to landscape. The mountain ascetics of Theodoret and others may be distant precursors of modern mountain engagement in some respects, but they are also utterly alien to it in others, and to many aspects of the classical tradition of mountain engagement too. Eusebius rejects the view from above, with all its connotations of territorial control, divine omniscience, satirical detachment, even pleasure; for him the mountainside is a place that demands uncompromising attachment to and immersion in the terrain at his feet, as a way of holding his attention on the divine.[47]

Pseudo-Nilus' *Narrations* and the Massacres at Mount Sinai

The saints' lives thus project a positive vision of mountain life. Often that involves expressing approval of the kinds of trial and humiliation and solitude that mountain terrains impose on their human inhabitants—sometimes in ways which seem quite alien to a modern audience, despite their superficial similarity with our own ways of idealising human mountain experience. In other cases it involves acceptance of the way in which living in the mountains often in practice involves a complex relationship with surrounding village and urban communities. However, all of the ascetic individuals and monastic communities represented in the saints' lives are very different from the one Dio portrays for us, because of their status as outsiders and incomers to mountain terrain. When it comes to the indigenous populations of mountain regions a lot of early Christian writing replicates or even intensifies standard Greco-Roman attitudes of dismissiveness and denigration precisely in order to emphasise the achievement of Christian appropriation of the wilderness.

The early fifth-century *Narrations* of Pseudo-Nilus, whose narrative of the massacre of Christian ascetics around Mount Sinai we have glimpsed already in chapter 4, is a particularly shocking example. The text as a whole seems designed to question and undermine extremist models of ascetic isolation:[48] the first-person narrator is increasingly beset by doubts about the wilderness lifestyle that is initially an object of desire for him, and about the status of Mount Sinai itself as a symbol of divine protection standing above the ascetic communities at its base. The summit of Mount Sinai is represented as a place of holiness, and a place of special access to the divine. It is also the place where the narrator and his companions retreat to once the first attack is over: he tells us that the other monks 'ran through the ravines (διὰ τῶν φαράγγων), hurrying to get to the mountain—for they [that is, the barbarians] do not approach it, in the belief that God stood upon it and issued commandments to His people' (*Narrations* 4.4). In that sense Mount Sinai has a special power, as a place of refuge and prayer, free from the contaminations of barbarian violence which is so hard to escape from in the desert below. However, the narrator elsewhere complains about the absence of divine intervention on the summit, as if acknowledging that the mountain experience of the Old Testament prophets that he has fantasised about is a mirage: 'How can it be that the miraculous terrors of Mount Sinai stayed silent, rather than striking the transgressors with bursts of thunder and oppressive storm-clouds and immeasurable flashes of lightning.... Instead the pious ones fell helpless by the Burning

Bush itself and by the mountain of the law-giving like irrational beasts of sacrifice' (*Narrations* 4.8).[49]

The *Narrations* also subverts the portrayals of extravagant ascetic achievement that we find in other texts. Other authors talk in much more assured terms about the astonishing holiness of the monks of Mount Sinai, who seemed almost to blend into the mountainous land around them. Sulpicius Severus' *Dialogues* date from the more or less the same period as the *Narrations*. The first dialogue focuses on an ethnographic account by Sulpicius' friend Postumianus, who has travelled to see the ascetics of Egypt:

> I saw the Red Sea, the ridge of Mount Sinai, whose summit almost touches heaven, and cannot by any means be approached. Within its recesses there was said to be a certain anchorite, whom I was unable to see, despite searching for him for a long time and with great effort. Having been removed from human society now for nearly fifty years, wearing no clothes and being covered by the hairs of his own body, he is oblivious by divine grace to his own nudity. This man whenever devout men wanted to approach him used to avoid human contact by running off into trackless terrain. (Sulpicius Severus, *Dialogue* 1.17)

Here, as in the description of the monk Elias from the *History of the Monks in Egypt*, the ascetic is almost a part of the landscape, recessed within the mountain's walls, and able to melt away into the wilderness. By contrast, the ascetics of the *Narrations* are more human and more vulnerable, as we see especially in the massacre scenes, which are recounted in terrifyingly vivid terms. The romanticised notion that ascetics can inhabit the mountain-desert side-by-side with the brigands, appropriating their territory and their outsider status, perhaps converting them in the process, is brought up against a much more complicated reality. The barbarians are described 'wandering and being forced by the rough ground to go now one way and now another, circling round steep mountains (ὄρη ... ἠλίβατα) and passing through pathless and difficult ravines (ἀτριβεῖς καὶ δυσβάτους ... φάραγγας)' (5.10). At one point they find an ascetic living in the cave at the foot of a high mountain, with a makeshift wall of 'small stones' (λίθοις ὀλίγοις) around it to keep out wild animals.[50] They drag him out, 'place him on a rock (ἐπὶ τινος πέτρας) and kill him with stones (λίθοις ... κατακτείνουσι)'. Here the standard image of the Christian population of the desert immersed in and almost indistinguishable from the landscape they inhabit is rewritten in a way that emphasises their exposure to violence. The ascetic has lived his life surrounded by rock, immersed in the rocky landscape, and that is how he meets his death too.

Increasingly, too, the narrator and the other ascetics in the region rely on military and diplomatic intervention from the Roman authorities in order to save them, and towards the end of the text they find themselves back in an urban environment. After the narrator descends from Mount Sinai he retreats to the city of Pharan, which was the only city on the Sinai peninsula at that date, standing about thirty miles west of Saint Catherine's Monastery. It is there that he tells his tale. Once the telling is over, a slave arrives who has similarly escaped from the barbarians. He explains how he was travelling across the desert with his master, Magadon, a wealthy member of the Council of Pharan, together with the town's *stratēgos* (that is, probably its leading official). They too are captured by the barbarians and killed, together with Magadon's son. The slave witnesses several other murders, and then manages to escape, leaving the narrator's son still alive and with the barbarians. The authorities then decide to act: 'The council of those who inhabited Pharan therefore decided, after hearing our news, not to remain silent about the atrocity, but to make it clear to the king of the barbarians' (6.9).The envoys return with good news: the king (that is, the regional overlord given money and the title of phylarch by the Romans in exchange for preventing raids by local tribes) confirms that 'he did not want to dissolve the terms of the peace . . . since he cherished the treaty he had with the Pharanites because of the money he received from them'[51] (*Narrations* 6.11). The barbarians who have committed the atrocities are scared away by a detachment of soldiers. The barbarian 'king' makes an enquiry to find out what has been stolen, and order is restored to the desert. The mountain is brought back under the control of the city.

That concluding scene is in line with the later history of Mount Sinai, which during the succeeding sixteen centuries or so has been for the most part a thriving place, closely linked with the outside world. As we have seen already the region also had a vast tourist trade. Egeria's pilgrimage diary makes it clear that there was an established system for receiving guests and showing them round. Anastasius of Sinai, writing rather later, in the seventh century, describes his monastery catering for 600 visitors at a single meal, and mentions 'cooks, cellarers, stewards and servers' (Anastasius, *Tales of the Sinai Fathers* 1.12). The monastery was also integrated with the local economy. One surviving papyrus document gives us a vivid glimpse of that. It records the expenses of a trading company operating between Nessana (in the far north of the Sinai Peninsula), Mount Sinai and elsewhere, probably in the sixth or seventh century:

Paid as price for slave girl, 3 sol., plus camel worth 6 1/3. Total: 9 1/3.
As price for slave boy, 6 sol., plus camel worth 4 1/3. Total (including fee of man who drew up bill of sale): 10 1/3.
Paid to the Saracen escort who took us to the Holy Mountain, 3. sol.
Turned over to us by Abba Martyrius, 270 sol.
We went for prayer at the Holy Mountain and gave a blessing, 1 sol.
Expenditures for you, also purchase of fish and almonds, 1 sol.
Donation to the Holy Mountain on behalf of the group from your town: 10 sol., and on behalf of [. . . sos]: 7 sol. Total: 17 sol.[52]

—and so on at great length. Even at this period, after the Arab conquest, the monastery at the Holy Mountain seems to be closely linked with the people of this other town more than 150 miles to the north, and part of the traders' regular route. The traders leave a donation at the monastery, and the monks in turn give a vast sum of money to the traders (in exchange for what is unclear).

The *Narrations* thus dramatises the process of moving towards a more moderate, more realistic image of what life around Mount Sinai might involve, rejecting the allure of extreme isolation and asceticism and recognising the vulnerability of the Christian community there, and its inevitable entanglement with a wider urban and imperial culture, which largely reflects what we know of the situation on the ground. It performs no such service, however, for the Saracen population, who are portrayed throughout as bloodthirsty and merciless cannibals, in a way which echoes the colonialist denigration of indigenous populations that has been so crucial to later imperial discourse both in the Sinai region and in so many other parts of the world, and not just, of course, in the mountains.[53] In fact many of the nomads in this period were themselves Christian, and had a close relationship with the settled population, just as the monks themselves did.[54] But the narrator's portrayal of the barbarians in the *Narrations* uses all the old stereotypes of nomadic, pastoral people living outside civilisation. He says that they live without trade and without agriculture: they rely instead on pasturing their flocks. They hunt desert animals and rob people on the roads. They worship the morning star, and perform human sacrifice. When they kill a camel, they eat it like dogs, having cooked it barely long enough to soften its flesh, or if a camel is sacrificed (in the absence of young children, who are their preferred victims), they rush in to have a first taste of the blood, and rip out the entrails to eat them there and then. There are overtones of Cyclopean savagery here.[55] In his description of the first massacre, beneath Mount Sinai itself, the author equates them with animals and with the force-of-nature images that Ammianus too had used for barbarian invaders. They descend on the monks unexpectedly, 'like a hurricane' (καθάπερ θύελλα). The narrator tells us that he happened to be there too, having come down from the mountain with his son. The barbarians 'ran at us like mad dogs, plundering and shouting incomprehensibly' (4.1), before lining up the monks for execution and hacking some of them to death with their swords, 'turning their fiery-eyed glance from side to side' (4.2), before unaccountably letting the others go. Here the text uses images of irrational and animalistic frenzy in order to convey the savagery of the attackers, in contrast with the pathos and emotional complexity of the Christian narrator and his fellow victims.

The Life of Symeon the Mountaineer

There are many other examples of that kind of denigration of the non-Christian inhabitants of the mountains. Some of the most extravagant of these narratives involve the Isaurians, and again replicate very closely the kinds of negative language that is applied to them in the work of Ammianus Marcellinus. In a text titled *The Life and Miracles of Saint Thekla*, from the late fifth century, the saint protects several different towns from Isaurian raids; at one point she blinds the savage Isaurians with mist, allowing them to be killed by cavalry in their mountain hideouts.[56] Another text, the *Life of Konon of Isauria*, describes that saint's conversion of the Isaurians.[57] Among other things Konon prevents the highland people from making their annual pilgrimage to a mountain sacred to Apollo, to worship a statue in a cave 'full of shadow' at the base of a mountain that is 'sheer' and 'difficult to ascend on foot' (5), and with angelic help overpowers and converts two Isaurian brigands, who are described as 'lurking in the mountains like snakes', in a metaphor reminiscent of Ammianus' Isaurian sections. The text has sometimes been characterised as an attempt to salvage a positive version of Isaurian-Christian identity by emphasising their successful conversion, and the fact that Conon himself is an Isaurian, using his own knowledge of the mountain terrain to beat his Isaurian opponents at their own game, arguably contributes to that effect.[58] But any positivity about late antique Isauria would surely have come across as double-edged, not least because the forces of civilisation originate, as so often in representations of Isauria, from the Christian population in the plains. The text hardly goes out of its way to discard the old stereotypes of Isaurian savagery, or the old images of a split between highland and lowland populations.[59]

Perhaps most astonishing of all is the little-read life of the holy man 'Symeon the Mountaineer' in the Syriac text *Lives of the Eastern Saints* by John of Ephesus, set in Syria and written in the sixth century. The text offers us an intriguing image of the mountain ascetic choosing human engagement ahead of an isolated life at high altitude,[60] but it represents a very troubling variant of that narrative pattern because of its denigration of the mountain population Symeon interacts with. Ultimately they are transformed from a state of uneducated ignorance into a Christian community, but the processes by which that conclusion is reached involve a ruthless suppression and rejection of their native culture, so much so that it is hard to believe, from a modern perspective, that any contemporary reader could ever have come away with a positive impression of Symeon's actions. The text offers us a celebratory image of colonial mistreatment of mountain populations far more shocking than the portrait of urban interference that we have seen already in Dio's *Euboian Oration*.

The story of that conversion process is embedded within a plot pattern very much like the one that is so common in the work of Theodoret and others, where the ascetic moves from a solitary lifestyle to a more engaged, urban way of living. Symeon at first spends his time in marginal places, cutting himself off from society as far as he can: we hear that he 'used to go about on the mountains like the wild beasts' (John of Ephesus, *Lives of the Eastern Saints*, p. 229),[61] although he comes down to a lower level in winter, in a way which replicates the movements of pastoral transhumance: 'he used to spend eight months on the mountains among caves and rocks, and for the four severe winter months he would come down to a monastic convent which he knew to be convenient for his occupation, on account of the hardness of the winter and the severity of the snow' (p. 232). There is an extraordinary parallel in the life of the ascetic Addai, earlier in the collection. He too retreats to the hills, but comes down to lower levels in winter:

> And so he departed and went up to the rugged, towering mountains in the east of that district, in which nothing except great beasts is to be found on account of their inaccessibility.... But he, on account of the ruggedness of the mountains and the unbounded amount of snow that covered them, went down to the neighbourhood of a certain hamlet that was situated among these same mountains... (pp. 128–29)

Addai hides in the mountains from those who want to come and see him. The author tells us that he himself several times went in search of Addai, together with a companion, and he gives a long account of one of those expeditions in particular. Like Symeon, in fact much more extravagantly, Addai is described here in animal terms. They hide behind some trees and wait for him to arrive:

> When he had approached to about half a furrow's-length from us . . . as if he scented the smell of us, he checked himself and halted, waiting a long time, while we on our side did not stand up and were not seen by him; and, as if he had become aware of us in his spirit, he thereupon like a wild beast turned aside, and set his face to go down the mountain-side at a run. (pp. 131–32)

Addai here has become immersed in his surroundings after twenty-five years in the mountains, so much so that he comes close to throwing off his human identity.

It is striking, however, that this preference for solitude does not stop either of these saints from intervening on behalf of the communities around them. Symeon later comes face to face with a more communal mode of mountain life which changes his whole approach:

> But once, while going round from mountain to mountain, he chanced to be on rough mountains near the river Euphrates . . . and he saw that, though these mountains were rugged and towering, houses and domestic brood-animals(?) were scattered over them all. . . . The blessed Symeon was amazed to see in what a rugged mountainous district human beings were living, and moreover that they possessed houses and cattle and were settled there in confidence (one being three miles distant from his neighbour, and another five and another two according to chance), and he was also astonished that all the mountains were so full of people [with] great houses and substantial dwellings. (pp. 232–33)

This mountain community thus has many of the trappings of civilisation, much to Symeon's surprise. But it also soon becomes clear that they are still in some ways outcasts from the world, and in that sense they represent a challenge which the saint deals with decisively. Symeon interrogates them and they confess that they pay no attention to Christian observance, admitting that with a few exceptions 'none of us has entered a church since he was born; but we live on these mountains like animals' (p. 235). The holy man is shaken: 'his bones shook with fright and his tears gushed out' (pp. 233–34). The rest of the text recounts his missionary work there: he converts this from a place which has superficial marks of civilisation—the houses and the farms—to a real Christian community in the mountains. His tactics are so extravagant that they might be almost comic if it were not for the fact that they echo countless abuses and suppressions of local populations from modern colonial history.[62] Symeon locks some of the children in the church, having enticed them with the promise of presents, and tonsures them en masse, in a scene which must have been meant to remind its readers of sheep-shearing, given the pastoral nature of this mountain population, and which therefore contributes to the impression of conversion from animal to human identity.[63] When the parents of two of the children complain and try to take them away, he predicts that the children will be struck dead, and when his prediction is fulfilled the whole population comes under his power. It is clear that the mountains are no longer wilderness places by the end of the text: 'thenceforward loud choirs were to be heard at the Service, and all these mountains also had been brought into subjection, and they trembled to commit any breach of order, lest the old man should hear it and separate them from the fellowship of men, or that he should curse them' (p. 246).

As in so many of the other saints' lives, the project of asserting a paradoxically positive vision of mountain life had severe limits, in the sense that it was possible only within a Christian framework, which often involved reinforcing or even intensifying the kind of denigratory stereotypes of indigenous populations that were so widespread elsewhere in Greek and Roman literature. That is clear for the 'Life of Symeon the Mountaineer' not least in its use of animal imagery, which is one of the most shocking features of the text. As I have suggested already it is sometimes tempting to see positive aspects in the way in which the saints' lives embrace animal imagery for their ascetic heroes, as in the case of Symeon and especially Addai. That manoeuvre in some respects anticipates current ecocritical interests in its challenge to the hierarchies between human and animal.[64] But it is important to stress that that phenomenon exists side by side with a much more upsetting version of the blurring between human and animal, where marginal peoples are associated with animals in order to justify conquest or in this case conversion.[65] The continuing importance of that strand of ancient thinking about mountain peoples in the saints' lives is a powerful reminder of the risks of oversimplification and idealisation in our quest for ancient precursors to modern attitudes to the environment.

Mountain Retreats in Jerome's *Life of Hilarion*

One final text from early in the hagiographical tradition, Jerome's *Life of Hilarion*, which was written in Latin in 390, memorably encapsulates the challenges of maintaining an idealised vision of solitary mountain asceticism in the face of the encroachment of human society.[66] Jerome was one of the first writers to imitate the *Life of Antony*. His saints' lives were themselves very influential, especially this text and another, the *Life of Paul of Thebes*, written in the mid 370s. Hilarion, like Antony, in Jerome's account retreats very early in his life from civilisation. He was born, Jerome tells us, to a pagan family in Palestine, and received a good education in Alexandria. But at the age of fifteen, having fulfilled his desire to meet the famous Antony, he sets out himself into the desert: not mountainous desert but the marshy coastal wilderness along from Gaza which was renowned for its banditry. He lives on a punishingly frugal diet: 'from the time he was 21 until he was 26, for three years he ate half a pint of lentils soaked in cold water [presumably Jerome means each day] and for the other three years he ate dry bread with salt and water. Then from the time he was 27 until he was 31, he sustained himself with wild herbs and uncooked roots of certain shrubs' (Jerome, *Life of Hilarion* 5.1–2).[67] When he is threatened by robbers he succeeds in converting them. His reputation for holiness spreads. Then one day, after twenty-two years there, he starts to get visitors: first a childless woman who comes to ask for his blessing, and later conceives, then a whole stream of others, so much so that Hilarion spends much of the rest of his life, according to Jerome's at times almost comical account, trying to escape from the attention. At one point we read that he longs to escape into solitude but his fasting has made him too weak to walk (paradoxically the techniques of fasting which should bring release from the world thus make release more difficult). When he finally gets hold of a donkey to facilitate his escape, a crowd of 10,000 gathers to stop him from leaving; only a hunger strike finally persuades them to let him go.[68]

Jerome is fully aware, then, of the way in which the ascetic is pulled in two directions, both towards and away from civilisation. It may be that this reflects something of Jerome's own ascetic experience: he spent some years in retreat in the deserts of Syria near Antioch.[69] Clearly his time there was far removed from the city lifestyle he was used to. But it is also clear that he was not cut off from the realities of civilised life quite so much as we would expect—certainly much less so than his exaggeratedly self-isolating hero Paul of Thebes, whose life he wrote around that time. He undertook regular correspondence by letter, and spent much of his time on scholarship, with his whole library and slaves to copy books for him. He even found himself being drawn repeatedly into theological controversies within the church. In his later life Jerome clearly had a very ambivalent relationship with the ideals of ascetic withdrawal that were given such prominence in the *Life of Antony* and in so many later texts, and clearly they continued to hold a great attraction for him, but he was also acutely aware of their difficulty and even their undesirability, and that ambivalence surely exercised a formative influence over the *Life of Hilarion* and his other biographical writing.[70]

There are two mountains in the text, both of which contribute to exploring that contrast between idealised isolation and human intrusion. Both of them are highly stylised and artificial. Jerome knew Apuleius' *Metamorphoses* well and refers to it repeatedly in the *Life of Hilarion* and he seems to be imitating Apuleius' extravagant mountains in both of these passages.[71] It may be that Jerome was attracted to Apuleius as a model partly because he found the *Metamorphoses*' dramatisation of different possible ways of imagining landscape and geography unusually promising as a framework for giving expression to his own exploration of the contest between conflicting conceptualisations of Christian geography.[72] Like Apuleius, he seems to be aware that the implausibly rocky and lonely summits he idealises as places of monastic isolation are in the end unrealistic, in the sense that they give a misleading impression of the ascetic's relationship with the wider world. The first mountain is Antony's. Hilarion returns there after Antony's death, and his description of the site recalls the equivalent description in the *Life of Antony*, but restores some of the lushness that Athanasius had stripped away from the *locus amoenus* traditions he inherited: 'A rocky and high mountain, extending for about a mile, gushes out water at its base; some of the water is absorbed by the sand, some of it flows down to lower ground and gradually comes together to form a stream, above which, on both banks, countless palm trees make the place very charming and full of advantages' (*Life of Hilarion* 21.2).[73]

The second mountain is Hilarion's own retreat, on Cyprus, where he spends the final years of his life, and which is clearly meant to recall Antony's mountain home:

> Arriving there he contemplated this place which was indeed very terrible and isolated. It was surrounded here and there by trees, with water pouring down from the brow of the hill, and a delightful little garden and very many fruit trees, whose fruit he never ate. But it also had nearby the ruin of a temple from which, as he himself used to tell and as his disciples confirm, the voices of countless demons used to echo day and night, so many that you might have thought there was an army of them. He was delighted at the idea of having his enemies nearby, and he lived there for five years. He was often cheered in this last period of his life by the visits of Hesychius, for

owing to the roughness and difficulty of the place and the large number (so it was rumoured) of ghosts, no one or scarcely anyone was able or dared to make the climb. (*Life of Hilarion* 31.4–5)

This is clearly a mountain in the Apuleian tradition, with a desperately steep approach, and water flowing from the top, just like the robbers' hideout in *Metamorphoses* Book 4.[74] But it is different in being more pleasant: it combines *locus amoenus* (the delightful garden and the stream) and *locus horridus* traditions (the demons and the jagged rocks, which strike fear into the surrounding population), as if to demonstrate the paradoxical power of Christianity to turn places of fear and wilderness into places of habitation and desire. It is hard, too, to miss the allegorical overtones, which cast further doubt on the realism of the description. The approach to the mountaintop, crawling on hands and knees, is surely a metaphor for the self-abasement and struggle which brings one close to God; and the mountaintop garden itself is an image of paradise.[75] The atmosphere of allegory is enhanced by Jerome's reference to the fruits of Hilarion's 'delightful garden' (*hortulum peramoenum*), which he refrains from eating. That detail casts Hilarion's self-denial in Edenic terms, while also incongruously recalling the Apuleian passage where Lucius refrains from eating roses in the 'pleasant garden' (*hortulum amoenum*) of *Metamorphoses* 3.29.[76] Hilarion is associated with Apuleius' absurd hero in ways which have the potential to be comical and undignified, but which probably signal more his ability to take on debased, marginal models and turn them paradoxically into positive resources for Christian identity.

It seems then that Hilarion has at last found the proper place for his spiritual disciplines. And yet even here it turns out that this idealised, allegorised place of freedom from the world is not secure from intrusion. First Hilarion heals a paralysed man who has somehow or other made it up the steep mountain path (it is not specified how). And from then on the familiar stream of visitors starts up again—'once this became known, the need of many overcame even the difficulty of the place and the pathless journey' (*Life of Hilarion* 31.9)—and the local inhabitants start to make plans to prevent him from escaping. Even in death Hilarion is not left alone: he is initially buried in obedience to his death-bed instructions, but his body is then stolen from Cyprus and taken to Palestine, to the city of Majuma: 'and there Hesychius laid it to rest in the ancient monastery, with all the monks and crowds of townspeople accompanying the body in procession' (*Life of Hilarion* 32.7).[77]

Jerome's text is in many ways quite alien to the ways of interacting with mountain landscapes that were familiar in earlier Mediterranean culture, and even more so to the dominant cultures of mountain life and leisure in the post-classical world.[78] At the same time, however, it is structured around a tension that has been central to human experience and representation of mountains over many millennia. Once again we have two different images of mountain life jostling against each other, one involving isolation, the other integration. Jerome draws our attention to that conflict, in showing us the real world of the surrounding community, and the public, processional life of the city, in that final image, breaking in upon Hilarion's idealised mountain retreat.

Epilogue

LATE IN 2020, when I had finished a draft of these chapters, I took the day off and went for a walk in the hills. I had hoped to go to Greece, but that wasn't possible, with the coronavirus travel restrictions in place. I parked in the Glen Doll car park, then went up to Corrie Fee through the woods; from there, up the steep path at the head of the corrie to the summit plateau, and on to the two Munros, Mayar and Driesh; and then down again on the even steeper descent along the Shank of Drumfollow.[1] It was only a short trip—just a few hours. I didn't feel I was particularly close to the mountains of the Mediterranean here. The news stories I had listened to on the radio in the car were going round and round in my head. And besides it just felt too close to home. This is a place I have been to maybe ten times in my life. I have lots of memories attached to it. I remember seeing a mountain hare up on the plateau, with the patches of white still in its fur matching the snow patches on the ground in late spring. I remember my children swimming and playing in the streams and pools that meander down through the meadow on the corrie floor, and a disastrous wild camping trip here where we were driven home by clouds of midges. I remember turning my ankle over running down the rocky path on my birthday a few years ago, then bathing it in the cold water.

As I walked up through Corrie Fee, I thought a lot about why I like being in the mountains. It was a beautiful, windless late autumn day. I could see the bright orange colour of the larches everywhere. I felt cushioned and safe, enveloped almost, with my GPS watch and my comfortable shoes and the well-made path beneath my feet. Certainly it gave me pleasure to be there. Spending time in the mountains was never something we did much of on family holidays when I was growing up, although I do remember climbing a hill on holiday in Wales when I was eight or nine, in the very early 1980s. It was somewhere in Pembrokeshire, just a few hundred metres high. I wish I could work out from the photos which hill it was. We planted a homemade paper flag on the summit. Then at school, from the age of fourteen or so, we used to be bused off to the mountains in Snowdonia several times a year and released into the wilderness, with old military rations and badly fitting army boots. In my memory it is always raining. I guess that must have been a common experience for English private-school boys at that time. I remember once sleeping on the summit of Snowdon so that we could get up before sunrise to do a hike over most of the peaks in Snowdonia; and then sixteen hours later coming down off the final mountain more or less in tears, with blisters the size of jam jar lids on my feet.

In some ways I have reacted against those experiences—or at any rate I have learned how to take pleasure from being in the mountains much more than I ever did then. One of the good things about living near to the Scottish Highlands is that you can wait for the sunny days. But I'm also aware of how much I have been shaped by them, and by ways of thinking about mountains that have had such a powerful hold over Western culture. I love climbing to summits and looking down. I love spending time in the mountains with just a few friends or family, and sometimes on my own, on the assumption that solitary time away from 'civilisation' can be a way of understanding yourself and having the freedom and the space to think. Some of the most memorable days of my life are days I have spent in the mountains, especially the kind of trip where you're miles from the nearest road and you don't meet any other human beings all day. I love timing myself—knowing how long I have taken on a particular route, and how far I have travelled. I love walking and scrambling and running in the hills because of the way they make me tired; sometimes that can be uncomfortable or stressful, but it gives a kind of pleasure too, not just in retrospect but even at the time, a sense of being challenged and alert.

I know that all of those ways of reacting are culturally determined, even if I have my own particular versions of them. The idea of the summit position has been a very powerful one within modern mountaineering culture.[2] At various times over the last few centuries the idea of conquering mountain summits has even been entangled with imperialist ideals.[3] The image of the solitary wanderer walking and scrambling in the fells is inherited from Romantic engagement with the Lake District by Coleridge and Wordsworth and others, and connected with idealising images of solitary creative or intellectual activity.[4] The pleasure I take in viewing mountain scenery is linked with ways of envisaging landscape that have an elitist history, where the ability to appreciate and access places of beauty and sublimity has been a marker of social distinction.[5] The enjoyment that many people today take from experiencing physical challenges in difficult mountain terrain is the legacy among other things of late nineteenth-century developments within mountaineering culture, which increasingly came to value bodily discomfort and exhaustion for its own sake.[6] In all of these ways mountains have often been used as landscapes for the exercise of an elite, white, able-bodied, male identity (though with plenty of exceptions, more and more so today), and that has often involved importing an outsider perspective that elides the experience of those who live and work in the mountains.[7] There is still a common story that these are new phenomena in human history. The image of mountains as places where we act out our own modernity[8] may even be one of the reasons why some people invest in these habits so heavily and so viscerally, as practices that are tied up with their own senses of pleasure and identity,[9] as they certainly are for me.

I am more self-conscious than I used to be about the way in which those traditions have shaped me. I'm also aware that my own ways of interacting with mountains have changed over time. That's partly just because I don't have as much time to spare as I used to: some years I only manage to go to the Highlands for a few days. I suspect that my capacity to care about mountains is less dependent on being there in person than it used to be. But I can also see that I have been influenced by changing ways of talking about landscape. I think much more than I would have done thirty years ago about how we can widen access to mountains and to other wild landscapes. I understand more clearly than I ever did that there is no such thing as wilderness removed from human culture—no such thing as a pristine landscape, especially now with the fear of climate change everywhere around us. I also think more and more about the way in which being in the mountains makes me experience my body as intertwined with the terrain I am moving through—rather than just as an opportunity for acting out a comically unrealistic fantasy of athletic prowess—as a way of understanding human vulnerability to and dependence on the environment that we inhabit.[10] The ways of spending time in the mountains that I have inherited are not set in stone: my own responses to them have changed over time, and will continue to change in the future. But I also know that I wouldn't want to shake off those inherited ways of acting entirely, when the pleasures I take from them are so deeply rooted.

As I went on farther—out of the sun now, on the muddy track leading up the head of the corrie—I started to think after all about the mountains of the ancient Mediterranean, and about what on earth they have to do with my experience of the Scottish Highlands. To me the Highlands feel very different from those places, not just because these Scottish mountains are so different as landscapes—wetter and greener—but also perhaps because they feel more removed from history. Of course that's not right: the Highlands have their own complex and important history too.[11] It's just that the history of the Greek mountains is sometimes easier to sense when they have the remains of ancient altars on their summits and famous battlefields on their slopes—or maybe it's just that I'm particularly obsessed with those things myself, having read so much about them.

What do I gain then from looking back to the mountains of ancient Greek and Roman culture? What does it have to do with this time I spend in the mountains myself? One of the things that fascinates me is the possibility that modern pleasures and habits associated with the mountains might have a much longer history than we usually realise. It has become increasingly clear to me that the traditional narrative of a watershed between premodern and modern engagement with mountains is oversimplified.[12] Of course some things changed in the eighteenth and nineteenth centuries. But what we do in the mountains also has many more continuities with the premodern past than we usually realise. Modern ways of responding to mountains and to landscape more generally were in many respects shaped by engagement with classical texts. Many early climbers and mountaineers, just like many of the most influential eighteenth- and nineteenth-century thinkers on landscape aesthetics, were steeped in a classical education. The story of classical influence over nineteenth- and early twentieth-century mountaineering has still not been told except in passing.[13] But I also turn to the ancient world to see something different, attracted by the prospect that I might find ways of interacting with mountains that are alien to our own. That process might give us models or inspirations for a different kind of future. It might also expose some of the arbitrariness and strangeness and cultural specificity of our own habits in turn.

For me that tension is central to what we gain from studying the ancient world at all. We find in ancient literature and ancient history precursors of our own ways of living and our own experience. That might sometimes involve the startling experience of recognition, as we see moments of continuity or influence between ancient and modern that we have not suspected; or in other cases resemblances that stop short of full equivalence and that may not be straightforwardly explicable by a genealogical connection. Of course that perception may sometimes be in part a symptom of our own needs and desires to draw connections and to enter into a relationship of kinship with the past. At the same time, often equally startlingly, we find things that are strange to us—although that may be in part a result of our own exoticising fantasies of estrangement. The never-resolved tension or oscillation between these two different kinds of reaction is one of the things that gives me the desire to keep reading ancient texts. And these are the kinds of realisation that have grabbed my attention over and over again in my attempts to understand how ancient Greek and Roman writers depicted the mountain landscapes of the Mediterranean.

The ancient world shares with us, for example, an awareness of the symbolic power of mountains as places of spiritual as well as literal ascent; of the aesthetic power of mountains as places of the sublime; of the status of mountains as places of fascination and enigma, puzzles for interpretation, in scientific writing and beyond. It shares with us an awareness of the role of mountains in regional and local self-definition, and of their position on the edge of human culture, as places of work and habitation, and as wilderness spaces that nevertheless turn out on closer inspection to be shaped by human activity and control. Ancient texts have a tendency to denigrate mountain communities—and sometimes in the same breath to exalt them as exemplars of natural virtue— often through traditions of environmental determinism that have a long history also in nineteenth- and twentieth-century writing. They also have an interest in advertising mastery over mountain landscape that has had a formative importance for modern engagements too. That phenomenon is regularly linked with the idea of viewing from above, and with the idea of good generalship in difficult conditions in battles and expeditions. That latter concept reflects the existence of specialist expertise in dealing with mountain terrain in military contexts in the ancient world, which again has many recent parallels. Side by side with those images of mastery, ancient Greek and Roman literature is also interested in using mountains as vehicles for thinking about the value of human intervention in the environment, for example through reflections on the value of landscape alteration. It has a sustained interest in the power of mountains to overwhelm human bodies and identities, in ways which can reveal human vulnerability to environmentally unstable or threatening landscapes: that experience is for the most part viewed negatively but occasionally, as in some early Christian texts, it is appropriated and treated as a positive phenomenon. Ancient writing about mountains, like its modern equivalents, is thus fascinated by the tension between different scales of mountain viewing—between distant viewing, and more close-up, haptic modes of engagement—and that tension lies at the heart of a lot of modern mountain writing too. Ancient and modern culture even share a sense of mountains as places of bodily performance, for example in the mountaintop sacrificial rituals which represent very distant ancestors of the increasingly strong strand of performativity within modern mountain engagement.[14] Running through all of those phenomena there is a recurrent sense that mountains are both within and beyond human control for ancient authors, and that insight too strikingly anticipates modern interests. That may be partly a reflection of what people really thought about mountains in the ancient Mediterranean, but it is also, for ancient as for modern authors, a matter of literary mastery: what many of these authors are grappling with is the difficulty of representing mountains, of bringing them under textual control.

At the same time, in the specifics of that engagement, we find things that are almost completely alien to us. The ancient experience of mountaintop ritual is almost impossible for us to recapture now in any of its details; that difficulty is related to the broader challenge we face in any attempt to understand ancient religion, which routinely envisages religious significance and divine presence in places and practices we would naturally see as secular. The enigmatic, metaliterary mountains of ancient art and literature were loaded with symbolic associations that are sometimes hard for us to appreciate, partly because we are used to thinking about visual and literary portrayals of mountain landscapes as unmediated representations of places that are to be valued precisely because of their realness and physical presence. The heroes of the early Christian saints' lives are precursors in some ways of modern ideals of immersion in the environment, but they are also at the same time utterly strange to us, as they were also to their original audiences. Ancient writing about mountains also has gaps. Most strikingly there is, of course, very little sense of the problems associated with environmental crisis that preoccupy so many of those working in mountain studies from scientific and geographical perspectives today, even if we find every so often fleeting and intriguing resemblances. Perhaps most importantly of all, the intratextual styles of representation that are so prominent in ancient engagement with mountains can take some time to adjust to. It is easy to see why a casual reader might think at first glance that ancient authors have very little interest in mountains: there is relatively little ancient writing that matches the kinds of extended, set-piece description of mountain landscapes and mountain experiences that we have become used to over the last few centuries. But in fact ancient Greek and Latin texts tend to think through the role of landscape and mountains specifically through a kind of cumulative, intratextual engagement, based on the generation of internal correspondences and contradictions between successive images, that is often every bit as sophisticated as its modern equivalents. Through that technique, individual mountains and mountain scenes are often connected implicitly with a network of others, both in literary terms and also by implication in the real world of Mediterranean geography. That way of engaging with landscape potentially represents a powerful resource for modern environmental engagement too, which might help us to move beyond our obsession with the local in fictional narrative and towards a more global perspective.

Looking back to the classical past helps me to see that what I am doing on these mountains has a long history, much longer than we have often thought, with links back to human practices that have been going on for many millennia. The idea that climbing a mountain involves retracing the steps that others have traced before, standing in a relationship of community with the past, is itself an ancient idea, exemplified by the practices of mountaintop sacrifice. At the same time looking back also confronts me with the oddity and the alienness of past responses to mountains. It makes me realise that the things I am doing now may themselves seem just as strange to some future historian. It also makes me wonder whether there are things we can take from the ancient world as resources for our own thinking about mountains in the present. I think, for example, about all those images of human immersion in the environment. I think about the donkey Lucius trudging through the mountains of Greece and I wonder whether that is an image I can use to measure up against my own experience, to help me understand my own human vulnerability in relation to the world around me. I kept thinking about these things as I went over the summit plateau, first down from Mayar, then up the steep climb to Driesh. I was back in the sun now. There were views north towards Lochnagar, with just a few first snow patches in the distance, and south to the smaller hills of Fife. There were quite a few people up on the summit, maybe ten or fifteen, eating their packed lunches or taking photos of each other. I didn't hang around: I had to get back to pick up my children from school.

I also wondered about that image of mountains as a network that needs to be understood as a whole, through its interconnections, rather than just through single peaks and single images. It is tempting to use the summit view as a stage for thinking about that phenomenon. One of the pleasures you can get from standing on a summit in the Highlands, if you have spent a lot of time in the mountains there, is the pleasure of seeing other peaks away in the distance: you can see how they look from unfamiliar angles, and how they connect with each other and with the summit you are standing on.[15] Many of the nineteenth-century travellers to Greece were aware of the pleasures that come from that kind of view. For them it had the added attraction of giving them access to an interconnected vision of the countless landmarks of classical history laid out before them, as they looked down from the summits of the mountains they had read about in ancient Greek and Roman mythological and historiographical texts.[16] The problem is that you often can't see a thing from the summit, if you end up in the cloud.[17] And perhaps the challenge anyway is to generate that kind of interconnected vision even within the experience of being immersed in a single landscape. I realised as I started to come back down that that is one of the things I can do a bit better now, thanks to all the ancient texts I have read. Ancient literature often imagines close-up views of mountain terrain, but those images tend to stand side by side with an awareness of a wider, interconnected system of mountains, reminding us that each mountain is local and specific, but also part of a bigger world. I can't see any of those other Highland peaks now as I go down: the descent is very steep and I feel that I am being swallowed very quickly into the valley and then into the forest below, which cuts short my vision even more. But I can still see in my mind's eye the glimpse I got from the summit just half an hour before of distant hills and coastline. I also feel I can hold those Mediterranean mountains in my imagination better now, more so than I could a couple of hours ago: I can see a bit more clearly how they are connected with the place I am in now, as part of a wider network of mountains that has a central role to play in the future of human relations with the environment. The image of the world's mountains as a network is becoming more and more widespread in current mountain studies too, from a realisation that we need to join up the problems faced by different mountains and mountain communities around the world if we want to make any difference to them.[18] Ancient literature is teeming with mountains and with images of interaction between humans and the environment in mountain settings. It invites us to view them together as well as separately, and to understand how they are connected with each other, just as the wild territories of the Alps and Spain in Strabo are ultimately part of a bigger vision of the possibilities for mountain landscape that includes also the urbanised mountains of Italy and Greece; just as each of Homer's mountain similes immerses us in a particular moment and a particular landscape, while also taking its place in a vision of the vastness and variety of the earth's environments.

NOTES

Preface

1. See Hughes (1991), 96–107.
2. On the upper sanctuary, see Romano and Voyatzis (2014); Belis (2015), I, 124–34; also Romano and Voyatzis (2010) for accessible overview of initial results from the Mount Lykaion project as a whole, up to 2009 (available at http://penn.museum/documents/publications/expedition/PDFs/52-1/zeus.pdf; last accessed 13/7/21); Romano (2019); the excellent project website at http://lykaionexcavation.org (last consulted 13/7/21); and further bibliography in chapter 1, including discussion of the excavations on the lower slopes.
3. Braudel (1972), 25–53, for example, at 25, where he writes that the Mediterranean is 'above all, a sea ringed round by mountains. This outstanding fact and its many consequences have received too little attention in the past from historians' (25). See also chapter 14, later, for subsequent critiques of his work, especially in reaction to Braudel's characterisation of mountain peoples as primitive.
4. For example, see Hammond (1967) on Epirus; Langdon (1976) and Fowden (1988) on Attica; McInerney (1999) on Parnassos; Horden and Purcell (2000), which includes discussion of a number of different mountain microregions, and general discussion of 'mountains and pastures' at 80–87; Roy (2009) on Arkadia; Robinson (2012) on Mount Helikon; Bersani (2019) on the Alps; also collections of essays in Fabre (1992) and Bersani (2001).
5. However, see http://parrhasianheritagepark.org (last consulted 13/7/21) for the recently founded Parrhasian Heritage Park.
6. See Buxton (2013), 9–32; also earlier versions in Buxton (1992) and (1994), 81–96.
7. However, see Borca (2002), which is one of the best and most extensive studies of classical mountains, but not easily accessible; also Hooley (2012); Barton (2017), 20–47, for a useful survey; Williams (2017), 23–71, on the tradition of writing about Etna in classical literature; and now the wide-ranging collection of essays in Taufer (2019).
8. The main exception is the *locus amoenus* tradition, which was in some cases grafted on to mountain descriptions in ancient literature, but often in slightly awkward ways: I discuss that phenomenon further in chapter 5.
9. On intratextuality in ancient literature see Sharrock and Morales (2000) and Harrison et al. (2018) but with very little reference to landscape descriptions.
10. For example, the mountains of Greek myth and especially Greek tragedy are treated relatively briefly, as one of the few areas already discussed at length in the existing scholarship: esp. in the work of Richard Buxton already discussed earlier in n. 6, and now Bray (2021).

11. See Price (2015) for a good introduction.

12. See esp. Stephen (1871), 1–78.

13. Nicolson (1959), esp. 38–40, for brief discussion of classical precedents which is almost entirely dependent on Hyde (1915): like Hyde she acknowledges that the ancient Greeks in particular had something approaching a modern feel for the sublime; by contrast she suggests that 'the Latin attitude . . . remained almost consistently adverse' (39).

14. Of those some mention Nicolson's work explicitly: examples include (among many others) Tuan (1971), 70–74; Thomas (1983), 258–60; Porter (2000), 34–36; Rigby (2004), 131–40; Isserman and Weaver (2008), 27; Walsham (2011), 391; S. Bainbridge (2020), 11; others tell a version of the same story without any mention of Nicolson: most influential over public perception has been MacFarlane (2003), esp. 137–67, which was an important early inspiration for this project, but also made me want to think more about how one might extend the history of human engagement with mountains back into classical antiquity; and see also Thacker (1983), for example, 3–4; Mitchell (1998), 4–6; Ring (2000), 7–25; Bates (2000), esp. xvii–xviii and 1–11; Fleming (2000); Hiltner (2015), xv; Dhar (2019), 345, in the opening section of an excellent account of mountain travel writing (among very many other examples). See Hollis and König (2021b), 17, notes 8 and 16, for earlier, briefer versions of these lists.

15. See König and Hollis (2021b), 2–5; Hollis (2019), who argues that the denigration of premodern mountain engagement is due to the way in which it was 'deeply implicated within discourses of modern exceptionalism', especially 'in the construction of ideas of Romanticism and post-Romantic literary criticism, and in the community-forming narratives of the self-declared "first mountaineers" of the Alpine Club' (3); compare Hansen (2013), esp. 1–9, for discussion of the work of Leslie Stephen and then Nicolson, as part of a wider argument about the notion of 'the summit position', the idea of the individual on a mountain summit, which he sees as a central feature in the development of the idea of mountaineering as a quintessentially modern pursuit; also Koelb (2009), who takes issue with the simplistic claim that classical and biblical writers viewed mountains negatively, pointing among other things (for example, at 446–47) to the problems in Nicolson's assumption that figurative representation of mountains in ancient literature implies indifference or dislike; and W. Bainbridge (2020), 34–35. See also Barton (2017) and Korenjak (2017), both of whom issue a partial challenge to the standard narrative by arguing for an earlier starting date for 'mountain glory', in the early modern period; and similarly Mathieu (2005) and (2011), esp. 120–22: 'the change in the late eighteenth century did not consist of a simple reversal from negative to positive but rather of a dramatic new weighting of earlier ideas and assessments' (122). Mitchell (1994), 8, takes issue with the idea that appreciation of landscape more broadly is an exclusively modern phenomenon.

16. See among many others Fleming (2000); Ring (2000); MacFarlane (2003); Hansen (2013); McNee (2016); Anderson (2020); S. Bainbridge (2020); W. Bainbridge (2020); Schaumann (2020); also Debarbieux and Rudaz (2015) for changing uses of the idea of the mountain in political contexts over roughly the same period.

17. On an alternative strand in modern writing about mountains which sees classical narratives of mountain climbing in a continuum with their postclassical equivalents, see Ireton (2021) on Josias Simler and W.A.B. Coolidge; also Freshfield (1904), a remarkable rebuttal of dominant views about the novelty of modern fascination with mountains by an important figure in the history of mountaineering.

18. See Borca (2002), esp. 7, on the importance of putting aside anachronistic assumptions and taking an anthropological approach to ancient mountains.

19. The word *oros*, the Greek word for mountain, shows how careful we need to be to avoid reading ancient mountains anachronistically. It has a very different range of connotations from the English equivalent. Absolute height is not always a major factor; even quite low hills can be described by the word *oros* if they stand out from the plains around them: see Buxton (2013), 9–10. More importantly it is used not just for specific summits, but also for a particular kind of terrain, which was in many respects distinct from the civilised territory of the city in the Greek imagination. We see an extreme example of that in the early Egyptian saints' lives of the fourth and fifth centuries CE and in other Egyptian documents where *oros* is used almost as an equivalent of the English word 'desert' to describe elevated terrain separate from the cultivated territory of the Nile valley: see further discussion later, in chapter 16. Compare Debarbieux and Rudaz (2015) on the constructed and culturally variable nature of the concept of the 'mountain' in the modern world.

20. Compare Porter (2016), 50, n. 132, for an incredulous response to Nicolson's claim that the eighteenth-century 'discovery' of the natural sublime was part of a profound intellectual 'revolution', and that 'the ancient Greeks and Romans lacked an aesthetic or some other appreciation of 'the power of hills': 'In response one can only reel off a series of names and nouns, mouth agape: Olympus? Ida? Parnassus? Helicon? Cithaeron? Pelion and Ossa? Soracte? Etna? The *Aetna* poet? The pseudo-Aristotelian work *On the Cosmos*?'

21. See della Dora (2011), (2016a), and (2016b).

22. For an excellent survey of the latter, see Rollinger (2010).

23. See also Ireton and Schaumann (2012) for another publication that looks across the traditional eighteenth-century watershed, with a focus on the representation of mountains in German culture, from the medieval period to the twenty-first century; also now Ireton and Schaumann (2020); and along similar lines Mathieu and Boscani Leoni (2005), Cosgrove and della Dora (2009), Kofler et al. (2010), and Kakalis and Goetsch (2018); and for studies focused on medieval mountain representation, with a similar goal of moving beyond stereotypical dismissal of premodern engagement with mountains, see Thomasset and James-Raoul (2000), Société des historiens médiévistes (2004), and Carrier and Mouthon (2011).

24. Esp. Hollis and König (2021a).

25. Compare Simpson (2019) for a valuable survey of recent work on modern mountain history, emphasising among other things the way in which mountains are absorbed within modernity but also resistant to that absorption.

26. See further discussion later, in part IV.

27. For example, see Ellis (2001); Debarbieux and Rudaz (2015).

28. See further discussion later, in part III.

29. For forward-looking accounts that summarise previous developments in ecocriticism while also attempting to map out some new directions, see Buell (2005); Clark (2011) and (2019); Garrard (2012) and (2014).

30. Most notoriously, see White (1967), in a publication which has been enormously influential in environmental studies, arguing, with only very cursory discussion of the ancient evidence, that our current willingness to exploit the natural world for human advantage is rooted in the anthropocentric assumptions of early Christianity.

31. For example, see Hughes (1983) on deforestation, arguing partly on the basis of literary evidence that the Roman Empire was responsible for massive clearance of forests across the Mediterranean, and that we see signs of that in the literary evidence, and more recently Hughes (2014) for a much broader account from a similar perspective; and Rackham (1996) for criticism; also now Harris (2013b); and further discussion later, in chapter 14.

32. Compare König (forthcoming a) for discussion along similar lines; also Coates (1998), 12: 'We are hard pressed to find a single doctrine of man-nature relations in any era. . . . A number of attitudes, notions and orientations invariably coexist in often messy contradiction'.

33. For example, see Schliephake (2020), 4–6.

34. See Schliephake (2017a) and (2020) for some groundbreaking initial attempts; also Burrus (2018), discussed in more detail later, in chapter 16; Hunt and Marlow (2019); Armstrong (2019); Usher (2020); Schlosser (2020).

35. See Armbruster and Wallace (2001).

36. For the tradition of claiming ancient authors were uninterested in describing the natural world, see Hurwit (1991), 34–35, with reference to Schiller, Humboldt, and Ruskin among others; also Schliephake (2017b), 5–6, on Humboldt; and see further chapter 1, n. 25.

37. See Clark (2019), 111–36, on ecocriticism and new materialism; Bosak-Schroeder (2020) for a recent account of ancient Greek ethnography from this perspective, focusing especially on Herodotus and Diodorus Siculus, and arguing that these texts are interested in exploring ways of living which challenge clear-cut dividing lines between human culture and the more-than-human world; also Chesi and Spiegel (2019) on posthumanism and antiquity, with important caveats in Goldhill (2019) on the way in which posthumanist approaches to classical literature can end up falling short of their own claims to novelty, in restating things we have always known about (for example) the erosion of boundaries between human and non-human in ancient myth; and further bibliography later, for example, chapter 2, n. 63, on new materialist and posthumanist approaches to Homer.

38. See Ghosh (2016), esp. 3–84; also Buell (2005), 62–96; Heise (2008), esp. 205–10; Clark (2019), 78–110, esp. 97–99.

39. See esp. Cosgrove (1984).

40. See de Jong (2018) and (2019).

41. See Schama (1995).

42. See della Dora (2016a), esp. 1–29, suggesting that the idea of 'place', rather than 'landscape', is particularly useful for understanding classical and Byzantine culture; also good brief discussion along similar lines in Gilhuly and Worman (2014b), 4–6.

43. For a clear and helpful introduction, see Rose and Wylie (2011).

44. There has been an increasing interest in space and landscape in classical literature over the last decade or two, including some important discussion of the different ways of viewing and experiencing that I outline in this paragraph, but relatively little of it is on mountain landscape: for example, see Gilhuly and Worman (2014a); the exception is the excellent chapter by Rood (2014) on Xenophon's *Anabasis*, discussed further in chapter 11; also Rosen and Sluiter (2006); and Fitzgerald and Spentzou (2018), which derives from a conference on urban psychogeographies. By contrast McInerney and Sluiter (2016) includes several discussions of mountain landscapes, by Buxton (2016), König (2016), Robinson (2016), and Williamson (2016).

45. See S. Bainbridge (2020), esp. 1, for summary, on the importance of embodiment in mountaineering experience even in the early nineteenth century; and McNee (2016) on the way in which haptic experience became particularly important in late nineteenth-century mountaineering.

46. See Wylie (2007), esp. 1–16, on the tension between these two different strands in modern scholarship on landscape.

47. The title is also at the same time intended as an acknowledgement of Jeremy McInerney's (1999) book *The Folds of Parnassos*, which broke new ground in making sense of one ancient region, Phokis in northern Greece, against the backdrop of its mountains.

48. See Homer, *Iliad* 11.77, for the phrase 'folds of Olympus', discussed further in chapter 2. The Greek word πτύξ has some of the same ambiguity between physical and literary connotations as the English 'fold': as well as signifiying a glen or valley, it can refer to the folds in a piece of clothing and the plates of metal or leather in a shield; alternatively, to the folds of a writing tablet, or even, in one metaphor from Pindar, the 'folds' of song (Pindar, *Olympian* 1.105).

49. See Hansen (2013).

50. See esp. Schama (1995), 383–513.

51. As long as you have a stick to deal with the sheep-dogs; see Hammond (1966), 39: 'I walked through the gorge of the Aoi Stena from Kelcyrë (in Greek Kleisura) to Telpenë on 12th July 1931. My speed was not more than three miles an hour, as I had a stiff leg after being bitten by a sheep-dog'.

Chapter 1. Summit Altars

1. Throughout the book I generally choose to avoid Latinate spelling for Greek names, except in cases where the Latinate spelling is so familiar that the alternative would look odd (for example, 'Olympus'), or in cases where I am discussing named mountains within Latin texts (for example, in my discussions of Latin texts in chapter 8).

2. All translations are my own unless otherwise specified.

3. See Janko (1994), 206.

4. In what follows I refer every so often to standard labels for different periods of classical antiquity, roughly as follows: archaic (776–480 BCE); classical (480–323 BCE); Hellenistic (323–30 BCE); imperial (30 BCE–284 CE); late antique (284 CE and following).

5. For useful overviews of the religious associations of mountains in ancient Greek culture, see Langdon (2000); Accorinti (2010).

6. See Buxton (2013) and earlier versions in Buxton (1992) and (1994) for the best survey of those phenomena; also helpful introductory surveys of mountains in myth in Quantin (2005) and Létoublon (2008).

7. See Mathieu (2006); also Bernbaum (1997), 243–44, on mountaineering and the sacred.

8. For example, see Mathieu (2006), 348, and (2011), 124, on mountains as 'cathedrals of the earth'.

9. See della Dora (2016b), 27, for the power of mountains to astonish; also on the tension in our understanding of mountains between two different ways of interacting with holiness, between 'respectful stewardship and speechless terror', which anticipates my comments later on

similar tensions between the antiquarian and the miraculous in responses to mountains by authors like Pausanias and Egeria; those reflections introduce della Dora's wide-ranging chapter on 'Mountains, the holy and the diabolic (27–71), which covers many different periods and cultures.

10. See Mathieu (2006), 346, and (2011), 123.

11. On the broader Arkadian context, see among others Jost (1985), esp. 179–83 on this site, (1992) and (1994), all of which offer an overview of Arkadian religion; and see further discussion later, in chapter 14, of the connection between rural and urban sanctuaries in Arkadia; also Romano (2019) and Nielsen (1999) on Arkadian identity; however, see also Morgan (1999), 408, who notes that 'there is no strong evidence to suggest that Mt. Lykaion played a regional role before ca. 500 at the very earliest, and even then, the clues are equivocal'.

12. Pausanias, *Periegesis* 8.38.5 (Pan); 8.38.2 and 8.38.8 (Apollo).

13. See Romano (2019).

14. See Nielsen (1999), 27; Roy (2013), 32–35.

15. For results of excavations on the lower slopes, see Romano and Voyatzis (2015).

16. See Romano (2014), 184–87, on the Lykaia; also Nielsen (1999), 27–29; Jost (1985), 267–68, in the context of a wider discussion of the importance of the sanctuary for Arkadian identity.

17. Pliny the Elder, *Natural History* 7.205.

18. Pindar, *Olympian Odes* 7.84, 9.97, 13.108; *Nemean Ode* 10.45–48.

19. *Inscriptiones Graecae* V, 2, 549–50.

20. See Nielsen (1999), 27–29 and 61–62; Pretzler (2009), 93–94.

21. Compare Buxton (2013), 20–21; and more generally on the association between mountains and antiquity in many different eras, see König and Hollis (2021b), 8–10.

22. See Langdon (2000), 468–69.

23. Ingold (1993).

24. See Pitches (2020).

25. For example, see Hyde (1915), 76, with approving quotation of Gilbert Murray and John Ruskin; Nicolson (1959), 38; Cosgrove (1984), 18–20: 'The insider does not enjoy the privilege of being able to walk away from the scene as we can walk away from a framed picture or from a tourist viewpoint' (19); also Forbes (2007), 389, for an anthropologically sensitive version of that claim, pointing out that the twentieth-century inhabitants of rural Methana in the Peloponnese tended to show very little interest in describing the experience of ascending to mountain shrines to celebrate festivals, despite the fact that these occasions were very important to them individually and communally.

26. See Forbes (2007), 18–44, for criticism of phenomenological approaches, which in his view tend to impose an outsider's viewpoint rather than helping us to access the lived experience of local populations.

27. For the summit shrines of Greece, the most comprehensive study is Belis (2015), which includes a full catalogue, with detailed description of all the Greek sites described in this chapter.

28. The catalogue in Belis (1995), volume II, includes 88 sites.

29. See Belis (1995), II, 174–77.

30. See the enormous three-volume work by Cook (1914–40), especially appendix B in vol. II, 2, 868–987, which includes detailed collections of ancient testimonia for cult worship of Zeus at many different sites; also brief overview by Dowden (2006), 57–61.

31. See Cole (2000), esp. 474–75, and (2004), 178–97.

32. See Bernbaum (1997) for many examples.

33. See Langdon (2000), 462–65; Sporn (2013). Dio Chrysostom *Oration* 12.61 associates worship of mountains with barbarians.

34. See Clarke (1997); Belis (2015), I, 31–33; also later, chapter 7, for some rare examples of personification in Greek art and literature in relation to Mount Helikon; and Lichtenberger (2021), 136–54, for an excellent survey of the evidence.

35. See Belis (2015), I, 85–95.

36. See Peatfield (1983) and (2009); Kyriakidis (2005); Belis (2015), I, 7–29.

37. See Belis (2015), I, 10–13.

38. For a brief overview, see Mitchell (1993), 21–22.

39. Strabo, *Geography* 12.3.40.

40. Appian, *Roman History* 12.66; and see Williamson (2014), and further discussion later, in chapter 14.

41. See Mitchell (1993), 22; Munn (2006), esp. 73–75.

42. For Jebel Aqra, see the chapter by Lane Fox (2008), 255–72, who reports a brief visit to the ash altar on the summit within the militarised zone, and who takes the mountain as a focus for discussion of intersections between Greek and Near Eastern religious traditions; and Williams Reed (2020), esp. 90–92, on Near Eastern traditions, and throughout on the formative influence of the mountain's environment over the religious activity associated with it. For another brief report of the ash altar on the summit, see Schaeffer (1938).

43. See Hunt (2015); Giorcelli Bersani (2019), 166–71, in the context of a wider discussion of Alpine religion at 139–90; also Jourdain-Annequin and Le Berre (2004), 210, in the context of a wider discussion of Alpine religion at 198–243.

44. For Mount Albanus and the worship of Jupiter Latiaris, see Smith (2012). On the nearby sanctuary of Diana at Aricia, see Green (2007), esp. 3–7, on the site's mountainous setting. For discussion of a range of other mountain sites, in the wider context of rural sanctuaries in Italy, see Edlund (1987), esp. 44–48 and 56–58; also Moralee (2018) on the Capitoline hill in Rome as a place of memory.

45. See Belis (2015), II, 64–68.

46. See Langdon (2000), 462; Buxton (2013), 9–10; and earlier, preface n. 19.

47. Pausanias 4.3.9.

48. Plutarch, *Aratus* 50.

49. Pausanias 4.33.1.

50. See Belis (2015), II, 16–22.

51. See Belis (2015), II, 29–31, and Rupp (1976).

52. Pausanias 2.25.10.

53. For a brief summary of recent finds of Mycenean material on the summit, see http://www.archaeology.wiki/blog/2013/01/18/a-mycenaean-sanctuary-on-proph-ilias-at-mt-arachnaion-in-the-argolid/ (last consulted 14/7/21).

54. Compare Langdon (2000), 468–69.

55. *Sylloge Inscriptionum Graecarum* 1107.

56. Important for the mountaintop sites of Attica is Langdon (1976), which includes a useful appendix B (107–12) giving an overview of evidence for mountaintop worship of Zeus on a small selection of other peaks outside Attica (including Mount Arachnaion and Mount Olympus); also Parker (1996), 28–33. For Mount Hymettos, see also Belis (2015), II, 52–57.

57. See Alcock (1994), 253–56.

58. Solinus, *Polyhistor* 8.6.

59. Plutarch, fragment 191; Augustine, *De Genesi ad litteram liber unus imperfectus* 1.14; compare Mythographi Vaticani 1.192 for another mention of worship of Zeus on the summit.

60. *Supplementum Epigraphicum Graecum* 56, 732–34.

61. Most of the material is now in the Archaeological Museum at Dion.

62. For evidence for sacrifice on Mount Olympus, see Kyriazopoulos and Livadas (1967); Höper (1992); Voutiras (2006), esp. 340–42; Belis (2015), II, 159–62; Lichtenberger (2021), 96–101. On the importance of the worship of Zeus and of Mount Olympus for the city of Dion, see Lichtenberger (2021), 104–11; also Voutiras (2006), esp. 340–42, for the argument that the cults of Zeus at Dion and on the Agios Antonios peak must have been connected.

Chapter 2. Mountains in Archaic Greek Poetry

1. See Clay (1989a) for the classic statement of that argument for the Homeric hymns; also Graziosi and Haubold (2005).

2. Compare de Jong (2012c) for a more generalising statement of the use of space in the Homeric hymns.

3. See Buxton (2013), 21, for that phrase, and for Aphrodite's union with Anchises as one example.

4. See Clay (1989a), 171; Faulkner (2008), 32–33 and 149–52; Brillet-Dubois (2011), 109–10; Olson (2012), 174–75.

5. The same goes for Aphrodite's transformative impact on the animals of Mount Ida, whose fawning is utterly different from the standard human experience of threatening mountain animals in the Homeric similes we will look at further later: see esp. Olson (2012), 176–79.

6. See Clay (1989a), esp. 166–70 and 198–201.

7. See de Jong (2012c), 41, for a list.

8. For example, see *Hymn to Hermes* for Hermes' birth and subsequent actions on Mount Kyllene; *Hymn to Dionysus* (1) 8–9 and *Hymn to Dionysus* (26) 3–10 on the imaginary Mount Nysa as birthplace and territory of Dionysus.

9. For example, see *Hymn to Artemis* 4–8; also later in this chapter on the *Hymn to Pan*.

10. See Faulkner (2011b), 21–22, for a nuanced discussion.

11. See Clay (1989a).

12. For good discussion of this passage, see Faulkner (2008), 179–81.

13. There is very little evidence for worship of Aphrodite on Mount Ida, and no mention later in the poem to suggest that we should take it as a narrative explaining the origins of such a cult: see Faulkner (2011b), 22.

14. See Buxton (2013), 22–25, for brief reflections on the relationship between mountain myth and ritual.

15. See Thomas (2011), 169–71.

16. See Thomas (2011), 152–55, for excellent discussion of the way in which the poet builds up here an impression of unrestrained movement.

17. See Thomas (2011), 153, for the suggestion that Pan moves here 'like the paradigmatically free-ranging goat and the pursuing goatherd, both of whose spirits he embodies'.

18. This passage was picked out by Nicolson (1959), 39, as a relatively rare exception to what she saw as the overwhelming lack of interest in mountains as places of pleasure and exhilaration in classical culture. Certainly she is right that the hymn offers a memorable counter-example to that view, but what she fails to see is the way in which this passage is itself part of an enormously rich exploration of the different possibilities for representing mountain terrain in archaic and classical epic more broadly, an exploration that is already quite self-conscious about the contrast between 'gloom' and 'glory'.

19. For other examples, see *Iliad* 9.15 (Agamemnon's weeping like water pouring from a cliff), 15.273 (a wild goat or stag takes refuge from hunters on a steep rock), 15.619 (the Trojans unable to break through the Greek lines, which stand firm like a steep sea cliff), 16.35 (Patroklos accuses Achilles of hard-heartedness, saying that the sea and the steep cliffs bore him); *Odyssey* 10.88 (description of the harbour of the Laestrygonians), 13.195 (description of the sheer cliffs of Ithaca before Odysseus recognises them); by contrast the word is generally used from a divine perspective with a positive spin in the other Homeric hymns to describe scenes that are beautiful or useful: for example, *Homeric Hymn to Aphrodite* 267 (description of tall and beautiful trees associated with the Nymphs); *Homeric Hymn to Hermes* 404 (description of the cave of Hermes); the only obvious parallel from the *Iliad* and *Odyssey* is *Iliad* 13.63 (Poseidon launches into flight from a cliff face).

20. See Clay (1989a), 101–2.

21. See Thomas (2011).

22. For example, see *Hymn to Hermes* 95–96 for the remarkable sense of speed in Hermes' travel; one detail in particular measures that up against a more human perspective, where Hermes says to Apollo in self-defence that 'I was born yesterday, my feet are soft, and the ground beneath them is rough' (*Homeric Hymn to Hermes* 273); see also Clay (1989a), 117–27, on the way in which Hermes' divine identity emerges increasingly as the hymn goes on.

23. See Brockliss (2018a).

24. See Petridou (2016), 216–17, for discussion of Hesiod's text in the wider context of ancient narratives that link divine epiphany and poetic inspiration, many of them in mountain settings.

25. See Lamberton (1988a), 27–37, for overview, with good discussion of the real-life topography of Askra and Mount Helikon.

26. Belis (2015), II, 48–51, includes a useful brief discussion of the uncertain evidence for worship of Zeus on Mount Helikon; see also Langdon (1976), 109–10, and Aravantinos (1996).

27. See Robinson (2012), 230–32, and further discussion later, in chapter 3, in relation to Pausanias.

28. See Lamberton (1988b), 494–97.

29. See later, chapter 8.

30. For a survey of the range of modern scholarly views about the relationship between the opening lines of Hesiod's *Theogony* and Hesiod's personal experience, and a list of parallels for mountaintop inspiration in the Hebrew Bible, see West (1966), 158–60.

31. However, see Petridou (2016), 219, pointing out that 'the pious majority of both Archaic and Classical Greece would not think of encountering a deity on a mountain as impossible, let alone as a literary construct'.

32. For the idea that Hesiod's move from local to Panhellenic status parallels the Muses' move to Olympus, see among others Nagy (1990), 36–82, esp. 57–61, and (2009), esp. 277–78; compare Clay (2003), 72.

33. See Eidinow (2016) and Schliephake (2020), 29–30, for general discussion of ancient myth in these terms.

34. See Lichtenberger (2021), 25–44.

35. See Graziosi (2013), 30–31, on the way in which these parallel the divine powers of vision associated with the gods themselves; Purves (2010a), esp. 4–5 and 33–35, on the way in which the poem hints at a parallel between the gods' viewing from above and the viewpoints of the poet and his audience, while also stopping short of giving us access to this kind of divine, 'eu-synoptic' vision in practice: 'despite scholars' observations about the occasional panoramic standpoint of the Homeric narrator, we are rarely afforded a sustained bird's-eye view' (34).

36. See Lichtenberger (2021), 19–23.

37. See Whitmarsh (2015), 110–13, on various ancient versions of the story that Bellerophon offended the gods by attempting to fly up to Olympus on the winged horse Pegasus.

38. See Sale (1984), 13–14, citing two parallels from the *Odyssey* for the location of the Homeric Olympus in Thessaly: *Odyssey* 5.50 and 11.315–16.

39. Sale (1984) goes so far as to suggest that the poet is combining two quite separate strands, an older tradition which places the gods on a mountain summit and a later one where they are located in a separate heavenly realm, generally referred to as Ouranos, but occasionally as Olympus. That case seems to me to be overstated, but Sale's account does make it clear that there is a certain amount of inconsistency, and a tendency to lose sight of Olympus' identity as a physical mountain which makes it quite different from the other mountains of the poem.

40. See Lateiner (2014), 68–69, for a concise summary; and Tsagalis (2012), 140–47, for an account of all the key spaces associated with the gods in the poem, including Olympus at 140–43.

41. First at *Iliad* 1.18 (Ὀλύμπια δώματ' ἔχοντες).

42. First at *Iliad* 1.402 (ἐς μακρὸν Ὄλυμπον).

43. First at *Iliad* 1.44, where Apollo comes down 'from the heights of Olympus' (κατ' Οὐλύμποιο καρήνων).

44. First at *Iliad* 1.499, where Zeus sits 'on the highest peak of ridged Olympus' (ἀκροτάτῃ κορυφῇ πολυδειράδος Οὐλύμποιο). See also 1.420 for the one occurrence of the phrase 'much snowed-on Olympus' (Ὄλυμπον ἀγάννιφον).

45. See Clay (2011), 3–6; de Jong (2018), 24–27; also de Jong (2019) for that Homeric tradition and its reuse in later epic. Just occasionally we see heroic mortals having access to god-like vision from a mountain. In a fragment of the non-surviving epic poem the *Cypria* (fragment 12, preserved in the scholia to Pindar, *Nemean* 10.114, which tells the same story), Lynkeus, one of the Argonauts, climbs Mount Taygetos and from there sees the twins Kastor and Polydeukes hiding in a hollow oak tree in the distance; he descends the mountain to kill Kastor.

46. See Lateiner (2014), 70–71, on the contrast between divine and human travel.

47. See Mackie (2014) for a wide-ranging article on the role of Mount Ida in the poem, esp. 6–7, on the differences between Ida and Olympus.

48. See Woronoff (1983), 88–89, on this and other passages attesting to worship of Zeus on Mount Ida in the *Iliad*, esp. *Iliad* 16.603–7, for mention of Onetor, a priest of Idaian Zeus, whose son Laogonos is killed on the battlefield.

49. See Woronoff (1995), esp. 216, on the way in which both the Greeks and the Trojans pray to 'Zeus who rules Mount Ida' (3.276 and 3.320) before the duel between Menelaus and Paris.

50. See Krieter-Spiro (2018), 143–44, including discussion of the range of possibilities for identifying the Gargaros peak mentioned at 14.292 and elsewhere in the poem; also Cook (1914–40), I, 949–52.

51. See Woronoff (2001), 40, with reference also to *Iliad* 8.75–76, which describes Zeus's thunder and lightning on the crests of the mountain almost immediately after his arrival there, and 8.170–6, where further thunderclaps from Zeus are correctly interpreted as a sign of support for the Trojans by Hector; also Kelly (2007), 113–15, for discussion of these moments as part of a wider pattern of thunder and lightning omens.

52. See Woronoff (1983), esp. 90.

53. The most famous statement of that is *Odyssey* 6.42–45; compare chapter 1, n. 59.

54. See Bocchetti (2003), esp. tables 1 and 2.

55. Pausanias mentions the tomb of Aipytos, and this passage of Homer, at *Periegesis* 8.16.3.

56. Also relevant is *Odyssey* 13.152, where Poseidon expresses his desire to cover the city of the Phaiacians with a mountain (an outcome that has been prophesied, according to Alcinous at 8.569) in punishment for the help they have given to Odysseus, with Marks (2008), 52–55, for discussion of the textual problems here. That passage is perhaps intended to take to a horrifying extreme the usually positive image of mountains performing sheltering and identity-forming roles for the cities they are close to; compare *Odyssey* 5.279–80 for the 'shadowy mountains of the land of the Phaiacians' (ὄρεα σκιόεντα γαίης Φαιήκων). The image of civilised human communities close to mountains is inverted in the *Odyssey* in the characterisation of the Cyclops as a figure outside this orderly relationship with the mountains, so much so that Polyphemus is himself compared with a mountain peak beyond human civilisation: 'That was the sleeping place of a giant man, who grazed his herds far off, alone; nor did he have contact with others, but lived far away in lawlessness. He was a monstrous marvel; he was not like a grain-eating human, but like a wooded peak of the high mountains, which is visible isolated from the others' (*Odyssey* 9.187–92). See Williams (2018) on mountains in the *Odyssey* Books 9–12, esp. 71–74 on the mountains of Ithaca and 74–80 on the Cyclopes and Polyphemus, emphasising especially the way in which mountains are depicted as places of isolation in these books; and further discussion later, in chapter 14; also Aguirre and Buxton (2020), 47–48, pointing out that Polyphemus himself does not live at altitude, unlike the other Cyclopes.

57. See Mackie (2014), 1–2.

58. Compare Mackie (2014), 2, on the economic importance of Ida for Troy in the *Iliad*. See also 21.448–49 for brief mention, by Poseidon, of the way in which Apollo was forced by Zeus to pasture cattle on Mount Ida for Laomedon for a year, another sign of the way in which Mount Ida has much greater potential than Olympus to be a zone of contact between human and divine.

59. Compare Scott (1974), 100–101, on the two worlds in the similes, one a world 'of peace and permanence', the other a world of 'sudden and threatening events' (101).

60. There has been a vast industry of scholarship on the similes' role in the poem over the last 100 years or more. A significant subsection of that field examines together similes which

share the same subject matter—for example, see Scott (1974), 56–95, and (2009), but in both cases without taking mountain similes as one of his main categories; also Fränkel (1921) for an influential example of that approach. In some cases that involves analysing them in relation not just to other similes but also to comparison points in the main body of the poem (so for example a bird simile might be juxtaposed not just with other bird similes but also with mentions of birds in the main narrative): for example, see Muellner (1990) on the crane simile of *Iliad* 3.1–9; Rood (2006) on the vulture simile of *Odyssey* 16.216–19; also Purves (2010b) on the representation of wind both in similes and in the main narrative. It is puzzling in that context that very little attention has been given to the intratextual relations between the mountain similes and the mountains of the main narrative, Olympus and Ida especially, despite the fact that intratextual reading methodologies have generally been central to Homeric criticism over the last century and more (if 'intratextual' is the right word for poems that arise from a tradition of oral poetry) (but for one exception, see Elliger [1975], 81–91). That is just one of the most striking examples of the general lack of attention to the intratextual character of ancient landscape description already discussed earlier in the preface. See also de Jong (2012c), esp. 21, for an overview of space in the *Iliad* and *Odyssey* more broadly, stressing the way in which the poems at first sight seem to give little attention to space, but on closer inspection use relatively brief details of setting very powerfully; compare Andersson (1976), 15–37, for a similar approach.

61. See esp. later, notes 75, 77, and 87, for examples from Tsagalis (2012), 271–345, who discusses the way in which similes within the same 'visual unit', in other words successive similes within the same segment of the main narrative, tend to have a shared setting.

62. See Redfield (1994), 190.

63. For example, see Holmes (2015); Purves (2015) on the figure of Aias in the *Iliad* and the way in which the poem resists any clear separation between his human identity or agency and the material objects he is in contact with, drawing on new materialist approaches; Brockliss (2018b); also Cooper (2020) and Schultz (2009) for ecocritical approaches to the *Odyssey*, both of them in different ways stressing the inextricable entanglement between human actors and the more-than-human world in the poem; Goldwyn (2018), 1–2, for an anecdote about how engagement with the Shield of Achilles in *Iliad* 18 in a teaching context prompted him towards new, ecocritical engagement in his research; also Brockliss (2018a) on Hesiod already discussed earlier, n. 23. Elliger (1975), 29–156, and Bonnafé (1984) are still valuable older studies of the natural world in the Homeric poems.

64. However, see the opening paragraphs of Payne (2014) for one exception.

65. See Ghosh (2016), 55, on 'awareness of the precariousness of human existence' as a staple of premodern literature, quoted by Cooper (2020), 123, n. 22, in relation to the *Odyssey*.

66. See Dimock (2008), 72–76.

67. See earlier discussion in the preface; also Kerridge (2014), 369, with reference to Heise (2008), 76–77, on the 'breaks, interruptions and switches of viewpoint and register' in Modernist literature, and the way in which they offer 'possibilities for the representation of ecological relationships that go beyond the range of local place and individual perception'.

68. For good examples using the same word λᾶας for 'stone', see *Iliad* 4.521 and 7.268.

69. Earlier, in 17.742–45, Meriones and Menelaus have been compared with mules hauling wood over a mountain track, in rescuing the corpse of Patroklos from the battle. The presence of Meriones in both passages ties them together, reminding us that the Greeks have entered

simile space in Book 23. There is a good parallel in *Odyssey* 19.426–66 in the story of the boar hunt on Mount Parnassos where Odysseus was wounded as a young man: that passage is the only extended Homeric description of hunting in the mountains outside the similes.

70. See later, chapter 14.

71. Compare celebration of human control in many of the poem's woodcutting similes: for example, 13.389–91; 16.482–84.

72. The battlefield scenes in that book also have a particularly intense concentration on the theme of human bodies immersed in and intertwined with their environment: see Brockliss (2018b).

73. Hainsworth (1993), 229, points out that ἕκηλοι can mean 'at ease' in other contexts, for example, at *Odyssey* 13.423, but here takes it to mean primarily 'not involved'.

74. The Greeks, by contrast, are at that moment as far from restful as they could be in making their push to break through the Trojan lines. That contrast is made all the more acute by the fact that the Greeks and Trojans have just been compared to reapers working in a rich man's field (11.67–69), an image which might make us all the more inclined to think that they too need to be released from their toil.

75. See Tsagalis (2012), 307–9, for a more detailed analysis of this progression.

76. Compare 15.271–76 for a similar example.

77. See Tsagalis (2012), 316–20, on all three similes as part of a long series within the same 'visual unit', all with mountain or field settings.

78. See Weil (2005), esp. 26–27, who discusses the way in which the more-than-human force of the simile world overwhelms the battlefield too, dehumanising victor and victim alike.

79. I am grateful to Chloe Bray for sharing a draft of her article on 'Time and human fragility in the landscapes of the *Iliad*', which includes analysis of several of the mountain similes I discuss here.

80. See Halliwell (2019); also Ready (2011), 5: 'the defining feature of a simile is the dissimilarity between tenor and vehicle', and more detailed discussion at 14–15, with further bibliography at 14, n. 9.

81. See Halliwell (2019), 8, on the comparison of Polyphemus with a mountain at *Odyssey* 9.190–92, and 8–9, on the comparison of Penelope's tears to the melting of snow in a mountain landscape in *Odyssey* 19.204–8: 'the imaginative movement of thought effected by the simile—from the almost claustrophobic human scenario in the firelight of the hall to the expansive view of a mountain range—exploits a perspective of physical distance to generate a temporary estrangement from the all-too-emotional immediacy of the situation itself' (9).

82. See Phillips (2015a) for a survey of the problems and proposed solutions, pointing out that the lack of a perfect fit between simile and what it describes is typical of the tradition Homer is working with.

83. For the latter suggestion see Panegyres (2017), 484–85.

84. See Panegyres (2017).

85. See Clarke (1997), esp. 70, on this simile. Clarke's discussion is not mentioned by either Phillips (2015a) or Panegyres (2017).

86. *Iliad* 16.3–4, echoing 9.14–15, where exactly the same lines are used to describe Agamemnon.

87. See Tsagalis (2012), 323–36, on the connections between these two similes as part of the same visual unit, pointing out especially that 'Patroklos and the Myrmidons are visualized similarly, for they are and always will be together throughout *Iliad* XVI' (326).

88. *Iliad* 24.507–12.

89. *Iliad* 22.347.

90. See Halliwell (2019).

91. See Halliwell (2019), 10.

92. De Jong (2018), includes both *Iliad* 4.275–82 and 5.770–72 in a list of examples of mortal *oroskopia*, but without any discussion of their significance for the poem.

93. See Kelly (2007), 406–7, for debate about the text in relation to lines 557–58, which some have viewed as an interpolation on the grounds that they recur word for word in another simile, at 16.299–300.

94. See Kelly (2007), 371–72, on the way in which the shepherds of the similes are usually to be identified with specific human actors: in this case he argues that there is an implied identification with Hector rejoicing at the Trojan advances, but also with good discussion of alternative possibilities in 372, n. 7.

95. See Clay (2011), 6–7; de Jong (1987), 131–34.

96. See later, chapter 5, for further discussion of ancient versions of the sublime in relation to mountains.

97. Porter (2016), 360–81.

98. See Longinus, *On the Sublime* 9.5, with Porter (2016), 162–63 and 361; Halliwell (2019), 7–8.

99. Compare Redfield (1994), 225–26.

100. See Janko (1994), 364–66, on this image and its relation to other portrayals of the justice of Zeus in the poem; also Ready (2018), 216–18, discussing these lines as part of a series of river similes. Other good examples, where the involvement of Zeus is explicit in weather similes, include 2.781–83, 5.87–92, and 11.492–95. However, see also Graziosi and Haubold (2005), 88–89, on the way in which the *Iliad* and especially the *Odyssey* tend to downplay divine involvement in weather and other natural phenomena.

101. Most often, however, the reactions of human onlookers in the similes are not specified. In Book 4, for example, the sounds of the two armies fighting are compared with the clash between two streams in flood: 'As when winter-flowing rivers running down from the mountains to a meeting point throw together the mighty waters from their great streams within a hollow ravine, and from far off in the mountains a shepherd hears their din' (4.452–55). Here once again the sense of distance and perspective is striking; it has an estranging function which brings a new dimension to our understanding of the human activities the simile describes: see Halliwell (2019), 10. It comes less than 150 lines after the goatherd-cave simile, and that proximity invites us to see the two as closely linked: see Kirk (1985), 384–85. It also leaves open the question of how exactly we should imagine the shepherd's response: the poet's silence about his reaction, as in other similar passages, can act as a question or an invitation. There is no explicit endorsement of the view that he sees this as a manifestation of the divine or as something approaching the natural sublime as it has been imagined in post-classical literature, but it leaves those possibilities open, and certainly the natural world is not portrayed here explicitly as hostile.

102. See later, chapter 5.

103. See 5.351, where Ares promises to make Aphrodite 'shudder at' war if she does not leave the battlefield; 12.208 for the Trojans shuddering (ἐρρίγησαν) in response to an omen involving an eagle and a snake, which is said to 'indicate the will of aegis-bearing Zeus' (12.209); 15.34, where Hera 'shudders' in response to Zeus's angry criticism of her; 16.119, where Telamonian Aias shudders in realising that Zeus is giving his support to the Trojans; by contrast the same verb is used of a reaction to human characters and events at 3.259, 4.148, 4.150, 11.254, 11.345, 12.331. It is also used twice in the *Odyssey*, in both cases again in reaction to the divine: once of Calypso's response to Zeus's demand, conveyed by Hermes, that she should send Odysseus home (*Odyssey* 5.116); and then a few lines later of Odysseus' reaction to Calypso telling him that she will help him to leave (5.171). There is one particularly interesting parallel in *Iliad* 5, where Diomedes encounters Ares on the battlefield and 'shuddered' 'as when a helpless traveller after a long journey over the plain stands before a fast-flowing river pouring out to the sea, seeing it roaring with foam, and runs back again the way he has come' (5.597–99). It is not specified that the traveller of the simile is afraid, but certainly there is an awareness of his helplessness (ἀπάλαμνος) here, and so a recognition of the limitations of human power: see Ready (2018), 216. In that passage a reaction of helplessness in the face of natural forces is equated with a reaction to a god on the battlefield, and a reader who keeps in mind the goatherd-cave simile of Book 4 at the same time as this one might be more inclined see that too as a reaction to the divine.

104. The verb occurs thirty-three times in the *Iliad* and *Odyssey*; of those, fourteen are in response to gods or divinely sponsored happenings: see *Iliad* 7.189 for Aias' reaction to the drawing of lots to decide who will fight Hector, immediately preceded by a prayer from Agamemnon to Zeus for a good outcome; 8.378 for Athene sarcastically anticipating Hector's 'joy' at her anticipated arrival, along with Hera, on the battlefield; 16.530 for Glaukos' joy at receiving help from Apollo; 24.321 for response to an omen; 24.424 for Priam's reaction to the news that the gods have kept the corpse of Hector intact; compare *Odyssey* 8.199, 13.226, 13.250, 13.353, 22.207, and 24.504, all cases of Odysseus' responding to Athene in disguise; and *Odyssey* 15.165, 20.104, and 21.414 for response to omens, the last two of Odysseus responding to thunder from Zeus.

Chapter 3. Pausanias: Mythical Landscapes and Divine Presence

1. See Tuan (1990); Robinson (2012), esp. 251, for application of that notion to the Valley of the Muses below Mount Helikon; compare Robinson (2016) for a similar reading of both the Valley of the Muses and the sanctuary of Apollo at Delphi, but using instead the notion of 'charisma of place' (229) rather than topophilia; also della Dora (2016a) for the importance of place in classical and Byzantine literature, with brief mention of Tuan's notion of *topophilia* at 3, n. 4.

2. Compare B. Zimmermann (2019) for discussion of the importance of Kithairon as almost a co-actor in the play, and as a constant background presence; also Finglass (2019) along similar lines on Kithairon in Sophocles' *Oedipus the King*.

3. Compare Buxton (2013), 26–27, on the way in which Dionysus' control over the mountain overflows into the built environment of the city.

4. See Taplin (2010), esp. 238–40, for vivid discussion: 'the great majority of the audience in fifth-century Athens would surely have known Cithaeron at first hand' (239). I have also

learned a great deal from Bray (2021), who argues that the bodily character of the play's mountain scenes would have had the capacity to stimulate the audience's tactile, corporeal memories of their experiences of mountain landscapes, both on Kithairon and elsewhere, in a way which would have encouraged identification with the events which unfold in front of them; she also shows at length the importance of reading the mountains of the play intratextually: the descriptions of Kithairon are interwoven with mention of a series of other mountains, for example Olympus, Parnassos and Nysa, the mythical birthplace of Dionysus.

5. See Buxton (1991), 39–48, for good discussion, with attention to the play of repetition and difference between the landscape descriptions in the successive messenger speeches.

6. See Buxton (2013), 27.

7. The play seems to have been written in Macedonia, during Euripides' time at the court of Archaelaos I of Macedon, and the question of whether Euripides was drawing on special knowledge of manaedic ritual in the mountains of Macedonia has long been debated: for example, Dodds (1940).

8. See R. Bradley (2000), esp. 20–28, on the way in which the Pausanias' account parallels archaeological evidence from prehistoric cultures for the use of natural features as sacred places.

9. See Hawes (2014).

10. See Hutton (2005b), 8, esp. n. 22, and (2005b), 293, esp. n. 7, with reference to Pausanias' 'participation in religious cults and his observance of religious taboos'.

11. See Elsner (1995) on the way in which this element stands in tension with Pausanias' antiquarianism, esp. 130 and 151–52: 'To signify the impossibility of enunciating the Other World, the holy, is to reveal that the kind of discourse inherent in ordinary Pausanian viewing cannot control the other world and is insufficient to it' (151).

12. Compare Hawes (2014), 193–94: 'Pausanias is not interested in unifying his approach to myth; his myths do not belong to a singular or discrete category. The diverse facets of mythology in antiquity are reflected in the *Periegesis*, not least in the ways in which these different kinds of material prompt particular modes of interpretation'.

13. For example, see König and Whitmarsh (2007).

14. See König (2005), 186–204, for one version of what it means to read Pausanias' text consecutively, focusing on his account of Olympia in Books 5–6; also among others Elsner (2001); Hutton (2005a); and Konstan (2001) for brief reflections on the pleasures of Pausanias' text.

15. See König and Hollis (2021b), 8–10.

16. On that stereotype, and its limitations, see among others Pretzler (2004), 215–16; Hutton (2005b), 294; also further later, n. 20.

17. Compare della Dora (2008) on corporeal engagement with mountain landscapes as a key part of antiquarian experience in the experience of nineteenth-century travellers to Greece.

18. For example, see 9.30 on the bones of Orpheus, or 9.38 on the bones of Hesiod.

19. I am grateful to Christopher Schliephake for sharing his not-yet-published work on Pausanias as 'nature writer'.

20. See Jost (1996), 722–30, and (2007), 106–10, on the way in which Pausanias' account in Book 8 reflects the experience of travelling, for example in his use of the word *oros* ('mountain') even for relatively low hills in cases where they have significance prominence from the perspective of the road; also Jost (1996), 730–38, on some of the challenges caused for the location of particular mountain sites by Pausanias' subjective ways of describing mountains. See also

Pretzler (2004) for more general discussion of what we can construct of Pausanias' experience of travel from the work as a whole; and (2007), esp. 32–72, on Pausanias' work in the wider context of travel writing in the Roman Empire; also Elsner (1995), 134–37, for the profoundly experiential nature of Pausanias' account, which reproduces Pausanias' movement from place to place albeit without discussion of his experiences on the road.

21. Jost (2007), 104.

22. See Akujärvi (2005), 131–66, for extensive discussion of both effects through the work as a whole.

23. See Frazer (1898) for detailed topographical commentary, drawing both on his own experience of travelling in Greece and on accounts by other nineteenth-century travellers, esp. IV, 194–96, on this passage.

24. Compare Alcock (1993), 119–20, on the role of sanctuaries as boundary markers which were sometimes subject to dispute, in Pausanias and beyond.

25. See further discussion later, in chapter 14.

26. For example, 8.7.4 for a mountain that holds the remains of a camp used by Philip II of Macedon during a trip to the Peloponnese after his victory at the Battle of Chaironeia in 338 BCE.

27. See 8.14.1 on signs of the flooding of the Phenean plain still visible on the surrounding mountains.

28. On Pausanias' interest in local religious traditions for Book 8 as a whole, see Jost (2007), 114–19.

29. See Alcock (1993), 200–210, on rural cults in Pausanias and in Roman Greece more broadly, making clear that some of the sites Pausanias records were in ruins, but also stressing that much of the evidence suggests a 'continuing civic commitment to rural cults, and thus to the countryside' (206); compare Baleriaux (2017), esp. 142–45, on the way in which Pausanias' account reflects Roman interests in archaising approaches to Arkadian myth after their 'brutal conquest' (142) of the region, and the changes to Arkadia's religious topography in the Roman period.

30. See Porter (2001).

31. Compare earlier, chapter 1; and see Rutherford (2001) and Hutton (2005b), 293–96, for careful discussion of the degree to which Pausanias' travel can plausibly be equated with pilgrimage, both drawing on the influential account of Elsner (1992).

32. See Cook (1914–40), I, 124–48, esp. 137–39, on Mount Sipylos.

33. The Niobe rock is mentioned again at 8.2.7, discussed later.

34. For example, in his report of the local tradition that the mountain was the place where Zeus was brought up (8.38.2–3).

35. For example, a sanctuary of Pan with a grove of trees around it (8.38.5) and a shrine of Parrhasian Apollo on the eastern side of the mountain (8.38.8).

36. See Pretzler (2004), 215: 'The whole *Periegesis* contains only one single reference to a good view from a place'. This passage is not mentioned by de Jong (2018) in her survey of mountaintop views from Greek literature.

37. See Elsner (1992), 24: 'here, briefly but memorably, we see the other world penetrating this world—we see one aspect of the sacred in action'. That detail connects this passage with a series of others in the work which collect stories from the past about punishments for people

who enter sacred space illicitly: compare 8.5.5 for the story that Aipytos was blinded for entering the sanctuary of Poseidon at Mantineia, which Pausanias says is still forbidden 'in our own time'; and see Elsner (1995), 144–50, who includes this detail within a wider category in the *Periegesis* of sacred things that are hidden, esp. 148, on the way in which this description of Mount Lykaion follows on from 8.36.2, which describes the prohibition on entry into the shrine of Rhea on Mount Thaumasios for all but women sacred to the goddess; also 149 on the secret object of the Messenians buried by Aristomenes on Mount Ithome at 4.20.4.

38. One way of interpreting this is to see it in the light of a number of other passages where Pausanias keeps quiet about certain religious rituals or places out of piety. For other examples of religious silence, see Elsner (1992), 21–25; Hutton (2005a), 8, n. 22, and (2005b), 293, nn. 7 and 9.

39. The Arkadians had a reputation in the ancient world for being a people of great antiquity. Pausanias endorses that view: he describes how Lykaon, son of Pelasgos, founded both the city of Lykosoura (which is later in Book 8 said to be the oldest city in the world) and the Lykaian festival (founded, he suggests, before the festival of the Panathenaia in Athens, but not before the Olympics), both on the slopes of Mount Lykaion.

40. On this passage see Hawes (2014), 215–16, who sees this as an example of the way in which Pausanias' standards for judging truthfulness shift according to the local context of the stories he is assessing: in Arkadia the continuities of population and ritual between the present and the very ancient past make these marvellous happenings more likely. See also Baleriaux (2017), 144. For a passage that complicates the impression of Pausanias' more positive attitude to the literal truth of divine marvels in Arkadia, see 8.8.3, where he explains that his visit to Arkadia converted him from a sceptical attitude towards stories about the gods, when he realised that some of them were in fact riddling expressions of wisdom: 'therefore, concerning the divine, I will make use of the stories that are told'; however, see Hutton (2005a), 303–11, and (2014), 182–83, who stresses the difficulty of drawing firm conclusions from this passage about Pausanias' changing views, in response to those who have taken it as evidence for a 'conversion' to allegorical thinking; also Hawes (2014), 191–93, for a reminder that Pausanias is talking here only about a particular category of divine stories, for which an allegorical approach was especially suitable. See also Hutton (2005a), 273–75 and 303–11.

41. It is mentioned, however, at 2.2.7.

42. See Hawes (2014), 203–4.

43. See Jones (2001) on Pausanias' mention of guides repeatedly throughout the work.

44. See Belis (2015), II, 74–75; also I, 57–58, on the Daidala, with further bibliography.

45. For example, Mount Hypatos, which has 'a temple and image of supreme Zeus' (9.19.3); Mount Ptous, with 'a temple and image of Dionysus that are worth seeing' (9.23.5) (that phrase 'worth seeing' is one of Pausanias' favourite terms of praise); Mount Phix, the home of the Sphinx, the riddling monster destroyed by Oedipus, rationalised by Pausanias as a pirate who 'seized this mountain and used it for plundering expeditions, until Oedipus overwhelmed her by the size of his army' (9.26.2); Mount Libethrios, which has images of the Muses and the Libethrian Nymphs (9.34.4); Mount Laphystios, which has a statue of 'bright-eyed Herakles', at the place where Herakles is said to have ascended from Hades with Kerberos, the guard-dog of the underworld (9.34.5); a cliff known as Petrachos, where they say that 'Kronos was deceived, receiving from Rhea a stone instead of Zeus, and there is a small image of Zeus on the summit of the mountain' (9.41.6).

46. See Rocchi (1996), esp. 17–22.

47. For an excellent discussion of the sanctuary, see Robinson (2012), including a reconstruction of the architecture of the site and a full account of the evidence for the artwork; also along similar lines, Robinson (2016), 231–36; Hurst and Schachter (1996) for a wide-ranging collection of essays on archaeological and literary evidence for the mountain and the Valley of the Muses; and Schachter (1986), 147–79, on development of the cult of the Muses by Thespiai.

48. See Robinson (2012), 236–41.

49. See Robinson (2012), 231 and 241–42, with further bibliography.

50. See Robinson (2012), 242–47, for detailed commentary on Pausanias' itinerary through the site.

51. See later, chapter 8, for further discussion; also Robinson (2012), 247–51, on the site and its literary associations.

52. For alternative explanations, see Calame (1996) for the suggestion that the cuts are intended to remove those sections of Hesiod's work that represent the Muses as Panhellenic rather than local figures; and Lamberton (1988b), 502, for the suggestion that this might be a sign that the local inhabitants clung to 'a purist position' about the original content of the poem, in reaction to a contemporary culture inclined to invent traditions and add interpolations in order to increase the prominence of Hesiod and his work; he cites as a parallel Plutarch's rejection of *Works and Days* 646–62, a passage which seems to guarantee the authenticity of the tripod supposedly dedicated by Hesiod himself and on show in the Valley of the Muses.

53. The same goes for Athens in Book 1, or Olympia in the central two books, Books 5 and 6: it is no accident that these three great historical and religious centres get such prominent positions within the overarching structure of the work: see Elsner (2001), 6. Delphi dominates within Book 10 to such an extent that Pausanias neglects some important routes through the territory of Phokis, in his eagerness to emphasise the roads that lead out from the city in all directions, and in some cases that involves focusing instead on routes that lead over quite rough mountain terrain: see Hutton (2005a), 86–88, for example, with reference to 10.33.3, which recommends a path to Lilaia 'across Parnassos' (διὰ τοῦ Παρνασσοῦ).

54. See Robinson (2016), esp. 236–47.

55. See Amandry (1981a), (1981b), and (1984).

56. See Jacquemin (1984).

57. Plutarch, *The Oracles at Delphi No Longer Given in Verse* 1, 394f.

58. The repetition of the phrase 'an active man' points up the contrast: the climb from Delphi is one thing; the journey onwards to the high mountain quite another. Compare 10.5.5: 'the main road from here to Delphi becomes more steep and more difficult even for an active man'; and 10.5.1, where Pausanias tells us about an alternative route up to the 'heights of Parnassos' which is less difficult than the route from Delphi but which he nevertheless chooses not to follow.

59. See Belis (2015), II, 172–73.

60. Plutarch, *De primo frigore* 18.

61. On the Thyiades and Mount Parnassos, and on the tension between order and wilderness in the landscape around Delphi, see McInerney (1997), 263–83; also Bremmer (1984) for a useful attempt to reconstruct the ritual.

62. See further later, chapter 10.

63. The incident involving Poseidon is another example of the way in which Pausanias seems more willing to contemplate divine intervention in Arkadia than elsewhere, but it is not a passage that is often included in discussions of Pausanias' attitude to rationalisation, for example in Hawes (2014), which are usually focused purely on mythical rather than historical events.

64. At 10.1.11, Pausanias describes how 500 Phokians attacked the Thessalian camp at night in whitewashed armour; that example of fabricated divine involvement stands in contrast with what Pausanias views as the genuine happenings in response to the Gauls; for a similar effect in Book 8, see earlier in this chapter, on 8.2.6–7.

65. See later, chapter 11, on the influence of Herodotus on this passage.

Chapter 4. Egeria on Mount Sinai: Mountain Pilgrimage in Early Christian and Late Antique Culture

1. For an overview, see 'Mountains', in Ryken et al. (1998), 572–74; also Barton (2017), 48–58.
2. Exodus 19:10–13.
3. Biblical translations in this chapter are from the New Revised Standard Version.
4. See della Dora (2016a), 152.
5. See Deuteronomy 32:49 for God's instructions to Moses and 34:1 ('And the Lord let him see all the land').
6. See esp. earlier, chapter 2, on the battle between the Olympian gods and the Titans in Hesiod, *Theogony* 617–735.
7. See later, chapter 15, including discussion there of parallels from modern mountain studies, which is similarly preoccupied with the interaction between antiquity and modernity in relation to mountains.
8. See Cogan (2000), 184–85, for discussion of the difficult Hebrew word *bama*, which is usually translated as 'hill-shrine' or 'high place'.
9. 1 Kings 13:2.
10. 1 Kings 13:33.
11. 1 Kings 18:17–40.
12. See Cogan (2000), 456–57.
13. 1 Kings 19:1–18.
14. 1 Kings 22:43.
15. See Alter (2019), 428–29.
16. For example, Isiaiah 40:9, 52:7.
17. For example, Isaiah 2:1–4.
18. For useful summaries, see Elsner (1995), 336, n. 78, and in more detail Ceschi (2019).
19. On mountains in the Gospel of Matthew, including a useful overview of precedents from the Hebrew bible, see Donaldson (1995).
20. Matthew 5–7.
21. Matthew 17:1–8.
22. Acts 1:10–12.
23. However, see della Dora (2016a), 153, on the way in which Jesus' divinity is made manifest to the apostles in the Transfiguration, in contrast with the impenetrability of God's appearance to Moses on Mount Sinai.

24. See Lee (2019).

25. See Elsner and Rubiés (1999), 8–20, on the growing prominence of allegory in late antique travel writing.

26. Methodius, *Symposium* pr. 5–8; and see König (2012), 156–59, on the allegorical character of the setting.

27. See Elsner (1995), esp. 108; della Dora (2016a), 152–53.

28. Bradbury (2004), letter 43 (p. 72).

29. Libanius *Oration* 18.172.

30. For the background to Julian's philosophical thinking and his views on sacrifice, see (among many others) Smith (1995) and Bradbury (1995), esp. 332–41, on the intellectual justifications for sacrifice, and debates over their validity, within Neoplatonism.

31. In another work, Libanius praises Julian for having restored sacrifice both 'to Zeus on the mountaintop and Zeus in the city' (Libanius, *Oration* 15.79). Less flatteringly, Ammianus Marcellinus tells us that in the months before his Persian campaign 'with excessive frequency he drenched the altars with much blood of victims, sometimes sacrificing 100 oxen at once, and countless flocks of various other animals, and white birds' (Ammianus Marcellinus, *Res Gestae* 22.12.6).

32. See Petridou (2016).

33. See Lane Fox (1986), 102–67.

34. See Petridou (2016), 210–14.

35. See Petridou (2016) 195–228.

36. Herodotus, *Histories* 6.105.

37. There are also precedents for divine signs from Zeus in response to mountaintop sacrifice, not least on Mount Kasios itself: for example, we hear that the Hellenistic King Seleukos I Nikator sacrificed to Zeus on the summit and then watched as an eagle took a piece of the meat, flew away, and then dropped the meat in the place where his new city of Seleukeia was to be founded: Malalas, *Chronicle* 8.12 (199).

38. Homer, *Odyssey* 19.177–78, with Schol. ad *Od.* 19.179; compare Plato, *Laws* 624a–b; the location of these conversations in the cave of Zeus, presumably the one on Mount Ida, is specified at Plato, *Minos* 319e; and see Petridou (2016), 336–37.

39. Philosophers like Iamblichos, who influenced Julian heavily, and before him Porphyry, made elaborate attempts to explain how exactly ritual could lead to communication with the gods. Some philosophers went beyond theory by involving themselves in ritual practices, collectively known as theurgy, which were specially designed to make the gods present, often with the goal of self-perfection through unity with the divine. These developments led to a large number of popular anecdotes about the supernatural powers of philosophers, for example in Eunapius' *Lives of the Philosophers and Sophists*. Julian seems to have gone further than most both in theorising that process and in putting it into practice through his combined regime of prayer and sacrifice. Julian's friend Sallustius claims in his work *Concerning the Gods and the Universe* that prayers without sacrifice 'are just words, whereas those with sacrifice are animated words' (Sallustius, *Concerning the Gods and the Universe* 16), and everything we hear about Julian's religious practices suggests that he felt the same way.

40. Julian, *To the Cynic Herakleios* (Oration 7), 230c–232d.

41. Libanius certainly suggests as much elsewhere in the funeral oration in representing the incident on Mount Kasios as a sign of Julian's special status: 'it would take a long time to tell of

his other conversations [with the gods]. . . . If therefore it were possible for a human to share heaven with the gods, he would have done so with them, and they would have made space for him. But given that his physical body did not allow that, they came to him, as instructors in what he should and should not do' (Libanius, *Oration* 18.172–73).

42. On Julian's rewriting of Matthew 4:8–10 in this text, see Greenwood (2014).

43. See Whalin (2021), in the context of a wide-ranging survey of late antique responses to mountains.

44. For the late antique evidence from Hymettos, see earlier, chapter 1; Langdon (1976), 73–74, 76, and 94–95; also Fowden (1988), 55 and 56–57, for similar developments in other religious sites in Attica.

45. See earlier, chapter 1.

46. For the late antique coin evidence from Olympus, see Kyriazopoulos and Livadas (1967), 13–14.

47. See Fowden (1988), 57, on *Inscriptiones Graecae* II² 4831 (= *Supplementum Epigraphicum Graecum* 37.140).

48. See further in chapter 16.

49. On Christian pilgrimage on the Sinai peninsula, see Hobbs (1995), 217–40; also Caner (2010), 17–39, which also contains an extensive selection of translations from late antique texts about Mount Sinai; and della Dora (2016a), 162–65, for the later Byzantine tradition.

50. See Hobbs (1995), 32–53.

51. *P.Colt.* 31, in Kraemer (1958), 27–28.

52. See Finkelstein (1981).

53. See Hobbs (1995), 106–19, on the climb to the summit.

54. Anastasius, *Tales of the Sinai Fathers* 1.4; and see Stone (1986), esp. 106–8, on the Anastasius passage, pointing out that pilgrimage of Armenians in large numbers seems to have been common, and that it was common to visit Mount Tabor as well as Mount Sinai.

55. For the full series, see Anastasius, *Tales of the Sinai Fathers* 1.1–6.

56. Procopius, *Buildings* 5.8.

57. Theodoret, *Religious History* 6.12, with Caner (2010), 19.

58. See Elsner (1995), 88–124, for a reading of Gregory of Nyssa and the Mount Sinai mosaics along these lines in order to illustrate the move 'from naturalist expectations towards the symbolism inherent in mystic contemplation' (88); for example, see 109: 'the Moses panels proclaimed the viewers' condition as initiate climbers on a spiritual ascent'; also Elsner and Wolf (2010), 50–58, for good discussion along similar lines; Paterson (2018); Caner (2010), 20, who suggests that the 'radiant image' of the mosaic 'affirmed expectations that God's "energy" could still be experienced here, on Mount Sinai, as it had been in Old Testament times'; and della Dora (2016a), 165, on John Climacus.

59. See della Dora (2016a), 152.

60. See Campbell (1986) on this absence of the marvellous; Elsner (1995), 155, on the lack of any conception of the distinction between sacred and secular in Egeria's writing; compare Sivan (1988), 71, on Egeria's lack of interest in miracles associated with monks. For one parallel, see the much briefer account of the Piacenza Pilgrim, *Travelogue* 37–39, who describes visiting Mount Sinai in the late sixth century, but with mention of a Saracen sacred stone that changes colour at the time of their festival, and a lion and panther that graze together with goats and deer and other animals without attacking them.

61. See Caner (2010), 73–135, for introduction and translation.

62. See Morgan (2015).

63. See further discussion of this passage later, in chapter 16.

64. See Caner (2010), 81–82.

65. That phrase and variants of it are repeated several times in what follows, including twice more in remarkably quick succession in the next few lines (2.6 and 2.7), but the main purpose of these mentions seems to be to identify the mountain unequivocally, rather than to raise any prospect of a repetition of that phenomenon of divine epiphany in the present.

66. For good overviews, see Sivan (1988a); Palmer (1998), 40–45; Dietz (2005), 44–54. For translation, with notes, see McGowan and Bradshaw (2018), in English, and Brodersen (2016) in German.

67. See Caner (2010), 212, for translation of Peter the Deacon's abridged summary of the opening sections, which includes regular mention of mountains.

68. See Caner (2010), 18–19, on Christian appropriation of Sinai's heritage from the Hebrew Bible.

69. On the absences of surprises in Egeria's account, see Campbell (1986), 22: 'the logic of her universe allows her to infer the authenticity of what she sees ... from the theological necessity of its being there'.

70. See Spitzer (1949) for still very valuable observations on Egeria's repetitive style and its appropriateness to her pilgrimage narrative; also Campbell (1986), 23–24 and 26.

71. See Leyerle (1996), 126–29, drawing parallels with the way in which modern tourists similarly often gain satisfaction above all from their encounters with the markers of particular sights, which make it clear that they have reached a significant place, as much as from the sights themselves; also Hunt (2000) on the role of the resident monks in identifying these places of scripture, esp. 46–50 on the passages describing Mount Sinai and Mount Nebo.

72. For example, see Westra (1995), 100, on *IE* 4.4.

73. For Egeria's relationship with her intended recipients, see Sivan (1988b); also Westra (1995), 95; and Palmer (1998), esp. 49–51, on Egeria as 'an instrument of "remote sensing"' (49) who appeals to all of the senses in her account in order to make it more vivid to her recipients.

74. However, see Schubert (2019), 323, on the importance of the first-person plural for Egeria on Mount Sinai, in her role as just one representative of a pilgrimage group.

75. De Jong (2018), 38, includes only a brief account of Christian uses of the motif of *oroskopia* (naturally not including this passage, given that her focus is on Greek texts).

76. See Elsner and Wolf (2010), 48.

77. See Hansen (2013) on the importance of first ascents in modern mountaineering history; also Bainbridge (2020), 72–128.

78. See della Dora (2008); König (2021).

79. Campbell (1988), esp. 20–33, takes Egeria as her starting point for the development of first-person travel writing in the European tradition, but she also stresses repeatedly, and in my view with undue negativity, the alienness of the *IE* by later standards: 'nothing ... could seem more remote from the modern experience of travel, or even of experience, than the monotonously litanized itinerary of Egeria's ideal pilgrim'.

80. For an excellent survey of the claims made about Petrarch's modernity, see Hansen (2013), 12–22; also Hollis and König (2021b), 4–5.

81. For the idea that Petrarch's use of allegory separates him from modern responses to mountains, see Nicolson (1959), 49–50, and MacFarlane (2003), 146–47; also Schama (1995), 419–21, on the tension between experience and allegory in Petrarch's account, and Durling (1974), who argues that the whole account is intended as a critique of the allegorical worldview of Augustine's theology.

82. See Schubert (2021), esp. his summary at 323–24, for a detailed account of the way in which Egeria alternates between narrative and descriptive passages in the work: the latter slow down the pace of the narrative, in a way which potentially prompts a meditative response, as does the prevalence of reference to biblical passages, but without diluting the personal quality of her account.

83. See Colley (2010), 101–44; Roche (2013); Louargant (2013); McNee (2016), 37–41; Anderson (2020), 70–76 and 186–94; König and Hollis (2021a), 14–15; also Debarbieux and Rudaz (2011) and (2015), 229–34, on the potential role of women (not yet fully activated in their view) in sustainable mountain development.

84. For text, French translation, and notes, see Maraval (1997), 321–49.

85. See Elsner and Rubiés (1999), 19, on the allegorical quality of this passage.

86. See later, part III.

87. See Leyerle (1996), 126.

88. See Westra (1995), 98.

89. White (1967) has been particularly influential.

90. See Westra (1995), 95, for brief but suggestive comments along similar lines.

91. For similar observations on this passage, see Elsner and Wolf (2010), 49; della Dora (2016b), 109–11.

92. Deuteronomy 32:48–52 and 34:1–4; and see Egeria's own references to that incident at *IE* 10.1.

Chapter 5. Mountain Aesthetics

1. See esp. Clytemnestra's speech describing the progress of the flame at Aeschylus, *Agamemnon* 281–316; and for evidence for military use of mountaintop fire beacons, both classical and Byzantine, see Pattenden (1983); also Polybius 10.42–47.

2. See de Jong (2018); also della Dora (2016b), 107–38, and (2018) for accounts which trace the importance of mountaintop viewing from the ancient Mediterranean right into the twentieth century; also further discussion earlier, chapters 2 and 4.

3. Hyde (1915) more or less accepts that view, although he also collects what he represents as occasional counter-examples; as noted already earlier, the influential views of Nicolson (1959) on mountains in Greek and Roman literature seem to be formed almost exclusively from her reading of Hyde's article. Barton (2017) and Korenjak (2017) argue for an earlier start date for modern aesthetic appreciation of mountains, backdating it to the Renaissance, drawing in Barton's case on the evidence of neo-Latin literature.

4. That phenomenon is a recurring theme in the chapters in Hollis and König (2021a), especially Hooley (2021), Jordan (2021), and König (2021).

5. Compare Goldhill (1984), 38–39, on the passage discussed earlier; also 11–12 on the tension between clarity and confusion in the watchman's initial mention of the beacon in the opening lines of the play.

6. Nydal (2018).

7. For example, see W. Bainbridge (2020) for extensive discussion of this issue in relation to nineteenth-century British travellers in the Dolomites.

8. See Doran (2015) for a detailed discussion of all three and of other key figures in addition.

9. For one recent attempt to define the sublime (not just the natural sublime), see Porter (2016), 5–6, and 51–53 for a long list of what he takes to be markers of the sublime in Longinus and in antiquity generally, including among other things 'immense heights' or profound depths', 'sudden or extreme, often violent, motions or changes', 'large masses and quantities and surfaces', 'moments of intense and vital danger, risk, and crisis', 'natural, mythical, divine, or literary phenomena embodying any of the above', for example 'Etna's deadly volcano'.

10. See Cosgrove (1984).

11. See Andrews (1989), 3–23.

12. See Elsner (2010) for that association with Pausanias; also Stoneman (2010), 145–46.

13. See discussion earlier, in chapter 3.

14. See Andrews (1989), 41–50, on ruins and the picturesque; compare Stoneman (2010), 141–42.

15. Price (1810), I, 51.

16. See Stoneman (2010), 136–47, on the association between Greece and the picturesque more broadly; compare della Dora (2016b), 158: 'unlike the Western Alps, Hellas' peaks were not perceived as sublime or chaotic, but rather as inspiring poetic objects, as beautiful, well-defined landmarks for orientation ... and as privileged nodes within a complex web of memory'. On some accounts the picturesque properly involved cultural or historical associations, although that was a debated matter. Uvedale Price viewed it as a purely aesthetic phenomenon; by contrast Richard Payne Knight took the picturesque to be partly dependent on intellectual associations in his work *Landscape: A Didactic Poem*: see Stoneman (2010), 140, for summary.

17. See esp. Porter (2016).

18. See Doran (2015), 18–19 and 83–88, esp. 88: 'Chapter 35 is one of the most iconic and consequential parts of *Peri hypsous*. It leads directly to the appropriation of the concept of sublimity by the aesthetics of nature in the late seventeenth and eighteenth centuries'; also many of the essays in Costelloe (2012), esp. Potkay (2012).

19. See Duffy (2013), esp. 9–10, on the concept of 'classic ground': 'time and again in the texts which I consider here, this concept is invoked to characterize the encounter with the "natural sublime" as involving either a landscape or an environment which already exists as what might be called "classic ground" in the European cultural imagination, that is, which already possesses a range of culturally determined and topographically specific associations, or which is in the process of becoming "classic ground", that is, of acquiring the associations which it often continues to possess to this day, of being inscribed upon Europe's cultural map of the world'.

20. See König (2021) on the writings of Edward Dodwell set in the wider context of nineteenth-century travel writing from Greece.

21. For example, see Thonemann (2020), 87–89, for a selection of passages from Artemidorus' *Oneirocritica* where dreaming about mountains and other uncultivated landscapes is said to have negative connotations.

22. Very few of the passages in the rest of this section are mentioned by Barton (2017) in his survey at 20–47.

23. See *Eclogues* 1.83, 5.8, and 10.32 on mountains as the natural habitat for Virgil's poet-herdsmen, with Barton (2017), 44–45; also further discussion later of the motif whereby poets are imagined as herdsmen receiving inspiration in the mountains, for example, in *Eclogues* 6.64–73 or in Theocritus, *Idylls* 7.91–95.

24. See Wallace-Hadrill (1968), 87–91, pointing out that this passage is relatively unusual in patristic writing for its praise of wild nature; della Dora (2016a), 171–72, in the context of a wider discussion of the idea of mountain as earthly paradise in Byzantine literature; Ludlow (2020), 105–15; Whalin (2021), 93–95; and Silvas (2007) for an attempt to reconstruct the site of Basil's retreat.

25. Two mentions of the pleasure of the view: οὐκ ἐλάττονα τέρψιν..,παρεχόμενον ἢ τοῖς ἐκ τῆς Ἀμφιπόλεως τὸν Στρύμονα καταμανθάνουσιν ('giving no less pleasure than to those who observe the river Strymon from Amphipolis'); ὄψιν τε ἡδίστην ἐμοὶ καὶ παντὶ θεατῇ παρεχόμενος ('providing a most pleasant view to me and to every observer').

26. See Ludlow (2020), 108–9.

27. See Ludlow (2020), 114–15.

28. See Koelb (2006) for the influence of classical traditions of ekphrasis over Romantic place descriptions.

29. Text in Spengel (1853–56), II, 118; translation in Kennedy (2003), 45–46.

30. Text in Rabe (1913), 15; translation in Kennedy (2003), 81; see also Webb (2009), 64.

31. See Webb (2009), 156, with reference to Menander Rhetor, *Treatise* 2.2.20, 383; also 159 on speeches in honour of the emperor, which should include description of places where the emperor has performed military feats, including mountains and plains, with reference to *Treatise* 2.1.22, 373.

32. See also later, chapter 11, on debates about the appropriateness of extended mountain descriptions in historiography.

33. The landscapes of Atlantis are implicitly compared with those of Attica 9,000 years before (esp. at *Critias* 110d–111e), which is said to have been a land of high hills covered with rich soil, which has then gradually been eroded in the succeeding centuries (on that image of erosion, see further later, in chapter 14).

34. Compare Aelius Aristides, *Panathenaicus* (*Oration* 1), 22–23, for a good parallel.

35. See Libanius, *Oration* 11.22–27 and 198–201.

36. It sounds as if Strabo is looking westwards here, past the luxurious buildings of the Campus Martius in the foreground, and over the Tiber to the Janiculum and Monte Mario, rather than eastwards towards the city with its seven hills; alternatively one might imagine him standing on the west of the Tiber, looking eastwards over the river towards the city.

37. See Roller (2018), 255–59, on 5.3.8, discussing among other things the influence of Stoic ideas over Strabo's description, and parallels for ancient mentions of the beauty of the Campus Martius.

38. Compare MacDonald and Pinto (1995), 181–82, on the views from Hadrian's villa at Tivoli; for example, the so-called Tempe terrace (*Historia Augusta, Hadrian* 26.5), named after the famously beautiful valley near Mount Olympus in Greece, had views of the Monti Tiburtini. For a more extreme example, where mountains are actively shaped to become part of a villa landscape, see the description of the villa of Pollius Felix in Campania in Statius, *Silvae* 2.2, esp. lines 54–59: 'Here there used to be a mountain where now you see level ground, and wilderness

where now you enter beneath a roof; where you now see tall woods, there was not even land; the occupier has tamed it, and the land rejoices as he shapes cliffs or destroys them, following his lead. Now see the rocks learning to bear the yoke, and the buildings as they enter, and the mountain which has been ordered to withdraw', with Bergmann (1991), esp. 57–59; Spencer (2010), 104–13; Newby (2012), 353–55; and König (forthcoming a), setting this passage against the tension between positive and negative judgements in ancient writing on landscape alteration more broadly. See also chapter 14, later, for farms sited on mountains for agricultural reasons.

39. See Andrews (1999), 59, on the interest of one Renaissance villa owner in this letter: 'this must be one of the first intimations of the Picturesque habit of using landscape paintings as the standard of beauty in assessing real scenery'.

40. See Borca (2002), 28–30; Koelb (2009), 454–57.

41. See Porter (2016), 360–81; 411–12, on Longinus' analysis of 'nature as a sublime object' in Homer; and further discussion earlier, in chapter 2.

42. See also Porter (2016), 339–41, for other relevant passages from the play; and see brief further discussion of lines 351–72 later, in chapter 6.

43. For the influence of the *Prometheus Bound* over Shelley, see Zillman (1959), 58–66.

44. See Koelb (2009), 458–62.

45. See further discussion later, in chapter 11.

46. See Schrijvers (2006), esp. 104–6, on Silius Italicus, *Punica* 3.477–99 as 'an interesting moment in the history of aesthetic reactions upon first seeing the Alps, an outstanding example of the natural sublime' (104); broadly speaking, however, he agrees with Nicolson (1959), 39, wrongly in my view, in characterising Latin engagement with mountains as 'almost consistently adverse', and sees Silius' account, and also the description of mountains in Petronius' 'Bellum civile' poem, lines 144–51 at *Satyrica* 122, which seems to have influenced Silius, as rare exceptions.

47. See Wilton (1980), 26–27; Schama (1995), 458–59.

48. The classic statement of the importance of fear in the sublime is in Kant, *Critique of Judgement* 28; see Porter (2016), 466–71, on the way in which the works of Kant, and also Edmund Burke, are reminiscent of and probably influenced by Lucretius in their views on this topic; and Doran (2015), 42–43 and 74, on the role of terror in Longinus; 134–36, on the way in which John Dennis draws on Lucretius and Longinus in making terror central to his conception of the sublime; and 145–46, along similar lines for Burke; but also Halliwell (2012), 332 (esp. n. 11), 334–35, 353 (esp. n. 55), and 361, who demonstrates that only certain types of fear are relevant to the sublime in Longinus. I am grateful to Stephen Halliwell for sharing draft material from his forthcoming commentary on Longinus, which makes it clear there is no particular prompt in *On the Sublime* 35.4 to take the verb ἐκπληττόμεθα as related to fear; compare Wilton (1980), 27–28, on the importance of Aristotle's claim that 'fear is central to the experience of divine art' (28), but also stressing that some commentators felt that 'it was a special *kind* of fear which was present in the sublime experience' (27).

Chapter 6. Scientific Viewing and the Volcanic Sublime

1. For useful collections of essays on volcanoes in the ancient Mediterranean not discussed at length later, see Foulon (2004) and Balmuth et al. (2005).

2. Porter (2016), 450–54.

3. See Sigurdsson (1999); Hine (2002). For other non-volcanic associations between mountains and scientific observation in ancient Greek and Roman culture, see Barton (2017), 41–42, citing Petronius, *Satyrica* 88, and Philostratus, *Life of Apollonius* 2.5, who mention ancient scientists Eudoxus, Anaxagoras, and Thales ascending mountains to observe the heavens; also Pliny the Elder, *Natural History* 25.1 on discovery of new plants in the mountains; Dueck (2012), 81–82, with further bibliography; Cajori (1929), esp. 482–93 on ancient attempts to determine the heights of mountains.

4. For example, see Robbins (1987); Hevly (1996); della Dora (2016b), 165–89.

5. For that tension between scientific and mythical explanation in relation to Etna in particular, see Williams (2017), 23–71, and Buxton (2016), and further discussion later in this chapter in relation to the *Aetna* poem; and for the richly mythological approach to volcanoes of one ancient author not discussed further in this chapter, see Johnston (1996) on Virgil.

6. For example, see Hollis (2020); Duffy (2021).

7. See Connors (2015), 126–27.

8. For example, see Clark (2019), 49.

9. See Williams (2012), 217–18, on the way in which Seneca evokes the move from serenity to panic.

10. See Connors (2015), 125–26; Williams (2006), esp. 125–26; and compare Walter (2017) for a similar example of ancient attempts to explain the natural disaster of an earthquake.

11. See Sigurdsson (2002), 32–33. For vivid accounts of the history of human responses to Vesuvius from antiquity to the present, see Scarth (2009) and Darley (2011); and for a useful collection of ancient responses, see Sebesta (2006).

12. See Connors (2015), 122–25.

13. For excellent surveys of ancient responses to Mount Etna, see Buxton (2016) and Williams (2017), 24–71; also Manni (1981), 79–81, for a useful list of some of the most important mentions in classical literature.

14. It is possible that the account of Typhoeus in Hesiod, *Theogony* 857–68, refers to Etna, but the text is debated: see Buxton (2016), 31–32; Williams (2017), 29.

15. See Buxton (2016), 26–28; Williams (2017), 26–33.

16. Porter (2016), 528.

17. See Williams (2016), 26; Hine (2002), 69–72, suggests that even in Pindar we can see traces of speculation about the causes of volcanic activity.

18. See Phillips (2015b), 150–52, on these lines.

19. For one very forceful rejection of mythical explanations of Mount Etna in favour of scientific speculation, see Philostratus, *Life of Apollonius* 5.16–17.

20. However, see also Buxton (2016), 36–38, on the way in which Strabo gives a more open-minded reaction to the Empedocles story at 6.2.10; also later, chapter 12, on Strabo's account of Vesuvius.

21. Pliny the Younger, *Letter* 6.16.

22. Pliny the Elder, *Natural History* 2.110; also Connors (2015) on Pliny's account of Vesuvius and the Phlegraean Fields in Books 2–3.

23. On another occasion, 'when he was sacrificing on Mount Casius, having climbed the mountain for the sake of seeing the sunrise, a storm arose and a lightning flash came down and blasted both the victim and the attendant' (*Historia Augusta, Hadrian* 14.3).

24. See Porter (2016), 473–83.

25. See Porter (2016), 475.

26. See Porter (2016), 477–78, on the oddity of the way in which the author talks about the earthly sublime with such enthusiasm in what follows, having expressed a preference for heavenly phenomena at the beginning.

27. Borca (2002), 30, stresses the similarities between this passage—or at least the equivalent passage from the Latin version of this text, usually ascribed to Apuleius (*De mundo* 296)—and the passage from Cicero's *De natura deorum* 2.98–100, discussed earlier, chapter 5.

28. See Glauthier (2016), 263–66.

29. See Buxton (2016), 28–30.

30. Outlined in Aristotle, *Meteorology* 2.8.

31. See Glauthier (2016), who argues that the closing cataclysm of the play (lines 1080–93) is intended to recall a volcanic eruption.

32. Lucretius, *De rerum natura* 639–702.

33. For two discussions that redefine Lucretius as an entirely typical representative of widespread ancient interest in mountain aesthetics, see Porter (2016), 450–54; and Koelb (2009), 458–62, including discussion of the way in which the 'disastrously inaccurate' (459) translation of *vastus* by phrases connected with the English word 'waste' has led to unduly negative accounts of his view of mountains; also briefly Nicolson (1959), 40.

34. Characteristically he enlists traditional mythical and religious imagery in support of his rationalising vision of the world: for example he uses the gigantomachic associations of Etna to characterise the philosopher Empedocles' assault against superstition and divine order, although that gives way to a more rationalising approach in Book 6: see Williams (2016), 38–45; compare Buxton (2016), 32–33, on the way in which Lucretius' rationalising account describes Etna in anthropomorphic terms associated with mythical language.

35. See Garani (2009), esp. 120–21, for the argument that Theophrastus is a particularly important influence; and Goodyear (1984) for extensive discussion of the poet's sources.

36. See esp. *Aetna* 94–101.

37. See Williams (2017), 59–68; also Toohey (1996), 188–92; Buxton (2016), 33–35; Porter (2016), esp. 512: 'what follows . . . is, however, strangely reminiscent of the mythical tales just told, not in all their idiosyncratic detail, but in their grim force and energy'; Taub (2008), 45–55, and (2009).

38. He also proclaims his own preference for following an 'unfamiliar path' (*insolitum iter*: *Aetna* 8), drawing on the image of the untrodden mountain track which had long been associated with authorial originality in Greek and then Latin poetry: see further discussion later, in chapter 8.

39. This passage follows from a question about causation: 'Now my work demands who is the maker and the cause (*artificem . . . causamque*) of the fire' (*Aetna* 189–90); the implication initially is that the answer is plain—presumably because it should be clear to any reader by now that the answer lies in the underground winds—but his mention of Jupiter then playfully raises an alternative possibility.

40. My reading here builds on recent work that has begun to draw out the literary sophistication of the *Aetna*: for example, Volk (2005); Welsh (2014); Kruschwitz (2015).

41. See Welsh (2014), 123–26, on the poem's relationship with Lucretius' account of Etna. The poem was written perhaps in the first half of the first century CE: at any rate it is usually

dated rather speculatively before the eruption of Vesuvius, on the grounds that it makes no mention of that event.

42. For a list of key passages see Welsh (2014), 120, n. 60.

43. Compare later in this chapter for a similar attitude in Seneca, drawing on Lucretius.

44. Soon enough he returns to the language of self-evidentness, for example at 332: 'the region [of Etna] itself will bring facts before your eyes and will force you to deny it' (*res oculis locus ipse dabit cogetque negare*). He is arguing here against the idea that the winds enter the volcano from above, through the crater, by observing that there is no sign of the worshippers who go up to the summit being disturbed by breezes (look at them, he says: *cerne, Aetna* 341); compare Pausanias, *Periegesis* 3.23.9, who describes offerings being lowered down into the crater of the volcano. In the process, however, he also emphasises in passing at least the theoretical possibility of error in this process of inference from observation: 'if I am wrong, appearance (*species*) is on my side' (*Aetna* 349).

45. Compare Welsh (2014), esp. 120–22, who emphasises the fact that the poet's repeated injunctions to look at Etna are in tension with the extreme shortage of visible evidence for the phenomena he discusses; for Welsh that gap draws attention to the indispensable role of the poet in guiding the reader, and so to the inextricability of science and poetry in this text. He also points out (121) that the poet's claims about the impossibility of missing the significance of the visible evidence are undermined in 203–6, discussed already earlier, where Jupiter misreads the eruption as a sign of the continuing threat from the Giants and from the underworld.

46. For example, see later, chapter 9, and repeatedly in relation in military narratives in part III.

47. See Hollis (2020), 323, on this passage and on the poet's exploration of vision and knowledge more broadly.

48. See Porter (2016), 516–17, on the way in which incomprehensibility is central to the poet's vision.

49. Compare 51.10, for the claim that soldiers from rough terrain (*ex confragoso*) are better than those from the town.

50. For volcanoes in Seneca's *Natural Questions*, see Dupraz (2004).

51. Compare Williams (2012), 213–57, on Seneca's account of the earthquake in Campania already discussed earlier, arguing that Seneca avoids a popular version of the natural sublime, characterised by awe, and replaces it with an alternative, more Lucretian vision of the sublime which involves responding actively and asserting control and understanding over nature, esp. 222–23, on resemblances between Seneca's account and the passages already discussed from Longinus, *On the Sublime* 35.2–5, and Lucretius, *De rerum natura* 6.608–737, both of which mention Mount Etna among other natural wonders.

52. See esp. Nicolson (1959), 184–270; MacFarlane (2003), 22–65, esp. 22–31, on Burnet; but also now Hollis (2020), esp. 310–12, and (2021) on the way in which Burnet and his contemporaries were thinking about ancient precedents; and della Dora (2016b), 146–55, on deep time in mountain history more broadly, including 150–52, on nineteenth-century responses to Mount Etna.

53. See Hine (2002), 60–63.

54. The logic of the transition is quite compressed, but Seneca's point seems to be that wisdom, unlike literary achievement, is fundamentally non-competitive: 'when you get to the summit (*cum ad summum perveneris*), it is a draw; there is no room for going further, it is at an end' (79.8).

55. Compare Gowers (2011), 169: 'it seems that Lucilius' rather grand posting to Sicily poses a potential threat to Seneca, one that he needs to cut down to size. This he does first by making Lucilius the superficial voice of Sicilian *megaloprepeia* / "magnificence", to force a contrast with his own deeper pursuit of wisdom'.

56. For good brief discussion of this passage, see Montiglio (2006), 568–69, pointing out among other things the parallel between *ascendas* in 79.2 (of Lucilius' projected ascent of Etna) and *ascenditur* in 79.8 (of the ascent to wisdom).

Chapter 7. Mountains in Greek and Roman Art

1. Compare CTHS (1991) for a wide-ranging collection of discussions of mountain images over many centuries, including several chapters on ancient art.

2. See later, chapter 8.

3. For good discussions of the relatively unobtrusive presence of landscape in ancient vase paintings by comparison with modern landscape painting, see Hurwit (1991) and Cohen (2007), esp. 321, on mountains.

4. See Taplin (2007), 39, for general comments on the stage equipment, and pot no. 18 (pp. 80–82), for the Prometheus image; also pot nos. 60 and 61 (pp. 178–80), for similar images of Andromeda.

5. See Hedreen (2001), 183, for brief discussion.

6. See Hedreen (2001), 183–87, for a series of examples.

7. Compare Dietrich (2010) on trees and rocks in vase paintings, arguing that they function not like landscapes in a modern sense, but more like other types of object that are used in vase painting to characterise the figures they are associated with; and see 552 for brief parallels from figures depicted together with rocks in sculpture, and 553 for Greek tragedy as the best literary parallel, rather than the Homeric poems, with their more extended landscape descriptions. In some cases, especially where several different images are displayed together, mountains also help to tie different stories together, in much the same way as the intratextually elaborate mountains of ancient Greek and Roman literature; for example, see Cohen (2007), 310: 'It has recently been argued that landscape elements in vase painting may have even served to link events and scenes that were temporally and spatially separated. For example, the presence of a palm tree may have forged narrative links between depictions of Ajax' suicide and his game of dice with Achilles at an earlier time'.

8. See Hedreen (2001), 182–220, and also 1–21, for discussion of the broader claim that settings 'often provide information that helps to explain why stories turn out in the ways that they do' (1).

9. See Vout (2012), 129–30, on this coin and one parallel, but in the course of a discussion of the relative absence of depictions of the hills of Rome, at 121–33.

10. See figure 14.1 later, and further discussion in that chapter. On these images, and also personifications of Mount Tmolos on coins, see Vout (2012), 125–26, with reference to 'Montes' in *Lexicon Iconographicum Mythologiae Classicae* 8.1, 856–60; 'Argaios' in 2.1, 584–86; and 'Tmolos' in 8.1: 44–45; and on Mount Tmolos, see also Foss (1982), 184.

11. Compare Vout (2012), 122–23, for the suggestion that conquered territory is more likely to have been represented in these terms than the hills of Rome themselves, with reference to

Tacitus, *Annals* 2.41, who tells us that the triumph of Germanicus included 'images (*simulacra*) of mountains, of rivers, of battles', discussed further later, in chapter 10.

12. See further discussion later, in chapter 10, with example image at figure 10.1.

13. On this image and its theological, iconographic, and archaeological context, see earlier, chapter 4; also della Dora (2016a), 48–58 and 153–55, on the way in which these effects were extended within the later Byzantine icon tradition, where the stylisation of mountains enhances their symbolic and spiritual potential rather than diminishing it.

14. On non-narrative landscape painting generally, see Ling (1991), 142–49.

15. See Ling (1991), 142. Compare Vitruvius, *De architectura* 7.5.2, for mountains as a standard feature of scenic wall painting, along with other landscape features like rivers and groves, although he also mentions that these are often combined with mythological themes.

16. The image has been widely reproduced and discussed, but I am not aware of any treatments which mention the background landscape except in passing.

17. See Hodske (2007), esp. Tafel 41–50, for a full account of the many similar Narcissus images from Pompeii.

18. I am grateful to Abigail Walker for pointing that out to me. For a good example, see Hodske (2007), 171, on Taf. 49, Kat. 140, Abb. 5 and 6, from the Casa della Regina Margherita.

19. See Mazzoleni (2004), 81, for a good example from the antechamber of the bedroom in the Villa of Publius Fannius Synistor at Boscoreale.

20. For further discussion of the images discussed in this section, see Bergmann (1999) and Newby (2012). See also Ling (1991), 112–28, for discussion of panel paintings with mythological subjects; and for surveys of landscape in mural painting, including accounts of all the paintings discussed here, see Dawson (1944) and Peters (1963); also Croisille (2010) and Hinterhöller-Klein (2015) for two other important recent studies on the wider context of Roman landscape painting.

21. See Bergmann (1999), 96–99, with all four images reproduced together at 97, but with the wrong image printed for 'Hylas and the Nymphs'; Newby (2012), 374–75; Dawson (1944), 77–81. None of the paintings survives in good condition and in situ: we have to rely for the most part on copies and descriptions from the late nineteenth century.

22. On the mountain setting of this image as a place of divine presence beyond human control, see esp. Newby (2102), 375: 'in the background a sharp crag and dark forest suggest the untouched spaces of nature which in literature are often the haunts of divine beings. . . . In the foreground we see the figure of Hylas, standing in a pool of water and being seized by amorous Nymphs who appear almost as extensions of the natural world, wearing vegetation in their hair'.

23. Compare Bergmann (1999), 98, for the co-ordinating function of the mountains in the room to the north; 101, on the similarities between this process of co-ordinated viewing and the rhetorical principles of *similitudo* which informed literary practices of intratextual reading; and 103, for the habit of drawing connections between adjacent images in ancient literary depictions of viewing artworks.

24. See Bergmann (1999), 93–96, with all four images reproduced together at 94.

25. See Bergmann (1999), 95: 'the two "quiet" opposing scenes [Hercules and Hippolytus] focus on an enclosure in the mountains defined by a vertical axis'.

26. For a systematic account, see Hodske (2007) and Dawson (1944), 116–72, who look at multiple versions of each subject together.

27. Many publications now emphasise the importance of analysing together different images from the same room—for example, see Lorenz (2008); also Newby (2012); Bergmann (1999) already discussed, esp. on the kind of arrangement which involved 'three or four panels in small rooms used by individuals or groups for extended periods of relaxation, where the scenes invited prolonged comparisons from wall to wall and across the space' (81).

28. There is another mountainous Actaeon image in the Casa del Frutteto: see Leach (1988), 324–29; and for that image in the context of the other images in the room, which cover a range of different landscape types, see Newby (2012), 377–79; also Bergmann (1999), 85–89, who sees Cithaeron in this image as a place of divine presence: 'Diana's body is enormous and blends with the milky color of the rocks—this is her space' (88).

29. For example, see Bergmann (1999), 88, on Ovid, *Metamorphoses* 3.247–50 in relation to the Diana and Actaeon scene from the Casa del Frutteto; 102–3, for discussion of a range of other authors, and also more on Ovid: 'No work comes closer to the painted ensembles in the patterns of thematic association and contrast than Ovid's *Metamorphoses*, which was inspired by a multitude of sources, including earlier texts, performances, possibly even paintings like these' (102); compare Newby (2012), 376–77. On mountains in Ovid, see further later, chapter 8.

30. For good examples, see Philostratus, *Imagines* 1.9 (an image of marshland ringed by mountains), 1.18 (Pentheus and the Bacchants on Mount Kithairon), 1.22 (Midas' capture of a satyr in the mountains of Phrygia), 1.26 (the birth of Hermes), 2.14 (Poseidon breaking through the mountains surrounding the plains of Thessaly), 2.18 (Polyphemus and Galatea).

31. See esp. Bergmann (1999); also (2001), esp. 162–63, drawing parallels between these effects and the kinds of absorption into mythological landscapes that we are prompted to by Pausanias' *Periegesis*; and Newby (2012).

32. See Newby (2012), 379: 'through their placement as fictional views out of the house the paintings are implicitly brought into the house-owner's experience, evoking the types of mythologized landscapes which were recreated within elite villas and giving the house-owner a share in the villa experience'.

33. Newby (2012), 374.

34. See Bergmann (1999), 85, on the Casa del Frutteto, and 95 on the Hippolytus scene in V, 2, 10; also 82, for the point that many of these scenes 'are striking within the ancient tradition of mythological representation in that the main interest is as much the place where fates play out as the figures themselves'.

35. Compare Bergmann (1999), 88, on the way in which the viewer is put into the position of voyeur in gazing at Diana in the Diana and Actaeon painting.

36. See Ling (1991), 108–11, including 111, on the uncertain date of the images.

37. See Ling (1991), 110.

38. See Ling (1991), 108: 'the painter's aim is to give the impression that the landscape of each scene passes almost imperceptibly into that of the next'.

39. *Odyssey* 10.81, 87–88, 97, 113, 121–22.

40. See Leach (1988), 36–44, for discussion of the way in which the artist fills in the many gaps in Homer's representation of space and landscape with realistic detail; in doing so, she argues, it is hard for him to reproduce the Homeric sense of vastness in the Laestrygonians and the terrain they inhabit, but that is made up for by the way in which that allows a more intimate

depiction of their savagery which is 'conferred upon them by the wild nature of the landscape, with its bristling trees and threatening rocks', so that the Laestrygonians come to 'assume an elemental brutality that appears to derive from the earth itself' (44).

41. See Connors (2015), 123–24.

42. See Simone (2011), arguing that Vesuvius was indeed viewed as a manifestation of Dionysus, partly because of the fertility of its vines, and presenting evidence for cult worship of Dionysus around Vesuvius.

43. See *Lexicon Iconographicum Mythologiae Classicae* 4.1, 573, no. 1, 'Helikon'; inscriptions at *Inscriptiones Graecae* VII, 4240; good introductory discussion by Robinson (2013), 182–84, with further bibliography at 182, n. 51.

44. See Robinson (2013), 182.

45. See Robinson (2013), 184.

46. Pausanias, *Periegesis* 9.31.4.

47. It has even been suggested that this is meant as a plea by the dedicator to his fellow citizens at a time of economic hardship in the Hellenistic period: one ancient source tells us that the inhabitants of Thespiai were not interested in agriculture, and therefore suffered poverty: Heraklides Lembos, fragment 76, in Dilts (1971), 8.

48. See Hurst (1996), 69, on links between the image and representations of mountains in the *Theogony*.

49. Compare Hurst (1992), 62–63.

50. However, see Hurst (1996), 66–67, for some literary parallels; Robinson (2013), 182, esp. n. 56 for Tmolus in Ovid, *Metamorphoses* 11.173–79, and for related coin images; compare earlier in this chapter; also good parallels in Philostratus, *Imagines* 1.14 (Kithairon 'in the form of a man' lamenting the misfortunes that he knows will occur on his slopes), 1.26 (Olympus rejoices in the birth of Hermes with an almost-human smile), and 2.4 (mountains in the form of mourning women lamenting the death of Hippolytus); and earlier chapter 2 for further discussion.

51. Korinna fragment 54, Campbell (1992). On links between Korinna's poem and the Euthykles stele, see among others Veneri (1996); however, see also Berman (2010), 46–47, for debate over whether Helikon really is intended as a personified mountain in the poem, or instead as a human actor who later gives his name to the mountain, expressing a preference for the latter option.

52. See Clarke (1997), 72–73: 'all this seems temptingly like a survival from a more primitive age of myth-making' (73).

53. See Vergados (2012), for a thorough survey of the poetic influences Korinna is drawing on, arguing that she deliberately modifies the dominant Hesiodic tradition in dissociating the Muses from Helikon.

54. See Robinson (2013), 182, for good description and further bibliography on the figure's appearance.

55. See Robinson (2013), 84–88, for good introductory discussion, esp. 85, on date and on the range of possible contexts for the image.

56. Compare Pollitt (1986), 15–16, characterising this as an example of the way in which Hellenistic art was influenced by the scholarly tendencies of Alexandrian literature, which led to 'the creation of works that were designed to be appreciated simultaneously on an immediately

apparent level, to be grasped by all who saw them, and on a less obvious, learned level designed for the few who were qualified to understand'; compare Zeitlin (2001), 199–200.

57. For example, see Newby (2007); and Robinson (2013) for a good survey of the different possibilities, with further bibliography.

58. Lichtenberger (2016), who identifies the mountain as Olympus on the grounds that it is the only mountain that combines the presence of Zeus on the summit, the presence of the Muses, and the presence of a sanctuary of Apollo; he also points out that that would make this the only securely identifiable ancient visual representation of Olympus as a mountain.

59. See Robinson (2013), 187–88, on this mixture of Hesiodic and Homeric as typical of Roman literary culture.

60. See among others Smith (1991), 187; Robinson (2013), 186.

Chapter 8. Mountain Landmarks in Latin Literature

1. Leigh Fermor (1977), 94–95.

2. For example, see Nicolson (1959), 47: 'the dominant tendency of medieval literature was toward abstraction and moralization, so far as most nature imagery was concerned. Indeed, so powerful was the negativistic influence of the Latin classics and Christian allegorization that even theologians and poets who lived among them seemed to see mountains not as they were but as tradition and convention had made them seem'.

3. See Koelb (2009), 447, criticising the way in which Nicolson (1959) dismisses premodern figurative mountains as 'mere allegories and symbols'.

4. See Hunter and Fantuzzi (2004), 51–54; Robinson (2013), 179–80; Worman (2015), 194. See also Petridou (2016), 214–21, for examples of imitation of the Hesiodic verses in other post-Hesiodic Greek poetry, esp. 217, on Theocritus, *Idyll* 7.91–5, where Theocritus says that 'the Muses have taught me, too, many good songs, while I was pasturing my cattle on the mountains', and 218, esp. n. 132, on two later accounts of Pindar, who began writing poetry after falling asleep while hunting on Mount Helikon and dreamed that his mouth was full of honey; and Argoud (1996), esp. 32–42.

5. See Hunter and Fantuzzi (2004), 52, for summary of the evidence.

6. On Roman imitation of that passage and more generally the way in which Latin poets describe themselves on mountainsides as a way of expressing their poetic identity, see Hunter (2006), 16–28; Robinson (2012), 247–50, and (2013), 188–89.

7. *Certamen Homeri et Hesiodi* 13.

8. See Hunter (2006), 18–20: 'the Heliconian grove is therefore a place where poetry which sings of agriculture and peaceful pursuits . . . is celebrated and from which Homer is excluded, but without damage to his reputation and primacy' (20). However, see also lines 1–3 of the preface to the *Satires* of Persius, who rejects these traditions in turn in defining himself as a satirist: 'I did not wash my lips in the horses' spring [that is, the Hippocrene], nor do I remember having dreamed on two-headed Parnassus, so as to become a poet all of a sudden'; and compare further later on Ovid, *Ars amatoria* 1.27–29. For a Christian version of that kind of rejection, see Heath (2020), 187, on the way in which Clement of Alexandria in *Protrepticus* 1.2.1–4 summons his readers away from Helikon and Kithairon and encourages them to move across to Mount Zion, in imitation of the transfer of Hesiod's Muses to Mount

Olympus: Clement thus asserts the primacy of his own Christian poetics over its Greco-Roman equivalents.

9. See Worman (2015), 78–80 and 214–16.

10. See Robinson (2012) and (2013).

11. I move to latinate spelling of Helicon and other equivalent names here, in moving on to discussion of Latin texts. On Propertius's Helicon imagery and his engagement with Callimachus in 3.1 and 3.3, see Hubbard (1974), 72–81; Hunter (2006), 20; Cairns (2006), esp. 120–31, for the possibility that Propertius may be drawing on now lost scenes of poetic initiation in the work of his predecessor Gallus, in 3.3 and elsewhere; Heyworth and Morwood (2011), 112–16 and appendices A–E and G–J, for text and translation of important poetic precedents; Robinson (2013), 189. See also Virgil, *Eclogues* 6.64–73 for an image of the poet Gallus encountering the Muses on Mount Helicon, with Robinson (2012), 249–50; also Clausen (1994), 200, and Saunders (2008), 64–65, on the way in which Gallus' physical elevation there stands for his elevation from a lower to a higher kind of poetry.

12. See Skutsch (1985), 149–50; Robinson (2012), 248–49, and (2013), 188–89; Lucretius, *De rerum natura* 1.117–18; Propertius 3.3.6.

13. See Koning (2010), 144, counting twenty-six later passages.

14. See Koning (2010), 144–47, for an overview; and on Plato's responses, see Folch (2018), 315–16.

15. See Phillips (2018b), 265–70, on this and other related passages, including 268 on the way in which 'Pindar often uses the imagery of height to conceptualize his poetry's affective force'.

16. See Porter (2016), 356, for both passages, and also for other parallels for summit imagery in Pindar's work; also earlier, chapter 6, n. 18, on the metapoetic implications of Pindar's description of Mount Etna in *Pythian* 1.

17. For example, it lies behind the description of progress to wisdom in Seneca, *Letter* 79.8, discussed already in chapter 6: 'when you get to the summit (*cum ad summum perveneris*), it is a draw; there is no room for going further'.

18. Compare Galen, *On the Diagnosis and Cure of the Errors of the Soul*, K5.89, mentioning Hesiod by name, for criticism of those who want to take shortcuts to the truth.

19. For example, see earlier on the opening of Methodius' *Symposium* and on Gregory of Nyssa's *Life of Moses*.

20. See Koning (2010), 145.

21. For example, see Worman (2015), 237–40 and 242–44, on the image of the mountain hike in the literary-critical works of Demetrius.

22. For example, see Worman (2015), 240–42, on Dionysius of Halicarnassus' characterisation of Thucydides' style as rugged and 'broad-striding', 'so that Thucydides resembles a strapping warrior or hiker moving across expanses' (241).

23. Compare Koning (2010), 146, with n. 83, for the possibility that this and other equivalent passages in Lucian indicate that Hesiod's words were used to articulate the idea of philosophical progress by the Stoics.

24. The mountain imagery is expanded quite elaborately later in the work, especially at *Professor of Public Speaking* 6–9; see Worman (2015), 244–46.

25. See de Jong (2018), esp. 39–41, on mountaintop viewing in Lucian's *Charon*; also Cyprian, *Epistles* 1.6, for a Christian version of the mountaintop as a place to view human failings; and an earlier version in Lucretius, *De rerum natura* 2.7–10.

NOTES TO CHAPTER 8 349

26. However, for one intricately allegorical, metapoetic mountain in imperial Greek epic, see Maciver (2007) on the mountain of *Arete* in Quintus of Smyrna, *Posthomerica* 5.49–56, esp. 262–64, on Quintus' use of Hesiod's rough path imagery.

27. However, see Thalmann (2011), 152, for the point that mountains have much less prominence in the poem than rivers.

28. Apollonius, *Argonautica* 1.547–58; see de Jong (2018), 27–28, in the context of a discussion of post-Homeric divine *oroskopia* at 27–30, with further examples among others from Valerius Flaccus, *Argonautica* 1.574–86 (Boreas watching the voyage of the Argo angrily from Mount Pangaeus), and Statius, *Thebaid* 9.678–725 (Diana watching the battle from Mount Cithaeron).

29. On Mount Dindymon in Apollonius' *Argonautica*, especially the view at 1.1112–16, see Williams (1991), 79–92; Thalmann (2011), 3–8; de Jong (2018), 36–37.

30. Compare Koelb (2009), 462–64.

31. Mention of the Cretan Mount Ida at *Aeneid* 3.112.

32. Compare Leach (1988), 70, pointing out the increased complexity of Aeneas' landscape descriptions as he gets closer to Italy.

33. See Scarth (2000), esp. 601–3, on the defeat of Cacus, in the context of a wider discussion of the way in which Virgil draws on contemporary knowledge about volcanoes, suggesting that he differentiates between different types of eruption; also Manioti (2019) on volcanic knowledge, in relation to the volcano Inarime on the island of Ischia in Campania, in the *Aeneid* and other Latin epic.

34. There are also close verbal echoes between the Athos/Eryx/Apennine image and the simile at 12.4–9, where Turnus is compared with a raging lion (but not in a mountain context), in a way which is likely to leave the impression of contrast between the two men (although it might also leave us with a fleeting impression that it is hard for Aeneas to throw off the kind of uncivilised imagery associated with Turnus even at this moment of increased dignity towards the end of the book): *se attollens* at 12.703 echoes *attollitque animos* at 12.4; *gaudetque* at 12.702 echoes *gaudetque* 12.6; *fremit* 12.702 echoes *fremit* at 12.8.

35. For a rather different version of the story of Lykaon's cannibalism and metamorphosis, see Pausanias 8.2.3, discussed earlier, chapter 3.

36. Compare Ovid, *Metamorphoses* 2.217–26 for the much longer catalogue of mountains set on fire by Phaethon, with McPhee (2019).

37. See Hinds (2002) on landscape in the *Metamorphoses*, esp. 130, on the tension between 'the beautiful setting and the sufferings which befall most of the characters who inhabit or enter it'.

38. Compare Euripides, *Hippolytus* 215 for Phaedra's much less extravagant version of the same request—'take me to the mountain' (πέμπετέ μ' εἰς ὄρος)—which gives a glimpse of the way in which Seneca has increased the prominence of the mountains in his version.

39. See earlier, chapter 2.

40. See earlier, chapter 4.

41. On Mount Pindus, see Nisbet and Hubbard (1970), 147, who suggest that this is a reference to Virgil, *Eclogues* 10.9–12, where Pindus is associated with the poet Gallus.

42. Compare Worman (2015), 264.

43. See Leach (1988), 231–32.

44. Virgil, *Georgics* 1.16–18.

45. Diehl (1949–1952), fragment 90 = Lobel and Page (1955), 338.

46. See Barton (2017), 18, who takes this poem as typical of the way in which 'the mountain [in the ancient world] is an object almost always identified by being seen'.

47. Edmunds (1992), 26–28, intriguingly suggests that the mountain is represented by Horace as something to be rejected not just because of its coldness and harshness, but also because it was viewed by Romans as an alien place, through its associations with death and untraditional religious practices of augury, but there is perhaps a risk of over-reading in that suggestion, given that there is very little in the poem to point us towards it explicitly.

48. See Nisbet and Hubbard (1970), 117, for debates about the linking of the storm in stanza three with the scene in stanza one.

49. Vessey (1985), 36, by contrast, rejects the connection, as do some others; compare Edmunds (1992), 105, for the debates about that issue.

50. See Clay (1989b) for that reading, pointing out that 'most philologists . . . come from Northern Europe' (116), and suggesting that standard readings of the poem may be importing assumptions about snowfall that are implausible for the Italian winter.

51. Compare Fitch (2009), 24–26, on the way in which nature is used by Horace as a standard for human life, and on the importance of intratextual reading processes in the *Odes* for appreciating that: 'What we as Horace's audience learn to do—and it is a cumulative process—is to make that connection for ourselves, between the passing seasons and the brevity of our lives'.

52. See Vessey (1985), 38: 'What then is the ode about? We should not expect an answer. . . . The sweep of the six stanzas is broad and any reductive approach demeans it. The text is both encompassed and lost in each reading and re-reading, and it always surpasses them'.

53. Edmunds (1992), 25–26, makes the same point, but in a way that perpetuates old stereotypes about the lack of interest in mountains in Roman culture, drawing on Hyde (1915).

Chapter 9. Mountains and Bodies in Apuleius' *Metamorphoses*

1. This chapter is an expanded and updated version of König (2013).

2. Compare Shumate (1996), esp. 7, 13–14, and 325–28, on the *Metamorphoses* as 'simultaneously a satire of credulity and a seductive evocation of religious belief' (7).

3. For surveys of Apuleius' depiction of landscape, see de Biasi (1990); Krabbe (2003), 90–121.

4. See earlier, preface, with reference to Wylie (2007).

5. See K. Bradley (2000).

6. See Brockliss (2018a), drawing on the concept of 'dark ecology' from Morton (2016), on the way in which human immersion in the environment would often have been viewed by ancient readers in pessimistic terms rather than as something to celebrate, esp. 5: 'If Morton is correct, ancient listeners familiar with the harsh environments of the Greek world would have been inclined to view such interweaving in a negative light, not as a celebration of an integrated ecology, but as a challenge to attempts to separate the human from other categories of living thing'.

7. Most of the passages I discuss from the *Metamorphoses* in this section have no equivalent in the *Onos*; all exceptions are noted.

8. See Zimmerman (2002), esp. 91–96; compare Bakhtin (1981), 120.

9. See esp. later, on *Met.* 4.6; also de Biasi (1990), 248–53, on landscape in Apuleius' *Florida* (esp. *Florida* 1, 10.4, 11, and 21).

10. See Webb (2009), esp. 87–106.

11. See Webb (2009), 167–91.

12. See Shumate (1996), 67–71, on links between ekphrasis and artificiality in the work.

13. Millar (1981) has rightly discussed the realistic quality of Apuleius' depiction of Roman provincial life in some parts of the text; compare Fick (1991). However, that realism is in tension with ostentatiously unrealistic pictures of wild landscape elsewhere in the novel, which are disorientatingly cut free from any kind of topographical markers: see Zimmerman (2000), 11, and Slater (2002), 173. The *Onos*, by contrast, is much more precise about topography: see Graverini (2002), esp. 58–59.

14. See O'Brien (2002), esp. 10–15, on the *De Platone*. Admittedly, that argument is complicated by the fact that the narrating voice has several different layers. In many passages in Books 1–10 we look at landscape through Lucius' eyes as he experienced it at the time: see Zimmerman (2002), esp. 81–86 and 95. In other cases, however, particularly in some of the lengthier passages of ekphrasis, we seem to be hearing the voice of the narrator speaking with hindsight, showing off his rhetorical skills: see Paschalis (2002) on 2.4, with reference also to 4.6, 5.1, 6.14, and 10.32–33; also Van Mal-Maeder (1997a). That need not mean, however, that we should see these ekphrasis scenes as irrelevant to Lucius' perception of the world at the time. In practice it is often difficult to separate *actor* and *auctor* securely (compare later, on 4.6). We might anyway feel that the narrator is trying to reproduce for us, through these set-piece passages of rhetorical description, the world of false perceptions which his own former self had moved through. Alternatively—and more unsettlingly—we might even take this as a sign that he is still mired in that world of false rhetoric, and keen to indulge in it even after his conversion in Book 11.

15. See Shumate (1996), esp. 14, for the claim that 'according to this pattern of crisis and conversion, a perception of the collapse of familiar cognitive constructs precedes the convert's reconstruction of a new world and world view along religious lines'; and 43–90, on the way in which Books 1–4 in particular are full of a sense of the instability of the physical world as Lucius perceives it.

16. See esp. the essays in Kahane and Laird (2001).

17. See Harrison (1990) on the last of those options, with summary of the debate.

18. For example, see Boschi (2016) for the argument that each of these three locations stands for one of the gods—Mount Hymettos for Zeus, the Isthmus of Corinth for Poseidon, and Taenaros for Hades—and that the reference is to their father, Saturn; intended among other things to signal that this is a 'Saturnine' narrative, concerned with the temporary reversal of hierarchies between slave and master, followed by the restoration of elite status.

19. *Met.* 1.24.

20. See Clarke (2001), 104; Innes (2001), 113–14; Boschi (2016), 147–48.

21. The word 'path' is not specified in the Latin text, which uses a neuter plural adjective without any accompanying noun in all four phrases.

22. See Keulen (2007), 97–100.

23. See de Biasi (1990), 201–2; Merlier-Espenel (1999), 163–64; Zimmerman (2002), 79–80; also Keulen (2007), 96, on overlaps with *Florida* 21.3.

24. See Zimmerman (2002), 91–96, on the role of that tradition in the novel as a whole.

25. See Krabbe (2003), 92.

26. Compare Krabbe (2003), 109–10.

27. See Keulen (2007), 96–97 and 100–104.

28. Other key passages include 1.3.1, 1.8.4, 2.5.4–7.

29. See Van Mal-Maeder (2001), 58–61; Shumate (1996), 50 and 60–61.

30. See Paschalis (2002), 138–39.

31. For that suggestion, see Penwill (1990), 8; compare Shumate (1996), 56–60; Van Mal-Maeder (2001), 59.

32. See esp. *Met.* 4.3 and 8.17–18.

33. See Newby (2012), esp. 361–62, on this passage of Apuleius.

34. For example, see *Met.* 1.19, with de Biasi (1990), 219–22; Merlier-Espenel (1999), 162–63; Mattiacci (2001), 847–53; also *Met.* 8.18–19; and Hijmans et al. (1977), 28–29, for a full list.

35. See Merlier-Espenel (1999); Mattiacci (2001).

36. See Mattiacci (2001), 853–58, who shows that Apuleius' version involves a much more complex play with *locus amoenus* conventions than the equivalent scene in *Onos* 17; and compare Hijmans et al. (1977), 28–36; de Biasi (1990), 216–19.

37. See Trinquier (1999), 268, esp. n. 58. We seem to be hearing here the voice of the post-conversion narrator, especially when he informs us that he wishes to use the description as a display of his talent (*ingenium*). That said, Apuleius also makes it clear, in his desire to let the reader know 'whether I really was a donkey in my understanding and my faculties of perception' (4.6.2), that the description has at least some connection with Lucius' pre-conversion view of the world, being based on the details he stored away in his mind at the time: see Trinquier (1999), 270–71; de Jong (2001), 209.

38. See Krabbe (2003), 93, for a good example.

39. See de Biasi (1990), 210–14.

40. See Schiesaro (1985), esp. 214–19.

41. See Walsh (1970), 57–58; Schiesaro (1985), 215; Trinquier (1999), 267.

42. See Keuls (1974), 267; de Biasi (1990), 215; Trinquier (1999), 269–76; Mattiacci (2001), 845–46.

43. See Keuls (1974), 267; also Merlier-Espenel (2004), 218, who takes this detail as a sign that the inaccessibility of the brigands' hideout is an illusion, and points out that it prefigures the ease with which they are in the end defeated.

44. For example, the huts of Philemon and Baucis in Ovid, *Metamorphoses* 8.629–30, or the hut in Pseudo-Virgil's *Moretum* 60–61: see Trinquier (1999), 271–72.

45. See Trinquier (1999), 270–71. See also Keuls (1974), 266–67; Schiesaro (1985), 214–15; and Trinquier (1999), 269–70, on the relevance of Lucian's *How to Write History* 19–20 (to be discussed later, in chapter 11), which is critical of those who pad their histories out with excessively long landscape descriptions.

46. Maaike Zimmerman, among others, has shown how Lucius' landscape descriptions often reflect his own perception of the situation in which he finds himself; she focuses, however, on the mental rather than the bodily impact of the roads Lucius travels along: see Zimmerman (2002), esp. 81–86 and 95; compare Bakhtin (1981), 120. For other aspects of Apuleius' fascination with bodies in the *Metamorphoses*, especially on the repeated images of dismembered bodies in the text, see König (2008), esp. 135–36, and Benson (2019), 149–83.

47. For reasons of space, it has not been possible to give close attention here to the landscapes of the Cupid and Psyche story, but it should be clear at once that they fit in with many

of the patterns I have been discussing. Psyche encounters landscapes which are highly literary and stylised: for example, see Harrison (2002), 48–52, for their literary character; and on *locus horridus* stereotypes in the cliff of 6.14.2–4, and its close links to the earlier description of the robber's cave, see Schiesaro (1985), 211–12 and 219–22; de Biasi (1990), 229–30; Merlier-Espenel (1999), 165–67. At the same time they are brutally physical landscapes (see further examples later in this section). Those themes play a key role in the work's depiction of Psyche's immersion in the realm of earthly experience: see Kenney (1990), esp. 184–85, Edwards (1992), and Harrison (2000), 256–58, on the Platonic distinction between spiritual and earthly in the famous scene in *Metamorphoses* 5.24 where Psyche falls back to earth. In all of those respects, Psyche parallels Lucius: see Frangoulidis (2008), 120–24, on general parallels between Lucius and Psyche; also 6.13.4 and 6.16–20, with Harrison (2002), 51–52, for Psyche's encounters with infernal landscape, which parallel the repeated use of infernal imagery for the landscapes Lucius moves through (on which see Nethercut [1969], esp. 101 and 103–4, and O'Brien [2002], esp. 32–35 and 104, n. 53).

48. See Hall (1995).

49. See Ingold (2004) on the way in which the experience of contact between the feet and the ground has been elided within elite Western culture from the classical period onwards, and for the claim that 'a more grounded approach to human movement, sensitive to embodied skills of footwork, opens up new terrain in the study of environmental perception' (315).

50. *Onos* 42 mentions only a 'hard road'.

51. Compare *Onos* 43.

52. Compare *Onos* 44.

53. Compare *Onos* 19.

54. See de Biasi (1990), 236–37; and compare similar comments at 230 on 6.26, discussed later in this paragraph.

55. Compare *Onos* 22.

56. Compare *Onos* 23 for a much briefer version.

57. In *Onos* 26, by contrast, the bandits are tied up and led away to the governor.

58. That fascination has, to my knowledge, never received any sustained critical attention, with the exception of König (2013). However, see brief discussion of rocky deaths in Nethercut (1969), 105–6, and Smith (1998), 72–73.

59. Compare Cohen (2016) for the long history of ideas about the agency of stones and rocks: Apuleius' *Metamorphoses* does not feature in his text, which does not deal at length with ancient Greek and Roman literature, but it has a lot in common with many of the works he discusses.

60. See also later for even stronger hints in the retransformation scene in 11.13.

61. See Frangoulidis (2008), 162.

62. See Van Mal-Maeder (2001), 60.

63. Compare *Onos* 27, but with no *locus amoenus* imagery and no mention of roses.

64. Compare *Met.* 9.32.4, where he eats lettuce which has rotted into a 'bitter mess of muddy juice' (*amaram caenosi sucus cariem*).

65. Much of the material discussed in this paragraph is close to *Onos* 29–31, although some of Apuleius' most memorable phrases (for example, the image of the 'pit or window' in *Met.* 7.17.4 or the description of the bank 'slippery with muddy slime' in 7.18.8) have no equivalent there.

66. Compare *Met.* 4.5.7, where Lucius rolls in dust, for a more pleasurable version of the image of voluntary immersion in landscape.

67. On the prominence of bodily concerns in Books 1–10, see (among others) Schlam (1970); de Filippo (1970); Penwill (1975), esp. 59–66; K. Bradley 2000.

68. See Holzberg (1995); also Fusillo (1999), 61, for a list of examples of that usage from earlier scholarship, whose approach he rejects.

69. See Millar (1981); also Mattiacci (2001), 843–85, and further discussion earlier, in n. 13.

70. Compare Rimell (2002), 12–15 and 123–24, on Petronius, criticising Auerbach (1953) and others for too straightforwardly applying the vocabulary of realism to the *Satyrica*; also Morales (2004), 128–30, on the way in which Achilles Tatius' descriptions of the physicality of emotional reactions are so detailed that they block any sense of realism, having instead an alienating effect.

71. For example, Chesi and Spiegel (2020) for posthumanist approaches to classical literature, esp. Korhonen (2020) for discussion of the *Onos* that has a certain amount in common with my account here.

72. Compare Gianotti (1995); K. Bradley (2000), esp. 114.

73. See Trinquier (1999), 262–67.

74. For example, see Shumate (1996), 35: 'Lucius' environment is one that is radically defamiliarized by changes that rupture its previous unity; it is marked by every kind of instability. His world is one where matter itself is unstable and where familiar ontological and cultural categories—death and life, human and animal, male and female, for example—merge unpredictably into one another'.

75. Oddly not discussed by de Biasi (1990).

76. See Zimmerman (1993), 148. There is a close parallel for this scene in Strabo, in his story of the bandit Selouros who terrorised the regions around Mount Etna; after his capture, Strabo tells us: 'I saw him torn apart by wild beasts at gladiatorial games in the Forum; for he was placed on a high stage, as if on Mount Etna, and the stage suddenly broke apart and collapsed, and he too was carried down into the fragile cages of wild beasts that had been built on purpose in this way beneath the stage' (Strabo, *Geography* 6.2.6). For Strabo, this is yet another in his long series of images of domesticated, urbanised mountains, made safe within the boundaries of human civilisation; for more detailed discussion of that theme, see chapter 12.

77. See Zimmerman (2000), 404.

78. See Finkelpearl (1991), 231–32.

79. See Zimmerman (1993), 146, n. 9; Krabbe (2003), 96.

80. To my knowledge that point has gone more or less unnoticed in recent Apuleius scholarship.

81. Compare Schlam (1970), 484–85; Zimmerman (1993), 159–61; Merlier-Espenel (1999), 171–72; Finkelpearl (1991), esp. 225–26.

82. See Zimmerman (2000), 367; compare Krabbe (2003), 95 and 109.

83. See Zimmerman (2002), 80–81.

84. See Nethercut (1968), 111–13; Krabbe (2003), 473–519; Frangoulidis (2008), 217–32.

85. Compare 6.14 for *procerus* applied to a mountain.

86. Krabbe (2003), 96–98, points out that many of the mountain images of Books 1–10 are transformed in Book 11 to other uses: for example, the 'wooden platform' (*tribunal ligneum*) of

11.24.2 echoes the wooden mountain of 10.30–34, and the word *iugum*, used repeatedly of mountain ridges in Books 1–10, is now used to describe the 'yoke' of servitude to Isis, willingly accepted by Lucius (11.15.5 and 11.30.1); see also Van Mal-Maeder (1997b), 97–98, on the way in which Isis' control over the world stands as a superior equivalent to the magic of Meroe, who similarly exercises control over landscape in 1.8; compare Frangoulidis (2008), 193–95.

87. See Krabbe (2003), 102–5, for a full survey of the word *lubricus* and related vocabulary in the novel.

88. Compare Zimmerman (2002), 87–89; Keulen (2007), 98.

Chapter 10. Warfare and Knowledge in Mountain Territories

1. For example, see Breeze (2011), 133–45, on mountain frontiers in the Roman Empire, and their importance for control over communication routes.

2. For example, see Southern (1996), who uses comparative evidence from campaigns as late as the eighteenth century to reconstruct the likely extent and duration of the Roman army's advances into the Highlands of Scotland: 'Until the 18th century the problems of terrain, communications and supply were much the same for any army' (371); also Burn (1949), 314, 316, and 318–19 on twentieth-century military uses of mountain transit routes in mainland Greece that had also played an important role in ancient battles, esp. at Thermopylai and on Mount Helikon.

3. See later, nn. 19–21, on the route taken by the Persians at the battle of Thermopylai, and chapter 11, nn. 62–63, on Hannibal's route over the Alps; also Campbell (2014) for an accessible recent summary of the extensive debate about the location of the battle of Mons Graupius in Scotland, as described in Tacitus, *Agricola* 29–38.

4. Compare Mitchell (1994) on the relationship between landscape representation and imperial ideology in the modern world.

5. See esp. later, chapter 11, on Herodotus.

6. Compare Simpson (2019), 580, with reference to Ghosh (2016): '[mountains] have always compelled some sense of the uncanny and have seemed to elude complete mastery by human agency. They have rarely if ever seemed lifeless or inert, and no variant of modernity has flattened them through entirely subsuming them into universal schemes. Acknowledging nature as an agent—something Ghosh terms "unthinkable" in modern arts, humanities, and sciences alike—has long and widely been understood in the mountains'.

7. See further discussion later, in part IV.

8. For example, see Simpson (2019), 553: 'recent scholarship across a range of historical sub-disciplines shows that uplands are where many forms of modernity are both crafted and overwhelmed. Maintaining multiple tensions—between assimilation and distinction, between projections of power and material and human resistance, and between knowledge and elusiveness—is essential to the modernities crafted in mountain spaces'; also 554–55, on the way in which mountains provide 'the resistance without which there is no power; the disarray without which there is no order; the archaic without which there is no modern'.

9. Compare Simpson (2019), 556–58, on the way in which 'new and old, modern and pre-modern' remain 'substantially entangled' from the nineteenth century onwards, with special reference to the works of Leslie Stephen.

10. See Bainbridge (2020), esp. 129–61.
11. See McNee (2016), esp. 109–88.
12. See Thompson (2008), 203–5.
13. See Davis (2011).
14. See Shelton (2003) and Jenkins (2003).
15. We also have evidence for training in mountain warfare even for non-specialist troops, for example in Vegetius, *De re militari* 1.27, who suggests that soldiers should be required to practice moving both up and down in hilly terrain in their monthly training marches; and for advice to generals on tactics in mountain warfare, see esp. 1.22, 3.6, 3.9, 3.10, 3.13, 3.19, 3.20, 3.22; compare Onasander, *Strategikos* 6.5, 7, 11.1, 21.3, 31; also Gilliver (1996), 57, on advice in military treatises about the possession and location of high ground in battle situations.
16. Compare Appian, *Civil Wars* 4.10.79, for another similar incident where the Romans observe the way in which some of their allies 'were climbing up through the crags' (διὰ τῶν κρημνῶν ἐπετροβάτουν ἄνω), and follow after with difficulty.
17. Compare Plutarch, *Camillus* 26.3; *Fabius Maximus* 7.2; *Sertorius* 12.7; Diodorus, *Bibliotheca* 5.39.3 for other uses of the same vocabulary.
18. See Gilliver (1996) on Agricola's use of auxiliaries on difficult ground in the battle of Mons Graupius, with parallels from other battles at 61–62; Anders (2015), esp. 301–2, for the Roman habit of using auxiliary troops on difficult ground.
19. For example, see later, chapter 11, on Plutarch's *Cato the Elder*.
20. For the topography of Thermopylai and Mount Kallidromos, see Burn (1951), and (1949) for similar discussion of high-altitude transit routes on Mount Helikon; also Wallace (1980) and Pritchett (1982), 176–210, for detailed follow-up discussion on Thermopylai.
21. Burn (1949), 315.
22. Compare Dionysius of Halicarnassus, *Roman Antiquities* 1.47, for the story that the Trojans and people from other surrounding cities took refuge on Mount Ida after the sack of Troy.
23. See Pausanias 4.9.1 for the decision to retreat to Mount Ithome from their cities on the plain, after several years of fighting.
24. See Pausanias, *Periegesis* 4.17.10, for the move to Eira; 4.20.5–21.1 for the informant.
25. Thucydides, *History of the Peloponnesian War* 1.103.
26. See Shaw (1990), situating the case of the Isaurians in the wider context of relations between mountain- and plains-dwellers, with quotation from Braudel (1972), at 199–200; also Shaw (1986) for comparison between Isauria and the similar situation in the mountainous region of Mauretania Tingitana; and Lenski (1999) for related discussion of Isauria.
27. See Lenski (1999), 413–15, for more detail on the region's topography.
28. See Shaw (1990), 223–26.
29. For example, see Shaw (1990), 227–30, on the use of this strategy in the late Republic, but also on the way in which even these local dynasts sometimes struggled to control the populations they were nominally responsible for; compare Lenski (1999), 418–20.
30. On this passage, see Shaw (1990), 263.
31. See esp. Lenski (1999), 431–39, who goes further than Shaw in seeing that 200-year period as a time when the Isaurian uprisings were largely brought under control; despite his difference of emphasis, however, Shaw (1990) is similarly very much aware of the depth of Isaurian acculturation, for example, at 200: 'there was an element of illusion in this idea [that is, the idea

of a clear dividing line between mountain- and plains-dwellers], since montane societies, even if they rejected political and military forces directed against them, seem to have been open to, and permeable by, various cultural and economic forces stemming from the lowlands'; also 266–67.

32. See Lenski (1999), esp. 446–55 and summary at 456, emphasising the way in which the resistance of the late antique period was 'led by a sedentarized, wealthy and sophisticated elite which had been fostered in the relative peace and prosperity of the high empire'.

33. Shaw (1990), 261, talks about 'a zone of permanent dissidence located wholly within the outer frontiers of the empire'.

34. See esp. Livy 39.54, with Giorcelli Bersani (2019), 37–40. The representation of the Alps as barrier in Greek and Roman writing over a long period is a major theme of Borca (2002), 101–57; compare Tarpin (1992), 98–100 and 105–10, on ease of crossing as the primary goal in Roman conquest of the Alps.

35. This paragraph is indebted to Dyson (1985), 87–125, who refers to Roman military engagement with Liguria as a 'grim and perpetual treadmill' (104).

36. See Dyson (1985), 87–88, for a more detailed account of the topography.

37. See Dyson (1985), 90.

38. See Dyson (1985), 90–91, suggesting that this fragmentation was so pronounced that there were no opportunities for the Romans to give their support to client rulers as in Isauria.

39. See Dyson (1985), 100–102, 104–8, 114–23.

40. See Dyson (1985), 104; and more generally Jourdain-Annequin (2011) on the development of Greek and Roman knowledge of the Alps, including extensive discussion of Liguria.

41. Caesar, *Gallic Wars* 3.1–6, with Borca (2002), 130.

42. See Giorcelli Bersani (2019), 46–54.

43. See Borca (2002), 107–11; Artru (2016).

44. Giorcelli Bersani (2019), esp. 71–100.

45. See Rollinger (2014), esp. 607–18, for a parallel phenomenon in inscriptions recording conquest of mountain territories by Assyrian kings from the eleventh to eighth century BCE.

46. For commentary, see Cooley (2009), 222–23; generally on the *Res Gestae* as a document that links imperial power and geographical knowledge, see Nicolet (1991), 15–27; also Borca (2002), 113.

47. See Borca (2002), 112; Giorcelli Bersani (2019), 53–54 and 75–76.

48. Partially surviving as the inscription *Corpus Inscriptionum Latinarum* V, 7817.

49. See Jourdain-Annequin (2011); also Diodorus Siculus, *Bibliotheca* 4.19.3–4, on Herakles' road building in the Alps; and discussion by Borca (2002), 131–32; Barton (2017), 22–23; also DeWitt (1941) and Knapp (1986) on the so-called Road of Hercules over the Alps and its strategic significance for the Romans in the late Republic.

50. See Giorcelli Bersani (2019), 25–35.

51. Compare Ovid, *Tristia* 4.2.37; and further discussion earlier, in chapter 7.

52. See Breeze (2011), 133–37, on the topography of Dacia; and earlier, chapter 7, figure 7.7.

53. See Nicolet (1991) on the links between cartography and imperial power, esp. 98–111, on the so-called map of Agrippa; also Dilke (1987) on 'maps in the service of the state'; and Brodersen (2012), 107–10, for a more sceptical account; on maps and power in the modern world, see Harley (1988).

54. See Debarbieux and Rudaz (2015), esp. 143–51: 'colonization meant projecting on to the coveted lands a type of spatiality (characteristic of the modern map), a type of geographical rationality, and a finality that capitalized on that comparability of knowledge acquired on a global scale' (144).

55. See de Jong (2018), 31–36, including discussion of Thucydides, *History of the Peloponnesian War* 5.6–10, also treated by Greenwood (2006), 26–30; also Philo, *Life of Moses* 1.41, 228–29, for another example not discussed later (and not mentioned by de Jong); and further discussion later, in chapter 11, for Hannibal.

56. On this passage, see Riggsby (2019), 189; and on military mapping more generally, Sherk (1974).

57. For example, see Riggsby (2019), 172–201, esp. 173, n. 64, with further bibliography; also Salway (2012); Diederich (2018) and (2019) for a comprehensive collection of references to maps and map consciousness in ancient texts; Janni (1984) and Brodersen (2003) for important studies of the relative absence of maps in ancient culture.

58. See Irby (2012) on mapping traditions in Greek geographical writing, with regular mention of mountains; and Dilke (1985), 93–96, on mountains in land surveying, with good examples of illustrations from the text of Hyginus Gromaticus in plates 9 and 10.

59. See Jones (2012), 127.

60. However, see the preface to Book 2 of Ptolemy's *Geography* for brief acknowledgement that some of the locations he enters are approximations in need of further exploration.

61. See Talbert (2010), 106–7.

62. See Talbert (2010), 142–44.

63. The most extensive recent account is by Talbert (2010), esp. 142–57, who argues that the map is meant for display purposes, and speculates about the possibility that it was designed with imperial backing in the tetrarchic period of the late third/early fourth century CE to celebrate Rome's mastery over the Mediterranean world; also Talbert (2012b); and Salway (2005) for another comprehensive reassessment of the evidence for the map and the traditions lying behind it, arguing for a primarily 'decorative or commemorative' (131) function rather than a practical one.

64. See Murphy (2004), 148–54, esp. 148–50, on the way in which mountains in Pliny stand in opposition to rivers, restraining them and containing them; and Debarbieux (2009) for eighteenth-century parallels for the idea that mountains provide a structuring framework for the earth's surface.

65. See Murphy (2004), esp. 154–60, on the way in which Pliny's parading of mountains and rivers parallels the celebration of geographical conquest in the Roman triumph; and 160–63, on Pliny's quotation of numerous sources that 'represent the expansion of Roman military power as the pre-eminent source of new discoveries, and geographical exploration as the achievement of great conquerors' (163), for example *Natural History* 5.11 and 5.14 for exploration of the Atlas mountains.

66. See Murphy (2004), 132–33, suggesting that looking at a place from on high is 'logically prior to owning or conquering it' (132).

67. Compare Purves (2010a), esp. 119, on the importance of cartographic thinking for Greek historiography even in the relative absence of physical maps.

68. See Borca (2002), 51–99, for comprehensive discussion.

69. See Debarbieux and Rudaz (2015), 29–31 and 72–87, but with no discussion of premodern precedents; for example, at 72–74, they discuss the move from denigration to celebration in portrayals of the Highlands of Scotland in the eighteenth and nineteenth centuries; also 160–61, on the rather different approach characteristic of modern colonial, as opposed to nationalistic, engagement with mountains: 'the situation was different in the colonies. In general, the construction of the otherness of the "native" was necessary for the colonial project' (160). See also S. Bainbridge (2020), 3–10, on changing uses of the word 'mountaineer' from 'mountain inhabitant' to its modern sense.

70. See Dench (1995).

71. See Woolf (2011), 59–88, esp. 81–85, taking issue with Murphy (2004).

72. See Woolf (2011), 60 and 86; and for the links between mountain exploration and imperialism in the late nineteenth and early twentieth centuries, see Ellis (2001); Bayers (2003); Debarbieux and Rudaz (2015), 139–61.

73. See Giorcelli Bersani (2019), 15, in the context of similar views expressed elsewhere both in the *Natural History* and by other authors; also Borca (2002), 11–12.

Chapter 11. Mountain Narratives in Greek and Roman Historiography

1. Compare Granius Licinianus 36.30–32, who claims that Sallust should be viewed as an orator rather than a historian, citing among other things his repeated inclusion of landscape descriptions.

2. See Polybius 5.21, on the importance of local description for the historian, including description of mountains and other landscape features, and on the influence of positioning over the outcome of warfare; but also 29.12.4, for criticism of historians who offer excessively elaborate descriptions of places, with discussion by Rood (2012), 182, and further later on Polybius' criticism of those who offer unrealistically spectacular portrayals of the Alps. In my view Lendon (2017) understates the importance of landscape description for some ancient military writing, for example, at 45–46 and 49, in the latter case talking about 'indifference to terrain'.

3. See Clarke (2018), 72 and 109–14, pointing out, however, that mountains are less prominent in the *Histories* than rivers; also Prontera (2019), who similarly suggests that rivers are more important as landmarks, but also points out that mountain passes in border zones play an important role in Herodotus' account. For a good general introduction to geography in Herodotus, see Harrison (2007); however, see also Purves (2010a), 118–58, on Herodotus' ambivalent relationship with the idea of mapping.

4. See Clarke (2018), 71–72, on this passage.

5. See Clarke (2018), 71.

6. See König (forthcoming a) for longer analysis and further bibliography; also Clarke (2018), esp. 171–218; Bosak-Schroeder (2020), 32–56; Romm (2006) 186–90.

7. See Lateiner (1989), 126–35.

8. See Clarke (2018), 192–93.

9. See Clarke (2018), 214–16, on the negative character of Xerxes' actions at the Hellespont.

10. See Baragwanath (2008), 254–65, for discussion of the doubleness of Herodotus' account, and particularly of the possibility that there are ways of viewing Xerxes' desire for magnificence as a positive trait; compare Bridges (2015), 56–57. Herodotus tells us that Xerxes

'ordered the canal to be dug out of arrogance (μεγαλοφροσύνης), and wanting to display his power and leave behind a memorial' (7.24.1); the last of those motives recalls Herodotus' goal, stated in the opening sentence of the work (1.1), of preventing people's achievements from losing their glory over time.

11. See Clarke (2018), 198–200.

12. Not dealt with at length in König (forthcoming a). On the theme of 'natural miracles', including the examples discussed here where the Greek land resists the Persians, see Harrison (2000), 92–100.

13. See della Dora (2011), 26, on Athos as a landscape of fear for the Persians.

14. For example, see the repetition of the word ἀπορραγεῖσαι in both Herodotus, *Histories* 8.37, and Pausanias, *Periegesis* 1.4.4.

15. See also de Jong (2018), 32–33, on the way in which Herodotus repeatedly associates Xerxes with quasi-cartographic authority by describing him viewing from mountains, but also in a way that characterises him as hubristic by his association with moments of divine viewing in the *Iliad*.

16. The Persians' success in mountain campaigning is reversed in Herodotus' description of the decisive Greek victory at the Battle of Plataia in Book 9, which includes a lengthy account of preliminary troop movements over a period of about two weeks on the slopes of Mount Kithairon: see Taplin (2010), 236–37; and *Histories* 9.59, where the Persian general Mardonios fails to see the Athenian troops 'because of the hills' (ὑπὸ τῶν ὄχθων).

17. See Rood (2014), 89–90, contrasting Herodotus with Xenophon, Polybius, and portrayals of Alexander.

18. See Lendon (2017), 54–56, on ancient generals' fear of disorder, and its reflection in military writing; also 42, esp. n. 4, on the way in which some modern military accounts offer us an immersive experience that tracks the perspective of particular combatants and allows us to share their confusion.

19. See Rood (2013), for example, at 77, on the text's 'complex web of internal allusions'; and 79, 'Descriptions of landscape . . . are most detailed in sections where the Greeks face military obstacles that prevent them making that sort of steady progress—and they are often first given not directly by the narrator, but as seen by the character "Xenophon" . . . Xenophon sees more than other generals and it is this capacity to see more that leads the Greeks to safety'; also M. Zimmermann (2019) for conclusions along similar lines, with reference to Xenophon's other works too; Purves (2010a), 159–95, on the way in which the *Anabasis* dramatises the experience of immersion in a landscape that is difficult to read and difficult to move through, esp. at 177–79 and 194; and Balatti (2017), 195–205, on Xenophon's representation of the mountain people the Carduchians in the southeastern Taurus in the *Anabasis*.

20. See Harrison (2005); also Bridges (2015), 119–25, on the association between Alexander and Xerxes more broadly.

21. See della Dora (2011), 27–28; Schama 1995: 401–4; Lucian, *Pro imaginibus* 9; and Plutarch, *On the Fortune or the Virtue of Alexander* II, 2, 335d, for explicit contrast with Xerxes' treatment of Mount Athos. The anecdote in Vitruvius leads into his positive representation of more moderate versions of environmental engineering: Alexander does not dismiss Dinocrates; instead he employs him, and redirects his energies towards the foundation of Alexandria; then in the rest of Book 2, Vitruvius discusses at length the way in which architecture should work with natural resources.

22. Recent work on Plutarch has shown an increasing interest in his complex and careful representation of space and place—for example, see Georgiadou and Oikonomopoulou (2017)—but his battle landscapes have had relatively little attention. This section is an adapted version of König (forthcoming b).

23. See Duff (2011), 262, with further bibliography in n. 223.

24. Other examples of mountain-battle scenes in Plutarch's *Lives* where the themes of trickery and sensory confusion are prominent, in addition to those discussed later, include *Timoleon* 26–28: battle against the Carthaginians, with recurring scenes of mist and storm which make it hard to see; *Alexander* 24: Alexander is separated from his army in mountainous territory at night with a few companions, but succeeds in stealing fire from a barbarian camp; *Flamininus* 3–5: Philip V of Macedon is in a position of strength holding the high ground around the Apsos Gorge, and Flamininus outflanks him by sending a group of soldiers along a secret route with a local guide; *Flamininus* 7–8: the battlefield at Kynoskephalai is initially impeded by heavy mist.

25. Compare Xenophontos (2017) for the way in which behaviour in the military sphere is linked with character in other areas in Plutarch's *Lives*.

26. For example, see Becchi (2014), 76: 'philosophers differ from the majority of men in that they possess strong and solid judgement, which they uphold even in life's adversities', citing *Eumenes* 9.1–2: 'but the truly magnanimous and constant soul reveals itself rather in its behaviour under disasters and misfortunes'; and see also Plutarch, *On the Fortune or the Virtue of Alexander* I, 12, 333b–c: 'philosophers differ from common persons in having their powers of judgement strong and firm to face danger, since the common man is not fortified by conceptions such as these ... but crises destroy all his calculations in the face of danger, and the fantastic imaginings of perils close at hand dispel his powers of judgement'.

27. Compare discussion of this passage earlier, in chapter 10, for its reference to specialised mountain expertise.

28. Beck (2014b), 4, even goes so far as to suggest that Plutarch had been to Thermopylai himself to investigate the site, but that seems to me to be impossible to demonstrate. Plutarch also avoids the obvious approach of a detailed replaying of Herodotus' account of the battle against Xerxes on the same site, although he does make clear that this is one of the things on Cato's mind. For example, he tells us that Cato 'called to mind that Persian going-round and encircling' (τὴν δὲ Περσικὴν ἐκείνην περιήλυσιν καὶ κύκλωσιν) (13.1), and that detail has resonances with Plutarch's discussion of Cato's knowledge of Greek literature in 2.3–6, and with Plutarch's broader interest in the benefits of Greek *paideia* for Romans. However, Plutarch does not seem to be taking the obvious route of replicating Cato's imitation of Herodotus within his own prose (and that is in line with his relatively infrequent use of Herodotus in his work generally): see Russell (1973), 60. Chaplin (2010) similarly shows that Livy avoids the obvious path of imitating Herodotus in his account of the battle.

29. There are other differences too: Livy (36.16.6–8) goes into detail on Antiochos' knowledge of the story of the Persians: the fear of being caught out in the same way leads him to ask the Aetolians for help with guarding the pass; Plutarch cuts out that detail, suggesting that it is Cato rather than Antiochos who knows the story of the Persian invasion, and in doing so he focuses our attention much more exclusively on the state of mind of Cato and his soldiers; Livy also makes it clear that Cato is a subordinate here, whereas Plutarch elides that detail; see Chaplin (2010), 54 and 57–58, stressing the difference between Livy and Plutarch; also Appian, *Roman*

History 11.18, who similarly portrays Cato as subordinate, and describes his flanking movement in half a sentence.

30. For example, from Book 1 of the *Strategemata* see 1.2.8, 1.4.5, 1.4.7, 1.5.3, 1.5.8, 1.5.21, 1.5.28.

31. One of the other remarkable features of Plutarch's account is the way in which Plutarch enhances his description through epic overtones: see König (forthcoming b) for more detailed illustration, focusing especially on the way in which Plutarch compares Cato's activity systematically to the night expedition of *Iliad* Book 10.

32. Scientific 'digressions' are certainly not confined to passages of landscape description in the *Lives*: see Hamilton (1969), 95, for a list.

33. See García Moreno (1992), 142–43. Others suggest that Posidonius is a likely source, given the meteorological details discussed further later: see Konrad (1994), liv.

34. Compare Chrysanthou (2018), 5–6 and 66–102, for that technique.

35. Compare Duff (1999), 78–82, for parallel discussion of the philosophical overtones of Plutarch's use of the vocabulary of reason elsewhere, esp. with reference to the word λογισμοί.

36. That kind of narrative pattern (initial *aporia*; confusion inflicted in turn on one's enemies) recurs frequently enough in the *Lives* to suggest that it is a particular interest of Plutarch's, rather than something he has inherited passively from his sources, although this may sometimes be a case of Plutarch heightening what he finds rather than inventing it.

37. Compare Theophrastus, *Weather Signs* 37.

38. Compare García Moreno (1992), 143, on the importance for Plutarch of anecdotes that 'recount extreme situations in which the protagonists reveal the authentic nature of their psyche, their vices or virtues', with particular reference to the role of paradoxography in the *Sertorius*.

39. For example, the guests in that text regularly discuss the qualities of particular naturally occurring substances, in a way which parallels Plutarch's characterisation of the soil and the wind here: see *Sympotic Questions* (*Quaestiones convivales*) 1.9 and 4.2 for examples involving discussion of soil.

40. On processes of conjecture and explanation in the *Sympotic Questions*, see König (2012), esp. 66–71.

41. For the general point that natural-science digressions in the *Lives* are often linked with characterisation of his biographical subjects, see the introduction to Meeusen and Van der Stockt (2015), 21–22, and essays in that volume by Lesage Gárriga (2015) and Ferreira (2015). The latter is particularly important as a precedent for my analysis here: she draws attention to the way in which natural phenomena, described with scientific language, are used as indices of the character of Plutarch's heroes; many of her examples are from battle contexts, and many of them show military leaders exploiting the natural world to their own advantage: 'a certain educational agenda lies behind these passages, promoting the idea that a true politician must possess a rational mentality and the right cognitive powers to face (natural) adversity calmly' (22).

42. For example at *Aemilius Paulus* 15.2, where he discovers, after testing every possibility, that there is one unguarded passage available to him.

43. For example, see *Aemilius Paulus* 4.3.

44. See König (forthcoming b) for a longer account, with reference also to Aemilius' interpretation of a lunar eclipse at *Aemilius Paulus* 17.9.

45. For example, see *Aemilius Paulus* 17.1–5, where Aemilius resists the impatience of his young officers.

46. Compare Plutarch, *Pompey* 32.2–3, for another very similar example of a general using his observational skills to find water in a mountain setting, with Tatum (2013), 379.

47. Aemilius' digging of wells is reported in several other accounts, but the scientific speculation is almost certainly Plutarch's addition (although it is impossible to be absolutely certain, given that Polybius' account does not survive); certainly there is no trace of it in Livy: see Tatum (2013), 380–81.

48. See Tatum (2013) for excellent detailed discussion.

49. Compare Jacobs (2018), 299–301, on other aspects of Aemilius' military virtue, including careful planning and adaptation, based on 'rapid calculation' in the course of battle; and see index p. 464, under 'paradigms for generals/in developing strategies/adapting to the situation' for a series of other examples of the importance of calculation and good judgement in successful generalship.

50. See Duffy (2013), 56–59.

51. Compare Petronius, *Satyrica* 122–23, for Julius Caesar depicted along similar lines as a Hannibal figure in the Alps, first looking down from a mountaintop over Italy at lines 153–54, then conquering the terrifying ice and snow of the Alps, at lines 183–209.

52. On Livy's account of Hannibal's crossing, see Levene (2010), 136–55, comparing it extensively with that of Polybius; Fabrizi (2015), with further bibliography, esp. 136–43, on Livy's Alps as an extravagant *locus horridus* landscape, with repeated mention of coldness and steepness and narrowness, as often in Latin literature, and 127–29 and 137, n. 71, on differences from Polybius; Giorcelli Bersani (2019), 32–35. For other even more extreme accounts of the horror of the landscape and the mountain peoples Hannibal faces, see the descriptions in Silius Italicus, *Punica* 3.477–646, discussed along with Livy's account by Barton (2017), 31–34, and Borca (2002), 134–40; also earlier, chapter 5, on the way in which some of these passages have been viewed as precursors of the modern mountain sublime.

53. That is not the case in Livy's brief account of Cato at Thermopylai, as we have already seen earlier in this chapter; however, see Livy 33.7–10 on the battle of Kynoskephalai for a good counter-example: it gives an even more detailed description of the obscuring effects of fog than the equivalent discussion in Plutarch, *Flamininus* 7–8; compare Eckstein (2014), 412–16, on the way in which Livy stresses confusion and chaos in this battle much more than his source Polybius.

54. Livy rejected some aspects of Polybius' approach quite conspicuously: see Levene (2010), 149–55.

55. Compare Rood (2012), 193.

56. See Levene (2010), 154, on Polybius' equation of himself with Hannibal; also Rood (2012), 193; Niccolai (2019).

57. For example, see McNee (2016), 151: 'The haptic sublime involves an encounter with mountain landscapes in which the human subject experiences close physical contact—sometimes painful and dangerous, sometimes exhilarating and satisfying, but always involving some kind of transcendent experience brought about through physical proximity to rock faces, ice walls, or snow slopes. Like the eighteenth-century sublime, it is to some degree an aesthetic of mastery, of overcoming a threat or difficulty'.

58. For example, see Bayers (2003), 99–114, on John Hunt's account of the 1953 Everest expedition—Hunt (1953)—as an 'imperial adventure narrative'; and for the language of

conquest in twentieth-century mountaineering, but also British ambivalence about that language, see Hansen (2001), 185–202.

59. Polybius tells the story of the Gallic crossing of the Alps and invasion of northern Italy in *Histories* 2.21–31.

60. See esp. 3.49.2 and 3.61.4–9, with Davidson (1991), 19.

61. See Rood (2012), 190–91, on other factors in the vagueness of some of Polybius' topographical descriptions, suggesting that Polybius finds it more helpful to refer to particular types of landscape feature in generic terms than to attempt a more detailed description.

62. I am grateful to Nicolas Wiater for discussion of this issue. On Hannibal's route through the Alps, see among many others Walbank (1957), 382–91; Jourdain-Annequin (1999).

63. Compare Fabrizi (2015), 118–19, for similar comments on Livy, who is notoriously inaccurate in his account of Hannibal's crossing and many other incidents.

64. Compare earlier in this chapter, on Plutarch's use of the same word in *Sertorius* 17.8; and see Rood (2012), 192–93, on the way in which Polybius' narrative is often focalised through Hannibal in order to convey his ability to 'recognise spatial possibilities' (192).

65. See Fabrizi (2015), 140–42, on the closely equivalent description in Livy 21.35.6–9, but also noting some differences of emphasis from Polybius; compare de Jong (2018), 35; de Jong also discusses at 35–36 the famous example of failed *oroskopia* in Livy 40.21.2–22.5, where the king Philip V of Macedon climbs Mount Haimos, in the expectation that he will be able to see vast amounts of territory from the summit; and see also 23–24, on Petrarch's reference to this incident in his famous account of his ascent of Mount Ventoux; compare Jaeger (2007), who associates the obstruction of Philip's vision on the summit with the hubristic 'blindness' of his leadership more generally, which is contrasted with Livy's acknowledgement of his own lack of omniscience; also Falcone (2019) on the techniques Livy uses in portraying this as a failed expedition.

66. Polybius' work had an engagement with geography which was quite intense even by the normal standards of ancient historiography: we know that he wrote a whole book (Book 34) on geographical topics, although it does not survive.

Chapter 12. Strabo: Civilising the Mountains

1. See Pothecary (2002) for the argument that Strabo was writing exclusively under Tiberius, between 17 or 18 CE and 23 CE, esp. 398–99, for discussion of Strabo's reference at 4.6.9 to Tiberius' Alpine campaign of 15 BCE.

2. For an earlier version of the discussion in this chapter, see König (2016); also König (forthcoming a) on Strabo's representations of landscape alteration specifically.

3. See Connors (2011), 143–49, on Strabo's conception of the geographer's gaze.

4. There has been a striking increase in attention to Strabo over the last few decades—major landmarks include Dueck (2000); Dueck et al. (2005); Dueck (2017)—but even so it is still surprisingly rare to find publications that analyse the experience of reading Strabo from end to end, in a way that maps the ebb and flow of recurring themes: much of the scholarship on Strabo still seems to be interested primarily in generalisations about his procedures and his politics which draw very selectively on particularly relevant passages, or else in closely focused readings of particular regions.

5. That contrast has been recognised before, but has not to my knowledge been discussed in relation to Strabo's interest in the theme of human alteration of the physical landscape. The best discussions rightly draw attention to the complexity of Strabo's categorisations: see Almagor (2005) on the way in which Strabo tends to define barbarian identity in opposition to civilisation, although also stressing the fact that his usage is far from uniform; Van der Vliet (2003) on the way in which the civilised-uncivilised dichotomy relates (never entirely straightforwardly) to the other dichotomies Strabo uses, for example, between Greek and barbarian or between Greek and Roman (and see esp. 255–56, on the way in which Strabo maps it onto a distinction between mountain-dwellers and plains-dwellers); Clarke (1999), 210–44, discussing among other things the conflict between a Rome-based and an Asia-Minor-based focalisation in Strabo's work, which complicates any simplistic view of Rome as protector of civilisation (see further later on Pontus); Jacob (1991), esp. 159–66; Thollard (1987). One particularly important passage is Strabo 13.1.25, where he refers to Plato's description, in *Laws* 3.677a–682e, of the three stages of civilisation after the flood, the first in the mountains, portrayed as simple and wild, including the Cyclopes in their summit caves, the second in the foothills, as humans gained the courage to descend farther, and the third in the plains.

6. Compare Borca (2002), 35–45, for analysis along similar lines, stressing at 38–39 that the equilibrium between mountains and other landscape types is crucial to the positive nature of human-environment relations in Italy.

7. Nicolet (1991) has argued influentially in favour of that view, for example, at 47: 'Strabo's intentions, in writing his geography, are clearly political. His description of the world, when seen as a whole, is constructed so as to lead to Rome's pretended universal domination'; however, see Woolf (2011) for a more sceptical account of the relationship between ethnography and empire, esp. 78–79, on Strabo.

8. See König (forthcoming a).

9. Compare Bosak-Schroeder (2020), esp. 1–9, on the way in which ancient ethnography, with its interest in representing entanglements between human culture and the environment, can be a powerful resource for modern environmental thinking, despite its potential to be linked by ancient readers with imperialist and racist assumptions in some contexts.

10. Frequency statistics for the use of ὀρεινός (in all its different forms) are as follows (all figures from *Thesaurus Linguae Graecae*): Strabo, 4.3 per 10,000 words; Ptolemy, 7.2; Pausanias, 0.6; Polybius 0.4; Herodotus, 0.2. Figures for ὄρος (nominative/accusative singular only) are as follows: Strabo, 6.8 per 10,000 words; Ptolemy, 49.1; Pausanias, 5.0; Polybius 0.5; Herodotus, 2.1.

11. However, see also Clarke (1999), 295, pointing to the alternative Herodotean tradition, which associates hard, mountainous lands with imperial dominance and soft lands with an inability to rule (esp. in *Histories* 9.122, discussed earlier, in chapter 11), and arguing that Strabo resists that model in taking Rome's geographical position as one of the factors in its success.

12. However, Strabo sometimes uses that kind of perspective too, particularly when he describes views of the land as if from the sea, drawing on the ancient tradition of *periplous* texts which described sailing routes: mountains were crucial landmarks for travellers by sea as well as by land: examples from Strabo include (among many others) 2.5.32, 'if one turns to the west from Indike, keeping the mountains on one's right'; 3.1.7, referring to Mount Kalpe, 'which is high and steep, with the consequence that it appears from a distance to be an island'. And see

Salway 2012, 193 (with further bibliography in n. 3), on the compatibility of hodological perspectives with map-based thinking.

13. See Irby (2012), esp. 101–2; Salway (2012), 197, on the standard division of the inhabited world by a line running eastwards from the Pillars of Herakles along the Taurus mountains, used also by Strabo at 2.1.1; Lasserre (1966), 23, on the way in which the passage just quoted, from 3.1.3, draws on both Eratosthenes and Posidonius. Strabo also regularly criticises those who misuse those traditions: for example, see 1.2.10 for criticism of chroniclers of Alexander who relocate the Caucasus to India; or 7.3.6 for criticism of those who write about the non-existent Mount Rhipaia.

14. Compare Strabo 7.5.1, where he corrects Polybius' claims about the view from Mount Haimos (although he makes no claim to have been there himself).

15. Discussed briefly by de Jong (2018), 36.

16. However, for a good parallel see earlier, chapter 10, on Pliny the Elder.

17. For equivalent use of γεωγραφεῖ, again with 'mountains' as the subject, see 4.1.11; and for equivalent passages with ὑπογράφειν, see (among others) 3.2.13, 5.1.2, 8.1.3, 12.3.42.

18. For example, 1.1.16.

19. For example, see Lasserre (1966), 195.

20. Strabo's repeated mention of mines in mountainous areas—which are so frequent that some commentators have assumed that he must have had some involvement in the mining industry himself: for example, Roller (2014), 12–13—is the obvious exception to his characterisation of these regions as infertile and economically unproductive. However, mineral wealth rarely seems to translate into wealth for the local population; 3.2.3 is a good example: 'the areas that have mines are necessarily rough (τραχέα) and rather poor'.

21. Compare Sodini (2019) on Strabo's association of the peoples of the Alps with brigandage.

22. For other similar references to Augustus exercising control over mountainous regions, see 3.4.20, 4.6.6, and 4.6.10; and 4.6.9 for Tiberius, discussed already earlier.

23. See also Pothecary (2005), esp. 169–73, for the point that Strabo's account largely ignores Roman provincial divisions in the Alps.

24. See Dueck (2000), 126–27, on that connection.

25. See Glacken (1969), 104.

26. For example, see 3.3.1 for the city of Moron 'well situated on a mountain' (εὖ κειμένην ἐν ὄρει).

27. Luna (5.2.5); Volaterrani (5.2.6); Poplonium (5.2.6); Cossa (5.2.8); Feronia (5.2.9); Antium (5.3.5); luxury cave dwellings along the Kaiatian gulf (5.3.6); Rome (5.3.7); Labicum (5.3.9); Venafrum (5.3.10); Praeneste (5.3.11); Foruli (5.3.11); Tusculum (5.3.12); Alba (5.3.13). Book 5 also contains a number of examples of cities built around water—for example, Ravenna built around the marshes and 'intersected by streams' (5.1.7).

28. It has never to my knowledge been analysed in relation to that wider theme in the text as a whole. However, see Purcell (2017a) for an account which does, unusually, read this passage as part of a wider series of representations of cities in Strabo's work, esp. 22, for explicit statement of the importance of reading intratextually. Vout (2010) mentions Strabo a number of times (for example, 9–10, 57, 80) in the context of other ancient writing about the hills of Rome, but without noting that this is an important moment in Strabo's long narrative of the

domestication of mountain territory, although her suggestion at 57 that the acquisition of the hills 'was an early model for imperial expansion' seems particularly appropriate to Strabo's text.

29. To my knowledge the only parallel is Dionysius of Halicarnassus, *Roman Antiquities* 1.79.12 for the Aventine and 2.50.1 for the Caelian. *Roman Antiquities* Book 1, which was written not long before Strabo's *Geography*, under the reign of Augustus, contains some of the best parallels for Strabo's image of the absorption of the hills of Italy into civilised Roman culture.

30. See Langdon (1999); Latin authors, by contrast, tend to use *mons* over *collis* for the hills of Rome. On the history and topography of the hills of Rome as described in Strabo's account, see Roller (2018), 253–55.

31. See Strabo, *Geography* 5.4.8 for Vesuvius; 6.2.3 for Etna; and compare earlier, chapter 6.

32. On Posidonius' Stoic ideas about the links between imperial good fortune and the blessings of Italian geography, and their influence over Strabo, see Swain 1996, 205, with reference to this passage and others.

33. For example, 5.2.9 on the rituals practiced in Feronia at the foot of Mount Soracte; 5.3.2 for the foundation of Alba on Mount Albanus by Ascanius.

34. For example, 5.2.6 for Volaterrani, occupied by the opponents of Sulla and then besieged for two years; or 5.3.5 for the piracy of the inhabitants of Antium, later curtailed by the Romans; 5.3.11 for Praeneste, where Strabo tells us that Marius was killed while being besieged.

35. See also earlier, chapter 9, for discussion of this passage in relation to the stage-set mountain of Apuleius' *Metamorphoses* Book 10.

36. For example, Argos (8.6.7), Epidauros (8.6.15), Athens (9.1.16), various cities of Aitolia (10.2.4).

37. Pausanias and Strabo are often contrasted with each other, but actually Book 8 of Strabo is in some respects very Pausanian. See Pretzler (2005a) for the differences between Strabo's global vision and Pausanias' localism, but also 149 for acknowledgement that Strabo's Greek books are more Pausanian than others.

38. Compare Madsen (2014), 82–86, on the way in which the inhabitants of Pontus are categorised by Strabo neither as Greeks nor as uncivilised barbarians.

39. For example, see 11.5.6, 11.7.1, 11.9.1, 11.13.3, 11.13.6, 11.4.4.

40. For example, see 11.8.4.

41. Compare Clarke (1999), 228–44, who is cautious about ascribing a conspicuously Pontic perspective to Strabo, but nevertheless points to some of the complexities and ambiguities of this section of the text, for example the way in which Strabo complicates any simple civilised-uncivilised dichotomy here by his mention of Roman involvement in piracy; also Braund (2005) on the prominent role of the Black Sea region in the text, although on the whole stressing the supportive character of Strabo's account of Roman imperialism in the region.

42. On Strabo's family connections with Mithridates, see Clarke (1997), 100; Lindsay (2005), 187; Braund (2005), 224.

43. For example, see 12.3.28, 12.3.31, 12.3.38; also 14.5.7, 16.2.18 for other nearby examples.

44. On the Stoic overtones of that pairing, see Lindsay (2005), 186–87; for the same pairing for other cities, see 5.3.8 on Rome, and 12.3.11 on Mithridates' capital Sinope, with Clarke (1999), 235–36, and Dueck (2000), 63.

45. However, see Purcell (2017a), 29, pointing out that Amaseia replicates the combination of natural advantages with human forethought in Strabo's Rome. Lindsay (2005) does draw a link with the other rock-built dwellings in Strabo's account of the Pontus region, but makes no reference to other sections of the text.

46. Mathieu (2011) both charts and exemplifies that enterprise.

Chapter 13. Ammianus Marcellinus: Mountain Peoples and Imperial Boundaries

1. See esp. Shaw (1990), 240–44, who sees the pattern of consolidation followed by revolt as one that was repeated in Isaurian interactions with Rome over many centuries; Lenski (1999) who argues, by contrast, that the Isaurians had been relatively peaceful for the previous two centuries, before this outbreak of more concerted aggression. On this incident see also Matthews (1989), 355–67; Hopwood (1999), 200–203, including excellent description of the geographical details of the region, based on personal investigation; Honey (2006).

2. Echoes of Hannibal's struggles are not always pessimistic, however: the Alps are mentioned at 15.10, in the context of Ammianus' description of Gaul, as an example of a mountain region with desperately difficult and dangerous terrain which has nevertheless been brought under control through a series of road-building enterprises, by Hannibal among others.

3. See Hopwood (1999), 203–4, and also 204–5, on the Isaurians' final appearance in the text at 27.9.6–7.

4. For example, see Lavan (2017), 23, on images of motion and disturbance to describe revolt in Roman sources, especially *turbare* and *turbidus*, both of which are widely used by Ammianus; 24–25, on the language of eruption, especially using the word *erupit*; and 26, on the way in which Tacitus especially uses the notion of unruly landscapes, where revolt seems to emerge almost as a natural phenomenon from the land itself.

5. For example, see Kelly (2004), 163, esp. n. 107, with special reference to Pacatus and Claudian; also 164 for an example from Themistius.

6. For good examples, see 19.11.1, on the Sarmatian Limigantes, and 28.2.11, on the Maratocupreni.

7. For example, at 27.5.3–4, the Goths retreat to the mountains of the Serri in the Carpathians, but some families are captured before they get there; at 27.12.11, the Armenian ruler Papa hides from the Persian king Sapor in the mountains; at 29.4.5, Macrianus, king of the Alamanni, escapes from Valentinian by hiding in the hills; at 30.5.13, the Quadi watch for Valentinian's arrival from the high mountains, to which they had withdrawn because of their uncertainty about the situation; at 31.3.7, Athanaricus, chief of the Theruingian Goths, takes refuge from the Huns in the mountains; at 31.4.13, Athanaricus again withdraws to the high mountains, having driven out the Sarmatians, motivated by his wariness towards the emperor Valens; at 31.10.12, the Lentienses retreat to the mountains; Gratian advances, attempting to blockade them, and at 31.10.15, the Lentienses retreat again to even higher mountains.

8. For example, at 29.5.44, Theodosius advances against the tribe of the Iubaleni, but is stopped by fear of the high hills, which are well suited to ambushes.

9. At 27.1.1, the Alamanni renew their strength and overleap (*persultabant*) the frontiers of Gaul; at 28.5.1, there is an outbreak of the Saxons (*erupit*); at 28.6.2–4, the Austoriani are

subdued for a time, but then return to their natural turbulence, like beasts aroused by madness; at 29.6.1, there is a new outbreak of the Quadi from beyond the Julian Alps (*perruptis Alpibus Iuliis*).

10. See Weil (2005), and discussion earlier, in chapter 2.

11. See Barnes (1998), 108–10, on animal imagery, applied to both barbarians and Romans; also Wiedemann (1986), 196–201; Matthews (1989), 258–59, on animal, especially snake imagery for 'hostile or aggressive officials' (258).

12. For a good example, see 27.7.4 for Ammianus' account of Valentinan's anger, which 'bursts out gradually more freely' (*paulatim licentius erupit*) after initial concealment.

13. See Wiedemann (1986), 196; Ross (2016), 68.

14. Discussed earlier, chapter 8.

15. For good examples of storm imagery applied to members of the imperial court, see 28.3.4–5 on Valentinus; 29.3.2 on the emperor Valentinian.

16. See Seager (1986), 48–49, on imagery of rivers and tides, in the context of a broader discussion of Ammianus' interest in many different kinds of excess.

17. However, see Sidwell (2010), 51–57, for the argument that Ammianus tends to differentiate between the negative anger of barbarian forces and more positive manifestations of anger in the Roman army.

18. Compare Kagan (2006), 23–95, for characterisation of Ammianus as a 'face-of-battle' narrator interested in the experience of battle; and Crump (1975), 80–81, on Ammianus' selective approach to topographical description of battles, but also noting a number of exceptions, including the battle at Solicinium discussed here.

19. By contrast, for a successful river crossing by Roman troops, see 24.6.7, with Ratti (2007), 187–88.

20. It has not to my knowledge been treated in relation to that wider theme except in passing; however, for excellent discussion from other perspectives, see Kelly (2004), with 142, n. 3, for a survey of the earlier scholarship.

21. Details at Kelly (2004), 142, n. 3.

22. Compare Kelly (2004), 159–66, for discussion of the metaphorical significance of the passage, among other things in prefiguring the 'flood' of the Gothic invasion, citing Lepelley (1990–91), esp. 364–66, as a precedent.

23. Ammianus' description of the earthquake at Nicomedia, in 17.7, with its vast landslides, has similar implications.

24. See Kelly (2008), 79–87, on this passage, including 83 on possible candidates for the peak from which Ammianus is viewing, and 87 for the argument that Ammianus moves from an eyewitness persona to a historiographical persona in offering these close-up details: 'being a historian involves possessing a sharpness of vision that leads you to being able to see and portray more than simply what you have witnessed'. By contrast Weisweiler (2015), 115–21, argues that Ammianus uses this incident to draw attention to the unreliability of claims to historiographical authority.

25. Other examples of geographical passages where mountains play a prominent role include 14.8, on the eastern provinces, and 22.8 and 27.4 on Thrace, with Sundwall (1996), 628 and 636–37; and more generally Merrills (2005), 6–20, on the intertwining of history and geography in late antiquity.

26. Ammianus has often been in the past viewed as an author with little geographical knowledge or expertise; more recently, however, a number of reassessments have offered more positive views of his geographical digressions: for example, see Drijvers (1999), esp. 171, for brief summary of the history of that debate; also Sundwall (1996), who argues for the sophistication of Ammianus' geographical engagement, but also emphasises its difference from the more strictly cartographic standards of modern geography, given the scarcity of maps in the ancient world.

27. See Kulikowski (2012) for the argument that Book 31 was written separately before being grafted on to the other thirty books; Kelly (2008) for a different view.

28. For example, see Kulikowski (2012), 83–86, on cross-references to the earlier books.

29. See Kulikowski (2012), 86–87, on ways in which the ethnographic digressions on the Huns and the Alans differ from equivalent passage in the earlier books.

30. However, see Kulikowski (2007), 124–26, on the likelihood of oversimplification in Ammianus' account; also den Boeft et al. (2018), 11–13, with further discussion of specific details in the commentary that follows.

31. See Ratti (2007).

32. For reconstruction, see Austin (1979), 75–76; Kulikowski (2007), 138.

33. See Burgersdijk (2016), 122, on Ammianus' use of natural-force imagery in these passages.

34. See Kulikowski (2012), 81–82.

35. Kelly (2007) argues for a pessimistic reading of the ending of Ammianus' work, suggesting that Ammianus takes a negative view of the reign of Theodosius after the end of his narrative; see esp. 231, notes 44 and 45, for an account of the extensive debate over that issue, with further bibliography; and esp. 236–37: 'the final image of the Goths wandering the Balkans at will (*licenter*) depicts a situation which had endured for the dozen or so years before Ammianus wrote. The official line, closely reflected in the panegyrics of Themistius and Pacatus, stressed Theodosius' achievement of peace in 382, and his success in turning the Goths into farmers. Not all were convinced'; also Kelly (2008), 24–29, for discussion along similar lines.

36. For example, Kulikowski (2012), 94–98; Kelly (2007), 238–39, on genocide as a positive alternative.

37. For other studies that emphasise the importance of reading Ammianus intratextually, see Kelly (2008), esp. 214 and Marcos (2015).

Chapter 14. Mountain and City

1. See also earlier, chapter 2.
2. See Williams (2018), 74–80.
3. Jameson (1989) offers a short survey of mountain-city relations in classical Greece.
4. See earlier, chapter 2, with reference especially to Bocchetti (2003) and Williams (2018).
5. See esp. Braudel (1972), esp. 25–53; Shaw (1986) and (1990), with further discussion earlier, in chapter 13; also Leveau (1977), 205, for skepticism about the usefulness of that distinction for Roman north Africa: 'Le thème oppositionel plaine-montagne doit donc être banni de l'étude géographique de la romanité en Afrique du Nord. L'impérialisme romain s'est intéressé aux régions les plus riches, qui n'étaient pas toujours les plaines'.

6. See Shaw (1990), esp. 199–200; Lenski (1999).

7. See Wickham (1988) on medieval Italy; Mathieu (2009) for refutation of the idea of the Alps as underdeveloped and unconnected to the lowlands from 1500–1900; Perlik (2019) on the effects of urbanisation and globalisation on mountain regions in the present; also Anderson (2020) on the way in which the development of mountaineering, especially in the late nineteenth century, was shaped by the urban priorities of its practitioners.

8. See Douglas (2020) on Himalayan history for a good recent example.

9. The journal *Mountain Research and Development*, founded in 1981, has been an important forum for those discussions; see also Price (2015), esp. 43–65.

10. See esp. Shepherd (1977), 76–89, and 80 for this quotation.

11. Campbell (1964).

12. Du Boulay (1974). More recently, see Forbes (2007) on peasant life in Methana in the Peloponnese.

13. That does not mean that we can reconstruct fully or effectively for ancient mountain communities the kind of 'dwelling perspective' that a lot of recent anthropological work on landscape has aimed for, in emphasising the immersion of non-elite human populations in the land they live in and work in: for example, see Ingold (1993) for the notion of 'taskscape' discussed earlier, chapter 1.

14. For a cross-cultural approach to mountain adaptations, see Beaver and Purrington (1984).

15. See the pioneering work of Horden and Purcell (2000), esp. 80–87, on 'Mountains and pastures'; and critique of the oversimplifications of Braudel (1972), at 36–43.

16. See Walsh (2014), 242–79; also Balatti (2017), 303–26, for the Near East.

17. For example, see Walsh (2014), 265–66, on evidence from the Pyrenees; Pelisiak (2018).

18. See Walsh (2014), 244–46, on zonation.

19. For example, see Walsh (2014), esp. 7–8 and 268–79: 'What we see now in the archaeological and palaeoenvironmental data from European, Mediterranean mountains are clear demonstrations of how traditional, environmentally determined hypotheses are untenable. . . . [K]nowledge of, and attitudes towards, these landscapes has fluctuated over time. Furthermore there is little evidence to suggest a diachronic, incremental evolution of such environmental knowledge' (268–69 for this quotation).

20. For example, see Walsh (2014), 255.

21. See Walsh (2014), 246–47.

22. For example, see Walsh (2014), 255, on woodland clearance in the Apennines in the fourth and third millennia BCE.

23. See Rackham (1996), reacting against the oversimplifications of Hughes (1983); Horden and Purcell (2000), 328–41, on the importance of avoiding a simplistic view of catastrophic deforestation, including 331–32, for criticism of standard treatments of the deforestation passage from Plato, *Critias* 110d–111e; Walsh (2014), 6, on the importance of moving beyond a 'Fall from Eden' narrative, which assumes 'the culpability of humanity in the destruction of a once supposedly pristine landscape'; but also Harris (2013b), who convincingly reasserts the idea of a significant degree of deforestation, with a thorough collection of the evidence.

24. See König (forthcoming a) on the importance of understanding the complex and conflicted nature of ancient literary portrayals of environmental damage.

25. See Roy (2009) for more detailed discussion; also Pretzler (2005b) on Arkadian identity, including discussion of the way in which the region's mountainous qualities were sometimes represented positively for the way in which they bred frugality and hardiness.

26. See Jameson (1989), 14–15.

27. See Pretzler (2009) on the development of Arkadian identity in the fourth century BCE and the way in which some Arkadian cities exploited the links with Mount Lykaion and its festival in their coinage.

28. Compare McInerney (2006) on the role played by sanctuaries in enabling the incorporation of border regions into the city's territory.

29. See Jost (1992), 61, with other Arkadian parallels; Belis 1, 58–63, for a thorough survey; also Baleriaux (2017), 150, on the way in which processions to rural shrines acted out a sense of unity and territorial identity, but also on the way in which actual procession into the countryside became less important under Roman rule, with less likelihood of conflict between neighbouring cities, and was replaced by civic versions of those old rituals.

30. See Debarbieux and Rudaz (2015), esp. 45–71; Hollis and König (2021b), 11–12.

31. See Debarbieux and Rudaz (2015), 53–55.

32. See Debarbieux and Rudaz (2015), 54–55.

33. See earlier, chapter 11.

34. See earlier, chapter 10.

35. See Horden and Purcell (2000), 81: 'That explains why mountain zones unexpectedly—and even paradoxically—become regions with wide internal coherence and close contact and interchange across what appear, to the outside, to be formidable physical obstacles'.

36. McInerney (1999).

37. Williamson (2014).

38. See Novičenkova (2008), esp. 287: 'From a modern point of view it seems unlikely that a mountain ridge could unite a population into a single ethnic group instead of splitting it into several distinct segments. Yet our evidence from Antiquity suggests the opposite'.

39. See Osborne (1987), 162–64. See also Rousset (1994) for a comprehensive survey of inscriptions recording confirmation of and arbitration over borders in frontier territory, esp. 117, on the prominence of mountains in these inscriptions; and for general discussion of ancient surveyors' techniques for marking boundaries in the mountain territory, see Campbell (2000), 469–70, and frequent references in the texts Campbell translates (see under *mons* in 'Index of Latin Words,' p. 544, for a full list).

40. For example, see Debarbieux and Rudaz (2015), 45, on friendly agreement between Switzerland and Italy to modify their shared boundary in 2009, and 48–49, for British arbitration in a dispute between Chile and Argentina in 1902.

41. See 'Argaios' in *Lexicon Iconographicum Mythologiae Classicae* 2.1, 584–86.

42. See DeRose Evans (2011) for all of those instances.

43. For example, see Horden and Purcell (2000), esp. 81–82, suggesting that that phenomenon 'makes some of these areas a curious analogue of the sea. Points where the mountains debouch into the coastlands can parallel the significance of great gathering ports' (82); also Roy (1999) for an extensive survey of the evidence for the economy of Arkadia; and McInerney (1999), esp. 40–47, on Mount Parnassos and the region of Phokis.

44. See Osborne (1987).

45. See Lane Fox (1996), but with some qualifications, pointing out for example that hunting is not exclusively a mountain activity for ancient authors.

46. See Columella, *De re rustica* 1.4.10–1.5.2, for both of those advantages; also Cato, *De agricultura* 1.3; and the land-surveying treatise *Casae Litterarum* for numerous examples, translated by Campbell (2000), 232–39.

47. For example, Theophrastus, *History of Plants* 3.3.2. Still useful on the timber trade is Semple (1932), 261–96, drawing heavily on Theophrastus and on a wide range of other authors.

48. See Veal (2013), (2017a), and (2017b); also Olson (1991) for a vivid account of the charcoal-burning industry in classical Attica.

49. See Veal (2013), 38–40.

50. For example, see Purcell (2017b), 89–91; Giorcelli Bersani (2019), 116–20.

51. See Goette (2002).

52. See Fowden (1988).

53. See Langdon (1976), 95, and further discussion earlier, in chapter 1.

54. See Fachard (2017), esp. 37–38, on *polis* control.

55. See Giorcelli Bersani (2019), 112–16, on ownership regulations, including 115–16, on disputes; also Forbes (1996) for modern parallels for dispute over uncultivated land, but also stressing gaps in our knowledge about ancient use-rights.

56. See Horden and Purcell (2000), 130–32.

57. See Thonemann (2011), 239–40: 'The interconnective geography of plains, valleys and roads, would seem at first sight to create natural links between Heraclea and Aphrodisias to the south, Attouda and Laodicea to the north. Yet the Carminii of Attouda chose to pursue their careers at Aphrodisias, not Laodicea; the Heraclean nobility chose to pursue theirs at Laodicea, not Tabai or Aphrodisias. In both cases, small-town elites undertake their municipal careers not in the nearest big city, but in the city on the far side of a substantial mountain range'.

58. See Cole (2000).

59. See Fachard (2017), 54.

60. See Purcell (2017b), 82–87 and 99–101; and Roy (1999), 346–49, on mercenaries from Arkadia.

61. See Walsh (2014), 268–79, on variations in the degree of 'porosity' in mountain regions.

62. See Mathieu (2011), 81–82.

63. See Shaw (1986), 79, n. 58, with reference to Leveau (1984) on survey evidence for the influence of Roman rule over the economic landscape of the mountains of Mauretania.

64. See Novičenkova (2008), 295–98.

65. *Corpus Inscriptionum Latinarum* XIII, 38, with discussion by Purcell (2017b), 90.

66. On the evidence from Varro, see Garnsey (1998), 201.

67. On the evidence from the Biferno valley, see Barker et al. (1978), esp. 46–48.

68. See Horden and Purcell (2000), 85; Halstead (1987), esp. 79–81, stressing the dangers of being misled by modern comparisons into assuming widespread transhumance in antiquity; also Skydsgaard (1988) and Georgoudi (1974) for surveys of the evidence.

69. See Barker (1989), 13; Garnsey (1998), 178.

70. See Garnsey (1998).

71. On the mixed farming of the Apennines, see Dench (1995), 111–25.

72. See Horden and Purcell (2000), 'there is nothing in any sense of the word primitive about pastoralism. It is subsequent to agriculture on any evolutionary time-scale: the agriculturalist was the first to domesticate animals'; Thonemann (2011), 197: 'specialised animal husbandry is only possible in the context of a relatively sophisticated market economy, which is able to support a distinct and dedicated pastoral class. Far from being a relic of a primitive, pre-agricultural mode of production, specialised pastoralism is in fact most often an offshoot of an agricultural economy at an advanced stage of development'.

73. See Thonemann (2011), 197–202, on the varieties of transhumance in the Maeander Valley region and the way in which medium-range transhumance involved complex networking.

74. See Georgoudi (1974), 173–81.

75. For example, see Dyson (1985), 88, on agreement about pasturage rights between Genoa and the Ligurians, in the so-called Tabula Polcevera, *Corpus Inscriptionum Latinarum* V, 7749, lines 32–35.

76. See Horden and Purcell (2000), 131.

77. Campbell (1964), 8.

78. See Cabanes (1992) on the complexity of pastoral practices and social organisation in the Pindos mountains in ancient northwest Greece, including discussion of *ethnos* organisation and summer interaction; McInerney (1999), 92–100, for a nuanced sketch of pastoralism in Phokis and its close co-existence with agriculture, as part of a wider argument about the influence of landscape and settlement patterns on the importance of affiliation to the Phokian *ethnos*.

79. On agreements between cities for reciprocal or shared use of pasture and related disputes, esp. *Hellenica Oxyrhynchia* 13.3, see Robert (1949), 152–60 ('Épitaphe d'un berger à Thasos'), esp. 155–57.

80. See McInerney (1999), 105–6.

81. See Robert (1965), 99–100; Robert and Robert (1983), 101–9; Fachard (2017), 40–41; also Robert (1937), 96, for *orophylakes* killed by brigands, and 108–10, for a vivid account of epigraphical evidence for border controls in another region of Mount Parnassos, involving a dedication to Pan and the Nymphs at the Korykian Cave by a troupe of border guards from the city of Ambryssos.

82. See Mack (2015); also Thonemann (2011), 196–97, for the Mykale inscription in the wider context of pastoralism in the region.

83. Translation by Mack (2015), 63–64.

84. See Thonemann (2011), 291, and Mack (2015), 53–54, on the relationship between Thebes and Miletos.

85. See Mack (2015), 66.

86. See Mack (2015), 66–67. For context, see Robert (1949), who offers a survey of mentions of shepherds in Greek epigraphy.

87. For conflict between Samos and Priene over Mount Mykale, see Thonemann (2011), 28–29, with further bibliography in n. 73, and 281–82.

88. Pausanias, *Periegesis* 5.7.5, with Thonemann (2011), 291, n. 147.

89. Mack (2015), 68–69, argues that the boundary decree is aimed at an internal audience within the city of Thebes.

90. On these two passages, see Georgoudi (1974), 167–70. That count does not include references to long-distance transhumance like the passage from Varro, *De re rustica* 2.2.9, already discussed earlier.

91. See further discussion earlier, chapter 12, n. 5, in relation to Strabo.
92. For example, see Buxton (2013), 20.
93. Plato quotes from *Odyssey* 9.112–15 at *Laws* 680b.
94. See Walsh (2014), 267, on the limitations of an evolutionary model in mountain history generally.
95. See Purcell (2017b), 101.
96. Nowicki (1999).
97. See earlier, chapter 1.
98. See Haggis (1999).
99. See Chaniotis (1995) and (1999b), esp. 192, on 'the interdependence between specialized pastoralism and specific demographic and sociopolitical conditions'; also further discussion of the economic importance of the Cretan mountains in Chaniotis (1991) and (1996a).
100. See Chaniotis (1999b), 198–99.
101. See Chaniotis (1999b), 199.
102. See Chaniotis (1996b), no. 5 B 33–68; translation from Chaniotis (1999b), 198.
103. See Chaniotis (1999b), 198.
104. See Chaniotis (1999b), 199–201.
105. See Chaniotis (1999b), 201–2.
106. See Chaniotis (1995), 70–71.
107. See Chaniotis (1999b), 202–5.
108. See also earlier, chapter 4.
109. See Nightingale (1993), 282–83.
110. Later in the dialogue, in a conversation about how to design athletic contests, the Athenian suggests that for one of the races 'an archer dressed in full archer's equipment will compete in a race of 100 stades to a temple of Apollo and Artemis through mountains and variable terrain' (833b).
111. Chaniotis (1999b), 208.
112. See Morrow (1960), 27–28, choosing between the three possible 'caves of Zeus' within walking distance of Knossos.

Chapter 15. Dio Chrysostom and the Mountains of Euboia

1. Williams (1973), emphasizing the way in which that idea has been used to justify and naturalise a range of social and political developments. See also Cronon (1991), who charts the ways in which the city of Chicago was intertwined with the countryside of the American West.
2. Cronon (1991), 17.
3. See Rosen and Sluiter (2006) for a collection of essays that discuss ways in which the city-country dichotomy was both reinforced and undermined in ancient Greek and Roman literature.
4. This chapter is a revised and expanded version of König (2019).
5. See Jones (1978), 135.
6. See Russell (1992), 9–13, on the connections between the two halves of the work and on the likelihood that the text as it survives is not an exact reflection of the speech as originally delivered.
7. See du Boulay (1974).

8. See Wickens et al. (2018), 29–30 and 61–66; compare Alcock (1993), 39.

9. See Goette (2012).

10. See Alcock (1993), 29–30, for careful discussion of that problem for Dio; also Day (1950), for an extensive survey of the evidence for the economy of Euboia, concluding that Dio's portrayal of decline is not a good reflection of conditions on the ground.

11. Compare Ma (2000), who argues along similar lines for Dio's representation of political culture in the Greek cities of the Roman Empire in this work.

12. See Anderson (2020), esp. 145, on nineteenth-century attempts to preserve traditional Alpine customs: 'Only by keeping the Alpenvolk poor, naïve and primitive could they provide the necessary "magic" to the emotionally impoverished urban tourist'; Huggan and Tiffin (2010), 66–69, for more general reflection on the way in which modern practices of 'ecotourism' tend to 'fetishise local communities' (68); Clark (2019), 140; and further discussion later of the characterisation of mountain populations as ancient.

13. See Russell (1992), 110, citing *Odyssey* 1.3.

14. At any rate that is what this kind of geographical detail seems to imply in one very similar later passage, where Philostratus (*Lives of the Sophists* 2.1, 552–54) describes Agathion, a rustic figure from the centre of Greece, who was an object of fascination for the sophist Herodes Atticus, and who is represented as a relic of the ancient Greek past. On this passage from Dio, see Whitmarsh (2001), 105–8; also Brunt (1973) on the Stoic origins of Dio's thinking, esp. 153–54, on his tendency to favour rural morality, following Xenophon.

15. A reference to the Homeric description of the Euboians as 'having long hair at the back' in *Iliad* 2.542.

16. See Debarbieux and Rudaz (2010), 31.

17. See Debarbieux and Rudaz (2010), 31, with reference to the work of Onésime Reclus, in the late nineteenth/early twentieth century.

18. See Anderson (2020), 139–74, which takes account of all those different strands in analysing urban engagement with Alpine communities in nineteenth-century mountaineering culture, esp. 140: 'Yet urbanites' application of the past to the countryside did more work than simply affirming their own modernities. By insisting on a temporal distance between their own lives and those who lived in the places through which they moved, walkers and mountaineers justified their anthropological gaze over rural people.... In England, Germany and Austria, often well-meaning urban people valorised rural communities, but in doing so, they appropriated their voices, categorised and prescribed their identities, judged their status against their own as modern individuals, and as we saw in the last chapter, wrote them out of narratives of "progress" in the mountains'.

19. See Simpson (2019).

20. See Alcock (1993), 87–88.

21. See Snyder (1990) for a cross-cultural study of the idea of the 'commons'.

22. Compare earlier, chapter 14.

23. See Horden and Purcell (2000), 204.

24. See Liddell-Scott-Jones, *A Greek-English Lexicon*, s.v. μεταμανθάνω, p. 1114.

25. At least in that respect Dio's description here is close to that of Plato, who similarly describes the primitive post-flood populations as harmonious and lacking in deceit: *Laws* 3, 678c–679c.

26. See Russell (1992), 127 and 130.

27. Compare earlier, chapter 14.

28. See Hughes (1996) for a reading along these lines.

29. On the literary texture of the work, see among others Highet (1973), on the influence of New Comedy, and Jouan (1977).

30. For example, see Alciphron, *Letters* 1.3.2 and 2.11, for good examples of pale, barefoot, impractical philosophers described from the perspective of country dwellers.

31. Compare König (2009), 54–55, for more detailed discussion of that paradox.

32. See Desideri (2000), 99–101, on the role of these scenes in Dio's broader critique of urban life.

33. See Hughes (1996), 97–98, on the land tenure regulations underlying the narrative.

34. See earlier, chapter 14.

35. See Day (1951).

36. See Hughes (1996), 97–98.

37. See Jones (1978), 59.

38. See earlier, n. 20.

39. Compare Corbier (1991), 226: 'Most cities had at their disposal a public domain which brought them revenue, but which the notables (who could guarantee its management) tended to monopolise or sell for private profit; the preservation or recovery of this land, to protect the financial interests of cities, was one of the major preoccupations of central government'.

40. See esp. Dio's use of the words καρπουμένων, κατανέμουσι, and ἔχοντες in the passage quoted earlier from 27–28, with Fachard (2017), 26: 'The verb ἔστι + genitive indicates ownership, while verbs like ἔχω, νέμομαι, and καρπίζομαι indicate possession or exploitation without implying lawful ownership'.

41. See Alcock (1993), 85–86 and 91, on the way in which less productive, marginal land would sometimes be recategorised as *agri deserti* in order to be shed as a tax liability; also Jones (1978), 58, on the way in which 'economic decline seems to have been accompanied by a widening of social divisions' in the unnamed city of the *Euboian Oration*.

42. See Bryen (2019), 132, with further bibliography and a list of key epigraphical sources at n. 9; also Alcock (1993), 91; Russell (1992), 120–21; Jones (1978), 60; and Galimberti (2013) for reflections on the kinds of agrarian reform Dio envisages here, against the background of difficult economic conditions in Roman Greece.

43. Compare Huggan and Tiffin (2010), 71–72, for a parallel from modern fiction: 'Development is largely filtered in the novel through economistic myths of progress. . . . At the heart of the community's objections to the development plans is the right to control use of their own land, but also important is the need to protect the commons'.

44. See Bryen (2019); also Russell (1992), 116–17: 'But the situation is hardly clear. If the land belonged to the rich man whose property had been confiscated, it would presumably have gone to the *fiscus* or *patrimonium Caesaris* [in other words effectively as possessions of the emperor]. How did the city have a claim on it?' The process by which public land was absorbed into imperial control, and sometimes then reallocated to elite, private owners itself led to increasing inequality in access to border lands: see Veal (2017a), 347–48.

45. See Jones (1978), 60; Russell (1992), 123.

46. See earlier, chapter 14, n. 60.

47. See Bryen (2019), 131, esp. n. 8.

48. Compare Hughes (1996), 89.

49. Compare Whitmarsh (2004), 460–63, on Dio's shifting persona in this work: 'In the course of the narrative, the role of the internal narrator "Dio" shifts from that of translator of an unfamiliar world—that is, a townsman interpreting the country for townsmen—to that of apologist for rustic values' (462).

50. See earlier, chapter 5.

51. See Corbier (1991), 221, on this passage and on the city's tax obligations as a key factor in Dio's positive representation of its territory; also 225–26: 'Disputes might also concern grazing land, water-springs, wasteland or scrub. . . . [I]n colonies the land which the surveyors left out of the centuriated zone was of considerable value in Mediterranean countries where the use of *saltus*, uncultivated land, was necessary for the pasturing of herds, or for acorns for the pigs to graze, let along the gathering of wild fruits'; and 238, on the way in which 'Roman taxation tended to reinforce the power of towns over their surrounding countryside'.

52. See Russell (1992), 140, on the way in which this echoes Plato's 'imaginary city-founding', with reference to the *Republic* rather than the *Laws*.

53. In that sense we might even view the transition between the two halves of the work—which looks so awkward and disjointed to modern eyes—in positive terms, as a good example of the way in which ancient literature was comfortable with moving sometimes quite abruptly between different geographical scales, using local problems as a way into thinking about global or universal challenges: see Ghosh (2016) among others, and further discussion earlier, in the preface, on the way in which modern fiction often struggles to articulate the global scale of our current environmental crisis, because of its focus on the local and the individual.

Chapter 16. Mountain Saints in Late Antique Christian Literature

1. See now Whalin (2021) on mountains and late antique hagiography; and for the later Byzantine material, della Dora (2016a), 147–75.

2. See Cadell and Rémondon (1967); also Hedstrom (2017), 121–22, on the use of the word 'mountain' (*toou*) in Coptic to mean 'monastery'.

3. For a vivid account of the harsh landscape of the Egyptian desert as a venue for ascetic withdrawal, and its power as a symbol of separateness from human civilisation, see Brown (2008), 213–40.

4. For further treatment of fourth- and fifth-century hagiography along similar lines, but with special reference to representations of fasting rather than landscape, see König (2012), 323–51, stressing especially the way in which ascetics, as they are represented in these texts, appropriated practices usually associated with social marginality.

5. See Hedstrom (2017), 140–41 and 168; and related discussion earlier, in chapter 4; also Theodoret, *Religious History* 3.1, for acknowledgement of the biblical precedents, with reference to Elijah and John the Baptist, and to Hebrews 11:37–38.

6. See Hedstrom (2017), 142–45.

7. Diogenes Laertius, *Lives and Opinions of the Eminent Philosophers* 9.1.3.

8. Brown (2008), li–liv, acknowledges, in the second edition of his influential book *The Body and Society*, that the original edition may have underestimated the degree to which the separateness of the desert is partly an imaginative construct of the writers of the early saints' lives.

9. For example, see Hedstrom (2017).

10. For the move from solitary to communal asceticism, both within the history of monasticism and often in the lives of individual ascetics, see Rousseau (1978), 33–55.

11. For example, see Rousseau (1985), 149–73, on the close relationship between Pachomius' monastic community, at Tabennesi in Egypt, and the surrounding community.

12. See Goehring (1999), esp. 45–52.

13. See Rousseau (1978), 56–67.

14. On Palestinian monasticism, see Binns (1994), esp. 79–147, on links between ascetics and the city.

15. See Binns (1994), 142–47, on Scythopolis.

16. See Cronon (1995); also Morton (2007) for related critique of the category of 'nature' within environmental discourse; Clark (2019), 31–37, on the impulse to move beyond fetishisation of 'nature' and the 'natural' in recent ecocriticism, with reference to concepts of wilderness at 32 and 37.

17. For example, see Urbainczyk (2002), 85, on athletic metaphors in Theodoret, who uses them particularly frequently.

18. On this tension between the alienness of the past and its status as a resource for environmental thinking in the present, see Burrus (2019), 1–2, citing Schliephake (2017b), 4.

19. See discussion of Simpson (2019), in chapter 15, earlier, in relation to Dio; also Hollis and König (2021b), 8–10.

20. See Buxton (2013), 20–21, and further discussion earlier, in chapter 1.

21. See more detailed discussion earlier, in chapter 4.

22. See della Dora (2016a), 162–65.

23. See Athanasius, *Life of Antony* 8–11, for the foundational example.

24. See Whalin (2021), 89 and 104–5, on Saint Thekla's campaign against pagan mountain shrines associated with Apollo and Athene.

25. For mountains as places of performance, defined broadly to include ritual in a range of historical contexts as well as in modern artistic and mountaineering cultures, see Pitches (2020).

26. See White (1967), discussed already earlier, preface, n. 30, and Burrus (2019), 2–4 in response.

27. See Burrus (2019), esp. 106–10, 128–35, and 140–42.

28. See Adler (2006).

29. For example, see Brockliss (2018a) on the pessimism inherent in many ancient accounts of that phenomenon, with further discussion earlier, in chapter 2.

30. Augustine, *Confessions* 8.6.14–15.

31. See della Dora (2016a), 126, on the way in which the geography of the *Life of Antony* sets it apart from earlier accounts of Christian asceticism; compare Hedstrom (2017), 147, although pointing out that the concrete details of the landscape were of little interest to Athanasius.

32. For the distinction between the 'outer desert', close to and even visible from the towns and villages of Egypt, and the more remote 'inner desert', see Hedstrom (2017), 81–82.

33. See Burrus (2019), 100–102, for eloquent discussion along those lines.

34. See Hedstrom (2017), 178, for discussion.

35. See also *Lausiac History* 20 for the mountain of Perme in Egypt, which Palladius tells us is home to 500 ascetics.

36. In other texts there is some self-consciousness about the risk that Nitria's high population will be incompatible with ascetic devotion: see Hedstrom (2017), 156, for the tradition that the monastery at Kellia was founded, by an ascetic called Amoun, as a retreat from the bustle of Mount Nitria.

37. See Urbainczyk (2002), 40–51, on Theodoret's relationship with earlier hagiography.

38. See Price (1985), xvii–xxiii.

39. See Finn (2009), 137.

40. See Price (1985), xx: 'Significant too is their location on frequented routes; contact with the outside world seems to have been cultivated rather than shunned'. Urbainczyk (2002), esp. 115–29, argues that Theodoret is interested in challenging standard perceptions of the Syrian monks as inhabitants of the wild places outside human culture, and in showing show that the Syrian holy men are ultimately under clerical control, in an attempt to bolster his own authority in the theological struggles between Antiochene and Alexandrian Christianity: 'Theodoret wanted to show that he was an extraordinary bishop with an army of remarkable monks behind him, the equal of any Egyptian. To the upper classes of these big cities these were wild men from the Syrian mountains. To Theodoret they were devoted and loyal' (9).

41. For other mountain dwellings near to towns and villages, see 11.1, 12.2, 18.1, 21.4, 23.2.

42. Compare *Religious History* 6.4, on Symeon the Elder, who settles on Mount Amanos (the same mountain as Theodosius) and displaces the pagan worship there.

43. Other examples include Eusebius of Asikha, who lives on a mountain ridge in the open air, and is 'frozen in winter and burnt by the sun' (18.1); Maris, whose hut is flooded by water from the local mountain (20.1); and John, who lives for 25 years on a 'jagged ridge, prone to storms and northward-facing' (23.1).

44. See Urbainczyk (2002), 80–88, on the tension between isolation and engagement in Theodoret.

45. See Price (1985), xxvii–xxix, on holy men as mediators in the *Religious History* and more widely.

46. Price (1985), 57, identifies this with the plain of Dana, 'dominated by Mount Barakat, on which had stood the great shrine of the semitic deities Zeus Malbachos and Salamanes'.

47. Compare Kleinkopf (2017) for extensive discussion of the way in which Theodoret's saints embed themselves in the landscapes they inhabit.

48. See Morgan (2015).

49. Compare brief discussion earlier, in chapter 4.

50. On 'hermit cells . . . set under cliff overhangs' around Mount Sinai, see Patrich (2015), 437, in the context of a discussion of the archaeological evidence for monastic dwellings in the region at 435–9.

51. For translation of this passage (slightly adapted for my own version here) and commentary, see Caner (2010), 121, esp. nn. 79 and 80.

52. Extract from *P.Colt.* 89, in Kraemer (1958) 251–60; the translation here is from Caner (2010) 267–68, who reproduces Kraemer's original translation with minor alterations.

53. See Ward (2015) on the use of negative stereotyping of the Saracen population around Mount Sinai, by Pseudo-Nilus and many others, including demonisation of their pastoral culture, as a means of reinforcing Christian control.

54. See Ward (2015), 17–41.

55. See König (2012), 306–7.

56. See Wood (2009), 132–33; Shaw (1990), 245–46; Johnson (2006), 123–30 and 130–35, stressing among other things the way in which Thekla is presented as having a natural affiliation with the region, in contrast with the pagan gods, who are represented as temporary interlopers: she is 'reconquering her homeland' (125); also earlier, n. 24, on discussion of this text by Whalin (2021), focusing on Christian appropriation of mountain holy sites associated with pre-Christian religion.

57. See Halkin (1985) for Greek text and French translation.

58. See Wood (2009), 134–36.

59. See Shaw (1990), 246–48.

60. On John of Ephesus and Symeon the Mountaineer, see Harvey (1990), esp. 95–97, arguing that Symeon's actions are typical of John's tendency to see missionary work as a part of the ascetic vocation.

61. All translations and page numbers are from *Patrologia orientalis* 17. For other ascetics in the mountains in this text see pp. 57, 161, 296–97, and 301.

62. Compare Estes (2017), 89–117, on the relevance of approaches from postcolonial ecocriticism to Anglo-Saxon hagiography, with its narratives of colonial and environmental dominance.

63. See also Symeon's speech on p. 238, which they respond to uncomprehendingly 'like some irrational animal': 'Wherefore, when God formed us in his image, do we on our part live animal lives outside the orderliness of men? Know you not that you are men, and not animals? Know you not that even the animals have a greater blessing than you? . . . Wherefore then do you make yourselves like the animals on the mountains?'

64. See earlier, n. 27, on Burrus (2019).

65. Compare Huggan and Tiffin (2010), esp. 6, for modern parallels.

66. See König (2017) for an earlier version of the section following.

67. See König (2012), 342, on this passage.

68. See König (2020) for more extensive discussion of these passages in relation to the challenges of representing solitude in ancient biography.

69. On Jerome's time as an ascetic in Syria, see Kelly (1975), 46–56; Rebenich (2002), 13–17; Koelb (2021), 112–17.

70. See Williams (2008), 125–36.

71. On Jerome's *Life of Hilarion* and its relationship with Apuleius' *Metamorphoses*, see Weingarten (2005), 81–163, esp. 94–97, on the mountain homes of Antony and Hilarion in the *Life of Hilarion*, stressing both their allegorical, paradisiacal connotations and also their close relationship with Apuleius' landscapes.

72. See König (2017) for further discussion of that possibility.

73. See Burrus (2019), 104–5, on the way in which Jerome, in this passage and also in his *Life of Paul of Thebes* 5–6, re-asserts the luxuriousness of the saintly *locus amoenus* in response to the equivalent scene in the *Life of Antony*; also Burrus (2004), 42–45, incorporating discussion of *Life of Hilarion* 31 in addition.

74. See also Weingarten (2005), 96–97, on close verbal parallels with the hostile landscape of the entrance to Hades in Apuleius, *Metamorphoses* 6.13–14.

75. Compare Weingarten (2005), 31–32, on similar paradise imagery in Jerome's *Life of Paul of Thebes*.

76. See Weingarten (2005), 96.

77. See Weingarten (2005), 145–52, on these scenes.

78. However, see Koelb (2021) and Jordan (2021) on the continuing attraction in the post-classical world of the models of mountain retreat that we find in late antique hagiography.

Epilogue

1. Corrie is the Scottish word for a cirque, an amphitheatre-like valley carved out of the mountainside by a glacier; Munros are Scottish mountains over 3,000 feet.

2. See Hansen (2013).

3. See Ellis (2001).

4. See Bainbridge (2012) and (2013).

5. See Cosgrove (1984).

6. See McNee (2016).

7. See Anderson (2020), 139–74.

8. See Simpson (2019); Anderson (2020).

9. Discussed in many of the chapters in part 2 of Musa et al. (2017), with summary in the introduction, Higham et al. (2017), 11.

10. Compare Schaumann (2020), 5–6, for interesting comments on the way in which 'recent theories of material ecocriticism allow us to conceptualize mountaineering as an intimate exchange between the human and more-than-human world' (5), and 197–203, on the role of vulnerability in modern mountaineering literature.

11. For example, see Mitchell (1998); Baker (2014) and (2020).

12. See Hollis and König (2021b); and compare discussion earlier, in the preface.

13. I have learned a lot from Jonathan Westaway's not-yet-published work on that topic; see also Westaway (2009), 591, for brief preliminary discussion along those lines in relation to late nineteenth-century British and German mountaineering.

14. See Pitches (2020).

15. Compare Lorimer and Lund (2016) on Munro-baggers looking from summits at other peaks they have climbed.

16. See della Dora (2008) and König (2021).

17. Philip V of Macedon famously discovered that on Mount Haimos, according to Livy's account: see Livy 40.21.2–22.5, and further discussion earlier, chapter 11, n. 65.

18. See Price (2015), esp. 116–18.

BIBLIOGRAPHY

Accorinti, Domenico (2010). 'La montagna e il sacro nel mondo greco', in Alessandro Grossato (ed.), *La montagna cosmica*, Milan: Medusa, 17–42.

Adams, Colin, and Jim Roy (eds.) (2007). *Travel, Geography and Culture in Ancient Greece, Egypt and the Near East*, Oxford: Oxbow Books.

Adler, Judith (2006). 'Cultivating wilderness: environmentalism and legacies of early Christian asceticism', *Comparative Studies in Society and History* 48: 4–37.

Aguirre, Mercedes, and Richard Buxton (2020). *Cyclops: The Myth and Its Cultural History*, Oxford: Oxford University Press.

Akujärvi, Johanna (2005). *Researcher, Traveller, Narrator: Studies in Pausanias' Periegesis*, Stockholm: Almqvist and Wiksell International.

Alcock, Susan E. (1993). *Graecia Capta: The Landscapes of Roman Greece*, Cambridge: Cambridge University Press.

Alcock, Susan E. (1994). 'Minding the gap in Hellenistic and Roman Greece', in Alcock and Osborne (1994), 247–62.

Alcock, Susan E. (1996). 'Landscapes of memory and the authority of Pausanias', in Jean Bingen (ed.), *Pausanias historien*, Entretiens sur l'antiquité classique 41, Geneva: Fondation Hardt, 241–76.

Alcock, Susan E., John Cherry, and Jaś Elsner (eds.) (2001). *Pausanias: Travel and Memory in Roman Greece*, New York: Oxford University Press.

Alcock, Susan E., and Robin Osborne (eds.) (1994). *Placing the Gods: Sanctuaries and Sacred Space in Ancient Greece*, Oxford: Clarendon Press.

Almagor, Eran (2005). 'Who is a barbarian? The barbarians in the ethnological and cultural taxonomies of Strabo', in Dueck et al. (2005), 42–55.

Alter, Robert (2019). *The Hebrew Bible. Volume II: Prophets, Nevi'im. A Translation with Commentary*, New York: W. W. Norton and Company.

Amandry, Pierre (1981a). 'L'Antre corycien dans les textes antiques et modernes', in *Bulletin de correspondance hellénique*, Supplément 7: 29–54.

Amandry, Pierre (1981b). 'L'exploration archéologique de la grotte', in *Bulletin de correspondance hellénique*, Supplément 7: 75–93.

Amandry, Pierre (1984). 'Le culte des Nymphes et de Pan à l'Antre corycien', in *Bulletin de correspondance hellénique*, Supplément 9: 395–425.

Anders, Adam (2015). 'Are you (Ro)man enough? Non-Roman *virtus* in the Roman army', in Geoff Lee, Helen Whittaker, and Graham Wrightson (eds.), *Ancient Warfare: Introducing*

Current Research, Volume I, Newcastle upon Tyne: Cambridge Scholars Publishing, 291–308.
Anderson, Ben (2020). *Cities, Mountains and Being Modern in Fin-de-Siècle England and Germany*, London: Palgrave Macmillan.
Andersson, Theodore M. (1976). *Early Epic Scenery: Homer, Virgil, and the Medieval Legacy*, Ithaca, NY: Cornell University Press.
Andrews, Malcolm (1989). *The Search for the Picturesque: Landscape Aesthetics and Tourism in Britain, 1760–1800*, Aldershot: Scolar.
Andrews, Malcolm (1999). *Landscape and Western Art*, Oxford: Oxford University Press.
Aravantinos, Vassilis (1996). 'Topographical and archaeological investigations on the summit of Helicon', in Hurst and Schachter (1996), 185–92.
Argoud, Gilbert (1996). 'L'Hélicon et la littérature grecque', in Hurst and Schachter (1996), 27–42.
Armbruster, Karla, and Kathleen R. Wallace (eds.) (2001). *Beyond Nature Writing: Expanding the Boundaries of Ecocriticism*, Charlottesville: University of Virginia Press.
Armstrong, Rebecca (2019). *Vergil's Green Thoughts: Plants, Human, and the Divine*, Oxford: Oxford University Press.
Artru, François (2016). *Sur les routes romaines des Alpes Cottiennes entre Mont-Cenis et col de Larche*, Besançon: Presses universitaires de Franche-Comté.
Auerbach, Erich (1953). *Mimesis: The Representation of Reality in Western Literature* (tr. W. R. Trask; first published in German in 1946), Princeton, NJ: Princeton University Press.
Austin, N.J.E. (1979). *Ammianus on Warfare: An Investigation into Ammianus' Military Knowledge*, Brussels: Collection Latomus.
Bainbridge, Simon (2012). 'Romantic writers and mountaineering', *Romanticism* 18: 1–15.
Bainbridge, Simon (2013). 'Writing from "the perilous ridge": Romanticism and the invention of rock climbing', *Romanticism* 19: 246–60.
Bainbridge, Simon (2020). *Mountaineering and British Romanticism: The Literary Cultures of Climbing, 1770–1836*, Oxford: Oxford University Press.
Bainbridge, William (2020). *Topographic Memory and Victorian Travellers in the Dolomite Mountains: Peaks of Venice*, Amsterdam: Amsterdam University Press.
Baker, Patrick (2014). *The Cairngorms: A Secret History*, Edinburgh: Birlinn.
Baker, Patrick (2020). *The Unremembered Places: Exploring Scotland's Wild Histories*, Edinburgh: Birlinn.
Bakhtin, M. M. (1981). *The Dialogic Imagination: Four Essays by M. M. Bakhtin* (ed. Michael Holquist; tr. Caryl Emerson and Michael Holquist), Austin: University of Texas Press.
Balatti, Silvia (2017). *Mountain Peoples in the Ancient Near East: The Case of the Zagros in the First Millennium BCE*, Wiesbaden: Harrassowitz Verlag.
Baleriaux, Julie (2017). 'Pausanias' Arkadia between conservatism and innovation', in Greta Hawes (ed.), *Myths on the Map: The Storied Landscapes of Ancient Greece*, Oxford: Oxford University Press, 141–58.
Balmuth, Miriam S., David K. Chester, and Patricia A. Johnston (eds.) (2005). *Cultural Responses to the Volcanic Landscape*, Boston: Archaeological Institute of America.
Baragwanath, Emily (2008). *Motivation and Narrative in Herodotus*, Oxford: Oxford University Press.

Barker, Graeme (1989). 'The archaeology of the Italian shepherd', *Proceedings of the Cambridge Philological Society* 35: 1–19.

Barker, Graeme, John Lloyd, and Derrick Webley (1978). 'A classical landscape in Molise', *Papers of the British School at Rome* 46: 35–51.

Barnes, Timothy D. (1998). *Ammianus Marcellinus and the Representation of Historical Reality*, Ithaca, NY: Cornell University Press.

Barton, William (2017). *Mountain Aesthetics in Early Modern Latin Literature*, Abingdon: Routledge.

Bates, Robert H. (2000). *Mystery, Beauty and Danger: The Literature of the Mountains and Mountain Climbing Published before 1946*, Portsmouth, NH: Peter E. Randall.

Bayers, Peter L. (2003). *Mountaineering, Masculinity, and Empire*, Boulder: University of Colorado Press.

Beaver, Patricia D., and Burton L. Purrington (eds.) (1984). *Cultural Adaptation to Mountain Environments*, Athens: University of Georgia Press.

Becchi, Francesco (2014). 'Plutarch, Aristotle, and the Peripatetics', in Beck (2014a), 73–87.

Beck, Mark (ed.) (2014a). *A Companion to Plutarch*, Malden, MA: Wiley Blackwell.

Beck, Mark (2014b). 'Introduction', in Beck (2014a), 1–9.

Belis, Alexis (2015). 'Fire on the mountain: a comprehensive study of Greek mountaintop sanctuaries' (2 volumes), PhD dissertation, Princeton University.

Benson, Geoffrey C. (2019). *Apuleius' Invisible Ass: Encounters with the Unseen in the Metamorphoses of Apuleius*, Cambridge: Cambridge University Press.

Bergmann, Bettina (1991). 'Painted perspectives of a villa visit: landscape as status and metaphor', in Elaine K. Gazda (ed.), *Roman Art in the Private Sphere: New Perspectives on the Architecture and Decor of the Domus, Villa, and Insula*, Ann Arbor: University of Michigan Press, 49–70.

Bergmann, Bettina (1999). 'Rhythms of recognition: mythological encounters in Roman landscape painting', in Francesco de Angelis and Susanne Muth (eds.), *Im Spiegel des Mythos: Bilderwelt und Lebenswelt*, Palilia 6, Wiesbaden: Deutsches Archäologishes Institut Rom, 81–107.

Bergmann, Bettina (2001). 'Commentary. Meanwhile, back in Italy . . . : creating landscapes of allusion', in Alcock et al. (2001), 154–66.

Berman, Daniel W. (2010). 'The landscape and language of Korinna', *Greek, Roman and Byzantine Studies* 50: 41–62.

Bernbaum, Edwin (1998). *Sacred Mountains of the World*, Berkeley: University of California Press.

Bersani, Silvia Giorcelli (2019). *L'impero in quota: I Romani e le Alpi*, Torino: Einaudi.

Binns, John (1994). *Ascetics and Ambassadors of Christ: The Monasteries of Palestine, 314–631*, Oxford: Oxford University Press.

Bocchetti, Carla (2003). 'Cultural geography in Homer', *Eras Journal* 5: 1–30.

Bonnafé, Annie (1984). *Poésie, nature et sacré. L'age archaique*, Lyon: Maison de l'Orient et de la Méditerranée Jean Pouilloux.

Borca, Federico (2002). *Horridi montes: Ambiente e uomini di montagna visti dai Gallo-Romani*, Aosta: Keltia editrice.

Bosak-Schroeder, Clara (2020). *Other Natures: Environmental Encounters with Ancient Greek Ethnography*, Oakland: University of California Press.

Boschi, Alessandro (2016). '*Quis ille? Saturninus sum*: l'enigma della *prosapia* nel prologo delle *Metamorfosi* di Apuleio', *Prometheus* 42: 144–62.
Bradbury, Scott (1995). 'Julian's pagan revival and the decline of blood sacrifice', *Phoenix* 49: 331–56.
Bradbury, Scott (2004). *Selected Letters of Libanius: From the Age of Constantius and Julian*, Liverpool: Liverpool University Press.
Bradley, Richard (2000). *An Archaeology of Natural Places*, London: Routledge.
Bradley, Keith (2000). 'Animalizing the slave: the truth of fiction', *Journal of Roman Studies* 90: 110–25.
Braudel, Fernand (1972). *The Mediterranean and the Mediterranean World in the Age of Philip II*, volume I (tr. Siân Reynolds; first published in French in 1949), London: Collins.
Braund, David (2005). 'Greek geography and the Roman Empire: the transformation of tradition in Strabo's Euxine', in Dueck et al. (2005), 216–34.
Bray, Chloe (2021). 'Mountains of memory: a phenomenological approach to mountains in fifth-century BCE Greek tragedy', in Hollis and König (2021a), 185–96.
Breeze, David J. (2011). *The Frontiers of Imperial Rome*, Barnsley: Pen and Sword Military.
Bremmer, Jan (1984). 'Greek maenadism reconsidered', *Zeitschrift für Papyrologie und Epigraphik* 55: 267–86.
Bridges, Emma (2015). *Imagining Xerxes: Ancient Perspectives on a Persian King*, London: Bloomsbury.
Brillet-Dubois, Pascale (2011). 'An erotic *aristeia*: the *Homeric Hymn to Aphrodite* and its relation to the Iliadic tradition', in Faulkner (2011a), 105–32.
Brockliss, William (2018a). '"Dark ecology" and the *Works and Days*', *Helios* 45: 1–36.
Brockliss, William (2018b). 'Abject landscapes of the *Iliad*', in Debbie Felton (ed.) (2018). *Landscapes of Dread in Classical Antiquity: Negative Emotion in Natural and Constructed Spaces*, London: Routledge, 15–37.
Brodersen, Kai (2003). *Terra Cognita: Studien zur römischen Raumerfassung*, Hildesheim: Georg Olms.
Brodersen, Kai (2012). 'Cartography', in Dueck (2012), 99–110.
Brodersen, Kai (2016). *Aetheria/Egeria: Reise ins heilige Land, Lateinisch-deutsch*, Berlin: De Gruyter.
Brown, Peter (2008). *The Body and Society: Men, Women, and Sexual Renunciation in Early Christianity* (2nd edition; first published in 1988), New York: Columbia University Press.
Brunt, P. A. (1973). 'Aspects of the social thought of Dio Chrysostom and the Stoics', *Proceedings of the Cambridge Philological Society* 19: 9–34.
Bryen, Ari Z. (2019). 'Politics, justice, and reform in Dio's *Euboicus*', *Transactions of the American Philological Association* 149: 127–48.
Buell, Lawrence (2005). *The Future of Environmental Criticism*, Malden, MA: Blackwell.
Burgersdijk, Diederik (2016). 'Creating the enemy: Ammianus Marcellinus' double digression on Huns and Alans (*Res Gestae* 31.2)', *Bulletin of the Institute of Classical Studies* 59: 111–32.
Burn, A. R. (1949). 'Helikon in history: a study in mountain topography', *Annual of the British School at Athens* 44: 313–23.
Burn, A. R. (1951). 'Thermopylae and Callidromos', in George E. Mylonas (ed.), *Studies Presented to David Moore Robinson on His Seventieth Birthday*, volume I, Saint Louis, MO: Washington University, 480–89.

Burrus, Virginia (2004). *The Sex Lives of Saints: An Erotics of Hagiography*, Philadelphia: University of Pennsylvania Press.

Burrus, Virginia (2019). *Ancient Christian Ecopoetics: Cosmologies, Saints, Things*, Philadelphia: University of Pennsylvania Press.

Buxton, Richard (1991). 'News from Cithaeron: narrators and narratives in the *Bacchae*', *Pallas* 37: 39–48.

Buxton, Richard (1992). 'Imaginary Greek mountains', *Journal of Hellenic Studies* 112: 1–15.

Buxton, Richard (1994). *Imaginary Greece: The Contexts of Mythology*, Cambridge: Cambridge University Press, 81–96.

Buxton, Richard (2004). 'Similes and other likenesses', in Robert Fowler (ed.), *The Cambridge Companion to Homer*, Cambridge: Cambridge University Press, 139–55.

Buxton, Richard (2013). *Myths and Tragedies in Their Ancient Greek Contexts*, Oxford: Oxford University Press.

Buxton, Richard (2016). 'Mount Etna in the Greco-Roman imaginaire: culture and liquid fire', in McInerney and Sluiter (2016), 25–45.

Cabanes, Pierre (1992). 'La montagne, lieu de vie et de rencontre en Epire et en Illyrie méridionale dans l'antiquité', in Fabre (1992), 69–82.

Cadell, H., and R. Rémondon (1967) 'Sens et emploi de τὸ ὄρος dans les documents papyrologiques', *Revue des études grecques* 80: 343–49.

Cairns, Francis (2006). *Sextus Propertius: The Augustan Elegist*, Cambridge: Cambridge University Press.

Cajori, Florian (1929). 'History of determinations of the heights of mountains', *Isis* 12: 482–514.

Calame, Claude (1996). 'Montagne des Muses et Mouséia: la consecration des *Travaux* et l'héroïsation d'Hesiode', in Hurst and Schachter (1996), 43–56.

Campbell, Brian (2000). *The Writings of the Roman Land Surveyors: Introduction, Text, Translation and Commentary*, *Journal of Roman Studies* Monograph 9, London: Society for the Promotion of Roman Studies.

Campbell, David A. (ed.) (1992). *Greek Lyric. Volume IV: Bacchylides, Corinna and Others*, Cambridge MA: Harvard University Press.

Campbell, Duncan B. (2014). 'The search for a lost battlefield: where was the battle of Mons Graupius?', *Ancient Warfare* 8: 47–51.

Campbell, J. K. (1964). *Honour, Family and Patronage: A Study of Institutions and Moral Values in a Greek Mountain Community*, Oxford: Oxford University Press.

Campbell, Mary B. (1988). *The Witness and the Other World: Exotic European Travel Writing, 400–1600*, Ithaca, NY: Cornell University Press.

Caner, Daniel F. (2010). *History and Hagiography from the Late Antique Sinai*, Liverpool: Liverpool University Press.

Carrier, Nicolas, and Fabrice Mouthon (2011). *Les communautés montagnardes au Moyen Age*, Rennes: Presses Universitaires de Rennes.

Ceschi, Giovanni (2019). 'La montagna nel Greco neotestamentario', in Taufer (2019), 287–302.

Chaniotis, Angelos (1991). 'Von Hirten, Kräutersammlern, Ephebern und Pilgern: Leben auf den Bergen im antiken Kreta', *Ktema* 16: 93–109.

Chaniotis, Angelos (1995). 'Problems of "pastoralism" and "transhumance" in classical and Hellenistic Crete', *Orbis terrarum* 1: 39–89.

Chaniotis, Angelos (1996a). 'Die kretischen Berge als Wirtschaftsraum', in Eckart Olshausen and Holger Sonnabend (eds.), *Stuttgarter Kolloquium zur historischen Geographie des Altertums* 5, Amsterdam: Hakkert, 255–66.
Chaniotis, Angelos (1996b). *Die Verträge zwischen kretischen Poleis in der hellenistischen Zeit*, Stuttgart: Franz Steiner Verlag.
Chaniotis, Angelos (ed.) (1999a). *From Minoan Farmers to Roman Traders*, Stuttgart: Franz Steiner Verlag.
Chaniotis, Angelos (1999b). 'Milking the mountains: economic activities on the Cretan uplands in the classical and Hellenistic period', in Chaniotis (1999a), 181–220.
Chaplin, Jane D. (2010). 'Historical and historiographical repetition in Livy's Thermopylae', in Wolfgang Polleichtner (ed.), *Livy and Intertextuality*, Trier: WVT Wissenschaftlicher Verlag Trier, 47–66.
Chesi, Giulia Maria, and Francesca Spiegel (eds.) (2019). *Classical Literature and Posthumanism*, London: Bloomsbury.
Chrysanthou, Chrysanthos S. (2018). *Plutarch's Parallel Lives—Narrative Technique and Moral Judgement*, Berlin: De Gruyter.
Clark, Timothy (2011). *The Cambridge Introduction to Literature and the Environment*, Cambridge: Cambridge University Press.
Clark, Timothy (2019). *The Value of Ecocriticism*, Cambridge: Cambridge University Press.
Clarke, Katherine (1997). 'In search of the author of Strabo's *Geography*', *Journal of Roman Studies* 87: 92–110.
Clarke, Katherine (1999). *Between Geography and History: Hellenistic Constructions of the Roman World*, Oxford: Oxford University Press.
Clarke, Katherine (2001). 'Prologue and provenance: *Quis ille?* or *Unde ille?*', in Kahane and Laird (2001), 101–10.
Clarke, Katherine (2018). *Shaping the Geography of Empire: Man and Nature in Herodotus' Histories*, Oxford: Oxford University Press.
Clarke, Michael (1997). 'Gods and mountains in Greek myth and poetry', in Alan B. Lloyd (ed.), *What Is a God? Studies in the Nature of Greek Divinity*, London: Classical Press of Wales, 65–80.
Clausen, Wendell (1994). *A Commentary on Virgil, Eclogues*, Oxford: Oxford University Press.
Clay, Jenny Strauss (1989a). *The Politics of Olympus: Form and Meaning in the Major Homeric Hymns*, Princeton, NJ: Princeton University Press.
Clay, Jenny Strauss (1989b). '*Odes* 1.9: Horace's September song', *Classical World* 83: 102–5.
Clay, Jenny Strauss (2003). *Hesiod's Cosmos*, Cambridge: Cambridge University Press.
Clay, Jenny Strauss (2011). *Homer's Trojan Theater: Space, Vision, and Memory in the Iliad*, Cambridge: Cambridge University Press.
Coates, Peter (1998). *Nature: Western Attitudes since Ancient Times*, Cambridge: Polity Press.
Cogan, Mordechai (2000). *1 Kings: A New Translation with Introduction and Commentary*, New York: Doubleday.
Cohen, Ada (2007). 'Mythic landscapes of Greece', in Roger D. Woodard (ed.), *The Cambridge Companion to Greek Mythology*, Cambridge: Cambridge University Press, 305–30.
Cohen, Jeffrey Jerome (2015). *Stone: An Ecology of the Inhuman*, Minneapolis: University of Minnesota Press.
Cole, Susan Guettel (2000). 'Landscapes of Artemis', *Classical World* 93: 471–81.

Cole, Susan Guettel (2004). *Landscapes, Gender, and Ritual Space: The Ancient Greek Experience*, Berkeley: University of California Press.

Colley, Ann C. (2010). *Victorians in the Mountains: Sinking the Sublime*, Farnham: Ashgate.

Connors, Catherine (2011). 'Erastosthenes, Strabo, and the geographer's gaze', in Sabine Wilke (ed.), *Literature, Culture and the Environment* (*Pacific Coast Philology* 46.2, special issue), 139–52.

Connors, Catherine (2015). 'In the land of the giants: Greek and Roman discourses on Vesuvius and the Phlegraean Fields', *Illinois Classical Studies* 40: 121–37.

Cook, A. B. (1914–40). *Zeus: A Study in Ancient Religion* (3 volumes), Cambridge: Cambridge University Press.

Cooley, Alison (2009). *Res Gestae Divi Augusti: Text, Translation and Commentary*, Cambridge: Cambridge University Press.

Cooper, Samuel (2020). 'Speculative fiction, ecocriticism, and the wanderings of Odysseus', *Ramus* 48: 95–126.

Corbier, Mireille (1991). 'City, territory and taxation', in John Rich and Andrew Wallace-Hadrill (eds.), *City and Country in the Ancient World*, London: Routledge, 214–43.

Cosgrove, Denis E. (1984). *Social Formation and Symbolic Landscape*, London: Croom Helm.

Cosgrove, Denis E., and Veronica della Dora (eds.) (2009). *High Places: Cultural Geographies of Mountains, Ice and Science*, London: I. B. Tauris.

Costelloe, Timothy M. (ed.) (2012). *The Sublime from Antiquity to the Present*, Cambridge: Cambridge University Press.

Croisille, Jean-Michel (2010). *Paysages dans la peinture romaine. Aux origines d'un genre pictural*, Paris: Picard.

Cronon, William (1991). *Nature's Metropolis: Chicago and the Great West*, New York: W. W. Norton and Company.

Cronon, William (1995). 'The trouble with wilderness: or getting back to the wrong nature', in William Cronon (ed.), *Uncommon Ground: Rethinking the Human Place in Nature*, New York: W. W. Norton & Company, 69–90.

Crump, Gary A. (1975). *Ammianus Marcellinus as a Military Historian*, Historia Einzelschriften 27, Wiesbaden: Franz Steiner Verlag.

CTHS (1991). *La montagne et ses images du peintre Arkesilas à Thomas Cole*, Paris: Éditions du Comité des Travaux historiques et scientifiques.

Darley, Gillian (2011). *Vesuvius*, London: Profile Books.

Dawson, Christopher M. (1944). *Romano-Campanian Mythological Landscape Painting*, Yale Classical Studies 9, New Haven, CT: Yale University Press.

Davidson, James (1991). 'The gaze in Polybius' Histories', *Journal of Roman Studies* 81: 10–24.

Davis, Wade (2011). *Into the Silence: The Great War, Mallory, and the Conquest of Everest*, London: Bodley Head.

Day, J. (1951). 'The value of Dio Chrysostom's *Euboean Discourse* for the economic historian', in P. R. Coleman-Norton (ed.), *Studies in Roman Economic and Social History*, Princeton, NJ: Princeton University Press, 209–35.

Debarbieux, Bernard, and Gilles Rudaz (2011). '"Mountain women": silent contributors to the global agenda for sustainable mountain development', *Gender, Place and Culture: A Journal of Feminist Geography* 19: 1–20.

Debarbieux, Bernard, and Gilles Rudaz (2015). *The Mountain: A Political History from the Enlightenment to the Present* (tr. Jane Marie Todd; first published in French in 2010), Chicago: University of Chicago Press.

de Biasi, Luciano (1990). 'Le descrizioni del paesaggio naturale nelle opere di Apuleio. Aspetti letterari', *Memorie della Accademia delle Scienze di Torino, Classe di Scienze morali, storiche e filologiche* 14: 199–264.

DeFilippo, Joseph G. (1970). '*Curiositas* and the Platonism of Apuleius' *Golden Ass*', *American Journal of Philology* 111: 471–92.

de Jong, Irene J. F. (2001). 'The prologue as a pseudo-dialogue and the identity of its (main) speaker', in Kahane and Laird (2001), 201–12.

de Jong, Irene J. F. (ed.) (2012a). *Space in Ancient Literature: Studies in Ancient Greek Narrative*, Leiden: Brill.

de Jong, Irene J. F. (2012b). 'Homer', in de Jong (2012a), 21–38.

de Jong, Irene J. F. (2012c). 'The Homeric Hymns', in de Jong (2012a), 39–54.

de Jong, Irene J. F. (2018). 'The view from the mountain (*oroskopia*) in Greek and Latin literature', *Cambridge Classical Journal* 64: 23–48.

de Jong, Irene J. F. (2019). 'From *oroskopia* to *ouranoskopia* in Greek and Latin epic', *Symbolae Osloenses* 93: 12–36.

della Dora, Veronica (2008). 'Mountains and memory: embodied visions of ancient peaks in the nineteenth-century Aegean', *Transactions of the Institute of British Geographers* 33: 217–32.

della Dora, Veronica (2011). *Imagining Mount Athos: Visions of a Holy Place from Homer to World War II*, Charlottesville: University of Virginia Press.

della Dora, Veronica (2016a). *Landscape, Nature and the Sacred*, Cambridge: Cambridge University Press.

della Dora, Veronica (2016b). *Mountain: Nature and Culture*, Chicago: Reaktion Books.

della Dora, Veronica (2018). 'Mountains as a way of seeing: From Mount of Temptation to Mont Blanc', in Kakalis and Goetsch (2018), 189–212.

den Boeft, J., J. W. Drijvers, D. den Hengst, and H. C. Teitler (eds.) (2007). *Ammianus after Julian: The Reign of Valentinian and Valens in Books 26–31 of the Res Gestae*, Leiden: Brill.

den Boeft, J., J. W. Drijvers, D. den Hengst, and H. C. Teitler (2018). *Philological and Historical Commentary on Ammianus Marcellinus XXXI*, Leiden: Brill.

Dench, Emma (1995). *From Barbarians to New Men: Greek, Roman, and Modern Perceptions of People from the Central Apennines*, Oxford: Oxford University Press.

DeRose Evans, Jane (2011). 'From mountain to icon: Mount Gerizim on provincial coins from Neapolis, Samaria', *Near Eastern Archaeology* 74: 170–82.

Desideri, Paolo (2000). 'City and country in Dio', in Swain (2000), 93–107.

de Simone, Girolamo F. (2011). 'Con Dioniso fra i vigneti del vaporifero Vesuvio', *Chronache ercolanesi* 41: 289–310.

DeWitt, Norman J. (1941). 'Rome and the "Road of Hercules"', *Transactions of the American Philological Association* 72: 59–69.

Dhar, Amrita (2019). 'Travel and mountains', in Nandini Das and Tim Young (eds.), *The Cambridge History of Travel Writing*, Cambridge: Cambridge University Press, 345–60.

Diederich, Silke (2018). 'Kartenkompetenz und Kartenbenutzung bei den römischen Eliten— Teil 1', *Orbis Terrarum* 16: 55–136.

Diederich, Silke (2019). 'Kartenkompetenz und Kartenbenutzung bei den römischen Eliten— Teil 2', *Orbis Terrarum* 17: 101–84.

Diehl, Ernestus (1949–52). *Anthologia lyrica Graeca* (3rd edition), Leipzig: Teubner.

Dietrich, Nikolaus (2010). *Figur ohne Raum: Bäume und Felsen in der attischen Vasenmaleri des 6. und 5. Jahrhunderts v. Chr.*, Berlin: De Gruyter.

Dietz, Maribel (2005). *Wandering Monks, Virgins, and Pilgrims*, University Park: Pennsylvania State University Press.

Dilke, O.A.W. (1985). *Greek and Roman Maps*, London: Thames and Hudson.

Dilts, Mervyn R. (ed.) (1971). *Heraclidis Lembi excerpta politiarum*, Durham, NC: Duke University.

Dimock, Wai Chee (2008). 'After Troy: Homer, Euripides, total war', in Rita Felski (ed.), *Rethinking Tragedy*, Baltimore, MD: Johns Hopkins University Press, 66–81.

Dodds, E. R. (1940). 'Maenadism in the *Bacchae*', *Harvard Theological Review* 33: 155–76.

Donaldson, Terence L. (1985). *Jesus on the Mountain: A Study in Matthean Theology, Journal for the Study of the New Testament*, Supplement 8, Sheffield: JSOT Press.

Doran, Robert (2015). *The Theory of the Sublime from Longinus to Kant*, Cambridge: Cambridge University Press.

Douglas, Ed (2020). *Himalaya: A Human History*, London: Bodley Head.

Dowden, Ken (2006). *Zeus*, Abingdon: Routledge.

Drijvers, Jan Willem (1999). 'Ammianus Marcellinus' image of Arsaces and early Parthian history', in Drijvers and Hunt (1999), 171–82.

Drijvers, Jan Willem, and David Hunt (eds.) (1999). *The Late Roman World and Its Historian: Interpreting Ammianus Marcellinus*, London: Routledge.

du Boulay, Juliet (1974). *Portrait of a Greek Mountain Village*, Oxford: Clarendon Press.

Dueck, Daniela (2000). *Strabo of Amasia: A Greek Man of Letters in Augustan Rome*, London: Routledge.

Dueck, Daniela (2012). *Geography in Classical Antiquity*, Cambridge: Cambridge University Press.

Dueck, Daniela (ed.) (2017). *The Routledge Companion to Strabo*, Abingdon: Routledge.

Dueck, Daniela, Hugh Lindsay, and Sarah Pothecary (eds.) (2005). *Strabo's Cultural Geography: The Making of a Kolossourgia*, Cambridge: Cambridge University Press.

Duff, Tim (1999). *Plutarch's Lives: Exploring Virtue and Vice*, Oxford: Oxford University Press.

Duff, Tim (2011). 'The structure of the Plutarchan book', *Classical Antiquity* 30: 213–78.

Duffy, Cian (2013). *The Landscapes of the Sublime 1700–1830: Classic Ground*, Basingstoke: Palgrave Macmillan.

Duffy, Cian (2021). 'Famous from all antiquity: Etna in classical myth and Romantic poetry', in Hollis and König (2021a), 37–54.

Dupraz, Emmanuel (2004). 'La représentation du volcanisme dans les *Naturales quaestiones* de Sénèque', in Foulon (2004), 231–58.

Durling, Robert M. (1974). 'The ascent of Mt. Ventoux and the crisis of allegory', *Italian Quarterly* 18: 7–28.

Dyson, Stephen L. (1985). *The Creation of the Roman Frontier*, Princeton, NJ: Princeton University Press.

Eckstein, Arthur M. (2014). 'Livy, Polybius, and the Greek East (Books 31–45)', in Bernard Mineo (ed.), *A Companion to Livy*, Malden, MA: Wiley Blackwell, 407–22.

Edlund, Ingrid E. M. (1987). *The Gods and the Places: Location and Function of Sanctuaries in the Countryside of Etruria and Magna Graecia (700–400 B.C.)*, Stockholm: Svenska Institutet i Rom.

Edmunds, Lowell (1992). *From a Sabine Jar: Reading Horace, Odes 1.9*, Chapel Hill: University of North Carolina Press.

Edwards, M. J. (1992). 'The tale of Cupid and Psyche', *Zeitschrift für Papyrologie und Epigraphik* 94: 77–94.

Eidinow, Esther (2016). 'Telling stories: exploring the relationship between myths and ecological wisdom', *Landscape and Urban Planning* 155: 47–52.

Elliger, Winfried (1975). *Die Darstellung der Landschaft in der griechischen Dichtung*, Berlin: De Gruyter.

Ellis, Reuben (2001). *Vertical Margins: Mountaineering and the Landscapes of Neoimperialism*, Madison: University of Wisconsin Press.

Elsner, Jaś (1992). 'Pausanias: a Greek pilgrim in the Roman world', *Past & Present* 135: 3–29.

Elsner, Jaś (1995). *Art and the Roman Viewer: The Transformation of Art from the Pagan World to Christianity*, Cambridge: Cambridge University Press.

Elsner, Jaś (2001). 'Structuring "Greece": Pausanias' *Periegesis* as a literary construct', in Alcock et al. (2001), 3–20.

Elsner, Jaś (2010). 'Picturesque and sublime: impacts of Pausanias in late-eighteenth- and early-nineteenth-century Britain', *Classical Receptions Journal* 2: 219–53.

Elsner, Jaś, and Joan-Pau Rubiés (1999). 'Introduction', in Jaś Elsner and Joan-Pau Rubiés (eds.), *Voyages and Visions: Towards a Cultural History of Travel*, London: Reaktion Books, 1–56.

Elsner, Jaś, and Gerhard Wolf (2010). 'The transfigured mountain: icons and transformations of pilgrimage at the Monastery of St Catherine at Mount Sinai', in Sharon E. J. Gerstel and Robert S. Nelson (eds.), *Approaching the Holy Mountain: Art and Liturgy at St Catherine's Monastery in the Sinai*, Turnhout: Brepols, 37–71.

Estes, Heide (2017). *Anglo-Saxon Literary Landscapes: Ecotheory and the Environmental Imagination*, Amsterdam: Amsterdam University Press.

Fabre, Georges (ed.) (1992). *La montagne dans l'antiquité*, Pau: Publications de l'Université de Pau.

Fabrizi, Virginia (2015). 'Hannibal's march and Roman imperial space in Livy, *Ab urbe condita*, Book 21', *Philologus* 159: 118–55.

Fachard, Sylvian (2017). 'The resources of the borderlands: control, inequality, and exchange on the Attic-Boeotian borders', in von Reden (2017), 19–61.

Falcone, Maria Jennifer (2019). 'Filippo sul monte Emo: note di lettura a Liv. XL 21–22', in Taufer (2019), 231–41.

Faulkner, Andrew (2008). *The Homeric Hymn to Aphrodite: Introduction, Text, and Commentary*, Oxford: Oxford University Press.

Faulkner, Andrew (ed.) (2011a). *The Homeric Hymns: Interpretative Essays*, Oxford: Oxford University Press.

Faulkner, Andrew (2011b). 'Introduction. Modern scholarship on the *Homeric Hymns*: foundational issues', in Faulkner (2011a), 1–25.

Ferreira, Ana (2015). 'The power of nature and its influence on statesmen in the work of Plutarch', in Meeusen and Van der Stockt (2015), 155–65.

Fick, Nicole (1991). 'Ville et campagne dans les *Métamorphoses* d'Apulée', *Revue belge de philologie et d'histoire* 69: 110–30.

Finglass, Patrick (2019). '*Iō Cithaeron*: high rhetoric and everyday discourse in Sophocles' *Oedipus the King*', in Taufer (2019), 131–40.

Finkelpearl, Ellen (1991). 'The judgement of Lucius: Apuleius, *Metamorphoses* 10.29–34', *Classical Antiquity* 10: 221–36.

Finkelstein, Israel (1981). 'Byzantine prayer niches in southern Sinai', *Israel Exploration Journal* 31: 81–91.

Finn, Richard (2009). *Asceticism in the Graeco-Roman World*, Cambridge: Cambridge University Press.

Fitch, John G. (2009). 'Nature in Horace', *Green Letters* 11: 23–35.

Fitzgerald, William, and Efrossini Spentzou (eds.) (2018). *The Production of Space in Latin Literature*, Oxford: Oxford University Press.

Fleming, Fergus (2000). *Killing Dragons: The Conquest of the Alps*, London: Granta Books.

Folch, Marcus (2018). 'Plato's Hesiods', in Loney and Scully (2018), 311–23.

Forbes, Hamish (1996). 'The uses of uncultivated land in modern Greece: a pointer to the value of wilderness in antiquity', in Shipley and Salmon (1996), 68–97.

Forbes, Hamish (2007). *Meaning and Identity in a Greek Landscape: An Archaeological Ethnography*, Cambridge: Cambridge University Press.

Foss, Clive (1982). 'A neighbor of Sardis: the city of Tmolus and its successors', *Classical Antiquity* 1: 178–201.

Foulon, Éric (ed.) (2004). *Connaissance et représentations des volcans dans l'Antiquité*, Clermont-Ferrand: Presses Universitaires Blaise Pascal.

Fowden, Garth (1988). 'City and mountain in late Roman Attica', *Journal of Hellenic Studies* 108: 48–59.

Frangoulidis, Stavros (2008). *Witches, Isis and Narrative: Approaches to Magic in Apuleius' Metamorphoses*, Berlin: De Gruyter.

Fränkel, Hermann (1921). *Die homerischen Gleichnissen*, Göttingen: Vandenhoeck and Ruprecht.

Frazer, J. G. (1898). *Pausanias's Description of Greece, Translated with a Commentary* (6 volumes), London: Macmillan and Co.

Freshfield, Douglas W. (1904). 'On mountains and mankind', *Popular Science Monthly* 65: 543–48.

Fusillo, Massimo (1999). 'The conflict of emotions: a *topos* in the Greek erotic novel', in Simon Swain (ed.), *Oxford Readings in the Greek Novel*, Oxford: Oxford University Press: 60–82 (first published in French in 1990).

Galimberti, Alessandro (2013). 'L'Eubea in età imperiale e l'"Euboico" di Dione di Prusa', in C. Bearzot and F. Landucci (eds.), *Tra mare e continente: l'isola di Eubea*, Milan: Vita e pensiero, 271–84.

Garani, Myrto (2009). 'Going with the wind: visualizing volcanic eruptions in the pseudo-Virgilian *Aetna*', *Bulletin of the Institute of Classical Studies* 52: 103–21.

García Moreno, Luis A. (1992). 'Paradoxography and political ideals in Plutarch's *Life of Sertorius*', in Philip A. Stadter (ed.), *Plutarch and the Historical Tradition*, London: Routledge, 132–58.

Garnsey, Peter (1998). 'Mountain economies in southern Europe: thoughts on the early history, continuity and individuality of Mediterranean upland pastoralism', in *Cities, Peasants and Food in Classical Antiquity: Essays in Social and Economic History*, Cambridge: Cambridge University Press, 166–79 (reprinted, with a brief addendum, from Whittaker [1988], 196–210).

Garrard, Greg (2012). *Ecocriticism* (2nd edition, first published in 2004), London: Routledge.

Garrard, Greg (ed.) (2014). *The Oxford Handbook of Ecocriticism*, Oxford: Oxford University Press.

Georgiadou, Aristoula, and Katerina Oikonomopoulou (eds.) (2017). *Space, Time and Language in Plutarch*, Berlin: De Gruyter.

Georgoudi, Stella (1974). 'Quelques problèmes de la transhumance dans la Grèce ancienne', *Revue des études grecques* 87: 155–85.

Ghosh, Amitav (2016). *The Great Derangement: Climate Change and the Unthinkable*, Chicago: Chicago University Press.

Gianotti, Gian Franco (1995). 'In viaggio con l'asino', in Fabio Rosa and Francesco Zambon (eds.), *Pothos: il viaggio, la nostalgia*, Trento: Università degli studi di Trento, 107–32.

Gilhuly, Kate, and Nancy Worman (eds.) (2014a). *Space, Place, and Landscape in Ancient Greek Literature and Culture*, Cambridge: Cambridge University Press.

Gilhuly, Kate, and Nancy Worman (2014b). 'Introduction', in Gilhuly and Worman (2014a), 1–20.

Gilliver, Catherine M. (1996). 'Mons Graupius and the role of auxiliaries in battle', *Greece and Rome* 43: 54–67.

Giorcelli Bersani, Silvia (ed.) (2001). *Gli antichi e la montagna: Ecologia, religione, economia e politica del territorio*, Torino: Celid.

Giorcelli Bersani, Silvia (2019). *L'impero in quota: I Romani e le Alpi*, Torino: Giulio Einaudi editore.

Glacken, Clarence J. (1969). *Traces on the Rhodian Shore: Nature and Culture in Western Thought from Ancient Times to the End of the Eighteenth Century*, Berkeley: University of California Press.

Glauthier, Patrick (2016). 'Playing the volcano: *Prometheus Bound* and fifth-century volcanic theory', *Classical Philology* 113: 255–78.

Goehring, James E. (1999). *Ascetics, Society, and the Desert: Studies in Early Egyptian Monasticism*, Harrisburg, PA: Trinity Press International.

Goette, Hans R. (2002). 'Quarry roads on Mount Pentelikon and Mount Hymettus', in Hans R. Goette (ed.), *Ancient Roads in Greece*, Hamburg: Verlag Dr. Kovač, 93–102.

Goette, Hans R. (2012). 'Die Topographie der Karystia in der *Euböischen Rede* des Dion von Prusa—Autopsie oder Fiktion?', in Gustav Adolf Lehmann, Dorit Engster, Dorothee Gall, Hans Rupprecht Goette, Elisabeth Herrmann-Otto, Werner Heun, and Barbara Zehnpfennig(eds.), *Armut—Arbeit—Menschenwürde: Die Euböische Rede des Dion von Prusa*, Tübingen: Mohr Siebeck, 167–89.

Goldhill, Simon (1984). *Language, Sexuality, Narrative: The Oresteia*, Cambridge: Cambridge University Press.

Goldhill, Simon (2019). 'Conclusions', in Chesi and Spiegel (2020), 331–42.

Goldwyn, Adam J. (2018). *Byzantine Ecocriticism: Women, Nature, and Power in the Medieval Greek Romance*, London: Palgrave Macmillan.

Goodyear, F.R.D. (1984). 'The "Aetna": thought, antecedents, and style', *Aufstieg und Niedergang der römischen Welt* 2.32.1: 344–63.
Gowers, Emily (2011). 'The road to Sicily: Lucilius to Seneca', *Ramus* 40: 168–97.
Graverini, Luca (2002). 'Corinth, Rome and Africa: a cultural background for the tale of the ass', in Paschalis and Frangoulidis (2002), 58–77.
Graziosi, Barbara (2013). *The Gods of Olympus: A History*, London: Profile Books.
Graziosi, Barbara, and Johannes Haubold (2005). *Homer: The Resonance of Epic*, London: Duckworth.
Green, C.M.C. (2007). *Roman Religion and the Cult of Diana at Aricia*, Cambridge: Cambridge University Press.
Greenwood, David (2014). 'A pagan emperor's appropriation of Matthew's gospel', *Expository Times* 125: 593–98.
Greenwood, Emily (2006). *Thucydides and the Shaping of History*, London: Duckworth.
Haggis, Donald C. (1999). 'Staple finance, peak sanctuaries, and economic complexity in late Prepalatial Crete', in Chaniotis (1999a), 53–85.
Hainsworth, Bryan (2003). *The Iliad: A Commentary. Volume IV: Books 9–12*, Cambridge: Cambridge University Press.
Halkin, François (1985). 'Vie de S. Conon d'Isaurie', *Analecta Bollandiana* 103: 5–34.
Hall, Edith (1995). 'The ass with double vision', in David Margolies and Maroula Joannou (eds.), *Heart of the Heartless World: Essays in Cultural Resistance in Memory of Margot Heinemann*, London: Pluto Press, 47–59.
Halliwell, Stephen (2012). *Between Ecstasy and Truth: Interpretations of Greek Poetics from Homer to Longinus*, Oxford: Oxford University Press.
Halliwell, Stephen (2019). 'Perspectivism and the Homeric simile' (The 2nd Martin West Memorial Lecture, Oxford, March 1st, 2019), http://media.podcasts.ox.ac.uk/classics/general/2019-04-03-classics-halliwell.pdf (last consulted 31/7/21).
Halstead, Paul (1987). 'Traditional and ancient rural economy in Mediterranean Europe: plus ça change?', *Journal of Hellenic Studies* 107: 77–87.
Hamilton, J. R. (1969). *Plutarch, Alexander: A Commentary*, Oxford: Clarendon Press.
Hammond, N.G.L. (1966). 'The opening campaigns and the battle of the Aoi Stena in the Second Macedonian War', *Journal of Roman Studies* 56: 39–54.
Hammond, N.G.L. (1967). *Epirus: The Geography, the Ancient Remains, the History, and the Topography of Epirus and Adjacent Areas*, Oxford: Clarendon Press.
Hansen, Peter H. (2001). 'Modern mountains: the performative consciousness of modernity in Britain, 1870–1940', in Martin Daunton and Bernhard Rieger (eds.), *Meanings of Modernity: Britain from the Late-Victorian Era to World War II*, Oxford: Berg, 185–202.
Hansen, Peter H. (2013). *The Summits of Modern Man: Mountaineering after the Enlightenment*, Cambridge, MA: Harvard University Press.
Harley, J. Brian (1988). 'Maps, knowledge and power', in Denis Cosgrove and Stephen Daniels (eds.), *The Iconography of Landscape*, Cambridge: Cambridge University Press, 277–312.
Harris, W. V. (ed.) (2013a). *The Ancient Mediterranean Environment between Science and History*, Leiden: Brill.
Harris, W. V. (2013b). 'Defining and detecting deforestation in the ancient Mediterranean, 800 BC–600 CE', in Harris (2013a), 173–94.

Harrison, Stephen J. (1990). 'The speaking book: the prologue to Apuleius' *Metamorphoses*', *Classical Quarterly* 40: 507–13.
Harrison, Stephen J. (2000). *Apuleius: A Latin Sophist*, Oxford: Oxford University Press.
Harrison, Stephen J. (2002). 'Literary topography in Apuleius' *Metamorphoses*', in Paschalis and Frangoulidis (2002), 40–57.
Harrison, Stephen J., Stavros Frangoulidis, and Theodore D. Papanghelis (eds.) (2018). *Intratextuality and Latin Literature*, Berlin: De Gruyter.
Harrison, Thomas (2000). *Divinity and History: The Religion of Herodotus*, Oxford: Oxford University Press.
Harrison, Thomas (2005). 'Mastering the landscape', in E. Dabrowa (ed.), *Titulus: Essays in Memory of Stanislaw Kalita*, Cracow: Jagiellonian University Press, 27–33.
Harrison, Thomas (2007). 'The place of geography in Herodotus' *Histories*', in Adams and Roy (2007), 44–65.
Harvey, Susan Ashbrook (1990). *Asceticism and Society in Crisis: John of Ephesus and the Lives of the Eastern Saints*, Berkeley: University of California Press.
Hawes, Greta (2014). *Rationalizing Myth in Antiquity*, Oxford: Oxford University Press.
Heath, J.M.F. (2020). *Clement of Alexandria and the Shaping of Christian Literary Practice: Miscellany and the Transformation of Greco-Roman Writing*, Cambridge: Cambridge University Press.
Hedreen, Guy (2001). *Capturing Troy: The Narrative Functions of Landscape in Archaic and Classical Greek Art*, Ann Arbor: University of Michigan Press.
Hedstrom, Darlene L. Brooks (2017). *The Monastic Landscape of Late Antique Egypt: An Archaeological Reconstruction*, Cambridge: Cambridge University Press.
Heise, Ursula (2008). *Sense of Place, Sense of Planet: The Environmental Imagination of the Global*, Oxford: Oxford University Press.
Hevly, Bruce (1996). 'The heroic science of glacier motion', *Osiris* 2: 66–86.
Heyworth, S. J., and J.H.W. Morwood (2011). *A Commentary on Propertius, Book 3*, Oxford: Oxford University Press.
Higham, James, Anna Thompson-Carr, and Ghazali Musa (2017). 'Mountaineering tourism: activity, people, place', in Musa et al. (2017), 1–15.
Highet, Gilbert (1973). 'The huntsman and the castaway', *Greek, Roman and Byzantine Studies* 14: 35–40.
Hijmans, B. L., Jr., R. T. van der Paardt, E. R. Smits, R.E.H. Westendorp Boerma, and A. G. Westerbrink (1977). *Apuleius Madaurensis Metamorphoses Book IV, 1–27: Text, Introduction and Commentary*, Groningen: Bouma's Boekhuis.
Hiltner, Ken (2015). 'General introduction', in Ken Hiltner (ed.), *Ecocriticism: The Essential Reader*, Abingdon: Routledge, xii–xvi.
Hinds, Stephen (2002). 'Landscape with figures: aesthetics of place in the *Metamorphoses* and its tradition', in Philip Hardie (ed.), *The Cambridge Companion to Ovid*, Cambridge: Cambridge University Press, 122–49.
Hine, Harry M. (2002). 'Seismology and volcanology in antiquity?', in C. J. Tuplin and T. E. Rihll (eds.), *Science and Mathematics in Ancient Greek Culture*, Oxford: Oxford University Press, 56–75.
Hinterhöller-Klein, Monika (2015). *Varietates topiorum: Perspektive und Raumerfassung in Landschafts- und Panoramabildern der römischen Wandmalerei vom 1. Jh. v. Chr. bis zum Ende der pompejanischen Stile*, Wien: Phoibos Verlag.

Hobbs, Joseph J. (1995). *Mount Sinai*, Austin: University of Texas Press.

Hodske, Jürgen (2007). *Mythologische Bildthemen in den Häusern Pompejis: Die Bedeutung der zentralen Mythenbilder für die Bewohner Pompejis*, Ruhpolding: Verlag Franz Philipp Rutzen.

Hollis, Dawn (2019). 'Mountain gloom and mountain glory: the genealogy of an idea', *Interdisciplinary Studies in Literature and the Environment* 26: 1038–61.

Hollis, Dawn (2020). 'Aesthetic experience, investigation and classic ground: responses to Etna from the first century CE to 1773', *Journal of the Warburg and Courtauld Institutes* 83: 299–326.

Hollis, Dawn (2021). 'The "authority of the ancients"? Seventeenth-century natural philosophy and aesthetic responses to mountains', in Hollis and König (2021a), 55–71.

Hollis, Dawn, and Jason König (eds.) (2021a). *Mountain Dialogues from Antiquity to Modernity*, London: Bloomsbury.

Hollis, Dawn, and Jason König (2021b). 'Introduction', in Hollis and König (2021a), 1–20.

Holmes, Brooke (2015). 'Situating Scamander: Natureculture in the *Iliad*', *Ramus* 44: 29–51.

Holzberg, Niklas (1995). *The Ancient Novel: An Introduction* (tr. Christine Jackson-Holzberg; first published in German in 1986), London: Routledge.

Honey, Linda (2006). 'Justifiably outraged or simply outrageous? The Isaurian incident of Ammianus Marcellinus 14.2', in Harold Allen Drake (ed.), *Violence in Late Antiquity: Perceptions and Practices*, Aldershot: Ashgate, 47–56.

Hooley, Dan (2012). 'Prelude: classical mountain landscapes and the language of ascent', in Ireton and Schaumann (2012), 20–32.

Hooley, Dan (2021). 'Gessner's mountain sublime', in König and Hollis (2021a), 21–36.

Höper, Hermann-Josef (1992). 'Zwei Statuenbasen als Reste einer Opferstätte auf dem Hl. Antonios, einem der Olympgipfel (Griechenland)', in O. Brehm and S. Klie (eds.), Μουσικὸς Ἀνήρ: *Festschrift für Max Wegner zum 90. Geburtstag*, Bonn: R. Habelt, 213–22.

Hopwood, Keith (1999). 'Ammianus Marcellinus on Isauria', in Drijvers and Hunt (1999), 198–208.

Horden, Peregrine, and Nicholas Purcell (2000). *The Corrupting Sea: A Study of Mediterranean History*, Oxford: Blackwell.

Hubbard, Margaret (1974). *Propertius*, London: Duckworth.

Huggan, Graham, and Helen Tiffin (2010). *Postcolonial Ecocriticism: Literature, Animals, Environment*, Abingdon: Routledge.

Hughes, Dennis D. (1991). *Human Sacrifice in Ancient Greece*, London: Routledge.

Hughes, J. Donald (1983). 'How the ancients viewed deforestation', *Journal of Field Archaeology* 10: 435–45.

Hughes, J. Donald (1996). 'The hunters of Euboea: mountain folk in the classical Mediterranean', *Mountain Research and Development* 16: 91–100.

Hughes, J. Donald (2014). *Environmental Problems of the Greeks and Romans: Ecology in the Ancient Mediterranean* (2nd edition; first published in 1994), Baltimore, MD: Johns Hopkins University Press.

Hunt, Ailsa, and Hilary Marlow (2019). *Ecology and Theology in the Ancient World: Cross-Disciplinary Perspectives*, London: Bloomsbury.

Hunt, E. D. (2000). 'The itinerary of Egeria: reliving the Bible in fourth-century Palestine', in R. N. Swanson (ed.), *The Holy Land, Holy Lands, and Church History, Studies in Church History* 36: 34–54.

Hunt, John (1953). *The Ascent of Everest*, London: Hodder and Stoughton.
Hunt, Patrick (2015). '*Summus Poeninus* on the Grand St Bernard Pass', *Journal of Roman Archaeology* 11: 265–74.
Hunter, Richard (2006). *The Shadow of Callimachus: Studies in the Reception of Hellenistic Poetry at Rome*, Cambridge: Cambridge University Press.
Hunter, Richard, and Fantuzzi, Marco (2004). *Tradition and Innovation in Hellenistic Poetry*, Cambridge: Cambridge University Press.
Hurst, André (1996). 'La stèle d'Hélicon', in Hurst and Schachter (1996), 53–71.
Hurst, André, and Albert Schachter (eds.) (1996). *La montagne des Muses*, Geneva: Librairie Droz.
Hurwit, Jeffrey M. (1991). 'The representation of nature in early Greek art', in Diana Buitron-Oliver (ed.), *New Perspectives in Early Greek Art*, Hanover, NH: National Gallery of Art, Washington, 33–62.
Hutton, William (2005a). *Describing Greece: Landscape and Literature in the Periegesis of Pausanias*, Cambridge: Cambridge University Press.
Hutton, William (2005b). 'The construction of religious space in Pausanias', in Jaś Elsner and Ian Rutherford (eds.), *Pilgrimage in Graeco-Roman and Early Christian Antiquity: Seeing the Gods*, Oxford: Oxford University Press, 291–318.
Hyde, Walter Woodburn (1915). 'The ancient appreciation of mountain scenery', *Classical Journal* 11: 70–84.
Ingold, Tim (1993). 'The temporality of the landscape', *World Archaeology* 25: 152–74.
Ingold, Tim (2004). 'Culture on the ground: the world perceived through the feet', *Journal of Material Culture* 3: 315–40.
Innes, Doreen (2001). 'Why *Isthmos Ephyrea*?', in Kahane and Laird (2001), 111–19.
Irby, Georgia L. (2012). 'Mapping the world: Greek initiatives from Homer to Eratosthenes', in Talbert (2012), 81–108.
Ireton, Sean (2021). 'Toward a continuity of Alpinism in antiquity, premodernity and modernity: Josias Simler's *De Alpibus Commentarius* (1574) and W.A.B. Coolidge's French translation from 1904', in Hollis and König (2021a), 73–88.
Ireton, Sean, and Caroline Schaumann (eds.) (2012). *Heights of Reflection: Mountains in the German Imagination from the Middle Ages to the Twenty-First Century*, Rochester, NY: Camden House.
Ireton, Sean, and Caroline Schaumann (eds.) (2020). *Mountains and the German Mind: Translations from Gessner to Messner, 1541–2009*, Rochester, NY: Camden House.
Isserman, Maurice, and Stewart Weaver (2008). *Fallen Giants: A History of Himalayan Mountaineering from the Age of Empires to the Age of Extremes*, New Haven, CT: Yale University Press.
Jacob, Christian (1991). *Géographie et ethnographie en Grèce ancienne*, Paris: Colin.
Jacobs, Susan G. (2018). *Plutarch's Pragmatic Biographies*, Leiden: Brill.
Jacquemin, Anne (1984). 'Lampes', in *Bulletin de correspondance hellénique*, Supplément 9: 157–65.
Jaeger, Mary (2007). 'Fog on the mountain: Philip and Mount Haemus in Livy 40.21–22', in John Marincola (ed.), *A Companion to Greek and Roman Historiography*, Malden, MA: Wiley Blackwell, 397–403.

Jameson, Michael H. (1989). 'Mountains and the Greek city states', in Jean-François Bergier (ed.), *Montagnes, fleuves, forêts dans l'histoire: barrières ou lignes de convergence?*, St Katharinen: Scripta Mercaturae Verlag, 7–17.

Janko, Richard (1994). *The Iliad: A Commentary. Volume IV: Books 13–16*, Cambridge: Cambridge University Press.

Janni, Pietro (1984). *La mappa e il periplo: cartografia antica e spazio odologico*, Rome: Giorgio Bretschneider.

Jenkins, McKay (2003). *The Last Ridge: The Epic Story of America's First Mountain Soldiers and the Assault on Hitler's Europe*, New York: Random House.

Johnson, Scott Fitzgerald (2006). *The Life and Miracles of Thekla: A Literary Study*, Washington, DC: Center for Hellenic Studies.

Johnston, Patricia A. (1996). 'Under the volcano: volcanic myth and metaphor in Vergil's *Aeneid*', *Vergilius* 42: 55–65.

Jones, Alexander (2012). 'Ptolemy's *Geography*: mapmaking and the scientific enterprise', in Talbert (2012a), 109–27.

Jones, C. P. (1978). *The Roman World of Dio Chrysostom*, Cambridge, MA: Harvard University Press.

Jones, C. P. (2001). 'Pausanias and his guides', in Alcock et al. (2001), 33–39.

Jordan, Alley Marie (2021a). 'Sublime visions of Virginia: Thomas Jefferson's Romantic mountainscapes', in Hollis and König (2021a), 131–46.

Jost, Madeleine (1985). *Sanctuaires et cultes d'Arcadie*, Paris: Librairie philosophique J. Vrin.

Jost, Madeleine (1992). 'La vie religieuse dans les montagnes d'Arcadie', in Fabre (1992), 55–68.

Jost, Madeleine (1994). 'The distribution of sanctuaries in civic space in Arkadia', in Alcock and Osborne (1994), 217–30.

Jost, Madeleine (1996). 'Le vocabulaire de la description des paysages dans les *Arkadika* de Pausanias', in *Comptes rendus des séances de l'Académie des Inscriptions et Belles-Lettres* 140: 719–38.

Jost, Madeleine (2007). 'Pausanias in Arkadia: an example of cultural tourism', in Adams and Roy (2007), 104–22.

Jouan, François (1977). 'Les thèmes romanesques dans l'*Euboïcos* de Dion Chrysostome', *Revue des études Grecques* 90: 38–46.

Jourdain-Annequin, Colette (1999). 'L'image de la montagne ou la géographie à l'épreuve du mythe et de l'histoire: l'exemple de la traversée des Alpes par Hannibal', *Dialogues d'histoire ancienne* 25: 101–27.

Jourdain-Annequin, Colette (2011). *Quand Grecs et Romains découvraient les Alpes*, Paris: Picard.

Jourdain-Annequin, Colette, and Maryvonne Le Berre (eds.) (2004). *Atlas culturel des Alpes occidentales*, Paris: Editions A. et J. Picard.

Kagan, Kimberley (2006). *The Eye of Command*, Ann Arbor: University of Michigan Press.

Kahane, Ahuvia, and Andrew Laird (eds.) (2001). *A Companion to the Prologue of Apuleius' Metamorphoses*, Oxford: Oxford University Press.

Kakalis, Christos, and Emily Goetsch (eds.) (2018). *Mountains, Mobilities and Movement*, London: Palgrave Macmillan.

Kelly, Adrian (2007). *A Referential Commentary and Lexicon to Iliad VIII*, Oxford: Oxford University Press.

Kelly, Gavin (2004). 'Ammianus and the great tsunami', *Journal of Roman Studies* 94: 141–67.
Kelly, Gavin (2007). 'The sphragis and closure of the *Res Gestae*', in den Boeft et al. (2007), 219–41.
Kelly, Gavin (2008). *Ammianus Marcellinus: The Allusive Historian*, Cambridge: Cambridge University Press.
Kelly, J.N.D. (1975). *Jerome: His Life, Writings, and Controversies*, London: Duckworth.
Kennedy, George A. (2003). *Progymnasmata: Greek Textbooks of Prose Composition and Rhetoric*, Atlanta, GA: Society of Biblical Literature.
Kenney, E. J. (1990). 'Psyche and her mysterious husband', in D. A. Russell (ed.), *Antonine Literature*, Oxford: Oxford University Press, 175–98.
Kerridge, Richard (2014). 'Ecocritical approaches to literary form and genre: urgency, depth, provisionality, temporality', in Garrard (2014), 361–75.
Keulen, W. H. (2007). *Apuleius Madaurensis Metamorphoses Book 1: Text, Introduction and Commentary*, Groningen: Egbert Forsten.
Keuls, E. (1974). 'Une cible de la satire: le "locus amoenus"', *Les études classiques* 42: 265–75.
Kirk, G. S. (1985). *The Iliad: A Commentary. Volume I: Books 1–4*, Cambridge: Cambridge University Press.
Kleinkopf, Katie (2017). 'A landscape of bodies: exploring the role of ascetics in Theodoret's *Historia Religiosa*', *Studia patristica* 96: 283–92.
Knapp, Robert C. (1986). 'La "via Heraclea" en el occidente: mito, arqueología, propaganda, historia', *Emerita* 54: 103–22.
Koelb, Janice Hewlett (2006). *The Poetics of Description: Imagined Places in European Literature*, New York: Palgrave Macmillan.
Koelb, Janice Hewlett (2009). '"This most beautiful and adorn'd world": Nicolson's *Mountain Gloom and Mountain Glory* reconsidered', *Interdisciplinary Studies in Literature and Environment* 16: 443–68.
Koelb, Janice Hewlett (2021). 'Erudite retreat: Jerome and Francis in the mountains', in Hollis and König (2021a), 109–29.
Kofler, Wolfgang, Martin Korenjak, and Florian Schaffenrath (eds.) (2010). *Gipfel der Zeit: Berge in Texten aus fünf Jahrtausenden*, Freiburg: Rombach Verlag KG.
König, Jason (2008). 'Body and text', in Tim Whitmarsh (ed.), *The Cambridge Companion to the Greek and Roman Novel*, Cambridge: Cambridge University Press, 127–44.
König, Jason (2009). *Greek Literature in the Roman Empire*, London: Bristol Classical Press.
König, Jason (2012). *Saints and Symposiasts: The Literature of Food and the Symposium in Greco-Roman and Early Christian Culture*, Cambridge: Cambridge University Press.
König, Jason (2013). 'Landscape and reality in Apuleius' *Metamorphoses*', in Michael Paschalis and Stelios Panayotakis (eds.), *The Construction of the Ideal and the Real in the Ancient Novel*, Ancient Narrative, Supplement 17, Groningen: Barkhuis, 219–42.
König, Jason (2016). 'Strabo's Mountains', in McInerney and Sluiter (2016), 46–69.
König, Jason (2017). 'Rethinking landscape in ancient fiction: mountains in Apuleius and Jerome', in Marília P. Futre Pinheiro, David Konstan, and Bruce Duncan MacQueen (eds.), *Cultural Crossroads in the Ancient Novel*, Berlin: De Gruyter, 275–88.
König, Jason (2019). 'Mountain and city in Dio Chrysostom's *Euboicus*', in Taufer (2019), 327–45.

König, Jason (2020). 'Solitude and biography in Jerome's *Life of Hilarion*', in Koen de Temmerman (ed.), *The Oxford Handbook of Ancient Biography*, Oxford: Oxford University Press, 295–308.

König, Jason (2021). 'Edward Dodwell in the Peloponnese: mountains and the classical past in nineteenth-century Mediterranean travel writing', in Hollis and König (2021a), 147–64.

König, Jason (forthcoming a). 'Ecocritical readings in late Hellenistic literature: landscape alteration and hybris in Strabo and Diodorus', in Jason König and Nicolas Wiater (eds.), *Late Hellenistic Greek Literature in Dialogue*, Cambridge: Cambridge University Press.

König, Jason (forthcoming b). 'Generic enrichment in Plutarch's mountain-battle landscapes', in T. E. Duff and C. S. Chrysanthou (eds.), *Generic Enrichment in Plutarch's Lives*, London: Routledge.

König, Jason, and Tim Whitmarsh (eds.) (2007). *Ordering Knowledge in the Roman Empire*, Cambridge: Cambridge University Press.

Koning, Hugo H. (2010). *Hesiod, the Other Poet: Ancient Reception of a Cultural Icon*, Leiden: Brill.

Konrad, C. F. (1994). *Plutarch's Sertorius: A Historical Commentary*, Chapel Hill: University of North Carolina Press.

Konstan, David (2001). 'The joys of Pausanias', in Alcock et al. (2001), 57–60.

Korenjak, Martin (2017). 'Why mountains matter: early modern roots of a modern notion', *Renaissance Quarterly* 70: 179–219.

Korhonen, Tua (2020). 'What is it like to be a donkey (with a human mind)? Pseudo-Lucian's *Onos*', in Chesi and Spiegel (2020), 73–84.

Krabbe, Judith K. (2003). *Lusus iste: Apuleius' Metamorphoses*, Dallas, TX: University Press of America.

Kraemer, Casper J. (1958). *Excavations at Nessana, Volume III: Non-Literary Papyri*, Princeton, NJ: Princeton University Press.

Krieter-Spiro, Martha (2018). *Homer's Iliad: The Basel Commentary, Book 14*, Boston: De Gruyter.

Kruschwitz, Peter (2015). 'Getting on top of things: form and meaning in the pseudo-Vergilian *Aetna*', *Habis* 46: 75–97.

Kulikowski, Michael (2007). *Rome's Gothic Wars: From the Third Century to Alaric*, Cambridge: Cambridge University Press.

Kulikowski, Michael (2012). 'Coded polemic in Ammianus Book 31 and the date and place of its composition', *Journal of Roman Studies* 102: 79–102.

Kyriakidis, Evangelos (2005). *Ritual in the Bronze Age Aegean*, London: Bristol Classical Press.

Kyriazopoulos, B., and G. Livadas (1967). 'Ἀρχαιολογικὰ εὑρήματα ἐπὶ τῆς κορυφῆς τοῦ Ὀλύμπου Ἅγιος Ἀντώνιος', *Deltion* 22: 6–14.

Lamberton, Robert (1988a). *Hesiod*, New Haven, CT: Yale University Press.

Lamberton, Robert (1988b). 'Plutarch, Hesiod, and the Mouseia of Thespiai', *Illinois Classical Studies* 13: 491–504.

Lane Fox, Robin (1986). *Pagans and Christians in the Mediterranean World from the Second Century AD to the Conversion of Constantine*, London: Viking.

Lane Fox, Robin (1996). 'Ancient hunting: from Homer to Polybios', in Shipley and Salmon (eds.), 119–53.

Lane Fox, Robin (2008). *Travelling Heroes: Greeks and Their Myths in the Epic Age of Homer*, London: Allen Lane.
Langdon, Merle K. (1976). *A Sanctuary of Zeus on Mount Hymettos*, Hesperia Supplement 16, Princeton, NJ: American School of Classical Studies at Athens.
Langdon, Merle K. (1999). 'Classifying the hills of Rome', *Eranos* 97: 98–107.
Langdon, Merle K. (2000). 'Mountains in Greek religion', *Classical World* 93: 461–70.
Lasserre, François (1966). *Strabon, Géographie. Livres III et IV*, Paris: Les Belles Lettres.
Lateiner, Donald (1989). *The Historical Method of Herodotus*, Toronto: University of Toronto Press.
Lateiner, Donald (2014). 'Homer's social-psychological spaces and places', in Marios Skempis and Ioannis Ziogas (eds.), *Geography, Topography, Landscape: Configurations of Space in Greek and Roman Epic*, Berlin: De Gruyter, 63–94.
Lavan, Myles (2017). 'Writing revolt in the early Roman empire', in Justine Firnhaber-Baker and Dirk Schoenaers (eds.), *The Routledge History Handbook of Medieval Revolt*, London: Routledge, 19–38.
Leach, Eleanor Windsor (1988). *The Rhetoric of Space: Literary and Artistic Representations of Landscape in Republican and Augustan Rome*, Princeton, NJ: Princeton University Press.
Lee, Dorothy A. (2019). 'Natural world imagery and the sublime in the Gospel of Matthew', *Australian Biblical Review* 67: 69–83.
Leigh Fermor, Patrick (1977). *A Time of Gifts*, London: John Murray.
Lendon, Jon E. (2017). 'Battle description in the ancient historians, part 1: structure, array, and fighting', *Greece and Rome* 64: 39–64.
Lenski, Noel (1999). 'Assimilation and revolt in the territory of Isauria: from the first century BC to the sixth century AD', *Journal of the Economic and Social History of the Orient* 42: 413–65.
Lepelley, Claude (1990–1991). 'Le présage du nouveau désastre de Cannes: la signification du raz de marée du 21 juillet 365 dans l'imaginaire d'Ammien Marcellin', *Kôkalos* 36–37: 359–74.
Lesage Gárriga, Luisa (2015). 'The light of the moon: an active participant on the battlefield in Plutarch's *Parallel Lives*', in Meeusen and Van der Stockt (2015), 155–66.
Létoublon, Françoise (2008). 'Montagnes grecques de la géographie aux représentations', *Cause commune* 3: 151–58.
Leveau, Philippe (1977). 'L'opposition de la montagne et de la plaine dans l'historiographie de l'Afrique du Nord antique', *Annales de géographie* 474: 201–5.
Leveau, Philippe (1984). *Caesarea de Maurétanie: une ville romaine et ses campagnes*, Rome: École française de Rome.
Levene, D. S. (2010). *Livy on the Hannibalic War*, Oxford: Oxford University Press.
Leyerle, Blake (1996). 'Landscape as cartography in early Christian pilgrim narratives', *Journal of the American Academy of Religion* 64: 119–43.
Lichtenberger, Achim (2016). 'Der Berg des Archelaosreliefs', in Holger Schwarzer and H.-Helge Nieswandt (eds.), *"Man kann es sich nicht prächtig genug vorstellen!" Festschrift für Dieter Salzmann zum 65. Geburtstag*, volume I, Marsberg: Scriptorium, 341–49.
Lichtenberger, Achim (2021). *Der Olymp: Sitz der Götter zwischen Himmel und Erde*, Stuttgart: Verlag W. Kohlhammer.

Lindsay, Hugh (2005). 'Amasya and Strabo's *patria* in Pontus', in Dueck et al. (2005), 180–99.
Ling, Roger (1991). *Roman Painting*, Cambridge: Cambridge University Press.
Lobel, Edgar, and Denys Page (1955). *Poetarum Lesbiorum fragmenta*, Oxford: Clarendon Press.
Loney, Alexander C., and Stephen Scully (eds.) (2018). *The Oxford Handbook of Hesiod*, Oxford: Oxford University Press.
Lorenz, Katharina (2008). *Bilder machen Raüme: Mythenbilder in pompeianischen Häusern*, Berlin: De Gruyter.
Lorimer, Hayden, and Katrín Lund (2016). 'A collectable topography: remembering and recording mountains', in Tim Ingold and Jo Lee Vergunst (eds.), *Ways of Walking: Ethnography and Practice on Foot*, London: Routledge, 318–45.
Louargant, S. (ed.) (2013). 'Lever le voile: les montagnes au masculin-féminin', *Revue de géographie alpine* 101-1, https://journals.openedition.org/rga/1973 (last consulted 31/7/21).
Ludlow, Morwenna (2020). *Art, Craft and Theology in Fourth-Century Christian Authors*, Oxford: Oxford University Press.
Ma, John (2000). 'Public speech and community in the *Euboicus*', in Swain (2000), 108–24.
Macdonald, William L., and John A. Pinto (1995). *Hadrian's Villa and Its Legacy*, New Haven, CT: Yale University Press.
MacFarlane, Robert (2003). *Mountains of the Mind: The History of a Fascination*, London: Granta.
Maciver, Calum A. (2007). 'Returning to the mountain of *Arete*: reading ecphrasis, constructing ethics in Quintus Smyrnaeus' *Posthomerica*', in Manuel Baumbach, Silvio Bär, and Nicola Nina Schmid-Dümmler (eds.), *Quintus Smyrnaeus: Transforming Homer in Second Sophistic Epic*, Berlin: De Gruyter, 259–84.
Mack, William (2015). 'Shepherds beating the bounds? Territorial identity at a dependent community (*IPriene* 361–63)', *Journal of Hellenic Studies* 135: 51–77.
Mackie, C. J. (2014). 'Zeus and Mount Ida in Homer's *Iliad*', *Antichthon* 48: 1–13.
Madsen, Jesper Majbom (2014). 'An insider's view: Strabo of Amaseia on Pompey's Pontic cities', in Tønnes Bekker-Nielsen (ed.), *Space, Place and Identity in Northern Anatolia*, Stuttgart: Franz Steiner Verlag, 75–86.
Manioti, Nikoletta (2019). 'The other Campanian volcano: Inarime in Flavian epic', in Antony Augoustakis and R. Joy Littlewood (eds.), *Campania in the Flavian Poetic Imagination*, Oxford: Oxford University Press, 61–73.
Manni, Eugenio (1981). *Geografia fisica e politica della Sicilia antica*, Rome: Giorgio Bretschneider.
Maraval, Pierre (ed.) (1997). *Égérie, Journal de voyage*, Sources chrétiennes 296, Paris: Éditions du Cerf.
Marcos, Moysés (2015). 'A tale of two commanders: Ammianus Marcellinus on the campaigns of Constantius II and Julian on the northern frontiers', *American Journal of Philology* 136: 669–708.
Marks, J. (2008). *Zeus in the Odyssey*, Cambridge, MA: Center for Hellenic Studies.
Mathieu, Jon (2005). 'Alpenwahrnehmung: Probleme der historischen Periodisierung', in Mathieu and Boscani Leoni (eds.), 53–72.
Mathieu, Jon (2006). 'The sacralization of the mountains', *Mountain Research and Development* 26: 343–49.

Mathieu, Jon (2009). *History of the Alps, 1500–1900: Environment, Development, and Society* (tr. Matthew Vester; first published in German in 1998), Morgantown: West Virginia Press.
Mathieu, Jon (2011). *The Third Dimension: A Comparative History of Mountains in the Modern Era* (tr. Katherine Brun first published in German in 2011), Cambridge: White Horse Press.
Mathieu, Jon, and Simona Boscani Leoni (eds.) (2005). *Die Alpen! Zur europäischen Wahrnehmungsgeschichte seit der Renaissance*, Bern: Peter Lang.
Matthews, John (1989). *The Roman Empire of Ammianus Marcellinus*, London: Duckworth.
Mattiacci, Silvia (2001). 'Riscritture apuleiane del *locus amoenus*', in Silvia Bianchetti (ed.), *POIKILMA: Studi in onore di Michele R. Cataudella*, La Spezia: Agorà edizioni, 843–59.
Mazzoleni, Donatella (2004). *Domus: Wall Painting in the Roman House*, Los Angeles: John Paul Getty Museum.
McGowan, Anne, and Paul F. Bradshaw (2018). *A New Translation of the Itinerarium Egeriae with Introduction and Commentary*, Collegeville, MN: Liturgical Press.
McInerney, Jeremy (1997). 'Parnassus, Delphi, and the Thyiades', *Greek, Roman and Byzantine Studies* 38: 263–83.
McInerney, Jeremy (1999). *The Folds of Parnassos: Land and Ethnicity in Ancient Phokis*, Austin: University of Texas Press.
McInerney, Jeremy (2006). 'On the border: sacred land and the margins of community', in Rosen and Sluiter (2006), 33–59.
McInerney, Jeremy, and Ineke Sluiter (eds.) (2016). *Valuing Landscape in Classical Antiquity: Natural Environment and Cultural Imagination*, Leiden: Brill.
McNee, A. (2016). *The New Mountaineer in Late Victorian Britain: Materiality, Modernity, and the Haptic Sublime*, Basingstoke: Palgrave Macmillan.
McNeil, J. R. (1992). *The Mountains of the Mediterranean World: An Environmental History*, Cambridge: Cambridge University Press.
McPhee, Brian D. (2019). '(*Adhuc*) *virgineusque Helicon*: a subtextual rape in Ovid's catalogue of mountains (*Met.* 2.219)', *Classical Quarterly* 69: 769–75.
Meeusen, Michiel, and Luc Van der Stockt (eds.) (2015). *Natural Spectaculars: Aspects of Plutarch's Philosophy of Nature*, Leuven: Leuven University Press.
Merlier-Espenel, Véronique (1999). 'Les représentations de la nature dans les *Métamorphoses* d'Apulée', in Christophe Cusset (ed.), *La nature et ses représentations dans l'antiquité*, Paris: Centre national de documentation pédagogique, 157–72.
Merlier-Espenel, Véronique (2004). 'La grotte des brigands dans les *Métamorphoses* d'Apulée', in Marie-Claude Charpentier (ed.), *Les espaces du sauvage dans le monde antique: approaches et définitions*, Besançon: Institut des Sciences et Techniques de l'Antiquité, 209–22.
Merrills, A. H. (2005). *History and Geography in Late Antiquity*, Cambridge: Cambridge University Press.
Millar, Fergus (1981). 'The world of the *Golden Ass*', *Journal of Roman Studies* 71: 63–75.
Minchin, Elizabeth (2001). *Homer and the Resources of Memory*, Oxford: Oxford University Press.
Mitchell, Ian (1998). *Scotland's Mountains before the Mountaineers*, Edinburgh: Luath Press.
Mitchell, Stephen (1993). *Anatolia: Land, Men, and Gods in Asia Minor. Volume II: The Rise of the Church*, Oxford: Clarendon Press.
Mitchell, W.J.T. (1994). 'Imperial landscape', in W.J.T. Mitchell (ed.), *Landscape and Power*, Chicago: University of Chicago Press, 5–34.

Montiglio, Silvia (2006). 'Should the aspiring wise man travel? A conflict in Seneca's thought', *American Journal of Philology* 127: 553–86.

Moralee, Jason (2018). *Rome's Holy Mountain: The Capitoline Hill in Late Antiquity*, Oxford: Oxford University Press.

Morales, Helen (2004). *Vision and Narrative in Achilles Tatius' Leucippe and Clitophon*, Cambridge: Cambridge University Press.

Morgan, Catherine (1999). 'Cultural subzones in early Iron Age and Archaic Arkadia', in Nielsen and Roy (1999), 382–456.

Morgan, J. R. (2015). 'The monk's story: the *Narrationes* of pseudo-Neilos of Ankyra', in Stelios Panayotakis, Gareth Schmeling, and Michael Paschalis (eds.), *Holy Men and Charlatans in the Ancient Novel*, Ancient Narrative, Supplement 19, Eelde: Barkhuis, 167–93.

Morrow, Glenn R. (1960). *Plato's Cretan City: A Historical Interpretation of the Laws*, Princeton, NJ: Princeton University Press.

Morton, Timothy (2007). *Ecology without Nature: Rethinking Environmental Aesthetics*, Cambridge, MA: Harvard University Press.

Morton, Timothy (2016). *Dark Ecology: For a Logic of Future Coexistence*, New York: Columbia University Press.

Muellner, Leonard (1990). 'The simile of the cranes and the pygmies: a study of Homeric metaphor', *Harvard Studies in Classical Philology* 93: 59–101.

Munn, Mark (2006). *The Mother of the Gods, Athens, and the Tyranny of Asia: A Study of Sovereignty in Ancient Religion*, Berkeley: University of California Press.

Murphy, Trevor (2004). *Pliny the Elder's Natural History: The Empire in the Encyclopedia*, Oxford: Oxford University Press.

Musa, Ghazali, James Higham, and Anna Thompson-Carr (eds.) (2017a). *Mountaineering Tourism*, London: Routledge.

Nagy, Gregory (2009). 'Hesiod and the ancient biographical traditions', in Franco Montanari, Antonios Rengakos, and Christos Tsagalis (eds.), *Brill's Companion to Hesiod*, Leiden: Brill, 271–311.

Nethercut, William (1969). 'Apuleius' *Metamorphoses*: the journey', *Agon* 3: 97–134.

Newby, Zahra (2007). 'Reading the allegory of the Archelaos relief', in Zahra Newby and Ruth Leader-Newby (eds.), *Art and Inscriptions in the Ancient World*, Cambridge: Cambridge University Press, 156–78.

Newby, Zahra (2012). 'The aesthetics of violence: myth and danger in Roman domestic landscapes', *Classical Antiquity* 31: 349–89.

Niccolai, Roberto (2019). 'I pericoli della montagna: la traversata delle Alpi e le frontiere dello storico', in Taufer (2019), 191–206.

Nicolet, Claude (1991). *Space, Geography, and Politics in the Early Roman Empire* (tr. Hélène Leclerc; first published in French in 1988), Ann Arbor: University of Michigan Press.

Nicolson, Marjorie Hope (1959). *Mountain Gloom and Mountain Glory: The Development of the Aesthetics of the Infinite*, Ithaca, NY: Cornell University Press.

Nielsen, Thomas Heine (1999). 'The concept of Arkadia: the people, their land, and their organisation', in Nielsen and Roy (1999), 16–79.

Nielsen, Thomas Heine, and James Roy (eds.) (1999). *Defining Ancient Arkadia*, Acts of the Copenhagen Polis Centre Volume 6, Copenhagen: Royal Danish Academy of Sciences and Letters.

Nightingale, Andrea (1993). 'Writing/reading a sacred text: a literary interpretation of Plato's *Laws*', *Classical Philology* 88: 279–300.

Nisbet, R.G.M., and Margaret Hubbard (1970). *A Commentary on Horace, Odes Book 1*, Oxford: Clarendon Press.

Novičenkova, Natalia G. (2008). 'Mountainous Crimea: a frontier zone of ancient civilization', in Pia Guldager Bilde and Jane Hjarl Petersen (eds.), *Meetings of Cultures in the Black Sea Region: Between Conflict and Coexistence*, Black Sea Studies 8, Aarhus: Aarhus Universitetsforlag, 287–301.

Nowicki, Krzysztzof (1999). 'Economy of refugees: life in the Cretan mountains at the turn of the Bronze and Iron Ages', in Chaniotis (1999a), 145–71.

Nydal, Anja-Karina (2018). 'A difficult line: the aesthetics of mountain climbing 1871–present', in Kakalis and Goetsch (2018), 155–70.

O'Brien, Maeve C. (2002). *Apuleius' Debt to Plato in the Metamorphoses*, Lewiston: Edwin Mellen Press.

Olson, S. Douglas (1991). 'Firewood and charcoal in classical Athens', *Hesperia* 60: 411–20.

Olson, S. Douglas (2012). *The Homeric Hymn to Aphrodite and Related Texts: Text, Translation and Commentary*, Berlin: De Gruyter.

Osborne, Robin (1987). *Classical Landscape with Figures: The Ancient Greek City and Its Countryside*, London: George Philip.

Palmer, Andrew (1998). 'Egeria the voyager, or the technology of remote sensing in late antiquity', in Zweder von Martels (ed.), *Travel Fact and Travel Fiction: Studies on Fiction, Literary Tradition, Scholarly Discovery and Observation in Travel Writing*, Leiden: Brill, 39–53.

Panegyres, Konstantine (2017). 'Ὄρεϊ νιφόεντι ἐοικώς: *Iliad* 13.754–755 revisited', *Mnemosyne* 70: 477–87.

Parker, Robert (1996). *Athenian Religion: A History*, Oxford: Clarendon Press.

Paschalis, Michael (2002). 'Reading space: a re-examination of Apuleian *ekphrasis*', in Paschalis and Frangoulidis (2002), 132–42.

Paschalis, Michael, and Stavros A. Frangoulidis (eds.) (2002). *Space in the Ancient Novel*, Ancient Narrative, Supplement 1, Groningen: Barkhuis Publishing.

Paterson, Andrew (2018). 'Climbing the invisible mountain: the apse mosaics of St. Catherine's monastery, Sinai, and their sixth-century viewers', in Kakalis and Goetsch (2018), 107–28.

Patrich, Joseph (2015). 'Monastic landscapes', in Luke Lavan (ed.), *Local Economies: Production and Exchange of Inland Regions in Late Antiquity*, Late Antique Archaeology 10, Leiden: Brill.

Pattenden, Philip (1983). 'The Byzantine early warning system', *Byzantion* 53: 258–99.

Payne, Mark (2014). 'The natural world in Greek literature and philosophy', in *Oxford Handbooks Online in Classical Studies*, https://www.oxfordhandbooks.com/view/10.1093/oxfordhb/9780199935390.001.0001/oxfordhb-9780199935390-e-001 (last consulted 31/7/21).

Peatfield, Allan (1983). 'The topography of Minoan peak sanctuaries', *Annual of the British School at Athens* 78: 273–79.

Peatfield, Allan (2009). 'The topography of Minoan peak sanctuaries revisited', in Anna Lucia D'Agata and Aleydis Van de Moortel (eds.), *Archaeologies of Cult: Essays on Ritual and Cult in Crete in Honor of Geraldine C. Gesell*, *Hesperia* Supplement 42, Princeton, NJ: American School of Classical Studies in Athens, 251–60.

Pelisiak, Andrzej, Marek Nowak, and Cyprian Astaloş (eds.) (2018). *People in the Mountains: Current Approaches to the Archaeology of Mountain Landscapes*, Oxford: Archaeopress Publishing.

Penwill, J. L. (1975). 'Slavish pleasures and profitless curiosity: fall and redemption in Apuleius' *Metamorphoses*', *Ramus* 69: 49–82.

Penwill, J. L. (1990). '*Ambages reciprocae*: reviewing Apuleius' *Metamorphoses*', *Ramus* 19: 1–25.

Perlik, Manfred (2019). *The Spatial and Economic Transformation of Mountain Regions: Landscapes as Commodities*, London: Routledge.

Peters, W.J.T. (1963). *Landscape in Romano-Campanian Mural Painting*, Assen: Van Gorcum.

Petridou, Georgia (2016). *Divine Epiphany in Ancient Greek Literature and Culture*, Oxford: Oxford University Press.

Phillips, Tom (2015a). '*Iliad* 13.754: ΟΡΕΙ ΝΙΦΟΕΝΤΙ ΕΟΙΚΩΣ', *Classical Quarterly* 65: 439–43.

Phillips, Tom (2015b). *Pindar's Library: Performance Poetry and Material Texts*, Oxford: Oxford University Press.

Phillips, Tom (2018). 'Hesiod and Pindar', in Loney and Scully (2018), 261–75.

Pitches, Jonathan (2020). *Performing Mountains*, London: Palgrave Macmillan.

Poiss, Thomas (2014). 'Looking for the bird's-eye view in ancient Greek sources', in Klaus Geuss and Martin Thiering (eds.), *Features of Common Sense Geography: Implicit Knowledge Structures in Ancient Geographical Texts*, Berlin: Lit Verlag, 69–88.

Pollitt, J. J. (1986). *Art in the Hellenistic Age*, Cambridge: Cambridge University Press.

Porter, James I. (2001). 'Ideals and ruins: Pausanias, Longinus, and the Second Sophistic', in Alcock et al. (eds.), 63–92.

Porter, James I. (2016). *The Sublime in Antiquity*, Cambridge: Cambridge University Press.

Porter, Roy (2000). '"In England's green and pleasant land": the English Enlightenment and the environment', in Kate Flint and Howard Morphy (eds.), *Culture, Landscape, and the Environment*, Oxford: Oxford University Press, 15–43.

Pothecary, Sarah (2002). 'Strabo the Tiberian author: past, present and silence in Strabo's *Geography*', *Mnemosyne* 55: 387–438.

Pothecary, Sarah (2005). 'The European provinces: Strabo as evidence', in Dueck et al. (2005), 161–79.

Potkay, Adam (2012). 'The British Romantic sublime', in Costelloe (2012), 203–16.

Pretzler, Maria (2004). 'Turning travel into text: Pausanias at work', *Greece and Rome* 51: 199–216.

Pretzler, Maria (2005a). 'Comparing Strabo with Pausanias: Greece in context vs. Greece in depth', in Dueck et al. (2005), 144–60.

Pretzler, Maria (2005b). 'Polybios to Pausanias: Arkadian identity in the Roman Empire', in Erik Østby (ed.), *Ancient Arkadia*, Athens: Paul Forlag Astroms, 521–31.

Pretzler, Maria (2007). *Pausanias: Travel Writing in Ancient Greece*, London: Duckworth.

Pretzler, Maria (2009). 'Arcadia: ethnicity and politics in the fifth and fourth centuries BCE', in Peter Funke and Nino Luraghi (eds.), *The Politics of Ethnicity and the Crisis of the Peloponnesian League*, Washington, DC: 86–109.

Price, Martin (2015). *Mountains: A Very Short Introduction*, Oxford: Oxford University Press.

Price, R. M. (1985). *A History of the Monks of Syria, by Theodoret of Cyrrhus*, Kalamazoo, MI: Cistercian Publications.

Price, Uvedale (1810). *Essays on the Picturesque, As Compared with the Sublime and the Beautiful; and on the Use of Studying Pictures, for the Purpose of Improving Real Landscape* (3 volumes), London: J. Mawman.

Pritchett, W. Kendrick (1982). *Studies in Ancient Greek Topography, Part IV (Passes)*, Berkeley: University of California Press.

Prontera, Francesco (2019). 'I monti nella geografia di Erodoto', in Taufer (2019), 167–73.

Purcell, Nicholas (2017a). '"Such is Rome . . .": Strabo on the "Imperial metropolis"', in Dueck (2017), 22–34.

Purcell, Nicholas (2017b). 'Mountain margins: power, resources and environmental inequality in Antiquity', in von Reden (2017), 75–114.

Purves, Alex C. (2010a). *Space and Time in Ancient Greek Narrative*, Cambridge: Cambridge University Press.

Purves, Alex C. (2010b). 'Wind and time in Homeric epic', *Transactions of the American Philological Association* 140: 323–50.

Purves, Alex C. (2015). 'Ajax and other objects: Homer's vibrant materialism', *Ramus* 44: 75–94.

Quantin, François (2005). 'À propos de l'imaginaire montagnard en Grèce ancienne', in Serge Brunet, Dominique Julia, and Nicole Lemaître (eds.), *Montagnes sacrées d'Europe*, Paris: Publications de la Sorbonne, 23–34.

Rabe, Hugo (1913). *Hermogenis opera*, Leipzig: Teubner.

Rackham, Oliver (1996). 'Ecology and pseudo-ecology: the example of ancient Greece', in Shipley and Salmon (1996), 16–43.

Ratti, Stéphane (2007). 'Le traverse du Danube par les Goths: la subversion d'un modèle héroïque (Ammien Marcellin 31.4)', in den Boeft et al. (2007), 181–200.

Ready, Jonathan L. (2011). *Character, Narrator, and Simile in the Iliad*, Cambridge: Cambridge University Press.

Ready, Jonathan L. (2018). *The Homeric Simile in Comparative Perspectives*, Oxford: Oxford University Press.

Rebenich, Stefan (2002). *Jerome*, London: Routledge.

Reden, Sitta von (ed.) (2017). *Économie et inégalité: ressources, échanges et pouvoir dans l'Antiquité classique*, Entretiens sur l'antiquité classique 63, Geneva: Fondation Hardt.

Redfield, James M. (1994). *Nature and Culture in the Iliad: The Tragedy of Hector*, Durham, NC: Duke University Press.

Rigby, Kate (2004). *Topographies of the Sacred: The Poetics of Place in European Romanticism*, Charlottesville: University of Virginia Press.

Riggsby, Andrew M. (2019). *Mosaics of Knowledge: Representing Information in the Roman World*, New York: Oxford University Press.

Rimell, Victoria (2002). *Petronius and the Anatomy of Fiction*, Cambridge: Cambridge University Press.

Ring, Jim (2000). *How the English Made the Alps*, London: John Murray.

Robbins, David (1987). 'Sport, hegemony and the middle classes: the Victorian mountaineers', *Theory, Culture and Society* 4: 579–601.

Robert, Louis (1937). *Études anatoliennes: recherches sur les inscriptions grecques de l'Asie Mineure*, Paris: E. de Boccard.

Robert, Louis (1949). *Hellenica: Recueil d'épigraphie, de numismatique et d'antiquités grecques VII*, Paris: Librairie Adrien Maisonneuve, 152–60.

Robert, Louis (1965). *Hellenica: Recueil d'épigraphie, de numismatique et d'antiquités grecques XIII: D'Aphrodisias à la Lycaonie*, Paris: Librairie Adrien Maisonneuve.

Robert, Jeanne, and Louis Robert (1983). *Fouilles d'Amyzon en Carie. Tome 1, Exploration, histoire, monnaies et inscriptions*, Paris: Diffusion de Boccard.

Robinson, Betsey A. (2012). 'Mount Helikon and the Valley of the Muses: the production of a sacred space', *Journal of Roman Archaeology* 25: 227–58.

Robinson, Betsey A. (2013). 'On the rocks: Greek mountains and sacred conversations', in Deena Ragavan (ed.), *Heaven on Earth: Temples, Ritual, and Cosmic Symbolism in the Ancient World*, Chicago: Oriental Institute of the University of Chicago, 175–99.

Robinson, Betsey A. (2016). 'Charismatic landscapes: scenes from central Greece under Roman rule', in McInerney and Sluiter (2016), 228–52.

Rocchi, Maria (1996). 'Le mont Hélicon: un espace mythique', in Hurst and Schachter (eds.), 15–25.

Roche, Clare (2013). 'Women climbers: a challenge to male hegemony', *Sport in History* 33: 236–59.

Roller, Duane W. (2014). *The Geography of Strabo*, Cambridge: Cambridge University Press.

Roller, Duane W. (2018). *A Historical and Topographical Guide to the Geography of Strabo*, Cambridge: Cambridge University Press.

Rollinger, Robert (2010). 'Berg und Gebirge aus altorientalischer Perspektive', in Kofler et al. (2010), 11–52.

Rollinger, Robert (2014). 'Aornos and the mountains of the east: the Assyrian kings and Alexander the Great', in Salvatore Gaspa, Alessandro Greco, Daniele Morandi Bonacossi, Simonetta Ponchia, and Robert Rollinger (eds.), *From Source to History: Studies on Ancient Near Eastern Worlds and Beyond*, Alter Orient und Altes Testament 214, Münster: Ugarit Verlag, 597–635.

Romano, David Gilman (2014). 'Athletic festivals in the northern Peloponnese and central Greece', in Paul Christesen and Donald G. Kyle (eds.), *A Companion to Sport and Spectacle in Greek and Roman Antiquity*, Malden, MA: Wiley-Blackwell, 176–91.

Romano, David Gilman (2019). 'Mt Lykaion as the Arkadian birthplace of Zeus', in Tanja Susanne Scheer (ed.), *Natur—Mythos—Religion im antiken Griechenland*, Stuttgart: Franz Steiner Verlag, 219–37.

Romano, David Gilman, and Mary E. Voyatzis (2010). 'Excavating at the birthplace of Zeus: the Mount Lykaion excavation and survey project', *Expedition* 52: 9–21.

Romano, David Gilman, and Mary E. Voyatzis (2014). 'Mount Lykaion excavation and survey project, Part 1: the upper sanctuary', *Hesperia* 83: 569–652.

Romano, David Gilman, and Mary E. Voyatzis (2015). 'Mount Lykaion excavation and survey project, Part 2: the lower sanctuary', *Hesperia* 84: 207–76.

Romm, James (2006). 'Herodotus and the natural world', in Carolyn Dewald and John Marincola (eds.), *The Cambridge Companion to Herodotus*, Cambridge: Cambridge University Press, 178–91.

Rood, Naomi (2006). 'Implied vengeance in the simile of the grieving vultures (*Odyssey* 16.216–19)', *Classical Quarterly* 56: 1–11.

Rood, Tim (2012). 'Polybius', in de Jong (2012), 179–97.
Rood, Tim (2014). 'Space and landscape in Xenophon's *Anabasis*', in Gilhuly and Worman (2014a), 63–93.
Rose, Mitch, and John Wylie (2011). 'Landscape—Part II', in John A. Agnew and James S. Duncan (eds.), *The Blackwell Companion to Human Geography*, Chichester: Wiley-Blackwell, 221–34.
Rosen, Ralph M., and Ineke Sluiter (eds.) (2006). *City, Countryside, and the Spatial Organization of Value in Classical Antiquity*, Leiden: Brill.
Ross, Alan J. (2016). *Ammianus' Julian: Narrative and Genre in the Res Gestae*, Oxford: Oxford University Press.
Rousseau, Philip (1978). *Ascetics, Authority and the Church in the Age of Jerome and Cassian*, Oxford: Oxford University Press.
Rousseau, Philip (1985). *Pachomius: The Making of a Community in Fourth-Century Egypt*, Berkeley: University of California Press.
Rousset, Denis (1994). 'Les frontiers des cités grecques: premières réflexions à partir du recueil des documents épigraphiques', in *Cahiers du Centre Gustave Glotz* 5: 97–126.
Roy, James (1999). 'The economies of Arkadia', in Thomas Heine Nielsen and James Roy (eds.), *Defining Ancient Arkadia*, Copenhagen: Royal Danish Academy of Sciences and Letters.
Roy, James (2009). 'Living in the mountains: Arkadian identity in the classical period', in Mercourios Georgiadis and Chrysanthi Gallou (eds.), *The Past in the Past: The Significance of Memory and Tradition in the Transmission of Culture*, British Archaeological Reports International Series 1925, Oxford: Archaeopress, 57–65.
Roy, James (2013). 'The Parrhasians of southwestern Arkadia', *Classica et Medievalia* 64: 5–48.
Rupp, David William (1976). 'The altars of Zeus and Hera on Mount Arachnaion in the Argeia, Greece', *Journal of Field Archaeology* 3: 261–68.
Russell, D. A. (1973). *Plutarch*, London: Duckworth.
Russell, D. A. (1992). *Dio Chrysostom, Orations VII, XII, XXXVI*, Cambridge: Cambridge University Press.
Rutherford, Ian (2001). 'Tourism and the sacred: Pausanias and the traditions of Greek pilgrimage', in Alcock et al. (2001), 40–52.
Ryken, Leland, James C. Wilhoit, and Tremper Longman III (eds.) (1998). *Dictionary of Biblical Imagery*, Downer's Grove, IL: IVP Academic.
Sale, William Merritt (1984). 'Homeric Olympus and its formulae', *American Journal of Philology* 105: 1–28.
Salway, Benet (2005). 'The nature and genesis of the Peutinger map', *Imago Mundi* 57: 119–35.
Salway, Benet (2012). 'Putting the world in order: mapping in Roman texts', in Talbert (2012a), 193–234.
Saunders, Timothy (2008). *Bucolic Ecology: Virgil's Eclogues and the Environmental Literary Tradition*, London: Duckworth.
Scarth, Alwyn (2000). 'The volcanic inspiration of some images in the *Aeneid*', *Classical World* 93: 591–605.
Scarth, Alwyn (2009). *Vesuvius: A Biography*, Princeton, NJ: Princeton University Press.
Schachter, Albert (1986). *Cults of Boiotia. Volume II, Herakles to Poseidon*, Bulletin of the Institute of Classical Studies, Supplement 38.2, London: Institute of Classical Studies.

Schaeffer, Claude F.-A. (1938). 'Les fouilles de Ras Sharma-Ugarit', *Syria* 19: 313–34.
Schama, Simon (1995). *Landscape and Memory*, London: Harper Collins.
Schaumann, Caroline (2020). *Peak Pursuits: The Emergence of Mountaineering in the Nineteenth Century*, New Haven, CT: Yale University Press.
Schiesaro, Alessandro (1985). 'Il "locus horridus" nelle "Metamorfosi" di Apuleio, *Met.* IV, 28–35', *Maia* 37: 211–23.
Schlam, Carl (1970). 'Platonica in the *Metamorphoses* of Apuleius', *Transactions and Proceedings of the American Philological Association* 101: 477–87.
Schliephake, Christopher (2017a). *Ecocriticism, Ecology, and the Cultures of Antiquity*, Lanham, MD: Lexington Books.
Schliephake, Christopher (2017b). 'Introduction', in Schliephake (2017a), 1–15.
Schliephake, Christopher (2020). *The Environmental Humanities and the Ancient World*, Cambridge: Cambridge University Press.
Schlosser, Joel Alden (2020). *Herodotus in the Anthropocene*, Chicago: Chicago University Press.
Schrijvers, Piet H. (2006). 'Silius Italicus and the Roman sublime', in Ruurd R. Nauta, Harm-Jan Van Dam, and Johannes J. L. Smolenaars (eds.), *Flavian Poetry*, Leiden: Brill, 97–112.
Schubert, Christoph (2019). 'Die Bergerzählungen im *Itinerarium Egeriae*: Phänomenologie und Funktion', in Taufer (2019), 303–26.
Schultz, Elizabeth (2009). 'Odysseus comes to know his place: reading the *Odyssey* ecocritically', *Neohelicon* 36: 299–310.
Scott, Michael (2014). *Delphi: A History of the Center of the Ancient World*, Princeton, NJ: Princeton University Press.
Scott, William C. (1974). *The Oral Nature of the Homeric Simile*, Leiden: Brill.
Scott, William C. (2009). *The Artistry of the Homeric Simile*, Hanover, NH: University Press of New England.
Seager, Robin (1986). *Ammianus Marcellinus: Seven Studies in His Language and Thought*, Columbia: University of Missouri Press.
Sebesta, Judith Lynn (2006). 'Vesuvius in classical literature', *New England Classical Journal* 33: 99–111.
Semple, Ellen Churchill (1932). *The Geography of the Mediterranean Region: Its Relation to Ancient History*, London: Constable.
Sharrock, Alison, and Helen Morales (eds.) (2000). *Intratextuality: Greek and Roman Textual Relations*, Oxford: Oxford University Press.
Shaw, Brent D. (1986). 'Autonomy and tribute: mountain and plain in Mauretania Tingitana', in *Désert et montagne au Maghreb: Hommage à Jean Dresch, Revue des mondes musulmans et de la Méditerranée* 41–42: 66–89.
Shaw, Brent D. (1990). 'Bandit highlands and lowland peace: the mountains of Isauria-Cilicia', *Journal of the Economic and Social History of the Orient* 33: 199–270.
Shelton, Peter (2003). *Climb to Conquer: The Untold Story of World War II's 10th Mountain Divison Ski Troops*, New York: Scribner.
Shepherd, Nan (1977). *The Living Mountain: A Celebration of the Cairngorm Mountains of Scotland*, Aberdeen: Aberdeen University Press.
Sherk, Robert K. (1974). 'Roman geographical exploration and military maps', *Aufstieg under Niedergang der römischen Welt* II, 1: 534–62.

Shipley, Graham, and John Salmon (eds.) (1996). *Human Landscapes in Classical Antiquity: Environment and Culture*, London: Routledge.

Shumate, Nancy (1996). *Crisis and Conversion in Apuleius' Metamorphoses*, Ann Arbor: University of Michigan Press.

Sidwell, Barbara (2010). *The Portrayal and Role of Anger in the Res Gestae of Ammianus Marcellinus*, Piscataway, NJ: Gorgias Press.

Sigurdsson, Haraldur (1999). *Melting the Earth: The History of Ideas on Volcanic Eruptions*, New York: Oxford University Press.

Sigurdsson, Haraldur (2002). 'Mount Vesuvius before the disaster', in Wilhelmina Feemster Kashemski and Frederick G. Meyer (eds.), *The Natural History of Pompeii*, Cambridge: Cambridge University Press, 29–36.

Silvas, Anna (2007). 'In quest of Basil's retreat: an expedition to ancient Pontus', *Antichthon* 41: 73–95.

Simpson, Thomas (2019). 'Modern mountains from the Enlightenment to the Anthropocene', *Historical Journal* 62: 553–81.

Sivan, Hagith (1988a). 'Who was Egeria? Piety and pilgrimage in the age of Gratian', *Harvard Theological Review* 81: 59–72.

Sivan, Hagith (1988b). 'Holy Land pilgrimage and Western audiences: some reflections on Egeria and her circle', *Classical Quarterly* 38: 528–35.

Skutsch, Otto (1985). *The Annals of Q. Ennius*, Oxford: Oxford University Press.

Skydsgaard, Jens Erik (1988). 'Transhumance in ancient Greece', in Whittaker (1988), 75–86.

Slater, Niall W. (2002). 'Space and displacement in Apuleius', in Paschalis and Frangoulidis (2002), 161–76.

Smith, Christopher (2012). 'Feriae Latinae', in J. Rasmus Brandt and Jon W. Iddeng (eds.), *Greek and Roman Festivals: Content, Meaning and Practice*, Oxford: Oxford University Press, 267–88.

Smith, R.R.R. (1991). *Hellenistic Sculpture: A Handbook*, London: Thames and Hudson.

Smith, Rowland (1995). *Julian's Gods: Religion and Philosophy in the Thought and Action of Julian the Apostate*, London: Routledge.

Smith, Warren S. (1998). 'Cupid and Psyche tale: mirror of the novel', in Maaike Zimmerman, Vincent Hunink, Thomas D. McCreight, Danielle Van Mal-Maeder, Stelios Panayotakis, V. Schmidt, and B. Wesseling (eds.), *Aspects of Apuleius' Golden Ass, Volume II: Cupid and Psyche*, Groningen: Egbert Forsten, 69–82.

Snyder, Gary (1990). 'The place, the region, and the commons', in *The Practice of the Wild*, San Francisco: North Point Press, 25–47.

Société des historiens médiévistes de l'enseignement supérieur public (ed.) (2004). *Montagnes médiévales: XXIV Congrès de la SHMES (Chambért, 23–25 mai 2003)*, Paris: Éditions de la Sorbonne, https://books.openedition.org/psorbonne/23225 (last consulted 31/7/21).

Sodini, Ivan (2019). 'Strabone e i popoli delle Alpi: poveri, nomadi e briganti', in Taufer (2019), 243–85.

Southern, Pat (1996). 'Men and mountains, or geographical determinism and the conquest of Scotland', *Proceedings of the Society of Antiquaries of Scotland* 126: 371–86.

Spencer, Diana (2010). *Roman Landscape: Culture and Identity*, Cambridge: Cambridge University Press.

Spengel, Leonhard von (1853–56). *Rhetores Graeci* (3 volumes), Leipzig: Teubner.
Spitzer, Leo (1949). 'The epic style of the pilgrim Aetheria', *Comparative Literature* 1: 225–58.
Sporn, Katja (2013). '"Der göttliche Helikon": Bergkulte oder Kulte auf den Bergen in Griechenland?', in Rupert Breitwieser, Monika Frass, and Georg Nightingale (eds.), *Calamus: Festschrift für Herbert Graßl zum 65. Geburtstag*, Wiesbaden: Harrassowitz Verlag, 465–77.
Stephen, Leslie (1871). *The Playground of Europe*, London: Longmans, Green and Co.
Stone, M. E. (1986). 'Holy land pilgrimage of Armenians before the Arab conquest', *Revue biblique* 93: 93–110.
Stoneman, Richard (2010). *Land of Lost Gods: The Search for Classical Greece* (2nd edition; first published in 1987), London: Tauris Parke Paperbacks.
Sundwall, Gavin A. (1996). 'Ammianus geographicus', *American Journal of Philology* 117: 619–43.
Swain, Simon (1996). *Hellenism and Empire: Language, Classicism and Power in the Greek World, AD 50–250*, Oxford: Oxford University Press.
Swain, Simon (ed.) (2000). *Dio Chrysostom: Politics, Letters, and Philosophy*, Oxford: Oxford University Press.
Talbert, Richard J. A. (2000). *Barrington Atlas of the Greek and Roman World*, Princeton, NJ: Princeton University Press.
Talbert, Richard J. A. (2010). *Rome's World: The Peutinger Map Reconsidered*, Cambridge: Cambridge University Press.
Talbert, Richard J. A. (ed.) (2012a). *Ancient Perspectives: Maps and Their Place in Mesopotamia, Egypt, Greece, and Rome*, Chicago: University of Chicago Press.
Talbert, Richard J. A. (2012b). '*Urbs Roma* to *orbis romanus*: Roman mapping on the grand scale', in Talbert (2012a), 163–90.
Taplin, Oliver (2007). *Pots and Plays: Interactions between Tragedy and Greek Vase Painting of the Fourth Century B.C.*, Los Angeles: J. Paul Getty Museum.
Taplin, Oliver (2010). 'Echoes from Mount Cithaeron', in Phillip Mitsis and Christos Tsagalis (eds.), *Allusion, Authority, and Truth: Critical Perspectives on Greek Poetic and Rhetorical Praxis*, Berlin: De Gruyter, 235–48.
Tarpin, Michel (1992). 'Frontières naturelles et frontières culturelles dans les Alpes du nord', in Fabre (1992), 97–120.
Tatum, W. Jeffrey (2013). 'Still waters run deep: Plutarch, *Aemilius Paulus* 14', *Classical Quarterly* 63: 377–86.
Taub, Liba (2008). *Aetna and the Moon: Explaining Nature in Ancient Greece and Rome*, Corvallis: Oregon State University Press.
Taub, Liba (2009). 'Explaining a volcano naturally: Aetna and the choice of poetry', in Liba Taub and Aude Doody (eds.), *Authorial Voices in Greco-Roman Technical Writing*, Trier: WVT Wissenschaftlicher Verlag Trier, 125–41.
Taufer, Matteo (2019). *La montagna nell'antichità—Berge in der Antike—Mountains in Antiquity*, Freiburg: Rombach Verlag.
Thacker, Christopher (1983). *The Wildness Pleases: The Origins of Romanticism*, London: Croom Helm.
Thalmann, William G. (2011). *Apollonius of Rhodes and the Spaces of Hellenism: Classical Culture and Society*, Oxford: Oxford University Press.

Thollard, Patrick (1987). *Barbarie et civilization chez Strabon: étude critique des livres III et IV de la Géographie*, Paris: Les Belles Lettres.

Thomas, Keith (1983). *Man and the Natural World: Changing Attitudes in England, 1500-1800*, London: Allen Lane.

Thomas, Oliver (2011). 'The Homeric Hymn to Pan', in Faulkner (2011a), 151-72.

Thomasset, Claude, and Danièle James-Raoul (eds.) (2000). *La montagne dans le texte medieval: entre mythe et réalité*, Paris: Presses de l'Université de Paris-Sorbonne.

Thompson, Mark (2008). *The White War: Life and Death on the Italian Front 1915-1919*, London: Faber and Faber.

Thonemann, Peter (2011). *The Maeander Valley: A Historical Geography from Antiquity to Byzantium*, Cambridge: Cambridge University Press.

Thonemann, Peter (2020). *An Ancient Dream Manual: Artemidorus' The Interpretation of Dreams*, Oxford: Oxford University Press.

Toohey, Peter (1996). *Epic Lessons: An Introduction to Didactic Poetry*, Abingdon: Routledge.

Trinquier, Jean (1999). 'Le motif du repaire des brigands et le topos du *locus horridus*: Apulée, *Metamorphoses*, IV, 6', *Revue de Philologie* 73: 257-77.

Tsagalis, Christos (2012). *From Listeners to Viewers: Space in the Iliad*, Cambridge, MA: Center for Hellenic Studies.

Tuan, Yi-Fu (1990). *Topophilia: A Study of Environmental Perception, Attitudes and Values* (2nd edition; first published in 1974), New York: Columbia University Press.

Urbainczyk, Theresa (2002). *Theodoret of Cyrrhus: The Bishop and the Holy Man*, Ann Arbor: University of Michigan Press.

Usher, M. D. (2020). *Plato's Pigs and Other Ruminations: Ancient Guides to Living with Nature*, Cambridge: Cambridge University Press.

Van der Vliet, Edward C. L. (2003). 'The Romans and us: Strabo's *Geography* and the construction of ethnicity', *Mnemosyne* 56: 257-72.

Van Mal-Maeder, D. K. (1997a). 'Descriptions et descripteurs: mais qui décrit dans les *Métamorphoses* d'Apulée?', in Michelangelo Picone and Bernhard Zimmermann (eds.), *Der antike Roman und seine mittelalterliche Rezeption*, Basel: Birkhäuser Verlag, 171-201.

Van Mal-Maeder, D. K. (1997b). '*Lector intende: laetaberis*: the enigma of the last book of Apuleius' *Metamorphoses*', *Groningen Colloquia on the Novel* 8: 87-118.

Van Mal-Maeder, D. K. (2001). *Apuleius Madaurensis Metamorphoses Book 2: Text, Introduction and Commentary*, Groningen: Egbert Forsten.

Veal, Robyn (2013). 'Fuelling ancient Mediterranean cities: a framework for charcoal research', in Harris (2013a), 37-58.

Veal, Robyn (2017a). 'The politics and economics of ancient forests: timber and fuel as levers of Greco-Roman control', in von Reden (2017), 317-67.

Veal, Robyn (2017b). 'Wood and charcoal for Rome: towards an understanding of ancient regional fuel economies', in Tymon C. A. de Haas and Gijs Tol (eds.), *The Economic Integration of Roman Italy: Rural Communities in a Globalising World*, Leiden: Brill, 388-406.

Veneri, Alina (1996). 'L'Elicona nella cultura tespiese', in Hurst and Schachter (1996), 73-86.

Vergados, Athanassios (2012). 'Corinna's poetic mountains: *PMG* 654 col. i 1-34 and Hesiodic reception', *Classical Philology* 107: 101-18.

Vessey, D.W.T. (1985). 'From mountain to lovers' tryst: Horace's Soracte Ode', *Journal of Roman Studies* 75: 26-38.

Vidal-Naquet, Pierre (1986). 'Land and sacrifice in the *Odyssey*', in *The Black Hunter: Forms of Thought and Forms of Society in the Greek World* (tr. Andrew Szegedy-Maszak; first published in French in 1981), Baltimore: Johns Hopkins University Press, 15–38.

Volk, Katharina (2005). '*Aetna* oder Wie man ein Lehrgedicht schreibt', in Niklas Holzberg (ed.), *Die Appendix Vergiliana: I Pseudepigraphen im literarischen Kontext*, Classica Monacensia 30, Tübingen: Gunter Narr Verlag, 68–90.

Vout, Caroline (2012). *The Hills of Rome: Signature of an Eternal City*, Cambridge: Cambridge University Press.

Voutiras, Emmanuel (2006). 'Le culte de Zeus en Macédoine avant la conquête romaine', in A. M. Guimier-Sorbets, M. B. Hatzopoulos, and Y. Morizot (eds.), *Rois, cités, nécropoles: institutions, rites et monuments en Macédoine*, Athens: 333–45.

Walbank, F. W. (1957). *A Historical Commentary on Polybius, Volume II*, Oxford: Clarendon Press.

Wallace, Paul W. (1980). 'The Anopaia path at Thermopylai', *American Journal of Archaeology* 84: 15–23.

Wallace-Hadrill, D. S. (1968). *The Greek Patristic View of Nature*, Manchester: Manchester University Press.

Walsh, Kevin (2014). *The Archaeology of Mediterranean Landscapes: Human-Environment Interaction from the Neolithic to the Roman Period*, Cambridge: Cambridge University Press.

Walsh, P. G. (1970). *The Roman Novel: The 'Satyricon' of Petronius and the 'Metamorphoses' of Apuleius*, Cambridge: Cambridge University Press.

Walsham, Alexandra (2011). *The Reformation of the Landscape: Religion, Identity, and Memory in Early Modern Britain and Ireland*, Oxford: Oxford University Press.

Walter, Justine (2017). 'Poseidon's wrath and the end of Helike: notions about the anthropogenic character of disasters in antiquity', in Schliephake (2017a), 31–43.

Ward, Walter D. (2015). *The Mirage of the Saracen: Christians and Nomads in the Sinai Peninsula in Late Antiquity*, Oakland: University of California Press.

Webb, Ruth (2009). *Ekphrasis, Imagination and Persuasion in Ancient Rhetorical Theory and Practice*, Farnham: Ashgate.

Weil, Simone (2005). 'The *Iliad*, or the poem of force', in Simone Weil and Rachel Bespaloff (2005), *War and the Iliad* (tr. Mary McCarthy; first published in French in 1940), New York: New York Review Books, 3–37.

Weingarten, Susan (2005). *The Saint's Saints: Hagiography and Geography in Jerome*, Leiden: Brill.

Weisweiler, John (2015). 'Unreliable witness: failings of the narrative in Ammianus Marcellinus', in Lieve Van Hoof and Peter Van Nuffelen (eds.), *Literature and Society in the Fourth Century AD: Performing Paideia, Constructing the Present, Presenting the Self*, Leiden: Brill.

Welsh, Jarrett T. (2014). 'How to read a volcano', *Transactions of the American Philological Association* 144: 97–132.

West, Martin (1966). *Hesiod, Theogony: Edited with Prolegomena and Commentary*, Oxford: Oxford University Press.

Westaway, Jonathan (2009). 'The German community in Manchester, middle-class culture and the development of mountaineering in Britain, c. 1850–1914', *English Historical Review* 124: 571–604.

Westra, Haijo Jan (1995). 'The pilgrim Egeria's concept of place', *Mittellateinisches Jahrbuch* 30: 93–100.

Whalin, Douglas (2021). 'Mountains and the holy in late antiquity', in Hollis and König (2021a), 89–107.
White, Lynn, Jr. (1967). 'The historical roots of our ecologic crisis', *Science* 155: 1203–7.
Whitmarsh, Tim (2004). 'Dio Chrysostom', in Irene J. F. de Jong, René Nünlist, and Angus Bowie (eds.), *Narrators, Narratees, and Narratives in Ancient Greek Literature*, Leiden: Brill, 451–64.
Whitmarsh, Tim (2015). *Battling the Gods: Atheism in the Ancient World*, New York: Alfred A. Knopf.
Whittaker, C. R. (ed.) (1988). *Pastoral Economies in Classical Antiquity*, Proceedings of the Cambridge Philological Society, Supplementary Volume 14, Cambridge: Cambridge University Press.
Wickens, Jere M., Susan I. Rotroff, Tracey Cullen, Lauren E. Talalay, Catherine Perlès, and Floyd W. McCoy (2018). *Settlement and Land Use on the Periphery: The Bouros-Kastri Peninsula, Southern Euboia*, Oxford: Archaeopress.
Wickham, C. J. (1988). *The Mountains and the City: The Tuscan Apennines in the Early Middle Ages*, Oxford: Oxford University Press.
Wiedemann, T.E.J. (1986). 'Between men and beasts: barbarians in Ammianus Marcellinus', in I. S. Moxon, J. D. Smart, and A. J. Woodman (eds.), *Past Perspectives: Studies in Greek and Roman Historical Writing*, Cambridge: Cambridge University Press, 189–201.
Williams, Gareth D. (2006). 'Greco-Roman seismology and Seneca on earthquakes in *Natural Questions* 6', *Journal of Roman Studies* 96: 124–46.
Williams, Gareth D. (2012). *The Cosmic Viewpoint: A Study of Seneca's Natural Questions*, Oxford: Oxford University Press.
Williams, Gareth D. (2017). *Pietro Bembo on Etna: The Ascent of a Venetian Humanist*, New York: Oxford University Press.
Williams, Hamish (2018). 'Mountains in the *Apologue*: figures of isolation in society, space, and time', *Scripta Classica Israelica* 37: 69–91.
Williams, Mary Frances (1991). *Landscape in the Argonautica of Apollonius Rhodius*, Frankfurt: Peter Lang.
Williams, Michael Stuart (2008). *Authorised Lives in Early Christian Biography: Between Eusebius and Augustine*, Cambridge: Cambridge University Press.
Williams, Raymond (1973). *The Country and the City*, London: Chatto and Windus.
Williams Reed, Eris (2020). 'Environments and gods: creating the sacred landscape of Mount Kasios', in Ralph Haüssler and Gian Franco Chiai (eds.), *Sacred Landscapes in Antiquity: Creation, Manipulation, Transformation*, Oxford: Oxbow Books, 87–96.
Williamson, Christina (2014). 'Power, politics and panoramas: viewing the sacred landscape of Zeus Stratios near Amaseia', in Tønnes Bekker-Nielsen (ed.), *Space, Place and Identity in Northern Anatolia*, Geographica Historica 29, Stuttgart: Franz Steiner Verlag, 175–88.
Williamson, Christina (2016). 'Mountain, myth, and territory: Teuthrania as focal point in the landscape of Pergamon', in McInerney and Sluiter (2016), 70–99.
Wilton, Andrew (1980). *Turner and the Sublime*, Chicago: University of Chicago Press.
Wood, Philip (2009). 'The invention of history in the later Roman world: the conversion of Isauria in the *Life of Conon*', *Anatolian Studies* 59: 129–38.
Woolf, Greg (2011). *Tales of the Barbarians: Ethnography and Empire in the Roman West*, Oxford: Wiley-Blackwell.

Worman, Nancy (2015). *Landscape and the Spaces of Metaphor in Ancient Literary Theory and Criticism*, Cambridge: Cambridge University Press.

Woronoff, Michel (1983). 'Zeus, maître de l'Ida', *Annales littéraires de l'Université de Besançon* 273: 83–93.

Woronoff, Michel (1995). 'De l'Olympe à l'Ida', *Ktèma: civilisations de l'Orient, de la Grèce et de Rome antiques* 20: 213–22.

Woronoff, Michel (2001). 'Zeus de l'*Iliade*, Zeus de l'*Odysée*', in Michael Woronoff, Simone Follet, and Jacques Jouanna (eds.), *Dieux, héros et médecins grecs: hommage à Fernand Robert*, Besançon: Institut des Sciences et Techniques de l'Antiquité, 37–52.

Wylie, John (2007). *Landscape*, London: Routledge.

Xenophontos, Sophia (2017). 'Military space and *paideia* in the Lives of Pyrrhus and Marius', in Georgiadou and Oikonomopoulou (2017), 317–26.

Zeitlin, Froma (2001). 'Visions and revisions of Homer', in Simon Goldhill (ed.), *Being Greek under Rome: Cultural Identity, the Second Sophistic and the Development of Empire*, Cambridge: Cambridge University Press, 195–268.

Zillman, Lawrence John (1959). *Shelley's Prometheus Bound: A Variorum Edition*, Seattle: University of Washington Press.

Zimmerman, Maaike (1993). 'Narrative judgement and reader response in Apuleius' *Metamorphoses* 10.29–34: the pantomime of the judgement of Paris', *Groningen Colloquia on the Novel* 5: 143–61.

Zimmerman, Maaike (2000). *Apuleius Madaurensis, Metamorphoses Book 10: Text, Introduction and Commentary*, Groningen: Egbert Forsten.

Zimmerman, Maaike (2002). 'On the road in Apuleius' *Metamorphoses*', in Paschalis and Frangoulidis (2002), 78–97.

Zimmermann, Bernhard (2019). 'Und der Kithairon tanzt—Der Berg als Mitspieler in Euripides' *Bakchen*', in Taufer (2019), 141–48.

Zimmermann, Markus (2019). 'Bergerlebnisse bei Xenophon', in Taufer (2019), 175–89.

INDEX LOCORUM

Aelius Aristides, *Panathenaicus* (*Oration* 1)
    22–23, 338n34
Aeschylus
    Agamemnon
        281–316, 336n1
    Prometheus Bound
        4–5, 105
        15, 105
        20, 105
        351–72, 112
        1080–93, 341n31
Aelius Theon *Progymnasmata*
    11, 101–2
Alciphron, *Letters*
    1.3.2, 377n30
    2.11, 377n30
Ammianus Marcellinus, *Res Gestae*
    14.2.1, 231
    14.2.2, 231, 236
    14.2.5–6, 232
    14.3.2, 235
    14.4.1, 235
    14.5.6, 235
    14.8, 369n25
    15.2.4, 235
    15.4.8, 236
    15.4.11, 236
    15.10, 368n2
    16.5.17, 236
    16.12.51, 237
    16.12.57, 237
    17.7, 369n23
    17.8.4, 236

18.6.21, 239
18.6.22, 239
18.7.2, 239
18.8.9, 238
19.11.1, 368n6
19.13.1, 233
22.8, 369n25
22.12.6, 333n31
23.6.28–9, 239
23.6.59–61, 239–40
24.6.7, 369n19
26.6.10, 235
26.10.15–19, 238
27.1.1, 368n9
27.4, 369n25
27.5.3–4, 368n7
27.7.4, 369n12
27.10.9, 237
27.10.11, 237
27.10.12, 237
27.12.11, 368n7
28.2.1, 368n6
28.2.5–9, 237
28.2.8, 237
28.3.4–5, 369n15
29.3.2, 369n15
29.4.5, 368n7
28.5.1, 368n9
29.6.1, 369n9
28.6.2–4, 368n9
29.5.44, 368n8
30.5.13, 368n7
31.2.1, 240

Ammianus Marcellinus, *Res Gestae*
(*continued*)
    31.2.4, 240
    31.3.7, 368n7
    31.3.8, 240
    31.4–5, 241
    31.4.6, 241
    31.4.9, 241
    31.4.13, 368n7
    31.8.9, 241
    31.10.12, 368n7
    31.10.15, 368n7
    31.10.21, 241
    31.12.17, 241
    31.15.2, 241
    31.16.7, 242
    31.16.9, 242
Anastasius of Sinai, *Tales of the Sinai Fathers*
    1.1–6, 334n55
    1.4, 334n54
    1.12, 295
Apollonius of Rhodes, *Argonautica*
    1.547–58, 349n28
    1.1112–16, 349n29
Apuleius
    De mundo
        296, 341n27
    Florida
        1, 350n9
        10.4, 350n9
        11, 350n9
        21, 350n9
        21.3, 351n23
    Metamorphoses
        1.1, 164
        1.2.2, 165
        1.3.1, 352n28
        1.8, 355n86
        1.8.4, 352n28
        1.19, 352n34
        1.24, 351n19
        2.1.3–4, 166
        2.1.4, 171
        2.5.4–7, 352n28
        2.5.7, 171
        3.23, 171
        3.24.4, 171
        3.29, 303
        4.2.1–2, 167
        4.3, 352n32
        4.5.3, 171
        4.6, 351n14
        4.6.2, 352n37
        4.27.4, 169
        4.5.4, 170
        4.5.7, 168, 354n66
        4.6.1–4, 163, 167
        4.6.4, 175
        4.12.8, 170
        5.1, 351n14
        5.24, 353n47
        5.27.3, 170
        5.27.5, 170
        6.1.4, 354n85
        6.13–14, 381n74
        6.13.4, 353n47
        6.14, 351n14
        6.14.2–4, 353n47
        6.14.6, 171
        6.16–20, 353n47
        6.25.4, 170
        6.26.6, 170
        7.13.6, 170
        7.14.5, 171
        7.15.1, 171
        7.15.3, 171
        7.15.5, 171
        7.17.3–4, 172
        7.17.4, 353n65
        7.17.5, 172
        7.18.2, 172
        7.18.8, 353n65
        7.20.2, 172
        8.17.4–5, 169–70
        8.17–18, 352n28
        8.18–19, 352n34
        9.9.1–2, 169
        9.10.5, 169
        9.32.4, 169, 353n64
        9.40.2, 170

INDEX LOCORUM

10.29, 174
10.30–34, 355n86
10.30.1, 161, 174–75
10.32–33, 351n14
10.34.2, 161, 175
11.1, 176
11.3, 176
11.13.5, 176
11.7, 176
11.15.1, 176
11.15.5, 355n86
11.16.2, 176
11.23, 176
11.24.2, 354–355n86
11.25.3–4, 176
11.26, 176
11.30.1, 355n86

Appian
Civil Wars
4.7.56, 185
4.10.79, 356n16
Roman History
11.18, 362–363n29
12.66, 319n40

Aristotle
Meteorology
2.6 (363b17), 210
2.8, 341n30
Problems
26.1 (940a19), 210

Arrian, *Anabasis*
4.18.7–19.3, 184–85, 204
4.21, 205
4.28–30, 205

Athanasius, *Life of Antony*
3.2, 288
8–11, 379n23
11.2, 288
49.17, 288

Augustine
Confessions
8.6.14–15, 379n30
De Genesi ad litteram liber unus imperfectus
1.14, 320n59

Basil of Caesarea, *Letters*
14, 101

Cato, *De agricultura*
1.3, 373n46
Certamen Homeri et Hesiodi
13, 347n7

Cicero
De natura deorum
2.98–100, 104–5, 341n27
Pro Cluentio
25 (67–8), 234–35

Clement of Alexandria, *Protrepticus*
1.2.1–4, 347n8

Columella, *De re rustica*
1.4.10–1.5.2, 373n46

Cypria
fragment 12, 322n45

Cyprian, *Epistles*
1.6, 348n25

Dio Chrysostom
Oration 7
1, 269
4, 269, 275
5, 275
6, 270
7–8, 275
11, 271
12, 271
13, 271
14–15, 101, 274
16, 272
19, 273
20, 273
24, 275
25–26, 275–76
27–28, 276
29, 276
30, 276
34, 276
37, 276
46, 273
47, 272
49, 279

Dio Chrysostom, *Oration* (continued)
    61, 279
    63, 279
    65–80, 273
    68–69, 273
    73, 273
    75, 273
    76, 273
    107–8, 281
  Oration 12
    61, 319n33
  Oration 33
    2, 102
    20, 102
  Oration 35
    13, 102, 281–82
Diodorus Siculus, *Bibliotheca historica*
    2.6.8, 185
    4.19.3–4, 357n49
    5.39.2, 356n17
Diogenes Laertius, *Lives and Opinions of the Eminent Philosophers*
    9.1.3, 378n7
Dionysius of Halicarnassus, *Roman Antiquities*
    1.47, 356n22
    1.79.12, 367n29
    2.50.1, 367n29

Egeria, *Itinerarium*
    1.1, 85
    2.3, 83
    2.5, 82
    2.6, 335n65
    2.7, 83, 84, 335n65
    3.2, 85
    3.4, 285
    3.8, 85–86
    4.4, 335n72
    5.3, 83
    5.8, 83
    5.11–12, 84
    10.1, 336n92
    12.3–5, 90

Euripides
  Bacchae
    704–8, 48
    751–54, 48
    1043–45, 49
    1051–53, 49
    1137–39, 49
  Hippolytus
    215, 349n38

Frontinus, *Strategemata*
    1.2.8, 362n30
    1.4.5, 362n30
    1.4.7, 362n30
    1.5.3, 362n30
    1.5.8, 362n30
    1.5.21, 362n30
    1.5.28, 362n30
    2.4.4, 208

Galen
  On the Composition of the Art of Medicine
    K1.224, 147–48
  On the Diagnosis and Cure of the Errors of the Soul
    K5.89, 348n18
Granius Licinianus
    36.30–32, 359n1
Gregory of Nazianzus
    Letters 4–6, 101
Gregory of Nyssa, *Life of Moses*
    1.46, 74
    2.158, 74

Hellenica Oxyrhynchia
    13.3, 260, 374n79
Herodotus, *Histories*
    1.1, 360n10
    1.203.1–2, 201
    2.81–2, 201
    3.60, 202
    3.117, 203
    4.23–25, 201–2

INDEX LOCORUM 423

    6.44, 203
    6.105, 333n36
    7.22.1, 203
    7.24.1, 360n10
    7.35, 203
    7.42, 203
    7.49, 203
    7.178, 203
    7.188, 203
    8.12, 203
    8.37, 203, 360n14
    9.59, 360n16
    9.122, 202, 365n11
Hesiod
    Theogony
        1–8, 27–28
        22–23, 27–28
        39–43, 26–27
        113, 26
        126–32, 26
        482–84, 26
        617–735, 332n6
        857–68, 340n15
    Works and Days
        232–33, 27
        287–92, 147
        509–11, 27
        639–40, 27
        646–62, 331n52
Hippocrates, *Airs, Waters, Places*
    24, 196
Historia Augusta, Hadrian
    13.3, 111
    14.3, 340n23
    26.5, 338n38
History of the Monks in Egypt
    7, 289
Homer
    Iliad
        1.18, 322n41
        1.44, 322n43
        1.235, 36
        1.268, 36
        1.402, 322n42

        1.420, 322n44
        1.498–99, 32
        1.499, 322n44
        1.530, 32
        1.591, 32
        2.455–56
        2.496–97, 34
        2.542, 376n15
        2.603–4, 34
        2.631–32, 34
        2.756–58, 34
        3.10–12, 96
        3.10–14, 37
        3.259, 327n103
        3.276, 323n49
        3.320, 323n49
        4.148, 327n103
        4.150, 327n103
        4.275–79, 37, 43
        4.275–82, 326n92
        4.279, 44
        4.452–55, 326n101
        4.521, 324n68
        5.351, 327n103
        5.557–58, 326n93
        5.770–72, 43–44, 326n92
        6.395–97, 34
        7.189, 327n104
        7.268, 324n68
        8.47–48, 3
        8.75–76, 323n51
        8.170–6, 323n51
        8.378, 327n104
        8.555–59, 43–44
        9.14–15, 325n86
        9.15, 321n19
        10, 362n31
        11.67–69, 325n74
        11.77, 317n48
        11.254, 327n103
        11.345, 327n103
        12.208, 327n103
        12.209, 327n103
        12.252–54, 33

Homer, *Iliad* (*continued*)
    12.331, 327n103
    13.17–19, 33
    13.63, 321n19
    13.389–91, 325n71
    13.754, 41
    14.169–72, 21
    14.225–30, 21, 32
    14.280–85, 21
    14.283, 21
    14.292, 323n50
    14.342–44, 3
    15.34, 327n103
    15.273, 321n19
    15.619, 321n19
    16.3–4, 325n86
    16.35, 321n19
    16.119, 327n103
    16.156–63, 42
    16.299–300, 326n93
    16.482–84, 325n71
    16.530, 327n104
    16.603–7, 323n48
    17.742–45, 324n69
    20.216–18, 34
    21.448–49, 323n58
    22.169–71, 33
    22.347, 326n89
    23.114–22, 38
    24.321, 327n104
    24.424, 327n104
    24.507–12, 326n88
  Odyssey
    1.3, 376n13
    5.50, 322n38
    5.116, 327n103
    5.171, 327n103
    5.597–99, 327n103
    5.279–80, 323n56
    6.42–45, 323n53
    8.199, 327n104
    8.569, 323n56
    9.112–15, 375n93
    9.113–15, 247
    9.187–92, 323n56
    9.190–92, 247, 325n81
    9.243, 25
    9.315, 247
    10.81, 133
    10.87–88, 133
    10.88, 321n19
    10.97, 133
    10.113, 133
    10.121–22, 133
    10.121–32, 169
    10.146, 274
    10.156–71, 275
    11.315–16, 322n38
    13.152, 323n56
    13.226, 327n104
    13.250, 327n104
    13.353, 327n104
    13.423, 325n73
    15.165, 327n104
    16.216–19, 324n60
    19.177–78, 333n38
    19.204–8, 325n81
    19.426–66, 325n69
    20.104, 327n104
    21.414, 327n104
    22.207, 327n104
    24.504, 327n104
  Schol. ad *Od.* 19.179, 333n38
Homeric Hymn to Aphrodite
  59–63, 21
  67–69, 21
  97–102, 22
  267, 321n19
Homeric Hymn to Artemis
  4–8, 320n9
Homeric Hymn to Delian Apollo
  22–23, 23
  141, 23
  144–45, 23
Homeric Hymn to Demeter
  272, 23
Homeric Hymn to Dionysus (1)
  8–9, 320n8

Homeric Hymn to Dionysus (26)
    3–10, 320n8
Homeric Hymn to Hermes
    95–96, 321n22
    273, 321n22
    404, 321n19
Homeric Hymn to Pan
    2–14, 24–25
Horace, *Odes*
    1.2.33, 156
    1.9.1–4, 144, 157–58, 159
    1.9.5–8, 158
    1.9.9–12, 158
    1.9.17–18
    1.12.1–8, 156
    1.16.5, 156
    1.17.1–2, 157
    1.22.5–8, 155–56
    1.21.5–8, 156
    1.23.1–3, 155
    3.4.21–22, 156–57

Jerome
    Life of Hilarion
        5.1–2, 301
        21.2, 302
        31, 381n73
        31.4–5, 302–3
        31.9, 303
        32.7, 303
    Life of Paul of Thebes
        5–6, 381n73
John Climacus, *Ladder of Divine Ascent*
    30, 79
John of Ephesus, *Lives of the Eastern Saints* (*Patrologia orientalis* 17)
    pp. 128–29, 298
    pp. 131–32, 299
    p. 229, 298
    p. 232, 298
    pp. 232–33, 299
    pp. 233–34, 299

    p. 235, 299
    p. 246, 300
Julian, *To the Cynic Herakleios*
    230c–232d, 333n40
Julius Caesar, *Gallic Wars*
    3.1–6, 357n41

Korinna
    fragment 54, 346n51

Libanius, *Orations*
    11.22–27, 338n35
    11.198–201, 338n35
    11.200, 102
    12.28, 148
    15.79, 333n31
    18.126, 75
    18.172, 333n29
    18.172–73, 334n41
Livy, *Ab urbe condita*
    21.35.6–9, 364n65
    33.7–10, 363n53
    36.16.6–8, 361n28
    36.18.8, 207–8
    39.54, 357n34
    40.21.2–22.5, 364n65, 382n17
Longinus, *On the Sublime*
    9.5, 326n98
    35.2–5, 342n51
    35.4, 99, 107, 339n48
Lucian
    A Professor of Public Speaking
        3, 148
        6–9, 348n24
    Hermotimus
        2, 148
    How to Write History
        19, 200
        20, 200
        19–20, 352n45
        57, 200
    Pro imaginibus
        9, 360n21

Lucretius, *De rerum natura*
    1.117–18, 348n12
    2.7–10, 348n25
    6.608–737, 342n51
    6.639–702, 341n32

Malalas, *Chronicle*
    8.12 (199), 333n37
Martial, *Epigrams*
    4.44
Menander Rhetor, *Treatises*
    2.1.22 (373), 338n31
    2.2.20 (383), 338n31
Methodius, *Symposium*
    pr.5–8, 333n26
Mythographi Vaticani
    1.192, 320n59

Onasander, *Strategikos*
    6.5, 356n15
    7, 356n15
    11.1, 356n15
    21.3, 356n15
    31, 356n15
Ovid
    Amores
        1.7.13–14, 153
        2.16.19–20, 153
    Ars amatoria
        1.27–9, 152
        2.185–86, 153
    Metamorphoses
        1.212–17, 153
        1.689–91, 153
        1.699–700, 153
        2.217–26, 349n36
        2.415–16, 153
        2.441–43, 153
        3.225–27, 154
        3.239, 154
        3.247–50, 345n29
        11.173–79, 346n50
    Tristia 4.2.37, 357n51

Palladius, *Lausiac History*
    7, 290
    20, 379n35
Pausanias, *Periegesis*
    1.4.4, 66, 360n14
    1.32.2, 16
    2.2.7, 330n41
    2.25.10, 319n52
    3.23.9, 342n44
    4.3.9, 319n47
    4.9.1, 356n23
    4.17.10, 356n24
    4.20.4, 330n37
    4.20.5–21.1, 356n24
    4.33.1, 319n49
    5.13.7, 55
    5.7.5, 374n88
    8.2.3, 56–57, 349n35
    8.2.6, 57
    8.2.6–7, 332n64
    8.2.7, 57, 329n33
    8.4.7, 54
    8.5.5, 330n37
    8.6.4, 53, 54
    8.7.4, 329n26
    8.8.3, 330n40
    8.10.9, 66
    8.12.8, 53
    8.13.1, 54
    8.13.4, 53
    8.13.6, 54
    8.14.1, 329n27
    8.15.9, 54
    8.16.1, 54
    8.16.2, 54
    8.16.3, 323n55
    8.17.1, 54
    8.17.5, 54
    8.18.7, 54
    8.21.4, 54
    8.36.2, 330n37
    8.36.8, 55
    8.38.2, 318n12

INDEX LOCORUM 427

    8.38.2–3, 329n34
    8.38.5, 318n12, 329n35
    8.38.6, 56
    8.38.7, 56
    8.38.8, 318n12, 329n35
    9.2.3–4, 58
    9.2.4, 57
    9.3.4, 58
    9.3.5–8, 59
    9.19.3, 330n45
    9.23.5, 330n45
    9.26.2, 330n45
    9.28.2, 61
    9.30, 328n18
    9.31.3–4, 62
    9.34.4, 330n45
    9.34.5, 330n45
    9.37.7, 52
    9.38, 328n18
    9.39.9–11, 52
    9.41.6, 330n45
    10.1.11, 332n64
    10.23.1, 67
    10.23.4, 67
    10.24.1, 67
    10.32.2, 65
    10.32.7, 65
Persius, *Satires*
    pr.1–3, 347n8
Petronius, *Satyrica*
    88, 340n3
    122, 339n46
    122–23, 363n51
Philo, *Life of Moses*
    1.41 (228–29), 358n55
Philostratus
   Imagines
    1.9, 345n30
    1.14, 346n50
    1.18, 345n30
    1.22, 345n30
    1.26, 346n50
    2.4, 346n50

    2.14, 345n30
    2.18, 345n30
   Life of Apollonius
    2.5, 340n3
    5.16–17, 340n19
   Lives of the Sophists
    2.1 (552–54), 376n14
Piacenza Pilgrim, *Travelogue*
    37–39, 334n60
Pindar
   Nemean Odes
    1.10–11, 147
    1.34, 147
    10.45–48, 318n18
    10.114, 322n45
   Olympian Odes
    1.105, 317n48
    7.84, 318n18
    9.97, 318n18
    9.107–8, 147
    13.108, 318n18
   Pythian Odes
    1.21–8, 110
Plato
   Critias
    110d–111e, 371n23
    118b, 102
   Laws
    624a-b, 265, 333n38
    625a, 265
    625b, 265
    625b-c, 265
    625c-d, 265
    677a-682e, 365n12
    677b, 263
    678c-679c, 376n25
    678e-679a, 263
    680b, 375n93
    833b, 375n110
   Minos
    319e, 333n38
   Phaedrus
    230b–c, 266

Pliny the Elder, *Natural History*
    2.110, 340n22
    3.2.4, 191
    5.11, 358n65
    5.14, 358n65
    7.205, 318n17
    25.1, 340n3
    35.116, 127
    36.1–2, 197–98
Pliny the Younger, *Letters*
    5.6.7–13, 104
    5.6.28, 104
    6.16, 340n21
Plutarch
    fragment 191, 320n59
    Amatorius
        1, 748f
    De primo frigore
        18, 331n60
    On the Fortune or the Virtue of Alexander
        I, 12 (333b-c), 361n26
        II, 2 (335d), 360n21
    Oracles at Delphi No Longer Given in Verse
        1 (394f), 331n57
    Sympotic Questions (Quaestiones convivales)
        1.9, 362n39
        4.2, 362n39
    Aemilius Paulus
        4.3, 362n43
        14.1–2, 211
        14.5–6, 211
        15.2, 362n42
        15.11, 210
        17.1–5, 362n45
        17.9, 362n44
    Alexander
        24, 361n24
    Aratus
        22, 206
        50, 319n48
    Camillus
        26.3, 356n17
    Cato the Elder
        2.3.6, 361n28
        13.1, 361n28
        13.2, 185
        13.2–4, 207
        13.7, 207
        14.1, 207
    Eumenes
        9.1–2, 361n26
    Fabius Maximus
        6–7, 206
        7.2, 356n17
    Flamininus
        3–5, 361n24
        7–8, 361n24, 363n53
    Pompey
        32.2–3
    Publicola
        22, 205–206
    Sertorius
        12.7, 356n17
        17.5–8, 209
        17.8, 364n64
        17.12, 208
    Timoleon
        26–28, 361n24
Polybius, *Histories*
    2.21–31, 364n59
    3.47.6–9, 214
    3.48.10–12, 214
    3.49.2, 364n60
    3.51.4, 215
    3.53.4–5, 215
    3.54.2–3, 216
    3.54.7, 216
    3.55.1–4, 217
    3.61.4–9, 364n60
    5.21, 359n2
    10.29.5, 186
    29.12.4, 359n2
Procopius, *Buildings*
    5.8, 334n56
Propertius, *Elegies*
    3.1.17–18, 146

3.3.1–4, 146
3.3.6, 348n12
Pseudo-Aristotle, *On the Cosmos*
    391a, 111–12
    392b, 112
    395b, 112
Pseudo-Hermogenes, *Progymnasmata*
    7, 102
Pseudo-Lucian, *Onos*
    17, 352n36
    19, 353n53
    22, 353n55
    23, 353n56
    26, 353n57
    27, 353n63
    29–31, 353n65
    42, 353n50
    43, 353n51
    44, 353n52
Pseudo-Nilus, *Narrations*
    4.4, 293
    4.8, 82, 293–94
    5.10, 294
    6.9, 295
    6.11, 295
Pseudo-Virgil
    Aetna
        2, 113
        8, 341n38
        94–101, 341n36
        179, 114
        180–83, 113
        189–90, 341n39
        192, 114
        193–96, 114
        203–6, 113, 342n45
        224–25, 114
        252–53, 114
        332, 342n44
        341, 342n44
        349, 342n44
        465–66, 114
        505–7, 114
        601–2, 115

Moretum
    60–61, 352n44
Ptolemy, *Geography*
    Book 2, preface, 358n60

Quintus of Smyrna, *Posthomerica*
    5.49–56, 349n26

Sallust, *Jugurtha*
    93–94, 186
Sallustius, *Concerning the Gods and the Universe*
    16, 333n39
Seneca
    Letters
        51.1, 115–16
        51.5, 116
        51.10, 342n49
        51.11, 116
        79.2, 343n56
        79.2–4, 116–17
        79.5, 117
        79.6, 117–18
        79.8, 342n54, 343n56, 348n17
    Natural Questions
        6.1.4–5, 109
    Phaedra
        2, 154
        4–5, 154
        22, 154
        54, 154
        69, 154
        233–35, 154
        613–14, 154
Silius Italicus, *Punica*
    3.477–99, 339n46
    3.477–646, 363n52
Simonides
    fragment 579, 148
Solinus, *Polyhistor*
    8.6, 320
Sophocles, *Oedipus the King*
    1133–39, 259

Statius
   Silvae
      2.2.54–59, 338–39n35
   Thebaid
      9.678–725, 349n28
Strabo, *Geography*
      1.1.16, 366n18
      1.2.10, 366n13
      2.1.1, 366n13
      2.5.26, 224
      2.5.32, 365n12
      3.1.3, 366n13
      3.1.7, 365n12
      3.2.3, 366n20
      3.2.13, 366n17
      3.3.1, 366n26
      3.3.5, 223
      3.3.8, 223
      3.4.20, 366n22
      4.1.11, 366n17
      4.6.6, 366n22
      4.6.7, 223
      4.6.9, 364n1, 366n22
      4.6.10, 366n22
      5.1.2, 366n17
      5.1.7, 366n27
      5.2.5, 366n27
      5.2.6, 366n27, 367n34
      5.2.7, 226
      5.2.8, 366n27
      5.2.9, 366n27, 367n33
      5.3.5, 366n27, 367n34
      5.3.6, 366n27
      5.3.7, 225, 366n27
      5.3.8, 367n44
      5.3.9, 366n27
      5.3.10, 366n27
      5.3.11, 225, 366n27, 367n34
      5.3.12, 226, 366n27
      5.3.13, 366n27
      5.4.8, 135, 367n31
      6.2.3, 367n31
      6.2.6, 226, 354n71
      6.2.8, 110–11
      6.2.10, 340n20
      6.4.1, 226
      7.5.1, 366n14
      8.1.3, 366n17
      8.6.7, 367n36
      8.6.15, 367n36
      8.6.21, 226
      9.1.16, 367n36
      10.2.4, 367n36
      11.5.6, 367n39
      11.7.1, 367n39
      11.8.4, 367n40
      11.9.1, 367n39
      11.13.3, 367n39
      11.13.6, 367n39
      11.4.4, 367n39
      12.3.11, 367n44
      12.3.18, 227
      12.3.28, 367n43
      12.3.31, 367n43
      12.3.38, 367n43
      12.3.39, 228
      12.3.40, 319n39
      12.3.42, 366n17
      12.8.17, 209
      13.1.25, 365n5
      14.5.6, 189
      14.5.7, 367n43
      16.2.18, 367n43
Sulpicius Severus, *Dialogues*
      1.17, 294

Tacitus
   Agricola
      29–38, 355n3
   Annals
      2.41, 192, 344n11
Theocritus, *Idylls*
      7.91–95, 338n23, 347n4
Theodoret, *Religious History*
      1.2, 291
      1.7, 291

INDEX LOCORUM 431

    3.1, 378n5
    6.4, 380n42
    6.12, 334n57
    10.1, 290
    11.1, 380n41
    12.2, 380n41
    13.1, 291
    13.4, 291
    13.7, 291
    18.1, 380n41, 380n43
    20.1, 380n43
    21.4, 380n41
    23.1, 380n43
    23.2, 380n41
    28.1, 291
    28.5, 291
Theophrastus
    History of Plants
        3.3.2, 373n47
    Weather Signs
        37, 362n37
Thucydides, *History of the Peloponnesian War*
    1.103, 356n25
    5.6–10, 358n55
    Valerius, *Letter in Praise of
        the Life of the Most Blessed
        Egeria*
    2, 88
    3, 88
    4, 88
Valerius Flaccus, *Argonautica*
    1.574–86, 349n278
Varro, *De re rustica*
    2.2.9, 258, 374n90
Vegetius, *De re militari*
    1.22, 356n15
    1.27, 356n15
    3.6, 192, 356n15
    3.9, 356n15
    3.10, 356n15
    3.13, 356n15
    3.19, 356n15
    3.20, 356n15
    3.22, 356n15

Virgil
    Aeneid
        2.696, 150
        3.112, 349n31
        5.252–53, 150
        5.448–49, 151
        6.234–35, 151
        7.785–86, 152
        8.193–267, 151
        10.158, 151
        12.4–9, 349n34
        12.523–25, 152
        12.523–28, 235
        12.684–90, 152
        12.697–703, 150
        12.702, 349n34
        12.703, 349n34
        12.923, 235
    Eclogues
        1.83, 338n23
        4.43–5, 175
        5.8, 338n23
        6.64–73, 338n23, 348n11
        10.9–12, 349n41
        10.32, 338n23
    Georgics
        1.16–18, 349n44
Vitruvius, *De architectura*
    2.pr., 205
    7.5.2, 344n15

BIBLICAL PASSAGES
Exodus
    19–34, 70
    19:10–13, 332n2
    19:18–20, 70
    33:21–23, 70
    33:22, 79
Deuteronomy
    12:2–3, 71
    32:48–52, 336n92
    32:49, 332n5
    34:1, 332n5
    34.1–4, 336n92

1 Kings
- 11:7, 71
- 13:2, 332n9
- 13:33, 332n10
- 14:23–24, 71
- 18.17–40, 332n11
- 19.1–18, 332n13
- 22:43, 332n14

Psalms
- 98:8, 72
- 114:1–4, 72

Isaiah
- 2:1–4, 332n17
- 25:6–8, 74
- 40:9, 332n16
- 52:7, 332n16

Ezekiel
- 33:28, 72

Amos
- 9:13, 72

Matthew
- 4:8–10, 77
- 5–7, 332n20
- 17:1–8, 332n21

Acts
- 1:10–12, 332n22

Hebrews
- 11:37–38, 378n5

GENERAL INDEX

Achilles, 3, 32, 36, 42, 321n19, 343n7; Shield of, 324n63
Achilles Tatius, 354n70
Acrocorinth, xvii, 206, 221–22, 226, 254
Acropolis (Athens), 254
Adrianople, Battle of, 241
Aemilius Paulus, 210–12
Aeneas, 21, 34, 150–52, 235
Aeolian islands, 110, 112
Aeschylus, *Agamemnon*, 95, 97; *Prometheus Bound*, 105, 112
Agamemnon, 36, 38–39, 42, 95, 321n19, 325n86, 327n104
agriculture, 8, 35, 139, 146, 247, 251, 255, 258, 289, 292, 296
Aias (Ajax), 39–41, 324n63, 327n103, 327n104, 343n7
Aigina, 17
Aktaion (Actaeon), 48, 57–58, 130, 132, 154, 166, 345n35
Alamanni, 236–38, 368n7, 368n9
Alban Hills, 12, 156
Alcaeus, 157, 158
Alexander the Great, 184–85, 199, 204–6, 360n17, 366n13
Alexandria, 85, 146, 301, 360n21
allegorical and symbolic uses of mountains, 3, 73–77, 79–81, 86–89, 96, 115–18, 119, 124–26, 143–59, 163–68, 174–78, 303, 309, 310, 314n15
Alps, xxvi, 4, 11–12, 105–6, 128, 153, 190–91, 196, 197, 212–17, 218, 223–4, 226, 227, 232, 248, 252, 312, 313n4, 337n16, 355n3, 359n2, 363n51, 376n12, 376n18

altars on mountain summits, xvii–xviii, xxvi–xxvii, 3–19, 22, 27–28, 33, 47, 56, 59, 72, 75, 91, 308
Amaseia, 11, 228, 253
Ambryssos, 260, 374n81
Amida, 230, 238
Ammianus Marcellinus, *Res Gestae*, 183, 218–19, 230–43, 247, 297
Anastasius of Sinai, 78–79, 295
Anaxagoras, 340n3
Anchises, 20, 21–23, 54, 150
Andromeda, 130, 343n4
anthropocentrism, xxiv, 35, 38, 39, 43, 45, 89, 92, 108, 163, 173, 178, 220, 287, 315n30
Antioch, 74, 102, 290, 301
Antiochos (Antiochus) III, 186, 206, 361n29
Aornos, rock of, 205
Apennines, 104, 150, 152, 184, 190, 193, 197, 226, 258, 371n22
Aphrodite, 20, 21–23, 120, 221, 327n103. See also Venus
Apollo, 5, 16, 23, 25, 55, 62, 65, 66, 140, 142, 146–47, 156, 252, 297, 323n58, 327n104, 327n1, 329n35, 379n24
Apollonius of Rhodes, *Argonautica*, 149, 150
Apsos Gorge, 361n24
Apuleius, *De Platone*, 164; *Metamorphoses*, 143, 155, 160–78, 183, 213, 216, 276, 302, 303
Arabia, 201
Archelaos relief, 140–43
Argos, 15–16, 367n36
Aricia, 319n44
Aristomenes, 330n37
Aristotle, 18, 339n48

Arkadia (Arcadia), xvii–xviii, 4–6, 25, 34, 53–57, 66, 76, 81, 122, 125, 151, 153, 156, 157, 251–52, 313n4, 372n43
Armenian, Armenians, 78–79, 84, 368n7
Arrian, *Anabasis*, 204–5
Artemidorus, *Oneirocritica*, 337n21
Artemis, 10, 48, 54, 55, 153, 256. *See also* Diana
ascent, imagery of, 79, 86–89, 147–49, 309
ascetics, asceticism, 78, 81, 101, 283–304; athletic metaphors for, 286, 291; tension between communal and solitary, 285–86, 293–97, 301–4
Askra (Ascra), 27, 29, 152, 321n25
Atalanta, 153
Athanasius, *Life of Antony*, 288–89, 301–2
Athene, 16, 120, 327n104, 379n24
Athens, Athenians 15–17, 49, 55, 66, 164, 254, 255–56, 263–67, 330n39, 331n53, 367n36
Atlas mountains, 358n65
Attica, 9, 16–17, 48, 60, 77, 154, 251, 256, 313n4
Augustine, 18, 336n81; *Confessions*, 288
Augustus, 127, 156, 191, 218, 219, 223–24; *Res Gestae*, 191, 196, 224
auxiliaries, 185–86

Baal, 11, 71, 72, 74
Bacchic ritual, 65–66, 87, 328n7.
Bacchus, 135–37. *See also* Dionysus
Baiae, 115–16
bandits, 163, 167, 169, 170, 171, 174, 175, 189, 223, 224, 226–7, 233, 260, 269, 276, 279, 284, 294, 297, 301, 303, 374n81
Basil of Caesarea, 101
beacons, 95
Bellerophon, 62, 130, 146, 322n37
Biferno valley, 258
Black Sea, 11, 149, 227, 253, 367n41
bodily engagement with/immersion in landscape, xxv–xxvi, 8–9, 23–26, 27, 37, 38, 45–46, 48–49, 51–53, 58, 67, 97, 114–15, 130, 162–63, 165, 166, 168–74, 176, 178, 182–83, 204, 212–17, 232, 236–38, 241, 243, 287, 289, 292, 294–95, 299, 307, 309, 310, 311
Boiotia, Boiotians, 34, 57–64, 68, 221

Boscoreale, 344n19
Braudel, Fernand, xviii
brigands. *See* bandits
Brown, Capability, 98
bucolic. *See* pastoral
Burke, Edmund, 97, 339n48
Burn, A. R., 187
Burnet, Thomas, 99, 117
Buxton, Richard, xix, 21
Byron, *Childe Harold's Pilgrimage*, 145

Caesarea in Cappadocia, 123, 253
Cairngorms, 248
Callimachus, *Aitia*, 146–47
Callisto, 153
Campania, 116, 338n38, 342n51
Campbell, John, 249, 259
Capitoline Hill (Rome), 319n44
Cappadocia, 101. *See also* Caesarea in Cappadocia
Carduchians, 360n19
Carpathians, 123, 192
cartographic perspective, 192, 196, 216, 220–22, 238–40
Casa del Frutteto, Pompeii, 345n28, 345n29, 345n34
Cassandra, 130
Cato the Elder, 206–7
Caucasus, 105, 112, 155–56, 158, 201, 366n13
caves, 25, 26, 37, 43, 44, 50, 72, 77, 82, 167, 200, 208, 209, 247, 255, 265–66, 294, 297, 298, 366n27. *See also* Korykian cave
Celts, 214
charcoal, charcoal burners, 255
Chorienes, rock of, 205
Christian responses to mountains, 4, 10, 69–92, 101, 148, 283–304, 309, 347–348n8, 348n25
Cicero, 189, 231
Cilicia, 189, 230, 290
Claudian, 368n2
climate change, 108–9, 248, 250, 307
Clio, 152, 156
Clytemnestra, 95

coins, xviii, 6, 18, 119, 122–23, 125, 251, 253–54, 257
Coleridge, Samuel Taylor, 306
commons, 376n21, 377n43
Constantius II, 234
Corinth, 206, 221–22, 253, 259
Corsica, 226
Crete, 10, 76, 144, 151, 262–66
Crimea, 253, 257
Cronon, William, 267
Cybele, 156
Cyclopes, 247, 259, 263, 273, 296, 323n56, 365n5. *See also* Polyphemus
Cyprus, 302

Dacian Wars, 123, 192
Daidala, 58–60
Danube, 241
dark ecology, 350n6
deforestation, 250–51, 316n31
della Dora, Veronica, xxii
Delos, 23
Delphi, 48, 64–67, 140, 203, 260, 327n1
Demeter, 23
Demetrius, 348n21
Dennis, John, 97
Diana, 130, 132, 153, 154, 156, 166, 319n44, 345n35, 349n28. *See also* Artemis
Dinocrates, 205
Dio Chrysostom, *Euboian Oration*, 71, 100–101, 262, 267–82, 293, 298
Diodorus Siculus, 316n37
Diogenes Laertius, 284
Dion, 18–19
Dionysus, 48–49, 62, 65, 320n8, 328n4, 330n45
Dionysius of Halicarnassus, 348n22
Dodwell, Edward, 337n20
Dolomites, 183–84, 337n7
du Boulay, Juliet, 249

earthquakes, 67, 188, 340n10, 369n23
ecocriticism, xxii–xxiv, 35–36, 41, 89, 173, 219, 281, 300, 324n63, 379n16, 382n10
Egeria, 69, 81–92, 95, 154, 285, 295
Egypt, 78, 85, 201, 284–85, 288–90, 294, 315n19

ekphrasis, 101–2, 163, 167–68
Elijah (Elias), 15, 18, 71–72, 73, 82, 88, 378n5
Empedocles, 111, 341n34
empire, 156, 184, 189, 190, 191, 192, 196–98, 201, 202, 204, 219, 223–24, 230, 241, 296, 306
Ennius, 146
environment. *See* human-environment relations
environmental determinism, 196–97, 234, 250, 309
environmental justice, 281
Epic Cycle, 20
Epidauros, 15, 253, 367n36
epiphany, 21–23, 27–30, 75–76, 153
Epirus, 313n4
Eratosthenes, 221, 366n13
Eros, 62, 130
Ethiopia (Aethiopia), 290
ethnic identity, 251, 252, 259
ethnography, xx, 193, 196–97, 200, 201, 218–19, 220, 227, 230, 240, 247–49, 269, 294, 316n37, 365n9
Euboia, 33, 249, 267–82
Eudoxus, 340n3
Eunapius, *Lives of the Philosophers and Sophists*, 333n39
Euphrates, 299
Euripides, *Bacchae*, 47–49, 57, 65, 97; *Hippolytus*, 154
Euthykles stele, 137–40
Evagrius, 288

Faunus, 157
fear, xx, 37, 44, 74, 98, 106, 109, 113, 175, 181, 207, 208, 303, 368n7
Feriae Latinae, 12
festivals, 4, 6, 14, 23, 28, 47, 54, 64, 140–42. *See also* Lykaia, Mouseia, Olympia, Pythian festival
first-person narrative, 29, 53, 55, 63, 85, 159, 160, 221, 268, 293
floods, 36, 40, 41, 44, 45, 231, 234, 235, 238, 263, 273, 326n101, 380n43
Frontinus, *Strategemata*, 207–8

Gabala (Jableh), 291
Gaia, 26
Galala Plateau, 289
Galatea, 132
Gallus, Flavius Claudius Constantius (Caesar) 234–35
Gallus, Gaius Cornelius (poet), 348n11, 349n41
gardens, xxiv, 73, 98, 100, 102, 127, 133, 167, 290, 302–3
Gaul, 230, 236, 368n2, 368n9
Gauls, 66–68, 91, 182, 203, 216
Gaza, 301
geographical writing, xx, xxiv, 49, 91, 149, 181, 191, 193, 196, 201, 202, 210, 217, 218–29, 239–40, 364n65
geology, xx, 117
Germany, 230, 236
Ghosh, Amitav, xxiv
Gibbon, Edward, 238
global and local scale, xxiv, 36, 220, 229, 311, 378n53
gloom and glory, xx–xxi, 45–46, 106, 321n18
goats, xviii, 24, 32, 37, 44, 65, 157, 161, 175, 185, 260–61, 272, 291
Goths, 233, 240–42
Gray, Thomas, 105–6
Great Saint Bernard Pass, 11, 191, 212
Greece, 12–19, 47–68, 224, 226–27, 228, 269, 312
Gregory of Nazianzus, 101
Gregory of Nyssa, 74, 77, 79, 348n19
guides, 59, 63, 82
Gurzuf Saddle Pass, 253, 257

Hades, 351n18. *See also* Pluto
Hadrian, 111, 255, 338n38
hagiography. *See* saints' lives
Halani, 241
Hannibal, 105–6, 116, 190, 191, 197, 199, 206, 212–17, 232, 363n51; route over the Alps, 214–15, 355n3
Hare, Augustus, 144–45

Hebrew Bible, 69–73, 78, 83, 90, 284, 285, 293, 321n30; Deuteronomy, 70–71; Exodus, 70, 73; 1 Kings, 71–2, 73; Psalms, 72, 80
Hector, 3, 33, 34, 38, 41–42, 326n94, 327n104
Helios, 76–77
Hellespont, 149, 203
Hephaistos, 32, 110
Hera, 3, 15, 21, 23, 32, 33, 43, 44, 58–59, 120, 327n103, 327n104
Heraclitus, 284
Herakles (Hercules), 121, 130, 147, 151, 191, 330n45
Hermes, 25, 54–55, 62, 76, 261, 320n8, 327n103, 346n50
Herodotus, *Histories*, 200–204, 210, 220, 225, 230, 239, 252, 316n37, 361n28, 365n10
Hesiod, 18, 20, 26–30, 62, 75, 137–40, 142, 145–49, 152, 157, 164, 177, 178, 328n18; *Theogony*, 62, 64, 139; *Works and Days* 62, 64, 139
Himalayas, xxvi, 183–84, 371n8
Hippocrates, *Airs, Waters, Places*, 196, 220
Hippokrene (Hippocrene) spring, 27, 62–63, 146
Hippolytus, 130, 154, 346n50
historiography, xix, xxiv, 109, 168, 178, 181–243, 269, 312
History of the Monks in Egypt, 284–85, 289, 294
hodological perspective, 192–93, 220
Homer, xix, 18, 20, 69, 75, 76, 81, 89, 92, 101, 105 141–42, 146, 149, 161, 312, 343n7; *Iliad*, xxiv, xxv, 24–25, 30–46, 70, 132, 151, 233–34, 248, 269–70; *Odyssey*, 25, 32, 41, 76, 100, 133–34, 247
Homeric hymns, 20–26
Homeric Hymn to Aphrodite, 20, 21–23, 76
Homeric Hymn to Hermes, 25, 320n8
Homeric Hymn to Pan, 20, 24–26, 37, 154
Horace, *Odes*, 144–45, 155–59
House of the Centenary, Pompeii, 135–37
House of Lucretius Fronto, Pompeii, 128–30, 132–33
House of Virnius Modestus, Pompeii, 130
hubris, 202, 204, 205, 212, 364n65

human-environment relations, xxii–xxiv, xxvii, 27, 30, 35–36, 45–46, 52–53, 108–9, 162–63, 200, 217–20, 231, 241, 249–51, 286–87, 309, 312
Humboldt, Alexander von, 316n36
Huns, 233, 240–41
hunting, 24, 40, 41, 154, 254, 272–73, 325n69
Hyginus Gromaticus, 358n58
Hylas, 130–31

Iamblichos, 333n39
Icarus, 130, 132
Inarime, 349n33
Ingold, Tim, 8
intervisibility, 9, 10, 15
intratextual reading, xix–xx, 30, 45–46, 50–51, 68, 71, 145, 152, 155, 178, 200, 205, 219, 228–29, 310–11, 324n60, 328n4, 343n7, 344n23, 350n51, 366n28, 370n37
Isauria, Isaurians, 189–90, 231–36, 240, 247, 257, 297
Isis, 160, 174–77
Italy, 11–12, 145, 151, 156–57, 190, 193, 197, 216, 224–26, 228, 312
Ithaca, 34, 323n56

Jerome, *Life of Hilarion*, 286, 300–304; *Life of Paul of Thebes*, 301, 381n75
Jerusalem, 78, 82, 90, 285; Temple, 71–73
Jesus, 73, 77, 79, 284, 288
John the Baptist, 284, 378n5
John Climacus, 79–80
John of Ephesus, *Lives of the Eastern Saints*, 298–300
Julian, 73–77, 82, 148, 235, 236, 239
Julian Alps, 242, 369n9
Julius Caesar, 12, 116, 191, 213, 223, 363n51
Jupiter, 113, 150, 153, 156; Latiaris, 12; Poeninus, 11. *See also* Zeus
Jura, 252
Justinian, 78, 123

Kant, Immanuel, 97, 339n48
Karystos, 275

Kastor and Polydeukes, 322,n45
Kelainai, 102, 280–81
Knossos, 265–66
Korinna, 139–40
Korykian cave, 64–65, 374n81
Kos, 17
Kronos, 26, 330n45
Kynoskephalai, Battle of, 361n24, 363n53

Laestrygonians, 133–34, 169, 232
land surveying, 358n58, 372n39, 373n46
landscape, xix–xx, xxiv–xxvi, 35–36, 95–106, 162–63, 165; alteration of, 200, 202–3, 309; appreciation of, associated with elite identity, xxiv, 8, 97, 98, 108, 306
late antique pagan activity at mountain sites, 10, 17, 18, 31, 65, 77, 255–56
Latium, 12
La Turbie, 191, 196
Lemnos, 32
Leto, 23
Libanius, 74–75
Libya, 201
Life and Miracles of Saint Thekla, 297
Life of Konon of Isauria, 297
lightning, xviii, 41, 44, 67, 79, 293, 323n51, 340n23
Liguria, 186, 190–91, 374n75
Linos, 62
Lipara (Lipari), 112
Livy, 106, 212, 213, 361n28, 363n47, 364n65
locus amoenus, 100–102, 105, 166–68, 171, 266, 274, 289, 302–3, 313n8
locus horridus, 168, 303, 353n47, 363n52
Lokris, Lokrians, 260
Longinus, 44, 99, 106, 111, 112, 337n9, 339n41
Lucian, 148–49; *Charon*, 348n22
Lucretius, 105, 107, 112, 113, 339n48, 342n51
Lykaia, 6, 47, 251, 330n39
Lykaon (Lycaon), 56–57, 153
Lynkeus, 322n45

Macedonia, 6, 328n7
Maeander river/valley, 209, 256, 260–62, 374n73
Magnesia beneath Mount Sipylos (Magnesia ad Sipylum), 55
Mantineia, 53, 54, 66, 330n37
maps, 123, 192–96
marble, 197, 255, 257
Marius, 116, 367n34
Marsyas, 132
Massif Central, 252
Mauretania, 290, 356n26, 373n63
meadows, 24, 25, 100, 101, 102, 161, 165, 171, 187
medieval responses to mountains, 78, 87, 106, 145, 248, 257, 283, 315n23
Megalopolis, xvii, 252
Megara, 17, 58, 253
Megaris, 60, 221
memory, xxvi, xxvii, 7–8, 12, 36, 47, 50, 73, 151, 162, 287
Memphis, 201
Menander Rhetor, 102
mercenaries, 257
Messene, Messenians, 12, 187–88, 330n37
Methana, 318n25, 371n12
Methodius, *Symposium*, 73, 348n19
microregions, 249–50, 251, 313n4
Miletos, 66, 261–62
military history, modern, 183–84, 355n2, 360n18
milk, 12, 211, 263
mining, 255, 366n20
Minoan period, 10
Minos, 76, 265
miracles, 78, 79, 81, 84, 287, 291, 293, 360n12
mist, 37, 43, 65, 96, 297, 361n24
Mithridates, 11, 227–28
Mnemosyne, 140, 142
monasteries, 283–86, 288, 289–90, 293, 295–96
Monastery of Saint Catherine (Sinai), 78, 123, 295
Mons Graupius, 355n3, 356n18
Monte Mario, 338n36
Monti Tiburtini, 338n38

Mont Ventoux, 86, 364n65
mosaics, 79–80, 123–26
Moses, 70, 72, 73, 74, 79–80, 81, 82–84, 87, 88, 90–91, 123–26
Mother Goddess, 11, 149
Mount Aigaion, 26
mountaineering, history of, xx–xxi, xxv, xxvi, 8, 31, 84–89, 97, 108, 182–84, 213, 217, 243, 270, 286, 306–8, 314n15, 314n17, 317n45, 371n7, 376n18
mountain peoples, representation of, 182, 196–97, 200, 218–43, 247–49, 257, 267–82, 293–300, 307, 309
mountains: as beautiful, 100–105, 112, 135, 159, 225, 280–81; as borders, 53–54, 201, 222, 252, 253, 256, 260, 261, 262; and cities, xx, xxii, 7, 11, 38, 50, 53–56, 58–61, 219, 224–27, 247–82, 303–4; conflict over resources and territory, 253, 260, 262, 264–65; and the divine, xx, xxii, xxv, 1–92, 120–26, 130–32, 135–43, 156–57, 283–304; economic connectedness of, 38, 181, 219, 220, 226, 248, 249, 251, 254–65, 268, 280, 284, 285, 289–90, 295–96, 309, 323n58, 357n31; as enigmatic, 96, 115, 118, 135–43, 145, 155, 157, 159, 164, 177, 206, 309, 310; and gender, 66, 69, 87–89, 153–55, 256; and military history, xix, xx, xxv, 12, 97, 181–243, 309; and modernity, 71, 181–83, 198, 270, 287, 307, 315n25; as objects of worship, 10, 11; and the past, xxvi–xxvii, 3–19, 50–51, 54–55, 57, 68, 71, 73, 81–84, 86, 182, 249, 263, 269–70, 287, 308, 311; as places of connection, 251–53, 256, 258–29; as places of refuge, 54, 73, 187–88, 233, 263, 293, 382n78; and science, xx, 96, 108–9, 110–12, 113, 116–17, 135, 177, 182, 209–12, 262
mountain studies, xx–xii
mountain warfare, specialised expertise in, 183–86, 309
Mount Albanus (Monte Cavo), 12, 226, 367n33
Mount Algidus, 156
Mount Amanos, 290, 380n42

GENERAL INDEX 439

Mount Anchesmos, 16
Mount Anchisia, 53, 54
Mount Apesas (Phoukas)
Mount Arachnaion, 15, 320n56
Mount Argaios, 123, 253–54
Mount Aroania, 54
Mount Athos, 23, 32, 95, 149, 150, 203–4, 205
Mount Barakat, 380n46
Mount Carmel, 71
Mount Chelydorea, 54
Mount Dindymon/Dindymos (Dindymus) (applied to multiple mountains), 11, 149, 156, 349n29
Mount Eira, 188
Mount Erymanthos (Erymanthus), 151, 156
Mount Eryx, 150, 156, 254
Mount Etna, 96, 99, 107, 109–18, 145, 152, 212, 226, 241, 313n7, 337n9, 340n5, 354n76
Mount Everest, xxvi, 363n58
Mount Gerizim, 254
Mount Geronteion, 54
Mount Gragus, 156
Mount Haimos (Haemus), 156, 227, 241, 364n65, 366n14, 382n17
Mount Helikon (Helicon), 27–30, 47, 61–64, 120, 122, 132, 137–40, 145–46, 156–57, 177, 221, 313n4, 315n20, 327n1, 355n, 355n3, 356n20
Mount Horeb, 72, 73, 82
Mount Hymettos (Hymettus), 16–17, 77, 164, 255–56
Mount Hypatos, 330n45
Mount Ida (Asia Minor), 3, 11, 20, 21–23, 32–35, 38, 41, 45, 81, 95, 102, 120, 130, 150–51, 161, 315n20, 323n58, 356n22
Mount Ida (Crete), 76, 144, 151, 265–66, 274
Mount Ithome, xvii, 12, 17, 188, 330n37
Mount Kadmos, 256
Mount Kallidromos (Callidromus), 186–87, 204, 207
Mount Kalpe, 365n12
Mount Kasios (Casius) (Jebel Aqra), 11, 74–76
Mount Kirphis, 260

Mount Kithairon (Cithaeron), 48–49, 57–61, 95, 97, 130, 132, 259, 315n20, 346n50, 347n8, 349n28, 360n16
Mount Krathis, 54
Mount Kyllene (Cyllene), 25, 34, 54–55, 153, 320n8
Mount Kynthos, 23
Mount Labus, 186
Mount Laphystios, 330n45
Mount Libethrios, 330n45
Mount Lucretilis, 157
Mount Lykaion (Lycaeus), xvii–xviii, xxvi, 4–7, 9, 12, 13, 15, 32, 47, 56–57, 64, 68, 122, 153, 157, 251–52
Mount Mainalos (Maenalus), 55, 153
Mount Mykale, 23, 260–62
Mount Nebo, 69, 70, 81, 90–92, 95, 335n71
Mount Neriton, 34
Mount Nysa (Nyssa), 112, 135, 320n8, 328n4
Mount Ocha, 275
Mount of Olives, 73
Mount Olgassys, 10
Mount Olympus, xix, 3, 18–19, 20, 21, 22, 25, 26–27, 30–35, 36, 39, 41, 43, 44, 45, 77, 81, 95, 105, 140, 149, 153, 156, 210–12, 315n20, 320n56, 323n58, 328n4, 338n38, 346n50
Mount Ossa, 149, 315n20
Mount Othrys, 16
Mount Pangaeus, 349n28
Mount Parnassos, 17, 64–68, 91, 140, 182, 221, 252, 260, 313n4, 315n20, 325n69, 328n4, 372n43, 374n81
Mount Parnes (Parnethus), 9, 16–17, 77, 255
Mount Parthenion, 53, 76
Mount Pelion, 23, 34, 149, 203–4, 315n20
Mount Pentelikon, 16, 255
Mount Phix, 330n45
Mount Pirus, 237
Mount Ptous, 330n45
Mount Rhipaia, 366n13
Mount Silpios, 102
Mount Sinai, 69, 70, 72, 73, 74, 81–86, 88, 89, 91, 95, 123–26, 285, 293–97
Mount Sipylos, 55–57

Mount Soracte, 144–45, 157–59, 367n33
Mount Tabor, 73, 79, 88, 334n54
Mount Taygetos, xvii, 322n45
Mount Thaumasios, 330n37
Mount Tmolos (Tmolus), 11, 343n10
Mount Trachys, 53
Mount Ustica, 157
Mount Vesuvius, 109, 135–37, 140, 193, 226, 342n41
Mount Vulture, 157
Mount Zion, 72, 347n8
Mouseia, 28, 61
Murray, Gilbert, 318n25
Muses, 18–19, 26–27, 27–30, 62, 64, 75, 120, 122, 137–42, 145–47, 152, 157, 330n45
Mycenean period, xviii, 10, 15
myth, xxvi, 4, 7, 17, 20–68, 71, 75–76, 108–9, 111, 112, 113, 115, 119–24, 128–34, 137–43, 149–55, 166, 191, 221, 226, 255, 312, 313n.10

Naples, 109, 115, 151, 193
Narcissus, 128–30, 133
nature, xxiii, 4, 36, 38, 39, 44, 89, 98, 99, 100, 101, 104, 107, 111, 114, 115, 128, 130, 151, 175, 197, 220, 228, 235, 267, 281, 379n16
Neapolis (Nablus), 254
Near Eastern responses to mountains, xxii, 10, 11, 42, 357n45, 371n16
Nemea, 13
Neolithic period, xviii, 258
Nessana, 78, 295
New Comedy, 377n29
new materialism, xxiv, 316n37, 324n63
New Testament, 73, 77, 292
Nicolson, Marjorie Hope, xxi, 314n15, 315n20, 318n25, 321n18, 336n81, 336n3, 339n46, 341n33, 342n52, 347nn2 and 3
Nile, 99, 107
Niobe, 55, 57
Nisibis, 238
Nitria, 289
Numidia, 257
Nymphs, 14, 21, 22, 24, 26, 54, 65, 130, 149, 153, 261, 321n19, 330n45, 374n81

Odysseus, 34, 39–40, 169, 232, 269, 274–75
Odyssey landscapes, Esquiline hill, 133–34
Oedipus, 48, 57, 259, 330n45
Old Testament. *See* Hebrew Bible
Olympia, 6, 18–19, 55, 328n14, 330n39, 331n53
Onos. *See* Pseudo-Lucian
Orchomenos, 53–54, 59
oreibasia. See Bacchic ritual
orophylakes, 260
oros (ὄρος), 220, 225, 271, 283–84, 288, 315n19, 328n20, 365n10
oroskopia. See viewing, from mountains
Orpheus, 62, 156, 328n18
out-migration, 256–57, 263
Ovid, 152–54; *Amores*, 155; *Ars amatoria*, 155; *Metamorphoses*, 132, 153–54, 166, 345n29

Pacatus, 368n2
palaeoenvironmental research, 250
Palestine, 78, 85, 90, 284–85, 301, 303
Palladius, *Lausiac History*, 289
Pan, 5, 24–26, 55, 65, 67, 76, 122, 125, 153, 157, 185, 329n35, 374n81
Panhellenism, 22, 30, 331n52
Paphos, 21
Paris, 37; Judgement of, 120, 124, 161–62, 174–75
pastoral activity, 11, 21, 24–5, 28, 35, 37, 48, 190, 232, 247, 249, 250, 256, 257–66, 271, 273, 296, 298, 300
pastoral/bucolic literature and art, 5, 98, 100, 132, 157, 168, 251, 265, 267, 268, 284
paths, symbolic significance of, 146–49, 165, 176–77, 341n38
Patroklos, 38, 42, 321n19, 324n69, 326n87
Pausanias, 5, 12, 14, 15, 17, 34, 47–68, 69, 77, 81, 89, 91, 92, 98–100, 110, 119, 139, 182, 203, 220, 221, 252, 262, 345n31, 365n10, 367n37
Payne Knight, Richard, 337n16
peak sanctuaries (Crete), 10, 264
Pegasus, 130, 322n37
Pentheus, 48–49, 57, 59, 65, 97
performance, 8, 287, 309
Persephone, 23

Perseus, 130
Persia, Persians, 156, 186–88, 199, 202–4, 206, 230, 235, 236, 238, 239
personification of mountains, 10, 42, 72, 129, 137–40, 203, 222, 343n10
Peter the Deacon, 335n67
Petrarch, 86, 364n65
Petronius, *Satyrica*, 354n70
Peutinger Table, 193–96
Phaethon, 349n36
Phaiacians, 247, 323n56
Pharan, 84, 88, 295
Pheidippides, 76
Pheneos, 53–54
phenomenology, xxv, 318n26
Philip II of Macedon, 329n26
Philip V of Macedon, 12–13, 361n24, 364n65, 382n17
Philo, 284
philosophy, philosophical writing 111–12, 115–18, 147, 148, 206, 210–12, 274–75, 284;
Philostratus, *Imagines* 132
Phlegraean Fields, 340n22
Phokis, Phokians, 64–68, 186, 204, 221, 252, 260, 317n47, 372n43, 374n78
picturesque, the, xx, 96, 98–100, 101, 104, 108, 177, 339n39
pilgrimage, 4, 13, 47, 55, 62, 64, 73, 77–92, 136, 295, 297, 335n74
Pindar, 6, 112, 147, 347n4
Pindos range (Pindus), 154, 156, 374n78
Plataia, 58–59, 61; Battle of, 57, 360n16
Plato, 348n14; *Gorgias*, 164; *Laws*, 262–66, 268, 273, 274; *Phaedrus*, 164; *Republic*, 378n52; *Symposium*, 73
Platonic, 163–64, 262–66; Neoplatonic, 76–77; Stoic, 281, 348n23, 367n32, 367n44, 376n14
Pliny the Elder, *Natural History*, 6, 196, 197
Pliny the Younger, 104
Plutarch, 18, 65, 66, 331n52; *Lives*, 205–12; *Sympotic Questions*, 210
Pluto, 113. *See also* Hades
poetic/musical inspiration, 27–30, 62, 64, 140–42, 146–47, 152, 156–57, 164, 177

Polybius, 366n14; *Histories*, 212–17, 360n17, 365n10
Polyphemus, 132, 247, 323n56
Pompeii, 127–33, 135–37, 140, 154, 166
Pompey, 116, 227
Pontic Alps, 10–11, 153, 227
Pontus, 11, 227–8
Porphyry, 333n39
Poseidon, 33, 34, 62, 66, 321n19, 323n56, 323n58, 330n37, 351n18
Posidonius, 222, 362n33, 366n13, 367n32
posthumanist approaches, 173, 316n37
Praeneste, 225, 228
Price, Uvedale, 98–99
Priene, 262
processions, 4, 8, 12, 17, 19, 58–60, 75, 160, 176, 177, 192, 252, 287, 303
Procopius, 79
Prometheus, 105, 112, 120
prominence, 12, 225, 315n19, 328n20
Propertius, 146–47, 152
Pseudo-Apollodorus, *Library*, 49
Pseudo-Aristotle, *On the Cosmos*, 111–12, 315n20
Pseudo-Lucian, *Onos*, 162, 163, 169, 354n71
Pseudo-Nilus, *Narrations*, 81, 293–97
Pseudo-Plutarch, *On Rivers and Mountains and Things Found in Them*, 49
Pseudo-Virgil, *Aetna*, 113–15, 315n20
Ptolemy, *Geography*, 192–93, 220, 365n10
Pyrenees, 154, 221, 252, 257, 371n17
Pythian festival, 48–49, 260

quarries, 255

rain, 15–17, 40, 44
Ras Shamra, 11
rationalising approaches to myth, 49–51, 52, 56–57, 58, 66, 67, 68, 108, 111, 112, 113, 330n45, 332n63
Renaissance, xxiv, 100, 103, 336n3, 339n39
Rhea, 26, 330n37, 330n45
Rhine, 236, 237
Rhodes, 6, 262

Rhosos, 290
rivers, 23, 34, 35, 40, 44, 45, 59, 88, 90, 101–5, 112, 127, 144, 156, 157, 161, 175, 176, 192, 196–97, 200, 205, 209, 211, 214, 216, 222, 223, 228, 233–36, 237–38, 241, 261–62, 274, 299, 338n25, 344n15, 349n27, 358n64, 359n3
road building/road networks, 53–54, 103, 190, 191, 251, 368n2
rock-climbing, 184–85
rocks/stones, 24–25, 37, 48, 49, 51, 56, 58, 66–67, 99, 105, 107, 110, 115, 120, 122, 125, 130, 133, 135, 148, 152, 154, 161–62, 167, 169–72, 174, 178, 185–86, 215, 223, 232, 233, 237, 289, 294–95, 298, 303, 343n7
Romantic representations of landscape, xix, 29, 96, 128, 267, 314n15
Rome, 12, 120, 123, 128, 140, 144–45, 146, 151, 157–8, 176, 192, 193, 214, 216, 367n44; hills of, 102–4, 122, 125, 128, 225–26, 228, 366n28
Rousseau, Jean-Jacques, 270
ruins, 55, 99
Ruskin, John, 316n36, 318n25

Sabine hills, 157
sacrifice, xvii–xviii, xxi, xxvi, 3–4, 8, 11, 12, 13, 15, 17, 18–19, 20, 22–23, 30, 33, 49, 57, 58–60, 62, 65, 72, 74, 76, 95, 142, 253, 260–62, 287, 291, 309, 311; human, xviii, 56–57, 296
saints' lives, xix, 78, 283–304
Sallust, 168, 208, 359n1
Samos, Samians, 202, 225, 261
Samothrace, 33
Saracens, 85, 296–97, 334n60
Sarakatsani, 249, 257, 259
Sardinia, 226
Sardis, 11
Saturn, 351n18
Schiller, Friedrich, 316n36
Scottish Highlands, 248, 305–12, 355n2, 355n3, 359n69
sculpture, 123, 126, 137–42, 166, 177, 343n7
Scythians, 201, 240
Scythopolis, 285
Seleukos I, 333n37

Semiramis, 185
Seneca, 168, 175; *Letters*, 115–18, 145; *Natural Questions* 109, 116; *Phaedra*, 154–55
Sertorius, 208–10
sheep, xviii, 28, 35, 65, 232, 247, 260, 261, 278, 281, 300
Shelley, *Prometheus Unbound*, 105
Shepherd, Nan, 248
Sicily, 6, 111, 114, 115, 150, 156, 254
Silius Italicus, 106
Silvanus, 257
similes, xxiv, 24, 35–46, 92, 96, 105, 132, 143, 149–52, 155, 234–35, 312
Sinai Peninsula, 78, 295
Sinope, 367n44
Skeironian rocks, 227
slaves, 160, 163, 174, 188, 260, 261, 295, 296, 301, 351n18
Smith, William, 106
Snowdonia, 306
Sogdian rock, 184–85
Solicinium, 236
Solinus, 18
solitude, xxvi, 73, 130, 284, 286, 288, 290, 293, 296, 299, 301–2, 306
Solomon, 71
Sophocles, *Oedipus the King*, 259, 262, 327n2
Spain, 208, 219, 220–21, 222–24, 226, 248, 312
Sparta, Spartans, 66, 186, 188, 263–66
stage-sets, 103, 120–21, 123, 126, 160–62, 174–85, 226
Stairway of Repentance (Mount Sinai), 78, 126
Stephen, Leslie, xxi, 314n15, 355n9
Stesichoros, 58
storms, 11, 27, 34, 37, 43, 44, 66, 88, 105, 112, 152, 158–59, 203–4, 231, 233–35, 236, 237, 240, 241, 293
Strabo, 10, 100, 102–3, 110–11, 115, 128, 218–29, 230, 239, 247, 248, 312
Studius, 127
sublime, the, xx–xxi, 4, 43–45, 73, 96, 97–100, 105–6, 107–8, 110, 111–12, 113, 118, 120, 151, 177, 306, 309, 314n13, 363n57

Sulla, 62
Sulpicius Severus, *Dialogues*, 294
summit position, 87, 88, 306, 314n15
symbol. *See* allegorical and symbolic uses of mountains
Symeon the Mountaineer, 298–300
Syria, 78, 284, 290–92, 298–300, 301

Tacitus, 168, 233
Tarsos, 102
Tartarus, 113
taskscapes, 8, 371n13
Taurus, 189, 360n19, 366n13
taxation, 271, 276–80
Tegea, 53
Tempe, 338n38
Thales, 340n3
Thebes (Asia Minor), 260–62
Thebes (Boiotia), 48–49, 59, 61, 259
Themistius, 368n2
Theocritus, *Idylls*, 100
Theodoret, *Religious History*, 79, 290–92
Theophrastus, 255, 341n35
Therapeutai, 284
Thermopylai, 67, 185, 186–88, 203–4, 206–8, 355n2
Theseus, 227
Thespiai, 28, 59, 61
Thessaly, 26, 32, 160, 265
Thetis, 32
Thrace, 224, 227, 241
throne of Pelops, Mount Sipylos 55
Thucydides, 348n22
thunder, 26–27, 44, 66, 150, 203, 235, 236, 241, 275, 293, 323n51, 327n104
Thyiades, 65–6
Tiberius, 218, 223
Tigris, 238
Titans, 26, 332n6
Tivoli, 338n38
topophilia, 47, 64
touch, 97, 114
tourism, 13, 55, 59, 61, 62, 64, 78–79, 90, 110–11, 115, 117, 146, 295, 335n71. *See also* pilgrimage

tragedy, xix, 47–49, 97, 105, 313n10, 343n7
Trajan's Column, 123, 126, 192
Transfiguration, 73
transhumance, 257–59, 264, 272, 273, 298
travellers in Greece and Italy, eighteenth- and nineteenth-century, 51, 86, 99–100, 144–45, 248, 311, 328n17, 329n23
Trophonios, 52
Troy, 3, 11, 21, 33–35, 95, 102, 120–21, 150, 356n22
tsunami, 238
Turnus, 150–52, 235
Tusculum, 226, 228
Typhos (also Typhon, Typhoeus), 110, 112

Valens, 241, 368n7
Valentinian, 236–37, 368n7, 369n15
Valerius, 87–89, 154
Valley of the Muses, 28, 61–63, 137, 146, 327n1
Varro, 258–59
vase paintings, 119–24
Venus, 150, 156, 161, 167, 175, 254. *See also* Aphrodite
viewing, xx, xxiv–xxv, 13, 37, 95–143, 144–45, 177–78; from mountains, 7, 22–23, 33, 43, 56, 59, 70, 77, 85–86, 90–91, 95–96, 114, 148–49, 192, 196, 216, 221, 239, 292, 306, 309, 311–12, 322n35, 364n65; of mountains from below, 8, 15, 22–23, 43–45, 59–61, 85, 95, 97, 157–58; obstructed, 37, 43, 70, 96–97, 182, 204, 206–7, 216, 312, 364n65. *See also* landscape
villas, 104, 127–28, 130, 140, 158, 166, 338n35, 339n39, 345n32
Virgil, 155, 168, 267, 340n5; *Aeneid*, 149–53; *Eclogues* 100; *Georgics*, 157
Vitruvius, 205
Vlachs, 257
volcanoes, 96, 107–18, 151, 177, 212, 253
votive offerings, xvii–xviii, 10, 12, 15, 17, 65

wall paintings, 119, 126–37, 140, 154, 166, 177
Walpole, Horace, 106

wild animals, 21, 24, 39–40, 42, 45, 49, 135–37, 153, 176, 231–35, 243, 276, 284, 289, 290, 294, 296, 298–99, 349n34

wilderness, xxii, 4, 5, 49, 70, 78, 88, 133, 155, 254, 274, 277–78, 292–94, 300, 303, 307; as human construct, 286

Williams, Raymond, 267

wood-cutting, 24, 27, 38, 39, 41, 251, 255–56. *See also* deforestation

wool industry, 261

Wordsworth, William, 306

Xenagoras, 210–11

Xenophon, 376n14; *Anabasis*, 204, 213

Xerxes, 199, 203–4, 205, 206

Zeus, xviii, 3, 9, 10, 12–13, 14, 15–17, 21, 23, 26–28, 30, 32–34, 40, 41, 43, 44, 55, 58–59, 61, 70, 74–76, 95, 105, 110, 120, 140, 142, 254, 265, 323n58, 327n103, 327n104, 330n45, 351n18, 38n46; birth of, 6, 13, 26; Lykaios, xvii, 5–6, 56, 122, 251–52; Ombrios, 16–17; Stratios, 11, 253. *See also* Jupiter

zonation, 250

A NOTE ON THE TYPE

This book has been composed in Arno, an Old-style serif typeface in the classic Venetian tradition, designed by Robert Slimbach at Adobe.

GPSR Authorized Representative: Easy Access System Europe - Mustamäe tee 50, 10621 Tallinn, Estonia, gpsr.requests@easproject.com

www.ingramcontent.com/pod-product-compliance
Lightning Source LLC
Jackson TN
JSHW021117080925
90632JS00001B/2